T0271383

ADJUSTMENT, STRUCTURAL CHANGE, AND ECONOMIC EFFICIENCY

SOVIET AND EAST EUROPEAN STUDIES

ADJUSTMENT, STRUCTURAL CHANGE, AND ECONOMIC EFFICIENCY

ASPECTS OF MONETARY COOPERATION IN EASTERN EUROPE

JOZEF M. VAN BRABANT

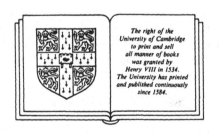

The right of the
University of Cambridge
to print and sell
all manner of books
was granted by
Henry VIII in 1534.
The University has printed
and published continuously
since 1584.

CAMBRIDGE UNIVERSITY PRESS

CAMBRIDGE

NEW YORK   NEW ROCHELLE   MELBOURNE   SYDNEY

CAMBRIDGE UNIVERSITY PRESS
Cambridge, New York, Melbourne, Madrid, Cape Town,
Singapore, São Paulo, Delhi, Tokyo, Mexico City

Cambridge University Press
The Edinburgh Building, Cambridge CB2 8RU, UK

Published in the United States of America by
Cambridge University Press, New York

www.cambridge.org
Information on this title: www.cambridge.org/9780521334556

First published 1987

A catalogue record for this publication is available from the British Library

Library of Congress Cataloguing in Publication data
Brabant, Jozef M. van.
Adjustment, structural change, and economic efficiency.
(Soviet and East European studies)
Bibliography: p.
Includes index.
1. Finance–Europe, Eastern. 2. Monetary policy–
Europe, Eastern. 3. Investments–Europe, Eastern.
4. Europe, Eastern-Commercial policy. 5. Europe,
Eastern – Economic integration. 6. Council for Mutual
Economic Assistance. I. Title. II. Series.
HG186.E82B7 1987 332.4'947 87-785

ISBN 978-0-521-33455-6 Hardback

For Anja, Katja, and Miyuki
in spite of it all . . .

Contents

Figures and tables

Preface

This monograph presents a systematic analysis of topics on which I have worked extensively during the past fifteen years. The project in its present state was first conceived in early 1984 against the backdrop of the arduous adjustment policies of several Eastern European economies during the early 1980s. From the outset, I had no doubt that turning the economic situation around toward economic recovery and regaining a sustainable higher-level growth path would require unwavering and far-reaching positive structural adjustment policies in these countries individually and in their groupwide concert.

From the project's inception, how best to come to grips with ongoing policy drifts in the area has entailed structural problems for this book. In recent years, top-level policy makers of several Eastern European countries have increasingly been entertaining measurable changes in institutions, policy instruments, development policies, and organizational behavior. Although these ambitions pertain foremost to some of the Eastern European economies in isolation, they have more than passing implications for their mutual economic cooperation. Even those that, for the time being, opt to eschew serious institutional and policy transformations will have to come to terms with and work off the indirect effects of ongoing changes elsewhere in their primary partner countries.

As the project was drawing to its first-draft state, the momentum of the movement toward changing economic mechanisms or even toward adopting explicit economic reforms of potentially wide-ranging portent accelerated markedly. With the hindsight of developments during the latter part of 1986, when the copy editing of the manuscript was being completed, the reform movement in Eastern Europe has been solidifying into a course that well transcends what I had anticipated when I embarked on the project. In this context, it is important to bear in mind a few dates associated with the evolvement of this product.

Because a working draft was at hand by late 1985 and a first polished draft by the second quarter of 1986, under the circumstances, I have had to face essentially a trade-off between moving forward with the project as it had been maturing or revising it in line with ongoing changes in Eastern Europe. The latter choice would have entailed inevitable, possibly considerable delays to take more fully into account the implications of the evolving transformations in Eastern Europe. I have opted for the first alternative basically for three reasons. First, I have been naturally reluctant to recast an offspring that has been germinating for so long. Second, because the economic and political trends in the area are far from clear, even at this stage (year-end 1986), it is essentially a matter of speculation when the drift toward more comprehensive economic reform will crystallize, or be rejected as in the past. Third, and principally, the chief focus of this inquiry was on the functions and role of indirect coordination instruments in fostering or deterring regional economic cooperation in Eastern Europe. Although changes in individual countries are bound to have repercussions on Eastern European economic cooperation as a whole, it remains as yet unclear what precisely may emerge on that front. Under the circumstances and because a thorough analysis of past setbacks may be instructive in devising feasible alternatives, I opted for moving ahead with the project "as is," taking essentially a raincheck on the future even beyond what I have already been able to assess in my most recent book (Brabant in press, d).

Most of the ideas developed here were first broached in lectures, discussions, seminars, or a friendly chat with colleagues. Some of these travails were published earlier in journals on both sides of the Atlantic (particularly *Osteuropa-Wirtschaft, Documentation sur l'Europe Centrale, Jahrbuch der Wirtschaft Osteuropas–Yearbook of East-European Economics, Soviet Studies, Journal of Comparative Economics,* and *Comparative Economic Studies*) as well as in a number of collective works. Other topics were given extensive treatment in two of my earlier books (Brabant 1977a, 1980). This book builds extensively upon these two earlier monographs, although it is a self-contained research product.

The protracted research of which the present volume is one of the fruits has been possible in good measure because of generous financial support from numerous institutions and the unstinting professional assistance of many colleagues, as well as secretaries, statistical clerks, and library aides, in a diverse lot of European and North American institutions.

Many people share in what is good in this book. Although I have not cited friends and colleagues, or critics for that matter, by name, I trust my indebtedness to particular individuals will be clear from the parts of the text in question. But I would be grossly remiss if I did not at the very least express my gratitude to all of them collectively. Responsibility for not always heeding the advice or admonitions of colleagues and editors, for misrepresenting information gleaned from them, or for factual errors in reporting Eastern European events is, of course, solely mine.

Although I have been a full-time staff member of the Department of International Economic and Social Affairs of the United Nations Secretariat in New York, the views expressed here are my own and do not necessarily reflect those of the United Nations Secretariat.

Finally, a word of thanks to the three women in my family. If it were not for their demands on my "spare" time, this volume simply could not have been written.

Jozef M. van Brabant

December 1986

Note on transliteration, referencing, and units

Cyrillic language publications or names of persons from Cyrillic-script countries or regions are transliterated according to the so-called scientific transliteration system advocated by the USSR Academy of Sciences. A distinction is made between the three Russian *e*'s and, in the case of Bulgarian sources, the Russian šč is replaced by št. Whenever possible, names of writers, personalities, or places are spelled according to the convention of the home country, possibly followed by transliteration as indicated. The affiliated organs of the CMEA are normally referred to by their Russian names, because in most cases the official or working language of these organizations is Russian.

For brevity's sake, bibliographical references in the text are identified by author and date of publication. In the absence of a name, the reference consists of a simple acronym of the organization sponsoring the publication or one key word from the title. Because they are meant to be codes to the bibliography, where full details are listed, name prefixes are deleted from the code in the text. References to publications with up to three authors are cited in full the first time; from the second reference on or for publications with more than three author's, et al. follows the first author.

Throughout the volume, a billion is understood to be equal to a thousand million, and all dollar magnitudes are expressed with reference to the U.S. dollar. References to the currency denominations of the Slavic countries, other than the ruble, follow the standards of the countries in question; that is, the inflection of the currency denomination depends on the precise magnitude of the preceding number. For Rumanian currency, a unit is called leu but the plural is lei. All dates are specified according to European custom: 1.4.70 means 1 April 1970.

Abbreviations

BIS	Bank for International Settlements
BTPA	bilateral trade and payments agreement
BWS	Bretton Woods system
CC	convertible currency
CCO	Central Committee
CCP	Conference of First Secretaries of Communist and Workers' Parties and of the Heads of Government of the CMEA Member Countries
CCS	Central Committee (secretaries)
CIF	cost, insurance, and freight
CMEA	Council for Mutual Economic Assistance
COCOM	Coordinating Committee for Multinational Export Controls
Comecon	Council for Mutual Economic Assistance
Cominform	Communist Information Bureau
Comintern	Communist International
CP	Communist Party
CPE	centrally planned economy
EC	European Communities
ECU	European currency unit
EFC	external financial convertibility
EMS	European monetary system
EPU	European Payments Union
ER	exchange rate
ERP	European Recovery Program
FOB	free on board
FTO	foreign trade organization
FTR	financially convertible transferable ruble
GATT	General Agreement on Tariffs and Trade
GDR	German Democratic Republic
IBEC	International Bank for Economic Cooperation
IBRD	International Bank for Reconstruction and Development
IEO	international economic organization
IIB	International Investment Bank
IMF	International Monetary Fund

xvii

IMS	international monetary system
IPS	independent price system
ISDL	international socialist division of labor
LIBOR	London interbank offered rate
ME	market economy
MFN	most favored nation
MFT	monopoly of foreign trade and payments
MPE	modified planned economy
MTPA	multilateral trade and payments agreement
NEM	new economic mechanism
NIC	newly industrializing country
NIEO	new international economic order
PE	planned economy
SCEP	Standing Commission for Economic Problems
SCFQ	Standing Commission for Currency and Financial Questions
SCFT	Standing Commission for Foreign Trade
SDR	special drawing right
SEI	socialist economic integration
TR	transferable ruble
UNCITRAL	United Nations Commission for International Trade Law
UNCTAD	United Nations Conference on Trade and Development
WMP	world market price

Introduction

Overall sociopolitical backdrop

The evolution of the doctrine of "commodity–money" relations under socialism is a checkered one. Its bearing on planned economies (PEs) and on their reciprocal economic relations is still largely an unexplored aspect of socialist economic thought. There is not even a generally accepted definition of what this notion precisely means. Usually, commodity–money relations are identified as the opposite of traditional central planning, and they are therefore frequently equated with the operation of market categories and their supporting institutions. Applied to PEs, neither the selection nor the sphere of operation of these policy instruments and institutions coincides with the familiar resource allocation processes of market economies (MEs), however. As a result, equating commodity–money relations in PEs with free-market mechanisms could be a very misleading approach.

Socialist economies are centrally planned and managed. Many economies profess to be socialist, although they are not centrally planned, just as there are economies with central planning that are by no means socialist. The economies I have in mind are essentially those belonging to the core of the "socialist world economic system," as this notion was coined in the years following World War II. My particular focus here is on the seven active European members (Bulgaria, Czechoslovakia, the German Democratic Republic (GDR), Hungary, Poland, Rumania, and the Soviet Union) of the Council for Mutual Economic Assistance (CMEA). In fact, CMEA, Eastern Europe, socialist countries, PEs, and so on are here used interchangeably, unless explicitly stated otherwise. I am aware that, strictly speaking, the Council comprises members from three continents. This geographical extension may at times be a crucial political bonus, and it is occasionally slotted as a prominent argument in political debates, but it is not very relevant to most aspects of socialist economic integration (SEI) that form the core of this investigation. Albania (an active member until 1961), Mongolia (a full member since 1962), Cuba (a full member since 1972), and Vietnam (a full member since 1978) are relatively small,

1

underdeveloped economies.[1] They are far removed from the center of power – and the focal points of the Council's principal tasks as well! For these reasons, there is little of acute relevance to the role of money and finance in the process of SEI that is lost by ignoring these countries in most of what follows.[2]

The PEs traditionally subordinate most market-type categories to comprehensive central planning. That is, quantitative incentives and targets are instrumental in formulating, guiding, and controlling these economies, whereas commodity–money relations are, on the whole, reserved a distinctly less significant role in the formulation and execution of plans. Those goals and instruments are, for all practical purposes, set by national policy makers at the center of the Communist Party (CP). The latter forms the exclusive societal power nexus in each country, but its influence on regional and international affairs depends very much on the specific country and time period under review. Seen in a more cumbersome but, hopefully, more accurate frame of reference, commodity–money relations can be defined as the set of economic policy instruments that help to coordinate economic decisions indirectly. This does not necessarily imply, however, that economic decisions are exclusively or even mainly subordinated or pegged to the indirect indicators of economic efficiency. In other words, the socialist doctrine regarding commodity–money relations should focus on how market-related concepts can help formulate and implement centrally conceived objectives and thus reduce the bewildering complexity of nationwide planning in great physical detail. For want of a more accurate terminology, I shall frequently refer to commodity–money relations as "instruments of indirect economic coordination" or, for short, "indirect coordination instruments."

In the past two decades or so, socialist policy makers and influential spokesmen of PEs have been seriously concerned about the possibilities of harmoniously combining central planning with instruments of indirect economic coordination. The debate was triggered in the smaller PEs as long ago as the mid-1950s. The economic malaise that followed upon the near-feverish pace of growth typical of the first industrialization wave led to an in-depth investigation of the efficiency and long-term growth prospects of these economies. At the heart of these inquiries was the question of how to infer accurate and operational policy conclusions, particularly regarding increasing economic efficiency under central planning. The alternatives considered were quite diverse. They ranged from a cybernetic system of overall central planning by an interconnected powerful computer network to a full-fledged imitation of the market suitably adapted to socialist conditions. It was quickly realized, however, that this diversity of theoretical solutions should realistically be pared to a manageable few of practical import. The following three general questions merit most attention. First, how can one identify the fields of decision making in which market-type policy instruments might be rendered compatible with overall planning? Second, how can these instruments be employed while preserving the virtues of socialist planning? Third, to what extent can these instruments help coordinate allocatory decisions in the process of formulating and implementing central plans more flexibly?

The central concern of Eastern European policy makers favorably inclined toward reforms has been primarily how their economies can be liberated from the fetters of detailed, statewide planning and the quantity ideology so as to make them more receptive to structural and institutional changes and to foster productivity growth on the basis of hidden reserves that not even an astute central planning board could locate and mobilize. There has also been a parallel, but in some instances quite esoteric, debate on the reconciliation of market-based concepts with the dominant Soviet interpretation of the basic Marxist–Leninist doctrines. But this rather eclectic ideological discussion should not overly concern us here.

The fate of the so-called economic reform era in Eastern Europe – basically the mid-1960s – is too well known to be reexamined here in detail. Suffice it to recall that the measures designed to decentralize the decision-making processes to some degree were exceedingly modest in most cases. Planners were indeed more preoccupied with how to avoid introducing objectionable capitalist practices than with how to adapt their economies to the changing domestic and external constraints on economic growth. Moreover, each of these reforms was essentially conceived in isolation, largely in response to domestic growth conditions at the time of a malaise in CMEA relations for various reasons. Some countries, especially the USSR, resorted to reforms as a way to extricate themselves from the administrative reorganization and other legacies of the self-styled leadership typical under Nikita S. Chruščëv and his emulators in Eastern Europe. These included the major political disagreements about the objectives and means of fostering the so-called international socialist division of labor (ISDL), on which more shortly. Furthermore, even the measured reforms were launched against the vested interests of some powerful layers of the ruling elite and careerists, most of whom felt that the reforms tended to be viewed too much from the economic standpoint and not enough from the political and social ones. Finally, the reform attempts were interrupted or even reversed before the combination of indirect coordination instruments with national planning could take firm root and yield tangible results. The first wave of economic reforms was followed by a retrenchment. Decision-making authority was gradually recentralized, and many of the institutions created in support of the incipient move toward allocating resources in part on the basis of indirect efficiency indicators were dismantled. The only major exception was in the sphere of foreign trade, especially the extent to which links between the domestic and external sectors of the economy were allowed to affect the appropriation of scarce resources. For one, a substantial component of the trade reforms of the 1960s has survived until now. Even in terms of economic strategy, the order of the day since then, obviously with some wavering in this commitment, has been to experiment with alternatives in the foreign sector.

Two features of this experience are crucial to this investigation. First, the abrogation of the reforms, in spite of the inclination to pursue adaptations in the trade sector, was associated with an attempt to patch over the Czechoslovak trauma of 1968–1969 and its aftermath. This wrenching concern culminated in the promulgation of a broad policy document, indentified here as *Integration Program*,[3] and a commitment to pursue SEI. Economic integration is understood here, although this definition does not quite emerge from the aforementioned document, as a process aimed at leveling differences in relative scarcities of goods and services by consciously eliminating barriers to trade and other forms of interaction between at least two states.[4] Second, at the same time, each PE in isolation began to emphasize much more than before, albeit to a different degree, the role of economic and financial relations with MEs. The decision to borrow from MEs to finance substantial imports of advanced technology in support of productivity growth is beyond question. But this strategic choice was partly motivated by the expectation that such a technological fillip would boost domestic production, qualitatively as well as quantitatively, and thus engineer a sharp upswing in competitive exportables resulting in an increased potential for earning foreign exchange revenues, especially in convertible currency (CC) markets. At least in the beginning, these loans were believed to be self-liquidating. In retrospect, several strategic mistakes distorted this calculation. Some were already embedded in the logic of the choices that were made. Others arose only ex post when major unanticipated economic and political events at home and abroad invalidated crucial assumptions underlying this strategy.

The emergence of a new constellation of domestic and external economic constraints since the mid-1970s has engendered a broad-based economic malaise not only in East–West and intragroup cooperation but virtually in each CMEA member. Short- and medium-term plans have tended to be overtaken rapidly by ongoing events. Some of the latter, especially the world economic recession and the crisis of confidence in the global financial system, were short-term and, on the whole, remained well beyond the purview of the PEs individually or as a group. In the process, the need to seek positive structural adjustment, which in some PEs had already been felt since the late 1950s, was measurably exacerbated.

Modification in economic structures of the PEs has become the order of the day since the late 1970s. There are several interrelated reasons for this. Four clusters can be identified: (1) to bring decision making and planning generally in line with explicit economic calculations; (2) to adapt to sharp shifts in the mix of economic resources at the disposal of central decision makers; (3) to adjust to the structural shifts that have taken place in the overall supply from within the CMEA region; and (4) to conform gradually to the seminal changes in the global economic and financial networks that have erupted and taken root since the early 1970s. The energy crisis could undoubtedly be considered as one way of stylizing the adjustment requirements of the PEs also. But it would be fundamentally wrong to ascribe to it the entire range and character of the structural adaptations that confront Eastern Europe. The escalation of the oil price is only the tip, albeit perhaps a very visible apex, of the momentum of changes that may be in the offing or that should soon loom on the horizon if these economies are not to prolong their present economic malaise and thus further aggravate societal disenchantment, which has already had an impact on morale and, hence, labor productivity.

Essentially since the late 1970s, but with some interruptions due to the external pressures of 1981–1983, including reduced external demand and severe payment problems, nearly all of the Eastern European countries, including the USSR since 1983, have been exploring, once again, ways of rendering their economies more efficient in the use of primary and intermediate inputs. These incipient changes in "the economic mechanism," as these reforms are presently labeled, generally do not envisage the comprehensive exploitation of indirect coordination instruments. However, given the power of dialectics and the magnitude of the economic problems faced, a solution can undoubtedly be rationalized that would not jeopardize the primacy of planning in the economic mechanism. But to reinforce this in each economy and in the reciprocal relations of these countries as a group, it is necessary, as one recent commentary puts it, to explore "commodity–money relations and their organizational forms" (Lidvanova 1985, p. 76) much more effectively. The economic mechanisms may therefore well evolve in the near term chiefly in the direction indicated. But the breadth, depth, and speed of these institutional and policy changes remain to be determined.

For nearly forty years, the PEs have made policy choices that have often differed quite radically from the plausible alternatives embedded in inherited economic structures with the help of decision-making criteria that have only weak links with those ensuring static efficiency in the prototype ME. This deliberate choice to underemphasize the optimal exploitation of static efficiency has had a logic of its own in the context of PEs. Indeed, the crucial component of the forces motivating policy makers in socialist economies is not mainly economic. This is so despite the dominant materialist ideology, which leads socialist leaders to cling to the conviction that economic forces in the productive sphere bring about the essence of the "superstructure" in any society and that these "laws" become explicitly recognized only in socialist systems.

Admittedly, this component of the dominant ideology has been at substantial variance with the actual course of events in most PEs, especially the Soviet industrialization strategy of the 1930s. The socialist revolution was aimed at establishing a unique society based on a completely new political culture that cannot be created gradually. This transition toward a world where workers would not be alienated is fundamentally predicated on the moral transformation in individuals and society at large; this in turn determines the rest, including economic affairs.[5] Economic efficiency can be given a lower priority than social, political, and strategic objectives held by the socialist leaders, but at a price that *can* be approximated. Furthermore, the determined drive to restructure the Eastern European economies, in sharp contrast to their prewar situation, called for a different distribution of resources from the one that could possibly have been supported by market instruments.

National and regional economic progress

How to reconcile international economic relations with the themes dominating domestic economic policies provides a tangled web of vexing theoretical and practical problems. Their magnitude is particularly affected because the PEs hold on to national economic objectives in marked contrast to their allegedly international ideology. More specifically, the combination of social, political, economic, and strategic goals at home has had no readily identifiable counterpart in the international domain, not even in what appears to cement the regional cohesion of the CMEA members. The regulation of relations within a group of countries bent on safeguarding as much national sovereignty and domestic policy autonomy as possible is therefore not at all an easy task. An even touchier issue is the proper operational definition of the particular, and perhaps special, nature of such relations.[6]

Precisely because of the pronounced domestic orientation of socioeconomic policies, the PEs have been concerned more with economic affairs than, say, with politics or ideology in regional and international cooperation. This statement might appear paradoxical in light of the unconstructive role PEs at times have played in international relations. Although the Eastern European political regimes have unquestionably tried to export their communist ideology and to promote their own power–political stronghold abroad, these do not appear to have been the overriding motives in molding their own day-to-day economic interactions. Furthermore, in relations with other countries, the ideological fonts of the international vocation of communism have frequently been brushed aside, or rubbed out altogether, whenever economic imbalances compelled the PEs to participate in world markets more than was convenient in an atmosphere of political, ideological, and strategic rivalry and tensions.

In any case, it appears fair to say that, compared with the muted role of efficiency considerations in domestic affairs, the PEs have devoted a larger proportion of their priorities in foreign relations to the energetic pursuit of economic levers within their overall concepts of trade and cooperation. It is true that these countries have not taken advantage of all opportunities available in world trade. Yet, they have nearly fully explored, or even exploited, at times only on an experimental basis, the potential advantages within their overall concept of economic development. A redistribution of national income or value added is actively encouraged at home, particularly within the material sector. But it is deemed to be quite unacceptable in most foreign economic activities. The only exception, which has played an incidental role in foreign economic relations, is the granting of development assistance, especially when embedded in more comprehensive, planned trade and cooperation agreements. The disproportionate weight of economics in the gestation of relations among PEs arises because there is no consistent set of objectives and policy instruments at the international level that is directly comparable to those typical of individual PEs. As a result, foreign economic and other objectives are invariably subordinated to domestic policies, not the reverse.

Once the foregoing, perhaps tenuous, proposition is accepted, it becomes relatively easy to perceive the motives behind the second thrust for dovetailing market-type instruments with centralized planning. The application of instruments of indirect economic coordination in international relations of the PEs, especially within the context of the CMEA, has been a sensitive subject of topical discussions at the summit policy-making levels for nearly thirty years. The complex debate on this issue has been polarized since the 1970s because of at least two developments. Indirect economic coordination became a topical issue with the efforts to infer policy-oriented interpretations from *Integration Program*. This was particularly true with respect to the latter's ambiguous stipulations on the objectives and means of SEI and of how to mold them into concrete follow-up policy steps. Furthermore, the recent bout of attempts, which fundamentally remained uncoordinated, to weather external constraints in conjunction with sharp shifts in prices has added a new dimension to national and regional coordination instruments. It is precisely because the PEs insist on avoiding a potentially far-reaching intraregional redistribution of economic resources that the preservation of economic interests in regional cooperation continues to be such a controversial topic.

Although the PEs place a disproportionate emphasis on ensuring economic equivalence in their external economic relations, their actual behavior does not coincide with what stylized models of economic competition tend to suggest. Profits or financial rewards are not the main criterion molding the foreign economic relations of the PEs. One of the more cogent reasons for the intensive debate on the role and forms of commodity–money relations in and among PEs is that their socialist economic decisions are based on complex criteria. Because these economies are centrally planned, incentives and motivations necessarily differ from those common in MEs. The market indicators typical of their international economic relations must be at some variance with the yardsticks of nonsocialist world trade. To most economists, it might seem trite, or even naive, to draw attention to the influence of socialist ideology on the economic policies of PEs. Nevertheless, in some important instances, such as the imitation of market processes, these economies do take their ideology seriously, at least in some matters of relevance to the topics selected for the in-depth exploration that follows.

The impact of these so-called laws of socialism[7] on the gradual transformation of the SEI model becomes particularly apparent in a more precise formulation of how PEs can render their internal decision making more flexible, while preserving the essential elements of planning, so as to map the potential advantages of international processes. How this can be accomplished without a Copernican revolution continues to be a matter of strained debate. But the ideological convictions underlying the official interpretations and justifications of socialist economic policies still explicitly reject free competition on the premise that the unhindered mobility of commodities, services, and capital between countries "does not reduce, but reinforces the uneven economic development of these countries" (Koval'cev 1975, p. 15).

On the mechanisms of socialist economic integration

A key concept in analyzing SEI is the so-called mechanism by which integration is to be cultivated. This had a historical as well as a conceptual dimension. Regarding the first, elaborations differ considerably, depending on the analyst's view of what has been achieved in the CMEA and how it has been accomplished. Conceptually, the mechanism of SEI can usefully be placed against the backdrop of the protracted controversy between the "market" and the "plan" as the key vehicles to encourage regional cooperation.

The outlook on the achievements of CMEA economic cooperation can be divided into three broad categories. The first one denies that anything of note has been achieved. Because those observers refute any solid result from nearly forty years of close economic cooperation in the area, it would clearly be useless to inquire into the underlying mechanisms. Antipodal to this view is the one that claims that SEI has been quite successful and that further progress is guaranteed to emanate from the policies and instruments at hand. Even in most instances of detail, such assertions founder on the glaring reality of widespread dissatisfaction with the SEI results obtained to date. These proponents include not only uninformed or badly briefed observers, but there is also a layer of serious economists who have endeavored to prop up their claims by reference to quantitative success indicators. In between these two is the more nuanced interpretation that acknowledges that progress has been undeniably positive but that room for further improvement, and hence marked integration effects, remains considerable. Typical for the latter group, with which I associate myself, is the presumption that the potential for profitable integration can be activated only if the CMEA members resort to more flexible forms of economic cooperation, including indirect instruments of economic coordination. The perspective held by this group of observers will become clear as I proceed, because that is precisely one of the purposes of this inquiry. However, the second one needs to be examined more closely.

The definition of integration embraced here is the opposite of the views recently propounded by Vladimir Sobell, who must be counted among the more vocal Western observers belonging to the second group. He argues that the CMEA is essentially an international protection system created primarily to attain a maximum degree of economic stability (Sobell 1984, pp. 5ff). This is the opposite of the market-oriented approach geared to maximizing efficiency. The accomplishments of SEI in Sobell's views should be measured by the extent to which the mutual exchange of resources ensures steady expansion of production in the participating economies. Foreign trade plans and bilateral trade and payments agreements (BTPAs) are thus a necessary prerequisite, though not forcibly a sufficient one, for maximizing stability in a relatively self-contained system. Sobell is even willing to equate the enmeshing of bilateral ties of PEs as a halfway station towards the "single plan" that some have coveted for decades. The CMEA should accordingly be chiefly concerned with the "international management of the burden of inefficient production. . . . The spreading of the Soviet subsidy and the reduction of losses attributable to the devaluation of 'hard' into 'soft' commodities [are] the main engines of industrial co-operation and specialisation" (Sobell 1984, p. 6).

In my view, this interpretation of the CMEA's history ignores the political and economic debates of the past thirty years or at least brushes them contemptuously aside, it lacks operationality, and it misses the essence of the current state of affairs in Eastern Europe. Just one logical question concerning this misguided casuistry may help to underpin my critique at this stage. To the extent that the CMEA should indeed be concerned with managing inefficiency, the PEs still have to choose among alternative ways of accomplishing it. Could they be presumed to seek an efficient mode of managing regional inefficiency and of apportioning its burden? Surely it could not be left to each PE to absorb its "natural" share of the premeditated inefficiency! BTPAs and specialization protocols may provide one approach. But recent debates clearly suggest that the members hope to exploit to some degree many different instruments so as to raise the efficiency as well as the stability of their regional cooperation.

In connection with the preservation of a relatively self-contained regional protection system, which is the heart of Sobell's thesis, the primary yardstick should be economics rather than politics and ideology. Any type of constraint imposed on production, distribution, or consumption processes, if operative, is bound to entail a cost. It may be difficult to quantify this cost and to apportion it equitably according to its various causes. Inasmuch as the leaders of the participating countries are bent on shielding their individual and shared distinctiveness against "foreign competition," however, they should be made aware of the burden associated with the regional integration scheme. Moreover, decision makers should perceive this cost to be demonstrably inferior to the aggregate cost of protecting each participant separately. Whether one should call this a cost of inefficiency, protection, empire maintenance, exploitation, or some such designation is semantics and largely immaterial to the task at hand. Perhaps the second is the least politically loaded term.

From an economic point of view, the leadership of a regional economic union should vie to minimize this protection cost, at given preferences regarding the extent and comprehensiveness of the insulating cordon, and to seek an equitable distribution rule. To make these components more explicit, in my view, has been a major preoccupation of the attempts to reform the CMEA and the participating economies, as amply emphasized in recent discussions at the highest policy-making levels. Indeed, this has been the pivot of the debate on commodity–money relations and the crystallization of an SEI mechanism. In spite of the protracted evaluation of the alternative means by which SEI is to be enhanced, no uniform, cohesive, or clearly paramount position has emerged as yet. In fact, a serious clash of concepts stemming chiefly from the profound diversity of strategic aims has emerged in the process. The dispute about introducing a market-based mechanism, rather than planning, on an international scale has more dimensions than those readily apparent from the somewhat tautological discussions in the literature. In fact, efficient planning cannot exist without correct market-type indicators. This is being increasingly acknowledged in the Eastern European literature and political debates.

At the bottom of the complicated dispute about the appropriate integration mechanism lies the question of greater flexibility in planning, as distinct from the technocratic promulgation of "market incentives." The more liberal proponents argue that the SEI mechanism should be constructed organically on the basis of the policies and instruments deemed adequate in each PE. In the process, it is strongly suggested that only a regulated market mechanism suitably adapted to current conditions in the member countries can safeguard national interests and yet foster economic efficiency domestically as well as regionally. More specifically, there should be an organic interdependence between domestic and foreign trade prices of goods and services. Free regional factor mobility, on the other hand, is only rarely advocated. This concern about prices is more involved than simply reintroducing competitive markets.

The specific role of market-type instruments in guiding SEI and the goals such instruments serve differ in essential respects from those in conventional MEs. This stems partly from the unique features of the all-embracing socialist ideology and its implications for managing the PEs. It is also a consequence of the more important elements of their growth strategy and economic model. Price irrationality has been the most important reproach made by Western economists. Precisely because many of these observers too easily judge the merits and faults of planned "price irrationality" and the associated planned inefficiency, when contrasted with the profit rationality criterion of MEs, their analyses have fallen prey to brush-off criticism on the part of Eastern European commentators. To forestall such objections, I have tried to analyze the financial and monetary relations of PEs, relying on the general framework of policy making and development objectives of these economies.[8] This hopefully meets the more cogent points of such criticism.

Perhaps the crux of arguing the case for placing greater reliance on indirect coordination instruments, or market-type categories, is that they essentially generate, transmit, and analyze information about what kind of decisions should be invoked in the system; they coordinate the multitude of disparate pieces of information and decisions, and may provide the requisite material and other incentives to foster productivity. Market-type instruments can handle all of these tasks at a comparatively low transaction cost. They probably handle this best, at least in a microeconomic setting, under conditions where market forces can range freely. But they are less apt to generate equilibrium at the macroeconomic level in either a static or a dynamic setting. The wider use of indirect coordination instruments under guidance of suitably defined macroeconomic policies may solidify into a policy combination that achieves greater cohesiveness among the various micro- and macroeconomic spheres. In what follows I maintain that some of the instruments typical of MEs, suitably adapted to local conditions, could prove helpful in other social organizations too.

Objectives of this book

The basic features of SEI have been examined in the literature from a number of different economic, historical, and organizational angles. I do not propose to duplicate those efforts, especially since I have already had ample opportunities to state my views of the economics and organization of SEI elsewhere.[9] Many reasons could be adduced for presenting yet another book about the financial and monetary aspects of CMEA integration. Those that I wish to bring to bear here concern the currency and range of issues discussed in the most recent surveys of CMEA affairs in the context of ongoing national, regional, and global changes in economic structures and broad socioeconomic policies.

To the best of my knowledge, Brabant 1977a is still the most comprehensive and detailed independent study of CMEA monetary relations available. Much of its historical material has lost none of its analytical insight, institutional setting, or empirical accuracy when compared with newer studies and data disclosed since the underlying research was conducted. Thorough updating of the material could remove some of the statistical guesswork required in the mid-1970s and place the euphoria engendered by *Integration Program* in a more dispassionate context. Although I was rather skeptical at the time about the chances of the PEs implementing a new, indirect mechanism of SEI (as outlined in Section 7 of the program (Tokareva 1972, pp. 58–64) dealing with commodity–money relations), actual events have turned out to be even more detrimental to the realization of these intentions than I had anticipated. The experiences of the European PEs since the mid-1970s are bound to have a strong bearing on (1) the future of their integration activities; (2) their interest in actively pursuing SEI within the boundaries that all members have agreed upon de jure or de facto; (3) attitudes with respect to East–West economic relations; and (4) the chances of resuming a sustainable pace of economic growth in the years ahead. Many factors could be cited in support of this contention, but the following four figure most prominently among current policy concerns.

The first oil shock was initially diagnosed as a temporary aberration engendered by the military conflict in the Middle East in October 1973. At the latest since the second oil shock, Eastern European leaders have come to realize that seminal changes in world, including CMEA, markets have taken place in part as a result of the two shifts in oil prices. The PEs are now also accepting that the global recession and financial crisis of the early 1980s have changed the international economic environment within which national and regional growth must necessarily be pursued. Thus the shift in the interpretation of the price-setting principles for trade cleared in transferable rubles (TRs) combined with the considerable tightening of the restrictions on the volumes of oil and other key primary goods that can be procured from within the region have had very weighty consequences, especially for the Eastern European economies.

Second, the period of economic reforms of the 1960s and the subsequent economic and political détente yielded a sharp upswing in the volume of East–West trade and an escalation of Eastern Europe's CC debt. It was hoped that a substantial surge in East–West trade, particularly imported technology, would in and of itself foster a pronounced change in the PE's overall productivity level that would be sustainable in the medium to long run. Unfortunately, this strategy of self-liquidating external financing in the end miscarried because of domestic features of the PEs and unanticipated transformations in world markets. For these and other reasons, policy makers in Eastern Europe are now more cautious about resuming rapid growth in East–West relations. A brisk expansion is likely to be sought only if the PEs succeed in lifting their exports dependably. A resumption of relatively rapid economic growth in the area might therefore be contingent on the steady intensification of regional economic cooperation as the pivot of macroeconomic policies of the PEs.

Third, now more than ever it is incumbent to explore ways of bolstering exports to the MEs. This is particularly so for the trade-dependent PEs, even though the prospective trading environment is likely to be much more complex than that of the 1970s. Because the PEs failed even then to promote their exports as intended, it is worth investigating how and under what circumstances Eastern Europe can accelerate East–West relations in a balanced manner without forcibly jeopardizing profitable SEI endeavors. The differences stem from the rapid emergence of exporters of manufactures, particularly among the so-called newly industrializing developing countries (NICs); the slowdown in the pace of economic growth in developed MEs, and the latter's increasingly protectionist policy stance; the rising expectations with respect to product quality in intra-CMEA trade; and the need of the PEs to procure essential imports from world markets, owing to physical or other limits on effective supplies from within the CMEA that can realistically be counted on.

Finally, in spite of all the efforts made during the roughly forty years of cooperation in Eastern Europe, the aggregate degree of genuine integration there continues to be surprisingly low.[10] Now more than ever, these PEs need to emerge from their recent economic slump through common efforts. A realistic evaluation of the room for SEI must necessarily rest on a more comprehensive type of analysis than the delimiters set for Brabant 1977a. As the past fifteen years have amply documented, regional economic cooperation in the CMEA cannot flourish only on the basis of the traditional instruments of plan coordination and ex ante trade agreements. In the past several years, nearly all PEs have been experimenting with some type of incentive reforms. A more comprehensive recasting of policies, institutions, and instruments is more than likely to be in the offing. Essential ingredients thereof are reformulations of planning techniques, the scope and nature of central planning, the goals and methods of economic management, and the devolution of decision making. The latter especially presupposes the promulgation of an economic mechanism in which indirect instruments of economic coordination by necessity play a central role.

These are the essential reasons that motivate me to propose this survey of the actual and potential role of money and finance in Eastern Europe. In contrast to the focus on intra-CMEA cooperation in Brabant 1977a, the present tome is more comprehensive but at the same time less ambitious. Thus the historical details of the role of money and finance in the postwar environment for SEI are of lesser concern here than the bearing of prevailing policies, institutions, and instruments on the future of SEI. At the same time, this volume is more comprehensive. It assesses the actual and potential reform forces in Eastern Europe with special reference to the sharp internal and external adjustments since the early 1980s and the continued need to reformulate policies in line with the prevailing internal and external determinants of growth and to redesign economic institutions accordingly.

At this point, I shall clarify some terminology, especially buzzwords like "adjustment," "reform," "change in the economic mechanism," and other loaded terms that are frequently invoked in commentary on the current policy framework of the PEs. In what follows, structural adjustment is understood to mean policy changes within the basic parameters of the given socioeconomic system. Emergency adjustment in this context refers to the introduction of policy changes in response to sudden disturbances or shocks from within the economy or because of external pressures. Positive adjustment, on the other hand, implies that policy changes are deliberately sought, possibly in a planned manner, but still within the framework of the given system. The latter itself comprises state ownership of the means of production, far-reaching autonomy over the domestic economy, including its external trade and payments links, and the deliberate disregarding of some scarcities through centralized planning, administrative management, and control over society. However, conscious changes, such as those envisioned in positive structural adjustment policies, may become so ambitious and all-encompassing that they assume some of the prerogatives of a full-fledged economic reform by default. A reform in this connection means changing the principles governing the system and the system's institutional arrangements for generating, conveying, processing, and coordinating information about economic magnitudes. A reform is therefore much more ambitious in scope and fundamental in nature than positive structural adjustment could possibly be. But it does not necessarily, as Prybyla argues, mark the system's transformation in such a way that "the market and private property must become the dominant determinants of production, investment, and the distribution of income shares in the system" (Prybyla 1986, p. 22).

This definition of economic reform diverges in a number of respects from the evolving and vacillating connotation given in the PEs. During the first reform wave, the notion stood for relatively far-reaching changes in the economic model of the PEs. At that time, it was convenient to differentiate between comprehensive reforms and others that envisaged merely the streamlining of economic administration. After the Czechoslovak trauma of 1968, the term "reform" became anathema in socialist policy discussions, which reserved it largely to denote reprehensible deviations from established doctrine or corruption from abroad. With Michail S. Gorbačëv's recent usage of the term, most notably in his keynote address to the Twenty-seventh Congress of the USSR's CP, the notion is being hesitatingly revived in the policy vocabulary of Eastern European policy makers too, albeit with some trepidation.

A proper description of "changes in the economic mechanism" – a euphemism that in recent years has been very much in vogue in the PEs – is much more difficult than that of adjustment. Because it has become nearly completely a political slogan to assuage diverging interest groups in many of the PEs, and thus a term less loaded than "structural adjustment" and "economic reform," it is often devoid of real meaning. When used, this notion is meant to refer to a major policy measure that could be included in positive structural adjustment or economic reform policies.

There are two basic assumptions underlying the analysis here. First, I take it for granted that SEI has become a prime objective of the domestic, regional, and international economic policies pursued by the PEs. This important assumption should not be equated with the frequently voiced but inopportune opinion that the PEs have already agreed on a comprehensive and consistent long-term integration strategy or that they have already charted all essential ingredients of their integration model.[11] I only wish to preclude an extensive examination of the formidable political obstacles that have to be removed before any earnest integration strategy and model can be formulated. This does not signal that controversial topics will be dodged at all cost. Second, the officially held integration tasks and instruments are not formulated in a vacuum. They have crystallized as a result of the postwar evolution of CMEA cooperation. This proposition can be buttressed by hard facts. For example, *Integration Program* and subsequent documents do not fundamentally depart from past practices of regional cooperation.[12] They are basically reformulations of well-tried ad hoc methods of cooperation and a more systematic exposition of the formidable tasks the PEs have to come to grips with in the near future.

Outline

Not all aspects of the role of money and finance in the evolution of regional economic cooperation can be pursued here in equal detail. I

shall focus on how the PEs could resume faster output growth by enhancing their participation in the world economy on the basis of indirect
coordination instruments. As such, the volume consists of three parts.
Part I, Chapters 1–3, is meant to paint the historical and organizational
backdrop for the detailed study of indirect coordination instruments.
Chapter 1 provides a brief summary of the historical aspects of SEI and
the overall organizational features of the member economies as they have
evolved from the orthodox model of the centrally planned economy
(CPE) implanted in the late 1940s. This yields the rationale for a succinct
discussion of the first wave of economic reforms, the so-called modified
planned economy (MPE), and the recent attempts to come to grips with
bulging development constraints.

Chapter 2 is concerned with the overall organization of the CMEA as it
presents itself to date and the broad integration policies of the past ten to
fifteen years. Although a historical perspective is not altogether eschewed, the principal aim here is to summarize the existing literature on
how the CMEA as a regional organization blends into the process of SEI,
how it could assist the PEs in adjusting to changing growth opportunities,
and on the Council's likely role in the decade ahead.

The reasons for and the types of adjustment policies pursued in the
PEs are documented in Chapter 3. Here I examine the recent growth
performance of the PEs, the course of SEI and domestic economic policies during the period of adjustment to external payments pressures, the
prime vehicles for adjustment in CPEs and MPEs as contrasted with
typical adjustment programs of MEs, and the rationale for developing a
positive adjustment policy in the majority of PEs. The latter's compass is
determined by the eventual formulation of some type of comprehensive
economic reform, the opening of markets, the exploration of outside
trading opportunities, and the potential for fostering blockwide cooperation in the context of more intensive global trade and financial links in
the years ahead.

Part II, Chapters 4–11, presents the detailed analyses of selected indirect coordination instruments and supporting institutions. Chapters 4
and 5 deal with prices. I first examine the official theses regarding the
presumed relationship between lagged world market prices (WMPs) of
some reference period and current intragroup trade prices. Even if the
alleged relationship between world and CMEA prices conformed with
official principles, the PEs would have to come to grips with key problems
of managing resource allocation under multiple price systems that, generally speaking, are not–and cannot be–interlinked. The causal relationship rarely holds, however. The key features of these market buffers,
their implications for efficient resource allocation, and their empirical
manifestation are scrutinized here. Chapter 5 is essentially concerned
with domestic prices, price policies, and the relationship between domes-

tic and trade prices. A particularly important aspect of economic policies since the mid-1970s has been the disposition of socialist policy makers to resort to price changes, even in consumer markets. Trade prices have also been adapted both with regard to the way in which foreign commercial transactions are factored into domestic accounting and in the space and mechanisms for actual trade decision making with the CMEA and outside partners.

The next two chapters focus on links between a PE and the external environment. Chapter 6 zeroes in on the role of the exchange rate (ER) and surrogates in domestic decision making in the PEs. It also examines the importance of separating the TR payments zone from that in which CC plays a predominant role in order to understand both the complexity of foreign economic decision making and the formidable tasks ahead in integrating these segregated markets. It concludes with the more speculative aspects of the direction that prospective foreign exchange policies in PEs may take.

The actual and potential links of the PEs and the CMEA as a whole with the international monetary system (IMS) are the focus of Chapter 7. After a brief examination of the evolution of the attitude of the socialist countries toward the IMS and its two multilateral institutions, I detail the crucial components of the PEs' critique of the Bretton Woods system (BWS), their attitude toward the new international economic order (NIEO), their expressed preference with regard to a reform of the IMS, and the ways in which the PEs could more fully participate in the IMS.

Chapters 8–11 deal largely with the emerging capital market in Eastern Europe. Chapter 8 examines the characteristics of the TR clearing zone, bilateral and multilateral clearing, the role of the International Bank for Economic Cooperation (IBEC), the bank's contribution to SEI, and its links with nonmember countries. Chapter 9 first looks at labor mobility. It then discusses the recent experiences with so-called joint investment projects, explains their scope and nature, and evaluates their potential effects on present and foreseeable economic policies of the PEs. The next sequence of topics deals with the role of investment coordination in SEI and the more general aspects of the gradual emergence of a capital market in Eastern Europe.

Chapter 10 is concerned with the International Investment Bank (IIB). It explains the backdrop to the bank's creation, operations, and lending record. It also assesses the IIB's role in coordinating investments in the CMEA and the bank's actual and potential contributions to SEI. Chapter 11 is devoted to convertibility. After a brief rundown of the relationship among multilateralism, transferability, and convertibility, official statements and intentions regarding convertibility are summarized. This calls for a thorough clarification of the many possible meanings of convertibility and what the PEs may be aiming at, and the advantages and drawbacks they associate with convertibility. The issue of seigniorage is briefly touched upon as a prelude to the evaluation of the possibility of creating a financially convertible CMEA currency. The chapter concludes with an assessment of the direction in which the convertibility policy discussions might move in the medium term.

The widely held conviction that views SEI as distinct from, or even as antipodal to, East–West cooperation in the sense that an intensification of the latter necessarily weakens the former, and vice versa, forms the topic of Part III. Chapter 12 argues with reference to the prevailing growth conditions of the PEs that the possibilities of intensifying SEI with a view to strengthening East–West economic interdependence, and vice versa, should be explored. Greater harmony with better integrated merchandise and financial markets could improve the setting for assessing the limits and opportunities of CMEA collaboration. Chapter 12 spells out that framework, evaluates to what degree the various elements thereof are already operational or can be activated in the near future, and provides some forecasts of the direction of East–West economic cooperation under alternative scenarios of the continuing military, political, and strategic problems besetting the economic interdependence of MEs and PEs.

PART I

THE ENVIRONMENT OF SOCIALIST ECONOMIC INTEGRATION

1

Socialist economic integration in perspective

Close cultural, economic, military, and political ties among the countries of Eastern Europe started in the mid-1940s and have gradually been extended in breadth and in depth. Despite this long experience, it was only in 1971 that the CMEA members approved a comprehensive document on their intentions regarding the road to SEI. To assess SEI, I give a prominent place to the antecedents to this declaration of intent, because the official program itself does not amount to a completely new approach to tackling regional problems. Furthermore, in the fifteen years or so since the program's approval, many changes have occurred in the internal and external environment of the CMEA members. The "spirit" of *Integration Program* may still be alive, but its concrete prescriptions no longer act as the central guideline to SEI processes feasible at this stage.

This chapter draws major inferences for the pursuit of SEI from three aspects of Eastern European economic developments: (1) the circumstances surrounding the creation of the CMEA as the center guiding integration in Eastern Europe; (2) the economic development strategy sought in the various countries and the model instituted to support it; and (3) the Council's institutional setup and the key instruments guiding the integration process. But the broader setting of the evolution of the Council and its policies will be the focal point of attention in Chapter 2. Section 1.1 summarizes the settlements in the economic domain following World War II and the circumstances under which the Council was founded in 1949. The role of economic efficiency in and the contribution of economic policy to the Council's gestation form the subject of Section 1.2. A broad picture of the internal organization and economic policies in the PEs is presented next. Section 1.4 looks at the key features of the economic reforms of the 1960s. This sets the stage of the current environment of the economics of the PEs.

1.1 Origins of Eastern European economic cooperation

Trade and cooperation between the USSR and Eastern Europe in the interwar period remained exceedingly modest. These economies found their external markets primarily in Western Europe rather than within the region. This state of affairs may have stemmed from economic considerations, but the political and strategic determinants were undoubtedly overwhelming. Due to the precarious political, military, and economic situation after World War II, the USSR gained strategic control over Eastern Europe. This was solidified by the Cold War, which was perhaps the main force that eventually molded the region into a close, if not monolithic, political and strategic alliance.

Intraregional cooperation and trade in the interwar period were almost negligible, primarily due to latent or open hostilities among the Eastern European countries and between each of them and the Soviet Union. World economic instability, especially the beggar-thy-neighbor protectionist policies activated in the 1930s, only strengthened each nation's resolve to disregard the potential benefits of creating a regional pool of resources. Disenchantment with the dismal experiences of the recent past and the radical shift in the balance of power in the late 1930s played a critical role in the discussions concerning regional economic, cultural, and political cooperation during and at the conclusion of World War II. Several such cooperation schemes were negotiated, and some were at the point of being introduced. This was particularly the case for the Czechoslovak–Polish cooperation agreement and some of the variants of the Balkan federation plan.

The political turmoil in the immediate postwar period and the open hostility of Stalin and his associates to any kind of regional economic or other union, which eventually could oppose Soviet policy, nullified the chances of implementing the several projects hatched during and after the war. The smaller countries were actively dissuaded from forming any economic alliance among themselves, although the particular economic problems that these cooperation schemes were slated to address initially went unheeded by the USSR.

Today, as in the past, it is well-nigh impossible to pinpoint the exact reasons for the CMEA's creation and the circumstances under which it took place in early 1949. The decision to set up the Council is usually explained as a retaliatory political act, masterminded by Stalin or his associates, rather than as a momentous agreement with far-reaching implications. The end of the 1940s was unquestionably a very turbulent period for a variety of reasons. Chiefly, international efforts to revive the still war-ravaged economies went largely uncoordinated and lacked the essential measure of political reality. Furthermore, the de facto division of Europe was imminent. It resulted from the Cold War, which itself ensued from a combination of basically incompatible political, ideological, and other objectives pertaining to the "most desirable" course of "historical" development.[1]

Political and strategic considerations at the time were certainly the most important preoccupation of most Eastern European leaders. Although by the late 1940s the chances of implementing a continental or Eastern European subregional cooperation plan had become dim, the disappearance of these issues from the debating table did not eliminate the problems that such plans were intended to tackle. In fact, economic realities are treated here as one of the focal points that may help to explain the CMEA's origins. But international tensions, the economic disarray in Europe, and the imminence of a new global conflict were equally important. Let us briefly examine each of these forces.[2] They are not only of interest for their historical perspective. To some extent they are eminently relevant to help explain why the end of World War II as such provided a unique setting for regionwide economic policies. This opportunity was regrettably not grasped with as much determination as, perhaps only with hindsight, would have been desirable.

A wide range of possible motives may have prompted the Eastern European leaders to establish the CMEA in January 1949.[3] There is no uniform opinion on the chief objectives and instruments for enhancing postwar regional economic integration that may then have been contemplated and the reasons for the Council's inertia up to the mid-1950s. In spite of the many studies on the subject, the organization's genuine origins and early activities are still largely shrouded in secrecy. Much of the pertinent factual and conceptual information regarding the start-up of intensive economic cooperation among the PEs continues to be inaccessible. The genuine documents of the period, if the contemporary discussions were recorded at all,[4] are confined to central archives with highly restricted access, possibly because it has been held politic to avoid references to what became a discouraging enterprise.

The evidence that can be assembled tends to indicate that the Council's genuine origins, long-term development objectives, and agreed instruments of cooperation were apparently far more ambitious, complex, and challenging than what the mainstream of professional opinion in East and West alike typically takes for granted. The various authentic and circumstantial pointers drawn mainly from the Eastern European literature enabled me elsewhere (Brabant 1974a, 1979) to underpin five theses. Where references were far more abstruse, they at least permitted me to entertain the notion that the Council had initially been mandated with far more purposeful directives than the commonly accepted record tends to endorse. Indeed, the earliest plans called for action-oriented work in the field of regional economic cooperation. Rather than being created simply to counter or to imitate the propaganda forces that were perceived to be behind the Marshall Plan and the embryonic integration movement in Western Europe, the evidence that can be mustered tentatively suggests that the Council was set up intentionally to perform tasks pertinent to the gradual integration of a strong, solid economic bloc. This conjecture can be strengthened on the basis of evidence that has surfaced more recently, including the disclosure of the pact that the CMEA founders allegedly signed in January 1949.[5]

The motives behind the founding of a common regional organization ostensibly directed at fostering intensive economic cooperation in Eastern Europe are many. The most essential ones can be grouped under four headings: (1) to counter the economic, political, and military ramifications of the Marshall Plan; (2) to conclude the involved debates about subregional federations, confederations, or unions in postwar Eastern Europe; (3) to create an economic arm of the Communist Information Bureau (Cominform) in support of the ideological and political struggle against the West and the Yugoslav dissension; and (4) to provide an effective institutional link to galvanize tight regional relations also in the economic domain, in addition to the already existing ideological, political, and other affinities.

The rationale most frequently cited to elucidate the Council's origins by writers from East and West is the dispute about the Marshall Plan, especially its instrumental role in heightening the incipient Cold War ruffles.[6] Certainly, U.S. postwar foreign policy, which was abetted by most Western European countries, played an overwhelming role in the CMEA's creation in the sense that it challenged the USSR to develop a countermove. Was the American offer to assist European economic recovery simply seized upon as a welcome opportunity to implement the USSR's long-contemplated strategy with respect to the future organization of Eastern Europe? Or was it simply a poker bet calling for a hastily improvised response? These are moot questions, especially because so very little is known about Stalin's real intentions with regard to the future of Eastern Europe. Until genuine documentary material from Eastern European archives becomes accessible, it will unfortunately remain very difficult to draw a comprehensive picture of the USSR's postwar foreign policy designs. Nevertheless, the setting for the widely cited political origins of the CMEA can be summarized as follows.

In the aftermath of World War II, earnest attempts were made to prolong the alliance with the USSR in peacetime. The establishment of the United Nations and the signing of peace treaties were viewed as the necessary preliminaries for cementing more concrete forms of economic and political interdependence. Fundamental disagreements about reparation payments and the administration of the former enemy territories, however, sowed or activated deep-seated distrust among the allies. The American leadership perceived the Soviet Union as bent on thwarting any cooperation program that would subject national policies to any kind of "unilateral foreign influence." Foreign policy deliberations at the time appear to have been polarized by fundamental disagreements about the postwar organization of the world.[7] This was made quite clear in March 1946 in Churchill's famous Fulton address, which had the wholehearted, if tacit, support of President Truman. Although the speech is notoriously famous for its reference to the "descending iron curtain," Winston Churchill also advanced the chilling presumptions of dominance in world affairs by the "English speaking peoples" under the nuclear umbrella that "God had willed to the United States." He then also called for establishing "a unity in Europe from which no nation should be permanently outcast" (*The New York Times,* 6 March 1946, p. 1).

Motivated by communist ideology, the Soviet leaders naturally refused to endorse any collective undertaking that could weaken the USSR's position in Eastern Europe or strengthen Western Europe's capacity to resist communist penetration. The United States was steering exactly the opposite course but with the same goal of securing its own sphere of influence, albeit that this objective was allegedly motivated by concerns about safeguarding its own brand of democracy. Collision was unavoidable if both superpowers held on to their strategies. The proposal to revive all-European economic cooperation buttressed by the infusion of U.S. capital and other aid, under the circumstances, had increasingly become at variance with facts. Although the prospect of Eastern European participation in the European Recovery Program (ERP) was kept alive for a short while by Czechoslovakia, Hungary, Poland, and the Soviet Union, these hesitant signs crystallized briefly as a result of confusing Soviet diplomacy and, in retrospect, were not at all a genuine signal of a promising juncture in the East–West turn of events.

Regardless of the political animosities prevailing at the time or the fundamental responsibility for the rupture of mutual cooperation prospects that ensued in the process, economic reconstruction and recovery in Eastern Europe could have been measurably enhanced by the infusion of foreign economic aid. Eastern European participation in ERP was unquestionably foiled for political reasons. But this did not alleviate the need of these countries for outside assistance.

Second, well before the emergence of the postwar Western European cooperation programs, except the attempts to dovetail the economies of Belgium, Luxemburg, and the Netherlands, some type of subregional federation or economic union had been contemplated as one important vehicle for stimulating economic progress in postwar Eastern Europe and thereby averting a retrogression into the disastrous policies of the interwar period.[8] Although not completely devoid of political and strategic calculation, the immediate objectives of the subregionalization schemes were accelerating economic reconstruction and fostering steady economic growth as viable alternatives to the inward-turned and divisive beggar-thy-neighbor policies of the 1930s. Especially important components of these projects revolved around the encouragement of reciprocal trade and common investment policies with the aim of establishing growth poles around which the region could be more harmoniously interlocked.

None of the contemplated cooperation programs envisaged direct participation of the Soviet Union, perhaps in view of mainly political reasons. But economic interaction with the big neighbor would not be forcefully precluded. Economic realities did not argue in favor of the USSR's direct participation because Eastern Europe's growth rejuvenation efforts, which were largely self-reliant, were not predicated on far-reaching intercourse with the world economy. However, economic arguments carried little weight in big-power politics, and, under the circumstances, Stalin believed there was sufficient reason to squash all further efforts aimed at strengthening subregional cooperation. He is reported to have nurtured a profound distrust of Eastern European intentions, political or otherwise. He apparently feared that if the region were to fuse and bolster mutual cooperation, it might eventually crystallize into an anti-Soviet bulwark – not altogether an unreasonable expectation in view of the confusing wartime and postwar policies of these countries. On the other hand, perhaps the strongest argument in favor of displaying "socialist caesarism" was external: The deteriorating political situation on the continent and the presumed attitude of the United States in postwar negotiations.

Would a regional policy with the Soviet Union as equal partner or even as *primus inter pares* then offer an alternative? Most observers think not on the ground that, as argued by Peter Wiles, the USSR did not favor a regional economic policy that would permit the uninhibited exchange of ideas and traditions throughout the socialist world (Wiles 1968, pp. 311–313). Even if true *in se*, in my opinion, this line of thinking does not offer a convincing explanation of what germinated in late 1948 and early 1949. But it might help to rationalize various other features of Eastern European developments in the early 1950s, especially the region's subjugation to a stereotyped, instead of a creative, application of Soviet experiences. Unfortunately, it cannot clarify why a common organization was established at all, except for propaganda purposes – a rather weak argument.[9]

Third, a panoply of other ideological and political explanations of the Council's gestation has been exhibited in the literature. As an instrument in the diatribes typical of the Cold War, the overt demonstration of alleged unity in the socialist camp by creating an economic equivalent to the Cominform could have been one such motive. Also the sudden political and ideological rift with Yugoslavia could have urged the choice of a course envisaging the tightening up of relations within the rest of the socialist camp, which was apparently an important preoccupation of the early Council deliberations (see Kaplan 1977, 1979). Equally relevant was the need to check and to counter Western foreign policy moves.

On the other hand, whatever the political conditions under which the Eastern European countries were to unfold their postwar identity, the rapidly deteriorating political climate between East and West was very important. Among other implications, this growing discord threatened to undermine the resumption of the prewar pattern of trade and economic relations of the Eastern European countries. Yet, without intensive foreign economic ties these countries could not hope to normalize their economic activity, let alone tackle the basic roots of their underdevelopment. Because Eastern Europe's prewar trade had been cleared largely outside the region, World War II left a political and economic vacuum, which the West could not have immediately filled even if it had wanted to.

Shortly after the conclusion of hostilities, the USSR stepped in to relieve the desperate shortage of food by grain and other loans, and concluded trade agreements for the supply of raw materials and other essential products in exchange for whatever the countries had to offer. Through reparation claims, control over key activities, large-scale dismantling of factories, and BTPAs, the Soviet Union sought to strengthen its preponderance in the area and managed to do so. But these agreements had been concluded largely in response to immediate needs rather than as the beginning of a comprehensive cooperation effort. As internal conditions gradually reverted to normal, especially Czechoslovakia, Hungary, and Poland accelerated their trade with Western Europe. As a result, the USSR's share declined precipitously. Given that trade forms one important component of foreign policy, for the USSR to maintain its privileged position in the area it had to embrace an alternative course very soon. This certainly reinforced the need for changing gears engendered by the ERP and its ramifications, the Yugoslav crisis, and the stillborn subregionalization efforts.

The Soviet Union's first concrete reaction to the Marshall Plan debacle was a hastily improvised series of piecemeal trade and payments protocols, including credit agreements, grants in aid, remission of some reparation claims, and other such activities. This package of measures is sometimes referred to, with some exaggeration, as the Molotov Plan. Because this terminology is by no means standard and, in my view, quite misleading,[10] I shall avoid it here. These various types of economic assistance were certainly quite helpful. But this apparent retort to the Marshall Plan fell far short of the minimum aid required to bolster economic growth in the long run, mainly because the budding antagonisms between East and West were gradually spilling over into other domains. In particular, they had already started to impede buoyant interregional trade. The willy-nilly opposition to the Marshall Plan, the apparent solidarity against the Yugoslav road to socialism, and the region's general support in favor of the Berlin blockade – a most effective "reconnaissance in force" (Medvedev 1972, p. 479) – also strengthened Eastern Europe's isolation. The West imposed its export embargo and cut off capital exports, a policy later formalized with the creation of the Consulting Group's Coordinating Committee for Multinational Export Controls (COCOM). All this must have been particularly damaging to the three Central European countries still relying on extensive trade ties with the West, especially because they were probably viewing these commercial relations as essential building stones in their postwar reconstruction effort.

A reduction of trade below levels necessary to sustain recovery and economic stability could not but exacerbate the tensions already present in the region, which heightened the pressure on the Soviet Union. Under the circumstances, then, it seems logical to expect a program of mutual cooperation to be launched, possibly under the aegis of the Cominform.[11] More plausibly, however, the riposte had to encompass measures beyond those normally within the compass of an interparty agency. As argued by many Eastern European writers, the West's embargo and boycott were instrumental in spurring on the CMEA's creation. Beyond that, however, they are unable to clarify the organization's genesis for no attempt was made subsequently to come to grips with the region's genuine economic problems, apart from the diversion of trade to the USSR and the granting of some additional capital construction loans and recovery assistance.[12]

Fourth, there is little doubt that some Eastern European countries wished to participate in an interlocked regional or supraregional cooperation effort also in view of the prevailing internal economic conditions: Domestic recovery and steady economic growth required economic assistance on a large scale – if not from the West, then from some other source, possibly the USSR, though that country had to tackle a huge recovery problem itself. In addition to the unfavorable external economic environment and the need to reactivate the economies quickly, the magnitude of the region's economic plight should not be understated. It certainly should not be neglected as it has been in most literature about the CMEA's gestation.

Kindled largely by the strident nationalism of the successor states, the lingering disputes about controversies inherited from the past, and widespread irredentism throughout the region, the leaders of Eastern Europe after World War I prevented the implementation of a bold regional economic cooperation effort throughout the interwar period. This lack of cohesion in policy outlook measurably magnified the problems engendered by the abrupt liquidation of natural links with their former hinterlands. Certainly, the level of mutual interaction in economic and financial affairs within the region – not to mention broader

economic and related policies – fell far short of the degree of constructive cooperation needed to surmount the dislocations caused by World
War I, the ensuing divisive "peace settlements," and the sequence of
economic, trade, and financial crises. The depression of the 1930s
proved especially disastrous to the region's viability. In the wake of the
deteriorating East–West climate in the late 1940s, these countries could
hardly have been expected to overcome soon a burdensome level of
agrarian overpopulation, unemployment, and industrial backwardness
without broad regional cooperation.

In view of the postwar fusion of these countries under a single polity,
the region could have been governed from a common center with as
much mobility of capital and labor as the cost of structural redeployment
permitted or defense considerations allowed. In any case, a balanced
forward-looking policy could have exerted a highly positive influence on
the region's growth process. Admittedly, lasting success could have been
reaped only in the medium to long run, owing to the economic backwardness of some members, the general shortage of capital, and the
unavoidable dislocations that a reversal of established trade and financial
links would entail. Under the circumstances, it would therefore have
been logical to foster closer regional economic cooperation within the
parameters of a cohesive development strategy.

The above arguments admittedly fail to solve fully the riddle of why the
CMEA was set up. Certainly, the political motivation inspired by the perceived need to demonstrate, at least for foreign consumption, political and
economic unity under Soviet guidance against the challenges presented by
the Marshall Plan, the Yugoslav dissension, and the more general need for
regimenting and reinforcing regional cohesion was of overwhelming importance. However, exclusive reliance on political and strategic references
is not very helpful in assessing the CMEA's emergence and some of the
concurrent events of 1949–1950. Naturally, the CMEA could have become
an effective riposte to various disquieting international developments only
if the founders had intended to prop up their political commitment with
action-oriented, rather than perfunctory, initiatives, especially in economic
affairs. But failure to do so is not necessarily proof that no such course had
been contemplated in 1948–1949, if perhaps not premeditated several
years earlier.

In the absence of genuine documentary evidence, especially on the
Soviet Union's foreign policy strategies, arguments based on political and
related motives as explanations of why the Council was established at all
seem to suffer from conjecture. Exclusive reliance on them neglects the
crucial reality that the region's "environment" offered few chances for
swift economic growth without some kind of external support. Clearly,
the isolation of the Eastern European polity by its own design, though
bolstered by Western actions that were perceived to be quite hostile,

would seem to strengthen the logic of gradually working out a joint economic policy targeted at correcting the rapidly growing obstacles to interregional trade and improving in depth and in breadth the indigenous conditions for steady growth through industrialization.

1.2 Economic aspects of the inaugural debates

In addition to the economic difficulties engendered by the West's embargo and the harnessing of the region's resources in support of the boycott of Yugoslavia and the defense of socialism, other economic considerations seem to have been instrumental in the CMEA's foundation. The conjecture that the Council was also established in the hope that a comprehensive, purposeful regional economic policy would mature certainly does not represent the traditional view of what may have germinated in 1949–1950. Ironically, it is only in some recent Eastern European reports that a stronger emphasis on the economic aspects of the Council's early activities can be found and that oblique references to the basic continuity underlying the SEI processes are being replaced by more reliable details that fit in quite well with earlier, but highly disparate and incomplete, information.

Various arguments tend to firm up the impression that in 1949–1950 at least some of the Council members were sincerely concerned about promoting economic cohesion in Eastern Europe under the USSR's guidance (Brabant 1974a, pp. 195–205). Far-reaching economic interdependence was to be fostered by elaborating a socialist industrialization strategy patterned after the very important interwar experiences of the USSR. It was clear, however, that the swift inauguration of a harmonious development policy, nationally or on a regionwide scale, would crucially depend on the establishment of institutional links in support of intensive trade and cooperation within the region. Particularly relevant to this discussion was the research on the goals and means of plan coordination, common planning, and new trade and payments instruments tailored to the needs of economic interaction among PEs. The Council's Bureau[13] and various other agencies of the PEs were actively engaged in this search until at least mid-1950. A prominent place among the clear-cut terms of reference under which this staff work proceeded was reserved for finding ways and means to reduce disparities in relative economic scarcities in the region (Ausch 1972, p. 44; Faddeev 1974, pp. 130–1), that is, regional economic integration as commonly understood.

In spite of the complexity of formally inaugurating broad-based regional integration, several Eastern European countries were bent on dovetailing their production, commerce, and investment policies until circumstances forced them to abandon such ambitions. Under impact of the rapidly deteriorating global political and military situation and the lingering convulsions stemming from the struggles for gaining effective and exclusive political control in most of these countries, further work on the integration blueprint was discontinued. In fact, it was replaced largely by national development strategies and the "embassy system" of intensive bilateral cooperation under the direct supervision of the USSR, even in the context of the Council's Bureau and supporting staff.[14] From the evidence assembled to underpin the foregoing conjecture, it would appear that many observers have erroneously equated the post-1950 perfunctory activities in the CMEA until the late 1950s with the motives behind its creation – an unnecessarily misleading generalization.

This conjecture could be strengthened if further details were unearthed about the period debates and research that took place within the CMEA's Bureau and the highest organ, the Council Session. Unfortunately, few hard facts on the matter are available.[15] One exception, however, might be of considerable interest in revisiting the issue – namely, the long-rumored twenty years' economic pact regarding the basic goals and instruments of economic cooperation under the Council's aegis, which was allegedly signed in early 1949.[16] Before looking at the document, however, I shall amplify the relevant background.

When and where the final decision to create the Council was taken has remained enigmatic (as argued in detail in Brabant 1974a, pp. 194–201). Eastern European sources generally content themselves with some variation on "during an economic conference in January 1949,"[17] but confusion continues to be widespread.[18] Comprehensive details about the concrete topics dealt with during that conference, in which mainly economic chiefs of the socialist countries congregated in Moscow from 5–8 January 1949, are not available.[19] The evidence on hand indicates that the conference resolved to embrace economic cooperation through plan coordination and regional planning in which trade and specialization indicators would play an important role. The ultimate objective was to generate fast economic progress within a dovetailed regional economic structure. Normally, such a potentially momentous decision would have been heralded by signing an official document outlining in a comprehensive way the intentions of the participants. Unfortunately, the vaguely worded communiqué of 25 January 1949 is the only official indicator of what was allegedly hammered out in Moscow. It called for "exchanging economic experience, extending technical aid to one another, and rendering mutual assistance with respect to raw materials, foodstuffs, machines, equipment, and so on" (Tokareva 1967, p. 44) under the aegis of the newly established organization. The bold, aggressive nature of the Council as a countervailing force to the Marshall Plan and as an organ designed to obviate as far as possible the economic losses resulting from the West's embargo was explicitly included among the CMEA's tasks.[20]

Although the mystery of the CMEA's creation is far from solved, sev-

eral additional pieces of the highly complex puzzle have become available
in recent years; at any rate, their conjectured shape is less amorphous.
Especially important has been the growing evidence on draft documents
debated in 1948–1950. It now seems beyond doubt that the charter
members did indeed draft documents outlining the Council's organization in preliminary statutes, the tasks of regional economic cooperation,
and instruments to cement economic cooperation to be placed at the
Council's disposal. These background papers were prepared in late 1948
and tabled at the Moscow conference. Unfortunately, only some vague
glimpses of the overall directions of these documents have surfaced.[21]

Nevertheless, the written and other agreements arrived at in 1949
make it incontrovertible that the members then did not seek to confine
the CMEA's vocation simply to the coordination of national economic
plans, as this aspect of the SEI mechanism has since been commonly
understood. Plan coordination was stipulated as the Council's preeminent
task only in 1954. The initial agreements envisaged far more flexible
cooperation by combining comprehensive planning of macroeconomic
aggregates with a host of other, indirect coordination instruments. They
included, in particular, the essentials of a monetary and financial cooperation mechanism appropriate to economic intercourse between sovereign states, as illustrated in Part II. Apparently, the Council's founders
contracted to create the common economic organization initially for a
period of twenty years, starting 18 January 1949 (for details, see Brabant
1979). Without explicit termination notice, the agreement was to be extended automatically for another ten years. The formulation of a common economic plan for the harmonious development of the region as a
whole, including the USSR, was to be the prime task of this new regional
institution. This strategic goal was to entail the creation of broad-based
regional complementarity in economic profiles, planning approaches,
and institutions. To elaborate a realistic economic plan and to enhance its
implementation, the Council was endowed with plenipotentiary powers in
the economic domain. It was to help dovetail the member economies
through the establishment of joint enterprises, particularly to boost the
regional output of fuels, energy, and basic raw materials from newly
discovered deposits so as to accelerate supplies of the crucial inputs for
the region's industrialization. Through joint companies and the coordination of national economic plans, the Council was mandated to foster
standardization and regional complementarities, presumably to capitalize
on economies of scale. Also the exchange of scientific and technical information and the promotion of capital flows, including direct investments,
were to be allotted an active role in bringing about harmonious growth
through swift industrialization. Initially, accommodation would be sought
for whatever goods and services the member countries had to offer to the
rest of the region.

The Council's organization was to consist of a Secretariat General in Moscow endowed with an own fund to the tune of 100 million rubles[22] that was to be contributed by 1 April 1949. Half would be financed by the Soviet Union; the remainder would be contributed in equal shares by the five other founding members (Bulgaria, Czechoslovakia, Hungary, Poland, and Rumania). These subscriptions could be transferred in gold, CC, or rubles (the latter presumably applying only to the Soviet Union). As the executive arm of the Council Session, the Secretariat General was conceived as the organization's highest organ. The Session could be convened whenever necessary, but not less than once a quarter, to ensure smooth progress toward regional integration; any member could request a special convocation if circumstances warranted it. Meetings would be held in rotation in the varous countries to discuss the economic situation of each member and its relationships with the rest of the Council.

Starting in 1950, the national economic development plans of all participants were expected to be drawn up in full conformity with the Council's advice. In the interim and where possible, the members agreed to adapt their plans to regional requirements according to recommendations to be issued by the Secretariat General. This was to apply particularly to investment decisions for which the then operative plans still left some room for maneuver so that reallocations could realistically be undertaken to shorten the transition to a uniform approach to industrialization. Each member obligated itself to cooperate fully with the Council by releasing all relevant information (statistical and otherwise) and documents to facilitate adequate policy initiatives and responses by the Council and the Secretariat General. This information would also be accessible to observers and technicians whom the Council might choose to send on fact-finding missions in any signatory country upon the proposal of the Secretariat General or the Council Session or at the request of the member in question. The Secretariat General would be entitled to take any decision, subject only to ratification by the Council Session at its first subsequent meeting. Each member would in any case have to furnish the Secretariat General with monthly reports disclosing detailed documentary evidence on its economic and financial situation for the preceding month.

The document leaves no doubt about the Council having been conceived as a supranational organ charged with enhancing regional economic interdependence through a common economic plan.[23] Such a plan would be drawn up directly by the Council organs. It would also emerge indirectly through the instructions handed down by the Council Session and its Secretariat General to the national planning offices. The Secretariat General would actually be a regional planning agency with full access to pertinent information and entrusted with broad powers of decision making and control, with such decisions subject only to approval by the formal Council Session.

These powers were to exceed considerably the authority subsequently vested in the national planning agencies. Its stature would probably be enhanced because the relationship between the Secretariat General and the Session could not but differ from that between each national planning agency and its respective government (mainly the CP's Central Committee (CCO) or Politbureau). Or was it assumed that overall decision-making authority would be entrusted to the Soviet Union or the Cominform in order to ensure political supremacy over economic affairs? The Council Session was presumably to chart overall policy for the region and to formulate the key strategic goals of regional integration. The translation of these goals into concrete operative plan targets was to be entrusted in the first instance to the Secretariat General and, in a subordinate capacity particularly as regards concrete production, consumption, and trade details, to the national planning agencies.

The preceding brief summary of the wide-ranging historical events that could have led to the creation of the CMEA admittedly fails to solve fully the riddle of what the Council's original mission and powers exactly were. Certainly, the political motivation to demonstrate unity against Western policies was of overwhelming importance. But the subsequent isolation of the European PEs seems to strengthen the economic arguments for the elaboration of a comprehensive regional economic policy. The notion that economic factors were also instrumental in creating the common organization, or that they were at least sufficiently important to be mentioned alongside political considerations associated with that action, certainly does not reflect the traditional approach in East and West alike. In light of the then prevailing economic situation, one would have expected the Council to preoccupy itself with the construction of a comprehensive regional development program. This could have enabled the member countries to overcome isolationism, economic retardation in various regions, and self-perpetuating low-level development. It is paradoxical that, for all its underlying rationale, the Council then really did not become engaged in constructive practical economic measures from the perspective of the region as a whole. But this negative result was not apparently due to shortcomings in the Council itself.

Soon after the formal announcement on 25 January 1949 that the aforementioned six socialist countries had created a common economic organization, the Council Bureau started work on a grand design for Eastern European economic cooperation. Although many of the details are still inaccessible, informed observers suggest that these preliminary discussions had as objective the establishment of a preferential trade area with, from the present vantage point, moderately liberal capital and labor mobility within an own currency zone, and the free transfer of scientific–technical information. All this would be subordinated to the longer-term strategic aim of joint planning for rapid industrialization.

This interpretation reaches well beyond the official tasks announced in the founding communiqué quoted earlier. Naturally, the essence of the Council's tasks as formulated there is open to almost any interpretation. Indeed, it is no more than an extremely vague declaration of intent, which is so common in most of the bilateral friendship agreements signed by pairs of socialist countries. During the first year, however, the Bureau elaborated concrete proposals on how to advance close cooperation within a protective zone. These blueprints were discussed at the highest policy-making level and reexamined by the bureau. According to a well-informed source, only minor points of dissent remained in late 1949 for enacting a more formal, comprehensive agreement on a preferential trade zone, a common investment fund, and plan coordination. Specialization, multilateralism, and other such institutions, policy instruments, and development goals in support of rapid regional economic development could be envisioned if they were not already in the offing (see Brabant 1974a, pp. 196ff.; but Kaplan 1977 contests this). It was assumed by the Bureau and several Eastern European policy makers that, after redrafting the Bureau's proposals, formal documents could be drawn up sometime in mid-1950.[24] It was then decided rather suddenly – allegedly at the behest of Stalin personally – to cancel further negotiations on the redrafted project, to focus the members' policies on strictly domestic development concerns, to seek economic self-sufficiency by embracing the concept of all-round national economic development, and to bind the countries together with detailed BTPAs.

Because of the relatively small size of the individual markets and the inadequate domestic reserves of many fuels and industrial raw materials, regional cooperation was still sought in the context of the CMEA, but on a plane that diverged radically from what would have come to the fore under a regional development program. Rather than seeking multilateral cooperation within a preferential zone, the PEs retrenched to a tightly knit network of BTPAs under the direct supervision of the USSR, which was also to provide the focal axis of all these agreements. Naturally, this unexpected decision had profound implications for domestic economic policies, to which I now turn.

1.3 Internal economic organization and policies

Although the typical features of the PEs as they evolved after the war would probably have emerged even if a regional development strategy had been adopted, the latter's absence has had momentous implications for domestic policies. Because a regional approach was shunned in favor of a highly paternalistically supervised development path patterned after the experiences of the *primus inter pares* of the CMEA community, the PEs embraced a peculiar development strategy and underpinned it with the

policy instruments and institutions typical of CPEs. The most important
elements of much a strategy and economic model help to clarify the
background for later chapters, and hence a brief discussion of them here
may be useful.

Planned economies are distinguished from MEs chiefly by the implications of the political, social, and ideological doctrines and convictions of
their leadership. A specifically socialist economic model and an interesting long-term development strategy gradually emerged in the first set of
countries. In some respects, both were causally related to the failure to
opt for regional economic cooperation. Owing to the absence of an operational integration strategy, both features have continued to be molded
chiefly on the strength of domestic considerations. Although minor variations in the strategy and model in the several PEs should not be ignored,
the characteristic common elements are so important to an understanding of the conditions for SEI that I shall largely abstract from country
detail.

The first strategy of socialist economic development

A growth strategy is a complex of measures to ensure resource allocation
with a view to attaining one or more long-term development objectives.
Excepting the immediate postwar period, when most energy and time
were devoted to reconstruction and the consolidation of socialist supremacy, the socialist development strategy had as central aim the industrialization of backward, mostly agrarian economies. This objective was to be
implemented by manipulating key policy instruments, by transforming
the economic institutions, and by prescribing some behavioral rules that
together make up the model. Eastern European development processes
in the 1950s and early 1960s were overwhelmingly anchored to an economic policy of forced industrialization. This played a crucial role, even
to such an extent that decision making about the overall allocation of
resources was almost exclusively centered on the priority role of industry,
on whose advancement all economies were bent.

Socialist economic development has as its prime objective the elaboration of a more or less autarkic economic complex. Autarky here is not
synonymous with complete severance of all foreign contacts, although at
one time a narrowly defined economic self-sufficiency was certainly an
integral concern in the socialist concept of how best to allocate scarce
resources. The creation of a well-balanced, diversified industrialized
economy that can function relatively independently of foreign fluctuations and other disturbances propagated from abroad is predicated on
the establishment of *the* economic complex, which becomes the key focus
of economic policy. The strategy adopted by Soviet policy makers in the

1930s was for a long time the accepted example of how to achieve that goal. It was transplanted into Eastern Europe because it suited immediate Soviet interests and also because the chief mentor of economic policy in postwar Eastern Europe could not quickly adapt its own experiences and interests, which emanated less from ideology than from historical trial and error, to conditions that diverged substantially from those in the USSR. The practical implication of this stance was that even countries such as Czechoslovakia and the GDR, where the industrial sector in the presocialist period was already well entrenched, were required to transform their capacities so as to anchor industry to a strong metallurgical sector, which functions as a motor generating high growth rates elsewhere in the economy.

Socialist economic organization and strategic planning of the entire economy were first initiated in the Soviet Union when political expediency and ideological convictions took ascendency over the semifeudal Russian society in 1917. Lacking firm guidance from the Marxian classics or from experience, the planners had to fill an enormous theoretical and practical vacuum. The issues they had to come to grips with after the revolution surfaced again in the Eastern European countries, owing to their palpable differences in size, resource base, level of development, and so on. Although socialist economics was essentially of an empiricist character, despite the dogmatic rationalization of practical affairs in theoretical discourses, it was slow in adjusting itself to the actual requirements of the *Praxis*. This was so in part because the Marxian doctrines were congenial both to this way of thinking and to the theoretical validation of empirical matters.

The intellectual foundations of the socialist development strategy can be outlined in terms of three basic Marxist–Leninist "laws" of or propositions on economic development: (1) the eschatological goal of historical development, (2) the material–technical foundations thereof, and (3) the means gradually to solidify these foundations. These laws can be briefly put as follows (see Brabant 1980, pp. 63–9 for details).

First, the ultimate objective of a socialist economy is the realization of the so-called communist welfare state, a society in which every person is rewarded according to need and contributes according to ability. To make this objective of the dynamism of a socialist society feasible, even if only in a remote future, socialist planners feel impelled to aim at a high growth rate of material output and a diverse selection of products so as to firm the material and technical prerequisites of communism. Second, to embark on such a growth path, socialist managers must adhere to the "law of planned proportional development." To steer a smooth course toward the ultimate development goal, they must guide and control economic activity through strict central planning. The socialist doctrine of proportional development cannot be equated with balanced growth but must be viewed in the context of "disharmonious" development (Kornai 1971, 1972). The inherited economic structures first require an unbalanced economic policy to set the economy on the desired growth path. These consciously induced disequilibria create bottlenecks, whose elimination serves to sustain the next growth phase. Third, and especially important in this connection, is the so-called law of faster growth in the sector of producer goods and, within this first department of the Marxian reproduction scheme, the more rapid growth in the subdivision capital goods for the reproduction of capital goods.

Although these development principles are only a rationalization or justification of pragmatic choices, they in themselves suggest some important implications of economic policies, even aside from those associated with the dogmatization of the Soviet experiences of the 1930s. The growth strategy focuses on the most important links in the development process of backward economies. Under these circumstances, the strategic choices could be confined to a narrow range of priority processes and products: fuels, metals, basic machinery, and essentials for human consumption. The planning regime would support this makeup. In other words, by far the larger share of available investment funds is invariably channeled into extending industry in breadth, not in depth. In the immediate postwar years, this strategic decision was understood to imply that each socialist country should strive for a relatively self-sufficient economy, where growth is attained primarily as a result of the mobilization of capital and labor resources for creating new structures, especially to generate a modern manufacturing sector. Although each such venture is designed to be of the highest technical standards, it is normally not updated on a regular basis. Efficiency considerations as such were not very important in determining the economic structure of the typical CPE.

In retrospect, a pivotal place in the socialist growth strategy is reserved for amassing production factors in priority sectors and appropriating most of the current "surplus value" not for present consumption but for the financing of the expansion of selected production sectors at the expense of agriculture and services in particular. This strategy also implied that consumption levels not be raised by as much as productivity gains could have warranted. In fact, levels of living of the population could even decline for a few years, as evinced during the early stages of the industrialization drive in virtually all PEs. This attitude was reinforced by the model, which was to support the growth strategy.

The traditional economic model

A growth strategy must be buttressed by an appropriate economic model, which is a combination of institutions, behavioral rules, and policy instruments that help to implement planned economic development with a strong emphasis on forced industrialization. The prescriptions regarding behavior are, by definition, normative and are sanctioned as such. Just as the strategy adopted by the socialist economies can be explained in terms of Soviet aims during the 1930s, the same is true of the economic model, although the development experiences and the factor endowments to accelerate growth in these countries were very different and generally did not at all compare favorably with the USSR's. It is this particular set of model features that makes for a typical CPE.

The following eight characteristics of socialist policies are the most important components of the model of a traditional CPE: (1) central planning of nearly all economic activities; (2) virtually exhaustive nationalization of all production factors, including capital, natural resources, and, in some countries, land, with strict controls over the regulation of labor; (3) collectivization of agriculture; (4) subordination of fiscal, income, price, and monetary policies to the realization of the physical objectives of economic growth; (5) the need for informal initiative at all levels of production and consumption; (6) bureaucratization of production and consumption; (7) the transformation of the CP into an instrument to support the economic and other goals of the socialist society; and (8) rather rigid insulation of internal and external economic activities. To explain monetary cooperation in the CMEA in its proper setting, it will be useful to examine somewhat more closely some of these organizational features.[25]

a. Central planning. Planning means setting development targets and allocating resources to fulfill those aims as well as possible. The means used for allocating resources to priority sectors and the determination of the development preferences can be taken as substantial pointers in distinguishing among various planning systems. In a traditional PE, the planning instruments and objectives are determined by a select circle of party members, especially the Politbureau, on behalf of the CP as the vanguard of society. Resources are essentially allocated by central fiat. The plan endeavors to formulate instructions that leave no alternative to their execution with the objective of ensuring a close association and a particular interrelationship between political and economic functions. Whether such quantitative targeting was deliberately designed to coax economic agents rather than to command them, as argued in Bonin 1977, is a moot point. The issue is that questions concerning what is to be produced, how production is to be organized, what inputs are to be used, and so on, are, in principle, settled by the norms specified in the plan and not by the foresight, risk taking, and creative innovation of an entrepreneurial elite. Moreover, the latter's initiative and leadership, if present, are not to impinge on the priority of physical yardsticks.

The real world of production and consumption differs substantially from this ideal, however. For one, conscious human activities cannot be reduced to the simple act of pulling a lever. The plan has to reserve some scope for entrepreneurial decision making because the planning center cannot possibly cope with all details of the appropriate functioning of an increasingly complex economy. Uncertainty also is bound to arise from difficulties inherent in forecasting accurately all the complex relationships of an economy. In addition, activities in such sectors as agriculture and international trade are essentially unpredictable because the specification of some of their parameters depends on events that are largely outside the scope of the information at the disposal of central planners and, moreover, beyond their control. This uncertainty has to be resolved eventually either by introducing a flexible type of planning (such as continuous planning) or, more likely, by ad hoc solutions contrived by the ultimate economic agents.

Because the lower tiers of the planning hierarchy, including the final producer and consumer, may harbor other preferences (such as private income considerations or the promotion of local activities) than those of the central policy makers, their decision-making sphere coincides with the center's only by fluke. As a rule, therefore, the plan eventually has to be supplemented with proper criteria for guiding the decisions of economic agents as producers and consumers.

b. Efficiency considerations. The Soviet theory of central planning – and hence the leading thought behind the economic policy and organization in the other PEs – crystallized as one resting on quantity calculations, as distinct from value planning. Ideological precepts may have contributed to this choice. However, three crucial circumstances advocating the phrasing of central planning in terms of physical and dynamic results rather than in value terms may have been prevalent.

First, centralized control and guidance of the economy were embraced to support the forcible transformation of an agrarian economy into a diversified industrial society. If growth per se is the objective, it does not matter much which particular sectors are selected for growth. The pursuit of a fleshed-out, preconceived development strategy may merit the suspension or significant modification of market signals.[26] Second, since the socialist strategy and economic model were introduced without taking due account of each country's specific factors of time and place, real scarcity indicators would probably have failed to further the central objectives. Instruments of indirect economic coordination that may ensure static efficiency are too inflexible to facilitate the drastic changes necessary to bridge the gap between the presocialist and the industrial society. Finally, the introduction of central planning followed closely on radical transitions in political and economic power. Given the severe shortage of entrepreneurial talent in backward economies and the fact that economic responsibilities often reverted to people who were hardly familiar with the complexity of economic administration, it may have been desirable to allot only the narrowest degree of freedom to individual production units. This could not fully preclude "local initiatives" – at times with disastrous results.[27]

c. Market-type instruments and institutions. From the beginning of socialist economic organization, it has been accepted as axiomatic that socialism implies (1) the effective control of the economy, in particular of productive resources, by society in pursuance of its objectives by appropriate institutions, and (2) the planned steering by the state of the course of economic life. Without this being necessarily well articulated, the accepted premise of traditional planning has been that tools of indirect regulation are not dependable. Resource allocation in a CPE therefore proceeds to a significant degree other than by "price" signals. These measures are sometimes concealed, as illustrated by the open or discreet involvement of the political leadership in the selection of priority targets, the allocation of cheap but rationed credit and critical primary inputs, and the regional allocation of resources.

Socialist price policies are a case in point of the subordination of value criteria to physical targets. Prices are traditionally calculated by the center on the basis of average sectoral cost without making due allowance for capital and land scarcities. They are generally held unchanged for long periods. The deliberate choice to underplay value planning through the price mechanism was carried over to nearly all familiar instruments and institutions of economic policy in MEs. In fact, the organization of the economy and economic policy were simply to enhance the realization of priority goals expressed mostly in physical terms. Other policy instruments were not to interfere with the plan execution, although they did to some extent.

The CPE's fiscal policy is almost exclusively concerned with indirect taxation (that is, turnover taxes) to ensure some sort of equilibrium between demand and supply of consumer goods. Based overwhelmingly on the real bills doctrine, monetary policy has, at best, been passive. Credit policy is geared toward facilitating interenterprise transactions. Capital investments, usually financed through the budget, are undertaken without much regard for macroeconomic efficiency, and no scarcity levies are applied. The credit institutions are expected simply to finance the investment targets set by the center, regardless of how they are selected. A more active monetary policy to equate income with the planned value of the amount of consumer goods to be marketed is sporadically instituted to counter dangerous open or repressed inflation.

d. Foreign trade and cooperation. An integral element of the CPE model is the more or less complete disjunction of the domestic economy from external influences, especially in the microeconomic sphere. This choice might have been variously inspired by the fact that an ambitious growth path must be trodden without taking into account all relevant internal and external market conditions; policy makers do not use sophisticated plan techniques and instruments to guide and control plan execution by indirect means; and growth targets are not selected on the basis of real opportunities. For economies that cannot be autarkic because of size or resource endowments or both, severing domestic decision making from world market criteria has had several important drawbacks.

The selection of institutions and mechanisms for conducting trade was a direct consequence of the failure to adopt a regional economic policy in the late 1940s. Instead of anchoring economic development to an internally consistent, comprehensive regional program, each PE sought to isolate its national economy from the rest of the world, thereby protecting itself against foreign events and reducing the interaction with other economies – including other PEs – to the minimum still compatible with rapid industrialization. A state monopoly of foreign trade and payments (MFT) was expressly instituted to neutralize all influences from abroad, whether positive or disruptive.

Trade decisions in the CPE usually result from a combination of economic and other factors. The planning of the level and composition of trade, as of other economic activities, was largely intermeshed with the overall system of material balances. The question of whether to import or to produce domestically was usually answered by considering the domestic availability of inputs and the necessity to pay for imports. In any case, the central planner exhibits only a marginal interest in reaping the potential benefits of export-led growth or in minimizing the real economic cost of the preferred import substitution. The technique of material balances might be highly useful in ensuring that physical demand and supply in the economy even out. But it is hardly conducive to the exploitation of trade opportunities.

Trade is, by definition, a sector that eludes the complete control of one planning center and that can hardly be managed in quantitative terms only. To gain greater stability in domestic economic activity, the CPEs nevertheless also tried to forecast trade flows as accurately as possible. But not all activities and fluctuations abroad are predictable. Born out of necessity in the immediate postwar economic, political, and strategic situation, detailed ex ante BTPAs at relatively stable, if artificial, prices suited the administrative planning system fairly well. Furthermore, it facilitated the implementation of the political aspirations of some of the countries that would have been much more chancy in a multilateral trade network, even one set by comprehensive multilateral trade and payments agreements (MTPAs).

To the extent that trade cannot be forgone, the CPEs insulate domestic processes from direct interaction with agents abroad. They attempt to minimize indirect influences as well. Actual trade events can impact on the domestic economy, but usually not through price pressures, because domestic prices are set autonomously. The nominal gains and losses from trade are simply absorbed by fiscal means. But there are macroeconomic impacts. A disturbance from planned import cost and export return, if accommodated, affects the disposable budget, and ultimately consumer income, as well as the foreign exchange situation (see Chapter 3). Planners attempt to neutralize the impact of this perturbation by sterilizing trade results. Alternatively, they offset trade gains or losses through the variation of other budgetary expenditures and adjust the next plan accordingly. But this indirect influence did not play an overriding role in decision making, because the bulk of trade was, in any case, regulated within the confines of comprehensive BTPAs associated with rather autonomous prices.

A crucial implication of this trade model has been that macroeconomic decision makers have been unaware of the real economic cost of their import-substitution policies. From the planner's point of view, this did not matter much so long as autarky reigned supreme. But once a more active trade policy was to be explored, the existing trade model proved to be a formidable obstacle. There is a microeconomic equivalent to the lack of interest in trade results per se by central decision makers: Economic agents did not really know about the true scarcity cost of availabilities and requirements of world markets. Other features of the trade model and their repercussions will be introduced when needed.

1.4 Economic reforms of the 1960s and their legacies

It is in the nature of the principles of full control over productive resources and the planned steering of the economy that one can try to isolate the evolvement of central planning. For over a quarter century, the steady transformation of socioeconomic processes by the early emphasis on forced industrialization has been invalidating the simplifying assumptions of the methodology of physical planning and running the PE. This has led to an increasingly acute need for more refined techniques, more powerful policy tools, and a more dispassionate, economic approach to policy making. Considering the priority attached to industrialization so as to create a diversified economy, one should not be surprised to learn that most efforts designed to improve economic performance have fallen into two categories. Planners have searched for the nonessential elements of the growth strategy, particularly regarding the antitrade bias. They have also sought to define more precisely and with greater discrimination which elements of the model are really necessary to support the salient objectives of the socialist society. In this connection, it is of some importance to recall a truism: just as there might be more than one model to support the development strategy, several strategies might have been sustained by the centralized model. Each combination has its particular advantages and drawbacks. So when seeking to adapt the strategy and the model because they no longer fully satisfy policy makers, it is essential to separate as far as possible their necessary elements from their incidental.

Backdrop to the reforms

As the development record of the past thirty years or so suggests, the Eastern European industrialization strategy has been suitable for radically restructuring a relatively backward society into a moderately sophisticated economy, albeit at a considerable real cost. The same applies to the traditional model. A tightly centralized organization might have been the only platform that could support a fast transition of economic structures. The turbulent times, inexperienced management, a largely unskilled labor force, backward ways of thinking, unproductive economic relations, and other factors could well have prompted the adopted course of industrialization under strictly centralized control. Once these conditions fade away as a result of historical, social, economic, and political changes, however, the justification for maintaining these more incidental features of socialism becomes less and less persuasive.

There is little doubt that, over the years, socialist policy makers have been won over to the conviction that an extensive growth pattern is not an essential ingredient of economic development. The shift in strategy stressing productivity gains rather than the steady expansion of the supply of primary and intermediate inputs arose, in particular, from the growing labor shortage, which has become rather acute. The tightening of this constraint on development is conventionally taken to mark the end of the era in which the PE can raise industrial output simply by building new factories, expanding old ones, and pouring vast numbers of new workers into manufacturing. Since the early 1960s, there has been a rather steady, perhaps secular, decline in Eastern Europe's economic performance, despite the fact that accumulation (that is, net capital formation and inventory changes) was kept at high levels until the late 1970s or even the early 1980s in most countries. Furthermore, policy makers have gradually become aware that central planning of a complex economy inhibits technical progress.

The reasons for focusing policy more on intensive growth are complex. But a conceptual distinction might be drawn between the causes inherent in the strategy and those that can be ascribed to the model. With respect to the strategy, a dissipation of scarce resources over many sectors is not an immanent feature of socialist development, particularly in relatively small economies. Instead of fostering extensive growth, policy makers have tried to encourage "intensive" economic expansion by various means. Though these policy initiatives differ considerably from country to country, as a rule the political priorities of the central planners have become more realistic than they were in the 1950s, aimed as they are at achieving a more balanced and outward-looking economy.

Questions concerning the economic efficiency of autarkic development, rather than growth per se, gradually emerged as a focal point of economic and political investigation in the mid-1950s, when the smaller PEs slowly acquired a measure of sovereignty in economic affairs. These concerns culminated in the early 1960s in what became known as the era of economic reforms, which stressed the opening up of these economies by intensifying trade. Countries bent primarily on mobilizing domestic resources for maximum output growth frown upon the regional and interregional distribution of value added that might be entailed by the lack of adequate scarcity indicators. Trade efficiency and foreign economic cooperation therefore became the primary stimulus to a revision of economic policies and institutions.

Principal ingredients of the reforms

The economic reforms[28] of the 1960s incorporated numerous changes, which can be divided into three groups according to their most important impacts: changes in the organization of the economy, wider use of indirect coordination instruments, and shifts in trade policy.

a. The organization of the economy. Even if the model and strategy of development had been appropriate at the time of their inception, revisions should have been enacted at comparatively brief intervals to stay abreast of domestic and foreign developments. One key instance is the growing complexity of detailed physical planning for a fast-maturing economy and considerable shifts in the external environment. It bears stressing also that centralized physical planning is not really an indispensable element of what is needed to support the development strategy. Reforms in this context therefore focused on a more practical division of administrative and economic duties between the central and local tiers. Changes were sought so as to activate an enterprise policy that could facilitate "local" decision making by means of cost-benefit analyses and in recognition of market preferences, especially with regard to trade and cooperation.

With respect to the administration of the economy, one could observe a movement toward deconcentration as well as concentration of economic power. Almost without exception, enterprises were absorbed in or brought under the authority of much larger economic associations. Deconcentration emerged in the sense that ministries or central administrators no longer vied to determine enterprise policy unilaterally. The associations were invested with the responsibility of guarding the "social" interests of the firm, and the separate units obtained greater latitude in the formulation of an appropriate enterprise policy. The latter's goal was not only to reach the centrally prescribed targets but also to work out at the lower planning levels some of the norms previously dictated by fiat from above.

The logical outcome of the most determined reform would have been to invest central planning with the authority to guide and control microeconomic decision making. Enterprise activity would proceed essentially on the basis of indirect coordination instruments within the framework of medium- to long-term development goals set within the context of aggregate socioeconomic priorities. Detailed prescriptions of how much of what the individual enterprise should produce with given resources were to be suppressed and replaced by genuine enterprise decisions. The latter were to be guided by qualitative and quantitative macroeconomic policies so that the center could ensure that the gap between the precepts underlying the central plan and the motivation of agents entrusted with day-to-day local planning and decision making would not become forbidding. By disengaging itself from some of the detailed chores of instructing production units, the central planning board was henceforth expected to evolve a better selection of strategic decisions on the future of the socialist economy.

b. The role and scope of coordination instruments. When economic decisions are no longer the exclusive prerogative of central planners, coordination between the center and local executors becomes much more urgent and complicated compared to when it was chiefly a matter of dovetailing physical yardsticks. One of the key elements here is the improvement of relative prices, which has been envisaged since the mid-1960s. But a price overhaul is by no means the exclusive focus of the coordination instruments to be adjusted. Extensive use of selective price, fiscal, credit, and income policies that aim at inducing enterprises and households to act in accordance with overall plan objectives was to be fostered too. But authorities cling to direct control over a number of key economic processes.

For example, credit and interest rate policies were then intended to guide the allocation of capital funds. Instead of gratis budgetary appropriations, a greater role was to be reserved for banks, where individual enterprises could procure loans to finance nonessential improvements in their production capacities and where consumers could obtain temporarily the means to purchase durable goods. Bank financing is closely supervised by the central authorities, however. The interest rate policy associated with this devolvement of financial policies was to guarantee greater economic rationality in the allocation of investment funds. Key investment decisions, such as the establishment of new factories and their financing, were to remain an exclusive prerogative of the central authorities as none of the reforms envisioned the creation of autonomous financial markets in which local agents could decide about the mobilization of voluntary savings.

Enterprises obtained more authority, though by no means the exclusive right, to determine premiums, basic salary scales, the hiring and firing of personnel, and so on, to foster productivity. Exclusive authority could not be delegated to the production units because the objective of full employment, combined with other more social aims of socialism, remained vital elements of overall policies. Instead of many detailed prescriptions with regard to employment and wages, a trend emerged to confine control to a few norms and indirect regulators.

In the traditional CPE, the enterprise could control profits only by reducing nominal production costs below the planned level, provided entrepreneurial decision makers behaved as postulated by the center. With the advent of the reforms, enterprises were entitled to influence costs directly through a more careful selection of inputs and suppliers, by producing according to market demand, and, in some cases, by using their authority over price formation. Profits were to become more meaningful than they had been in the orthodox CPE and were expected to play an important role in the determination of premiums and social advantages to the workers, in providing the means for self-financing, and in guiding enterprise behavior more generally.

c. Foreign trade and economic cooperation. Transitions in the conception of the role of trade in economic development and in the authority of some microeconomic units to trade relatively independently are perhaps the most important points to be retained when recalling the economic reforms. The reforms sought to endorse trade as a crucial activity in propping up domestic growth. At the same time, trade operations were to be managed and coordinated with domestic decision making. The attention that the reforms devoted to trade and foreign cooperation may be underscored by the fact that, since the early 1970s, the processes of gradual change in enterprise organization and in the methods of planning and control have continued in the foreign trade sector, in marked contrast to the reform measures affecting most other sectors of the economy. Reforms in most nontrade sectors were reversed and most of them were eventually abrogated altogether in all but Hungary.

As noted, the determination of the volume, direction, and composition of trade by means of material balances yields nonoptimal economic results and may therefore be unsatisfactory. Even though trade is confined to acquiring noncompeting imports with little regard for the true cost, the central planner can still choose among alternative combinations of exports that have distinctly different results in terms of trade efficiency. Alternatively, at given exports several different import packages can be procured. The more autarky and domestic industrialization as the overriding objectives of economic development recede into the background, the more the central planner is compelled to face up to multiple opportunities in both the domestic and foreign trade sectors. In reaction, the CPEs began to explore various ways to stimulate more efficient trade relations without, however, completely abandoning their autonomous economic policies.

Because the level and composition of imports are largely determined by the economic strategy pursued, research in the CPEs was concerned primarily with export efficiency. Note, however, that the more general problem of how to minimize the domestic and foreign cost of exports for a given import bill cannot be solved unambiguously. This is especially so because prices based on average production costs do not really express true scarcity relationships, and may therefore be quite misleading if used in determining the composition of exports. Furthermore, the CPEs are not completely free to select the trade channels that afford minimum import costs at maximum export returns. Some reasons are the following: their bilateral trade policies, their specific preferences for domestic industrialization and development, the inconvertibility of their currencies, nonscarcity prices in intra-CMEA trade, and the fiat type of clearing imports and exports in CMEA markets. Precisely because of their dependence on the regional market, a more trade-intensive growth strategy might mature only if the CMEA partners are able to accommodate such shifts or if outside channels can be explored more intensively. Because the latter course was not considered advantageous in view of the Cold War and Soviet predilections regarding regional cohesion, since the mid-1950s there has emerged a much more positive attitude toward regional economic cooperation.

In the process of encouraging greater efficiency in trade, Eastern European economists have devised an apparently inexhaustible variety of partial and global indices relating, some quite ingeniously if extremely laboriously, a variant of approximate real internal costs to returns in foreign currency.[29] Although it is questionable whether these experiments have played a significant role in choosing development targets, policy makers have doubtless been concerned with the problem, and some of these efficiency criteria have been instrumental in solving partial problems of economic structure (such as within branches of industry) and in the formulation of trade decisions left at the discretion of foreign trade organizations (FTOs). Trade efficiency considerations have given helpful guidelines in deliberations on regional specialization agreements, especially since the late 1960s. But their actual role in selecting specialization projects remains enigmatic.

The previous sharp separation of the trade sector from producers and users became increasingly more difficult to justify in view of the necessity in most countries to give highest priority to the expansion of commerce in manufactured products. The prolongation of the practically complete disjunction between trade and production also became more and more wasteful with the greater dependence on trade. In consequence, there was a general trend toward reinforcing the organizational links between trade and production and strengthening the role of trade prices in domestic price reforms and, in some cases, actual price formation.

Types of foreign trade reforms

It is useful to distinguish between partial and comprehensive reforms. The latter were envisioned only in Hungary's new economic mechanism (NEM), in the aborted 1968 Czechoslovak model, and in the Polish strategy initiated under Edward Gierek. Reforms comprise changes in prices, ERs or conversion coefficients, trade norms, or the authority to trade. These measures are loosely connected in the partial reforms, which amount to an administrative streamlining. But in the comprehensive reform, such as in the NEM, all innovations in the trade sector are interlinked not only with each other but also with changes in other sectors and, hopefully, in time as well.

a. Price and exchange rate reforms. Forging a meaningful link between domestic and foreign prices represents one of the crucial steps in price reform and the foreign trade system. The CPE's ER is set arbitrarily and has virtually no real influence except in the sphere of direct spending by nonresidents. The reforms so far have not affected the official ER, although in some PEs it continues to exist only in law (see Chapter 6). Instead, conversion coefficients, "shadow ERs," or so-called commercial ERs have been established. In partial reforms, the field of application of these coefficients was much narrower than in the more comprehensive reforms. In the former, trade results were allowed to influence major decisions at the enterprise level. But a meaningful use of these coefficients is contingent on a more comprehensive price reform with the goal of harmonizing domestic prices with real costs, including export returns and import costs, and with foreign prices at least to some extent. These changes were sought more intensively in Czechoslovakia, the GDR, Hungary, and Poland than they were in other CPEs.

b Planning reforms. As noted, all reforms aimed at reducing the number of physical norms imposed by the central plan and at establishing direct contact between domestic and foreign markets. Despite this, material balancing and central supply allocation of key materials remained essentially intact in all but Czechoslovakia, Hungary, and Poland. But the gradual elimination of the nearly complete separation of foreign trade and internal decision making was of prime concern, even in the USSR. The only noticeable influence that has endured is the administrative linkup of trade with production or user. Foreign trade specialists in the ministries, branch units, or the enterprises have played a major role in drawing up the plans and in providing efficiency calculations for trade processes. One evident change has been fewer material balances in physical units, which directly affect the plans of the trade enterprises. Although in many countries, the results of FTOs have been evaluated in foreign exchange equivalents, it is not yet common practice to pass on fully the real results of trade to the domestic market. Nor do these modifications signal that the trader can freely select partners or tradables. Trade plans, however aggregated, continue to be assigned subject to limitations on the commodity composition and the geographical distribution of trade. In some PEs, these restrictions are imposed by administrative fiat, whereas in others instruments of indirect coordination combined with tacit adherence to administrative instructions have been given greater scope.

c. The authority to trade. One of the first steps in changing the institutional functioning of the MFT was taken in the 1950s, when direct trading rights were granted to selected industrial firms or associations. Czechoslovakia, the GDR, and Hungary were pioneers in this field. One of the most notable legacies of the reforms of the 1960s has been the decentralization of trade tasks: The number of enterprises permitted to engage directly in trade sharply increased, although with substantial differences from country to country. But nowhere has the MFT as such been eliminated, nor have overall controls been relaxed much, not even under the NEM, at least until the late 1970s. Instead, the reforms were primarily designed to strengthen the MFT, particularly as far as the control over trade and payments and the implementation of the overall plan are concerned. As a result, the competence of the MFT has remained as comprehensive, if not as detailed, as in the orthodox CPE. Enterprises are subordinated to the ministry, which can issue compulsory plan targets, but these are usually rather elastic and allow the FTOs a certain margin for thoughtful action. The ministry of foreign trade draws up the plan, is entitled to issue legally binding regulations, and grants permits or licenses for enterprises to trade. It can also issue directives on what must be traded, especially with other PEs, and on the extent to which the trade results can influence the internal market.

d. Cooperation and joint ventures. Trade and more general economic cooperation between East and West were allotted a prominent role in the reforms. Several countries instituted the legal framework for creating joint ventures by which they hoped to acquire not only foreign capital but also the know-how and technology to gain greater flexibility in trade and payments with MEs. Some CPEs adapted their legal framework in matters of foreign property, the transfer abroad of earnings, the amortization of investments, the residence of foreigners, and so on. Moreover, all entered into major cooperation agreements with Western firms, although the macroeconomic results to date have been disappointing.

Cooperation between two or more enterprises belonging to at least two PEs has been in the forefront of the discussions about the ways and means of SEI since the late 1960s. As to concrete results in terms of common enterprises and cooperation schemes actually in operation, it is difficult to come to an objective conclusion that is not a platitude. The least that can be said is that the PEs seem to be sincerely concerned with exploiting various types of interenterprise cooperation other than direct trade, including joint ventures. These are viewed chiefly as a complement to, but not as a substitute for, the traditional exchange of commodities (see Chapter 2).

1.5 Evolving toward a modified planned economy

The evolution of the CPEs during the economic reforms of the 1960s and since then as a result of more piecemeal shifts, except in Hungary, resulted in considerable differentiation in Eastern Europe. This has been particularly true so far as individual components of the economic model are concerned. But since the mid-1970s, it applies also to strategic choices. It is therefore no longer adequate to speak only of CPEs. Some countries, including Hungary, in many respects hardly behave like a traditional CPE, yet they retain important institutional and other features of that entity. Policies in such a changed environment are phrased differently than in a typical CPE. To place the following commentary in a proper setting, it is important to have a reference point to a stylized version not only of the traditional CPE, but also to one that has moved away from it in several important respects. The MPE has the following crucial characteristics.[30]

First, the central planning authorities focus on the main components of short- and medium-term economic activity of enterprises and devote particular attention to the comprehensive structure of the economy in the long run. The center continues to be involved in great detail with nonproductive activities, such as infrastructural investments and social services. Most producing enterprises no longer prepare detailed input and output plans in close consultation with the central authorities, if not on their explicit instruction. They are expected to formulate their own enterprise policy within a set of mostly macroeconomic constraints.

Second, although enterprises may decide to draft their own plans, central authorities discourage the use of quantitative success criteria for evaluating enterprise performance. Indeed, some measure of qualitative performance related to enterprise profits is likely to be endorsed, even though profit as a maximand is severely constrained within the consensus imposed by the chief "societal constituents" of the enterprise.

A third feature derives naturally from the preceding two: the creation of some interenterprise market as a major determinant of resource allocation. This market operates in some cases with flexible prices, as in an ME. But decisions are often formulated not only on the basis of prices but also as a function of other "bargaining" instruments. As a result, the profitability criterion, increased enterprise initiative, and greater scope for market forces are inextricably interconnected.

Fourth, instead of the center prescribing wage norms and the overall wage fund as a function of planned increases in employment, labor productivity, and plan fulfillment and overfulfillment, enterprises obtain greater leeway in determining the distribution and growth of wages for their employees in relation to profitability. Given the overall social objectives of the socialist economy, such freedom is subject to a number of centrally set parameters and social compacts.

Fifth, a necessary, if not sufficient, corollary to the greater scope of market relations is the devolution of authority over the flexibility and level of prices to lower planning organs or even to individual economic agents. Two of the most essential characteristics of the MPE are price liberalization and decentralization in the foreign trade sector. Price liberalization is far from complete, however. It applies generally to a number of traded goods. On most other goods and services, strict controls are maintained in some form. Serious distortions persist among liberalized prices, fixed prices, and prices that can only be changed infrequently or within well-determined limits or both.

However, the MPE is by definition a system in flux, and one of the basic commitments is that price distortions, where possible, are to be eliminated in the near future. There is therefore some encouragement being given to linking up domestic and trade prices, but the dichotomy between CMEA and East–West trade prices continues to be a most serious obstacle. The very existence of traded goods with fixed prices reduces the effectiveness of the more decentralized allocation of resources typical of the MPE. However, their multilayered price regime represents an essential compromise between two broad considerations. The authorities trade off the social and economic losses that they perceive to ensue from opening the economy to domestic and international competition, especially when there is only a limited number of large enterprises, against the economic and political gains that emanate from improved allocative efficiency, including in the external sector.

A sixth feature concerns the financing of capital formation. Instead of relying heavily on budgetary allocations, bank credits and self-financing by enterprises are meant to assume a much more important role. In some cases, there may even be some movement to loosen up the sharp separation between the producer and the household money markets. In fact, increased "privatization" of some well-selected segments of the economy (including handicrafts, and repair and catering facilities) may be actively encouraged.

When all is said and done, however, significant differences between PEs and MEs remain not only at various stages of the process toward an MPE but even at its logical terminus, which no country has as yet reached. A close correlation between political and economic functions is typical, and the nonprice impact of the former on the latter remains considerable. There are indeed a host of essential ideological and ethical features of a socialist system that necessitate retaining far-reaching direct controls over market transactions. One such crucial instance is the scope for price flexibility, the variety of sources calling for price changes, and the size of the national product whose price is not subjected to market pressures. Although reduced in comprehensiveness, the planners' interest in the stability of producer and retail prices for planning, equity, and control purposes remains quite extensive. The same holds for fiscal, income, and monetary policies, which cannot function autonomously. Nevertheless, a distinguishing characteristic of an MPE is the willingness and capacity of the central authorities to foster an institutional setup for macroeconomic management that relies more and more, albeit with some vacillation, possibly even temporary retrogression, on "neutral" or rule-guided income, fiscal, and monetary policies. An MPE is therefore by necessity an organism in flux.

2

The CMEA's organization and policy programs

Because the CMEA's activities in the 1950s were only of marginal relevance to the economic achievements of the members, the Council's existence from mid-1950 until about 1960 can be all but disregarded. As already indicated in Chapter 1, changes in the policies and model of the orthodox CPE have had measurable repercussions on the attitudes of these countries toward the regional organization itself, the goals of SEI, and the modus operandi to which the PEs are inclined to subscribe. The initial stirrings in Eastern Europe at the time of the New Course and the sociopolitical convulsions of the mid-1950s in some CPEs did not immediately impact upon the Council's organization and role in bolstering regional cohesion. But even these incipient changes left a legacy. Measurable movement toward greater SEI has been noticeable since then, and seminal transitions in the Council's organization have materialized.

Section 2.1 gives first a brief outline of the structure of the Council as it exists today with some historical background where useful for the proper perspective to Part II.[1] The next four sections summarize the chief programmatic policy documents and less formal policy guidelines as they have molded the major precepts in the evolution of CMEA cooperation in each of the decades since the Council's creation, although this requires some tinkering with time arithmetic. I then present a comprehensive, if not exhaustive, analysis of the so-called SEI mechanism, which is the cornerstone of the rest of this book, and a brief perspective on SEI.

2.1 The Council's organizational structure

The CMEA's charter, signed in 1959 and revised several times since, singles out the most important CMEA organs as the Council Session, the Executive Committee and its subcommittees (of which there are now four), the Standing or Permanent Commissions (of which there are presently twenty-three), and the Secretariat. In addition to these pinnacle levels, the Council comprises six formal and informal conferences, three

54

institutes, and many affiliated institutions that maintain tenuous links with the Council.

According to its charter, the highest official organ of the CMEA is the Council Session, in which national delegations are usually headed by the Prime Minister. Between these meetings, CMEA affairs are guided by the Executive Committee, which is composed of each member's permanent representative, who is generally a deputy prime minister. The day-to-day affairs are entrusted to the Secretariat. Before examining briefly the role and place of these official organs, I shall give a word on a key "unofficial" organ. The pivotal problems of CMEA cooperation are, in general, discussed first within the framework of interparty relations, with the real core of decision making being the preparation for and the occasional gathering of the informal organ known officially as the Conference of First Secretaries of Communist and Workers' Parties and of the Heads of Government of the CMEA Member Countries – a cumbersome title that I shall condense to CCP.

The CP of the various member states has always played a leading role in CMEA affairs. The weight of the CPs in charting CMEA cooperation began to be felt positively with the top-level CCP meeting of May 1958, although some of the earlier postwar summits should not be completely ignored (Brabant 1974a, 1976). It has been convened rather infrequently since. Owing to the CCP's informal nature, the range of topics for debate is, in principle, very wide and not necessarily confined to regional economic cooperation. However, some sessions have been exclusively devoted to the goals, instruments, and problems of SEI. In addition, decisions reached there have been critical for the evolvement of integration policies, regional institutions, and national policy actions, instruments, and institutional changes. Although the decisions reached by the CCP are formally not binding for the CMEA organization and, hence, SEI, they are routinely confirmed by the CMEA's appropriate bodies. Moreover, they have been peculiarly effective in invigorating the Council.[2] In view of the "role of these parties as the leading political force [of the PEs], the directives adopted by the [CCP] are in fact binding and the appropriate organs of the organization are only called upon to give them formal legal force" (Klepacki 1975, p. 50).

It is because of the supreme powers vested in the General or First Secretary of the CP of each socialist economy that these summit meetings can chart such authoritative political guidelines for CMEA cooperation. It should hence not be surprising that the directions and basic principles of CMEA activities are laid down by the CCP. These rather infrequent meetings, starting with that held in May 1958, should therefore be kept quite separate from other gatherings of CMEA leaders, including the Council Session or meetings of CCO secretaries (CCS). The latter can be deadlocked on the simple procedural ground that a delegation first has to clear substantive matters with the top leadership at home. It is true that each PE's Politbureau, CCO, or even the CCS usually has the opportunity to "examine" the agreements signed by the CP chiefs. But this is normally a mere formality.

The CCP has intervened in CMEA affairs only in special circumstances to formulate new guidelines for the Council's activities. It played an instrumental role in the endorsement of the ISDL, SEI, and scientific–technical cooperation programs. Its influence has echoed well beyond the simple "endorsement" of programmatic documents. It has been the instigator of the sprawling CMEA organization, has laid down the distinguishing provisions of the programmatic policy documents, and has, moreover, transformed the intangible attitude toward SEI in all forms. The latter especially has had a palpably positive impact on regional cooperation since the late 1960s. But the CCP has never concerned itself with the continuous steering of the Council. It has also become crystal clear that the ratification of documents as such may fail to bring about the hoped-for actions. This has been the case in the last few years, which have shown that certain periods of stagnation or crisis in the operation of intergovernmental organizations, such as the CMEA, cannot always be remedied by resorting to well-entrenched procedures and instruments. Instead, extraordinary actions appear to be required to reconfirm at the highest political echelons the firm commitment to enhance economic or other forms of cooperation.

The day-to-day affairs and the execution of policies whose principles are hammered out by the respective CPs are entrusted to the formal CMEA organs. The key rungs of the official CMEA hierarchy and the relations of subordination and interaction are blocked out in Figure 2.1. The highest official organ of the CMEA – its "supreme organ" according to article 6 of the charter – is the formal gathering of top government delegates known as the Council Session. Since 1970, this organ convenes regularly once a year in one of the capitals of the member countries.[3] But an "extraordinary" or "special" Council Session can be convoked, usually in connection with an economic summit, such as the June 1984 meeting, which was followed immediately by a "special" session to endorse the published and other summit agreements and to start implementing them. The Session examines the fundamental problems of cooperation and directs the activities of the Secretariat and its subordinate organs.

In between meetings of the Council Session, the CMEA's affairs are guided by the Executive Committee and its subsidiary specialized Committees. Set up in 1962 to replace the Conference of Representatives of the CMEA member countries, the Executive Committee is a nonpermanent organ presently convoked at least once a quarter, usually in Moscow. It is composed of high-ranking officials – a deputy chairman of the Council of Ministers at the very least. The functions of the Executive Commit-

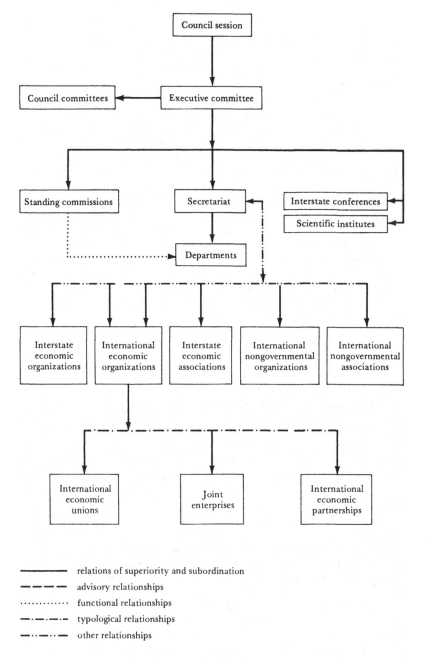

Figure 2.1. Formal hierarchical structure of the CMEA.

tee include implementing the decisions of the Session, directing the work program on plan coordination and scientific–technical cooperation, supervising the activities of the Standing Commissions, and overseeing and controlling the Secretariat. It can make decisions within its competence and submit proposals to the Session.

Although originally designed to assume the paramount responsibilities of a supranational planning center, the Executive Committee has largely remained a consultative organ concerned with the broad guidelines of national and regional macroeconomic policies. Since 1971, it has been assisted by four Committees (for planning since 1971, material–technical supply and scientific–technical cooperation since 1974, and machine building since 1984). These Committees are higher-level echelons for dealing with important target areas of the coordination of overall national plans, for finding ways and means of attaining greater consistency in production and consumption, and for furthering economic development through a more or less concerted effort to centralize and disseminate economic, scientific, and technical information. These Committees deal with the most crucial facts and figures regarding the dovetailing of economic policies, especially since top policy makers of the member countries participate in the deliberations.

The Standing Commissions are the real working organs of the CMEA. They were first set up in 1956 to replace the ad hoc working parties and subdivisions of the Bureau and the Secretariat. Their number and field of authority have fluctuated since. Starting with twelve commissions in 1956, their number gradually rose to a maximum of twenty-two in 1975. After the machine-building commission was replaced by a higher-level committee in 1984 and the commissions for cooperation in the field of new materials and technologies and in biotechnology in 1986 (*Svět Hospodářství*, 1986:22, p. 1) were added, their number now stands at 23 (Syčëv 1986a, p. 18), but with a slightly modified composition compared to the mid-1970s. Some are sectoral, and others deal with general economic issues. The Standing Commissions are important because it is here that concrete propositions on common activities are worked out, that the field of operation in various sectors is laid down, and that detailed documentation on the relevant sectors or general economic and organizational problems are disseminated. The national delegations in the Standing Commissions typically are headed by the ministers of the respective field or at least by senior civil servants of the ministries concerned. But this by no means guarantees that all, or even the most crucial, recommendations or informal decisions will be implemented. The commissions are in session at least twice a year, usually in Moscow.

The Secretariat in Moscow is the only permanent CMEA organ. It is headed by a secretary, who is invariably a Soviet citizen.[4] He has a number of deputies on the upper echelon and oversees a moderately large staff recruited from the various member countries. The Secretariat is officially responsible for organizing, contributing to, and servicing the meetings of the other CMEA organs, particularly the Council Session; it also guides the implementation of recommendations and decisions taken by itself and the other organs. Though it is not empowered to enact or to enforce recommendations on its own initiative, the Secretariat might still play a crucial role in charting the course of SEI. In short, it prepares the recommendations and decisions of the other organs and molds them into a practical form.

Among the other official organs, one should distinguish conferences, institutes, international economic organizations (IEOs), and miscellaneous ventures. Of particular importance for the gradual development of regional integration are the common enterprises and other such IEOs that have increased in number since the late 1960s, though at a greatly varying pace. Most do not formally belong to the Council. But their contacts with the pinnacle levels are intimate, and their routine operations are closely monitored by the relevant official Council organs. Some take the form of a common enterprise, a venture producing commodities, or an institution providing essential financial services, and thus are usually put on a self-financing basis (*chozrasčët*). Others are concerned, in essence, with producing services, or are entrusted with the coordination of production and research, and thus are normally financed by the central government budget of the participating PEs.

One cannot fail to note in connection with the CMEA's organization that, generally speaking, since the early 1970s the CMEA possesses, at least on paper, an adequate organizational structure to deal with nearly all the concrete problems involved in coordinating the members' economic development. The main organizational problem, as noted elsewhere in this book, is that many of the important Council organs were not really constituted to prepare or to make economic decisions per se. In this respect, it is symptomatic that the organizational and other reforms in the member countries, by and large, have not so far affected the CMEA. The Council's central role as a clearing house for overseeing and promoting SEI has, on the whole, remained unchanged since the early 1950s, despite the expansion of the CMEA's formal structure and the more systematic and up-to-date codification of cooperation principles. As Michail Gorbačëv stressed at the recently held Twenty-seventh Congress of the Soviet Union's CP (Gorbačëv 1986, cable 104): "changes are also required in the work of the [CMEA Secretariat so that] there is less armchair administration[5] and fewer committees and commissions of all sorts, that more attention is given to economic levers, initiative, and socialist enterprise . . ."

It is now ironic that thus far the CMEA's decisions typically fail to touch upon the key obstacles inherent in the internal organization of the member countries. Similarly, changes contemplated or inaugurated in the participating economies proceed without visible repercussions on the CMEA's organization and modes of behavior. Although this may seem contradictory, it really is not. The paradox is that country-specific needs are met through various channels that really remain outside the official Council structure and policies. BTPAs are the instrument par excellence in this case.

2.2 Official principles and methods of cooperation in the 1950s

Until 1962 the CMEA did not have a commonly agreed policy on how socialist cooperation was to evolve. At any rate, no such guidelines were publicized or appear to have motivated the external economic activities of the PEs. The only available documents from which one could infer official intentions were the vaguely phrased founding communiqué (1949) and the Council's charter (1959), which clarifies the legal position of the organization. It must be surmised that by late 1950 the "founding documents" of early 1949, including the elusive treaty, were no longer applicable, if they had been at all earlier!

The founding communiqué was not very informative about the structure, purposes, principles, and methods of the new organization. The goals of the Council as cited in Chapter 1 could be, and were, interpreted according to whatever suited the prevailing views on socialist internationalism, national development, and mutual cooperation. More specific tasks than those set out in the communiqué failed to be codified at that time. The provisions of the draft treaty discussed in Chapter 1 apparently did not play any significant role at all. Instead, the scope and content of socialist cooperation tended to be defined implicitly as the result of "historical experience."

As an organization, the CMEA was basically immobilized by the USSR's intransigence with respect to regional cooperation and the subsequent policy bent of the Eastern European partner countries, which was heavily nationalistic. The latter probably had neither the power nor the will to check the USSR's supreme role by warding off the worst effects of independent development. This is not equating all shortcomings of intragroup cooperation solely to the misguided outlook of the USSR. Eastern Europe's supine position, while doubtlessly resulting in part from the weight of the *primus inter pares,* also suited the then prevalent political elites.[6] The responsibility for the CMEA's decade-long rust must therefore not solely be thrust on the USSR's back, although the division of blame is by no means straightforward. The result of this collective disrespect for regionalism was, however, that for all practical purposes the

Council did not exist until the late 1950s, when the organization was expanded and an acceptable charter was finally drafted.

The first serious efforts to revive the Council and to stimulate regional cooperation were launched after Stalin's death, when industrialization per se at a breakneck pace was abandoned and, as a rule, a more balanced growth concept became the guiding beacon of practical economic policies. Because of the uncoordinated changes in domestic demand and the more open trade policy engendered by the so-called New Course in the smaller PEs, serious conflicts of interest in regional trade soon came to the fore and severely encroached upon the trade prospects of the more developed CMEA partners. To maintain regional economic and political stability, members, especially the USSR, looked more favorably upon groupwide cooperation. But economic affairs were certainly not the only impulse fueling this renewed interest in regional cooperation.

The Council's several sessions held in the mid-1950s, after a lapse of more than three years, focused on attaining a higher level of specialization, especially in branches where the PEs had been pursuing similar, if not identical, growth objectives. Although several agreements on intra- and interproduct specialization were signed as early as 1956,[7] opinion on their implementation and effects is none too favorable. To summarize matters: These agreements were slated for implementation precisely when seminal social, economic, and political events erupted. Although these shifts could not have been factored into the negotiations without the benefit of hindsight, their effect was such that the earlier commitments could no longer be honored. This failure provided a major incentive for reinforcing the Council's institutions, adopting a formal charter, and issuing the first broad policy document, which was to guide further concrete action.

The charter stipulates the purpose of the CMEA to be "the planned development of the national economy, the acceleration of economic and technical progress . . . the raising of the level of industrialization in the industrially less developed countries, a steady increase in the productivity of labor, and a constant improvement in the welfare of the peoples" (Tokareva 1967, pp. 45–6) of the PEs. This general task is specified to foster the most rational use of resources and to accelerate the development of the productive capacities of the members. All this is to be attained through plan coordination, the comprehensive examination of economic and scientific–technical problems, and the creation of common ventures in all spheres of interest to the members. But the charter is not entirely unambiguous about whether common or national advantage should be the principal criterion for CMEA decision making.[8] As an international organization motivated by these general objectives, the Council can only hope to discharge itself of its concrete tasks within rather narrow bounds, given that it is only empowered to prepare "recommendations," which the countries may or may not heed in policy guidelines. Certainly, it can decide upon measures pertaining to its own organization and administration. Since the changes endorsed in June 1979, which after ratification became operational in 1981, the member countries can also conclude so-called agreements on the implementation of synchronized measures of economic and scientific–technical cooperation. This is potentially an important modification. Because the agreement is specifically worked out by the members and delegates authority for the effective implementation of SEI measures on an ad hoc basis to the CMEA organs, the importance of the agreement should certainly not be overstated (as in Uschakow 1983b, p. 199). I shall return to it in Chapter 12.

The CMEA's charter cannot be regarded as a clear-cut statement of the principles, goals, and methods of cooperation, nor did it specify policy actions. Admittedly, the charter is not the most appropriate place to express such views. Since the early 1960s, the Council has been underpinned with policy documents, apparently with the aim of facilitating the regional mobility of goods and production factors. Special attention should be devoted to the two challenging documents on the goals and methods of the ISDL and SEI. It is true that these documents have given rise to much discussion, sometimes even to bitter and acrimonious debate. Nevertheless, they are specific on both the goals and purposes of the CMEA, they set forth the principles and methods of SEI endorsed by the members, and, in some cases, they provide the chief guidelines for concrete action during some period of time.

2.3 Principles and methods of cooperation in the 1960s

The centerpiece of the discussions on regional economic policy during the 1960s was a document (here referred to as *Basic Principles*[9]) elaborated in response to the political will to pursue SEI expressed by the first full-scale summit devoted to regional economic affairs. *Basic Principles* was signed in 1962 and led to an involved debate that questioned ab ovo the very meaning, purpose, and methods of socialist internationalism. This document places heavy emphasis on the following general principles of socialist cooperation: the inviolability of national sovereignty, the national independence of the members, unalloyed equality, mutual advantage, and so on.[10] In addition, for the first time ever the PEs collectively emphasized each country's need to map out its development plans according to its own conditions, while fully respecting the needs and potentialities of all countries as a commonwealth.

The objectives of socialist cooperation are more clearly defined in this document than in any other official policy declaration. In particular, it states that the CMEA aims at promoting the optimal allocation of resources according to regional, as distinct from national, tasks without overlooking the legitimate interests of the individual participants. The tendencies to create a self-sufficient economic complex in each national PE as well as to promote one-sided international specialization are recognized as unfruitful pursuits. Regional specialization according to comparative advantage is the theme underlying *Basic Principles*. A more efficient regional economy can be attained if plan coordination, as the basic instrument for implementing the ISDL, is improved and perfected. Bilateral and especially multilateral coordination of national plans should contribute to the realization of SEI. But nowhere is it stated how comparative advantages in the region ought to or could be assessed. The document also alludes to the strengthening of mutual economic ties through "the creation in the future of the world communist economy directed by the victorious masses of the proletariat according to one plan" (Tokareva 1967, p. 24). In accompanying and subsequent analyses and statements, this rather cryptic description of a veiled intention was interpreted as a definite signal to the effect that the ISDL would soon be the focus of a single plan for the region as a whole.

As noted, the key instrument to implement the ISDL is the coordination of the national socioeconomic plans, which eventually should be replaced by a common plan presumably drawn up by a supranational planning authority. Also the problems of bilaterialism and CMEA pricing were explicitly identified as important outstanding questions to be resolved on a high-priority basis. Multilateralism and appropriate prices were to serve as the main catalysts for furthering planned production specialization. Although the document pays lip service to the national interests of the member countries, it was the call for commonly solving shared problems, not only in trade but in economic development in general, that was at the forefront of the broad, at times acrimonious, debate that the PEs publicly engaged in shortly after the document was endorsed at the CMEA summit of June 1962.

Instead of carrying out the grand design of regional policies, strongly diverging trends surfaced shortly after the document was approved at the highest policy-making level under impulse of serious disagreements about the goals and means of uniform planning, the practical instruments of SEI that were left undefined by the document, and the realistic goals of SEI. Three such developments, in retrospect, were of seminal importance. First, a wave of economic reforms of varying intensity and scope started in several PEs and eventually encompassed the entire area. The nature of some reforms strongly inhibited the practical introduction on a regionwide scale of planning as practiced in the early 1950s in each CPE. Second, the mid-1960s provided a more reliable political and economic climate for cooperation between East and West, especially in Europe. Under these new conditions, each PE pressed the issue of more efficient international specialization in the context of the global economy and insisted upon doing so according to more precisely defined criteria of economic choice before entering into specific regional commitments. Third, a concentrated effort was made better to comprehend some of the fundamental problems of cooperation (such as price formation, mobility of labor and capital, or multilateralism), and some initiatives essayed to come to grips with the more practical aspects of the obstacles to fostering cooperation. If the effort had succeeded, it would have considerably weakened the case for unified regional planning. It did not, but the very debate engendered in the process obviated a determined attempt to implement standardized planning for the CMEA as a whole.

The Czechoslovak crisis in 1968–1969 must be seen as an important watershed in CMEA relations. The Warsaw Pact's invasion, the subsequent "normalization" of Czechoslovakia, including the redirection of its economic policies, and the ramification of these events for the other PEs, among myriad other changes, all led to a sharp retraction of the economic reforms, or at any rate to a forced slowdown in the pace of their implementation and a reconsideration of their scope, objectives, and modalities. Furthermore, the atmosphere for East–West détente deteriorated measurably under impact of the circumstances surrounding the "return to health"[11] of Czechoslovakia, initiated in August 1968, and, by analogy, other PEs that threatened to stray. Finally, proposals on economic integration as an acceptable term for cooperation in Eastern Europe surfaced and contributed in the end to the promulgation of a new cooperation strategy.

2.4 The doctrine on socialist economic integration and cooperation in the 1970s

Whereas previous policy documents referred vaguely to "international specialization" and "economic cooperation" as the goals of a common economic policy in the CMEA, the leading motive behind *Integration Program* is full positive integration. In other words, the CMEA members in 1971 apparently agreed to eliminate gradually the man-made obstacles to the free regional flow of goods, services, and, to some extent, production factors and to contain as much as possible the impediments due to natural obstacles by the purposeful coordination of all relevant aspects of economic policy. The full equalization of relative scarcities within the region is proposed as the basic objective of SEI even if somewhat ambivalently. But the specific needs of individual members should not be disregarded. This applies particularly to the construction of the national economic complex as an integral part of an optimal regional economy. Each CMEA member is entitled to decide freely whether and when to participate in a particular project. But lack of interest on the part of some countries should not impede other partners from carrying out their agreed projects.

The program stipulates two principal types of instruments for attaining SEI. The chief one is the coordination of national plans. The various governments are expected to submit drafts of their national economic plans to the other members and the CMEA organs. These still malleable blueprints are to provide the basis for discussions of each PE's most advantageous economic prospects. But no one can be compelled to withdraw a particular project even it if were to endanger cooperation and clash with the interests of SEI partners. Joint planning in especially important sectors was to be pursued in addition to plan coordination. Regular bilateral and multilateral consultations were to be held on matters concerning national and international economic policies in an attempt to specify the preferred areas for coordination and joint planning. Direct economic relations between the ultimate producer and user, as distinct from informal contacts, were not expected to play a key role in the process of formulating and implementing SEI.

The second type of instrument comprises policy instruments (including prices, ERs, and interest rates) and their supporting institutions (including multilateralism and banks) that help to coordinate economic decisions and activities indirectly. They are expected to underpin integration measures in the draft stage of the plans and to aid in the implementation of the coordinated plans. Economic criteria as such, however, are not to be allotted an exclusive or overriding role in selecting, formulating the broad contours of, or setting up common projects. Although it is slated to be sharply improved, the institutional setting within which such instruments operate is not to replace the conscious planning and centrally guided implementation of economic decisions. SEI was to be sought in accordance with comparative advantage, among other indicators, but chiefly within the framework of common planning.

Not only is SEI merely specified as an aim in *Integration Program,* the concrete means by which this is to be fostered have never been clearly defined. Methods of plan coordination and the scope for coordination instruments are still left vague, although they are recognized to need further refinement. Instead of providing an unambiguous solution, the program, for most issues raised, set deadlines for study and resolution – a significant departure from earlier commitments. The deadlines set for the steady improvement of the financial and monetary aspects of CMEA integration especially elicited very positive commentary. The details germane to this discussion are illuminated in Section 2.6 and especially in Chapter 11.

The program has little to say about how the Council was to function as the institution for promoting, steering, and overseeing integration. It prescribes the amelioration of traditional principles, methods, and tasks of economic cooperation and the study of a few new possibilities as areas in need of target attention. But no completely new forms or institutions of regional cooperation were slated for the duration of thᵉ program, which was expected to remain the principal policy statement charting the desirable course until at least the end of the 1980s. The PEs therefore anticipated bolstering SEI within the national and regional institutional frameworks as they existed around 1970. Neither the emergence of a market mechanism nor the erection of a clearly defined regional central planning agency was envisaged. Certainly, the program calls for amending the existing framework of the Council and of the separate planning centers with a view to enhancing their effectiveness. But it was doubtful from the start whether this vague commitment would suffice to elicit genuine integration on which some members had placed high hopes. Whatever the merits of the program's specific goals, the decision to keep the established institutional setup intact was by far the most significant program element, although also its most disappointing. For it is almost self-evident that unless each member country is voluntarily prepared to seek greater flexibility in internal planning, SEI cannot proceed very far.

Although none of the basic components of a proper, self-contained integration mechanism could be unambiguously agreed upon in the process of drafting *Integration Program,* the ensuing search for operationality in the numerous tasks slated for further study and negotiation was characterized very clearly by two features. First, the debate on the principles and methodology of plan coordination and joint planning on the one hand, and harmonizing monetary and financial coordination instruments with planning activities on the other, ran a stimulating course for a few years, roughly until 1974. But it failed to yield gradually acceptable solutions for any of the fundamental issues. To be sure, the deadlines for the 1970s incorporated into *Integration Program* were generally respected, at least from a purely formal point of view. But the solutions or revisions in the monetary and financial cooperation mechanisms then adopted fell far short of what could reasonably have been anticipated in the light of the expectations of policy makers revealed at the time the program was endorsed and in the ensuing debates. Second, parallel with the more detailed examination of principles and methods of SEI, practical matters began to be tackled more and more within the traditional framework of plan coordination. This major shift in emphasis on proper modi operandi thickened especially after the world price inflation, the raw materials shortage, and the recession in the developed MEs drastically curtailed the list of options available to the most market-minded PEs.

During the latter part of the 1970s, integration discussions focused nearly exclusively on improving plan coordination, especially for fairly detailed projects about which specific specialization or coordination agreements had been concluded. In this connection, two types of documents are of singular consequence for the evolving process of SEI. In 1975, the PEs endorsed the first Concerted Plan. Soon thereafter, beginning in 1976, the PEs started to formulate Target Programs, which were designed to mold the course of SEI for the next decade or so. The first three were adopted in mid-1978 and the other two in mid-1979.

The Concerted Plan worked out jointly in 1974–1975 was the first concrete, common integration plan of the PEs and aimed at very specific targets in a number of important economic activities to be pursued vigorously in conjunction with the medium-term plans for 1976–1980. Broadly speaking, these measures can be divided into five different classes. First, the plan contained concrete details regarding the material, financial, and, in some instances, labor transfers for the joint projects started in the mid-1970s. Second, a large number of mutilateral specialization and cooperation agreements, especially in the engineering and chemical sectors, were stipulated. Third, several scientific and technological cooperation projects were included, especially to improve and expand new sources of energy, fuels, and essential raw materials. Fourth, a special section was devoted to measures to enhance the development of Mongolia.[12] Finally, consequences of the common actions vis-à-vis third countries following from the Concerted Plan were drawn (Vorkauf 1977, p. 12). Also new in this respect was that the relevant parts of the Concerted Plan provisions for the individual participants were to become an integral component of the medium-term plans for 1976–1980 and had the force of law[13] in all participating countries through the annual implementation plans, which include a section on integration measures.

Planning tools such as a Concerted Plan certainly constitute an important innovation in CMEA cooperation in that they are explicitly directed at piecemeal improvements in SEI. But their significance should not be overrated. Because there was still no adequately formulated long-term development strategy or even a commonly accepted set of sound ideas about the preferred SEI path, the gestation of the first Concerted Plan was difficult and its formulation as such, as R. Nyers observed, "can be counted as a success" (Nyers 1977, p. 423). This positive evaluation stemmed in many ways from the fact that the Concerted Plan was intended greatly to alleviate the shortage of some goods on the CMEA market and to improve production specialization in a few well-defined fields. Nevertheless, the Concerted Plan was anticipated to be only an interim solution, pending the approval of dovetailed long-term programs of common action. These programs were to envisage the coordination of jointly funded or realized investments geared to framing complementary structures rather than isolated ventures (Biskup and Nosiadek 1978, p. 10).

2.5 Regional cooperation in the 1980s

The idea to embrace target programming germinated right after *Integration Program* was endorsed and took firm hold when the involved debates of 1970–1974 reached an impasse. Its chief purpose is to lay down jointly the desirable and binding common development path in selected fields. They were accepted in principle in 1975. The concrete formulation of such strategies preoccupied the member states during much of the second half of the 1970s. Focused on selected activities and with a time horizon set at about ten years, although this could be stretched up to twenty years, these programs were designed to come to grips with a number of important aspects of plan coordination that the PEs find difficult to accommodate within the framework normally available for the dovetailing of annual and medium-term economic plans.

Initially, five areas of special significance for long-term growth and the maturing of SEI were identified and agreed upon by the highest decision-making echelons. The goals of the target programs and the fields selected for intensive cooperation were (1) to solve the problems encountered in maintaining balance in energy, fuels, and raw materials; (2) to enhance regionwide specialization in existing engineering branches through modernization and structural change and to foster further expansion in a synchronized manner; (3) to improve the balance in basic food supplies in an effort to attain a higher degree of self-sufficiency in each PE and the region as a whole and to increase the effectiveness of agricultural output; (4) to improve the supply and quality of a wide range of industrial consumer goods not only to meet present and future market demand to an ever growing extent but also to promote greater regional self-sufficiency; and (5) to establish a fully integrated transportation system.

The actual conceptualization and formulation of the detailed programs was delegated to the CMEA organs and numerous national research institutes. Comprehensive drafts based on forecast demand and supply developments should have been available in mid-1977. Moreover, investment intentions as well as anticipated trade flows were to be coordinated in an effort to attain greater efficiency in the regionwide allocation of resources (Kormnov 1977). These results were to form the raw information on the basis of which the actual Target Programs and, later, the concrete multilateral and bilateral implementation agreements as well as the Concerted Plans were to be elaborated.

Intensive preparatory work followed upon the endorsement of these programs by the thirtieth Council Session in Berlin in July 1976. In the process, it transpired quickly that specifying concrete integration tasks of such a wide range and ensuring their operationality was a much more arduous task than had been anticipated. Though the blueprints were never published, there is sufficient evidence that the programs as endorsed in 1978 and 1979 were considerably scaled-down versions of what originally had been aimed at. They were focused especially on essential investment projects that would help to ensure the partial autarky of the region, which had been one of the several options in the discussions of the mid-1970s (Chodov 1976, p. 23). A number of important multilateral specialization agreements were concluded during the preparation of the medium-term plans for 1981–1985. Because these protocols were to be specified in detail in the context of the traditional annual and medium-term plans, the Concerted Plan was to become a recurrent planning instrument harmonized with the implementation of the Target Programs and with the associated bilateral and multilateral specialization agreements (Vorkauf 1977, p. 21).

Two important developments in the early 1980s appear to have changed drastically the outlook for SEI in the years ahead. One concerns the implementation of the first Target Programs. Target programming had been embraced as a policy tool compatible with the overall tone and intentions of *Integration Program*. However, since the latter's provisions were ambiguous and no new fundamental objectives of SEI were elaborated, the policy-making vacuum acted as a severe stricture on the concrete specification of the objects of target programming and perhaps even more so on the actual implementation of the adopted measures. The other concerns the considerable economic and social disturbances that erupted in several PEs in the early 1980s and the concomitant sharp slowdown in the pace of economic growth throughout the CMEA. They could be ascribed to capacity constraints and output bottlenecks only for a while. In fact, long-term growth obstacles as well as more transitory internal and external development constraints (see Chapter 3) were responsible for the slowdown in factor productivity growth, in spite of major modernization efforts, sizable technology imports from MEs, and related intensification policies.

Thus, the CMEA members were challenged to review their regional economic policies, as seen against the foregoing backdrop. To reach decisions of major political and economic weight and, hence, to endorse new forms and methods of joint planning that would stimulate in-depth cooperation, the CMEA members held an economic summit in June 1984 – the first since the full-scale Moscow meeting of April 1969. But the origins of this summit go back at least to 1980, when Ceaușescu first publicly asked for it (Brabant in press, a).

From the very beginning, the call for a summit made by Eastern European leaders had quite divergent motivations. Concerns about the promotion of SEI were only one of the several axes around which the debates revolved. Perhaps the foremost distinction to be made is among Rumania's policy stance, which was overwhelmingly motivated by its rapidly deteriorating economic fortunes; the USSR's, which endeavored chiefly to paper over some of the hindrances encountered in the process of implementing programs on which top-level leaders had apparently agreed – especially the Concerted Plan and the Target Programs; and Czechoslovakia's concern about the fundamental strategy of SEI and policy coordination in the CMEA. The precepts held by the other members were more ambiguous. Bulgaria was probably concerned mostly with the ramifications of any compromise on a more equal sharing of scarce industrial inputs. The GDR, in addition, emphasized the need for greater scientific–technical cooperation and specialization in manufactures. Hungarian policy pronouncements were, on the whole, defensive: In the absence of a real impetus to SEI, which could not be expected from any summit, it focused especially on keeping all avenues to foreign economic cooperation as uncluttered as possible. Poland did not participate much in the presummit debates, owing to its ongoing economic, political, and social malaise.

Several documents were endorsed at the summit,[14] of which two were published.[15] *Main Directions* merits most attention in this context, although the strong commitment to furthering all-round economic cooperation, particularly between East and West, expressed in *Preservation of Peace* (CMEA 1984a) should at least be mentioned. Before briefly pointing out the major SEI elements of *Main Directions* (CMEA 1984b), I will rephrase the chief objectives of the summit. This provides a broader backdrop to the achievements than what can be gleaned from the published documents.

Many pointers indicate that the summit was in the end convened to promulgate a new SEI document attuned to the prevailing external and internal economic circumstances in Eastern Europe. The debates of the early 1970s about pursuing SEI primarily through plan coordination or the guided market mechanism had underlined the lack of operationality of the criteria and goals originally agreed upon. Moreover, the serious deterioration in the world economy and the inability to embrace quickly appropriate adjustment policies in the PEs led to massive foreign borrowing that increasingly constrained the degree of policy flexibility, particularly in the smaller countries. Moreover, the insulation against world market fluctuations that the CMEA had provided for twenty-five years or so was seriously ruptured by three events. The adaptation of price-formation principles in January 1975 led, by normal CMEA standards, to very substantial upward price adjustments and hence threatened to disrupt the conventional bilaterally balanced trade approach. A much more significant fissure surfaced because steady increases in the regional supply of critical fuels and raw materials could no longer be counted on. Finally, the "new SEI strategy" for the 1980s that was gradually embraced in the second half of the 1970s had unraveled. Target programming as a means of enhancing the degree of integration through the strict administrative linking of medium-term plans did not get off the ground basically because of the same internal and external constraints that were complicating the realization of the national economic plans and the resumption of a more forward-looking growth policy.

The precise contours of such a new integration program have remained fluid until now. But a new strategy would evidently attempt to come to grips with (1) a more adequate pricing mechanism; (2) a greater role for monetary and financial instruments, including the TR; (3) more direct operational cooperation of enterprises; (4) paying much less attention to the specification in great detail of physical quantities and prices of most goods to be exchanged during the next planning period; (5) better dovetailing of policy instruments that may prop up steady productivity growth; (6) more efficient utilization of primary and intermediate inputs; (7) the enhancement of specialization especially in engineering and the upgrading of the scientific–technical parameters of specialized products; and (8) the coordination of East–West trade, finance, and technology policies. Perhaps the prime obstacle to innovation and its effective transmission emanates from the traditional planning and management systems of the PEs. Because regional regimentation along the well-tried lines followed in the component economies would be stymied by the same hindrances to production intensification as experienced in each PE individually, it is not surprising that the elaboration of proper supports for scientific–technical progress in combination with a more rational ISDL, especially in engineering, would be a core concern of furthering SEI.

Main Directions clarifies that the summit "concentrated attention on the solution of tasks stemming from internal and external conditions that have changed in recent years." It endorses many positions that affect short- and long-term cooperation policies of the CMEA, which can be discussed under four headings: short-term national and regional economic problems, the long-term goals of SEI, measures to enhance the formulation and implementation of concrete SEI measures, and other considerations. Items included under the short-term measures are (1) the potential expansion of trade beyond volumes agreed upon under the coordinated economic and trade plans for 1981–1985; (2) greater flexibility in the setting of TR prices, with the reference period to WMPs apparently being compressed for some goods, possibly starting with the next five-year plans;[16] and (3) readiness to increase deliveries of energy and industrial raw materials in exchange for high-quality manufactures.

With regard to the longer term, *Main Directions* identifies the most important tasks at the present stage in the areas of domestic and regional economic policies and cooperation mechanisms. Perhaps the most crucial component is the elevation of SEI to a new level by accelerating the transition to intensive growth policies so as to ensure structural changes through the more rational use of resources, nationally as well as regionally. Such changes, some to be elaborated at the CMEA level, should permit an export-oriented output structure that is versatile, technically up-to-date, reliable, and durable. Growth intensification policies must necessarily start at the national level. At the same time, however, Eastern Europe's leaders deem it necessary to improve measurably the coordination of all economic policies that affect the interests of CMEA partners directly or indirectly. Furthermore, interested members should explore new steps of coordinating selected sectoral policies. Holding summits on a more regular basis[17] should help to further these objectives.

As far as the mechanism of SEI is concerned, *Main Directions* underlines once again the primacy of plan coordination, but it also stresses that "the task of organically combining . . . plan activity with the active utilization of commodity–money relations retains its topicality." Accordingly, there would appear to be room for improvement in the regional price mechanism and in the functioning of the TR, but details remain to be worked out. It is particularly this rather obscure passus of *Main Directions* that has been receiving disproportionate attention in recent commentary. Plan coordination at the CMEA level needs to be reviewed, however, so as to enhance its effectiveness. In particular, it needs to be directed at the essential regional tasks and to be finalized before the implementation of the national five-year plans. The focus of plan coordination on the broad development of production cooperation could be enhanced importantly also by encouraging direct ties among enterprises and organizations, including the creation of joint firms on a cost-accounting basis. Also this summit issue has been receiving considerable attention in recent months.

The prime sectors for further policy actions envisioned in *Main Directions* are those earlier included in the Target Programs. But scientific–technical cooperation in general receives special emphasis in that the members committed themselves to the elaboration of a long-term program (for the next fifteen to twenty years) on that subject. More rational utilization of scarce inputs and higher production and trade levels, possibly through joint investments and industrial reconversion, should enable the group to solve its fuel, raw material, and foodstuff problems. Joint efforts in agroindustrial and fuel sectors receive special stress. But due attention needs to be paid to feasible output levels that can be sustained and the need to exchange hard industrial inputs for manufactures in short supply (including food, up-to-date industrial consumer goods, selected construction materials, and machinery and equipment of high quality required by the net exporters of fuels and raw materials).

Together with the gradual transition to intensive growth, the economic mechanisms of the PEs need to be rendered more effective so as to foster factor productivity in part through the ISDL. Emerging problems should be identified and tackled at the earliest possible occasion. At the same time, the interest of economic agents has to be strengthened, including with the aid of financial and monetary instruments. How these stipulations individually and in the aggregate will mutate SEI remains to be worked out.

Although they are very carefully phrased and leave the door wide open for subsequent action, the published documents suggest that the summit accomplished far less than what the various participants had been hoping for. It is somewhat disconcerting that the potential for beneficial action in the future is bound to be compressed by two key developments. The first is the insistence on "hardening" the export menu against which crucial industrial inputs are henceforth to be traded. Clearly, most of the Eastern European countries find it well-nigh impossible to attain this goal quickly. An up-to-date export pattern of high-quality goods can ensue only from a major modernization drive and a change in managerial styles. Both require time even if the current leadership were in principle prepared to act swiftly. Related to this is another worrisome development. At least for near-term practical purposes, the multilateral SEI approach envisioned in the early 1970s has been abandoned in favor of the wider exploration of bilateral relations. The strengthening of structural bilateralism implicitly called for in *Main Directions* and stressed in the recently concluded long-term agreements between the USSR and most of the other CMEA partners buttress this ominous turn of events. Whether these two modes are likely to prevail also under Michail Gorbačëv's stewardship remains to be seen, as indicated in Chapter 3.

In the extraordinary forty-first Council Session held on 17–18 December 1985, the CMEA member countries adopted the comprehensive program on scientific–technical cooperation[18] enunciated at the June 1984 summit. Whether the program is in line with the intramural summit decisions is uncertain.[19] There is little doubt, however, that the document is, as usual, quite expansive on general matters and intentions but very short on what concretely is to be done in the near future to carry out the slated goals. Perhaps this is not so remarkable given that the document is to remain valid until the turn of the century. But the absence of concrete decisions as to how these long-term processes are to be initiated, guided, and controlled is disquieting. The PEs are called upon to work out a mutually coordinated network of agreements and treaties about reciprocal scientific–technical cooperation that will be reflected in the prospective annual and medium-term plans.

The new program aims at speeding up the pace of scientific–technological progress, including its introduction into the productive sphere, in five broad areas: electronics, automation, nuclear energy, new materials and technologies, and biotechnology. By focusing on these broad endeavors, the CMEA members hope not only to catch up with existing know-how in these areas but to surpass it and to arrive at the knowledge frontier by the turn of the century, at the latest. These advances should permit raising the level of average labor productivity in the CMEA as a whole by a factor of more than 2 and reducing drastically the material content of aggregate national output, especially energy and critical raw materials.

The "electronization" of the national economies is to be achieved by supplying all production spheres with the most modern data-processing facilities as the foundation for a general rise in labor productivity, reducing the material intensity of production, accelerating the pace of scientific–technical progress, sharply curtailing research and development lags, and changing the nonmaterial sphere in several qualitative respects. The second area envisages the "complex automation" of selected economic branches, chiefly by substituting capital for labor through robots, numerically controlled machines, and other sophisticated equipment. The chief goal of the nuclear energy component is to change the composition of energy production and use, to assure greater reliability in the supply of electricity, and to reduce the use of organic energy carriers. A very important component of the acceleration of scientific–technical progress is the creation and manipulation of new materials and technologies. The goals envisaged are widespread and include rust-free materials, heat- and friction-resisting products, and the industrial technologies to obtain such goods. The component on advances in biotechnology is, in the first place, directed at curing human ailments, enhancing the output of foodstuffs, improving the supply of raw materials, opening up new and renewable sources of energy, improving the environment, and reducing wastage in production.

How these ambitious policy goals are to be realized remains unclear. The document calls for the usual concrete multilateral and bilateral agreements and protocols to be negotiated as soon as feasible.[20] These need to encompass the full science–technology–production–distribution cycle. It also calls upon the members to "pay particular attention" to the appropriation of the necessary material and financial resources so that the measures included in the program can be carried out as expeditiously as possible as part and parcel of the normal planning processes. Existing scientific–technological research in the PEs may have to be complemented with bilateral or even multilateral organizations set up specifically to tackle particular issues of accelerating technological progress in order to lift productivity. Perhaps the key clause of the implementation provisions is the emphasis on the effective realization of direct relations among enterprises, associations, and scientific–technical institutions not only within each signatory country but also among the various participants in concrete bilateral or multilateral protocols. Financing will be undertaken through regular budgetary appropriations and credits from IBEC and IIB; in addition, it is anticipated that special funds will be established for some of the concrete agreements yet to be worked out.

Specialization and trade are two potentially crucial aspects of the program to be considered even though the document does not even describe them at any length. Because one of the fundamental aims of the program is to create mutually compatible technologies throughout the CMEA area, additional room for production specialization and trade intensification will be created. Inasmuch as the bases for generating technological progress and factor productivity are being radically changed by the provisions of the program, if successfully implemented, one can anticipate important consequences for the traditional cooperation mechanism within the CMEA.

The single most important question, therefore, concerns the chances of the program being implemented quickly according to the established provisions. One crucial determinant derives from the considerable restrictions on the room for policy maneuver that linger into the near term. These are bound to limit the funds that can be mobilized for special components of the program. Not all provisions really require fundamental changes to be funded ab ovo, however. Indeed, making more effective use of the available resources in conjunction with a slight acceleration in appropriations for new ventures included in the program would go a long way toward alleviating the constraints on the room for policy maneuver.

Recent statements by high-ranking decision makers, including the CMEA's secretary (*Izvestija*, 22 March 1986, p. 1; Syčëv 1986a, 1986b), indicate that the program comprises ninety-three separate research projects. These programs are to be finalized in the next three years, and most should be regulated by concrete protocols during 1986 (Matějka 1986, pp. 1,4; Syčëv 1986b, p. 48; Syčëv in *Nedelja,* 1986:27, pp. 6,7). Each project will be supervised by a "head organization (*golovnaja organizacija*)." Each project englobes a number of smaller "topics" or subprojects and, at the still more decentralized level, an even larger number of "themes" or "targets." The latter are said to number several thousands (Lér 1986, p. 1). Unlike the scientific–technical coordination centers created throughout the CMEA chiefly in the first half of the 1970s as one feature called by *Integration Program*, the current nodal links are slated to be all Soviet entities invested with extensive executive powers (Syčëv 1986a, p. 17). Each head organization will be charged with working out the details of contractual arrangements that will form the linchpin of the program's implementation modalities. These contracts will be "instructed" to the counterpart organizations throughout the CMEA. In this way, direct and permanent intragroup links in research, development, and production are to be fostered. Although the creation of direct relations in the CMEA has been a key topic of SEI debates (see Abolichina and Bakoveckij 1986; Bakoveckij and Abolichina 1986; Editorial 1986; Možin 1986; Silvestrov 1986; Širjaev 1986a, 1986b; VK 1986b), especially since Brežnev first broached the idea in 1981 (see Brabant in press, a), the question of how this reorganization is to be realized and whether all PEs hold the same precepts on direct relations have not yet been resolved. Some commentators see this as a task that can be accomplished in the near term (see Epštejn 1985). Syčëv (1986a, p. 19) asserts that the realization of this program will require "serious changes in the structure of the CMEA and in the style and methods of its activities." If experience is any guide, however, a more skeptical attitude would appear to be warranted.

Nonetheless, since the endorsement of the program in December 1985, the CMEA members have undertaken a number of studies and initiatives. The concrete modus of implementing the provisions of the program is not yet fully in place, although the most recent forty-second Council Session (Bucharest, 3–5 November 1986) and the new CMEA economic summit, which was convened soon thereafter (Moscow, 10–11 November 1986), appear to have devoted considerable attention to the realization of the objectives of *Scientific–technological Cooperation.* Although comprehensive details of these meetings are still lacking at this stage, the implementation is likely to proceed according to the forms blocked out earlier. This adherence to the initial modi operandi has apparently received a fillip from what has turned out to be, in several respects, a rather disappointing economic performance during the first year of the new five-year plan period.

Even more than before, the priorities of phasing out antiquated products and production processes, of raising efficiency, and of accelerating growth were placed at the forefront of the policy discussions in Bucharest and Moscow. To reach the stated objectives in some form, all members apparently agreed there that new forms are urgently required to improve economic development and modes of economic cooperation in the CMEA. The latest Council Session emphasized once again the urgent need to establish direct links between the enterprises of different CMEA members and, indeed, between the CMEA and production units. In Nikolaj Ryžkov's view, this is the CMEA's most important political and economic task in the years ahead (*Pravda,* 4 November 1986, p. 1). Whether this will indeed transpire into concrete steps in management, organization, development policies, and expected behavior of economic agents remains to be seen, however.

2.6 On the mechanisms of socialist economic integration

When reading the official CMEA documents, it is disquieting that one searches in vain for a reference to the precise goals and methods of guiding SEI. It would seem that the most pivotal questions of CMEA cooperation have been acknowledged as problematical, which is progress indeed! Their resolution evidently remains contingent on the elaboration of principles to be drafted, discussed, and, if possible, agreed upon. This suggests that the mechanisms for fostering SEI continue to be ambiguous but in flux. The view that the mechanism of SEI can be reduced simply to bilateral agreements is too confining not only from the historical record but also when placed in the context of the conceptual debate that has been in process for nearly twenty years.

On the concept of the mechanism of socialist economic integration

Since the promulgation of *Integration Program* – in fact, since the demise of the first wave of economic reforms in the 1960s – a special meaning has been attached to the "mechanism" of SEI.[21] Its principal features, although not always crystal clear and variously emphasized by different authors, mirror those of the members' "model." The chief pillars of the SEI mechanism are usually seen as the economic, institutional–organizational, and legal facets of SEI. It has become a very fashionable terminology, although it is not always transparent what precisely is meant by it. In what follows, the legal mechanism, though doubtlessly very important, will not at all be examined. I shall focus the discussion instead on the economic means by which the PEs hope to foster SEI processes because the opportunities for intensifying cooperation and implementation agreements reached, in principle, at the political command level depend on the proper stimulation of SEI by economic means.

The economic mechanism of SEI is the set of interrelated measures comprising policy instruments, institutions, and behavioral rules to attain some regional development goals, possibly a formal SEI strategy, in harmony with the policies and institutions of the participants. As such, the mechanism parallels the economic model of the members. But it differs from it in major respects. The most important subsystems of the traditional PE economic mechanism comprise centralized allocation of resources; directive planning by one center of the activities of each economic agent, particularly in the production sphere, through mandatory plan indicators and associated gauges for measuring and rewarding plan fulfillment; centralized redistribution of income; administrative setting of material and other incentives; and others. This had led to the gradual emergence of a system of vested interests at the various producer and consumer levels, and thus has molded the behavior of economic agents such that it does not generally conform to the exigencies of an intensive development pattern (Pilat and Dăianu 1984, p. 254). These chief elements of the domestic economic mechanism of the participating economies are quite clear. But those to be included in the SEI mechanism are not. Little controversy arises in connection with the listing of the elements. It is when one tries to assess their relative importance with respect to encouraging regional cooperation that serious conceptual and practical problems crop up.

Components of the economic mechanism of socialist economic integration

It is instructive for this investigation to distinguish among the following five economic facets of the SEI mechanism: (1) economic policy consultations; (2) synchronization of plans and joint planning; (3) price systems; (4) financial and monetary cooperation systems, including interstate credit mechanisms; and (5) scientific–technical cooperation. I have separated the price system from the broader aspects of monetary and financial cooperation, and indeed from the system of indirect coordination instruments in general, because "prices" have continued to play such a crucial role in the gestation of SEI, even under directive central planning. This central concern, as argued here, would not diminish even if the other, more market-oriented, aspects of financial and monetary cooperation were to recede into the background in order to beat the joint planning drum.

a. The planning mechanism. It is in the very nature of the CMEA members that planning must play an important part, at least in the implementation modalities of a jointly formulated SEI strategy. The planning mechanisms are currently quite differentiated and range from simple ex ante trade agreements to complex joint plans, such as the Concerted Plan. Most of this activity concerns plan coordination, although there is a rapidly growing component that can be identified as joint planning, especially if the latter's meaning is not needlessly confined to the simple working out of an all-encompassing joint plan, which is not likely to materialize soon.

The PEs agreed that the harmonization of national economic plans should serve as the chief subset of instruments directed at promoting SEI, because the latter is inherently a process "regulated in a deliberate and planned way." The national central planning boards bear the responsibility for all plan coordination activities in "broad cooperation" with the official and other Council organs. The coordination of plans involves deepening common efforts in several directions simultaneously. First, the members resolved jointly to forecast future demand and supply policies as the basis for drawing up concrete regional cooperation plans. Second, the PEs decided to resort to long-term perspective planning, in the form of Target Programs with a horizon of ten to twenty years, to regulate the chief determinants of key economic activities. Plan coordination also includes compromises on the basic aims of economic policies, broadly defined, of each member economy. Third, the traditional methods of coordinating medium-term plans need to be improved in the sense that the compass of coordination is to be shifted more and more from the sphere of trade to that of production and investment strategies (including scientific–technical cooperation, production specialization in accordance with regional market forces, the joint construction of specific investment projects, and the scope and timing of reciprocal commodity exchanges). Finally, plan coordination is also sought in the form of joint planning of selected economic branches or specific production types.

However vaguely defined in *Integration Program*, joint planning is a distinct category inasmuch as it could become an embryonic form of regionwide planning with the special feature at this juncture of it being facultative. This is in some contrast to the obligatory nature of annual and medium-term plan coordination that follows from the CMEA charter and a number of resolutions adopted by the Council Session. Joint planning should properly be understood as consisting of three parts: (1) a coherent complex of linked documents, some of which may have been jointly prepared, covering the kind and volume of work being done, the necessary resources, the participation of individual countries and concrete executors responsible for individual components of the agreed projects, including the means of fulfillment, and the technical and economic terms of cooperation; (2) a set of legally binding agreements concerning the results of dovetailed work programs and covering the responsibilities of CMEA bodies, IEOs, or individual countries responsible for executing the accepted tasks; and (3) special parts of the national medium-term and annual socioeconomic plans that reflect the duty to execute the tasks of joint planning by each PE concerned (see Kerner and Trubač 1975, pp. 103–112). A particularly conspicuous place in plan harmonization is reserved for the promotion of scientific–technological cooperation (comprising research, development, and production specialization) with the assistance of planning and indirect coordination instruments. The elaboration of a "mechanism of scientific–technological" cooperation is held to be essential to foster technical progress and the intensification of production in each country and the region as a whole.

Second, plan coordination cannot be pursued in a vacuum. It should be concerned primarily with shaping the outcome of policy consultations at the highest level into operational plan tasks with the assistance of other policy instruments. An important role in SEI is in principle played by frequent bilateral and multilateral consultations on a vast array of national and international economic policies, not only on the government and planning level but by all those responsible for drafting and implementing plans. The levels, forms, and procedures of these consultations as well as the topics to be tabled are normally decided by interested members, who will commit themselves in principle to certain common targets. At the same time, they preserve the right in each case to determine what has to be done concretely, including the prerogative of opting out. It is in that light that one searches in vain for a broad institutional infrastructure in support of CMEA plan coordination in all its various meanings.

b. Instruments of indirect economic coordination. *Integration Program* devotes considerable attention to the means of coordinating economic decisions indirectly. Their crucial role in fostering SEI already in the draft phase of the plans and in assisting in the implementation of coordinated plans is acknowledged. Such monetary and financial instruments were not, however, to be allotted a key role in the stage of plan formulation or in the process of setting up common projects, for this is reserved for planning and plan coordination. But they are deemed to be of assistance in the concrete formulation and implementation of common and coordinated planning.

There is an entire array of indirect instruments of economic coordination as well as a variety of institutional supports. The most important are those pertaining to the price systems, the monetary instruments, and the credit systems (Špaček 1981, p. 15). I shall therefore give a brief indication of the TR, CMEA price formation, interest rate policies, stimuli of capital and labor flows, and ERs.

The collective currency. As the preeminent socialist currency, the TR was to be gradually transformed into a real international currency, at least with respect to intragroup economic relations, by improving a variety of economic and organizational conditions so as to enhance its role. These modifications were to be worked out gradually in order to meet the tasks arising at each stage of SEI. In particular, the PEs harbored high hopes about ensuring the TR's transferability and establishing realistic ERs for their collective currency. The fundamental prerequisite for improving the TR's role is a realistic and stable purchasing power for that unit. Proper price formation in its widest setting is crucial to accomplish this. Only by tackling the price system can conditions be improved sufficiently so that the TR could become a real currency unit capable of supporting trading as well as specialization, joint investment, research, and so on within the CMEA. This need not imply that decisions are at all times to be based solely on rational economic criteria.

On numerous occasions the CMEA members have committed themselves to measures to mutate the TR into something more useful than a simple regional unit of account. Its role is to be enhanced also so that it can eventually join other international currencies in global markets and reflect more adequately the position of the CMEA in the world economy. Foremost among the preliminary steps to effectuate this task is the elaboration of the conditions under which nonmembers can participate in the system of multilateral settlements in TR.

CMEA price mechanisms. For many years now the CMEA members have studied the feasibility of gradually reducing the substantial differences between retail and wholesale prices, to improve their regional price formation, and to enhance the links between domestic and trade prices. At the same time, virtually all PEs have emphasized the importance of adhering to the principle of fixing contract prices on the basis of past WMPs, albeit with modifications of the criteria by which prices are adjusted. The determination of adequate relative prices in regional trade is one of the preeminent preconditions for promoting efficiency in each member economy and hence SEI.

National, regional, and other exchange rates. Provided the PEs really intend to transform the TR into an international currency, realistic ERs for their own currencies and the TR need to be determined. This is especially important to make the CMEA system of multilateral settlements attractive to other countries without disturbing the required stability in national and regional economic policies. For the TR to perform the key functions of an international currency, it must have a "real" purchasing power for all potential holders. This can be accomplished only if the participants agree unanimously on the mechanism that sets and maintains a realistic ER, which can emerge neither from free market forces nor from unplanned competitive pressures exerted by real demand and supply forces of the member countries.

The ER issue should be seen first and foremost in the context of intraregional interchange. The present system of multiple ERs inhibits even the expedient dovetailing of partial plans upon which all members are in full agreement. National ERs for commercial transactions, as distinct from so-called nonmerchandise transactions, are to be set at an economically meaningful level and to be reduced to a single common denominator through actions on the domestic price front. This would permit the creation of an interrelated set of ERs for commercial transactions underlying SEI decisions. The same should be pursued in the context of nonmerchandise interchange. Then a uniform ER is to be declared at least vis-à-vis the TR and, at a later stage, also with respect to CCs. Whether these ERs should eventually be set under impulse of actual or simulated market forces with frequent fluctuations is a different matter. It depends crucially on the underlying exchange regime that the CMEA members are willing to support. It is a particularly important function of the degree to which each country decides to link domestic with foreign trade prices.

Interest rates. A crucial determinant of a number of features underlying any type of regional integration is the forward price of goods and services. This depends in an important way on a realistic time preference, which enables decision makers to allocate resources not only in space but also intertemporally. Moreover, such comparisons are of paramount importance in the establishment of an effective capital market, the institutionalization of a smoothly functioning system of multilateral settlements, and other aspects of regional cooperation.

Wage rates and related matters. If an effective regional interchange of workers with different skills is to be secured, not only is it necessary to provide the infrastructure to foster labor mobility but workers must be enabled to do so voluntarily through material and other incentives tailored to the principal goals of SEI.

c. Institutional supports for indirect instruments. An intensification of meaningful economic cooperation among the CMEA members depends in an important way on an appropriate organizational and institutional infrastructure. Among these instances in the context of indirect economic cooperation, I shall refer to the creation of direct ties between economic agents, the multilateralization of regional trade and payments, the institution of convertibility, the conditions for an effective capital market, labor mobility, and so on.

Decentralized decision making. Although the issue of letting enterprises of various PEs interact directly has been debated on and off since the mid-1960s, direct regional economic relations, as distinct from more informal contacts at the lower rungs of the planning hierarchies, are not expected to play a central role in plan coordination or in formulating and implementing concrete aspects of SEI. Because this depends essentially on the domestic organization of the PEs, there is little that the CMEA as a regional institution can do to foster direct contacts beyond involving key enterprises (such as the crucial *Kombinate*) in the early stages of discussions about scientific–technical cooperation and specialization plans. As *Integration Program* affirms, each country organizes its economy according to its own conditions by taking "steps to create within the framework of national economic planning and management systems the requisite economic, organizational, and legal conditions for the successful realization" (Tokareva 1972, p. 100) of *Integration Program*.

Multilateralization of trade and payments. Changes in the trade sector, especially the transition toward multilateralism, among others, by seeking greater flexibility in BTPAs and allowing for nonquota trade, less rigorous annual balancing, greater capital mobility, and so on, have been promised for many years now. At various times, the members agreed to improve sharply traditional principles, methods, and tasks of economic cooperation and to study a few new possibilities within the existing CMEA framework. Because very little appears to have transpired from these efforts to date, SEI needs to be fostered within the existing institutions of the PEs and with the methods presently available in the CMEA organization.

Multilateralization is largely contingent on the TR's role. Without guaranteeing the actual transferability of excess TR earnings, there is not much hope of eliminating regional bilateralism; there is even less hope of the MEs using the TR. Without eliminating bilateralism in a constructive way, the PEs cannot realistically hope that the TR will eventually help to solve other tasks of SEI (such as the improvement of contractual prices and the establishment of a capital market). It is, therefore, expedient to separate multilateralism from the more restricted task of the TR's transferability and its eventual convertibility. The TR's enhancement depends primarily on the creation of stable multilateral trade and the accumulation of reserve currencies to permit multilateral settlements.

Convertibility. Conceptually, convertibility of the national currencies and the TR should not be confused with transferability, although both are intimately related. Whether it is the aim of the PEs to render their currencies and the TR fully convertible or whether foreign exchange will be subject to some limitations is crucial to future relations of the PEs with each other and third countries. Though officials have talked about convertibility for the TR as well as for domestic currencies for nearly two decades, it has remained fundamentally unclear what particular type of convertibility is being envisioned and how realistic such a policy goal might be. *Integration Program* affirmed that the member countries would study and prepare the implementation of regional convertibility; the conditions and procedures for the introduction of convertibility and its sphere of application were to be jointly worked out according to what is suitable to each PE.[22] Although the official stipulations are consistent with various modalities, it is almost certain that the PEs are not aiming at full convertibility, nor is it their intention to abolish or to weaken the currency monopoly.

Capital mobility. It is useful in this connection to distinguish between credits and direct investment. Although both could be identical in a formal sense, they have definitely different effects and implications. Credits are particularly important in the functioning of the two CMEA banks and especially in the way in which these institutions could contribute directly to the enhancement of regional economic integration. In other words, the role of settlements and short-term credits regarding the IBEC and of investment credits regarding the IIB crucially depends on how the banks are allowed to operate within the context of plans elaborated on a quite different level.

A related, though different, set of issues concerns investment proper, for instance, various kinds of IEOs. In this connection there is an entire array of planning, management, and control issues that should be discussed, but this is not the proper place to do so. The PEs should work out the appropriate economic, legal, and organizational prerequisites so that these agreements are compatible with internal planning and regional plan coordination.

Labor mobility. In a world with free movement of capital and labor, in addition to goods, the gradual leveling of relative scarcities can be expected to proceed fastest and farthest. The PEs have so far severely restricted labor mobility for a variety of economic, ideological, political, and other noneconomic considerations. The prevailing variety of impediments should be seen chiefly against the background of the widespread isolation and the decision-making autonomy coveted by each PE.

2.7 Socialist economic integration in perspective

The arguments offered so far may help to explain the protracted process of SEI and the rather modest results derived from it after nearly forty years of institutionalized cooperation. It is yet unclear in which direction SEI may be heading. The current economic situation of the PEs and their near-term outlook, though improved over the recession levels of 1981–1983, remain unsatisfactory. This far from optimistic assessment derives from the backlog of needed adaptations that is being exacerbated now by the ongoing changes in CMEA cooperation called for by the USSR at a time when none of the required structural adjustments has been completed. In most cases, reforms have not even been fully charted and earlier tentative experiments have been slowed down, if not stifled altogether, by the bureaucracy's vested interests.

Especially crucial to the future of SEI would be the direction and impact of economic reforms in the Soviet Union. Any meaningful change in decision-making mechanisms, the planning and organization of enterprises, the earmarking and implementation of foreign trade, or in related planning routines would have immediate and, because of the USSR's weight, wide-ranging repercussion on the rest of Eastern Europe and the directions of SEI. Until current Soviet priorities become transparent, then, it is hard to forecast any major acceleration of SEI or even a shift in its direction. Perhaps the most important argument is that the PEs have held quite divergent views on a lengthy menu of immense problems that are at the heart of CMEA cooperation. The June 1984 summit may have obtained the undivided approval to tackle these fundamental issues and to prepare another basic policy document on SEI. But it is rather implausible that the answers are already known in sufficient detail to enable the members to pursue a weighty common strategy.

Finally, any agreement of top leaders that can realistically improve SEI and provide a substantial fillip to the region's growth prospects depends critically on the promulgation of institutional reforms in each PE. Traditional approaches to central planning through the mechanisms in place in most countries impede the implementation of any type of real integration on which agreement might be feasible. Domestic reforms have been debated only on the margin by the official CMEA organs because they cannot interfere with the domestic affairs of the membership. In reality the dilemma is precisely that the countries have not yet fully clarified the type of economic reform they might wish to pursue.

Under the above circumstances, then, CMEA deliberations can hardly muster consensus on a number of substantive aspects of SEI methods and strategies. That is not to say that they have not yet come to tangible achievements and inaugurated policy agreements that may become transparent only in the future. However, unless major policies that have not yet even been hinted at are currently being pursued, something more substantial is urgently needed if SEI is to contribute measurably to the acceleration of growth in the CMEA region in the next decade or so. Consequently, for us to assess the conditions for SEI in the late 1980s and beyond, it would seem crucial to come to grips with the lessons of past experiences. Both sets of instruments discussed in *Integration Program* and hinted at again in *Main Directions* have been the subject of frequent reform proposals, but so far without lasting results.

The early 1980s have amply demonstrated the painful adjustments that most PEs have recently had to enact. The major impetus to this attempt to change expenditure levels and the production structure originated principally in the external sector, including the lackluster global economic situation in 1981–1983, the sharp rise in interest rates and the dollar, the debt crisis, and the inability of the PEs to restructure their output patterns sufficiently to buttress an export drive with manufactures. The adjustment effort encompassed a combination of import cuts, export boosts, and a sharp compression in domestic absorption, particularly with regard to investment. On the whole, this involved emergency measures brought about by force of circumstance.

Nonetheless, a sobering reminder that the PEs did not incur sharp terms-of-trade losses with developed MEs helps to avoid placing the larger share of the blame exclusively on fortuitous external shocks in MEs. The largest adjustment burden has indeed gradually accumulated in intragroup relations. Not only have the importers of fuels suffered very large cumulative losses in their regional terms of trade, but the goods with which these PEs can hope to pay for the steadily rising import bill are to be improved considerably, in both quality and diversity. This structural adjustment need has not so far been met head on. Certainly, the PEs had been bent on a more specific regional cooperation strategy by means of target programming, but these programs were on the whole not implemented for a variety of reasons (see Chapter 3). Another important factor was the unsynchronized nature of the policy responses to the external payments pressures.[23] In fact, the CMEA as such had little to offer by way of easing the adjustment burden arising either from the financial and commercial ties with MEs or from sharp shifts in regional relations. Given the disarray in CMEA economic relations in the early 1980s, it is small wonder that attempts at a multilateral approach to SEI, although only of a planning type, foundered and were rapidly being replaced by strengthened bilateral ties particularly around the USSR as CMEA pivot.

It is evident that this retrogression to bilateralism is bound to entail knotty adjustment problems of its own. If tackled in the tried-and-true style of Eastern Europe, it is unlikely to rectify the deep-seated economic problems of the region. It may well be advantageous for the USSR to recoup some of the opportunity costs of trading with Eastern Europe by agitating for higher-quality goods. But these are not likely to come forth automatically or quickly, and they will be painful in any case. It would now be foolhardy to exact such a price only with the exigencies of the Soviet market in mind. Although large, the Soviet share in Eastern Europe's trade is well below half, although not for each individual partner.[24] Furthermore, given the physical limits on raising Soviet supplies of intermediate goods, the PEs can hope to sustain acceptable rates of growth only by a successful export promotion elsewhere.

In other words, the most urgent task ahead is not the strengthening of bilateral ties with the USSR, but a bold move to promote intragroup ties as a sine qua non for firming the foundations necessary to foster exports to MEs in the years to come. Such desirable developments cannot be pursued in isolation in response to a political commitment concerning the expansion of bilateral trade. Instead a common adjustment strategy needs to be put in place in part by changing the institutional environment. The latter, at the very least, should buttress productivity growth, direct links among enterprises at least domestically, the gradual expansion of these links to the international domain, decentralization of macroeconomic decision making with the central plan being concerned in particular about major directions of growth and the proportions in income distribution. In other words, a broad-based positive adjustment strategy appears to be called for. The reasons are legion. They will become more transparent in Chapter 3.

3

Adjustment policies in perspective

A basic premise of socialist economic policy is that the state's control over economic processes through central planning assures economic stability and rapid output growth. Economic policy should aim at maintaining balance among the various economic sectors. It should also generate a relatively high, but stable, pace of expansion. Another premise of socialist planning is that the state can decide autonomously which economic structure is to be attained through interventionist policies. By establishing institutions, prescribing sufficiently comprehensive behavioral rules, and supplying adequate policy instruments, structural change at a fairly rapid pace proceeds without measurably adverse effects, when measured in technicoeconomic terms (including factor productivity, the potential sustainability of growth processes, supply bottlenecks, and so on). Another crucial belief of socialist economic policy is that directive resource mobilization at full employment levels constitutes the key ingredient for promoting radical and rapid economic restructuring. Marxist–Leninist ideology is held to motivate economic agents to do their best, even without ample material rewards and adequate economic incentives. Workers are presumed to be imbued by psychological and moral bonds that encourage them to explore new avenues to "give to the best of their ability." Socialist ownership of the means of production and the CP's vanguard role in setting priorities and allocating resources in the best interest of society as a whole, which may or may not mesh with the aspirations of individuals, are nevertheless presumed to instill an unusual work ethic.

As a consequence of the PE's institutions, chosen policy design, and overall societal interests in reaching feasible decisions, it was fundamentally presumed for a long time that such an economy could insulate itself very largely against foreign economic perturbations. Such a caesura of domestic and external markets was held to facilitate domestic planning, to promote full and stable employment, and to enhance the overall environment for rapid output growth. The PE was accordingly assured to be able to opt deliberately for any desired output structure without being positively guided or adversely affected by outside markets. Comparative advantage was to be the outcome rather than one basic inspiration of economic policy making. Needless to say that reality has diverged in minor and major respects from this paradigmatic scenario.

The first section discusses how the traditional PE was able to ward off foreign influences and its implications for policy making. Section 3.2 summarizes the nature of Eastern Europe's recent disequilibria. This leads to an analysis of the concept of adjustment against the backdrop of the PE's economic situation. A stylized diagnosis of the various alternative needs for adjustment and their respective cures is presented in Section 3.4. Traditional adjustment measures, such as envisaged for members of the International Monetary Fund (IMF or the Fund, for short) and the International Bank for Reconstruction and Development (IBRD) are discussed next. The basic elements in adjustment efforts of CPEs and MPEs are outlined in Sections 3.6 and 3.7, respectively.

3.1 The socialist economies in a global perspective

As described in Chapter 1, two basic characteristics of socialist economic policies and supporting institutions are the considerable degree of central control over domestic price formation and the allocation of resources and the MFT, whereby the state assumes, in principle, full control over the foreign trade sector. These two elements enable policy makers to segregate the domestic market from the external market, which affords them the tools to segment trade markets into several layers and to separate the domestic consumer and producer sectors. Whereas communication among these various layers is not fully proscribed, the intermeshing occurs largely through other than market signals.

The central allocation of resources through mandatory plan instructions to enterprises insulates the producer sector against any disturbance that the planner chooses to neutralize. The planning authorities assume, as a matter of course, that entrepreneurs simply implement the plan and furnish accurate and complete information, though this is not necessarily so. The center's prescriptions regarding the availability of primary and intermediate inputs determine by and large to what extent the enterprise attains set output targets. Some degree of flexibility is built into the plan because the center is well aware that it cannot prescribe all parameters required by microeconomic agents. In addition, plan instructions are sometimes faulty or outdated by the time plan executors seek to implement them. By and large, however, in the traditional PE there is only very limited room for exploring adjustment in economic structures according to indirect economic indicators.

Consumers do react in two ways to marketlike signals. As wage providers, they are guided by central wage controls, though sovereignty in that respect is quite imperfect. Laborers really cannot freely choose not to work without adverse sanctions. But they can change occupation rather freely, decide to hold more than one job, volunteer for overtime, and determine the pace of work to some degree.[1] Similarly, though planners are in principle equipped with a fully malleable wage system, their degree of freedom is rather confined by sociopolitical imperatives. Nonetheless, there is undoubtedly some flexibility that permits practical decisions based on indirect coordination instruments that remain outside the norms prescribed by the plan. But such incentives are not really adjusted to attract more labor when required to fulfill the plan or to ease the effective supply of labor when plan priorities call for the pace of economic expansion to be moderated. Though planners, in principle, set the wage system autonomously, in fact the system of job security and socialist egalitarianism ensure downward inflexibility of the money wage, limited room for wage differentiation, and strict bounds on the erosion of nominal wages through price changes.

On the other hand, consumers can decide with considerable sovereignty how to spend or to save. Although such decisions are made chiefly in reaction to marketlike signals, the latter are only infrequently adjusted to ensure balance in partial consumer markets. The plan aims at overall equilibrium in consumer markets, ex ante surpluses in some partial markets are to be offset by deficits in others, and households are expected to substitute accordingly. Consumers may, however, decide not to spend because they cannot find adequate substitutes at a reasonable search cost, or they may voluntarily save for some future purchase, possibly because of earmarked savings accounts. Their choice in either case is simply between cash holdings or savings in the monobank system at comparatively modest interest rates that do not encourage a proper intertemporal allocation of resources.

It is useful to point out in this connection four interrelated features that differentiate monetary control in PEs and MEs. First, the institutional structure of financial markets, and therefore their nature, in PEs is much simpler than in most MEs. The PEs have a de facto monobank system, although the central bank may have several subordinated specialized agencies that deal with very specific, though broad, issues. Typically, there may be a construction, investment, foreign trade, or agricultural bank to alleviate the monobank system from the specialized activities associated with these particular economic tasks. Because there are no independent domestic or foreign commercial banks, the planners need not concern themselves with how to control their lending behavior with reserve or liquidity ratios or interest rates. Because credit is usually made available through the monobank system in order to implement the plan, there is no secondary credit expansion in response to changes in the monetary base.

A second set of issues derives from the range of financial assets offered in PEs. They are basically limited to cash, savings deposits, forced government bonds, and occasionally enterprise bonds.[2] There are generally no equity shares or debentures, no stock or broad bond markets, and little consumer credit; supplier credit is, in principle, excluded as well. Thus the planners need not worry about the prices and yields of financial assets, interest rates, their effects on expenditures, or open-market operations.

Third, the domestic monetary system of a PE is nearly completely insulated from external transactions, whether on current or capital account. Transactions with nonresidents are centralized in the foreign trade bank, if such a branch of the monobank system exists,[3] and otherwise in the external department of the national bank. Furthermore, there are no problems of controlling the operations of international banks and multilateral corporations because enterprises cannot independently borrow abroad, except perhaps in a strictly legal sense.[4]

Finally, monetary, credit, and fiscal policies in PEs are considerably influenced by the prevailing ideology. This has important implications for interest rate policies and, indirectly, for the degree to which active monetary, credit, and fiscal policies can be pursued. Credit in the traditional PE is essentially managed in line with the real bills theory of credit. This theory can be traced at least as far back as Adam Smith and was particularly in vogue by the Banking School in Britain in the nineteenth century. Accordingly, credit should reflect real flows, in which sense it becomes "productive." This was held to be conducive to monetary equilibrium and to forestall inflationary pressures. Although its alleged advantages are largely unfounded in actual practice (see Wilczynski 1978, pp. 114–16), its provisions have remained of paramount importance in the PEs. The five principal characteristics of this theory are that loans are extended for well-specified purposes, granted for fixed periods of time, secured by real assets, repayable, and centrally regulated (in the PE context, they are administered on a planned basis).

The segmentation of markets into financial and real flows is perhaps most conspicuous, though by no means the most significant, in the foreign trade sector. Moreover, real or financial foreign markets are further disaggregated into various trading zones with distinct currency denominations. FTOs are instructed to dispose of their imports at predetermined domestic prices, even of goods for which no domestic equivalent exists, and to acquire the exports at domestic fiat prices. This admittedly very rigid separation typical of the first postwar decades has more recently been relaxed, so there are now areas where the various trading and currency markets are no longer clearly identifiable. Nevertheless, the FTOs of nearly all PEs continue, in principle, to be instructed to acquire (and to dispose) of some combination of imports (exports) in predetermined markets, especially concerning intragroup trade. Although quantum adjustments are not precluded altogether, taut planning considerably restricts their latitude.

In their foreign relations, these organs do not normally control price setting. Most PEs are price takers, especially in Western markets. In CMEA trade, these countries have adopted own price-formation principles (see Chapter 4). Once the trade plans are signed, the scope for quantum or price adjustments there is generally quite limited. FTOs therefore acquire (dispose of) their imports (exports) at prices prevailing in world markets or agreed upon in the CMEA context. Relative external prices are in harmony with relative domestic prices, if both are unique at all, only by fluke. If they were to be called upon to behave as regular *chozrasčët* economic agents, subject to some basic constraints – that is, entities that can, in principle, finance themselves rather than depend on budgetary allocations – FTOs would reap (incur) windfall gains (losses) from the fiat pricing behavior and the central allocation of resources.

To counteract the transmission of the potentially adverse effects of these price dichotomies to domestic markets, such as through the bonuses that might be associated with the accounting profits of FTOs, price differences are offset by budgetary means. Price equalization, irrespective of where and in what form this accounting proceeds, is the central instrument through which the microeconomic effects of differences between domestic and trade prices are neutralized. The size and composition of these subsidies and taxes may or may not have been planned. Differences between the planned and realized physical trade flows cannot remain without effect on the economy. If imported quantities fall short of plan targets and current supplies cannot be maintained through inventory drawdowns, either domestic consumption, investment, or output, or a combination thereof, must be contracted. If exported quantities fall short of plan targets, either domestic inventories, consumption, or investment must rise. The converse is also true. In other words, disturbances abroad are propagated into the domestic economy primarily through quantum variations. But these are precisely to be avoided to the extent possible by offsetting actions resulting from ex ante or ex post macroeconomic decisions. In that case, the real adjustment will be deferred to a subsequent planning period.

Note that, in principle, planners are able to adjust the level of domestic consumption and investment as well as the pattern of production in response to unanticipated changes in exports and imports. The foreign trade multiplier and similar foreign trade adjustment mechanisms observed in MEs therefore do not exist in the CPE.[5] The real impact of deviations between planned and realized magnitudes manifests itself at least at the macroeconomic level. Because the budget acquires windfall gains or has to offset losses of the FTOs, the price-equalization account accumulates or loses financial resources. Unplanned inflows may provide a financial stimulus to budgetary expenditures, and losses may inhibit the implementation of some planned targets in the budget law. The reason for this is quite simple. The presumed independence of the domestic economy from foreign influences in the monetary sphere does not mean that feasible foreign trade decisions could be made in violation of the familiar requirements of foreign exchange balance. Usually, planners set their export targets according to what they perceive to be the imports implied by the selected output targets. Any inconsistency among these variables ex ante requires further iterations until a feasible interrelationship among output, trade, and consumption, and hence the external balance, results. A deviation from the ex ante targets could disturb the balance of payments. Although this could be counteracted in several ways, in principle it is rarely done so as to avoid disturbing the delicate balance of domestic planning.

If the authorities decide to absorb foreign disturbances without changing export and import quantities, the balance-of-payments effect of divergences between actual and planned prices is reflected in the foreign exchange situation. If the current account is in deficit, planners may decide to disburse foreign exchange[6] or to acquire loans from abroad to postpone the loss of foreign exchange. If there is a surplus, planners may simply decide to pay off foreign debt to reduce foreign exchange holdings, which is traditionally held to be "unproductive," owing to the profound antimercantilist bias in the CPEs' foreign trade policies.

In principle, then, planners attempt to safeguard trade targets as much as possible in order to implement the overall socioeconomic plan in as stable a domestic economic environment as possible. Strict adherence to the forecast export and import plans is only possible if foreign exchange reserves or external loans and capital transfers enable the country to finance its deficit or to neutralize an inflow of foreign exchange. The latter is usually possible.

The former was the case during most of the postwar period until about the early 1970s. Thereafter until the early 1980s, foreign capital markets provided this desirable flexibility in managing the PE. If real cutbacks in imports or the promotion of exports have to be enacted to preserve external equilibrium, their effect on the home economy will be qualitatively similar to that in MEs, including the familiar multiplier effect, until the authorities revise the plan. Because of market dichotomies and central inference, however, the size of the multiplier is bound to be smaller than in MEs.

3.2 Economic disturbances and stabilization in the early 1980s

In spite of the long experience with central planning and the powerful policy instruments at their disposal, the PEs have been facing significant disequilibria for over a decade. These imbalances have a complex origin and cannot solely be attributed to faulty policy options, although in some instances (including Poland and Rumania) costly mistakes were undoubtedly made as a result of inexpedient domestic development choices in the 1970s. For example, the roots of Poland's severe imbalances since 1979 must be traced back to the ill-conceived development strategy adopted in the early 1970s. Just as it did in the case of many developed and developing MEs, the appreciable drift and perturbations in global trading and financial networks since the first oil crisis in 1973–1974 considerably exacerbated these palpable imbalances. Nevertheless, the PEs adjusted very slowly, if at all, until the swift and drastic emergency operations called for by the convoluted external financial situation of 1981–1983. This delayed response stemmed in large measure from their domestic and regional policies, institutions, and economic mechanisms. The most important underlying causes of the sluggish economic performance include (1) the excessive energy and raw material intensity of production, which stems partly from the chosen structure of the PEs; (2) comparatively low factor productivity; (3) only lackluster success with the transition from an extensive to an intensive growth path sought since the mid-1960s; (4) stagnant or only moderately growing fuel, raw material, and foodstuff output levels and only modest gains with the promotion of exports of manufactures; (5) ambivalent success with fostering technological progress, even when up-to-date imported technology became available, presumably because "X-efficiency" in the PEs is not at all easy to mobilize; and (6) politically, organizationally, and economically it has proved more difficult than anticipated to reconcile the signals emanating from external markets with the success indicators typical of the domestic managerial paradigms. A better understanding of what has materialized in Eastern Europe since the late 1970s may be helpful in discussing adjustment policies in a more general setting in subsequent sections.

Eastern Europe's recent economic performance

The economic performance of individual PEs has recently fluctuated considerably, as illustrated by some key domestic macroeconomic indicators (see Table 3.1).[7] Especially in the context of the global economic recession and in contrast to the quite moderate advancement of developed MEs since the first oil shock, the CMEA region as a whole performed remarkably well throughout the first half of the 1970s, showed uneven growth in 1976–1978, registered a steady deceleration until 1983, and has since attained only a modest recovery. The uneven performance of the PEs stemmed partly from rather wide fluctuations in agriculture, with crop failures in a number of PEs contributing directly as well as indirectly to the overall slowdown. But it is evident that the deceleration has been much more extensive, enveloping also heavy industry

Table 3.1 *Selected macroeconomic indicators of recent economic performance in the CMEA region (average annual and annual percentage changes)*

	Net material product						
	1971–5[a]	1976–1980[a]	1981	1982	1983	1984	1985[b]
Bulgaria	7.8	6.1	5.0	4.2	3.0	4.6	1.8
Czechoslovakia	5.7	3.7	−0.1	0.2	2.3	3.5	3.1
GDR	5.4	4.1	4.8	2.6	4.6	5.5	4.8
Hungary	6.2	2.8	2.5	2.6	0.3	2.5	−1.4
Poland	9.8	1.2	−12.0	−5.5	6.0	5.6	3.2
Rumania	11.3	7.2	2.2	2.7	3.7	7.7	5.9
Eastern Europe	7.9	3.6	−1.9	0.1	3.9	5.3	3.6
Soviet Union	5.7	4.3	3.3	4.0	4.2	3.2	2.5[c]

	Gross industrial output						
	1971–5[a]	1976–1980[a]	1981	1982	1983	1984	1985[b]
Bulgaria	9.0	6.0	4.9	4.6	4.3	4.2	3.6
Czechoslovakia	6.7	4.7	2.1	1.1	2.8	4.0	3.5
GDR	6.5	5.0	4.7	3.2	4.2	4.2	4.4
Hungary	6.4	3.4	2.4	2.7	1.4	3.2	1.1
Poland	10.4	4.7	−10.8	−2.1	6.4	5.2	4.4
Rumania	12.9	9.5	2.6	1.1	4.7	6.7	4.9
Eastern Europe	8.7	5.6	−0.6	1.2	4.4	4.8	4.1
Soviet Union	7.4	4.5	3.4	2.9	4.2	4.1	3.9

Gross agricultural output

	1971–5[a]	1976–1980[a]	1981	1982	1983	1984	1985[b]
Bulgaria	2.9	0.9	5.9	5.2	−7.2	7.0	−10.8
Czechoslovakia	2.6	1.9	−2.5	4.4	4.2	4.4	−1.6
GDR	2.7	1.2	1.6	−4.0	4.1	6.2	3.0
Hungary	4.8	2.5	2.0	7.3	−2.7	2.9	−5.5
Poland	3.7	−1.7	3.8	−2.8	3.3	5.7	0.8
Rumania	6.4	3.8	−0.9	7.6	−1.6	13.3	0.1
Eastern Europe	3.8	0.8	1.8	1.6	0.9	6.7	0.1
Soviet Union	0.5	1.6	−1.0	5.5	6.1	−0.1	0.0

Gross investment

	1971–5	1976–1980[a]	1981[a]	1982	1983	1984	1985[b]
Bulgaria	8.4	4.0	10.5	3.6	0.7	0.3	2.6[c]
Czechoslovakia	8.2	3.5	−4.6	−2.3	0.6	−4.2	5.4
GDR	4.1	3.4	2.7	−5.2	0.0	−5.0	3.7
Hungary	7.1	2.2	−4.3	−1.6	−3.4	−4.3	−3.0
Poland	18.4	−3.0	−22.3	−12.1	9.4	11.4	5.7
Rumania	11.5	8.5	−7.1	−3.2	2.4	6.1[c]	0.7[c]
Eastern Europe	10.8	2.7	−7.1	−4.4	2.3	2.2	2.9
Soviet Union	7.0	3.4	3.8	3.5	5.6	1.9	2.5

[a] Average compound annual growth rates over the indicated period.
[b] Preliminary.   [c] Estimate.
Source: National statistics aggregated with weights based on relative country shares in data revalued on a comparable basis, but for different base years, for the CMEA region as a whole.

and construction. Even PEs like Bulgaria and Rumania that still possess appreciable reserves to sustain growth through factor inputs have been confronted with more confining development conditions. In addition to supply and capacity constraints, the feasible level of economic activity has recently also been adversely affected by shifts in internal and external demand and supply.

The recent slowing down in the pace of economic growth in Eastern Europe stems essentially from two different sets of factors. On the one hand, the majority of the PEs have been confronted with growing restrictions on factor availability and traditional macroeconomic redistribution options that are pertinent in designing effective policies for fostering factor productivity. The elements of the changing growth environment that would have come to bear on developments in the 1980s in any case will be examined briefly in Section 3.4 and more fully in Chapter 12. However, these fundamental restrictions on feasible development strategies have recently been compounded by growing domestic bottlenecks (including output constraints in basic sectors, capacity limitations in transportation, and inflexibilities in the generation of electricity in particular), sluggish performance in agriculture, and delayed policy responses especially to the worsening external economic environment.

The coincident emergence of the sharp deterioration in the terms of trade for nearly all Eastern European PEs, the slackening import demand of CC markets, and the already comparatively large external debt accumulated in the 1970s seriously complicated the formulation and implementation of effective economic policies. The latter had not been anticipated in the national economic plans and could not be quickly offset through policy adaptations; therefore it had a cumulatively disruptive effect in related sectors. In the event, the response to the global disturbances was neither quick nor decisive. Key components of economic policies in traditional PEs were simply kept in place perhaps in the hope that the worsening external environment would be a passing phenomenon. The delayed and muted response also emerged because of a number of institutional characteristics, including the specific arrangements for trade and payments within the context of the CMEA. Especially the CMEA pricing mechanism (see Chapter 4) eased the transmission of adverse global price developments. For example, when WMPs moderated and commodity prices were actually collapsing in the early 1980s, CMEA prices of raw materials continued their upward drift, relative to prices of manufactured products. These sizable changes in the CMEA terms of trade[8] severely curbed maneuverability in Eastern Europe's economic policies.

The worsening terms of trade had a particularly adverse impact because most of the small PEs were already exposed to pronounced external pressures and had run substantial CC balance-of-payments deficits.

To some extent, borrowing abroad had initially been a conscious policy decision to accelerate technology imports, to stimulate productivity, and to improve the quality and volume of exports so as to liquidate the debt in the near future; the loans were thus considered to be self-liquidating. However, the recessions after the two oil shocks and the subsequent disinflationary policies pursued by key MEs invalidated this strategy. The external problems of the PEs were also compounded by the import requirements associated with the technologies purchased in earlier years. This erosion of trade flexibility built into the strategy of the early 1970s had been inadequately anticipated in the planning process; it had especially debilitating consequences for Poland.

Changes in export and import quantum in Table 3.2 may help to clarify the particular problems of the small PEs. As the data illustrate, trade growth was very fast in the first half of the 1970s. It later slowed down markedly, but more so for imports than for exports. These magnitudes suggest that the deterioration in terms of trade together with the rapid growth of imports must have entailed payments problems. Although no precise data are available, the rough estimates of changes in price and quantum by broad partner grouping presented in Table 3.3 illustrate the problem. Admittedly the period averages mask the sizable annual fluctuations in prices and quantities, which have been more pronounced in East–West than in CMEA trade. The data indicate nevertheless that the smaller PEs sustained a sharp deterioration, especially in their regional terms of trade. Because the CMEA regional trade and payments arrangements do not normally allow countries to incur significant payments imbalances, the smaller PEs were unable to sustain their export momentum in the first place in trade with developed MEs. It is only as a result of a sharp cutback in import volume until 1985 that the situation has started to reverse.

The cumulative need for adjustment and stabilization has grown more on account of shocks that have emanated from the TR area than on account of other disturbances. This is not to deny that the PEs have been affected by many more shocks in a rather brief period from the MEs than from the CMEA area. However, the latter's cumulative magnitude and severity by far outweigh the former's impact. Two simple facts may illustrate this. First, Hungary's terms of trade with the dollar area improved considerably in most years since 1975, whereas its terms of trade with the ruble area sharply deteriorated: In 1984, the terms of trade in CC relations were virtually the same as in 1975, whereas the TR price index deteriorated by 20 percent.[9] Poland has been in much the same situation, in spite of the worsened East–West climate since 1979.[10] Although the precise magnitudes of the terms-of-trade shifts registered by the other members of the group may differ from Hungary's and Poland's, neither the direction of the shifts nor the broad size of the widening gap can

Table 3.2. Changes in trade quantum (annual percentage rates of growth)

Region	1971–1975[a]	1976–1980[a]	1979	1980	1981	1982	1983	1984	1985[b]
Exports									
Bulgaria	10.0	12.8	13.7	12.2	8.4	11.3	4.4	11.6	2.2
Czechoslovakia	6.3	6.3	3.2	4.7	0.5	6.1	5.7	8.5	2.6
GDR	9.0	6.0	8.9	3.6	8.4	5.4	10.6	3.7	1.7
Hungary	9.4	7.0	12.5	1.0	2.6	7.3	9.4	5.8	−0.3
Poland	10.7	4.0	6.8	−4.2	−19.0	8.7	10.3	9.5	1.6
Rumania	9.1	5.8	2.1	4.4	13.6	−7.6	0.9	16.5	1.6
Eastern Europe	9.0	6.5	7.6	2.9	1.2	5.5	7.4	8.4	1.7
USSR	5.0	4.9	0.6	1.6	1.9	4.5	3.3	2.5	−4.3
Imports									
Bulgaria	14.3	3.2	2.1	4.1	9.3	3.2	5.2	5.6	10.9
Czechoslovakia	6.5	2.9	2.2	−1.6	−6.9	2.9	2.0	4.8	4.6
GDR	7.2	5.1	6.5	5.1	−1.3	−4.7	5.3	5.7	2.3
Hungary	7.3	3.9	−3.3	−1.1	0.1	−0.1	3.9	0.1	1.1
Poland	15.4	1.7	−1.2	−1.9	−16.9	−13.7	5.2	8.6	7.2
Rumania	7.8	8.4	4.0	3.7	−7.2	−22.8	−5.0	9.6	10.3
Eastern Europe	9.5	3.9	1.7	1.2	−5.2	−5.8	3.4	5.5	5.7
USSR	10.6	5.7	1.1	7.5	6.4	9.7	4.0	4.4	4.0

[a] Average compound growth rates over the indicated period.
[b] Preliminary.

Source: With the exception of Rumania and the magnitudes for 1984–1985, the national data are derived from official indices. For Rumania, estimates have been prepared on the basis of the commodity group price indices by payments zone of other PEs, particularly Hungary. Some of the 1984 and all 1985 growth rates are preliminary. The aggregations use preceding year value weights.

have diverged much. Rumania is probably the only exception because it procures most of its imported oil from world markets. Second, several Eastern European countries have recently demonstrated that CC exports can be raised sharply without necessarily entailing sizably negative terms-of-trade effects.[11]

The sluggish export performance in CC trade during most of the 1970s was initially perceived to be purely temporary. In general, neither the magnitude nor the ramifications of the then emerging sharp changes in world markets, particularly fuel prices, were appropriately evaluated. Most PEs remained optimistic about the impact of the first oil shock in part because of the CMEA's institutional and policy arrangements and because energy was then an exceedingly small component of imports from nonsocialist countries. At the same time, their very energy-intensive, and by international standards energy-inefficient, production structures were not at all modified in response to changes in real marginal costs. Furthermore, most PEs were reluctant to revise ambitious social programs adopted in the preceding decade for implementation in the 1970s and beyond. Successive setbacks in agriculture, for instance, were offset mainly through imports rather than by compressing consumption. In short, some PEs borrowed to finance current consumption rather than, as initially contemplated, to foster more productive, export-oriented structures. As a result, they imported substantially more than had been planned while current export earnings trailed behind expectations. This apparent collision course and the eventual problems of financing current consumption from abroad were not taken as a cue to restrain imports.

The Soviet Union's situation differed palpably from Eastern Europe's. Most importantly, the USSR gained substantially from the change in WMPs of primary goods and could sharply lift import quantum without encountering adverse balance-of-payments effects. In particular, setbacks in agriculture could be accommodated without measurably constraining other imports or disturbing the balance of payments, but domestic food-stuff markets suffered to some degree just the same. Relative to the size of the USSR's output potential and even its trade level, the CC debt remained remarkably small. Nevertheless, by the second half of the 1970s the obstacles that inhibited a sustained output expansion in agriculture, fuels, and raw materials had become acute. As a result, rising domestic and CMEA import requirements competed with claims on resources to finance the USSR's imports of foodstuffs and machinery if borrowing in CC markets was to be avoided.

The response of the PEs in particular to the momentum of the world economic crises remained defensive at best. Initially, it encompassed short-term accommodation to what, in retrospect, turned out to be global structural shifts rather than temporary fluctuations. Fundamental changes in economic structures, policies, or implemenation modalities

Table 3.3. *Eastern Europe's trade prices and quantum by region, 1971–1984 (average annual percentage rates of growth between end-years)*

Region	1971–1975		1976–1980		1981–1984	
	Export	Import	Export	Import	Export	Import
Quantum						
Bulgaria						
CMEA	10	12	5	2	6	2
East–West	7	10	11	−2	9	11
Czechoslovakia						
CMEA	8	8	4	2	4	1
East–West	6	2	4	3	9	−2
GDR						
CMEA	10	7	3	0	4	−1
East–West	5	3	5	5	21	7
Hungary						
CMEA	12	10	7	2	6	1
East–West	6	5	7	5	6	1
Poland						
CMEA	13	8	16	3	4	−0
East–West	11	22	4	−4	−2	−12
Rumania						
CMEA	10	6	7	5	3	−0
East–West	14	8	5	6	9	−13

Prices

Bulgaria						
CMEA	4	5	6	9	5	10
East–West	8	12	9	7	−1	−1
Czechoslovakia						
CMEA	5	6	7	8	8	12
East–West	4	11	9	4	−5	−4
GDR						
CMEA	2	5	6	8	6	9
East–West	7	12	8	7	−4	−2
Hungary						
CMEA	4	6	−1	1	3	7
East–West	4	10	3	1	5	5
Poland						
CMEA	4	6	6	8	114	119
East–West	9	12	7	7	133	132
Rumania						
CMEA	3	5	6	8	34	35
East–West	9	13	9	13	39	42

Sources and methods: All data are estimates derived from local currency data in current prices divided into 10 commodity classes and Hungarian price indices suitably adjusted to reflect unsynchronized ER movements as well as discontinuities in the ER regimes of Hungary, Poland, and Rumania. Further details are available from the author.

were eschewed because the majority of PEs sought to cope most forcefully with the outward signs of these internal and external disequilibria
rather than their roots. As regards the external causes, this policy stance
may have been inspired in part because the global crisis was held to be a
temporary, reversible phenomenon. But adjustments called for by domestic circumstances were also evaded. In the event, imports were ruth-
lessly slashed and exports promoted in 1981–1984 to rectify the external
imbalance even if that meant curbing aggregate consumption (see Tables
3.2 and 3.3). Sectoral market imbalances even of comparatively scarce
goods were exacerbated in the process. Similarly, investment programs
were repeatedly revised, postponed, or shelved altogether, and various
overt and concealed changes in retail prices (see Chapter 5) were enacted
to blot up "excess" household money balances, which arguably improved
consumer market balances.

Rationale for the policy choice

The PEs seem to have directed little effort at clarifying and redressing
the root causes of their internal and external disequilibria by a comprehensive development program aimed specifically at regaining a more
satisfactory, balanced pace of expansion. When the relative weights of all
plausible determinants are duly ascertained, a better understanding of
the reason for the sluggish reaction of policy makers in PEs to emerging
and growing imbalances of the 1970s derives in an important way from
the typical economic mechanism of these countries. The disjunctions between domestic and foreign markets, on the one hand, and between
CMEA and outside markets, on the other, stand out. But the rather
primitive built-in adaptive ability of the CMEA region as a whole is important too.

Many characteristics of PEs and the CMEA have no counterpart in MEs
and their regional organizations. The single most important differentiation pertains to price formation (see Chapters 4 and 5). This is of particular significance for the PEs that have sought to utilize prices as allocatory
instruments in the guidance of decentralized decisions. Thus far the complexity of extraneous TR prices has been taken into account by neutralizing the effects of price differences through the traditional tax-cum-subsidy
transfers to and from the special budget account or a variation thereof in
all economies, at least for the bulk of their CMEA trade. Since the second
half of the 1960s, this is even true in Hungary, even though its policy
makers have clearly sought to improve the harmonization of TR prices
with other prices used in economic decision making. Because wholesale
prices of most primary and intermediate goods are not really flexible, all
countries have retained at least some key elements of the tax-cum-subsidy
equalization between domestic and CMEA trade prices and, in some in-

stances, with WMPs. To foster efficient decentralized decision making under the circumstances, these countries should set commodity-specific equalization subsidies and taxes without distortions. Seen against the backdrop of the hardy problems of centrally choosing accurate indicators for lower planning tiers, the various price dichotomies pose formidable obstacles to the exploitation of indirect signals by decentralized units.

Adjustment in the early 1980s and indirect coordination instruments

The recent bout of adjustment problems in the PEs came about largely because of a combination of faulty domestic planning, unforeseen adverse developments in trading markets, and shifts in financial markets that were without precedent. The nature and severity of the foreign exchange crises in several PEs since 1979 were determined importantly by external events beyond their control. Especially the loss of confidence by financial markets since 1981, which for some PEs still holds, has left a deep imprint on some CMEA members. Before 1981, commercial banks collectively had lent to the point where adjustments were postponed for an undesirably long period of time. They subsequently sought to reduce their exposure in ways that compounded the liquidity problems created by the adverse shifts in the foreign trade markets. PEs did not respond until the proportions became simply unmanageable. Their stance then took the form of the ruthless slashing of imports; the fast promotion of exports, even if at the cost of deteriorating terms of trade and aggravating domestic imbalances; the indiscriminate pruning of investment programs and projects in progress; and the compression of final consumption. Only in some instances, and then usually in a muted form, were these maneuvers anchored to shifts in enterprise guidelines of a more indirect nature or targeted at modified consumer behavior. Though some recalibrations of policy instruments were also undertaken to alleviate external payments pressures, it generally proved to be too cumbersome to enact swift adjustment by modifying indirect guidance mechanisms. The imposition of trade controls through explicit or implicit quantitative import restrictions proved to work much faster and more incisively than changing the domestic regulators, such as explicit and implicit internal ER(s), which are discussed in Chapter 6.

During the adjustment phase, policy makers resorted to direct as well as indirect policy instruments. Relatively large changes in domestic prices occurred, some attributable to devaluations, but most stemming from shifts in relative fiat prices enacted by the authorities as one means of curtailing budget subsidies and influencing the level and especially the composition of personal consumption demand (see Chapter 5). Similarly, several PEs tried to steer investments by more active interest rate and lending policies, as well as other indirect management criteria. These measures had been introduced as essential components of the devolution of economic decision making.

Changes in the "economic mechanisms" of PEs are inherently to be planned and dovetailed with medium- to long-term policy concerns rather than targeted at easing unexpected short-term external disturbances. As a result, adverse movements in the level of retail prices or in the relative price levels of the major segments of personal demand were generally compensated by additional social transfers and special income allowances. Some erosion in levels of living occurred as a result of meager wage gains, uncompensated price changes, involuntary product substitution, longer queues, or unplanned household savings. Nevertheless, the brunt of the adjustment maneuver has been borne by investments, in the form of a more cautious authorization of new projects, postponement or scrapping of projects already approved but not yet far along in their implementation phase, and changes in the direction of ongoing investment projects in mid-process in order to come to grips with the sharply risen cost of energy, shortages in regional supplies of fuels and raw materials, external constraints, and other adverse growth determinants.

At the start of the adjustment phase of the early 1980s, the majority of decision makers in Eastern Europe held that a slowdown in investment activity, in combination with a higher concentration of investment funds, better organization and management of the selected construction projects, and increased emphasis on modernization would stimulate capital productivity. Other decision makers and many economists contended, however, that higher capital productivity depends crucially on accumulation, which, if adroitly used, provides the means to eliminate disproportions, to raise the technical level of production, and to improve product quality. The recent experience with externally induced adjustments has confirmed the latter view chiefly because only a relatively small proportion of investment appropriations can be redistributed in the short run. A general cutback in investments tends to fractionalize allocations, results in additional projects in progress, and leads to bottleneck inventories, all contrary to policy intentions. There is therefore not likely to be a lasting reduction in marginal capital-output ratios at a time of austerity.

One prime characteristic of the recent bout of adjustment efforts has been strongly interventionist policies resorted to mostly on an emergency basis, in sharp contrast to the policy precepts declared since the early 1970s. In terms of curbing the CC deficit and winding down the piled-up debt, interventionism has yielded remarkable results. But the underlying crisis actions cannot provide the mainstay of a viable medium- to long-term growth strategy for a variety of reasons. Especially important is the fact that these measures were not well coordinated either internally or in the CMEA context, and adverse imbalances thus emerged in the process. There is then cause for concern about the medium- to long-term viability of these policies. Even if they had been harmonized with other economic proportions, the essentially negative bent of these policies calls for their repeal. An austerity policy conceived around the removal of inventories of consumer goods, the withholding of industrial inputs from the domestic production process to force up exports, and ruthless cutbacks in imports as means of attenuating the balance-of-payments constraints cannot provide a realistic medium-term strategy because it inexorably compresses feasible gains in per capita output levels, which is the very converse of one important trait buttressing socialist economic policies.

3.3 Adjustment at mid-decade

The quite comprehensive insulation of domestic markets from foreign contacts has been a key trait of the PE economic mechanism. It has facilitated a largely autonomous development course with "adjustments" that diverge markedly from what comparative advantage indicators would have called for. Rather than patterning the structure of their economies according to global demand and supply forces, and in line with other indicators of static economic efficiency, central planners regulated quite rigidly what was to be exported and imported, and set for themselves the compass within which these flows could directly stir up the domestic economy. Though policy makers can choose to offset external disturbances at the macroeconomic level or to manage changes in real magnitudes during plan implementation, *in se* the PEs are not immune to forces emanating from world markets or economic stringencies per se.

It would be a gross mistake, however, to equate the need for adjustment with the explosion of oil prices in the early 1970s, their gradual transmission into the CMEA pricing arrangements since then, or the severe external constraints in trade and payments relations with CC partners in the early 1980s. Although significantly exacerbated by these events, the "Eastern European economic crisis" finds its fundamental origin in phenomena that antedate the "oil crisis" and that were largely internal to either the group as a whole or the individual economies (Lavigne 1985b, p. 32).

The need for adjustment

Adjustment is, by definition, a relative concept. An economic system has to undergo small or large modifications, depending upon the gap between what decision makers envisage or have provided for and the prevailing reality. Because state ownership of the means of production and considerable control over the supply of labor at some wage scale are presumed to be prerogatives of central planners, the gap between what exists and what should be accommodated must necessarily be reflected in the foreign trade and payments sector.

Persistent deferral of adjustment to external pressures so as to sustain planned output levels is attainable only if the pressures are not too large and thus can be weathered through fluctuations in inventories or exchange reserves. Planners can also decide to offset the macroeconomic impact by cutting domestic absorption or by mortgaging the economy's future through foreign borrowing. The reckoning of the latter policy option will dawn forcefully if the nature of the initial inducement to adjust was not transitory but fundamentally structural, and foreign borrowing is not utilized so as to meet the deficiencies in underlying structures. Having procrastinated too long with the enactment of shifts in the traditional economic model in support of the planned strategy in its essential elements at a time of rapid transformations in trading and financial markets is the legacy that the PEs have to grapple with at this juncture.

It bears stressing, however, that the external reasons for adjustment have been considerably compounded by the pent-up need for a reconsideration of structural policies on account of shifts in policy objectives, less than full autonomy over the appropriation of production factors, and rising internal imbalances in the availability and allocation of resources. In short, the need for structural adjustment in the majority of PEs has now built up for over a quarter century. Its scope can be analytically blocked out into four areas: (1) to align economic structures with real factor scarcities, (2) to foster faster expansion of output chiefly through productivity growth, (3) to renew productive structures in line with shifts in trade prices since the mid-1970s, and (4) to come to grips with the mounting pressures within the CMEA to expand production capacities, to eliminate bottlenecks, to price goods and services realistically, and to upgrade the technological sophistication of more export-oriented productive structures.

Sources of disequilibria in the CMEA

As mentioned, the sources of the imbalances are the deformations in economic structures through extensive development policies; the inability of the PEs to initiate comprehensive economic reforms without serious wavering, stoppages, and retrogression; the systemic proclivity of PEs to import more than they planned for and to fall short on export targets, perhaps because of an "antimercantilist" bent of planners or because of their "saleability illusion" (Holzman, 1979, pp. 77–79), and the inadequate degree of progress achieved with SEI. If any of the basic assumptions underlying central planning, state ownership of capital and land, or control over the labor force is weakened as a result of shifts in the prefer-

ences of socialist society, there may be eminent cause for seeking adjustment for purely domestic circumstances as well. To the extent that these
problems can be tackled by devolving decision making, planners need to
make room for, at least piecemeal, adjustments in economic structures.
Such can be achieved through central planning or market processes, but
preferably by a combination of the two.

There is another important cause for adjustment that, though related
to the preceding, analytically differs from it. Structural changes in Eastern Europe were embraced in the postwar period without much regard
for static efficiency. This strategy worked admirably in backward economies with ample underutilized resources because it enabled planners to
pursue an autonomous pattern of growth anchored to the constant injec-
tion of new factors of production or the steady reallocation of factors
from one sector to another without necessarily depressing output capacity in the labor-shedding sectors. Central planning, in combination with
rather rigid market separation, has been a key buttress of such a policy.
This option of lifting output levels vanishes when all factors are mobilized, production factors can no longer be reallocated without depressing
output levels in the affected sectors, the growth of the effective labor
force slows to a trickle or becomes even negative, or the pace of capital
formation in production sectors must be curbed either because of limits
on overall capital formation or in recognition of other claimants on resources. When the combined factor input stream decelerates and compresses the pace of aggregate output growth, as indicated in Chapter 1,
planners normally attempt to bolster the trade sector and exploit it as an
alternative source of growth that they had previously downplayed. But in
order to participate more fully in world trade without inadvertently transferring a net amount of domestic value added abroad, greater harmony
between trade and domestic efficiency indicators needs to be achieved in
the plan or through market guidance. This is normally attainable only if
changes in domestic structures are enacted also in the real sphere.

The final set of adjustment requirements stems from structural and
other transformations in world markets. Just as when individual PEs
eventually run out of steam with an extensive growth strategy, seminal
changes in world markets have a macro- or microeconomic impact on
PEs. The first case occurs when the mechanisms typical of the CPE still
constitute the predominant mode of decision making, and the disturbances can be accommodated in the short run through shifts in inventories
or exchange reserves. A different resource allocation pattern will emerge
later within the context of subsequent plans and with the instruments
normally available to central planners. Unplanned disturbances are, in
principle, not to affect domestic production and consumption. When
reserves no longer permit further delays, a positive adjustment policy
needs to be formulated and implemented without procrastination. But in

the interim, planners may have no alternative but to come to grips with the most immediate of the foreign exchange pressures by way of emergency measures.

Basic growth determinants in the CMEA region

The crucial determinants for revitalizing the PEs and stabilizing their pace of growth at the socially desired level differ markedly from country to country, particularly in the short to medium run. The strategic long-run development determinants exhibit greater uniformity, however, because they are generally much less favorable to extensive development policies.

a. Domestic growth determinants. In contrast to the comparatively ample expansion in capital and labor through the first half of the 1970s, annual increments in primary factor supply have slowed down sharply since, and the prospects for a sustainable resumption of a faster pace are not encouraging at all. Though numerical factor availability could, in principle, be augmented through international mobility, the chances of doing so are not encouraging. Labor migration cannot be much more than a relatively short-term palliative because of fundamental precepts of socialist policies. Furthermore, the scope for capital inflows is rather confined because the PEs do not permit equity investment and are reluctant to raise their CC debt levels (see Chapter 9).

Labor availability is affected by past demographic trends, but also by social variables (including participation rates,[12] pressures for retirement, education policies, annual leave, sick benefits, length of the working week, and the like) that on balance have slowed down the expansion of effective labor services throughout the region. In most developed PEs, there is little prospect of growth in real terms in the years ahead, although demographic trends have recently improved and will be yielding new labor cohorts.[13] Others can still anticipate net additions to the labor force, although at a more moderate rate than during most of the postwar period. Moreover, further reductions in the working week, longer training periods, limited possibilities for an intersectoral relocation of labor at a tolerable cost (see Chapter 12), and so on, are likely to prevail in the near future too. Furthermore, shifts in consumer demand toward a broad range of services need to be gradually reflected in actual planning. Because such service sectors are as a rule substantially more labor intensive and less productive than, say, most industrial activities, at least in the short to medium term, such a shift may further accentuate the relative labor scarcity in Eastern Europe.

Also the evolution of the feasible net accumulation of capital from internal and external sources is likely to show a more moderate trend.

Consumption levels can hardly be compressed further without provoking social discontent. There is therefore only limited room for boosting macroeconomic savings behavior. Yet claims on new investment resources keep rising. Perhaps foremost is the sharp shift in real relative prices of intermediate inputs relative to finished products. The transformation in relative WMPs has measurably reduced the real economic value of the available capital stock, particularly of energy-inefficient production processes. As a result, the pressure for rejuvenating capital equipment in the material sphere has been mounting, but it has been encountering severe competition from other claimants. The investment strategies pursued in the recent past confront most PEs with sharply risen claims on resources that do not directly augment the "productive" capital stock. Even this more slowly growing investment fund will be appropriated mostly for capital-intensive projects with long gestation lags and will therefore not quickly increase capital services. Finally, because of the prevailing external payments conditions, instead of attracting more capital, most PEs have been experiencing a net outflow of funds in order gradually to work off their CC debt.

b. Key changes in the external environment. The most important features of the transformed external environment for growth, especially for the smaller PEs in view of the USSR's resource endowments, debt levels, and trade intensities, are (1) a sharp shift in the price of fuels in terms of manufactures; (2) large debt-service requirements; (3) slow growth in the aggregate import demand of MEs, still slower expansion in the import demand for traditional manufactures in MEs, and mounting competition for these markets mainly on the part of the NICs; (4) sluggish progress with SEI, even with the expansion of regional supplies of primary inputs; (5) growing reluctance on the part of enterprises of MEs to enter into joint projects on the rather confining terms offered by the PEs; and (6) much more discriminating financial markets than those that prevailed in the 1970s.

The PEs as a group could attempt to counteract the negative effects of the aforementioned external pressures through broad import substitution, vigorous export promotion, or raising the external debt. In principle, a conscious inward-turning process that magnifies the import curbs enacted since the late 1970s could help to relax the external constraints. Surely, this could be only a temporary option, for it would eventually curtail the feasible pace of economic growth and hence the long-term development potential of the PEs.[14] As such, it is neither a very useful nor a viable policy alternative, except perhaps in the short run to accommodate ineluctable shifts in the direction of development policies.

Owing to their market size and specific resource base, most of the smaller PEs need to diversify the markets where they procure fuels and raw materials. This requires first a solid improvement in their capacity to generate export revenues. Regional production of key fuels and raw materials in the years ahead, in the aggregate, is likely to show modest gains at best, even if present constraints on output capacities can be lifted. Furthermore, output levels can be sustained only at sharply rising costs. The only viable strategy is all-round export promotion on the basis of factor productivity growth. This option requires that structural adjustments enable the PEs to exploit trade advantages not only by marshaling opportunities for regional cooperation but also by seeking a proper global trade profile in general.

Towards a positive adjustment policy

Coming to grips with prevailing and expected economic scarcities in the years ahead constitutes a very ambitious agenda, whose implementation must proceed gradually even if the key authorities were to decide unambiguously on promulgating measures that can enhance factor productivity growth. One avenue would be to expose the PEs to the "economic shock" by creating institutions and setting behavioral rules that require agents to account for real economic scarcities. Given the magnitude of the needed adjustment, such a policy course could be realistically entertained only if the sociopolitical fabric of the PEs could withstand a deep recession with sharp cuts in levels of living. The slow or negative growth experience of 1978–1983, especially in Poland, has clearly underlined that, socially and politically, such a course is simply not viable. The alternative is gradualism, to promote the exchange of primary goods for manufactures, to upgrade steadily specialization in products and technical levels of manufacturing activities, to expand regional foodstuff production, and to borrow technology from the West selectively in combination with intragroup cooperation in science and technology as an integral component of regional output specialization. The PEs therefore need to formulate a positive adjustment policy and to blend it with the intended drive towards intensive growth.

3.4 Origins, symptoms, and remedies of imbalances

Constraints on the pace and direction of growth in a typical PE usually emerge from the availability of capital, labor, and intermediate goods. Foreign trade in an orthodox CPE is mostly concerned with mopping up marginal shortfalls and exploring quite obvious comparative advantages. Foreign exchange constraints on growth, on the other hand, are typically not perceived to be a problem (Fitzgerald 1985, p. 5). This may have been the case until the early 1970s, with some obvious exceptions, precisely because at first the PEs deliberately ignored the potential contribution of trade to growth and later on they could avail themselves of buoyant trade and financial markets in MEs. It clearly has not been so since then as the adjustment efforts of the past five years or so have amply demonstrated.

There is no coherent theory that permits systematic analysis of the origins and consequences of external or internal imbalances under the highly institutionalized environment of a PE. In contrast to the vast literature on their institutions and the planning processes, relatively little has been written on the nature and mechanisms of adjustment in such economies. It would certainly be useful to focus on well-defined features of an abstract model involving a monolithic, omniscient, all-pervading central plan, if only because "there is nothing more practical than a good theory" (Fedorenko 1984, p. 6). However, because I aim at a consistent, if perhaps not exhaustive, economic explanation of Eastern Europe's performance in the past ten years or so, the pay-off of such an approach is not likely to be sufficiently rewarding. This is so in part because the recent perturbations emerged quite abruptly and forcefully, for which there is no precedent in the postwar period. On the other hand, it is well-nigh impossible to give the complex reality of existing PEs its full due. In what follows, then, I shall resort to abstract PEs and contrast them with stylized MEs when this helps to concentrate on one or a few aspects of the adjustment process of PEs. Otherwise the discussion proceeds against the backdrop of the existing CPEs or MPEs.

Symptoms of imbalances

Macroeconomic imbalance may emerge variously. Typical symptoms are external payments difficulties, open inflation in the home market, large-scale shortages of goods, severe bottlenecks that disrupt the production process, a shift in demand towards foreign goods, a rapid rise in the volume of ongoing capital projects, rationing, rapid accumulation of inventories of some goods, a rise in involuntary savings, and other phenomena. In such circumstances, a program of structural adjustment is called for. Given the complexity of the microeconomic distortions that prevail in the typical PE, the macroeconomic adjustment program may in the end be directed to a significant extent at rectifying the microeconomic sphere. But the first steps have to be set at the aggregate level by key decision makers. Just as the symptoms of maladjustment may be various, so are its underlying causes and the cures.

Economywide disturbances usually stem from a combination of exogenous and endogenous factors. Among the former, mention should be made of a shift in the terms of trade, natural calamities that idle or destroy productive capacity, a serious harvest setback, failure of projected export markets to materialize for reasons of competition or abruptly sagging activity levels, or a sudden rise in the price of key intermediate imports. Some may be of genuine extraneous origin in the sense that they are beyond the reach of policies anywhere. Others may originate in policies adopted abroad and may require policy coordination among countries.

Macroeconomic imbalances may also be propagated by various inappropriate domestic policies. It may consist of an excess of investment over savings, runaway government expenditures, trade and payments regimes that discourage exports, overtaut planning in the sense that growth targets are slated deliberately above levels that the economy is capable of achieving or sustaining, and others. These features are usually associated with distortions in the microeconomic sphere, including inappropriate price policies, insufficient export incentives, unrealistic interest rates, distorted profit calculations, erroneous ERs, and others.

Cures for imbalances

Just as symptoms of macroeconomic imbalance may surface differently in alternative economic environments, so do the cures to rectify the imbalances. However, the underlying targets of redress consist in reducing aggregate demand or absorption (D), increasing production, and stressing export production. From the familiar relation of macroeconomic aggregates, D consists of consumption (C), investment outlays (I), and government expenditures (G):

$$D = C + G + I \tag{3.1}$$

Total supply (S) comprises domestic production (Y) and imports (M) minus exports (X):

$$S = Y + M - X \tag{3.2}$$

Hence ex post equilibrium requires

$$Y = C + I + G + X - M \tag{3.3}$$

If now domestic absorption D exceeds domestic production Y, the external balance (B) is

$$B = X - M < 0 \tag{3.4}$$

The foregoing national accounting identities require that

$$Y - D = X - M = B \tag{3.5}$$

This imbalance must be worked off by either increasing Y or decreasing D, yielding an increase in X or a decrease in M, thus generating a surplus on the current account in a subsequent period, provided financing is available in the short run. If equation 3.4 cannot be realized, changes in Y or D must emerge immediately through stabilization measures.

On the process of adjustment

Stabilization requires that total demand equals total supply ex ante. Restoring balance involves measures to contain domestic expenditures at levels that both curb import demand and release significant resources for export. To reduce aggregate expenditures of households, enterprises, and government and to switch their expenditures in favor of domestically produced goods and sevices, such a program must envisage actions on both the supply and demand sides. To bring this about, authorities need to alter the weights they attach to conflicting objectives, emphasizing economic efficiency, possibly at the cost of economic security. An immediate compression of imbalances is usually required, even if at the cost of not reaching preconceived sectoral proportions.[15] The rate of growth of supply should in any case exceed that of domestic and import demand. It is of special importance to transfer resources to the most efficient export sectors and branches producing import substitutes. Inefficient, and therefore oversized, import-substituting sectors need to be restructured and reduced. Supply adjustments may include the absorption of idle resources in the production process, more complete mobilization of appropriated funds, and resource reallocation by mandatory instructions or indirect incentive guidelines.

The restraining of demand involves the better management of final consumption through measures that particularly control wage and bonus rates, prices (including ERs), taxes, interest rates, and social transfers; the compression of investment activity directly or through indirect means; and the control of intermediate consumption. On the supply side, policies need to ascertain whether there is full employment. If so, remedial actions should foster a reallocation of productive factors in favor of import substitutes and exportables. If there are idle resources, they need to be mobilized. At the same time, factor productivity must be stimulated through direct as well as indirect policy actions. Direct actions comprise shifts in policy emphasis so that resources are appropriated for more productive uses, unutilized or underutilized resources are properly identified and put to productive use, and productivity levels are spurred on through the better utilization of the available capital stock and inventories, and by providing material and other incentives to labor.

When considering demand adjustment, we must distinguish between measures that simply suppress demand and those that seek to restructure it. In the first case, imbalances are bound to resurface once the suppressive forces are removed. In the interim, they may distort the economy in various other ways. Other measures aim at engineering real changes in the level and structure of demand. Demand essentially consists of household, enterprise, and government demands for final and intermediate products. Each in turn has different components that are not equally susceptible to policy action.

Final consumption demand is a function of wages and related premia, prices for consumer goods and services, interest rates and other parameters affecting savings behavior, government transfers, and nonpecuniary services. The government can mandate curtailment of the latter two, but broad social commitments made earlier by policy makers may compress its latitude. Wages and premia are the chief determinants of household revenues. Prices, on the other hand, are a determinant of expenditures. Interest rates and other incentives for private savings form another set of important parameters that influence the distribution of income. Improving the attractiveness of financial instruments for households may significantly change how they trade off consumption against savings explicitly or implicitly.

Another important component of domestic absorption is investment over which policy makers usually have considerable direct as well as indirect control. Private demand for investment goods depends to some degree on the rate of interest, which in turn determines the financial requirements for investment purposes. There may, however, be many other factors, including marketing practices, relative prices, taxation systems, and limits to the permitted extent of private ownership. Governments have more direct control over enterprise investments and over their own expenditure pattern.

Modifications in demand and supply, particularly in trade-dependent economies, should be undertaken in the most efficient way so as to minimize their adverse effect on growth, yet shift resources to the external sector. The latter may be more difficult to achieve than a purely internal reallocation of resources, especially if the export sector is to be placed on a greater profitability footing. Just like domestic adjustment, shifts in the external sector may be accomplished by suppressing imports or by fundamental changes in external demand and supply. When the problem is tackled chiefly from the trade side through administrative channels, the authorities are not likely to achieve a more efficient pattern of trade than the one that led to imbalances in the first place. Fundamental adjustment requires that the problem be cast in the context of absorption and supplies so that domestic balance is restored in a way consistent with the most efficient use of resources, and the corresponding modifications should permit the restoration of equilibrium in the external accounts as well. This cannot be accomplished solely by rescaling plan targets. The latter must indeed be complemented with an improved incentive system.

The preceding sources and symptoms of disequilibria suggest that the relation between internal and external balances is fundamentally the same in MEs and PEs. There is nothing peculiarly systemic about any of the causal factors discussed, given that the need to adjust arises, in essence, in similar circumstances in both PEs and MEs, although its precise manifestation may differ significantly. The same holds for the cures. The broad outline mentioned also provides the areas in which socialist economic managers have to look for corrective actions, starting from socioeconomic goals that admittedly are bound to have different weights from those typical of MEs. Unlike the stylized ME, however, the orthodox CPE and, because of its legacies, the MPE lack a flexibly appropriate mechanism by which the myriad price and quality shifts necessary to move the economy to a new general equilibrium can be accomplished swiftly and efficiently. Because of the complexity of central management of the enterprise sector and because the main socioeconomic goals of the PE historically have biased policies away from adjustment of wages, employment, and consumer prices, one might expect that a greater burden be placed on supply adjustment, in contrast to MEs, where such policies primarily envisage changes in the level and structure of demand.

3.5 Adjustment in a traditional setting

The role of the Fund in the world economy and the possible benefits of Fund membership to PEs are discussed in Chapter 7. A few stylized aspects of adjustment policies typically embraced by MEs under Fund surveillance or conditionality at this juncture may help the reader understand some of the root causes of the mixed relationship between these multilateral financial institutions and the PEs, which are dealt with in Chapter 7. By juxtaposition, it also facilitates the explanation in the next section of how traditional PEs go about adjusting to external or domestic pressures.

The common adjustment measures envisaged in Fund policies focus on austerity so as to cut demand through a variety of policy moves that are apt to promote indirect or market incentive mechanisms, epitomized by the slogan "getting the prices right." A typical adjustment program in an ME consists of a combination of measures aimed at improving the current account through stabilization policies and efficiency through target adjustments. Usually such a program is supported by financing from abroad arranged by official institutions, at varying degrees of conditionality, or private banks (or a combination of the two) and comprises three phases: the implementation of the preconditions for adjustment – otherwise banks would not be inclined to loan funds required for smoothing the adjustment process; the fulfillment of quantitative and qualitative policy targets upon which further disbursement of the loans agreed upon in the adjustment package is conditioned; and actions that governments commit themselves to undertake, although they do not normally stipulate sanctions for noncompliance. These areas for policy action are primarily concerned with demand management. The Fund has recently increasingly turned also to ways of stimulating supply, however.

The above suggests that there is normally a tie-in between additional loans and the implementation of adjustment measures. Participants in the negotiations normally select a quantum target as well as a time sequence for improving the current account. The decision on the amount by which the current account needs to be improved during a given period of time is a function of the volume and timing of the inflow of foreign capital from official and private institutions. Because it is constrained by conditions in international capital markets, the Fund does not have complete discretion in choosing the depth and speed of a country's adjustment. But it can nevertheless exert considerable leverage over the concrete terms on which commercial banks may be willing to keep lending. The second step in an adjustment program concerns domestic balance and stabilization. Domestic demand needs to be set at a long-term sustainable level without aggravating imbalances and inflation. If prices are not moving flexibly in response to shifts in demand and supply, inflationary pressures tend to be disguised or repressed. But they leave an imprint on the economy just the same. Stabilization usually requires a cut in total absorption so that real expenditure shrinks, which normally also entails a drop in real incomes. Austerity usually has a disproportionate impact on investment, which by lowering the growth of capital reduces the capacity to produce over time.

Demand management can take on various forms. The primary objective is to reduce expenditures by controlling nominal flows to various actors in the economy and cutting their purchasing power. In the household sector, wage levels are more strictly controlled, thereby possibly reducing household income and expenditure. In the enterprise sector, the reduction in aggregate credit supply from the banking sector curtails investment outlays. Government expenditures need to be compressed, and net indirect taxes are normally increased by cutting government subsidies. This direct reduction of government demand alleviates pressures on credit and money markets. Furthermore, the government normally curbs the rate of growth of money supply.

Expenditure switching is aimed at bolstering exports and discouraging import demand. A substantial devaluation raises the price of both imports and exports in domestic currency, and thus can be expected, after dissipation of the factors behind the familiar J-curve effect, to reduce domestic demand and divert it to domestically produced substitutes for imports. Domestic suppliers on balance tend to divert goods from the domestic market to exports.

Supply measures of the adjustment package can take on various forms as well. They mostly consist of enhancing resource allocation by direct and indirect policy means. Direct instruments are in the sphere of tariffs, ERs, interest charges, and, in many cases, key product prices, including energy and foodstuffs. Indirect instruments are contingent on changes in the underlying institutions, such as the liberalization of the trade and payments regime, or the imposition of control over nominal variables. Better management of aggregate credit and the money supply also improves the setting of financial markets and thus indirectly affects aggregate investment and inflation.

Stabilization and adjustment policies need not depress levels of economic activity, unless the imbalance originated in the first place from output levels that exceed long-run capacity. Nevertheless, recent experience has stressed unambiguously that adjustment usually entails a contraction of economic activity, which may in fact counteract the improvement in economic efficiency that the adjustment program was intended to bring about. This conflict between economic efficiency and the need to improve the current account may stem from a variety of sources. The most important are (1) "overkill" or excessive adjustment measures causing a contraction in economic activity; (2) optimistic assumptions of domestic market flexibility, thus overstating expenditure switching; (3) import cuts affecting not only final consumption but also intermediate and capital goods for which no substitutes from domestic production are available in the short run; and (4) the compression engineered in domestic absorption that may fall disproportionately on investments, possibly entailing a weakening of future production capacity levels.

Adjustment programs such as those enacted in the 1980s under the aegis of the IMF rely overwhelmingly on policy instruments that are appropriate in a free-market setting and that have their largest impact on aggregate demand. The recent bout of externally induced adjustments suggests that, in an environment where there are serious rigidities in markets or where markets are not fully free by policy design, output losses are entailed that far exceed any efficiency gains from better resource allocation. There is therefore a real trade-off between the two that is often neglected. This would seem to apply in particular to the PEs. Relatively distinctive ways generate, transform, and finally bring under control macroeconomic imbalance in CPEs and MPEs. Because macroeconomic problems and stabilization programs in MPEs can satisfactorily be assessed and monitored only if the specific policy and systemic antecedents of these economies in the classical CPE are clearly understood, I shall first discuss the latter's adjustment policies.

3.6 Adjustment in a traditional centrally planned economy

Policy instruments in a CPE overwhelmingly take the form of direct intervention by administrative means. In principle, the authorities control aggregate investment and its distribution, foreign exchange mobilization, wage rates, to some extent overall employment, the allocation of intermediate goods of domestic and foreign origin, and domestic prices either directly, by regulating commodity prices, or indirectly, by setting the rules by which enterprises are entitled to construct prices. This is true in all CPEs, although the degree of control varies. In theory, then, administrative instruments provide planners the tools they need to control the macroeconomic aggregates of key concern to adjustment regulators, such as the Fund or private commercial banks, and to allocate resources accordingly.

In the stylized ME model of economic theory, the adjustment of demand to supply is instantaneous. Full knowledge with timeless adjustment ensures balance in markets ex ante as well as ex post. This is clearly not true in reality. Similarly, if the planner were omniscient, he would know perfectly the desired reallocation of resources and restructure production and uses accordingly by simple administrative means. In practice, however, the authorities of a PE do not have this information any more than actors in an ME. They must therefore resort not only to direct resource reallocation but also influence the behavior of economic agents with the objective of inducing them to bring about adjustment rather than to circumvent it. Unsatisfied ex ante consumer demand, although having little effect on supply and retail prices in a CPE, may eventually discourage the supply of labor and thus exert a negative impact on production. It may also have other adverse social consequences. Similarly, in the socialized sector, planning authorities do not possess full information about all possible alternatives available at the enterprise level. The timely manipulation of an appropriate incentive system to enable enterprises to initiate a multitude of minor adjustments with a salutary impact on the economy as a whole affords CPE authorities crucial sources of initiative and information.

In principle, stabilization in a traditional CPE is a fairly simple operation: The authorities mandate in the plan the shift of resources required to foster exports, to promote import substitution, and to cut back total domestic absorption through quantum changes. Because the planners do not fully control trade prices, the extent of the required adjustment is a function of the terms-of-trade effect engendered in the process. This package of measures is almost certainly embraced on an emergency basis with immediate repercussions on trade with MEs, but delayed effects on CMEA partners. Because violations of BTPAs are by no means exceptional, the transmission of adjustment effects to CMEA partners may be more immediate than the institutional framework of these economies suggests at first glance. Whether the measures have a more permanent impact so as to forestall the recurrence of the imbalances that initially led to the stabilization program depends critically on the nature, origin, and depth of the disequilibria.

Among the instruments to be used most intensively in comprehensive adjustment are those that help to promote greater efficiency in the allocation of resources. To the extent that this can be accomplished with the traditional instruments of the command economy, chiefly the planning process, adjustment can be guided by changes in the level and structure of output targets. But direct policy actions leading to different plan targets need to be coupled with incentives such as bonuses, taxes, capital levies, and the like to ensure that the immediate improvement that is feasible can be sustained by "normal" policy means into the future as well. Such improved incentives in conjunction with better targeted sanctions may be exploited also in a more general way to boost production quantitatively as well as qualitatively. Profitability guidelines, elimination of undesirable taxes and subsidies, stressing financial discipline, and utilizing the profit lever more intensively for enterprise decisions can be very important other instruments.

The familiar monetary approach to the balance of payments focuses on accounting identities and behavioral relationships. From the accounting point of view, given a stable demand for money, the improvement in the balance of payments is equivalent to the change in the money supply minus the change in net domestic credit. Thus, when credit is controlled, autonomous adjustments in prices and the balance of payments occur, so the demand for money is satisfied. The physical adjustment process is mirrored in an increase in domestic savings by the household sector, the government, and enterprises. Because these categories also exist in a CPE, it has been argued that progress of the adjustment effort in a CPE can be monitored "through the use of financial indicators in broadly the same way as in [MEs]" (Allen 1982b, p. 417). Demand must be lowered by cutting private consumption, investments, or government demand. The financial aspects of a reduction in household demand in a PE, at least ex post, could follow a pattern quite comparable to the typical adjustment process of MEs provided money commands goods legally and in practice. This can be seen as follows.

A stabilization program for a CPE can ensure consumer market equilibrium only if the growth target for the household money supply is set realistically, which requires a better understanding of the money stock demand function and the flow adjustment function for households. Related to this is the need to examine more rigorously the variety of responses by households to excessive accumulation of liquidity and to improve methods for distinguishing between macro- and microeconomic imbalances in the consumer market.

The flow supply of money to the household sector (dM_h) consists of wage revenues (WN), government transfers (T), the change in the gross credit extended to households (dC_h), and the value of consumer goods and services actually purchased by households (P_cQ_c),

$$dM_h = WN + T + dC_h + P_cQ_c \tag{3.6}$$

where W is the commercial wage per hour, N is the effective supply of man-hours, P_c the consumer price column vector, and Q_c the row vector of goods and services in the retail sector. This flow supply of money must be equal in monetary terms to the sum of changes in the banking sector's net claims on the public sector (dNC_g) and enterprises (dNC_e), the change in the gross claims on households (dC_h), and the change in international reserves (dR),

$$dM_h = dNC_g + dNC_e + dC_h + dR \qquad (3.7)$$

The supply of money to households can be controlled directly by affecting the right-side variables of equation 3.7 or by declaring a strict ceiling on the domestic banking system's net accumulation of claims, because net household hoarding equals dishoarding of governments and enterprises plus the net accumulation of claims on the rest of the world:

$$dM_h - dC_h = dNC_g + dNC_e + dR \qquad (3.8)$$

The deviations between planned and actual magnitudes may suggest ways in which imbalances can be worked off. Priming the differences between actual and planned magnitudes yields

$$(dNC_g)' + (dNC_e)' = (WN)' + T' + (P_cQ_c)' - (dR)' \qquad (3.9)$$

If full adjustment has to be borne by consumption, Q_c' must be negative. A buildup of household liquidity and a decline in enterprise deposits could be avoided if producers of consumer goods cut back their wage bill $(WN)'$ by the full value of the shortfall in production $(P_cQ_c)'$, which requires a reduction in the average wage, employment, or both. Producers could also be permitted to raise prices by an amount sufficient to offset the change in quantity delivered. Finally, they could draw down inventories. The authorities could also permit a reduction in exports or increase imports, thus leading to a deterioration in the foreign currency trade balance, offset by some combination of above-plan subsidies or bank credit. This will not change household money supply.

Another key component of absorption that needs to be pruned is investment, over whose level and distribution authorities in CPEs have considerable control. But it is not exhaustive even for economic agents that come under the umbrella of the central plan. In addition to planned investment, whose level and distribution are sensitive to direct plan instructions, there is a growing component of autonomous enterprise demand. There is also private investment for productive (such as in agriculture and crafts) and nonproductive purposes (such as residential construction). Finally, the magnitude of investment under the control of planners depends on the resolution of competing claims for resources. Only the projects deemed essential for the economy should be authorized for start-up.

Private investment demand is rarely regulated by realistic credit ceilings and interest rates that discriminate properly among alternatives. Instead, in a traditional CPE the rationing of private investment is accomplished predominantly by physical means. Capital goods and construction inputs placed on the market determine to what degree private demand for investment goods or construction materials is satisfied. A proper adjustment effort should be directed at monitizing these regulations.

The level of planned investments or of project authorizations is a key policy tool. Planning authorities need to limit their demand for the funding of ongoing and new projects to the capacity of the economy to supply capital resources, giving competing domestic and foreign claims. Certain projects, including for defense, may be so politically important that no compression can realistically be entertained. Otherwise, projects should be authorized mainly on the strength of economic considerations. To make proper intertemporal choices, the planners should make an own rate of return the major criterion governing their investment decisions. This requires downplaying two other factors that normally influence investment decisions: filling gaps in the economy's production structure in response to shortages, and attaining a rounded economic structure in the long run. When economic stabilization becomes a priority, however, investments that are not profitable when evaluated at "correct" prices or will become so only in the long run must inevitably be compressed. Foreign supply should be explored as the principal alternative source. In any case, a proper rate of return could be critical in making policy makers fully aware of the implicit cost of trading off current against future savings.

Enterprise investment demand is a third important component, which can be regulated directly as well as indirectly. Direct measures essentially suppress the demand by refusing to take it into account in scheduling central investment decisions and by prohibiting its expression in decentralized investments. Modifications of the level of budgetary grants, bank credits, and fiscal regulations governing profit retention can also restrict enterprise demand.

A final component is demand for intermediate goods. This provides a separate issue in CPEs because enterprise production levels are set largely independently of the manager's evaluation of demand prospects. The center's output targets do not automatically curb enterprise demand for inputs, which may be marshaled to produce largely for inventory formation. Enterprise demand for excessive inputs of materials and labor tends to be particularly pronounced at times of taut planning. The ensuing shortages and inflationary pressures are reflected in a deterioration of the financial situation of enterprises. In some countries, the growing stocks consist more and more of goods that are outmoded or have become unsalable for other reasons. But they must be financed from bank loans, retained profits, or funds diverted from other purposes. At a time of adjustment, such excess stock formation and cost pressures have to be discouraged. Aside from simply compressing allocations of intermediate resources, greater financial discipline of which enterprises are made fully aware can be achieved through incentives that tie the manager's remuneration to the enterprise's financial rather than physical results.

Because one of the chief purposes of the adjustment program is to generate additional savings, greater attention to financial results should not be confined to enterprises. Savings may emerge from households through larger savings deposits, from local and central governments through larger budget surpluses, and from enterprises through larger bank deposits and profits. In some sectors, including agriculture and households, traditional instruments of fiscal and monetary policy can be applied to a considerable extent. In the state sector, however, the independent scope of such policies depends on the degree of financial discipline exerted by the plan in the socialized sectors.

In a CPE, the behavioral relationships associated with monetary policies are much less clear than they are in an ME context. Given the prevalence of administrative controls, there is asymmetry in the effects of restricted and excessive liquidity. If liquidity is sufficiently restricted, consumers reduce their purchases and enterprises may be unable to engage in transactions they might otherwise wish to undertake. Thus, financial stringency may have an effect on real behavior. Because excess liquidity in the hands of consumers and enterprises cannot spill over to the foreign sector, the balance of payments may be improved without eliminating excessive domestic liquidity. To the extent that consumers and enterprises are obliged to hold larger cash balances than desired, financial discipline tends to be undermined with ill effects on output performance. In other words, at a given level of economic activity there is a certain minimum demand for money. Credit ceilings can thus serve to ensure that monetary expansion on balance does not undermine the other measures taken to alleviate external payments pressures.

The financial levers mentioned can promote greater efficiency only if prices, including such special levies as interest charges and ERs, are not too distorted. If properly set, these scarcity indicators may play a pivotal role in the enactment of an adequate adjustment program. In any case, the more correct the structure of prices – all other things being equal – the more efficient and effective the adjustment process is likely to be. Prices are set correctly when they reflect opportunity costs and, therefore, the relative scarcities prevailing in the economy. Most CPEs have ample access to foreign markets, so these provide the ultimate opportunity costs. An appropriate price structure should therefore reflect WMPs to some degree. One way would be by letting prices fluctuate freely to levels compatible with WMPs. But this is unlikely to be a satisfactory solution because CPE preferences diverge measurably from those molding demand in world markets. Another avenue might be to parametrize exactly the desired differences between domestic and trade prices, to maintain this separation in line with policy priorities, and to let prices adjust freely otherwise.

The proper selection of the level and structure of prices is undoubtedly an important tool in enacting structural adjustment. However, the CPE price system is usually so distorted that rectifying the situation is intimately bound up with a comprehensive economic reform. A period of emergency adjustment because of sudden external or internal constraints does not normally provide the proper setting for such a venture. But emergency adjustment measures of the type discussed earlier may well help to stabilize the CPE, even if at much less than maximum efficiency. Once reached, the authorities may tackle more fundamental issues with a greater portent. Such a comprehensive positive adjustment program could be directed at a variety of socioeconomic problems of managing and steering the CPE.

3.7 Adjustment in a modified planned economy

Even though some PEs have passed through major reforms that have widened the scope for interaction through indirect policy instruments, the role of traditional administrative regulators is still pervasive. Everywhere elaborate controls over enterprise behavior severely limit their action radius. These include extensive interferences through a host of tax and subsidy schemes, and direct controls over investment, employment, wage, and output decisions. Enterprise profit is therefore by and large a function of government prescriptions rather than of own production and investment decisions.

Conditionality conditions worked out, possibly by private or official financial institutions, in the context of explicit or implicit adjustment programs based on the underlying assumption that a PE behaves like an ME may yield unexpected, perhaps even perverse, results. Because actors do not respond to price signals and prices do not react to market pressures, as they are presumed to in the neoclassical paradigm, alternatives to market incentives need to be explored. Variants of conditionality that better reflect the economic structure, policies, and institutions of the PE about to undergo adjustment are therefore in order.

What PEs have in common is considerable. But there are palpable differences in institutions, policy priorities, and social systems, and it would be a serious mistake to assume that all PEs operate in the same way. For example, though PEs are in principle fully in control of investment decisions at the aggregate and sectoral levels, recent experience has shown that this is far from absolute and it varies in individual countries.

Especially in 1981–1983, investments were drastically slashed and planners hoped to check the propensity to invest, to reverse the negative trends in the efficiency of investment and of capital in general, and hence to lift output-capital ratios. However, the bout of adjustment programs proceeded chiefly by administrative means and accomplished very little by way of protecting viable and desirable projects at the expense of uneconomic ones. Instead, projects in motion were delayed, and potentially high-yielding new ones were blocked and dispersed. Thus the squandering of investment funds on account of local and regional political interest groups was not halted.

This brings me to the point of adjustment programs embraced for reasons other than emergency external constraints. The efforts of the past decade and a half demonstrate that it is easier to agree upon temporary stabilization policies than on more fundamental changes in the functioning of the economy, such as price, ER, and interest rate policies. External regulators therefore face formidable obstacles in attempting to design and to enforce conditions that render resource allocation in PEs more flexible and efficient without taking sides in domestic political struggles over reform attempts.

The presumed greater room for maneuver available to the authorities in an MPE with respect to wage regulation and the decreased reluctance to alter relatively frequently administered prices, including interest charges and ERs, may facilitate the introduction of adjustment programs. Reduced government intervention, more comprehensive enterprise autonomy, and greater emphasis on financial discipline raise at least the possibility that authorities can pursue a more active monetary policy than in a CPE, where it was frequently designed to "accommodate" the lending system's assets in accordance with real and fiscal variables. With few exceptions, the enterprise and household monetary sectors do not interact, however, thereby lessening the impact of a flexible interest rate policy on restoring equilibrium in various parts of the economy. Furthermore, the downward inflexibility of the money wage, job security, and retail price stability, combined with the difficulty of central administrators to undertake quickly the required changes in wages, employment, and prices place a disproportionate burden of adjustment on the consumer sector. Without essential freedom of both interest rates and the price of consumer goods, however, it is difficult to imagine how household consumption patterns, saving preferences, and enterprise profitability calculations could be dovetailed effectively so as to yield equilibrium simultaneously in consumption and investment goods markets. Providing for smooth intermediation between enterprises and households through the banking system at market-clearing interest rates could significantly lessen the authorities' control over the basic "proportions" of the economy, widen social inequalities, and fuel excess demand if such movements were not closely monitored according to firm policy prescriptions.

The MPE normally pays considerable attention to foreign trade as a source of output growth and regulator of a more efficient allocation of resources. But with price and interest rate controls still in effect it is difficult to dispense with physical controls on both trade and payments. Continued expansion of the scope for flexible pricing of tradables is required. The ER in an MPE plays some role in price formation and the allocation of resources, and thus becomes a potentially significant instrument for macroeconomic stabilization because it may, in principle, relieve the burden placed on credit and fiscal policies. The instruments by which authorities attempt to move an MPE to internal and external balance differ in nature from those used in a CPE. Parametric approaches are now possible. However, given the less direct nature and possibly ambiguous effects of such approaches in the quasi- markets of the MPE, the authorities may be tempted, at least temporarily, to revert to the more direct, interventionist instruments of quantitative control typical of the orthodox CPE. This may be seen by taking a brief look at the potential role of the ER in an MPE, which is discussed more fully in Chapter 6.

As discussed in Section 3.5, a standard recipe to overcome structural balance-of-payment difficulties includes changes in relative prices, expenditure reduction, and, especially, expenditure switching by means of changing the ER or one of the key ERs. Clearly, the ER plays not much of a role in the CPE and therefore cannot be manipulated to righten the external payments position. In an MPE, however, one or a few ERs are operative in some aspects of micro- and possibly macroeconomic decision making. It is therefore legitimate to inquire into the potential of adroitly manipulating the ER so as to help restore external balance, even if strictly limited to the room for foreign transactions chosen by policy makers. Three questions spring to mind: Because the MPE normally operates with a wide variety of ERs, which ER is to be chosen for adjustment purposes? Because none of the ERs really operates freely, what is the precise room for maneuver reserved for ER manipulation? How is adjustment to proceed in an environment that segregates rather rigidly between TR and CC transactions?

Although it is theoretically possible that the external imbalance stems from disturbances in one currency regime only, and hence remedial measures should be confined to that particular set of ERs, the reality of the past few years has been one of external disequilibria in all main external payments zones of PEs. This has had a major bearing on policy maneuverability accessible to policy makers, including the targets chosen by international organizations such as the IMF–IBRD, the collective organ that negotiates on behalf of sovereign governments (Paris Club), and by ad hoc groups of influence-bearing regulators, such as the representative negotiators of private commercial banks (London Club).

The experience with forced adjustment in the early 1980s demonstrated quite clearly the limits of weak market-type instruments in helping to bring about desirable economic adjustments, especially in the external sphere. At the same time that the advantages of adjusting in the short run through traditional central planning were being appreciated, the rather pronounced drawbacks of the inflexibility of the central planning system in a longer time perspective came to the fore stronger than before. In other words, recent experience has underlined once again the need for reforming these economies from within without further delays and preferably against the backdrop of greater integration within the global financial and trading networks.

To overcome imbalances and especially to stimulate economic growth, buoyant trade is a crucial component of adjustment programs in MPEs. Precisely because foreign trade operations exhibit far greater uncertainty than any domestic sector, authorities are not wont to relax administrative control over foreign trade and payments to a large degree. Although the MPE does not maintain full market segmentation, this critical feature of the CPE is definitely not abolished altogether. This holds not only in "real" terms but also with regard to indirect decision-making criteria, especially effective surrogate ERs. But so far they have at best provided useful overall guidelines in drawing up essential plan proportions, in the planning by lower organs, in the establishment of new fiat prices, possibly in the clearing of foreign transactions by FTOs (even though the latter do not always have discretionary authority over the volume of traded goods or prices), and, under some conditions, in formulating useful indicators for choosing trade volume and determining profitability. These surrogate ERs could provide useful criteria for resolving trade problems in planning and management if the PE were to be realigned with relative world scarcities. But this is not likely to be the planner's intention.

It is therefore legitimate to inquire into what is likely to happen in the foreign trade sector in the near future. Inasmuch as a sizable share of each PE's total trade and the bulk of imported industrial inputs are transacted within the CMEA, the adjustment problem is far more complex than simply changing one or more applicable "prices." Domestic price liberalization and harmonization of domestic prices with WMPs are both incompatible with TR prices, unless volume and price of all three elements of the equation can be adjusted. This is evidently not so for the bulk of TR transactions because the PEs have not yet decided to open up their borders to free international competition and to expose their economies to the vagaries of the international business cycle. Shifts in enterprise behavior in response to changes in foreign prices result either in the violation of CMEA trade contracts or in unfulfilled demand or supply constraints, and they must be averted. Measures will therefore have to be taken to insulate against CMEA markets that continue to operate as a CPE. One way of coming to grips with this vexing problem is discussed in Chapter 12 in the context of the future of SEI under foreseeable global economic conditions.

PART II

INDIRECT COORDINATION INSTRUMENTS AND SUPPORTING INSTITUTIONS

4

Socialist trade prices and CMEA cooperation

There is arguably no issue about which more has been written and less is known than the mechanism of CMEA pricing and the gamut of problems associated especially with the links among CMEA trade, domestic, nonsocialist world trade, and East–West trade prices. This chapter addresses only selected aspects of the price system in the "world socialist economic system" sui generis and its links with WMPs. Chapter 5 deals with domestic prices.

In principle, there should be a strong relationship between CMEA prices and WMPs. The theory underlying this price-formation principle and how it has been emulated in practice are examined below. Section 4.1 sets the stage and briefly discusses the rationale behind the elaboration of a different price regime. The evolution of the price-formation principles in CMEA trade is examined next. The major conceptual determinants of actual CMEA trade pricing, as they emerge from the range of practical problems entailed by the various competing – in some cases even contra-dictory – principles embraced since 1958, are analyzed in Section 4.3. A morphology of generally differing pricing environments is built up on that basis in Section 4.4. This leads to a broad discussion of the impact of the actual, particularly the bilateral, trading environment on the applica-tion of the price-formation principles in Section 4.5. Next is a discussion of how some of the propositions elaborated here could be tested empiri-cally. Section 4.7 clarifies why a careful examination of the CMEA price-formation process can at best help to reduce the range of uncertainty associated with the setting of actual transaction prices, even if ample information on the latter were readily available.

4.1 The setting and rationale of CMEA prices

When the world socialist economic system was established after World War II, it was felt that the nature of that group called for the implemen-tation of socialist principles also in the members' reciprocal relations.[1] Its rationale hinges importantly on the precepts of domestic price formation in these countries; it is therefore addressed in detail in the Chapter 5. As far as trade pricing *strictu sensu* is concerned, at one point or another over the past forty years virtually all PEs have debated a range of contentious issues on how to apply general intragroup pricing principles that would be consonant with their particular features. Ideology, politics, and expediency have been crucial determinants of the price systems used in the intragroup trade of the PEs. The intermittent debate on desirable improvements in the formation of socialist trade prices has not so far been satisfactorily resolved, although actual trade prices, however derived, have continued to affect the course of plan formulation, the broad determinants of macro- and microeconomic decision making, and trade transactions. In the process, much bad blood has been shed without fostering either the type of economic development preferred by any member country or the type of SEI that at least a majority of PEs have coveted for quite some time.

The transformation of the present pricing principles into a mechanism that would suit the actual economic conditions in PEs, with few interruptions, has been a policy priority since the mid-1950s at the latest. But the debate has not been a smooth one. It has been strained especially since the sharp deterioration in economic performances in the second half of the 1970s. The major shifts in relative WMPs of the 1970s and the reformulation of the CMEA price-reference base in 1975 have engendered knotty adjustment problems for the energy-dependent PEs of Eastern Europe. But not all outstanding issues can be ascribed to the misalignment of prices, as argued in Chapter 3.

Ever since the mid-1970s, Eastern European planners and policy makers have pointed out the desirability of modifying their trade price system in due course. With the changed leadership in the Soviet Union now apparently bent on correcting some economic ills, the greater attention being paid to fostering economic efficiency in nearly all PEs, and the need for joint action to stimulate these economies individually and as a group, a major transition in the SEI mechanism, including price determination, may well be in the offing. A seminal change in price formation, if not in the underlying principles, is likely to materialize at the latest by the end of the current decade, when the impact of the new five-year plans for 1986–1990 on SEI can be assessed. But the changeover may commence even sooner, possibly in the context of the implementation of the recommendations on major aspects of CMEA economic cooperation that may have been endorsed at the June 1984 economic summit, but have not yet been published (see Chapter 2). The debate of the subject with explicit references to the summit has been raised several notches since the ascent of Michail S. Gorbačëv to the Soviet leadership.

It is against this backdrop that it appears useful to reexamine the regional price issue in some detail, though I shall not attempt to survey the many suggestions regarding desirable price reforms proffered intermittently since the mid-1950s. Instead, the accent here is on the principles and the actual determination of regional prices. The need for a more suitable alternative price formula emanates from the difficulties encountered with the present system and its domestic counterparts. A more in-depth examination of the particular configuration of alternatives is therefore considered in the context of possible modifications of the national and regional cooperation mechanisms in Chapter 5.

There is by now sufficient evidence to affirm that prices in intra-CMEA trade are not uniform, that they differ markedly from those observed in trade with other countries, MEs as well as PEs, and that they bear only a tenuous relationship with domestic prices in any of the CMEA members. This situation stems to some degree from principles that have varied over time in part because of numerous problems of interpretation and application. The major culprit, however, is the double inconsistency of this peculiar price system. On the one hand, uniform prices within a given region are *in se* incompatible with bilateralism, whenever the latter is operative, and even less so with structural or commodity bilateralism (Brabant 1973, pp. 27–54). Certainly, the potential for arbitrage at least between CMEA and East–West trade, which is embedded in the typical trade model but whose degree differs for each pair of PEs, has also been highly relevant.

In spite of what the voluminous literature and endless debates about the world socialist economic system might suggest, the principles and forms of cooperation within that second "global market" evolved largely from the practice of trading in a highly constrained environment. Marxist–Leninist ideological underpinnings may at times have codetermined the accent placed on observing as much purity as possible in the establishment of actual trade prices. Their impact on the trade system and its evolution has been minimal, however. Before describing the evolvement of the CMEA pricing principles, I shall look briefly at the reasons for the emergence of a special price system for trade among PEs.

The genesis of the peculiarities typical of the rather inflexible CMEA trade model starts with the particular dislocations caused by World War II and its aftermath. Especially the changeover from a war-economy footing to a peacetime civilian economy in Eastern Europe, as elsewhere, played a pivotal role. In some cases, this environment was compounded by major shifts in the political backdrop to the macroeconomic policy mechanisms, institutions, and objectives that were then promulgated. Whereas most MEs gradually promoted flexible market mechanisms also in their trade, the PEs actively evolved their trade model and policy in line with centralized economic control. Their becoming full-fledged CPEs had a major impact on the CMEA pricing mechanism.

One of the essential features of planning in the typical CPE has been the unambiguous preference for as much stability as possible within the typical planning periodicity. One instance of this is the policy of keeping domestic prices unchanged during long periods of time (see Chapter 5). Aside from ideological and other noneconomic reasons, stable trade prices were deemed to be highly desirable to support detailed central planning especially in trade-dependent PEs. Price inflexibility became an especially crucial feature in the context of BTPAs that almost by definition cannot accommodate substantial clearing facilities or CC flows to settle imbalances periodically.

To minimize the degree of confusion that may arise from the multitude of factors that underlie CMEA prices in theory and practice, I believe it will be instructive to distinguish among base, reference, contract, and transaction prices, although these four levers do not necessarily manifest themselves in each trade relationship at any time. The base price is the actual WMP that the PEs select as the starting point for the construction of a reference price. The latter is the average WMP of a predetermined period and relevant market(s) that partners agree upon bilaterally, although such prices are conceivably drawn up multilaterally. The contract price is the one that partners settle upon in the process of negotiating the actual annual or multiyear (usually, the quinquennial) BTPAs. The transaction price is the one at which actual trade is invoiced. It could coincide with the contract price. In some cases, negotiators may decide to postpone the fixing of contract prices until delivery time, thus resulting in identical contract and transaction prices. The transaction price is rarely the same as the reference price, and it definitely does not coincide, save by fluke, with any base price under consideration.

4.2 The evolution of CMEA price-formation principles

This section provides a succinct guide through the confusion that exists in the literature on the nature, validity, and application of the CMEA contract price systems. I shall distinguish basically among three broad regimes: current prices, stop prices, and lagged average WMPs. Neither this subdivision nor the exact periodization specified in what follows is standard. The different versions upheld in the specialized literature probably reflect the diversity of heterogeneous price-setting procedures embodied in the strategies adopted by individual PEs in negotiations about BTPAs.

Until about mid-1950

Prior to the commodity price boom in the early 1950s, which was triggered chiefly by the sudden shift in global demand and supply that followed upon the eruption of the Korean War, the PEs traded among themselves on the basis of physically detailed BTPAs.[2] Most were anchored in principle to current WMPs or to an average of WMPs of the preceding year. Before the negotiations about the 1949 annual trade protocols and the long-term trade agreements then under discussion, there were no generally applicable, formal principles about how trade prices for PEs should or could be determined. The particular prices chosen were those of main world markets either at the time of the signing of the trade agreement – usually the year preceding actual trade flows – or at delivery time. In the former case, prices were fixed for the duration of the agreement, but in the latter case prices probably could move in tandem with current WMPs. However, in the context of the rather convoluted political, ideological, and economic situation in 1945–1948, strict adherence to a uniform set of pricing principles in Eastern Europe was probably not a high priority in interstate economic relations. In some cases, prices were expressly designed to reflect goals unrelated to the properties of traded goods per se.

Precisely in view of the disarray in price levels and structures that emerged and the widely diverging approaches to the practical selection of WMPs, an important point on the agenda of the Council Session since the CMEA's creation through late 1950 was the proper determination of reciprocal trade prices (see Brabant 1974a, pp. 200–204). There was apparently firm agreement, on the adoption of general principles, including the validity of average WMPs, price stability, reciprocal advantage, and price uniformity. These were debated in some format at the second Council Session (Sofia, August 1949). But the questions were not fully settled, for the Council's Bureau and subsequent meetings of the Council Session continued to be preoccupied with the issue well into the 1950s (Hegemann 1980, pp. 59ff.) and, in fact, even now.

With the 1949 trade agreements, a two-year period of ex ante annually fixed trade prices set in. These were generally based on WMPs of the year preceding the implementation of the agreement. However, it often proved difficult to specify contract prices together with traded quantities. Similar price references were envisaged in the negotiations about the long-term trade agreements that were to become the paramount outgrowth of the initial debates about fostering SEI. Prices should normally have been set as a crucial component of the bilateral negotiating process about quantities to be exchanged during some period of time. Very often, however, the complexity of arriving at proper WMPs and modifying them to suit the needs of the CMEA members made it imperative to defer the fixing of contract prices to subsequent negotiations when other considerations than average WMPs of the preceding year could and did come into play.

Although the principles apparently agreed upon in 1949–1950 have remained deliberately vague, three additional features of CMEA pricing at that early stage are worth recalling. First, once any pair of partners selected an individual contract price for a particular product that in the process was clearly identified, including the precise direction "from-to" (more on this later), it remained valid for the entire duration of the trade agreement. In other words, stable prices fixed in BTPAs became the norm regardless of what materialized in alternative trade relations, including with other PEs. Given that this provision could lead to profitable arbitrage, proper execution of the quantities agreed upon sometimes called for price revisions during the implementation phase.

Furthermore, it became generally established at the time that proper reference WMPs, suitably identified "from-to" and averaged over an agreed reference period, would only provide a reference platform for the bilateral negotiations about contract prices – an "inherently pragmatic rationale" (Kraus 1985, p. 9) of the CMEA price system that has endured until this day. In other words, the actual terms at which members committed themselves to exchange prearranged quantities did not usually coincide with the reference prices, because the latter were but one of many determinants of contract prices. Deviations between the proper WMP and the contract price, let alone the actual transaction price, emerged for a variety of economic and other reasons. Perhaps the best-known esoteric rationale for a substantial deviation was used in determining the notorious price of Polish coal exported to the Soviet Union.[3] Similar, though less onerous, considerations prevailed in the transfer of uranium ore from Eastern Europe to the Soviet Union and generally the whole range of products emanating from joint-stock companies (see Chapter 9), whose trade prices were almost certainly not fixed on the basis of current WMPs.

Perhaps the most important feature of this early experience was the explicit recognition of the benefit of using modified WMPs in clearing CMEA trade. The price mechanism that evolved later is usually justified with reference to the need for equivalent exchange (see "The Bucharest principles" subsection) in trade among socialist countries. In the context of the postwar economic dislocations, the dollar shortage, widespread bilateralism in world trade, and other features of foreign exchange controls at that time, however, even purified average WMPs can hardly have been indicative of anything but short-term economic scarcities very broadly defined.

Stop prices before 1959

The commodity boom that erupted with the uncertainties around the Korean War considerably complicated the informal arrangements that had governed commerce among the PEs in the preceding five years. On the one hand, prices fluctuated greatly, which complicated the stabilization of prices in the BTPAs, and commodity prices tended to fluctuate much more than those of manufactures.[4] Further, because of the Cold War environment, all PEs felt compelled to redirect their trade to the Soviet orbit, which made it more urgent to work out a dependable pricing mechanism agreeable to most participants. Also in connection with this inward turning, a degree of informal dependence on each other's products came about which called for some form of incentive prices or at the very least for more predictable pricing guidelines. Finally, it was precisely at that juncture that the PEs intensified their first socialist industrial leap forward. As argued in Chapter 1, this policy could not possibly have been sustained by means of prices – it certainly could not have been brought about through prices – even had socialist policy makers been bent on utilizing such a mechanism.

The then nascent economic system and the concurrent shifts in policy formulations and development objectives called for distinguishing rather rigidly between domestic and trade prices, on the one hand, and CMEA and world prices, on the other, for two reasons. As the principle of equivalent exchange could hardly have been upheld under wildly fluctuating prices, countries felt the need to cleanse prices of monopoly rents and short-term fluctuations. In addition, it would have been practically impossible to support rapid physical growth in industry on the basis of the bilateral trade mechanism, unless the PEs were to resort to a system resembling pure barter. But the latter was clearly unrealistic when placed against the prevailing development objectives.

a. Unchanged prices, 1950–1953. For these and undoubtedly many other reasons, the PEs selected to hold prices at the average preboom[5] levels of 1949 and part of 1950.[6] This decision was taken sometime in the middle of 1950[7] and endorsed at the third CMEA Session in November 1950, without the members having agreed upon a comprehensive set of principles governing the determination of stop prices, except in the case of products exchanged on a recurrent basis in the same bilateral relation. The PEs apparently resolved to implement the multiyear trade agreements then in force at unchanged prices to guarantee continuity and stability in their trade relations at a very difficult juncture of their economic cooperation (Hegemann 1980, p. 60). However, as the years went by, new products gradually emerged in CMEA trade, potential competition from MEs intensified and hence created room for profitable arbitrage, and other events unfolded, including, not in the least, Stalin's demise in early 1953 and the subsequent political upheavals of the mid-1950s in Eastern Europe. As a result, the price freeze, which in retrospect officially held until the end of 1956, was frequently disregarded especially in the case of key products whose WMP had changed perceptibly.

Bilateral price adjustments were therefore undertaken with an eye to eliminating the most glaring inequities without, however, jeopardizing the bilateral balancing requirement. In fact, the uniformity and orderliness in pricing principles then allegedly observed was little more than a chimera. Price changes were nonetheless generally limited, and their overall impact on terms of trade and bilateral balances remained rather small. In other words, the general proportions in price levels and relative prices of the late 1940s and 1950 were, on the whole, kept intact.

b. Marginal adaptations, 1954–1956. As the price problems caused by the Korean War subsided, the PEs began to conceptualize a concerted approach to price formation according to current WMPs. As a result of ad hoc bilateral negotiations, prices different from the 1949–1950 averages were progressively adopted, possibly by revising long-term trade agreements within the bilateral balancing constraints. This was especially important for a dozen or so key traded goods, including cellulose, cereals, coal, iron ore, sawn timber, and so on (Kiss 1971, p. 219). These efforts, however, went largely uncoordinated and did not affect all bilateral negotiations. Price divergences occurred not only because of bilateralism, but mainly because there was no regionwide agreement on proper procedures to justify adjustments. Even during 1954–1956, few changes in absolute price levels and in the broad structure of relative prices emerged, owing to the absence of a built-in mechanism to deal with major shifts in the terms of trade or the regional balance of payments. Changes were therefore piecemeal trade-offs; in some cases, quantum adjustments by diverting trade to MEs proved to be the only means of dealing with sticky prices.

c. Special adjustment, 1957–1958. In view of these and other circumstances mainly related to the political differentiation then emerging in Eastern Europe, the PEs sought to conduct a full review of reference prices for the 1957 trade agreements. Actual contract and transaction prices would continue to be set bilaterally for the duration of the BTPAs with some reference to "averages of recent WMPs." Serious efforts were to be made to achieve greater price uniformity, after duly allowing for variations in product quality and transportation costs. Similar provisions applied to the 1958 trade protocols, although it is doubtful that all PEs reviewed trade prices in line with WMPs of 1957. In fact, the evidence that adjustments were limited to key goods, which obviously varied from pair to pair of partners, is rather persuasive.

The Bucharest principles

As noted in Chapter 1, several transformations occurred in the mid-1950s in the smaller PEs. The key forces behind the promulgation of more systematic pricing principles for intra-CMEA trade were (1) the rancorous allegations about the unequal exchange that had allegedly been rampant during the Stalin era; (2) the search for an economic model that could accommodate trade more flexibly and for a nonautarkic development strategy; and (3) the newly emerging channels for economic cooperation with MEs that magnified the scope for profitable arbitrage. In addition to promoting mutually satisfactory relations, it was envisaged in particular that such rebased prices would also foster the ISDL much more than had been the case up to then.

Common pricing principles, however, were not solely promulgated as a result of theoretical discussions. The negotiations about annual price revisions of 1957–1958 and the bitter experiences of earlier years, which only then could come to the fore, were central. Especially as the annual price revisions unfolded, the PEs found it expedient to revert to common principles on which to erect their reciprocal trade prices. This became an especially important item on the agenda of the eighth Council Session (Warsaw, 18–22 June 1957) in connection with the discusions about revising the then valid medium-term trade agreements (1956–1960) for 1958–1960 (Faddeev 1974, p. 295; Hegemann 1980, pp. 120–23).

Unfortunately, the price documents[8] approved during the ninth Council Session (Bucharest, 25–30 June 1958) and the subsequent refinements formulated by the Standing Commission for Foreign Trade (SCFT) in 1960 (Neustadt 1974, p. 10) have never been released in extenso. The same applies to the documentation used as basis for the research on the creation of an independent price system (IPS). These studies were conducted under the aegis of the Standing Commission for Economic Problems (SCEP), mostly in the first half of the 1960s, and later by the Council's Executive Committee (see Chapter 5).[9] An accurate assessment of the accomplishments is therefore rather difficult. Nonetheless, secondary sources[10] suggest that CMEA members[11] somehow codified a number of principles in an attempt to rationalize and legitimize ex post practices that had evolved since the late 1940s. It was believed at the time that such an agreement would help to eliminate prices that were deemed to be inconsistent with trade among equal partners or obstructing multisided regional production specialization, which had just then been launched in earnest.

The literature is generally bewildering about the broad principles, and particularly the concrete details, on which the PEs agreed in Bucharest. Near unanimity, if not consensus, exists about the acceptance, for the time being, of some "competitive WMPs" that would be stable and uniform to the mutual advantage of all participants. However, stability was not to be equated with absolute fixity. Price adjustments would be permitted in principle when economically justified, even after the conclusion of price and volume agreements. But the bilateral setting of actual contract and transaction prices was formally kept in place. The participants would periodically search for a mutually acceptable new reference base or application period, or both, in a multilateral agreement. Neither was to be rigidly fixed. The members agreed in 1958 only upon a reference base for the immediate future, possibly up to 1960 (Hegemann 1980, p. 187), pending study of the desirability and feasibility of establishing a mechanism for developing an IPS for the CMEA. The latter task was entrusted to the newly created SCEP.[12]

There is more ambiguity as concerns the determination of (1) reference prices for products with a "complex character," presumbly to take into account quality differences in the broad sense or possibly the deliberate modification of properly identified reference prices in order to mitigate the effects of changes in the price bases on the commodity composition of trade and BTPAs; (2) relational prices in exceptional cases; (3) preliminary prices; (4) the price regime for "above-plan" traded goods; (5) the need to hold price adjustments to within some band to ensure reasonable effects on the bilateral balance of payment; (6) a transition period for price adjustments; and others. I shall summarize the principal features of each rule to the extent that the available information permits.

a. Transformed WMPs. The rock on which CMEA reference prices are built is the following proposition: After suitable adjustment for various conjunctural, speculative, monopolistic, and other market characteristics, WMPs provide useful indicators of actual values of goods and services. This pivotal contention is not simply a pro forma statement. It derives from a theoretical and methodological principle of central relevance to the better understanding of the CMEA price system and associated policies. Domestic prices in PEs are generally set so as to promote various planning and social objectives involving, at least implicitly, an important redistribution of value added (see Chapter 5); but this is explicitly rejected for international transactions. Domestic prices cannot normally serve a useful purpose in clearing trade because they would violate the doctrine of equivalent exchange – a fundamental concept of Marxist economic theory and socialist ideology.

The concept of equivalent exchange finds its roots in the Marxian labor theory of value. It is said to prevail if the full labor values of the goods exchanged against each other are equal. Whether this ought to apply to each and every transaction or only to the mutually agreed upon balanced trade for a conventional period is not unambiguous. The debate about whose values to apply in international transactions has by now become very involved indeed. Although there is no clear majority for any of the several competing positions, in what follows, an exchange is deemed to be equivalent when equal amounts of socially necessary international labor are involved, as indicated by world technological conditions (Ivanova and Zacharčev 1974, p. 121). Under such conditions, all trade partners are said to benefit equally from international trade. Socialist economists believe that, as the center around which national values are distributed (Bautina 1972, p. 143), international values reflect socially necessary labor outlays. Because WMPs are volatile, international *value* is only attainable as a most general trend. After the "distortions" mentioned earlier are eliminated, "it is usually possible to crystallize the objective essence of this category so that it becomes practically possible to utilize [WMPs] as the basis for contract prices" (Mitrofanova 1977, p. 117) in the CMEA. Clearly, labor values are not the terms at which alternatives are offered in world markets. The basic leap from value to price in socialist economic theory is that properly defined competitive WMPs over a given period of time reflect true labor values. It is therefore deemed necessary to purge average WMPs of monopolistic influences, exploitative features, and cyclical, conjunctural, and speculative fluctuations because these things may reflect short-term changes in demand and supply that are fundamentally unrelated to the "true" labor value content.

b. Stability in reference prices. A second basic premise is that WMPs must be averaged over some period. As an interim solution, it was decided to set prices for the renegotiated three-year trade agreements (1958–1960) on the basis of average 1956 or 1957 prices, but the members apparently hoped to average WMPs over a multiyear period, starting with 1957–1958. Averaging WMPs over several years removes the effect of price fluctuations unrelated to what are taken to be true shifts in value. Furthermore, average past WMPs can be documented comparatively easily. This enables the members to guarantee the effectiveness and mutual advantageousness of collaboration "even if there is some time lag between the physical and the value forms involved in the exchange" (Mitrofanova 1977, pp. 117–18).

To understand better the recent evolvement of the CMEA recommendations with respect to trade prices, it is important for us to remember that no specific time frame for the averaging was agreed upon in Bucharest. Initially a one-year period was adopted. Average WMPs for some combination of the years 1956–1958 were actually applied until 1964–1965 inclusive for reasons to be discussed later. Only then was it decided to adopt a five-year reference basis, which, with the exception of 1975, has remained a key operating guideline until today. However, each time the base is shifted a multilateral agreement by the CMEA's Executive Committee is required because the Bucharest principles do not incorporate provisions for automatic adjustments according to standardized criteria.

Price stability also in regional trade was perhaps the chief objective envisaged in the Bucharest agreement. CMEA reference prices would remain applicable for years. Although it was not explicitly specified as such in Bucharest,[13] the common target time frame at which the CPEs should aim, as eventually[14] interpreted, was synchronized medium-term BTPAs based on stable reference and contract prices; to the extent possible, stable transaction prices were also to be fostered, but with some exceptions. However, the formula allowed for periodic revisions particularly in the event of major changes in world markets. In the case of new products emerging as a result of supplementary trade protocols, "contemporary prices" (see "Miscellaneous other principles") were to be adopted. The time horizon of reference prices could be prolonged if the members so desired or if they could not agree upon a mutually satisfactory revision.

Although not explicitly included in the Bucharest price clause, stability was in practice understood to imply relatively small changes in prices from one reference base to another. If major changes were called for, the terms-of-trade effect and the adjustment of individual product prices were in practice to be absorbed over a transition period of at least two years. In practice, however, price stability became a fetish. There are ample indications that, at least until the mid-1970s, the level and broad structure of CMEA prices were by and large still the stop prices that evolved at the time of the Korean War! This emerged as a result of the relatively small range of goods for which new prices were negotiated over time.[15] Even after the fundamental fissure enacted in 1975, few price revisions have been introduced, and even then the changes have generally been kept within a relatively small band (Klawe 1976, p. 95); energy products have been obvious exceptions.

c. **Prices of main world markets.** It is obviously very difficult to identify WMPs in the abstract. Although the venue for the deliverance of the Bucharest price principles did not provide the proper forum for the full specification of whose WMPs should be averaged, the PEs did apparently agree upon utilizing the prices observed in main world markets or of main producers after making proper allowance for quality differences. Prior agreement needs to be reached on what are sufficiently representative reference markets. This generally calls for selecting one of a few main world markets or leading manufacturers in the world from which the PEs would import – prices are in principle molded by the importer without, however, violating the interests of the potential exporter – if the CMEA did not exist (Faude, Grote, and Luft 1976, p. 201). Such prices can be documented on the basis of stock exchange and commodity market quotations, auction prices, price catalogs of major representative producers, actual prices in CMEA trade, East–West trade prices, and similar sources.

Because of their proximity to Western Europe, but also their ambivalent economic relations with Japan and especially North America until at least the maturation of economic and political détente in the early 1970s, the former's producer and market quotations were held to be most pertinent (Neustadt 1974, p. 10). In the case of iron ore, for example, Swedish prices played a formative role; for petroleum and oil products, reference was usually to Eastern Mediterranean and Persian Gulf quotations, in the ratio 40:60, at least until the price changes of the mid-1970s, when the Saudi Arabian marker crude price was apparently adopted as reference (Faude et al. 1976, p. 201); for many nonferrous metals, quotations of the London Metal Exchange are closely scrutinized (Huschke 1984, p. 43); for engineering products, the price lists and actual prices of leading firms mostly in France, Italy, Japan, the United Kingdom, and West Germany are determinants of the reference prices (Faude et al. 1976, p. 121).

d. Price uniformity. The Bucharest principles call for price uniformity, after allowing for quality variations and transportation costs.[16] The latter were defined as half of the transport cost that would have been incurred if the CMEA did not exist and the product had to be imported from outside the CMEA area minus the actual costs, if any.[17] However, the fictive transport cost markup had been a long-standing CMEA practice, especially in the case of bulk goods. It was apparently first instituted in 1947 as a constituent of the "principle of reciprocal advantage" applied in the then negotiated medium-term trade agreements.

To obtain a uniform set of prices, all members must agree ex ante upon unique reference prices that, after proper weighting and averaging, form the basis of trade negotiations and BTPAs. Because this has not been done, actual CMEA transaction prices as well as contract and reference prices diverge to a smaller or larger degree from pair to pair of CMEA relations. This circumstance has been perhaps the knottiest source of cooperation impediments encountered ever since the principles were first promulgated.

e. Mutual advantage. Reference WMPs should be mutually advantageous on the seemingly logical principle that the benefits ensuing from the existence of a socialist world market should be shared by both parties. Similarly, the losses that may be incurred because the PEs cannot trade freely with third markets, or when they do not deem it to their ultimate advantage to do so, should be distributed fairly. This principle is usually invoked to explain the phantom "transport rule," although its relevance in that context is not altogether obvious.[18]

f. Economically justified adjustments. Although striving for price stability, the PEs also want to keep in touch with "secular changes" in WMPs, as distinct from cyclical or other temporary perturbations, hence the principle of reciprocal advantage. Accordingly, the PEs decided that if it was felt that fundamental shifts had occurred in reference prices during the implementation phase of the medium-term BTPA, another reference price could be set in bilateral negotiations on the initiative of the exporter. This would then presumably have become applicable to all potential CMEA partners in order to safeguard the principle of price uniformity. How to reconcile price stability with competitiveness without frequent multilateral agreements about reference prices, however, has been a major dilemma in CMEA relations. It is also central to explaining the absence of price uniformity.

g. Bilateral contract and flexible transaction prices. Regardless of the uniform principles that may prevail in the selection of reference prices, the CMEA members agreed to determine contract and transaction prices bilaterally. Reference prices were to be adjusted for quality differences between the actual commodity to be traded and the reference good agreed upon, and the transportation charge. However, other considerations could and did come into play, but these are considered next and in Section 4.3.

h. Miscellaneous other principles. As noted, it is by no means clear to what extent these "other" principles were formally included in the Bucharest documents. Several had at one point or another been major determinants of trade price policies in the postwar period. At the very least, they must therefore have been discussed at some length during the Bucharest high-level meeting.

First, "new" products, however defined, introduced after the conclusion of the BTPA were to be transacted at "relational" prices: the original contract price is to be adjusted by a coefficient derived from the proportion between the original and the new reference price. Second, partners might consider it advantageous to foster mutual trade and therefore could set incentive prices for commodities they cannot or do not wish to acquire from third markets. How exporters were to be weaned of this presumably temporary protection subsidy is not at all clear. Somewhat paradoxically, some writers emphasize in this connection the need for "incentive prices" especially for products with a pronounced seasonal character, presumably to avoid arbitrage driving these products off the CMEA market. Third, preliminary prices could be set for ad hoc deliveries on short notice until negotiators can come up with mutually acceptable reference prices. Fourth, prices should be set in a "complex" way presumably to take into account a number of economic and other factors not necessarily pertaining to the transaction in question.[19] Finally, above-plan deliveries, which normally differ from ad hoc transactions, were to be effected at current prices.

A recent restatement and a reference map

A seminal change in the interpretation, but not the precise principles, of the Bucharest price guidelines was enacted in 1975. Instead of keeping average WMPs for reference purposes unchanged for years, henceforth reference and contract prices were to be recomputed annually on the basis of the preceding five years starting in 1976; for 1975 the preceding three years were to be used. In spite of numerous objections, this price formula was reconfirmed for the duration of the medium-term trade agreements for 1981–1985 and 1986–1990. The aforementioned time frame of the major stages in the evolution of CMEA pricing rules is summarized in Table 4.1, although as already suggested by the exceptions in the table footnotes, this reference guide can be no more than a rough-and-ready tool that may help to focus the discussion of a much more convoluted reality.

A brief evaluation

The principles just discussed are generally quite straightforward, and some make good sense in the context of chiefly physical planning of nearly all economic activities. It is in the interpretation and, even more so, in the application of these principles that formidable problems arise. In fact, one ends up with a peculiarly complex, quasi general-equilibrium model with individual commodities identified by producer, importer, transaction time, and other attributes. Needless to say, this makes for a rather unwieldy, if not completely unmanageable, environment. In other words, if all conditions of each transaction are taken into account, some kind of ex post market with real demand and supply schedules theoretically exists. But each of these markets is so fragmented that one can hardly speak of "atomistic" behavior. What is more, there is no such market in an ex ante sense, for the prices that appear are not exactly the terms at which alternatives are really offered. Even if partners wished to do so, some of the commodity attributes cannot possibly be transferred on a routine basis from one transactional relationship to another in some suitably modified form. It is precisely this feature that has been the root cause of the failure of any automatic type of multilateral clearing with or without the TR (see Chapter 8).

In summary, the CMEA price practice has rested, at least according to official claims, on basic WMPs that are transformed into CMEA reference prices. Four such modifications are important to recall: (1) Conjunctural, cyclical, seasonal, and other fluctuations in competitive WMPs are to be removed by averaging the prices that are deemed to be free of monopolistic, speculative, and other distortions. (2) Quality differences between the reference product of world markets and the corresponding CMEA

Table 4.1. *Evolution of price-formation reference points*

Type	Approximate application period	Reference period
Current prices	1945–1948	Ad hoc current WMPs
	1949–1950	Average WMPs of $t-1$[a]
Stop prices	1951–1953	Average WMPs of 1949 and part of 1950
	1954–1956	Average WMPs of 1949 and part of 1950 with ad hoc modifications
	1957–1958	Average WMPs of $t-1$
Bucharest rules	1959–1964 or 1965[b]	Current WMPs of 1957–1958
	1965/1966[c]–1970/1971 or 1966/1967[d]–1970/1971	Average WMPs of 1959–1964
	1971/1972–1975[e]	Average WMPs of 1965–1969
	1975	Average WMPs of 1972–1974
	1976–present	Average WMPs of the preceding five years

[a] $t-1$ = year before the application year.
[b] 1959–1965 for Bulgaria, Hungary, and Mongolia.
[c] The first changes were implemented in 1965 and the remainder in 1966 except for the countries in note b.
[d] The first changes were implemented in 1966 and the remainder in 1967 for the countries in note b.
[e] Half of the price adjustment was implemented in 1971 and the second half in 1972. But for some PEs (including Bulgaria), price adjustments were enacted only in the case of new products (Pěnkava 1975, p. 652). This rule was originally slated to remain in force until 1975, but it was suddenly abrogated in January 1975.
Source: Modification of Czechoslovakia's experiences as related in Pěnkava 1975, p. 652.

commodity call for target adjustments. (3) For goods that are not quoted in competitive markets or for which no direct trade prices can be located, the negotiators attempt to transform wholesale or retail prices into FOB trade prices. (4) Half of the fictive transportation charge is added to the price. In addition to these "regular procedures," actual intra-CMEA contract prices are obtained after various other modifications. Three are important. First, price shifts are to be kept within manageable proportions. It may therefore be necessary to smooth the passing through of substantial price changes over more than one period. Second, it may be deemed essential to procure certain goods from within the CMEA rather than from world markets. This applies in particular to specialization and cooperation agreements or when it is deemed warranted to encourage production of very scarce goods in the region by way of incentive prices. Finally, commodities are combined in "package deals" or *iunctim* transactions that aim at bilaterally balanced trade and allow some scope for special considerations of an economic or other origin, possibly the passing through of development assistance (Kuznecova 1985, p. 158).

These pricing principles are obviously much too vague to enable officials from planning offices and ministries to arrive at ready-made pricing criteria. A CMEA price research center could have been critical in identifying and averaging WMPs according to uniform guidelines, in monitoring temporary and basic shifts in WMPs, in formulating criteria for applying intra-CMEA trade surcharges or rebates, in cleansing WMPs, and in performing related tasks. The establishment of such a Secretariat organ was apparently entertained during the debate of the Bucharest principles. It was again in the limelight of cooperation discussions in the early 1960s, when the CMEA members explored the possibility of creating their own IPS in order better to reflect regional demand and supply (see Marciszewski and Rutkowski 1976, pp. 11–12 and Rutkowski 1977, p. 7).

4.3 Major determinants of intra-CMEA prices

Although one may try to survey the very wide range of factors that in one way or another impinge upon the selection of actual prices, they can logically be divided into three categories: (1) the management systems of the participants and their peculiar development strategy, which are the principal forces that explain the differential domestic and external prices in PEs; (2) the confluence of interests of PEs in ex ante trade determination, which is chiefly responsible for the existence of a separate CMEA price system; and (3) the peculiar features of the trade model of PEs, which is at the root of the heterogeneity of their pricing principles and behavior. Whether this neat separation holds in practice too is a different matter. Nevertheless, a brief look at each set may be useful.

Socialist planning for structural change

The implications for trade prices arising from the specifics of physical planning have already been alluded to in Section 4.1. It is important to remember that (1) socialist planning is discrete (mostly at one- or five-year intervals), and stability during the implementation phase is to be ensured to the extent possible to avoid ad hoc adjustments; (2) plans are generally implemented not by way of microeconomic indicators, such as prices, but by mandatory targets and rationed allowances of primary and intermediate inputs; and (3) domestic wholesale and retail prices fulfill distinct functions that, as a matter of principle and policy, are not directly related to cost and profitability considerations of individual markets.

From these factors follow a number of incentives for the creation of an MFT and the price-equalization mechanism.

Perhaps of equal importance is the socialist planner's growth vocation. Especially in the first two postwar decades or so, planners felt compelled to pursue competing development objectives that all derived from maximizing the physical growth tempo, with only marginal attention being paid to the quality of growth. These objections were generally pursued without taking into account static or dynamic comparative advantage indicators of global scarcities. Neither did planners attempt to implement their goals through conventional allocatory policy instruments. From this it follows that domestic prices have played a subsidiary role in both the selection of development goals and the implantation of mechanisms that enable planners to activate their socialist growth biases (see Chapter 5).

A socialist world market

The commonly held preference for fast growth through forced structural changes with the support of detailed physical plans facilitated rapid expansion in the reciprocal trade of the CMEA members by means of ex ante BTPAs. These BTPAs enabled the individual PE not only to achieve greater realism and to ensure a considerable measure of dependability in the national planning process, but they also provided these countries with the means to ward off temporary disturbances in world markets better than each PE individually would have been able to muster. More important, perhaps, reciprocal trade negotiations at a high level permitted planners to take into account micro- and macroeconomic objectives and to pursue various noneconomic goals. Comprehensive trade agreements, in principle, could have provided the necessary infrastructure for harmonizing domestic economic policies, and indeed they could have stimulated SEI, if other, economic as well as noneconomic, considerations had not inhibited the crystallization of these forces into adopting SEI as a solid objective of economic policy.

The bilateral trading world

The most important determinant of CMEA prices is, without doubt, bilateralism as it has been practiced in Eastern Europe for nearly forty years. The broad pricing principles agreed upon are too vague to permit a selection of concrete prices, as argued earlier. How then are prices determined?

Bilateral trade negotiations, by definition, resemble a monopoly–monopsony situation that is tempered by, on the one hand, concessions in the form of clearing or swing credits, capital transactions, reexports, and the like and, on the other hand, by the opportunities for arbitraged trade, especially with partners that do not impose bilateral balancing constraints. Generally speaking, the more competitive the reciprocal tradables of bilateral partners and the smaller the share of their mutual trade, the narrower the range for "full price" flexibility. In the extreme opposite, it is simply their actual demand and supply strengths at negotiation or, if revisions are feasible, at transaction time that are the key factors behind actual prices.

The greater the determination of negotiators to reduce the terms on which alternatives are offered to explicit monetary values, for given flexibility with third partners, the more prices will satisfy a priori notions of effectiveness. This would permit the selection of a range of prices situated between actual WMPs and some variant of domestic prices of the exporter country, depending upon the type of products and the state of the markets in which these goods are normally traded. Because the bargaining on prices has traditionally been conducted at a relatively high rung of the planning hierarchy, rather than by agents concerned mostly with "private" benefits and costs, the notion of overall trade benefits (including the total gains from trade and how they can be equitably divided between exporter and importer, the balancing of export and import values, the availability of priority goods, and so forth) is inevitably taken into account. The MFT permits each country to make trade decisions in line with aggregate economic policies; the most important microeconomic characteristics are generally handled through the familiar price-equalization mechanism and specific enterprise plans.

If planners decide to engage in trade beyond simply plugging deficits and disposing of surpluses in national material balances for a given time period, it becomes necessary to set up decision-making criteria conducive to specialization. To the extent that countries adapt WMPs and can forecast their evolution reasonably well, specialization on the basis of WMPs would be a feasible proposition. However, PEs also consciously wish to maintain some separateness in their reciprocal relations, even if only for noneconomic reasons. As a result, national assessments are arrived at. Regardless of the degree to which they are based on traditional socialist price-formation principles, these "local" evaluations inevitably influence actual regional prices (Kraus 1985, p. 10). Such trends are especially likely to emerge in the case of specialized nontraditional manufactures for which it is usually difficult to construct mutually acceptable WMPs in bilateral, let alone regionwide, economic relations. In the context of comprehensive economic reforms, some PEs have gradually adopted wholesale prices and price policies that aim at price stability, when absolutely necessary, in combination with periodic price adjustments, whenever warranted by shifts in domestic and foreign economic conditions. Especially for the trade-dependent PEs, it is therefore not obvious whether a coincidence between transaction and domestic wholesale prices reflects the utilization of transformed WMPs directly in trade relations or indirectly through the reference base of home prices.

On the basis of the various logical propositions set forth here, full prices in the CMEA appear to reflect the de facto state of markets. This may seem paradoxical, but it is not. Transaction prices, and even worse unit values, are not necessarily indicative of the state of markets because of several macroeconomic balancing aspects of trade negotiations, the particular time frame of the negotiations, the nonprice factors that impinge directly upon the size and distribution of trade gains, the full range of product attributes, and so on.

A regional price system?

Although the CMEA members officially profess to adhere to the fundamental principle of WMPs as the basic guide for regional trade prices, this claim often amounts to little more than paying lip service to the ideological underpinnings of equivalent exchange. Paradoxically enough, the latter calls for, and in fact mandates, a gamut of proper price adjustments that implicitly contribute to the establishment of a considerable degree of regional price autonomy in the CMEA (Faude, Grote, and Luft 1984, pp. 197–8). Some CMEA commentators actually regard it as a consciously designed autonomous price system operated as such (Kunz 1982, pp. 142–6). In addition to the price adjustments justified on the basis of centralized planning and equivalent exchange, bilateral bargaining about individual contract prices and expedient adjustments for transaction prices are two forces that have also measurably contributed to the gestation of a relatively autonomous price system. At given ERs, this differs markedly from WMPs with regard to both the level and structure of prices. Thus in the course of the years emerged comparatively stable price relations for a series of processed goods and parts and components that have no readily identifiable counterpart in world trade. The central problem in the CMEA now is that these prices do not reflect relative scarcities, they cannot generally be adjusted in line with shifts in market conditions, they cannot be harmonized to a uniform "price list" for the region as a whole, they do not really encourage adjustment in either demand or supply, and they certainly fail to foster regionwide specialization.

In accordance with the foregoing propositions, the determinants of prices can be divided into two categories: those that are inherent in traded goods, and the specific organizational arrangements under which those various goods are transacted. The latter give rise to an entire morphological array of possible combinations to be examined in some detail in Section 4.4. The former determine the availability and acceptability of WMPs, however, and, so to speak, are perforce the rock upon which the CMEA price system can be erected. Five different types can be distinguished: (1) homogeneous goods, including most fuels and raw materials; (2) finished products from processing industries; (3) intermediate processed products, including subassemblies, parts, and components of finished products; (4) individualized finished products; and (5) services, including wage products. Pricing matters are much more complex in the latter three cases because there are no readily identifiable WMPs for such goods.

a. Homogeneous goods. These goods are generally traded in relatively open world markets, commodity exchanges, and so on. The problem of arriving at proper base and reference prices is chiefly technical, namely the selection of accessible reference markets and the proper averaging techniques. The main market is supposed to be the leading one worldwide that would be the source of supply in the absence of a CMEA market (Brendel and Faude 1973, p. 1287). However, because only a few firms determine world prices of standard goods (such as diamonds, copper, and oil) or governments interfere in markets (as in agricultural products), such prices need to be purified in order to identify the competitive base price that acts as the reference for the construction of the CMEA price (Bogomolov 1980, pp. 120–1). This may considerably complicate the process of identifying proper "competitive prices" without at least one partner actively participating in that market. How daily price quotations are to be averaged, especially the selection of weights, has never been satisfactorily explained in the Eastern European literature.

b. Finished products. Processed products are as a rule priced with reference to catalogs, quotations, actual prices, tenders, price lists, and other types of information from producers in MEs with the highest technical and scientific standards and the lowest cost (Brendel and Faude 1973, p. 1287). Certainly, this may entail knotty problems in ensuring competitive quotes and in identifying products on a one-to-one basis. Nonetheless, for a wide range of standard manufactures some WMP can be obtained. To simulate a wholesale or retail price list into FOB WMPs is quite a different matter, however. But the long experience of skilled negotiators probably helps to cut through the red tape.

Given the shifts in productivity and the dynamics of international trade, especially the changes in real comparative advantage, it rarely pays to average a price over a long period of time and to keep it unchanged for possibly an even longer period of time if it is to play any allocatory role at all. It is known that "equal exchange" is one such key requirement. Prices are therefore shaped largely on the basis of the particular interests of the trading partners and tend to move in line with the exporter's home prices, which may be tailored according to the price catalogs of a few big firms of MEs (Knyziak 1974, pp. 180–1).

c. Individualized processing products. Together with goods not obtainable elsewhere or not to be procured from outside the CMEA area for practical purposes, custom manufactures are traded at ad hoc prices. Although some product components may be priced with reference to concrete WMPs (for example, a standard engine for a custom-made trawler), domestic prices of the exporters must inevitably play a formative role in the determination of reference prices. In this case, proper ERs also come into play, and PEs are likely to enact internal ERs that reflect some relation between domestic wholesale and some trade prices (see Chapter 6).

d. Intermediate processed products. These products are normally traded within large corporations, and there are therefore no competitive WMPs. As a rule, the PEs have promulgated ad hoc solutions for the derivation of reference prices. In some cases, the most celebrated being the joint production of different parts and components for the Žiguli car, the relative catalog prices of Western firms were used (Fiat in the case cited), which is discussed in Kormnov 1972, pp. 202–10. There has recently been considerable emphasis on the existence of a broad proposal on the pricing of goods coming under cooperation and specialization agreements. This document was apparently prepared in 1980 by the SCFT and has been refined several times since then (VK 1985a, p. 1).

e. Services. By definition, services are rarely generic, and their "prices" are therefore difficult to adapt from one market to another. The PEs have tried to imitate lists of service tariffs of Western firms or organizations. These tariffs include air, rail, and shipping freight, in particular (Šanina 1976, pp. 169–73). Though similar arrangements have been made for insurance and related charges, there is still quite a gap for other services, whose prices are by necessity codetermined by nominal or transformed domestic costs. The uncertainty is considerable in part if, as recently emphasized, the PEs also attempt to average such tariffs and service charges in world markets over a five-year period (Koz'menko 1986, pp. 25–26).

In addition to the type of traded good, as noted, the form under which it is traded, which can sometimes coincide with the product type as with specialized parts and components, appears to be a significant determinant of CMEA contract prices and often of transaction prices as well. This gives rise to a wide variety of price determinants, ranging from competitive price behavior to price indeterminancy, as in bilateral monopoly.

4.4 A morphology of separate pricing environments

Without standard practices, the setting of CMEA trade prices has become an intricate art with almost unique results. Nevertheless, it is useful to distinguish among different regimes in an attempt to unravel the mystery that continues to shroud this price policy and, by implication, that causes havoc and tensions in CMEA economic relations. Table 4.2 summarizes the regimes that are of general importance, but it does not try to cover each and every difference in the set of rules that underlie the formation of contract or transaction prices. The table is a mongrel in that it combines general rules with key features of price practices that are explained later. Finally, no attempt is made to cover all possible configurations of price rules that may have occurred in the postwar period; the focus here is on the last fifteen years.

There are undoubtedly alternative approaches to the specification of mutually exclusive situations in which different sets of pricing rules may, but need not, apply. Nevertheless, the following hierarchy may be useful, especially with regard to the evolution of apparent pricing determinants in the CMEA since the early 1970s: (1) currency of accounting or actual settlement (TR or CC), (2) type of trade agreement (regular, supplementary, and ad hoc), (3) type of transaction (regular exchange, specialization, and joint investment), and (4) market tension (giving rise to a very wide range of commodities from very soft to very hard goods). Admittedly, this particular configuration does not offer mutually exclusive situations nor does each and every combination of the four levels exist in actual practice.

Perhaps the most fundamental distinction is the currency of payment, closely followed by the type of trade agreement. Because CC transactions already embody a higher degree of hardness in comparison to TR transactions, they usually entail markedly different prices. This is especially true if mutual transactions are not kept in separate clearing accounts but give rise to actual payment flows.[20] Regular commercial transactions in CC can be planned and included in regular BTPAs; they could be paid for at actual costs. Such transactions can also be regulated in supplementary agreements that are planned (for example, Hungarian deliveries of foodstuffs to the USSR in the 1976–1980 and 1981–1985 trade plans) and probably involve mutually satisfactory current WMPs comparable to what could be earned in CC markets. Supplementary agreements can also be concluded outside the framework of regular trade negotiations, when they probably command a higher price. Single transactions[21] are usually conducted at whatever the market will bear.

Because the CC denomination is normally resorted to in recognition of goods that are judged to embody a superior degree of hardness, it may appear paradoxical that some deliveries of soft goods could occur at CC. Because this situation is admittedly exceptional, it is deleted from Table 4.2 on the asssumption that the degree of price difference is an adequate gauge. But it is not per se a theoretical curiosum, especially in the context of the transshipment of goods through ME intermediaries, including PE trade companies in the West. It may be rational to obtain soft goods for

Table 4.2. *Morphology of price determinants in intra-CMEA trade*

	Regular commerce		Specialization transactions		Joint investment	
	Soft	Hard	Soft	Hard	Soft	Hard
TR transactions						
Regular (planned)	PC	PC	< PC	> PC	< PC−	≤ PC
Supplementary						
Planned	< PC	> PC	< PC?	< PC?	< PC?	< PC?
Unplanned	< PC−	> PC+	n.a.	n.a.	n.a.	n.a.
Ad hoc						
Planned	n.a.	n.a.	n.a.	n.a.	< PC	≤ PC
Unplanned	< WP	≥ WP	n.a.	n.a.	n.a.	n.a.
CC transactions[a]						
Regular (planned)	≤WP		≈WP?		≈WP?	
Supplementary						
Planned	≤WP		≤WP?		≈WP?	
Unplanned	≥WP		≥WP		n.a.	
Ad hoc						
Planned	≈WP		n.a.		≈WP?	
Unplanned	≈WP		n.a.		n.a.	

Notes: n.a., probably not applicable; PC, Bucharest price principles; WP, current WMP; ?, sign and size uncertain; −, the magnitude of the change is smaller than normal; +, the magnitude of the change is larger than normal.
[a] In CC transactions, the CMEA price obtained by reference to current WMPs, including deviations for differences in quality, should as a rule adequately reflect the hardness or softness of goods. No distinction is therefore made between hard and soft goods in CC trade.

CC if the exporter grants a substantial discount on the true TR cost. Such transactions may be included in formal medium-term supplementary agreements or end up as planned or unplanned ad hoc transactions that remain unique.

Similar provisions probably apply to trade resulting from specialization agreements or jointly financed investment projects: For hard goods, the CMEA trade price is likely to approach closely the current WMP obtainable by the exporter. WMPs may be averaged for deliveries planned in the context of either regular or, more likely, supplementary agreements, and ad hoc transactions may even involve incentive prices to reflect the true marginal cost of ensuring delivery over some mutually agreed period.

Matters are very different for the bulk of trade conducted in TR. Regular trade protocols attempt to adhere to the Bucharest price principles for goods that have a more or less identifiable WMP (especially fuels, industrial raw materials, and some agricultural products). For most engineering products and many durable consumer goods, the problem of finding a proper WMP as reference is probably resolved bilaterally. Once the base price is agreed upon, averaging presumably prevails in order to obtain reference and possibly contract prices. Regular transactions conducted in the framework of supplementary or ad hoc agreements are more likely to be cleared at whatever price the situation can bear. TR prices will probably be attuned more to current WMPs and, occasionally, current domestic production costs of exporters transformed in some fashion into TRs.

The aforementioned situation is even more likely to prevail in the case of specialized products or the exchange of goods emanating from jointly financed investment ventures on TR account. Some guidance in prescribing the negotiation range may be provided by current WMPs or price relations, but the actual terms at which the goods move basically ensue from bilateral negotiations in which the production situation of participating countries is bound to play a determining, if not an exclusive, role.

4.5 The effects of the traditional trade model and price reforms

Everything that has been discussed in the preceding section is compatible with many different types of interstate trading. It is now necessary to place these comments within the context of the role of the trade strategy and its supporting model in the overall economic policies of the PEs, because they may significantly affect the type of prices that are obtained. But I cannot here provide more than a basic outline of the impact of bilateralism and structural bilateralism (for details, see Brabant 1973).

As already outlined, the PE's particular strategy and model imposed constraints on the degree of price flexibility that could be accommodated

and that policy makers wanted to embed in their economies. Strict bilateralism was resorted to not only as a means of economizing on scarce
foreign exchange in the postwar environment of structural disequilibria
but also as a strategic component of the overall planning framework that
these countries have gradually perfected. Certainly, the particular variant
of bilateral trade policies pursued by the PEs evolved out of experience
and short-term practical needs, especially in response to their shared
requirement to blend foreign trade with rigid central planning at home.
However, the USSR's experience in the interwar period demonstrated
that, even without the presence of a number of economies with perceived
similar needs, the MFT would have called for comparatively far-reaching
trade controls.

Particularly important has been the vocation of planners to eliminate as
much as possible the uncertainty normally associated with a variety of
economic processes. In trade, this aspiration found its reflection in binding BTPAs in support of the MFT. As a rule, governments of MEs find
their authority over trade matters limited to the creation of the mechanisms and conditions through which enterprises, on the basis of private
cost and benefit considerations, are motivated to engage in profitable
trade. Precisely because a PE is in a much more commanding position to
commit its future national output in almost minute detail, the existence
of a group of PEs has had formative consequences for the concrete shape
of bilateralism.

As discussed in Section 4.1, central planners engage in external commerce not as a direct means to maximize the micro- and macroeconomic
trade gains, but as one channel to assist in the implementation of preset
national economic plans or the realization of the economic development
priorities held by top policy makers. In such an environment, individual
commodity prices do not matter much in terms of the overall success
criteria of traditional PEs for as long as the trade sector is commanded by
the MFT. It is only when policy makers are entrusting enterprises with
individual trade targets, including profitability goals, that commodity
prices have to be scrutinized more carefully.

In other words, the policy maker's preference for greater certainty in
trade, the role of trade in the implementation of the typical socialist
industrialization strategy, and the rather rigid separation of domestic
from trade markets have had very important implications for the practical aspects of CMEA price determination.[22] Concrete individual commodity prices, as a result, have been negotiated bilaterally not mainly in order
to maximize profit from such transactions but as a means to the realization of a set of "higher" goals. In addition to the overall objectives already
discussed, the specific conditions of CMEA bilateralism itself necessitated
price deviations to secure approximate balance during a mutually agreed
period to obtain goods that otherwise would have had to be procured in

"unfriendly" markets, to promote bilateral collaboration, to transfer what is, in effect, development assistance, to reduce the impact of price revisions on the state of the bilateral balance of payments, and to accommodate other circumstances.

Although the PEs have unquestionably tried to observe some degree of reference price uniformity, at least for one country's exports to two or more CMEA partners, it is in the nature of the bilateral trading process to yield individualized contract and, even more so, bilaterally differentiated transaction prices. The greater the "distance" between domestic producer (or user) and the foreign user (or producer), and the stricter the enforcement of the MFT through government means, *ceteris paribus*, the greater the disparity in individual prices and the harder it is to identify the actual determinants of individual trade prices.

The particular type of CMEA bilateralism that has been strengthened during the past forty years or so allows only marginal room for price flexibility. As a result, the actual scarcity of individual goods or commodity groups has been expressed increasingly through nonprice commercial conditions (including special purpose credits, ex post capital flows to regularize bilateral trade imbalances, reexports, CC payments, combined or tied-in sales of hard and soft goods, conditional specialization agreements, and many others). Especially important has been the emergence of a panoply of hard and soft goods which has given rise to a particular type of structural or commodity bilateralism that continues to be a crucial determinant of the CMEA trade model.

Structural bilateralism tends to emerge when the price mechanism cannot or is not allowed to perform its allocatory function. Under such conditions, concrete prices result from, possibly very complex, negotiating positions. It is therefore difficult to determine how individual transaction prices are set. The magnitude of the problem depends not only on the variety of economic and other price determinants but also on concrete negotiating stances, which belong at the very least to the category "commercial secrets." Actual transaction prices are therefore difficult to document for all but those most intimately involved in the concrete bilateral negotiating positions for which documented prices are desired.

In addition to the serious problems associated with isolating individual commodity prices, identifying how these prices are derived is also a comparatively useless exercise because the normal transaction price is not the full price charged; that is to say, the burden of "scarcity competition" between alternative markets or products does not mainly fall on prices. If one did not seek to clarify as much as possible the other conditions that set the stage for bilateral negotiations and transactions, identifying concrete commodity prices would be nearly pointless. It would be especially difficult to draw meaningful inferences from such purely empirical evidence.[23]

The paucity of concrete information on contract and transaction prices in individual CMEA commercial transactions is a serious impediment to the better understanding of the nature and portent of SEI. It has been beyond doubt for quite a long time, however, that there is a great lack of clarity about pricing procedures and a wide margin for discretionary adjustment of relative prices. In spite of the fact that CMEA policy makers have serious reservations about the ability of the traditional price mechanism to guarantee equivalent exchange, to bolster economic growth, and to assist in undertaking structural transformations so as to promote a more coherent ISDL, very few changes in the actual modes of price determination have been enacted to date. In some instances, this persistence of unsatisfactory policy instruments – they are certainly not efficient – can be attributed to the fact that it is not at all expedient to tackle the price mechanism in isolation. Furthermore, because the latter necessarily yields de facto benefits to some partners, it is difficult to reach even a clear majority in favor of piecemeal changes or unpredictable and vaguely defined overhauls.

4.6 Empirical issues

Although the identification of individual CMEA prices is very difficult and would not be apt to yield a meaningful general inference with respect to the applicability of the formal pricing rules, it could still be of more than passing interest to spell out the means by which one can construct or isolate more or less precise information regarding CMEA trade pricing. At the least this would be a preliminary step in a more comprehensive assessment of the trade criteria used in fostering SEI. There are several ways in which one might specify such empirical inquiries, although each exercise is bound to be fraught with its own identification and interpretation problems. For our purposes here, the various alternatives could be separated into those focusing on absolute price levels as distinct from those testing changes in price levels over time.

Regarding price levels, the type of CMEA bilateralism anchored to the ruble or, since 1964, the TR as clearing unit may logically, and in fact does, yield a price level that diverges, possibly very markedly, from that in world markets. There are various reasons for this: the mechanism for creating reference prices, the bilateral determination of contract prices, the logic of arriving at expedient transaction prices, bilateralism, the fictive transport charges, and a host of other factors described earlier. Empirical information on the precise degree of price divergence is highly inconsistent. But estimates of "20 percent or even more" (Gadomski 1974, p. 44) or of a "normal" disparity between 20 and 30 percent (Kisiel 1974, p. 230) on average are not at all uncommon; the dispersion of individual commodities in any given relation may be much wider. For our purposes, it suffices to be aware of two facts: CMEA prices are not uniform, and they differ from absolute and relative WMPs.

Several CMEA institutions (including the Secretariat, research institutes, SCEP, SCFT, the Standing Committee for Currency and Financial Questions (SCFQ), and others) have attempted to quantify some of the differences in price levels on a number of occasions since the first comprehensive studies on the feasibility and desirability of creating an IPS for the CMEA as a whole. Ausch and Bartha (1969) and Ausch (1972, pp. 84ff.) summarize the main findings: Relative to average WMPs of 1957–1961, prices among the six Eastern European countries aggregated with CMEA trade weights for 1963 exceeded WMPs on average by 25.9, 15.4, and 1.7 percent for machinery, raw materials, and agricultural products, respectively. Another exercise, apparently undertaken under the direction of Oleg Tarnovskij (Kalčev 1974, p. 69) although not published in full, details price relations in 1971, but the corresponding WMP reference base is not known. This reportedly arrived at a decline in the overvaluation of machinery to 19 percent and an undervaluation of raw materials and foodstuffs by 8 and 19 percent, respectively (Cvetkov-Golubarev 1974, p. 54; Kalčev 1974, p. 69). There have been other measurements usually involving pairs of PEs, but I shall not review them here.

Since the late 1950s, Western scholars have attempted to measure the level and direction of differences between CMEA and world prices or of what PEs could hope to obtain if they were to redirect their trade to third markets. Most of these studies had as object "price discrimination" in the CMEA and were therefore most concerned with the implicit transfer of regional taxes and subsidies than with the issue of price differentiation per se. Because these efforts have recently been quite critically reviewed in Marrese and Vaňous 1983 against the background of their own exhaustive approach to the subject, I shall refrain from repeating these findings here.

All of these studies have tried to prepare aggregate inferences from individual commodity studies and a variety of commodity and country group weights without really attempting to ensure individual commodity comparability, representativeness, and proper sampling for its own sake. In my view, this has been a serious shortcoming because perhaps the knottiest empirical problem common to all of these exercises is the absence of information about individual commodity prices. This critique is given in full awareness of the empirical problems endemic to PEs that well transcend the issues related to the lack of commodity value and quantum information for some PEs or the selectivity of published details for others. At best, one occasionally finds an individual price quotation in the literature, particularly for various types of energy in recent years. Even when point estimates can be prepared, it is frequently impossible to specify precisely whether it is an average price, a unit value, an average

of CC and TR denominated transactions, or something else. For petroleum, for example, quotations are further complicated because some PEs,
until recently, obtained the goods at a special fixed price negotiated at
the time these countries invested in the expansion of production capacity
in the USSR. This can certainly be confusing (Brabant 1984a; Lavigne
1983). To document prices over at least a few years, the best one can
hope for is unit values of a select number of traded goods. Without
opening Pandora's box, suffice it to note that it is very difficult to distinguish the information regarding prices that may be derived from unit
values from the distortions attributable to the special features of intra-
CMEA trade and possibly the specific composition of the commodity
groups under consideration.

Perhaps more significant than considerations about absolute price levels is the measurement of the direction and magnitude of relative price
changes over time. Assuming that nonprice trade conditions and the
composition of the individual commodity group remain unchanged, do
the direction and approximate magnitude of CMEA price shifts closely
mirror changes in reference prices? The nature of the CMEA trade system would appear to argue for the validity of this change *on average*, at
least for the type of commodities whose WMP can be identified (see
Hewett 1974, pp. 91–110 for the 1950s and 1960s). With some commodities (basic fuels, homogeneous raw materials, and some crucial agricultural goods, in particular), one would even expect that movements in
individual commodity prices be synchronized more or less tightly with
changes in WMPs after the proper averaging and lagging as per the basic
CMEA pricing principles examined in Section 4.2.

Published trade data suffer from a number of shortcomings. Furthermore, the interesting details of actual trade negotiations and individual
commercial transactions are virtually never disclosed; when they are, it is
very difficult to verify them. For these and other reasons, it is nearly
impossible to test, with the aid of standard statistical techniques, many
plausible hypotheses regarding the relationship between CMEA and
world prices. An exception can probably be made for trade cleared in TR
(see Brabant 1984a, 1985b).

To test more generally whether the CMEA pricing principles are applicable, one must examine individual commodity prices in CMEA and
world trade over a number of years. With some exceptions, there is no
systematic information on individual commodity prices that would permit
standard statistical inference over a fairly long time. Some PEs (Czechoslovakia, Hungary, Poland, and the USSR) publish quantum and value
data in their general statistical or trade yearbooks. Unfortunately, the
unit values that can thus be obtained for some selected years are not very
good surrogates of prices required for the above test mainly because of
the mixture of TR and CC pricing in CMEA trade, the heterogeneity of

the "commodities" or commodity classes listed, and the different regimes under which identical goods are traded in any given bilateral relationship. The best statistical information that can be accessed is the Hungarian commodity price indices in ruble-denominated trade, although the precise parameters of these data are unfortunately not known. This considerably complicates the derivation of the corresponding WMPs. Nevertheless, for some products a plausible series of WMPs can be constructed that permits TR prices to be compared with what should have prevailed if the pricing principles had been applied consistently. This does not mean that PEs constantly scrutinize all individual prices for any minor changes in reference prices, however. Because TR prices, in principle, are uniform, the Hungarian experience should be indicative of CMEA developments.

4.7 The empirical relationship between CMEA prices and world market prices

The WMPs can be averaged according to the CMEA price principles and converted into a common currency, say the TR, at alternative ERs. In principle, the following relationships should hold exactly:

$$PC_t = PR_t = \frac{1}{k} \sum_{i=t-1}^{t-k-1} WMP_i \quad \text{for } t \geqslant 1975; \quad \begin{array}{l} k = 3 \text{ for } t = 1975 \\ k = 5 \quad t > 1975 \end{array} \quad (4.1a)$$

$$= \frac{1}{5} \sum_{i=\bar{t}-1}^{\bar{t}-6} WMP_i \quad \text{for } 1965? \leqslant t < 1975 \quad (4.1b)$$

where PC is the actual TR price, PR the average of the reference WMPs, $\bar{t}$ the first year under the old price regime in which the new price base was implemented, t the current time, and k the number of years over which the averaging is to be computed. In view of what has been said, the right side of equation 4.1 is not easily quantified and is subject to negotiation. Instead of an exact relationship, perhaps

$$PC_t = f(PR_t) \quad (4.2)$$

holds, with the precise functional form being essentially unknown. However, target research (Brabant 1984a, 1985b, 1985c, in press, c) indicates that a stochastic relationship exists between PC and PR, possibly

$$\log PC_t = a + b \log PR_t + u_t \quad (4.3)$$

where the error term, u_t, is assumed to have mean zero and constant variance. This model essentially posits that proportional changes in WMPs are transmitted into the CMEA price formula. Although the principles suggest that TR prices are patterned after absolute WMP levels, proportional transmission is more plausible chiefly because (1) prices, particularly for "standard" goods, have evolved from what gradually emerged in the first postwar decade when the precise formative role of WMPs was far from transparent; (2) prices are hammered out bilaterally, and one basic guideline in the negotiations must be the transmission of broad changes in WMPs; (3) especially for many bulk and primary goods, the half-freight charge is applied with some flexibility; and (4) the stage of processing, the specific characteristics of the goods under investigation, the volume of the transaction, and other important commercial parameters are likely to affect the price level but not necessarily its variations, except when the processing costs of extracting the components itself changes.

The logic of the Bucharest principles would suggest a conversion of WMPs at average annual ERs of the TR. However, there has never been a clear-cut official statement to that effect, and experiments tend to indicate that end-year ERs yield, though marginally, better results than those obtained from series converted at average annual rate.[24] Owing to this uncertainty, alternative ERs for the TR and the Soviet ruble were explored in the set of experiments that are summarized here.[25]

Against the foregoing backdrop, equations similar to equation 4.3 with alternative specifications for converting WMPs into TR or rubles were run for periods starting in 1971 or 1975 through, most recently, 1985. The first observation point was dictated by empirical constraints (Brabant 1985c). Even if a longer series could have been constructed, it was felt necessary to test for a break in the "sample structure," among others on account of the newly agreed interpretation of the "Bucharest principles" in early 1975 and the very sharp changes in absolute and relative WMPs sustained in the 1970s. I conjectured that these seminal shifts motivated the PEs to scrutinize more closely the application of the formal pricing principles particularly for rather well-defined goods for which WMPs are publicly quoted in international commodity exchanges. Provided WMPs have been correctly identified and averaged, adherence to the Bucharest principles should yield near unity as the estimated value of the elasticity parameters. Offhand, the relationship for the period since 1975 should be better, because the reinterpreted Bucharest principles have probably been observed much more closely for the former than for the latter period. The computations show that, in several cases, the foregoing expectations are far from being confirmed.

One of the most crucial points of the entire empirical investigation concerns the proper identification of WMPs. Because this is not at all a straightforward matter, the experiments were undertaken in two clusters. In the first one, an attempt was made to match individual commodities traded within the CMEA according to the Hungarian trade statistics with price quotations in world commodity exchanges. This necessarily limited the size of the sample to a comparatively small number of products. The second cluster basically conjectured that the experience with prices in East–West trade must be an important determinant of CMEA pricing. I therefore identified products traded in both East–West and CMEA trade, according to Hungarian foreign trade statistics.[26] Although this yielded a larger sample, the requirement that significant volume be transacted in both relations for a comparatively long time considerably impinged upon the selection process.

The commodities selected for empirical analysis using TR and world prices are all among the primary ones for which standard price quotations are available. They fall into four categories: foodstuffs, fuels, metals, and nonfood agricultural products. Good relationships were obtained for some commodities, especially for the long series even in some instances where the elasticity value turns out to be insignificant or not different from zero. The strongest relationships hold for the various kinds of fuel in the sample, and an adequate fit is obtained for most metals and nonfood agricultural raw materials; for the remaining commodities, however, the relationships are not very robust, particularly in the short observation period. The divergence of the determination coefficient from unity signals that there are other determinants of the TR price, in addition to the identified WMP, which may, but need not, indicate a violation of the official pricing principles. This may stem from various circumstances. In the past fifteen years or so, for example, the WMPs of these goods have greatly fluctuated, but these substantial moves are not necessarily, and at any rate not immediately, incorporated into the CMEA price formula. Furthermore, particularly for agricultural products, prices have continued to be subject to special regimes that are not necessarily mirrored in the CMEA. But there need not be a close relationship between the standard product and the corresponding CMEA good for various other reasons.

The values obtained for the elasticity parameter clearly exhibit a wide spectrum and in many instances they significantly diverge from unity – the value that ideally should have been obtained. Frequently, however, the estimated elasticities do not differ from it in a statistically significant sense, especially when allowance is made for the "half-freight principle," which applies to nearly all of these commodities (Šanina 1976, pp. 169–73).

According to the Bucharest principles and their extension, the estimation should have been performed on

$$\log PC_t = a' + b' \log(PR_t + F_t) + u_t' \tag{4.4}$$

where F_t stands for the "half-freight" charges incorporated in TR prices. Depending upon the initial values, the elasticities of equations 4.3 and 4.4 may be quite different. However, in many instances in the 1970s, WMPs clearly surged ahead faster than transportation charges. Hence, even if the estimated elasticity of equation 4.4 were close to 1,

$$b \gtreqless b' \quad \text{if } \dot{P}R_t \lesseqgtr \dot{F}_t \tag{4.5}$$

where the dot over the variable signals growth rates. This may be one of the explanations for why many elasticities are smaller than unity.

Perhaps the most surprising result is that the pricing principles do not appear to have been observed more closely since 1975. One would have expected the elasticities to be closer to unity and to be more significant than what is observed for the longer series. These expectations are fulfilled only in a few cases out of the ten estimations for which different series could be analyzed. Nonetheless, the estimated equations are generally significantly better for well-defined products traded in established world markets. CMEA prices for agricultural products do not seem to move closely with WMPs possibly for a variety of reasons, especially the fact that "incentive prices" are frequently negotiated for key agricultural products.[27] Given the persistent foodstuff shortages in the PEs in recent years, severe problems in global food trade since the early 1970s, and sharp price fluctuations in the 1970s, it is not surprising that there is no simple one-to-one relationship. CMEA prices appear to be determined largely by movements in WMPs, but the latter's proportional changes are apparently asynchronously transmitted to the CMEA. With metals and minerals, the results are strongly mixed.

The second cluster of experiments was basically designed to test whether, for Hungary, prices experienced in East–West trade can be suitably adapted according to the CMEA price-formation principles to be a major determinant of CMEA prices. Clearly, after eliminating all the goods that are not traded in both directions and for which insufficient time series are available, the size of the experiments could be increased to thirty-nine exportables and thirty-three importables, but there are very few overlaps between the two series. The equations were run as specified in equation 4.3. In addition, the series starting with 1971 were also rerun with a kink in order to test directly for the significance of the shift in price base in 1975. The results were generally not as good as those included in the first group of experiments. Because a wider array of products could be tested, somewhat more general inferences could be drawn. Although it would be premature to attempt definitive conclusions at this stage, there was sufficient evidence of price divergence for some goods to maintain the hypothesis that some CMEA prices are probably not derived from East–West prices, which differ from WMPs for a variety of reasons. But as for WMPs, East–West prices are used at times as a handy reference in trade negotiations and may be indicative of trade opportunities in world markets.

The foregoing key results of much broader empirical investigations indicate that CMEA pricing is not a straightforward matter. The broad verification of the applicability of the CMEA pricing guidelines reported on here has yielded mixed results.[28] On the whole, no evidence at all could be found of a close correspondence in price levels, not even for commodities whose WMPs have changed dramatically and should therefore in principle have been closely scrutinized in the last decade or so. The relationship between proportional changes in CMEA prices and WMPs or, alternatively, East–West prices, works very well for some standard commodities, moderately well for most metals, nonfuel minerals, nonfood agricultural product, and not at all for a number of foodstuffs. Finally, with few exceptions no evidence could be found to buttress the proposition that since 1975 the CMEA countries have watched WMPs much more closely than when CMEA reference prices remained unchanged for long periods of time.

These results are, however, tentative because of several problems with the design of the experiments as well as the statistical verification. Perhaps the central lesson to be learned from these exercises is that pricing in CMEA trade continues to be beset by complex conceptual and practical problems. Even so, there would appear to be sufficient evidence to cling to a healthy degree of skepticism, in some cases in combination with agnosticism, as far as the emulation of averaged WMPs in the CMEA is concerned. The linkup of CMEA prices with WMPs, on the one hand, and with domestic prices, on the other, therefore remains an important task for target adjustments, if not comprehensive economic reforms.

5

Domestic prices, structural adjustment, and economic reform

An ME is by definition anchored to properly functioning markets. Positive structural adjustment there, if required, is directed at rectifying whatever has been inhibiting the return to balancing accounts that is in the nature of the market system. There may be good social or other reasons to interfere occasionally with that mechanism. The pivot should be the market, however, with flexible prices and quantities, inasmuch as this, in principle, ensures the best static and dynamic allocations of resources according to prevailing tastes. In the stylized model of economic theory, equilibrium implies that there are no unsatisfied consumers and no producers with excess supplies at the price level where supply and demand balance ex post. If not, movements in relative prices ensure the restoration of balance in a comparatively short time, usually by some combination of quantum and price movements. The speed of change of supply and demand depends essentially on the flexibility with which resources can be disengaged, elasticities of demand, the availability of substitutes, and other such factors. This is very different from decision making in a PE.

This chapter is devoted to the entire complex of domestic pricing policies and practices in Eastern Europe, including what may emanate in that respect from any fundamental change in economic mechanisms. Given the theme of this volume, particular emphasis is given to the implication for the foreign trade sector of present and future price systems within the PEs. The basic price components of a generic PE are set forth in Section 5.1. Next I explain the original rationality behind such a price system. Evidently, several important changes in socialist preferences have materialized in the past thirty years or so, and this shift in the structure of rationality underlying socialist prices is taken into account in Section 5.3. The relationship between domestic producer and consumer prices, and their link with trade prices, which is the subject of Section 5.4, is crucial for understanding the problems faced by PEs when they attempt to exploit the advantages embedded in the detailed information of economic agents. How all of these factors bear on the issue of comprehensive economic reforms in the context of a positive adjustment program is debated in Section 5.5. The last section is devoted to the potential reform of the CMEA price mechanisms as seen from the perspective of domestic prices.

5.1 Basic components of socialist price systems

Because prices are considered to be the paramount reference point for effective decision making, it is instructive at this juncture to examine more closely the various price tiers that exist in the PE, and to what extent these components have been weakened or strengthened by the modifications in the economic mechanisms introduced over the past twenty years or so. I shall first look at the bases of the price system. The next subsections discuss the determination of producer and consumer prices and the rationale for the dichotomies between the two. The final subsection examines more closely the relationship between domestic and trade prices.

On the bases of the price system

The complexity of the price system and pricing policies in a PE is of a different order of magnitude from that under the ME paradigm and indeed of that typical of developed MEs. It is at the same time more complex and controversial because it is not only a matter of economics but eminently one of ideology, politics, and social objectives. Being a value category, prices cannot be dissociated from labor, which for ideological reasons is taken to be the sole source of value. However, to reach simultaneously several competing social targets, socialist policy makers deliberately differentiate prices from their underlying value essentially for political reasons.[1] This has crucial ramifications for domestic and external economic, social, and political decisions.

The socialist concept of value is steeped in the Marxian labor theory of value, which posits that a product's value equals the amount of socially necessary labor it embodies. For each product,

$$V = C + L + S \tag{5.1}$$

where V is value, C is the constant cost of capital expenditure or embodied labor, L is the variable cost of live labor, and S is the surplus value. The latter can be determined variously. The orthodox definition is

$$V_1 = C + L(1 + s) \tag{5.2}$$

where s is the average profit markup on direct labor expenditures. An alternative definition, the so-called production price, is derived by setting the surplus value in another way:

$$V_2 = (L + C)(1 + s') \tag{5.3}$$

where s' is the average markup to live and embodied labor combined. Finally, the third variant, which provides the value category underlying the two-channel price, is defined as

$$V_3 = C(1 + s'') + L(1 + s''') \tag{5.4}$$

where s'' is the markup on embodied labor and s''' is the one on live labor.

In actual practice, it is recognized that prices "normally" deviate from their reference values because of temporary disequilibria between demand and supply for goods and services. In addition, prices need to be deliberately deflected from their true reference values to foster a variety of objectives, including the allocation of resources according to macroeconomic priorities and sociopolitical preferences. It is against this backdrop that one should rationalize the emergence of a relatively autonomous two-tier system of producer (or wholesale) and consumer (or retail) prices in the PE with both steered rather separately from trade prices. The disparity between the prices paid to the producers by the state and prices paid by consumers for retail goods and services is considerable and derives not only from commercial margins and the government's fiscal needs but one price system is largely independent of the other. Each is usually determined and modified according to criteria that are deemed suitable to reach specific objectives either in the social sphere or in the sphere of plan formulation, implementation, and control.

Different types of prices

The socialist policy maker has several degrees of freedom in setting prices. He or she might ignore values altogether and set prices randomly or according to extraneous criteria that are at least consistent. But the PE's price manager is likely to be motivated by one of the formulae of values discussed earlier. Decisions are required essentially on three degrees of freedom: (1) the determination of embodied labor and at what rates (capital depreciation, land rent, rent on nonrenewable resources, and other) the value of these resources are to be factored into value and price; (2) the precise magnitude of the surplus value levy; and (3) the method of calculating surplus value. The last two are not independent of each other. Before discussing the parameters of these degrees of freedom, I believe a terminological note will be helpful.

As in any ME, there are numerous prices for a given product depending on the complexity of its market. Distribution channels as well as the actual degree of market control of the producer over the product's price may be crucial in determining the various price categories. To avoid unnecessary confusion about terminology, it may be helpful to specify the

Price category		Definition
Producer price (also known as factory price)	⟶	average branch cost of labor and capital, plus a profit markup
Industry price	⟶	producer price plus turnover tax or minus turnover subsidy
Wholesale price	⟶	industry price plus a wholesale margin, including a wholesale profit markup
Retail price	⟶	wholesale price plus a retail margin, including a retail profit markup

Figure 5.1. Basic price types in a socialist economy.

most important components of the key alternative price categories that one regularly encounters in a socialist economy. Figure 5.1 blocks out the scheme for industrial goods. In the traditional CPE, wholesale prices of consumer goods are normally established before the imposition of turnover taxes or subsidy grants. Most economies have since gradually moved to the scheme outlined here. In the former case, the industry price would normally coincide with the producer price. Prices of agricultural products and foodstuffs more generally may be set differently, however, depending on the organization of agriculture, the specific goals the government intends to pursue with its procurement prices, and the center's influence over free peasant markets.

The determination of wholesale prices

For all practical purposes, the period of reconversion, stabilization, and reconstruction, as well as the voluntarism of the early 1950s, should be ignored in this connection. Policy makers at that time were essentially concerned with mopping up excess liquidity in circulation, controlling the transfer of the surplus from agriculture to industry, and the promotion of heavy industry. But we should not ignore the fact that the historical antecedents of more recent price reforms can frequently be found precisely in the disequilibrium situation of the immediate postwar period.

From the point of view of effective economic administration, it is important to understand the relationship between the two broad domestic price systems. Because both derive their essential traits from the calculation of average production costs, the question of how the latter are set has a crucial bearing on how "informative" administrative prices are likely to be. As already indicated, there are various ways in which average production costs can be determined, with the variations essentially hinging on the definition of surplus value, the magnitude of the surplus value levy, and the assessment of embodied labor.

The basic approach to the setting of wholesale prices is the one blocked out in the preceding subsection: average branch costs of life and embodied labor plus some markup. Critical in this connection is the determination of cost elements at the initial stages of the production process, because the actual outlays for intermediate goods in combination with the factor rewards embodied in them are a basic constituent of the entire wholesale price system. A defect of traditional pricing in PEs in that respect has been the relative disregarding of the scarcity cost of land, capital, and nonreproducible natural resources. Proper evaluation of the contributions of capital and land in the form of rents is usually eschewed, and amortization rates are generally well below those that would be economically justified. Similarly, the true domestic cost of imported intermediate goods is rarely accurately factored into the cost computation. Because average costs are inferior to marginal costs with an upward sloping supply curve for the branch as a whole, the pricing rule in a PE suggests that there are always firms that lose money and others that gain.

In the CPE, accumulation was typically financed by the budget, and no capital scarcity factor was imposed on the computation of fiat prices. In traditional Marxist labor theory, interest on capital is viewed as a claim on a share of the surplus value, which itself is produced solely by labor. Such a claim can only be legitimate in social systems that function around the transformation of money into capital, which is itself regarded as a form of socioeconomic exploitation. Because this is considered reprehensible, the orthodox socialist economy eschews the interest category. Similarly, amortization rates were based on historical capital values with absolutely no allowance for replacement cost. Strictly regulated by the center in an administrative accounting framework, amortization rates have tended to be very conservative in the sense that they rarely reflect the probable "economic" life of an asset. Finally, no land or natural resource rents were factored into the cost computations.

The principal argument for not factoring land and natural resources into prices was that, according to the labor theory of value, "natural goods" cannot have value or price if no human labor is expended (Dochia 1984, p. 139). Furthermore, because land and natural resources are social property they cannot be traded in socialism; hence no price needs to be established. This misconception of the composition of costs in an economic sense led, in particular, to a significant downward bias in the wholesale prices of commodities with very little transformation relative to those for processed goods, manufactures in particular. This was especially blatant for agricultural products. Through a very own procurement policy, the state was bent on obtaining what Preobraženskij called "primitive accumulation" and to mobilize it for industrial expansion.

Certainly, some of these factors, such as amortization schedules, could have been corrected at the higher stages of transformation. However, the "wrong" price of most intermediate goods has palpably affected the level and structure of prices in general. It has also had side effects on price policies and remedial measures that economic agents have had to embrace to cope with incomplete plan instructions or to bridge differences between plan targets and actual data. The relative neglect of true scarcities and its implications for decision making are a natural consequence of an axiom of the orthodox socialist economy that there cannot possibly be room for a discrepancy between how economic agents act and the policy actions of state and party officials in response to the perceived economic interests of their agents.

Consumer prices

It is of more than passing interest to recall that consumer prices in a PE fall into distinct categories, whose importance varies not only according to the country under scrutiny, but it also depends on the time frame considered. Most consumer goods and services are subject to price regulations affecting socialized retail outlets. But an important consumption component, especially foodstuffs, derives from more or less "free" peasant markets. Finally, handicraft, several types of service, unique, and scarce products are priced privately. The latter category may include second-hand goods (such as used car exchanges) or goods owned privately, usually of foreign origin, that are resold through special retail outlets. Especially during the 1970s, there was a sprawl of foreign currency shops, whose prices are regulated by the state (in most cases under the aegis of the MFT) but directly in function of the real foreign exchange cost. Both are exceptional categories and are ignored in what follows.

In the early phase of the PE, there was a clear tendency to restrict retail trade to the socialized sector, where prices are set by central fiat. Of course, private peasant markets were too important in ensuring adequate availability and distribution of some essential goods to be abolished altogether. Although some attempts in that direction were made, authorities exhorted private traders to observe self-imposed restrictions on the degree of price flexibility that could be condoned socially and politically. Inasmuch as the latter pricing policy was explicitly defined, it derived importantly from the state's official pricing behavior and priorities in the socialized sector. In what follows, then, I shall focus on this aspect of consumer prices.

Wholesale and retail prices are normally separated by turnover taxes, budget subsidies, and trade markups or discounts (including normal insurance, handling, and transportation charges). In countries where, in addition to fiat prices, there are contract prices or prices that allow room for negotiation about the influence of product quality and modernity on actual prices, the relationship between the two sets of prices is further compounded. An essential component of recent developments, regardless of the progress towards price liberalization already made, is the parametrization of the links among wholesale, retail, and trade prices.

The basic differences between retail prices and enterprise wholesale prices is the turnover tax, which is levied in accordance with the center's preferences. This possibly constitutes the principal source of government revenue. Taxes are imposed on goods in short supply or on goods whose consumption the authorities hope to discourage. Conversely, other goods benefit from government subsidies because it is felt that their consumption ought to be fostered. In most PEs, this tax is imposed as an absolute value, with the percentage rate being applied only to local industry where central price regulation does not hold. It has become increasingly recognized, however, that this procedure is too much divorced from production conditions. Countries have therefore been resorting more and more to an ad valorem specification of turnover taxes.

A parallel cause of some of the differences between wholesale and retail prices is the subsidy, which is an important outlay of the government's budget. In some countries or sectors, the subsidy is directly granted to the producer side. Thus in Bulgaria and Rumania, the bulk of retail subsidies are the indirect result of wholesale price subsidies. These used to be set, like the turnover tax, in absolute value, but increasingly countries have been moving to a percentage definition. One might in principle expect that for an absolute value there would be no difference as far as the relationship between retail and wholesale prices is concerned, but this is not so. For instance, other charges that keep wholesale and retail prices apart are added in proportion to the wholesale price, and they may therefore amplify the subsidy.

The level of retail prices should exceed that of wholesale prices in consequence of positive costs arising in transferring goods from the producer to the consumer sector. Curiously, the reverse relationship emerged in Hungary in the early 1970s as a result of the very extensive system of retail price subsidies. During the NEM's earlier phases, it had been planned to abolish this negative differential in the first half of the 1970s. But it was not until the sharp price revision of October 1979 and subsequent price adjustments that the painful bullet was bitten.

The size of the turnover tax in a PE is usually determined by the level of retail prices required so that supply equals demand in partial markets. Supply is highly regulated by the planners. By contrast, demand emanates from consumer preferences and household budget constraints. As a result, turnover taxes and subsidies need to be flexible and highly differentiated to maintain balance in partial consumer markets. They are therefore the most powerful instrument to separate prices and to implement the sociopolitical preferences of government and party authorities. The system of turnover taxes is particularly important in the regulation of levels of living of the population through the redistribution of money incomes that is implied in the differentiated turnover tax system. Unlike the graduated income tax system typical of most developed MEs, in the PE the major fiscal regulator is the combination of indirect tax and subsidy schedules.

Consumer price stability has been a stalwart of the socialist credo for many years and continues to be a very explosive social issue indeed in most PEs. In fact, Marxist economic theory as viewed by Soviet policy makers in the early phases of revolutionary industrialization posited that consumer prices should exhibit a steadily declining trend. Prices are held to be the monetary expression of the value of goods and services determined by the socially necessary expenditures of labor. The latter tend to decline as a result of technical progress, the growth of labor productivity, and rising efficiency in the exploitation of the means of production. These tendencies individually or in combination should be mirrored in a gradual downward trend in price levels (Miastkowski 1980, pp. 896–7). The declining real cost of production can be reflected in declining prices, rising factor rewards, or some combination thereof. The effects of the method chosen to pass on efficiency gains to the production factors are very different. Thus lower prices, in principle, benefit all consumers, especially the "anonymous owners of money," but the factors that are responsible for the efficiency gains are not sufficiently rewarded for their effort. For a very long time this doctrinaire view prevailed at least in policy discussions. But retail price stability was held de rigueur for both ideological reasons and very practical planning requirements. Domestic price stability was deemed useful so as to facilitate plan implementation, chiefly in the case of wholesale prices, and to buttress social welfare and income distribution measures, particularly for consumer prices.

As a result of keeping retail prices unchanged from the early 1950s at least until the late 1960s or even more recently, the "economic romanticism" (Miastkowski 1980, p. 909) developed that the currency of a PE is extremely stable, inflation is alien to the PE, and price revisions, if required, are invariably planned in an orderly fashion, introduced gradually, and fluctuate around a downward trend (Mujżel 1974). Planned or unplanned subsidies or taxes, as the case may be, help to bridge differences in the interim. This policy myth encompassed not only the level of prices but also the stability of consumer prices and therefore particularly ignored shifts in the relative costs of production in favor of manufactures and against foodstuffs and services. A very bothersome by-product of this policy practice and ideological exhortation has been the reluctance of consumers to tolerate any type of price change, even if initially fully offset by compensatory income allowances. The sequence of societal upheavals in Poland over intended price changes and the tedious preparations of the population by government, party, and trade union officials in the case of Hungary illustrate this proposition.

A very important axiom underlying the socialist economy, as noted, is that there can be no conflict between social and private preferences, and that the state can plan nearly all foreseeable actions. As a result, economic agents need only execute plan instructions. This has been a fallacious presumption with dire consequences, especially in consumer sectors. Economic agents do indeed assess their present and future prospects and formulate a strategy to promote their own private interests independently of official projections and simulations, although the two may at times coincide. Furthermore, private agents are able to act in accordance with such a strategy, even if in doing so they violate official expectations and policies. There is finally some interaction—sometimes a clearly defined adaptive behavior—between private strategies and the expectations of these agents with respect to present and future official targets and policies.

The relationship between domestic and foreign prices

Perhaps much more important than the actual or desirable relationship between wholesale and retail prices is the one between domestic wholesale and foreign trade prices, especially in the context of the degree of autonomy in economic decision making coveted by PE leaders. The presumption that there ought to be as much "equal exchange" as possible pleads for this thesis. Accordingly, policy makers could set whatever level and structure of domestic consumer prices they deemed to be consonant with their ideological, political, and other prerogatives. At the same time, they would be bent on marshaling all available resources, including the growth-stimulating function of foreign trade, for enlarging the economy's productive and reproductive capacities. It is in that light that the crucial role of the relationship between domestic and external prices should be viewed. It is also against that backdrop that the very serious problems associated with the dichotomy between CMEA trade prices and WMPs need to be studied.

According to the precepts of an autonomous system of centralized planning and administration, for more than two decades the link between trade and domestic prices remained exceedingly weak. To the extent that stable prices could not be attained, the PEs have found it extremely useful to neutralize as much as possible short-term fluctuations in trade prices through the "price-equalization account" also in the case of commercial relations, such as with MEs, that do not allow for a substantial degree of ex ante price stability. As described, the FTOs paid domestic producers and invoiced final users of imports at the domestic fiat price; if such was not extant, a calculative price was computed in line with domestic pricing precepts. There may have been some exceptions, for instance, for luxury consumer goods. On the whole, however, price developments in foreign trade could affect domestic producers and consumers only indirectly, usually in a muted form because of "the averaging" and the introduction of changes only with considerable delays.

Admittedly, this divorce of domestic prices from real export returns and import costs does not facilitate a rational allocation of resources and hence may yield inefficiency. But it has clearly been instrumental in eliminating by and large the microeconomic effects from abroad on domestic decision making. This can be thought of as a possibly constructive avenue to self-reliant growth certainly for temporary fluctuations and to smooth more permanent shifts in foreign economic relations over time so that orderly adjustments can be incorporated in the plans. Even in the more flexible decision-making environment created under impulse of the economic reform movement, the PEs have generally attempted to smooth the impact of foreign price fluctuations on the implementation of the aggregate output and consumption plans.

One negative consequence of this market divorce was the considerable weakening of the potential allocatory role of prices: A rise in foreign trade prices in foreign currency units should have encouraged exports and discouraged imports. These stimuli were exerted, if at all, only through the planning bureaucracy. Because the latter was not at all keenly interested in searching for more profitable export and import patterns, very soon domestic structures were well out of line with the degree to which policy makers really desired to insulate their local markets against foreign developments. Inasmuch as the price system provides the key incentive for the most rational use of material, labor, and financial resources of the national economy, there should be a close link – actual or simulated – between trade and domestic prices.

The desirability of price stability has an unquestionable trade-off in terms of feasible levels of economic efficiency. The more the latter becomes the explicit focus of economic policies, the higher is the social cost of upholding price stability as a policy instrument. Especially since the major shifts in WMPs in 1972–1974 and the respecification of the CMEA price formula in 1975, an increasing number of PEs have inquired into the precise trade-off of price stability that can be socially tolerated. Some have even expressed doubts about the wisdom of maintaining the postwar price system at any cost. Only Hungary took the logical first step of linking domestic and trade prices directly in the late 1970s and of expressing its preferences regarding the evolution of the CMEA trade price mechanism. But few of its partners have so far concurred in this position in principle, let alone in actual practice, and the price mechanism in CMEA relations therefore remains as convoluted as it was during the past quarter century or so after the war.

5.2 On the rationality of prices in a planned economy

One of the most conspicuous differences between a PE and an ME is the formation of prices, and thus price structures, mostly for systemic, policy, and institutional reasons. The marked differentiations in the relative prices of PEs and MEs are therefore not necessarily attributable to flaws in the former's economic policy or to their "irrational" pricing policies. Barring planners' unintentional errors, prices have certainly not been administered arbitrarily, in the sense that they have been selected randomly, for instance. Quite the contrary: Fiat prices have performed functions that are an integral part of the logic of the development objectives adopted by socialist economic planners and other decision makers. As such, they have had a rationality of their own that differs from that prevailing in an ME environment. Thus socialist prices have not been rational from the standpoint of fostering the efficient allocation of resources in general. Rather than to ensure market clearing, particularly in the traditional CPE context, the role of prices is subordinated to nationwide planning; this is especially true for producer prices. With respect to retail prices, they are also meant to ensure a greater degree of social equality and minimum welfare levels.

The rationality of prices in a PE must therefore be identified with the economic aims, development conditions, social priorities, development "laws," economic mechanism, or those factors and characteristics that set apart a typical PE from a standard ME. This cannot be taken to mean that all the current price relations in a socialist economy are automatically rational. It does suggest, however, that the transplantation of the price structures and mechanisms appropriate to an economic system whose policy aims and development conditions are markedly at variance with the ambitions of a socialist economy would be absolutely irrational (Fedorowicz 1975, pp. 276–302; Rutkowska and Rutkowski 1977, pp. 315–41).

5.3 Price systems in a centrally planned economy

The role of prices (here understood as referring also to wages, interest charges, and ERs) in a CPE needs to be assessed in the context of the development objectives and strategies of socialist planners. There are three sets of crucial formative elements: socialist ideology, the economic mechanism, and the growth strategy. All these need to be seen in their proper combination with societal preferences derived from socialist precepts. From a practical point of view, perhaps the last factor is the key determinant. But the special influence of the other two on policy making in the postwar period has been neither negligible nor constant, and it is therefore important to spell out succinctly each set of conditions.

Ideology and the labor theory of value

The way in which socialist ideology bears on economic policies and institutions of PEs is at best a murky subject. Although I shall not attach great practical importance to the direct formative role of Marxist–Leninist ideology in the gestation of the socialist economy, it would be equally short-sighted to deny any such influence. One of its roles can be gauged from the juxtaposition of the marginalist approach in the formulation of price policies and the typical cost averaging underlying nearly all types of prices in the socialist economy.

Models of a stylized ME suggest that economic efficiency is optimal when marginal cost coincides with marginal revenue. Socialist policy makers have exhibited an habitual aversion to marginalism, which has been held to be diametrically opposed to the precepts of "value" and "price" in a socialist economy. Both are directly related to Marx's labor theory of value, which is inextricably intertwined with his philosophical outlook on society; it also derives from the basic ideological precepts of socialism and communism in the real world but couched in the framework and against the views expounded by the founders of that creed. This sentiment against marginalism is also deep-grained in part because of the strong desire to forestall domestic inflation[2] and a reluctance to reward inframarginal firms with abnormally high profits. An important side constraint of this attitude is that if enterprises were to be asked to base their decisions on average prices, including an inframarginal ER, the external payments balance would be in perpetual deficit. This is one reason for the comprehensive foreign exchange controls typical of PEs (see Chapter 6). Even if marginalism were to be adopted in the spheres in which prices are habitually based on average costs as defined by socialist policy makers, prices would still not be a very good allocative guide. But would such a major shift in an entrenched position provide for relatively better guidelines? The answer is not at all straightforward, because it depends essentially on three questions: Are firms for a given product working in the downward phase of the cost cycle? Do policy makers insist on price uniformity for the branch as a whole and, if not, will there be room for larger adjustments so that inframarginal firms can expand capacities and have a feedback effect on the evaluation of cost components? Are marginal cost prices adjustable to shifts not only in demand and supply but also in technologies and societal preferences on a timely basis?

These crucial questions are associated with debates revolving around one type or another of economic reform.

The economic mechanism

The economic mechanism implanted from the USSR into Eastern Europe after World War II emulated what were believed to be doctrinally and ideologically "correct" policies and institutions; such a mimicry was at least deemed to be necessary to marshal all resources for fast industrialization. Socialist managers originally chose to mobilize their resources through detailed physical planning. This naturally called for giving a much larger emphasis to nonprice policies, including the very active involvement of the political leadership in the selection of priority projects and the direct allocation of cheap, but rationed, credit and critical inputs.

From the very outset of socialist economic policies in Eastern Europe, it has been accepted as axiomatic that socialism implies the effective control of the economy by society in pursuance of its social, economic, political, and strategic objectives. Full control over productive resources is perceived as a prerequisite of socialist economic policies to be buttressed through an appropriate layer of institutions, behavioral rules, and policy instruments. Among the latter, the planned steering by the state of the course of economic activity has been a pivotal precept. There are clearly several ways in which the state can formulate central planning. The Soviet theory of the central planning mechanism evolved essentially around the anchor of detailed physical calculations, as distinct from value planning, and physical distribution arrangements. The plan is the expression of the center's goals in regulating economic activity and therefore allows a tight synchronization of political and economic functions. The premise is that tools of indirect economic coordination are not sufficiently dependable in pursuing the broad goals of the socialist economy.[3]

In orthodox CPEs, precise specifications of physical input entitlements and output objectives substitute for both the relative price structure and the microeconomic decision making typical of an ME. Although workers usually receive their wages in money and consumer goods are generally distributed through several, possibly disconnected, market layers, incentives in various forms (including special material and other privileges) are frequently used to reward certain groups of workers. For enterprises, prices and costs have little impact on allocation. The allocation of resources is changed by direct decisions when planners respond to severe quantity imbalances to ease social and economic frictions, and politically harmful and socially disruptive consumer dissatisfaction. Nevertheless, the planner's main role is to design and manipulate a pattern of sectoral and subsectoral imbalances in line with plan priorities. The operations of financial institutions and the tasks of fiscal and monetary authorities are closely regulated to ensure support for the plan objectives, including the associated prices.

Given the overall development objectives of socialist policy makers, planners are called upon to engineer distortions in the system of relative prices consistent with the strategic development targets instead of striving for prices that reflect current demand and supply, even if confined only to the domestic market. The original distortions are quite simple: The domestic market is severed from markets abroad, and domestic consumer or retail prices are subjected to different conditions from those applicable to domestic producer or wholesale prices. Again reflecting the Marxist labor theory of value and the innate sense of socialists to strive for greater equality in profit levels, as noted, wholesale prices are in principle derived from average sectoral production costs plus a markup. Another fundamental feature of pricing is stability. The administratively set prices are revised infrequently according to prevailing market conditions, especially when consumer market imbalances become chronic or when major bottlenecks and shortages manifest themselves by hampering the implementation of the plan.

Socialist planners are aware that prices are not good indicators of real scarcities. Prices have therefore a sharply curtailed allocative role in the CPE. Their main function, for producer prices, is the accounting required to formulate, to implement, and to control the plan, and for consumer prices, the blotting up of incomes and the redistribution of such incomes in accordance with societal preferences. Because the responsiveness of enterprises to price changes in the short run under planned economic conditions is limited, if the central authorities want to bring about major shifts in supply, they are achieved directly by an appropriate investment policy. This underplaying of value planning through the price mechanism was carried over to nearly all indirect policy instruments and associated institutional supports.

Development strategy and social preferences

Finally, the PE typically attaches a particularly high priority to social and economic objectives that would not be recognized as such by the free operation of market forces. Specifically, the CPE aims at the full mobilization of available resources and at their redistribution in ways so as to resemble eventually those allocations in the most advanced industrial countries. The goal is not to imitate MEs per se. Instead, socialist planners are bent on accelerating development and enhancing the future international competitiveness of their economy by maintaining a highly protective environment in which a more or less self-reliant economic complex can be elaborated by the proper marshaling of available resources. A very important role in this proclivity for autarkic policy choices in Eastern Europe was played by the imposing example of the previous successes in the USSR of the 1930s. But also the convoluted dogmatism that crystallized around these achievements exerted a major influence, particularly with respect to the creation of a bland facsimile of Soviet institutions and policies.

The strategic precept of growth propulsion in the socialist stand on industrialization focuses primarily on the acceleration of a few crucial economic sectors especially as a result of injecting capital goods made possible through involuntary savings. The strategy envisages the promotion of a comparatively modern manufacturing sector that is favored and drains resources from the traditional sector. Accordingly, the CPE's growth efforts are directed at steadily enlarging the various sectors of heavy industry producing energy, metals, chemical products, construction materials, and machines. The reallocation of resources necessary to stimulate investment in industries believed to be growth promoting is achieved by manipulating sectoral imbalances in demand and supply, and relative prices. Thus, higher investment levels than would be financed voluntarily are channeled to industries that are intensive in capital and skilled labor, as against the traditional sectors (agriculture and labor-intensive manufacturing). The state-operated segment providing nontradables (with education, culture, basic health, and administration as the main expenditure components) is also typically promoted. The importance attached to these elements derives to a large extent from the socialist ideology as it has been interpreted from basic Marxist–Leninist elaborations.

The authorities in CPEs associate several disadvantages with equilibrium pricing (Gudac 1984, p. 42). They tend to affirm that such policies would jeopardize three alleged benefits of disequilibrium pricing: (1) the dynamic gains from the development strategy incorporated in the plan, which eventually may lead to allocative efficiency in the long run; (2) the distributional benefits that can be attained through skewed pricing policies; and (3) the advantages associated with the social and political arrangements pertaining to central control over physical flows. These three ostensible advantages of a distorted price regime cannot be sustained by manipulating relative prices. Such goals, if explicitly recognized as worthwhile societal objectives, could be pursued through other instruments, including income transfers, graduated fiscal policies, and special target social transfers (such as student stipends and family allowances). But this refinement of the central planning mechanism at a very early stage was not even contemplated.

Once the potential for extracting the surplus from the traditional sector is exhausted, the range of policy options in the CPEs increasingly resembles that in their market counterparts. In particular, economies stand to benefit, including politically, from improved immediate allocative efficiency and from reduced imbalances, which makes it possible to relax coercive redistribution imposed by the state.

5.4 Economic reforms and the role of prices in a modified planned economy

As noted in Chapter 2, an MPE uses price, fiscal, credit, and monetary policies that aim at inducing microeconomic agents to act according to the plan objectives. The latter are therefore pursued more and more in a marketlike framework. By definition, however, the indirect instruments and underlying institutions of even the most market-minded PE typically entail significant, if concealed, elements of nonprice resource allocation, with a disproportionate weight in overall preferences being accorded to social preferences of the ruling elites.

Perhaps the most important of the instruments that need to be improved when planners decide to devolve decision-making authority to the lower planning tiers is pricing, again seen in a holistic perspective. Interest charges to guide the allocation of capital resources and to spur on domestic savings; a proper ER to guide the acquisition and disbursement of foreign exchange; proper wage rates and capital charges to foster productivity gains; and the establishment of wholesale and retail prices that are indicative of relative scarcities prevailing in the economy, relative to both domestic as well as worldwide indicators, are essential ingredients of the transformation of the planned economic mechanism to one suitable for an MPE.

There are three components to be stressed in this connection: the liberalization of the price regime, the formation of "informative" prices by the center, and the linkup with foreign trade prices. All three need to be placed in their proper institutional context for liberalization should not be equated with freely fluctuating prices. Prices in an MPE can assume three functions: (1) an accounting tool for aggregating targets expressed in physical units or for controlling the performance of enterprises, associations, and ministries by synthetic criteria, rather than the physical success yardsticks typical of the classical CPE; (2) a means to transmit information between the center and the periphery of decision making in the context of the planning network; and (3) a key parameter conveying information about real scarcity relationships as a basis for microeconomic decisions.

The liberalization of the price regime

This is to be understood as moving prices closer to relative scarcities. It says nothing about the timing of this operation or about whether planners intend to maintain prices in line with real scarcities on a timely basis or only intermittently. This issue is frequently misunderstood. Thus, a comprehensive price revision is not likely to move prices closer to real underlying costs unless the proper computation of production costs is first specified, and it is here that the MPE differs from the orthodox CPE. Even if properly recomputed at a certain point in time, prices in a CPE are bound to fall out of line with real economic proportions in a comparatively short time because of shifts in either domestic production conditions or world markets. In the first case, I shall speak of "informative prices" at the time when they are calculated, but their allocative function in time remains highly confined. This is not so with more comprehensive price reforms, even if not yet based on true scarcities.

Regardless of the chief aim of the price reform, actual calculations can proceed in many different ways. Even in the most conservative CPE, the spirit of reform brought about the revision of administratively set prices, not only to realign them with the erstwhile price-determining factors – essentially average live and embodied labor expenditures. Policy makers were also bent on prices that better reflected the true scarcities of capital and land by adding preset capital charges and land rent, and of foreign trade by translating prevailing import costs expressed in foreign prices at an ER that approximates the average domestic cost of foreign exchange, given the preestablished trade patterns by commodity groups and geographical direction. Furthermore, the era of reforms brought about the better accommodation of noncompeting imports and domestically produced goods outside the socialized sector. Nonetheless, proposals to institutionalize scarcity pricing have not been received as favorably as might have been hoped for.

Regarding prices *strictu sensu*, marginalism continues to be spurned. Furthermore, cost elements are not properly evaluated. Although some PEs have made an attempt to approximate the "value" of natural resources by estimating their reproduction cost – in other words, some shadow price concept – this cannot be implemented easily. Natural resources and land continue to be undervalued, although less so than in the orthodox CPE. Regarding the ER, the continued rejection of marginalism in ER determination has had important consequences. Because this issue is intimately related to the link between internal and external prices, it is examined later.

Somewhat greater movement has taken place in the evaluation of embodied labor and the scarcity of capital. Instead of regarding interest charges as a reprehensible claim on labor's surplus value, it is now more and more viewed as a compensation for the limited availability of "materially embodied labor." Furthermore, claims on material assets exceed supply. A somewhat modified labor theory of value allows for viewing interest as a payment by borrowers to savers for the utilization of the latters' past labor. Nevertheless, the basic ideological objections to interest rates still linger and continue to hamper the claim of past labor on new income, which constrains the upward movement of the interest rate. To lend financial support to the priorities of the authorities and, hence, to discourage claims on funds by nonpriority sectors, several PEs maintain a differentiated interest rate structure. But there is not usually a clear-cut economic relationship among the various interest rates.

The timing of price revisions, regardless of how prices are set, has also undergone changes. Indeed, if prices are to be accorded any active role at all, the authorities must see to it that they are periodically adapted to fluctuations in domestic and foreign demand and supply. Most reforms have therefore aimed at greater flexibility in administrative price formation so that prices continue to convey meaningful information to the plan executors as a result of more frequent recalculations of centrally set prices and the delegation of more authority over price formation to the lower planning tiers. Regarding the variation of interest charges and ERs, the PEs have practiced rather different policies. The issues related to the ER are discussed in detail in Chapter 6. Interest rate policies continue to be hemmed in by ideological considerations in several PEs. The rates are therefore generally low, certainly far below the productivity of capital, or remain highly differentiated for sociopolitical reasons. In other countries, a more active interest rate policy has been put in place. But authorities are reluctant to modify this policy sufficiently to reduce aggregate credit demand to what the economy can support and to shift the structure of credit demand, particularly for capital formation, toward the highest-yielding endeavors.

Another issue directly related to the preceding is the degree to which centrally set or "market" prices are held to be one key guideline for enterprise decision making. Firms may have no direct control over price formation, although they are expected to react to the parameters issued by the central pricing authority. In still fewer countries do prices provide feedback to planners on the state of partial markets. In some economies, enterprises have some ability to adapt prices from time to time in response to changes in costs. But in all PEs, including those in which price adjustments are now a quasi-continuous process rather than a once-and-for-all major undertaking, price movements are permitted only within preset, narrow margins. This does not mean that they are rigidly controlled by the central pricing authority, although that is so in most PEs. In other words, until very recently, price stability because of the need for a stable plan environment or for more social reasons has endured as a top priority of socialist economic policies.

The informative role of prices

All CPEs have gradually made room for a more active role of prices in production and distribution processes, though these parameters continue to be set by central fiat. In almost all PEs, prices continue to act primarily as transmission channels for orders from the center to the lower planning units. It is only in Hungary and Poland that some prices provide market information, whereas elsewhere they continue to play the passive role of accounting units. But there are several exceptions: An attempt has been made by all PEs to allot a more active role to prices; and, in some cases, limited authority in setting prices has been extended to the enterprises or their associations. This is especially so in Bulgaria and Rumania, but the bulk of this is still kept within limited bounds or strictly controlled, and prices continue to play much the same role as before.

But even in PEs where prices are still fixed administratively, a serious attempt has been made to base them more closely on approximate real production costs. Rather than introducing scarcity prices, most price reforms have been confined to recalculating average costs, taking into account a capital charge, some rents, and an approximation of the real cost of imports. Occasionally, however, the rigidity and centralization of fiat pricing have been relaxed to restore better balance between demand and supply. One of the key elements of the reform consists in introducing greater price flexibility so that new developments can periodically be absorbed. Although it cannot be said that current prices fully reflect objective economic relations, they undoubtedly better approximate actual production costs, and sometimes they even react to changes in supply and demand.

The linkup with trade

Decisions in economies that depend on foreign trade for a substantial part of their aggregate product must be reached on the basis of information that includes key events in the foreign trade sector. The issues at stake concern the degree to which real foreign trade costs are reflected in domestic prices and the speed with which this transmission takes place. The majority of PEs have set pseudo-ERs and gradually accorded a more important role to real foreign trade opportunities when prices are centrally recomputed. Very few, however, have allowed foreign trade prices to influence domestic prices directly even if economic agents in the process have been accorded some latitude in the generation of individual product prices.

Price policy changes have not greatly improved the trade situation. Most countries have held onto the precept that structural changes in trade can only be attained as a result of programmatic adaptations of investment plans, certainly not in response to the voluntarism of domestic and foreign markets. In other words, prices continue to play a subordinate role in the basic decisions about structural transformations, even though the latter may be directly related to foreign trade. A sharp distinction should be drawn between using trade results in domestic allocation and in profit calculations. The former type of streamlining has been introduced in an attempt to motivate producers or traders to promote selected export and import contracts with segregated trade partners. But enterprises are not necessarily entitled to pass on real costs so that their decision making on matters not covered by the plan is necessarily confined to what appears to be profitable from the microeconomic point of view, unless the central authorities are willing to subsidize or able to tax, as the case may be. In any event, the connection between internal and external prices is still very loose and indirect in all PEs.[4]

Although foreign trade prices have undeniably exerted a growing influence on domestic pricing in most PEs, the price system has, on the whole, remained relatively inflexible. This rigidity is considerably larger for consumer prices than for producer prices. In the former, various subsidies and taxes buffer the domestic price system against socially undesirable changes in the cost of living. Although it ensures a high degree of stability, the rigidity inherent in setting prices administratively has come into sharp conflict with the desire to utilize prices as one of the key allocation levers at all levels of decision making.

Nevertheless, in the last decade or so there has been an unequivocal tendencey throughout Eastern Europe to pursue a more active price policy, possibly on an intermittent basis, at least for some goods and services. Instead of the erstwhile predictable landscape of constant retail prices with changes introduced on a comprehensive basis only after long intervals, the situation since the early 1970s has become increasingly differentiated. But retail prices have moved quite differently depending on the country and the type of goods. How current consumer price policies are being conceived and implemented are questions that cannot be answered unambiguously without an exhaustive study of laws, regulations, and, indeed, ad hoc administrative instructions. It may be useful in this connection to distinguish between the common principles and the more specific behavior with respect to prices (Górczak 1985, p. 9). In all PEs, administrative bodies designate a considerable portion of the prices, others are set in accordance with computational principles that are precisely specified by the pricing authorities, and the price trends of the remaining goods and services are at the very least carefully monitored and controlled. Second, prices in the state sector are more strongly regulated, and the decision-making authority there is less flexible than in other sectors. Third, the price systems of all PEs are heading more or less rapidly towards an effective decentralization of pricing authority. A typical breakdown is threefold: strictly regulated, centrally fixed, and contract prices. Where prices are established basically as a result of some operative market mechanism, the role of contract prices is considerable. Finally, all PEs are trying to implement a price system that will ensure better management, decision making, and participation in the ISDL. But different countries seek to achieve those aims to varying degrees and by different routes, depending upon the perceived dilemmas concerning which spheres of the PE should be managed directly and which indirectly in order to raise the overall socioeconomic effectiveness of management.

Because individual PEs have been experimenting with price changes, partly in view of external constraints but also in order to foster greater efficiency and rationality in the allocation of resources, it has become very difficult to identify precisely what rules a country may be pursuing at any time in any sector. One may confidently conjecture three distinct markers of the price landscape's relief, however.

First, some countries (Czechoslovakia,[5] the GDR, and the USSR) adhere, on the whole, to the traditional price policies. But they no longer hold onto absolute stability. Comprehensive price revisions in these PEs are ordinarily introduced together with the start (or in the beginning phases) of a new five-year plan, but the periodicity may still be even less frequent. In between such large-scale overhauls, revisions are sought perhaps on an annual basis, and they are normally implemented in such a way that their impact on the overall cost of living is minimal. In the course of the year, in case major imbalances develop or it becomes suddenly a policy priority to discourage consumption of target goods, individual prices of goods and services are revised on an exceptional basis. This is usually resorted to in the face of a serious harvest setback that cannot be offset through unplanned imports or if there are pronounced sudden balance-of-payments constraints (such as occurred for oil and oil products in the early 1980s). Under normal circumstances, however, prices in these PEs are not designed to maintain balance in partial consumer markets. The slack is taken up either by inventory accumulation, when supply exceeds demand, or by larger queues and involuntary product substitution, in the reverse case. This continued disequilibrium behavior with only discrete modifications undoubtedly constitutes a disincentive for labor morale. Whether it does influence to a significant degree the behavior of the labor force in terms of supply of effective labor has been a controversial topic in recent macroeconomic analyses of PEs.[6]

At the other end of the spectrum are countries, such as Hungary and Poland,[7] that endeavor to follow a more active price policy. There is no connection between consumer price changes and the five-year planning rhythm as such. Nevertheless, these countries do not normally condone a free-for-all and continue "to guide" prices for important goods and services. Revisions for such products are usually planned in conjunction with the annual socioeconomic plan. However, prices of a substantial proportion of consumer goods and services are subject to an upper limit or a margin for fluctuations "from-to" set by the central authorities. Finally, an increasing segment of the market is nominally free, although price variations are subject to self-imposed checks and balances to avoid socially undesirable changes that might induce policy makers to revert to central intervention. Price changes for all but goods with centrally set prices occur in response to autonomous changes in development conditions, including changes in foreign trading markets or pressures stemming from harvest fluctuations; factors that are not controlled as such but can be to some extent because they are essentially subject to probabilistic regularities, such as for price and income elasticities of demand; and policy priorities of central administrators.

Between the two extremes just discussed are the mixed cases – Bulgaria and Rumania. These countries profess to adhere to consumer price stability as an important sociopolitical advantage of the socialist economy by synchronizing price overhauls with the medium-term planning cycle. But substantial unplanned changes may be introduced on an interim basis, possibly in order to restrict the range of consumer frustrations over bare shelves, as in Rumania, or because the policy makers, as in Bulgaria, are tinkering with the economic mechanism on an experimental basis without as yet really harmonizing all contemplated measures in a consistent reform package.

In principle, the range of instruments at the disposal of socialist policy makers is sufficiently comprehensive to keep wholesale and retail prices of consumer goods and services completely separate. This aspiration may have prevailed during the early phases of socialist construction. In all PEs, there is now some nexus between the two price systems, but the relationship is not always very transparent, and often it is not at all a parametric one.[8] Similarly, the relationship between trade and domestic prices continues to be somewhat tenuous even in PEs, especially Hungary and Poland, that have attempted to introduce comprehensive reforms. Foreign trade prices are now directly factored into domestic price computations at a more realistic ER (see Chapter 6) in economies that continue to set at least the most important prices by administrative means. Since 1980, a rather comprehensive linkup between domestic and CC trade prices prevails in Bulgaria, Hungary, and Poland. Czechoslovakia has factored real import costs into the administratively set price reforms, the most recent one having been introduced in 1977. More timid attempts to utilize trade prices on a broader scale have been undertaken in the GDR and Rumania. But in the USSR the role of foreign trade in setting prices "continues to be negligible" (Górczak 1985, p. 9).

Second, though enterprises may not be in a position to recoup import cost changes by way of wholesale or retail price revisions, in some countries the direct cost is passed on by the FTOs and has an impact on enterprise profitability even if the enterprise itself has but little choice over what, how much, and where to export. In some countries, actual direct trading revenues and outlays may be reflected in interenterprise prices, but they cannot be passed on automatically into the retail price system. Finally, in some countries and for some goods, there is a direct parametric link between trade, wholesale, and retail prices.

5.5 Price formation and structural adjustment

Should the Eastern European countries seek to reequilibrate their economies by further liberalizing their trade and pricing regimes? Given their potential vulnerablity to events abroad, should they not instead pursue further refinements of the planning mechanism? The answer is not straightforward at all. Price flexibility is undoubtedly of decisive advantage if authorities reserve some room for adjustment of supply and demand forces. If, on the other hand, they opt for a considerable amount of central control, further reliance on the price mechanism is unlikely to return economic forces to a stable equilibrium.

For as long as domestic growth in the PEs could be generated without paying careful attention to the profitability of actual and potential trade processes, the drawbacks of SEI through a peculiar regional price system did not matter very much. In view of the serious slowdown in the pace of economic growth since the late 1970s and the dim prospects for a sharp reversal in the rate of change in factor availabilities in the near future, the Eastern European PEs especially have to seek ways and means of propping up their economic buoyancy through different channels. More effective trade participation through the efficient accounting of benefits and costs has been put forward as one potential growth source that may alleviate the present bottlenecks and constraints on the degree of policy maneuver accessible to these PEs.

Several PEs have in recent years enacted major changes in the level and structure of domestic prices for a variety of reasons, but most importantly in response to price shifts in trade. For one, policy makers have found it increasingly difficult to sustain large consumer price subsidies; to avoid passing on the basic changes in trade prices in CMEA relations and especially those incurred in relations with MEs; and to command production and consumption decisions through physical appropriations. In other words, circumstances, if nothing else, have compelled nearly all PEs to soften their pronounced preference for price stability. Some, including Hungary and Poland, have gone a long way toward redefining the precepts of consumer and producer price stability. A second major consideration has been the perception on the part of some policy makers that economic planning cannot be settled in detail on the central level, especially when the structure of the economy they are managing has assumed a certain complexity and policy priorities have become much more diverse than the simple call for maximum industrial growth per se. In some cases, the devolution of domestic economic decision making called for a reshaping of the way in which the MFT is called upon to control and regulate trade. Finally, in view of important shifts in world and CMEA prices, PE managers have become increasingly confronted with the problem of how to maintain stability without stifling economic activity.

The foregoing indicates occasions when central policy objectives and instruments of traditional PEs have undergone major perturbations. Unfortunately, these changes have not so far been part and parcel of a coherent, well-planned path toward structural change. The conservatism of socialist policy makers in commanding heights – basically, the political leadership – has in the past inhibited the formulation and implementation of far-reaching economic and other shifts in response to a thorough reevaluation of traditional precepts. With the growing strains in CMEA economic relations of late and the new leadership of the Soviet Union apparently bent on reversing the slowdown in the pace of economic activity, a thorough revision of the traditional cooperation mechanism may be in the offing. The importance of shifts in pricing policies and mechanisms, which has been recognized for many years, will be crucial components of such changes. Many reform proposals have been advanced in the process, but the shape of price reforms that may be in the offing remains as yet unclear.

5.6 Reform, adjustment, and CMEA prices

As noted, a properly functioning price system is one of the critical elements of a transformation in the economic mechanisms of the PEs, be it autonomously in response to flagging output performance or induced by internal or external imbalances. Regarding WMPs, there is little that the PE can do beyond improving its own allocation mechanisms, including adapting its domestic prices and allocative policies better to reflect international economic scarcities (read "socially necessary expenditures"). Certainly, socialist policy makers in the process need to relinquish some aspects of the large price autonomy that has been an integral part of their past experience, but they evidently need not directly imitate WMPs. For one, the preferences of socialist managers for greater stability than what typically prevails in world markets is very strong. A second reason is that PEs have different social priorities from those observed in most MEs. Because these priorities, in principle, are implemented, among other means, by consciously diverting prices away from underlying economic scarcities, there is a limit to the desirable degree of convergence between WMPs and domestic wholesale prices of a typical PE.

A real conundrum, however, is how to reconcile the sharp dichotomy between CMEA and world or East–West trade prices. One solution would be to strive for greater uniformity between WMPs and the prices of goods and services that the PE is trading with both areas or has not explicitly forbidden from being traded in both areas. Or a more general solution can be aimed at that takes advantage of a comprehensive reallocation of resources to the trade sectors. In this connection, two separate issues arise. First, given the dichotomy between CMEA and East–West trade prices, how can socialist managers hope to instill greater realism in domestic pricing without first bridging the gap in trade prices? Second, because most CMEA members have had serious complaints about the unsuitability of the CMEA price system for SEI, could the emergence of positive adjustment policies in the smaller PEs not be seized upon as a unique opportunity to revise the present CMEA price system?

There are few issues on which CMEA economists have maintained greater unanimity than on the drawbacks of the traditional CMEA pricing principles. All agree that the bilateral setting of prices inhibits trade, specialization, multilateralism, and the intensification of SEI. Patterning CMEA trade prices in some fashion after WMPs may be an expedient solution, but it fails to reflect true scarcities in the CMEA region. As a result, it cannot properly guide integration decisions, even if the latter are to be formulated and implemented through dovetailed plans. To the extent that WMPs are not really competitive prices but dominated by the oligopolistic and monopolistic practices of large firms in developed MEs,[9] they also funnel into the CMEA arena the issue of "exploitation," similar to the proposition held by socialist ideologists with regard to the relationship between "poor" and "rich" MEs.

The drawbacks of CMEA trade prices that have grown over the past forty years or so are largely the result of bilateralism. However, their general contours would also be manifest if the CMEA members could be found willing to adopt uniform prices on the basis of the Bucharest formula, as suitably modified in 1975, and instilled with greater realism in response to the trade criteria prevailing in the CMEA region. These trade prices are particularly troublesome for those PEs bent on investing the lower planning organs and economic agents with decision-making authority and on exploiting more comprehensively the advantages that can be reaped from international trade. Finally, the eclectic way in which trade prices are set, even if they were standardized for all CMEA members, inhibits higher forms of integration. These prices pose particularly grave obstacles to the improvement of the conditions for capital and labor mobility within the CMEA (see Chapters 9 and 10).

As argued in Chapter 1, the early debates about the Council's creation and the gradual fostering of SEI included a key provision regarding proper regional trade prices. Some proposals in the late 1940s argued the case for basing CMEA trade prices on some average of wholesale prices of the exporters. Such a solution would have been in perfect harmony with the then prevailing principles of domestic pricing: Instead of deriving producer prices as average branch costs plus some markups, trade prices – and by inference the wholesale prices of traded goods – would be based on average producer costs for the CMEA region as a whole plus a uniform markup. This alternative was rejected at the time mainly because internal wholesale prices were determined, as they continue to be, in different ways in various member countries and were thus not comparable. Second, this suggestion was aberrant because domestic wholesale prices were not only incomparable but also blatantly irrational, and the respective price systems were therefore in disarray.

By the second half of the 1950s, prices in the various PEs had undergone several transformations, although the improvement as measured by deviations from real scarcities was not very marked. At that time the CMEA members were formulating the ISDL's programmatic changes that were later narrowed down to what became known as *Basic Principles*. Because one of the latter's key provisions was the enhancement of production specialization, as distinct from market-based integration, an essential ingredient of the debate concerned the inauguration of an IPS (see Hewett 1974, pp. 158–75 for details). The Bucharest formula had been adopted in 1958 as an expedient for the rest of the 1950s (see Chapter 4). It was not believed to be very useful for guiding SEI in the longer run. Various proposals for the creation of an IPS in CMEA relations were launched at that time. Such a changeover would not only gradually affect trade but also domestic pricing and planning with a view to interlinking the PEs more effectively.

The first proposals for an IPS were rather simple: Derive some average of production costs of products flowing primarily among CMEA countries and use that average, instead of WMPs, to generate CMEA trade prices. Thus only price levels would change, not the pricing mechanism or the economic institutions that determine the CMEA trade and payments regimes. Most of the variants of these simple adjustments were tabled by the high-cost producers in the CMEA. Their export prices would improve without necessarily exerting an upward pressure on their import prices, given the considerable variations in the composition of exports and imports of manufactures that existed within the CMEA at that early phase of industrialization in most of Eastern Europe. They therefore stood to gain considerably from the terms-of-trade shifts that would inevitably come to the fore in the process.

Attempts to provide a quick fix that would not really improve the CMEA's pricing situation were rejected, especially by the PEs that would have had to foot the bill. But in the process nearly all CMEA members had become active participants in the debate. Many proposals emerged, and a vast amount of financial and intellectual resources was appropriated for further study. In fact, the issue of implanting an IPS for the region became one of the key preoccupations of a group of experts attached to the SCFT and subsequently the key area of work of the recently installed SCEP.[10] It would not only be impossible but also fruitless at this stage to go once again through the detailed history of these endeavors. The proposals advanced throughout the 1960s proved to lack a consensus on techniques for computing and averaging CMEA production costs, and thus they could not have been implemented even if agreement on other principles had been feasible. Furthermore, there were serious concerns about the fact that an IPS could strengthen the clamor for CMEA autarky and strictly central determination of all trade flows. As argued, both are major causes of the present deficiencies in CMEA economic relations.

There were undoubtedly serious problems associated with most of the proposals regarding the creation and operation of a proper IPS. But I am uneasy about the argument that none of the IPS proposals should have been implemented on the ground that an own price basis would have implied autarky and strict central determination of prices (Hewett 1974, p. 160). If that were so, it would be pointless to pursue the matter here. In my view, an IPS makes a lot of sense for economies that emphatically do not wish to integrate themselves fully into the world economy because they put a premium on warding off perturbations from world markets and on setting domestic prices relatively autonomously. After all, this is precisely what happens in regional integration schemes of MEs, although the instruments wielded there differ in many respects from those current in PEs.

The arguments for this position run quite parallel to those advanced earlier with regard to the domestic economic mechanism of the PEs. The introduction of a positive adjustment policy in order to resume a faster pace of growth than what has recently been possible hinges critically on the willingness and capacity of the PEs to adopt a quite different institutional setup than the hybrid one held over from the reform era. It would encompass macroeconomic management that relies on monetary, fiscal, price, and income policies that are as "neutral" as possible. Macroeconomic decisions ought to be guided by clear-cut rules in part so that policy makers are made explicitly aware of the probable economic costs associated with their societal preferences. Maintaining domestic price autonomy, for instance, has a cost in terms of postponing adjustments that can be approximated in quantitative terms. Similarly, the PEs would appear to have a strong liking for relative economic independence of fluctuations in world markets. If so, the central issue is not whether an IPS makes sense. The real kernel of the debate has been twofold. First, to what extent do the CMEA members consciously opt to safeguard their regional economic organization and their national independence in decision making? Second, because this preference by necessity entails a cost in terms of economic efficiency forgone, as measured by world standards, who will shoulder this cost and according to which rules will the burden be parceled out?

During the debates of the 1960s, the chief obstacles to the introduction of any IPS worthy of that name were perceived to be (1) estimating comparable product costs for each PE; (2) selecting proper weights for averaging national costs; (3) translating the national currency estimates into a common unit; (4) establishing standardized handling, insurance, and transportation charges; and (5) agreeing on the degree of the relationship between the IPS and WMPs. The hardy problems are clearly the first three, with the very first one being the least tractable. The selection of the degree to which WMPs should continue to influence CMEA prices also posed a vexing set of issues that had been already at the base of the concept of developing an IPS. It really requires that the CMEA members decide explicitly to what extent they want to be separate, in economic terms, from scarcities prevailing in world markets.

Though the literature of the 1960s is strewn with propositions on the properties of a feasible IPS, there are basically four variants around which all others were constructed. The first set hinged on the computation of averages of national industrial wholesale prices without turnover taxes. The second set envisaged three variants of the computation of average production costs net of all profits and taxes at all stages, or the sum of direct and indirect labor costs. The variants depend on the particular formula of the surplus markup chosen (see Section 5.1). It should be recalled that these were also the three basic alternative systems for setting domestic wholesale prices under consideration during the era of economic reforms.

Naturally, the computation of any of these variants was to involve also transportation costs, of which two alternatives were presented: the distance between the factory and the border multiplied either by the standard CMEA or domestic transportation charges. In addition, national costs had to be reduced to a common denominator at some ER. Though most propositions were far from explicit on that issue, the probable three alternatives considered were the commercial ER of the TR, the noncommercial ER rebased against the commercial TR, and a more appropriate variant of purchasing power. Furthermore, it was proposed that averaging should proceed with total product outputs as weights or, alternatively, with export volumes as weights.

This combination of four reference prices, with each two weights and transportation charges, converted at three alternative ERs gave rise to a "natural" combination of forty-eight basic alternatives! In practice, minor variations led to an even more bewildering number of proposals. This diversity of views may have startled decision makers, and indeed it may have been one main factor in abandoning the search for a practical IPS at that stage. Nevertheless, I contend that the real reason for the failure to erect an IPS was a much more fundamental one. A crucial objection to any of the variants was that the selection of basic price constituents varied greatly from country to country and that institutional provisions to curtail these divergences could not be worked out to mutual agreement. As a result, prices for the same commodity in different countries could not be compared without laborious prior recosting.

There are several major problems associated with the creation of an IPS. Those leading to the foregoing forty-eight alternatives are obvious candidates. So are the issues involved in determining the degree of autonomy the CMEA members voluntarily choose to support and to fund by common means according to some sharing rules. Perhaps the most pivotal issue, however, pertains to the computation of basic production costs. An essential ingredient of a meaningful and viable IPS is that the participants harmonize their domestic pricing policies. This could be done in two ways. The more desirable option would be to choose a certain set of prices based on an IPS convention; to introduce those prices into the domestic economy, at least to the degree that the individual participants refrain from imposing their own national preferences; and to let regionwide imbalances entail changes in quantities or prices, or both, at least on an intermittent basis. The other way would be by explicit agreement on principles for calculating production costs and introducing them in the traditional administrative fashion. This would require (see Rutkowski 1977, p. 3) that uniform principles be established for calculating land and natural resource rents, capital taxes or interest rates on enterprise assets, depreciation allowances, surcharges on wages, social outlays, and taxes, as well as for factoring import costs into domestic prices. Comparable pricing policies would not forcibly be contingent on each PE adopting identical prices, however. The precise contributions of labor and capital in physical units as well as intermediate goods to production costs need to be reflected in prices in order to avert inhibiting specialization in accordance with this particular choice of comparative advantage criteria.

Hewett claims that this first large-scale search for an IPS was abandoned because it had become absolutely clear that any IPS is a far more cumbersome price-determination process than that based on bilateral bargaining around some average WMPs, and thus proved to be even less satisfactory than the existing price system (Hewett 1974, p. 164). He also argues that the selection of WMPs would have been a better solution in any case because the resultant relative prices would have been more efficient than those derived from national prices. Given that East–West trade accounted for a significant proportion of overall trade of the PEs, he argues that it would have been counterproductive to ignore those prices (Hewett 1974, p. 165).

That proposition appears to suffer from several fallacies. For one, the composition of East–West trade varies significantly from that typical of CMEA relations. Some CMEA products are not at all traded with MEs for security or ideological reasons. Second, Hewett too readily presumes that East–West trade prices nearly coincide with WMPs, and that real scarcity indicators in world trade are thus transmitted to the CMEA. Apart from the dubious proposition that CMEA prices are indeed based on some reference WMPs, East–West trade prices diverge markedly from prices typical in trade among MEs (Brabant in press, c). In other words, if some products are nearly exclusively traded within the CMEA for whatever reason that the member countries want to rationalize, extraneous prices are hard to defend without further arguments being adduced. This proposition can be buttressed by the fact that prices allegedly based on WMPs have persistently failed to correct CMEA imbalances; in fact, it may have been one of the causal factors in the emergence of structural bilateralism. In my view, Hewett overstates the statistical difficulties per se of creating an independent IPS. I also fail to see why such a system should forcibly be predicated on a strictly autarkic economic region. As I see it, the real issue was then, as it is now, that trade prices or even domestic prices in the PEs are the symptoms of the real disease of these economies. It is indeed the economic mechanism as a whole, not only its price component, that should be commanding the intellectual resources of the CMEA economic community and the energy of the relevant decision makers.

A too rigid and absolute view of the IPS not only overdramatizes the problems faced by the PEs and indeed ignores or belittles those associated with the price system allegedly based on WMPs. It also misrepresents the intentions of the more cogent participants in the debates. The entire drift of the IPS as an economic issue would appear to have been to approximate to some extent prevailing scarcities in the CMEA on an intermittent basis without, at the same time, becoming completely divorced from world markets. A more explicit recognition of the indirect taxes and subsidies – regional tariffs, if you will – implied in this attitude could render a regional price system perfectly compatible with the aspirations of the PEs and their desire to continue to interact with world markets. This would at least reduce the paradox that PEs should pursue integration measures as indicated by conditions prevailing in rather different socioeconomic environments (Grinberg and Ljubskij 1985, pp. 100–1).

If the enhancement of SEI is seen in a realistic time frame of development of the PEs individually and in concert, the existing mechanisms of establishing trade prices for transactions coming under the provisions of the TR clearing regime may constitute a considerable drag on CMEA trade. It may be an even greater handicap in efforts to expand production and in other types of intragroup specialization. The transplantation to the CMEA arena of international market conditions will be less and less justified as progress is made in SEI. Furthermore, it could palpably hamper the development of economic cooperation among the PEs by imposing a nonequivalent, causal scale of values on the exchange of commodities. Consequently, the CMEA members must eventually adopt their IPS in regional economic relations. Such prices could be based initially on some formula of the production cost of the participants.

The emergence of an own CMEA price system that would be indicative for resource allocation is a function of the following conditions. First, individual PEs need to embrace similar, but not necessarily identical, principles for calculating costs and establishing domestic prices. This includes the computation of point prices as well as the flexibility of prices. It also requires agreement on the methodology for setting the various components of production costs, including the assessment of the accumulation elements to be factored into prices. But other substantive components of the equation are necessarily depreciation rates, capital levies, surcharges for wages, social contribution outlays, taxes, and myriad other parameters. Second, the member countries must jointly agree on priorities of economic policy for the whole community. This presupposes as an important component–the third condition–broad agreement on the relative insulation of the CMEA market against outside influences. Fourth, the participants need also to determine the purchasing power of individual national currencies to compare costs and an economically justified level for the TR and its management. Fifth, the PEs must agree to ensure that the establishment of common TR trade prices derived from national production costs need not forcibly imply that such trade prices are strictly binding on all CMEA members in all agreements and contracts. Countries must have the option of departing from these prices when this is in their own interest.

The computational difficulties of such an IPS, at first sight, would not differ measurably from those associated with any of the numerous propositions advocated in the 1960s. But this objection holds only if the endeavor were to administer regional, relatively inflexible, fiat prices. This would be a gross mistake, however. Regional trade pricing rules should be at least as flexible as the degree of malleability available in the most "liberal" member country. Other members of the group should be asked to rationalize, through concrete policy measures, the degree of protection against regional economic influences they appear to be endorsing implicitly; no member should be compelled to adopt such prices domestically. Comparable prices do not signify price uniformity because uniform national price components, especially direct production costs, would inhibit the exploitation of profitable lines of production specialization. But members should be compelled to parametrize their protective domestic regimes. This would at the very least clarify for policy makers the implications of their societal preferences that are being coercively imposed upon domestic economic forces.

The weak point of the present price system is that there are *in se* virtually no domestic goods and services that would not in some respect become the subject of international exchange in a well-functioning market, where it could proceed on the basis of comparative cost differentials. By establishing a uniform CMEA norm of domestic pricing, an IPS would be an earnest attempt to eliminate the most glaring distortions of the national price systems that inhibit the identification of proper costs. In conjunction with the ongoing reform attempts, more and more attention is being devoted to flexibility and, as an almost necessary corollary, the creation of direct "real relationships among associations and enterprises" of PEs (Grinberg and Ljubskij 1985, p. 101).[11] If such were to materialize, it would not be necessary to settle in detail on all of the constituents of production costs.

The traditional objection to any parametrization of decision making on a broad scale has been the fear of losing control over the consumption and production spheres. This is certainly a distinct possibility in principle. However, the trade-off between absolute charge over all economic processes and flexibility so as to foster productivity gains would seem to be tilting more and more in the latter's favor. Similarly the very frequent emphasis on strengthening the MFT (Konstantinov 1984; Němeček 1972, 1975) can be seen in two different ways, with emphasis on gaining more central control through cohesive macroeconomic policies definitely gaining ground. The further realization of flexibility in the years ahead through direct enterprise contacts and indirect coordination instruments may require a reinterpretation of traditional precepts so as to argue the case for the dialectical unity of planning and market mechanisms (Kazandžieva 1983, p. 32) and to justify it by labeling "reforms"[12] simply as "further developments of the economic mechanisms," which is the point argued in the Introduction. This would appear to be a small cosmetic price to pay, as examined at length in Chapter 12.

6

Exchange rates and foreign exchange policies

Rate targeting, efficiency of exchange markets, further liberalization of capital movements and integration of financial markets, Eurocurrency and offshore market regulations, macroeconomic policy coordination to support optimal ER fluctuations, and many other such crucial topics immediately spring to mind when dealing with the vital questions of ERs in MEs. A very different set of acute issues is embedded in the most pressing foreign exchange problems of PEs. Central policy topics there include the determination and uniformization of the ER; the role of the ER in micro- and macroeconomic decision making at the national and regional level; partial or full convertibility with respect to transaction types, partners abroad, and residents; transferability conditions; the activization and potential role of the TR; and others. Although none of these rather pedestrian topics may appear to transcend the art of elementary policy making, it is precisely these issues that have been widely debated throughout Eastern Europe.

This chapter provides a backdrop to the particular ER problems of the PEs, assesses the current state of affairs, speculates about what the situation might be in the late 1980s, and especially discusses how the chasm between what prevails now and what planners might covet for the foreseeable future might be bridged. Section 6.1 sets the stage for a discussion of the ER in the context of a PE. Its roles in a stylized CPE and MPE are outlined in Sections 6.2 and 6.3, respectively. Some perspective is given on the variety of situations that may characterize an individual PE, but it would simply be hopeless to try to cover the entire ground here. The multitude of ERs and, their derivation and application in TR transactions are discussed in Section 6.4. The same is done with respect to CC transactions in Section 6.5. The ER's actual and potential roles in present policy experiments in Eastern Europe, including the supporting instruments and institutions, are looked at in Section 6.6. An evaluation of the possible contribution of an ER in molding future economic developments and how to get there rounds off the analysis. Only in the latter setting shall I describe the ER's intrinsic role in a generic PE and how it ought to or could be realized in the light of the specific set of policy objectives sought by PEs. In that context it will also be useful to broaden the rather confined scope of the single country to the ER problems typical of the CMEA as a whole.

6.1 General notions about the exchange rate in planned economies

A country's ER is basically the price of foreign currency expressed in domestic currency or its inverse. As such, it should be determined as but one of many prices encountered in an economy by the demand for and supply of that foreign currency. However, in view of the importance of foreign economic transactions in ensuring economic stability, particularly in comparatively small open economies, policy makers are likely to pay special attention to the "proper" ER. They normally "monitor" foreign exchange markets more carefully than the price-formation mechanisms typical of most other activities. A variety of formal and informal obstacles prevent unhindered access to all domestic and foreign markets, which gives rise to a de facto network of ERs. Nonetheless, in most developed MEs, a uniform ER for a given type of currency (for instance, the spot dollar) is bound to ensue from domestic or foreign arbitrage.

The ER's role varies with the precise organizational arrangements of the home economy. As a rule, a country's foreign exchange regime comprises the institutions and rules that govern foreign currency trans-actions in domestic markets. An important component thereof is the set of explicit or implicit rules by which the authorities "guide" the acquisi-tion and disposition of foreign exchange in support of the implementa-tion of other socioeconomic policy goals. The extent and degree to which such transactions are regulated may range from fully uncon-trolled markets with freely fluctuating ERs for all types of foreign ex-change operations to complete proscription of any foreign exchange dealings by residents as well as nonresidents, except those benefiting from prior government authorization.

Although the aims underlying foreign exchange policy may well fail to be fully transparent even to the country's own monetary authorities, they generally derive from the perceived socioeconomic or political need to "protect" the domestic economy against unforeseen foreign economic disturbances. Usually the concerns center on the country's competitive position in world trade and the role of exports as a source of employment and growth, especially in small open MEs. In some instances, such preoc-cupations dominate official ER policies so overwhelmingly that exchange markets are suppressed altogether as the central policy makers them-selves assume complete control over foreign economic relations. This is so for the stylized PE, whose foreign exchange "markets" differ radically from those found in most MEs, including developing countries. For systemic reasons, PEs maintain a plethora of ERs, each of which is applicable to separate markets, and only limited arbitrage can occur among them.

Institutional and other characteristics of most PEs are responsible for relegating the ER to the status of a rather passive policy instrument. It is not among the key determinants of the basic features (namely, the overall level, commodity composition, and geographical distribution) of trade in a PE, not even in the MPE. It is true that the ER in Hungary is called upon to perform a more active role in some situations than, say, in the USSR. But that function is still not very large, as amply documented by the recent external adjustment efforts discussed in Chapter 3.[1] That is not to deny that some ER has some function to play in arriving at individual or collective economic decisions, and that its role has considerably increased in recent years. The major changes in economic policies in these countries since the abandonment of the very rigid development strategy of the early 1950s and the long history of economic reforms of varying intensity and scope have had some positive impact after all!

Because the ER regime of most PEs has been discussed at length in many studies, there is no need to rehash it. As discussed in Chapter 3, there is a pent-up need in all PEs to come more fully to grips, and promptly, with the major transitions in global and CMEA trade and finance. To accomplish these tasks, planners need to work out a positive adjustment policy in which indirect criteria of choice, including meaningful ERs and realistic prices, play a central role. Furthermore, the transition process toward a situation in which flexible decision making can be reconciled with the virtues of planning and the basic precepts of a socialist society needs to be examined in some detail. A brief recapitulation of past ER policies may provide a proper perspective on what may be feasible in the future.

6.2 Foreign exchange policies in a centrally planned economy

The two foremost determinants of foreign exchange policies in the CPE are the prevalence of far-reaching administrative controls over economic transactions and the great degree of autonomy over domestic pricing vis-à-vis both CMEA and world prices sought by central planners. As discussed in Chapter 5, there is no parametric link between domestic and foreign trade prices through one or more operative ERs, possibly in combination with conventional price buffers of MEs. Instead, policy makers in most CPEs deliberately enact only a macroeconomic connection through the price-equalization mechanism, regardless of whether such an accounting framework exists explicitly or results from a variety of taxes and subsidies.

Policy makers in CPEs have an inherent penchant to ward off uncon-trolled pressures emanating from unanticipated price changes abroad. As far as the economy as a whole is concerned, and economic activities are planned and implemented successfully, the precise level of the ER does not really matter very much. The chief exception is its role for bookkeeping purposes.[2] In other words, the ER is a purely passive policy instrument among the traditional modus operandi in CPEs. Changes in the overall level of the ER therefore have little bearing on the volume, the broad geographical direction, and the commodity composition of trade. Fluctuations in ERs induced by shifts in international financial markets do influence the specific geographical direction of trade, especially the distribution of the trade volumes earmarked for principal trade or currency zones in the central plan.

In the immediate postwar period, the CPEs tried to pursue a fully autonomous economic policy through rigid central planning and nearly exhaustive control over foreign transactions. A positive ER policy would, in the circumstances, have been redundant in any case. Inasmuch as it was intertwined with the aspiration of the authorities to confine the scope of foreign trade to what was absolutely necessary to foster rapid industrialization, the traditional CPE's passive ER policy tended to be implicit in the answers given by the central planner to the three basic trade questions. Note that within the predetermined commodity classes and partner groups (usually socialist and others, but possibly encompassing CMEA, other socialist, clearing trade with nonsocialist countries, and CC trade with MEs), actual trade can be neutral with respect to the ER only in the most rigid type of environment: FTOs are instructed to acquire and to dispose of certain goods in predetermined locations and at specified target prices, and they carry this mandate out to the letter. In such an economy, foreign transactions depend on prior plan decisions referring to input availability and output distribution in real terms, and are, as a result, not the consequence but the cause of financial flows. Given the institutional and policy characteristics of the CPE, the level of the ER, in principle, need therefore not be pegged at a "proper" level, and usually it is not.

To enhance the realization of these aspirations, the preponderant share of trade was traditionally appropriated for intragroup trade on the basis of strict BTPAs denominated in a conventional clearing currency. Actual trade prices under bilateralism are usually negotiable, and the ER becomes meaningless. Only the specific geographical distribution of the planned volume of trade with nonclearing partners could possibly be influenced by the ER. At fixed gold parities, however, the comparative evolution of prices in MEs, rather than the CPE's ER policies, was, in principle, one key guideline to identifying individual export and import markets within the volumes earmarked for, say, MEs.

The only major exception to the rule that the volume and the commodity composition of trade, and to some extent also its direction, are largely independent of the ER is the direct consumption of goods and services by foreign tourists, diplomats, foreign commercial or financial representatives, and beneficiaries of remittances (gifts, royalties, honoraria, and the like) from abroad. In other words, even in the most rigidly centralized CPE, the particular ER selected is not completely neutral. In fact, the aforementioned areas are where the ER in a CPE performs exactly the same function as it does in MEs. Only to the extent that the CPE allowed such other than merchandise and related transactions without prior government approval was a more positive policy required, although it did not emerge in most cases. Because the countries sought to discourage tourism and trade delegations, did not condone direct foreign investment, and resorted to capital flows only in highly exceptional cases, and then mostly in the form of tied real flows negotiated ex ante, a comprehensive positive ER policy was, on the whole, meaningless for as long as the authorities chose to hold on to the other aspects of their foreign exchange regime.

Even with regard to merchandise transactions proper, the rigidity embedded in the plan can rarely be adhered to in practice: Especially in relations with MEs, ex ante planning cannot be as comprehensive as in intra-CMEA relations and partner, and possibly product, substitution perforce occurs; planners cannot realistically regulate trade flows in minute detail even with other CPEs; and, finally, the primary concern of planners is to acquire imports[3] without jeopardizing the balance of payments.[4] It is therefore not surprising that the ER is not necessarily fully neutral even for merchandise transactions proper.

Regardless of how passive a policy instrument the ER is in the CPE, the correct price of foreign exchange can nevertheless be instrumental in fine-tuning planning and in conveying the proper incentives for microeconomic decisions. The latter is particularly important when trade cannot be completely circumscribed by ex ante planning, and "local management" is called upon to fill gaps or to resolve contradictions in plan instructions. The actual ER may also influence the results from trade for FTOs on which in some instances depend accounting profitability indicators and hence the premiums and other incentives distributed to those engaged in trade. Finally, for many imports there is no readily available domestic price, and the transaction price may be based on the landed or CIF cost at the official ER. These are a few of the instances in which the ER has real, as distinct from accounting, effects even in the case of merchandise transactions proper.

Precisely because there are so many and profound distortions between domestic and foreign decision-making rules, including relative prices, CPEs tend to regulate trade directly by proscribing certain activities, by tolerating minor deviations from what the planners had intended (such as the redistribution of some trade flows in accordance with "profitability" considerations), or by modifying the rules of the game by adding instruments to distinguish between the relative ease with which goods can be traded. If the ER threatens to operate in areas where the authorities fail to wield full control, corrective measures are announced whenever these contraventions are sufficiently weighty to the realization of other goals underlying the passive foreign exchange regime. In truly marginal cases, the authorities simply tacitly allow these limited markets to operate.

The exact guidelines underlying the determination of ERs in CPEs are quite obscure, and sources differ on their rationale (see Sections 6.4 and 6.5). Even if the original ER had been set in order to secure balanced external payments or to reflect purchasing power, the high degree of domestic economic autonomy, the drastic buffering of domestic producer from consumer prices, the insulation of domestic prices from movements in prices abroad, and the generally passive foreign exchange regime guaranteed that the ER quickly became unrealistic for allocatory decisions. Not only that, the degree of price autonomy achieved made it virtually impossible to select one single indicator of purchasing power parity or payments equilibrium, except in the purely statistical sense at a given moment of time.

Insulating domestic from foreign economic relations may be desirable at the time the PE takes off on a rapid and broadly based industrialization strategy. Nevertheless, changes in foreign economic relations or shifts in the attitudes of policy makers with respect to the organization of economic activity or the goals of development policies are as a rule contingent on paying closer attention to the ER's level and role. This is especially so once the planners start to exploit comparative advantage, including in tourism, as a potentially important source of growth. It will then become advisable to set a reasonable ER and to formulate a more active exchange policy to guide decentralized decision making.

The problem of setting the price of foreign exchange correctly is, on the whole, but one aspect of the more general issue of appropriate domestic price formation, as discussed in Chapter 5. Although CPE planners are keenly aware of the undesirable allocatory implications of operating with an improper ER, there is little that can be done in one sweep to realign the ER and the corresponding regime. The appropriate mechanism for linking the domestic economy with transactions abroad has been the subject of extensive debate, and some PEs have sought to reform their trade and exchange models to allow a more active exploitation of comparative advantage. With the exception chiefly of Hungary in recent years, however, the PEs have been extremely reluctant to revise basic domestic price policies that form part and parcel of socialist distribution precepts at the same time that major changes are sought in the foreign trade sector. To implement one without the other, planners had to work out a compromise by which the state MFT remained intact and the precise level of the ER would not generally matter. At the same time, however, surrogates for the ER by currency zone, and possibly also by type of economic activity, were enacted.

Depending upon the prevailing degree of price heterogeneity and the extent of pricing autonomy desired, the various PEs adopted quite different trade coefficients or multipliers that are sometimes quite ingenious. In the process, the official ER has become at best a notional bookkeeping magnitude and uniform denominator of statistics of foreign transactions. An integral element of this changeover was the efforts of decision makers to focus the foreign exchange policy not on the official ER, which remained as unimportant as during the heyday of the CPE, but on patterning surrogate ERs in support of the decentralized implementation of socioeconomic policies. But these reforms have generally fallen short of expectations because the leaders of CPEs have been quite reluctant to relinquish autonomy in domestic pricing and more general economic decisions.

6.3 The exchange rate and foreign exchange policies in a modified planned economy

Once authorities seek to delegate decision making to the lower planning tiers, to exploit foreign markets as a possibly essential means of buttressing relatively buoyant growth, or to approach tourism and other international services as active sources of foreign exchange, a more positive foreign exchange policy and operative ERs have to be elaborated. The crucial questions to be resolved at the time the transition to an MPE is initiated are not so concerned with determining and selecting *the* proper ER, which if understood to mean the computation of *the* equilibrium ER will undoubtedly entail knotty problems. The really pivotal issues pertain to the formulation of a foreign exchange policy that helps to ensure that the ER, perhaps after some transition, reaches a meaningful level and that this realism can be maintained without dispensing altogether with market separation or yielding too much of the economic autonomy so much prized in the CPE. In other words, if the authorities were to decide to tolerate a certain degree of freedom in price formation they could simply let the ER find its own level, possibly through discrete adjustments.

The ER policy that emerged under the impulse of attempts to reform the traditional CPE differed sharply between the various countries, as indicated, and it has changed perceptibly over the past twenty years or so. Generally speaking, all PEs have sought the benefit of a proper ER without yielding control over foreign economic decisions through the MFT. They therefore adopted an ER surrogate (a coefficient or multiplier) that was purported to reflect the average relationship between domestic wholesale and export prices in the TR, the CC, and, in some cases, the clearing regime with developing MEs. Because prices in each of these trade relations differ markedly and, except for CC transactions, are rather inflexible, average price ratios have had to be set as guidelines for trade policy decisions.

In this connection, it may be instructive to distinguish between the coefficient that relates the *valuta* price, which is the foreign currency price converted at the official ER, to the domestic wholesale price and the multiplier that is a direct surrogate for the ER. The former is identified here as the internal ER; the latter is referred to as the commercial ER if officially quoted, and as the trade multiplier otherwise. From an economic point of view, the former is undoubtedly the more important. For operational purposes, however, the internal ER is often disaggregated into different rates by trade partner (or currency zone), geographical direction (exports or imports), and commodity groups (especially fuels and raw materials, foodstuffs, manufactured consumer goods, and investment goods). Furthermore, these rates may, but need not, be applied in actual transactions, domestic pricing, macro- and microeconomic planning, or the calculation of enterprise results and bonuses. In some cases, as in the USSR (Šagalov 1986, p. 117), internal ERs are computed on the basis of expected prices, which may or may not be useful for planning purposes and decision making by economic agents in line with the expectations underlying the plan. The trade multiplier, on the other hand, is usually defined as an overall average ratio of domestic to trade prices of more limited use in plan formulation and implementation. In other words, the internal ER is a purely domestic category and can thus be changed unilaterally (Ljubskij, Suljaeva, and Šastitko 1978, p. 68), whereas the multiplier belongs in the set of international market categories.

The computation and practical application of internal ERs gained considerable momentum during the reforms of the 1960s. Although many of the latter's features have been abrogated since, the role of these coefficients as guides to macroeconomic resource allocation, enterprise decision making, and domestic pricing has been strengthened. They have been especially important in imparting greater realism to wholesale prices, in reducing the gap between consumer and producer price levels, and in modifying relative consumer prices, although to a far more modest degree than envisaged for producer prices.

As a rule, the internal ER is specified as the ratio between domestic prices of selected traded goods and the corresponding *valuta* prices per commodity group, trade direction, or currency zone, or a combination thereof. The foreign trade multiplier, on the other hand, is the ratio between domestic and actual foreign trade prices at some time and is therefore a surrogate for the ER. The advantage of keeping the two concepts separate is that foreign trade multipliers usually vary with shifts in the official ER, as in the case of the dollar since the early 1970s, whereas the internal ERs are kept constant for a comparatively lengthy period and are a domestic policy tool. In other words, the trade multiplier is usually a derived magnitude, whereas the internal ER is calculated at certain intervals, in most instances, as the ex post average domestic cost of earning a *valuta* unit in the export of some commodities or with some trade partners or both during a comparatively long time; once established, the internal ER tends to remain valid for a similarly long time.[5]

The policies underlying internal ERs have differed greatly from country to country because of two main reasons: The reform concepts at the root of the compilation of internal ERs were heterogeneous, and the application of the rates has diverged markedly from what was originally envisaged. These ERs were computed primarily to serve as microeconomic allocatory guides in nearly all economies and as major policy instruments for those in charge of macroeconomic choices in at least some PEs bent on going beyond simple economic streamlining. Whereas some confined the internal ER's role to experiments or the broad planning of trade, in others it filtered through into the actual trade accounting for decentralized units, domestic prices, and even the promulgation of structural adjustments. The policies pursued originally envisaged the periodic, but regular, recalibration of these rates (say, not more often than once a year) in order to benefit from stability in the economic regulators for enterprise decision making, to profit from shifts in comparative advantages, and gradually to pass on the real trade results to the microeconomic sphere. Only few have done so to date.[6]

The impact of the internal ERs on economic organization, policy formulation, and decision making in the various PEs has varied greatly. Originally all countries had slated those rates to be of major importance in rendering the fiat prices more realistic, transforming the trade sector into a pivotal source of growth, and guiding enterprise decisions. The checkered evolution of the economic reforms, however, has produced results that have varied from country to country and period to period. All that need be said at this juncture is that the uniform internal ER, if extant, has performed at best the role of an effective ER for a predetermined trade pattern. At worst, multiple internal ERs have assisted entrepreneurs to fill in gaps or to resolve contradictions in the plans, but they have had little impact on overall resource allocation. How much actual policies have differed from what was envisaged when the internal ERs were first introduced can be illustrated for Hungary. As noted, the ratios set in 1968 on the basis of out-of-date average prices remained unchanged until 1976, when the internal ERs were combined with the official ER to yield publicly quoted commercial ERs. Since then, both the ruble and the dollar commercial ERs have been adjusted with some periodicity, although much more flexibly for the dollar than for the ruble.

The precise role of the commercial ER in Hungary, at least since the sharp price adjustments of 1979, has been to relate directly domestic and import (or export) prices after adjusting for transportation costs, insurance charges, profit margins, and import duties or export subsidies. These factors play a role in both TR and CC transactions, although doubtlessly to a far larger extent in the latter area, where bilateral clearing at average prices is inherently irreconcilable with an active ER policy.

As far as ruble transactions are concerned, it is not exactly known how the redefinition of the commercial ER proceeds; in fact, in spite of sizable movements in CMEA trade prices, Hungary kept the ruble rate at twenty-six forints from November 1981 through early September 1985. The forint's devaluation since then has been insufficient to compensate for terms-of-trade losses, however. Earlier changes in the ruble rate were enacted to mitigate the average effect of the movement in CMEA trade prices on domestic transaction prices[7] rather than by concerns about redressing external balance. In view of the marked decline in Hungary's terms of trade vis-à-vis the ruble area in the 1970s, a depreciation of the currency would have been called for if the Hungarian authorities had desired to stimulate exports and to discourage imports by indirect means, including an active ER policy.[8] The appreciation of the forint helped to offset the differences between domestic and CMEA prices, but it could not compensate for the serious deterioration of Hungary's terms of trade with the TR zone until 1981 and certainly not since then.

Policy considerations regarding movements of the dollar multiplier or ER before 1979 were not unambiguous. In late 1972, Hungary apparently decided to move the dollar rate basically to offset on average the relative depreciation of foreign currencies to the forint stemming from different movements in domestic and CC trade prices during a comparatively long period of time.[9] In spite of frequent changes in the dollar multiplier and commercial ER, the revaluation of the forint has not been sufficiently large to offset differential changes in average trade prices.

Whereas Hungary has gradually moved toward a regime with a transparent link between domestic and trade prices, although it is by no means as smooth as it should be in principle (Brabant 1984b), other PEs have maintained formidable buffers in the form of sectoral, currency zone, or directional adjustment factors that take the place of multiple ERs. The commercial ER or trade multiplier in those countries tends to be a simple statistical average of price relations by currency zone that may convey some apposite information to planners; also, trade statistics are at times recorded at those rates rather than the official ones. But price formation and microeconomic decisions are influenced, if at all, by multiple multipliers or internal ERs derived from actual or anticipated future prices.

Until recently, the implementation of internal ERs and trade multipliers has had only marginal effects on the ER policies of most PEs. As noted, Hungary in 1976 started quoting ERs on a regular basis and suspended the official ER altogether. Poland followed suit in 1982. Rumania has held onto an independent policy with respect to the commercial ER, which as yet does not appear to be a fully operative decision instrument.[10]

Because the rates I have described relied upon some average relationship between domestic wholesale and trade prices of some reference period and predetermined trade pattern, even these surrogates could not help to regulate demand and supply of goods and services denominated in other prices. This applies particularly to retail prices for consumer goods and services for tourism, private remittances, expenditures of diplomatic and trade representatives, and so on. To the extent that such activities were to be encouraged, something had to be done about the distorted currency valuation. Again, instead of pursuing an active ER policy in general, most PEs intermittently compared domestic and benchmark foreign prices for consumer goods and services so as to select noncommercial premiums or surcharges. These are, however, rarely uniformly applied, they are ambiguously defined, and those that are activated are changed only infrequently in an effort to restore purchasing power in that limited range of activities. Only Hungary succeeded in bridging the gap between consumer and producer price levels by changing their structure in 1979–1981. This enabled the authorities in October 1981 to decree a uniform commercial ER applicable also to noncommercial CC transactions. Matters are very different regarding the TR.

Once the authorities want to move away from the foreign exchange rigidity typical of the CPE, different conversion coefficients and ERs for their currencies and the highly complex system of explicit and implicit bonuses and surcharges lead to substantial differentiation of the ERs of the same country in various types of transactions. Although the MPE may in time reach uniformity of the ER, the gradual abolition of the corrective system of bonuses and surcharges must be recognized as wholly unrealistic without additional policy measures. The authorities may strive to reduce the range of effective ER multiplicity, but they cannot entirely eliminate the need for differentiation because the objective conditions for establishing the price structure and price ratios in PEs differ from those in MEs.

Special issues derive from the fact that the PE not only works with two different types of domestic price systems but also with two heterogeneous sets of relative trade prices. This multiplicity has engendered critical practical problems whenever PEs seek to implement a cherished principle of regional or international economic cooperation. Rather than search for the roots of this type of problem, the authorities have almost invariably opted for ad hoc computations that can become very complex (Ondráček 1983, pp. 60ff.). As a result, most PEs have recently further exacerbated the already bewildering ER system. From the economic as well as the organizational and accounting point of view, then, one must distinguish rather rigidly between the network of ERs that link a PE with the CC world and those used for effecting various kinds of transactions within the CMEA.[11] Certainly, the "old" gold parity provides a formal connection between the two, but this nexus is only nominal and hence not very helpful in unraveling the separate economic relations of the CMEA countries.

6.4 Exchange rates and CMEA relations

It is useful to distinguish at least conceptually among the official, internal, notional commercial, effective commercial, noncommercial, tourist, joint investment, black market, and miscellaneous activity ERs. The determination, application, and realism of these various ERs is discussed in sequence in the following section.

The official exchange rate

The determination and role of the official ER of the TR and CC[12] are similar for all PEs. Until the gradual disintegration of the BWS, the PEs maintained perfect cross rates. This is still so for the national currencies of the PEs, including the TR; in many cases, official ERs are now quoted, if at all,[13] in a standard fashion against the TR proper only. My comments can therefore be restricted to the parities maintained against the TR.

The rationale underlying the determination of the gold parity is not unambiguous. Many Eastern European commentators claim that the official ERs when first established, mostly in the late 1940s or early 1950s, reflected purchasing power parities between the local currency and one or more reference CCs, usually the U.S. dollar. Some countries, including Bulgaria in 1962 and the Soviet Union in 1961, revised those earlier parities ostensibly on the basis of changed price relationships between transactions denominated in local currency and in CC. In most instances, however, the computations underlying the currency definitions of the late 1940s, as in virtually all later revisions, were not mainly motivated by a careful search for realistic "equilibrium ERs" or "purchasing power parities." Certainly, for some PEs such a comparison between the local and main international currency was attempted in the immediate postwar years[14] and at least the USSR's redefinition of the gold parity in 1961 was inspired by considerations about reducing the size of price-equalization transfers. Apart from these few instances, however, the valuation of the local currency appears to have been set largely by internal exigencies and, in some cases, by political prestige considerations without really impinging upon the basic factors underlying the determination of the gold content in the early postwar period.

Even if the original parities had been instituted on the basis of a careful purchasing power comparison, the disequilibrium conditions of the early postwar years could hardly have been conducive to the selection of an ER appropriate in subsequent years, even if only for notional purposes. However, because trade decisions especially in CMEA relations were overwhelmingly conditioned by the exigencies of central planning and did not directly affect domestic economic conditions, the precise level of the ER and its inertia in time proved to be largely irrelevant, as discussed in Section 6.2.

From the foregoing discussion, it can be concluded that the official ruble ER bears no relation whatsoever with reality, it is not utilized in economic transactions when it can be avoided, and it has been largely confined to that of a uniform accounting unit. Recent rates are shown in column 1 of Table 6.1.

The commercial exchange rate

The commercial ER in this context can have two distinct meanings. In some countries, it is the rate at which actual trade flows are recorded. Otherwise it has no realistic value, just as the official gold parity ER is meaningless. In others, however, it is the rate at which actual foreign trade values are translated into local currency units for transactions by the FTOs and local producers. This may or may not be the rate at which foreign economic transactions are evaluated in overall trade decisions (see column 2 of Table 6.1).

a. Pro forma commercial exchange rate. This applies only to the GDR. Since the early 1960s,[15] that country's trade statistics have been recorded at a special commercial unit (the Valutamark), whose initial value was set equal to the rate of the West German Mark and the dollar, or $0.238. But it has since moved to some extent relative to the dollar; the commercial rate to the ruble was originally derived as the official cross rate of the postwar gold parities of the mark. The exception is trade between the two Germanies, which is effected through a special clearing account for which the two marks are treated as being identical for accounting purposes. This entails inconsistent trade statistics, even for East–West trade.

b. Functioning commercial exchange rate. As noted in Section 6.3, there are presently three PEs that publicly quote a commercial ER:[16] Hungary, Poland, and Rumania. Further, Czechoslovakia used to set commercial rates for ruble- and dollar-denominated transactions. But these rates are more logically discussed under the heading internal ERs in the next section because they are not publicly quoted and their determination and application differ from those in the other PEs enumerated here.

The commercial ERs when first set reflected some statistical ratio between domestic wholesale and trade prices for the predetermined trade pattern with socialist and nonsocialist countries. It was usually confined to the exports of manufactures only and calculated over a multiyear period. As an export incentive, the commercial ER may even be slightly undervalued, and perhaps more so for the dollar than for the ruble because the ruble trade area is not really regulated by trade incentives and foreign exchange availability. Typical for these commercial ERs is the relatively sharp depreciation of the commercial ruble to the commercial dollar in comparison with the official cross rate. Inasmuch as the trade patterns of the PEs differ more or less sharply, the cross rates implied in the commercial ERs differ as well. This usually entails insuperable reconciliation problems in maintaining comparable foreign trade statistics over time.

The commercial ERs, when introduced, may have accurately reflected the relationship between domestic wholesale and dollar (or ruble) trade prices, although I have considerable doubts about this (see Section 6.3). How to maintain a realistic ER parity for commercial transactions has been a major problem, however. The ERs are not always adjusted properly – even not at some discrete intervals – in tandem with changes in relative domestic and trade prices, and are therefore not in all cases the rates used in economic accounting and macroeconomic planning. Though adjustments tend to differ markedly from one country to another, they generally follow the pattern of shifts in a basket of main currencies for the dollar ER (with other CCs being derived according to fluctuations in main financial markets). The ruble ER is adjusted at great intervals probably in line with changes in relative ruble trade prices, although the available information is not always unambiguous on that score.[17]

Rumania in 1981 and Poland in 1982 established commercial ERs that are expected to become fully operative links between trade and domestic wholesale prices. Whereas Rumania selected parity between the ruble and dollar (at 15 lei), the Polish devaluation of January 1982 to 80 złotych per dollar (from the "special" 34.9 in December 1981) did not entail an equivalent redefinition of the ruble parity, which was set at 68 (as against 44.4 before); it rose to 72 in March 1984, 77 in January 1985, 88 in June 1985, 91 in February 1986, and 95 in September 1986. However, whereas Rumania did not eliminate the dichotomy between commercial and noncommercial rates, Poland purports to have established uniformity, at least for CC transactions, but the validity of the claim is doubtful, as I shall argue in Section 6.5.

Table 6.1. *Intra-CMEA exchange rates*

Country	Official (per TR)	Commercial (per TR)	Cooperation coefficient[a,b]	Noncommercial[a,c] from:						
				1.1.56	1.4.63	1.7.71	1.3.75	1.1.78	1.1.81	1.1.85
Bulgaria	1.300	n.a.[d]	1.25	2.62	2.04	1.38	1.56	1.29	1.15	1.08
Czechoslovakia	8.000	[18][f]	2.25	5.40	4.10	2.77	2.88	2.38	2.13	2.01
GDR	2.470	4.67	1.46	6.00	4.40	2.98	2.98	2.46	2.20	2.07
Hungary	13.044	[35]y	3.07	4.10	3.42	2.31	2.60	2.15[i]	1.92[i]	1.81[i]
Poland	4.444	[68][g]	9.00	13.10	11.70	7.91	10.00[j]	8.25	13.77[k]	14.33
Rumania	6.667	[15][h]	2.62	5.60	4.23	2.86	[2.86][l]	2.36	2.11	1.99
USSR	1.000	n.a.	1.20	3.82	3.40	2.30	2.30	1.90	1.70	1.60

[a] Units of local currency per unit of official currency.

[b] This rate was agreed upon in 1973 and has been revised at least four times.

[c] The European date system is used, an explained in the introductory note.

[d] n.a., not applicable

[e] Commercial rate applied in the early 1970s. More recent ones are discussed in the text.

[f] Quotation of the official ER ceased in January 1976. The original trade multiplier was gradually revalued, starting with 35 in 1976 to reach 26 in 1982 (see Table 6.3 for time series).

[g] Ceased being quoted on 1 January 1982. The commercial rate then introduced was set at 68 but it has gradually been increased since early 1984 (see Table 6.3 for time series).

[h] Commercial rate introduced in trade statistics in 1981.

[i] Assuming the existence of the *deviza* forint at the parity quoted by partner countries.

[j] Effective 1 January 1976.

[k] Adjusted for the uniform devaluation of the noncommercial złoty in terms of other Eastern European noncommercial currencies by 55 percent enacted on 8 February 1982.

[l] Rate implied in later publications, although Rumania was not a signatory to the 1974 multilateral agreement.

Sources: Official rates – as published in many different ER tables, including those of *Statistická ročenka Československé socialistické republiky, 1984* (Prague: SNTL and ALFA, 1985), p. 174. Commercial Rates – as for the official rates or as detailed in the notes to Tables 6.2 and 6.3. Cooperation coefficients – as tabulated in the document cited in the text (also in Matejka 1974, p. 176). Noncommercial rates – 1956 and 1963 from Dülbokov 1965, p. 148; 1971 based on ruble coefficient as reported in *Vnešnjaja torgovlja,* 1972:10, p. 7; 1975 based on the noncommercial ERs reported in *Svět Hospodářství,* 1976:153, p. 4; 1978 based on noncommercial ERs as reported in *Hospodářské Noviny,* 1978:4, p. 10; 1981 based on the ruble coefficient reported in *Svět Hospodářství,* 1981:101, p. 5; 1985 based on the ruble coefficient reported in Špaček 1985, p. 1 and the changed rates for Poland as quoted in Soviet tables. Note that there have been frequent changes in the noncommercial złoty since 1982.

The precise methodology underlying the Rumanian commercial ERs remains unknown, although it too was probably based on a ratio of trade prices by currency zone and actual or anticipated domestic prices of the late 1970s, when these rates were being debated. In any case, Rumania has not yet fully eliminated the multipliers specific to some commodity groups and currency zones. The price reference base of the Polish commercial ERs, as envisaged in 1981 and utilized in the price reform introduced in 1982, was the average export price ratio of the first half of 1981 except for fuels, basic raw materials, and other materials. However, the ERs set in 1982 evolved as a political compromise between what economic calculations indicated and the perceived need for trade incentives (Wojciechowski 1982, pp. 6–7). These rates were all submarginal, because they implied losses for about 25 percent of exports. It was then decided to modify the rates whenever the underlying value of the currency basket changed by at least 5 percent because of differential movements of trade prices relative to the corresponding wholesale prices of selected exported manufactures (Wesołowski 1983b, p. 6). Adaptations since 1982 have, in principle, been based on shifts in a basket of nine currencies for CC transactions, but changes within the basket have been far more important than differential price movements in determining ER fluctuations for CC (Cipiur 1984, p. 8). The ruble rate has been changed infrequently, as discussed earlier in this section, but the precise methodological details are not known. In the case of Rumania the coefficient of 15 was kept unchanged until the end of 1982.[18] It was then gradually adjusted for the dollar from 17.5 to about 22–23; the ruble was kept at 17.5. In November 1984, the leu was abruptly revalued against both the dollar and the ruble; the reverse adjustment against at least the dollar suddenly occurred in March 1986.

In other words, the commercial ERs in Poland and Rumania convey some apposite information to planners, and trade statistics may be recorded at those rates rather than the official ones. However, these coefficients are only of limited use in reaching concrete decisions about trade and are probably a much weaker and less accurate link between domestic economic activity and foreign trade transactions than has been the case in Hungary since 1968. The chief reason for this will become apparent from a discussion of internal ERs.

Internal ER

The coefficient between domestic wholesale prices and the *valuta* or *deviza* values observed in trade or expected by price forecasters was established for the first time in the mid-1950s when the PEs began to explore trade as an active source of economic growth. Some created separate coefficients at least for ruble (or clearing currency) and dollar (or CC) transactions, but most eventually resorted explicitly or implicitly to an array of coefficients with the ostensible goal of influencing commercial decisions of selected enterprises involved with specific types of goods. Countries sought to tailor their rates specifically to economic branches, commodity groups, direction of trade, or currency zones. Some embraced the entire array of possible multiplicity enumerated here, and others attempted to restrict the number of coefficients to just a few. This multiplicity was resorted to in recognition of the serious distortions between domestic wholesale and CMEA trade prices, on the one hand, and CMEA prices and WMPs, on the other. Reluctant to embrace far-reaching price reforms, policy makers were compelled to tailor their decisions to relatively homogeneous products as a means of avoiding substantial windfall gains or losses for enterprises that would otherwise have had to be offset through a complex network of subsidies and taxes.

As noted, some countries combined the internal ERs with the official parity and created trade multipliers or even so-called commercial ERs. To the extent that reference is to the role of the coefficient in planning and entrepreneurial decisions, however, commercial and internal ERs should be kept separate. Although both normally have the same intrinsic starting value, policies regarding the periodic adaptation of these rates differ considerably and to varying degrees in the PEs that make use of them. In Hungary, for example, the dollar trade multiplier was periodically adjusted in line with parity changes in financial markets, but the initial values of the internal ERs were kept constant and the effective rates emerged implicitly from the frequent revisions in subsidies and taxes that were designed to keep enterprises or broad economic sectors profitable and to maintain domestic price autonomy. In Poland, however, no attempt appears to have been made to adjust the implicit multipliers in line with shifts in the official ER. Furthermore, the effective internal ERs emerged in a much more differentiated pattern than the two or three rates per currency zone tend to suggest. Subsidies and taxes were the main vehicles by which sector- or commodity-specific internal ERs emerged.

A surprising degree of inertia in adapting internal ERs to differential fluctuations in prices, not to mention considerable shifts in the commodity composition and geographical direction of exports, appears to be a feature of both the ruble and dollar commercial ERs for nearly all PEs. In ruble transactions, there are severe conceptual problems in the application of the internal ER. Not only do CMEA prices differ from domestic and world prices, the bulk of that trade is cleared bilaterally by government agencies. One may suspect therefore that the internal ERs for ruble transactions are not very good guides for economic decisions. In several PEs only the internal accounting of ruble trade proceeded at the ruble coefficient, but actual decisions relied on that rate only to a limited extent.

Effective internal ERs as unique policy instruments guiding trade decisions are usually not known.[19] In some PEs, including Rumania and the
Soviet Union, these rates are set not on the basis of actual prices of some
reference period but instead with reference to future plans for trade,
expected export returns and import costs, and the degree of shortage of
the particular currency in question (Šagalov 1986, p. 117). Nevertheless,
to the extent that they more or less correctly express relative price relations of a predetermined trade pattern of some period, they could be of
considerable use in obtaining realistic, if partial, purchasing power
parities.[20] But this is not the proper place to compile the discrete information that is sometimes cited in the pertinent Eastern European specialized literature. Some implicit overall dollar and ruble coefficients are
included in Table 6.3.

Noncommercial exchange rate

Access to CMEA markets is highly restricted and, for most purposes,
centrally controlled under the aegis of the MFT, which, as argued per-
suasively in Caffet and Lavigne 1985, should not necessarily be equated
with protectionism as commonly understood in MEs. However, PEs do
maintain at least minimal direct contacts with aliens, for instance, through
diplomatic, trade, and financial representations; family ties; tourism; student exchanges; private remittances; transfers of honoraria and royalties;
and so forth. Simple application of the official ER, although resorted to
in the postwar years, was not a very constructive solution because the
substantial differences in the level and structure of retail, wholesale, and
trade prices unavoidably entailed "nonequivalent exchange" among equal
partners.

Initially, the PEs opted to maintain special bilateral clearing accounts
for all forms of their mutual transactions not directly related to trade.[21]
Each country kept book of expenditures and receipts in each other's
currency, and periodically the imbalances were verified and eliminated,
usually by way of agreed deliveries of real goods (see Brabant 1977a, pp.
257–61). Because tourism was not at all actively encouraged and the
planners rigidly controlled market access, the sums involved remained
comparatively small. In any case, the windfall gains or losses were such
that they did not elicit strong pressure for reform.

Nevertheless, the issue became important from the mid-1950s on when,
under the lead of the USSR, the CMEA members worked out uniform
principles for the computation of bilateral noncommercial ERs. Imbalances on noncommercial accounts could in principle be converted at the
end of the calendar year into commercial units if the two PEs concerned
opted to do so (see Brabant 1977a, pp. 264–7 for details). The conversion coefficients were derived from a binary comparison of a market

basket of consumer goods and services that was bilaterally agreed upon. Such a basket involved component weights derived from the expenditure pattern of a "typical diplomatic family with four members." As a result, cross rates for noncommercial transactions were not uniform, and this divergence led to some friction during implementation. Also, it was agreed that the coefficients would be reviewed periodically. In particular, upon a change of 5 percent or more in the value of the reference basket, new coefficients were to be established automatically.

The gradually keener interest in fostering contacts among the PEs at a time of the discussions around *Basic Principles* made a uniform, consistent, and nearly automatic accounting of noncommercial transactions highly desirable. In 1963, twelve socialist countries (all present "traditional" socialist countries except Cuba and Yugoslavia) adopted a multilateral agreement that purported to set consistent noncommercial ERs. At the same time, a coefficient linking the Soviet domestic "consumer ruble" to the CMEA "commercial ruble" – later the TR – was created. This link permitted imbalances on noncommercial account to be settled, initially once a year but quarterly since early 1974 (Vincze 1978a, p. 22).[22] These rates were derived from a uniform sample of consumer goods and services evaluated in domestic prices of the participants and in CMEA trade prices.[23] The selected ERs, expressed relative to a unit of official currency, including the link for the Soviet ruble and the TR, are detailed in Table 6.1.

The 1963 system basically remained in force until early 1975[24] with two principal exceptions. First, in late 1971, another linking coefficient for the ruble (2.3 instead of 3.4) was introduced retroactively to 1 July 1971, though outstanding balances were to be converted at the old rate! Second, questions were occasionally raised as to whether "equivalent exchange" could be maintained by the original coefficients. Particularly the net exporters of tourist services felt almost from the beginning that they obtained the short end of the exchange because the standard sample reflected the expenditure pattern of tourists only inadequately. This shortcoming was expected to be gradually eliminated as the original agreement stipulated that the rates would have to be reviewed periodically to ensure equivalent exchange in time, and any change exceeding 5 percent from average prices in the base year should automatically trigger a revision of the coefficients. But no official revision could be agreed upon for years in spite of palpable changes in domestic and trade prices. The issue was on the agenda of several high-level meetings of the CMEA's SCFQ, but unanimity eluded the negotiators. Because the accounts were basically kept bilaterally and the balance could, but did not need to, be transferred to the commercial account at the IBEC from 1 January 1964 on, however, there was some scope for "ad hoc coefficients," and a number of PEs availed themselves of this opportunistic loophole (see VK 1986a, p. 4).[25]

In late 1974, Bulgaria, Czechoslovakia, the GDR, Hungary, Mongolia, and the USSR agreed upon the introduction of new coefficients on 1 March 1975.[26] Poland joined this system on 1 January 1976. Although not a signatory, Rumania appears to have joined the multilateral agreement implicitly as a result of bilateral agreements worked out in the spirit of the multilateral protocol (Špaček 1986, p. 14). The new rates were calculated on the basis of a revised methodology that, according to some, involved forty-five kinds of foodstuffs, twenty-six manufactured consumer goods, and twenty-one types of services all with specific weights (Vincze 1978a, pp. 75–76). Other reports (Špaček 1986, p. 12), however, suggest that those coefficients were derived from a dual purchasing power comparison. The "tourist" coefficient was established on the basis of a basket consisting of 83 items (45 foodstuffs, 19 manufactured consumer goods, and 19 services). The "diplomatic" coefficient, however, was derived from 114 items (56 foodstuffs and restaurant meal prices, 41 manufactured consumer goods, 16 types of services, and an unidentified item). Špaček states that these two coefficients were then aggregated in the proportion 65 percent for the tourist and 35 percent for the diplomatic coefficient, but that bilateral deviations were possible. This contradicts others, including Vincze (1978a, pp. 75–76), who contend that the new rates suffered also from serious bias. Although the PEs tried to improve the representativeness of the sample and approximate better the typical composition of noncommercial transactions within the CMEA area, the sampling procedures basically continued to favor the expenditure pattern of diplomats. The conflict in the cited and other reports probably stems largely from variations between recommended and applied methodologies and the particular time reference. These are unfortunately rarely specified to the degree of detail required.

In any case, many commentators have suggested that the bias in the coefficients towards diplomatic expenditures remained very marked. As a result, the new rates failed to meet the objections of the large net exporters of tourist services. It was therefore agreed that tourist transactions be treated separately from other noncommercial transactions, as discussed in the next section. For all intents and purposes, then, the system agreed upon in 1963 was kept intact with perhaps some fine tuning for other than tourist transactions proper. The members agreed too that any shift in national consumer prices exceeding 5 percent relative to the value of the basket adopted would have to be communicated to all signatories and new ERs would have to be established.

Since 1975, four further changes have been effectuated, although not all of them were agreed upon multilaterally. On 1 January 1978, the ruble-linking coefficient was reduced to 1.9,[27] in August 1981 to 1.7 – the latter becoming effective probably as of 1 January 1981, but the sources are ambiguous on that score[28] – and in January 1985 to 1.6. Further, in late 1981, the members apparently agreed upon new coefficients altogether. Unfortunately, the available information supports only major changes for the złoty, and other, minor changes appear to have been basically unsynchronized variations (Brabant 1985a, 1985d) on the old noncommercial parities to this day,[29] probably in view of the latitude for the wide margin around the central rates agreed upon. This bilateralization of ostensibly uniform "currency coefficients" continues to this day (Mrňa 1986).

Tourist exchange rate

It is very important to distinguish between organized and unorganized tourism, although in reality a mixture of the two is likely to prevail, especially in recent years. Organized tourism among PEs is usually regulated through bilateral agreements that specify the amount of local currency reciprocally placed at the disposal of official travel agencies. This is usually a subcomponent of the overall bilateral agreement on the amount of local currency to be made available during the year for noncommercial transactions and sometimes tourist transactions proper. Travelers pay the official travel agent in local currency and need to acquire the host country's currency only for out-of-pocket expenses. All kinds of unorganized interstate travel depend on the ability of individuals to obtain foreign currency officially or by stealth.

Organized tourist services are paid for in local currency and settled at the ministerial or banking level by official tourist organizations. Because of the inherent bilateral nature of the negotiations about the plan of the reciprocal exchange of tourist services for some period, effective ERs for such transactions are imprecise, subject as they are to pervasive bilateral bargaining. Because the effective ERs are really implicit in the reciprocal determination of available tour packages, they are not normally disclosed and will therefore not be further discussed here. It bears stressing, though, that organized tourism has traditionally accounted for the lion's share of the volume of intra-CMEA tourist transactions, although there may have been some slippage since the early 1970s.

Unorganized tourism has been highly circumscribed[30] by detailed passport controls and tight restrictions on the sums that can be freely exchanged for currency of another CMEA country (see Vincze 1978a, pp. 99–100). Although the currency of any signatory fraternal country, in principle, is available at the noncommercial ER (up to March 1963 at the bilateral and since April 1963 at the multilateral rates), actual tourist rates appear to depend heavily on the "tourist policy" of the individual PE concerned and, in particular, on the state of the bilateral noncommercial payments balance. The same holds with respect to the amount of currency that can be freely exchanged.

In late 1973, the CMEA members agreed upon a more flexible exchange regime that included a more generous maximum exchange limit,[31] new tourist ERs, and more comprehensive rules on the setting of such ERs. Together with the introduction of the new noncommercial rates in early 1975, the participating countries (including, since 1976, Poland and, implicitly, Rumania) can establish tourist ERs within a 10 percent band around the reference rates. In effect from 1 February 1980, this band can be expanded bilaterally to 20 percent around the central rate, at least for the countries that signed the multilateral agreement of late 1974.[32] Because such changes need not be coordinated with other partners, uniform cross rates for tourist transactions do not necessarily prevail. Note also that these rates are often not posted in published ER tables, so only direct participants may be apprised of the impact of the undisclosed actual policy measures.

Given the very confining controls on the ability of Eastern European citizens freely to acquire foreign exchange from other PEs and the frequent ad hoc adjustments introduced especially by the net exporters of tourist services, the tourist ERs are not even approximately accurate reflections of relative consumer prices in the various PEs. But they indicate actual relative prices of a select group of consumer goods and services in the benchmark period.

Joint investment exchange rates

Capital movements within Eastern Europe are usually conducted in real terms on a loan basis; repayment of principal and interest are also effected in real terms (see Chapter 9). In some cases, however, the PEs have deemed it profitable to establish common organizations either because no other form of exchange has proved to be acceptable,[33] other forms are simply not possible (such as in operating common banks), or it has been deemed desirable to enhance regional economic cooperation through joint organizations (for instance, Interatominstrument). To relax the complexity of arriving at a mutually satisfactory accounting for two PE partners (see Chapter 9), planners worked out the so-called Berlin method for evaluating the costs of joint investment or construction cooperation in 1964, and it has been periodically revised since. This method consists of disaggregating a project's total cost into various components. A sample of each is then translated into a common currency unit and aggregated.

With the establishment of the IIB in 1971 and the policy aim to foster SEI, also through common economic and other regional organizations, even the Berlin method as revised in 1972 proved to be too cumbersome to facilitate the creation and exploitation of joint undertakings. The PEs therefore explored the setting of special ERs for evaluating common

CMEA construction projects, which would help to promote SEI through production specialization possibly in joint ventures. Incidentally, *Integration Program* called for such ERs – a special form of internal ER for domestic currency per unit of "socialist currency" allocated to joint integration activities (see also Chapter 9). The first agreement on such special rates, endorsed in October 1973 (the Karl–Marx–Stadt agreement),[34] was to become effective in January 1974 "in order to raise the role of [the CMEA countries'] currency and financial relations, creating conditions for better determination of the efficacy of their economic relations, specialization and industrial cooperation, improvement of the mutual settlement of the accounts as well as possible introduction of the convertibility of the collective currency . . . and of their national currencies in future time."[35] The rates listed in column 3 of Table 6.1 could be used, if the members so decided, to ensure "equivalent exchange." Each member would notify the partners of a unilateral change in the internal ER of up to 5 percent either way, preserving the central cross rates with the TR. More substantial changes would have to be coordinated multilaterally among the partners.

The precise provenance of these rates has never been divulged satisfactorily, and it is therefore risky to assess unambiguously what these coefficients purport to measure and how realistic a guide they might be in deciding upon the potential for rational joint investments. Some commentators see these "investment ERs" as having been derived from the purchasing power parity calculations of traded goods (Konstantinov 1978a, p. 170; Válek 1984, p. 82). Vincze maintains that the SCFQ compared domestic producer prices and foreign trade prices of the "competitive, exportable parts of the national output" of the PEs (Vincze 1978a, pp. 71–73). However, for those (including Czechoslovakia, Hungary, Poland, and Rumania) known to have operated around that time with commercial ERs, overall reproduction coefficients, or internal ERs, it is beyond doubt that their "joint investment cooperation coefficient" coincided, but hardly fortuitously, with the internal ER established mostly in the late 1960s. These coefficients may have reflected realistic average price relations at the time they were computed, although that is not always beyond reasonable doubt (see Section 6.3). Nevertheless, they were already seriously out-of-date when introduced at home (such as in 1967–1968 in Czechoslovakia and Hungary) and could therefore not possibly adequately reflect current differences in trade and domestic price levels and structures. Even if these obstacles could have been overcome, the pronounced adjustments in domestic and especially in trade prices experienced since the mid-1970s quickly nullified whatever degree of realism these rates may still have reflected in 1973 (Válek 1984, p. 82). In fact, the original coefficients were so out of line with reality that soon after their promulgation considerable pressure arose to modify them.

New coefficients were worked out at least in 1975, 1977, 1981, and 1984 for introduction in the following year. Unfortunately, the precise magnitudes involved have not so far been quoted, but they are said to reflect changes in the "domestic wholesale prices in the individual countries and the contractual prices" (Janota 1985, p. 12). In any case, even the revised rates appear to have been applied in a "relatively small number of cases so far" (Válek 1981, p. 10), none of which has been divulged in the specialized literature. The same author notes in connection with the latest rates that further work on them is required in 1985 (Válek 1985, p. 11). It is therefore not surprising that these rates were, at best, applied "to a limited degree in 1975" (Vincze 1978a, p. 73), but later joint investment or production decisions have been based on bilateral rates that are themselves, more often than not, of multiple nature (see Georgiev, Kalčev, and Enev 1985, pp. 128–30). The daily operations of some IEOs, as often claimed in the Eastern European literature, might have been conducted partly on the basis of these rates. Because the field of operation of such organs has remained largely confined to plan coordination, however, nearly all operational expenses must have been incurred for wages and salaries. The standard recommendation has been to convert such expenditures at the noncommercial rate, which, when converted to the commercial TR, is far less favorable than the investment coefficient.

Miscellaneous exchange rates

Miscellaneous ERs include rates that may be highly important to very specific operations but can hardly be indicative of purchasing power parities or equilibrium ERs for all foreign transactions. They are only of parenthetical interest, and the discussion can therefore be very concise.

The black market ER is especially important as a source of foreign exchange to supplement the strictly limited amount of currency that can be acquired by residents for travel abroad or to purchase selected goods in special shops. Because there is no organized market, the rates fluctuate widely and can hardly be indicative of overall economic conditions. Second, many PEs have a private internal ER, which is especially important in foreign currency shops, where only coupons or vouchers can be used. These shops usually provide goods not otherwise available at rates that are more favorable than the official ones, but not quite as attractive as those obtainable by CC owners. Third, special-purpose shops in the PEs occasionally offer local products to holders of foreign currency at an especially favorable "special store ER."[36] This normally applies only to CC payments, however. Fourth, work crews from a fraternal PE are usually compensated at especially favorable rates (see Chapter 9) either to mask the rather high pay received in comparison with resident workers or to maintain sufficient incentives to attract such specialized skills to other PEs.[37]

Although apparently exceptional in itself, the special-purpose noncommercial ER for construction crews is not really that unique. It is rather a symptom of a much more convoluted system of regulations regarding the private exchange of currency that are in effect in the CMEA. Persistent problems with shopping sprees, excessive demand for tourist services, particularly in Hungary and the Balkan countries, problems with offsetting noncommercial imbalances, and other such issues have contributed to rendering any multilateral agreement about tourist ERs and foreign exchange limitations largely inoperative.

For a number of PEs that have invested heavily in a modern tourist infrastructure, tourism is really a "hard commodity" that should be traded only against equivalent goods or CC. Further, especially when retail markets are already strained as a result of production and import constraints, consumer goods and services, in general, become even harder and the authorities are therefore less inclined to tolerate shopping sprees by residents from soft currency countries. Instead of adhering fully to multilateral agreements, several PEs have fallen back upon the well-tried system of bilateralized settlements also for noncommercial transactions over which they have direct control, including tourism.[38] Although such arrangements are most inflexible, based as they are on cumbersome negotiations and distorted economics of the relevant transactions, bilateral agreements have proved to be a reliable means of controlling CMEA payments and receipts for tourist services and avoiding unexpected windfall losses. If, in the end, demand suddenly surges beyond the agreed upon limits, ad hoc target restrictions on travel, including special taxes on the exchange of a particular currency,[39] passport duties, and other such hindrances in effect severely compress "tourist demand."

6.5 Exchange regime for convertible currency transactions

In East–West trade, the PEs settle their foreign transactions in principle in CC. Because they do not utilize their own currencies abroad, the rate at which the national currency of a PE can be exchanged against currencies of MEs is a domestic matter of the PEs and not really subject to regulations that govern the currency ERs of MEs. This is a key characteristic to be retained for the discussion of the role of the PEs in the BWS or its successor (see Chapter 7).

Convertible currency is truly a "hard commodity" in Eastern Europe. Its exchange regime is generally much less diversified than that for the TR, which has no independent functions (see Chapter 8). It is perhaps in the very nature of clearing currencies to call for somewhat more complex regulations. Because by definition they deny the existence of a number of foreign exchange problems, transactions factored into the clearing regime must be dealt with by way of ad hoc adjustments. Furthermore, the absence of organized markets by necessity leads to a wide range of "hard" and "soft" goods and services, at least implicitly. It is useful to distinguish among the official, the commercial, the tourist, the internal, the support, and the travel ER. Each will be surveyed in sequence. Because overall exchange policies and general principles of ER determination have been discussed in the two preceding sections, the analysis here can be kept to the strict minimum.

The official exchange rate

The determination of the official ER for CC parallels that identified in Section 6.4: Until the gradual dissolution of the BWS, the gold parity fixed in the postwar period set the dollar ER and by inference all other ERs. The response of the PEs to the dollar devaluations of 1971 and 1973 and the floating parity regime since has been unsynchronized and mixed, as illustrated in Table 6.2. Generally speaking, most countries appreciated their currency after 1971 and 1973 in exact proportion to the changed dollar–gold parity, although in some cases with a considerable lag, which at least for a while entailed a de facto "sympathetic" devaluation. Since then, some have largely held on to the 1973 rates (the GDR until 1979 and, by and large, Poland and Rumania until 1977–1978); others pegged their ER at first to the dollar, but more recently to a basket of CCs (between nine and thirteen reference currencies are used by the PEs that have disclosed details). With the exception of the GDR and Rumania, all PEs have in the past three to four years gradually switched over to frequent (monthly, biweekly, and even weekly) ER quotations in line with the evolving conditions in international financial markets. But true revisions in the value of the currency basket have been rare (see Table 6.2),[40] and some PEs do not fully adjust the various currency ERs to shifts observed in international financial markets. In an ME, this situation would be quickly exploited by arbitrageurs. But there is only very limited room for this type of operation in the PE context, as examined in Chapters 1 and 2.

As for the reciprocal official ERs of the PE currencies, the official rates against CCs are practically without significance, except as noted for ruble-denominated transactions. The latter are especially relevant for PEs that have no special tourist ERs, as in the Soviet Union. In most instances, each PE's official ER, which by and large has remained measurably overvalued against CCs, applies only to the conversion of foreign trade statistics into a uniform but notional currency unit and, by implication in most cases, the price-equalization account. In the GDR and countries with proper internal ERs, even the price-equalization accounts have been based on one or more different ERs. In the past few years, a shift in recording trade statistics has emerged. First, Hungary transformed its trade multipliers into official commercial ERs in 1976 and started recording trade statistics at those rates. Second, Rumania followed the Hungarian example in 1981. Finally, with the devaluation of the złoty in 1982, Poland switched its trade statistics, beginning with 1981, over to the commercial quotations. As discussed, the trade multipliers implied a strong devaluation of the TR against the dollar. As a result, the transformation of the trade multipliers or internal ERs into commercial rates did not preserve the cross-rate uniformity typical of the official ER regime.

A related issue is the CC rate of the TR. This may be minor from an economic point of view, but the problem is obviously to be heeded in order to interpret correctly data furnished by a number of CMEA institutions and computations underlying pricing and other valuations for CMEA transactions (see Chapter 4). Initially, the TR was set equal to the Soviet *valuta* ruble. Although the relationship was not explicit, adjustments to dollar changes appear to have been synchronized with those of the Soviet *valuta* ruble until about 1974. With generalized CC floating, the TR is said to have been quoted at the "factual" value of foreign currencies, but in practice this amounted to little more than imitating Soviet quarterly and, since 1975, monthly quotations (Konstantinov 1978a, pp. 155–7; Beličenko and Matjuchin 1983, p. 103). The latter were at first based on the dollar, but beginning in November 1977 they were based on the simple arithmetic average changes of thirteen CCs (Konstantinov 1978a, p. 47). Starting with July 1978, but effectively introduced in IBEC's transactions only as of 1 January 1979, IBEC started to adjust the value of the TR, apparently on a monthly basis, in line with the weighted change in the value of the basket of thirteen currencies.[41] Because the weights of these currencies in TR transactions differ from those applicable to the USSR's foreign trade, a possibly significant gap between the dollar value of the TR and that of the Soviet ruble may emerge (Brabant 1985c). In January 1985, for example, this amounted to a 5.84 percent agio for the Soviet ruble.

The commercial exchange rate

The observations pertaining to the commercial rates of CCs parallel those applicable to the TR regime. That for the GDR was explained there as a peculiarly special case. In view of the inherently greater importance of proper accounting in CC than TR transactions and the role the economic reforms of the 1960s sought to allot to fostering trade with CC partners, the PEs generally developed internal ERs for the latter type of trade relations earlier, computed them with greater circumspection, and endowed the rules governing their behavior with greater flexibility[42] than

Table 6.2. *Official exchange rates of Eastern European currencies, 1970–1985*

Region	1970	1971	1972	1973	1974	1975	1976	1977
Bulgaria[a]	1.170	1.170	1.078	0.988	0.970	0.966	0.969	0.948
Czechoslovakia[b]	7.200	7.200	6.622	5.895	5.859	5.775	5.581	5.671
GDR[c]	2.223	2.223	2.061	1.868	1.842	1.842	1.842	1.842
Hungary[d]	11.740	11.740	10.812	9.620	9.148	[8.134]	8.604	8.026]
Poland[e]	4.000	4.000	3.680	3.365	3.320	3.320	3.320	3.320
Rumania[f]	6.000	6.000	5.520	5.062	4.970	4.970	4.970	4.970
USSR[g]	0.900	0.900	0.823	0.743	0.758	0.754	0.722	0.736
IBEC's TR[h]	0.900	0.900	0.823	0.743	0.758	0.754	0.722	0.737

Region	1978	1979	1980	1981	1982	1983	1984	1985
Bulgaria[a]	0.892	0.865	0.857	0.922	0.951	0.974	1.010	1.032
Czechoslovakia[b]	5.415	5.317	5.371	5.882	6.094	6.293	6.641	6.857
GDR[c]	1.842	1.842	1.747	1.757	1.826	1.874	1.927	i
Hungary[d]	[7.416	6.961	6.386	6.714	7.167	8.348	9.400	9.800]
Poland[e]	3.244	3.095	3.049	3.350	j	j	j	j
Rumania[f]	4.574	4.470	4.470	4.470	4.470	4.470	4.470	4.470
USSR[g]	0.681	0.656	0.649	0.719	0.726	0.743	0.816	0.837
IBEC's TR[h]	0.684	0.660	0.654	0.711	0.741	0.758	0.787	0.812

Note: A number of rate changes occurred either at the very end or at the very beginning of the calendar year. In most cases, no adjustments were made for the few days concerned.

[a] Time-weighted average of quotations in *Dúržaven vestnik*.

[b] Time-weighted average of quotations in *Hospodářské Noviny* and *Svět Hospodářství*.

[c] Gold parity as quoted in *Statistická ročenka Československé socialistické republiky, 1984* (Prague: SNTL 1985), p. 174, adjusted by the same relatives as for the commercial ER in Table 6.3.

[d] Time-weighted average of quotations in *Magyar Közlöny* and *Népszabadság*; since 1976, commercial rates adjusted by old internal ER. Because the latter are my inferences, I am enclosing them in brackets.

[e] Time-weighted average of quotations in *Tabela Kursów*, circulated by the Polish National Bank.

[f] Time-weighted average of quotations in *România Liberă* and *International Financial Statistics*.

[g] Time-weighted average of quotations in *Ėkonomičeskaja gazeta* and *Izvestija*.

[h] Time-weighted average of quotations mostly in *Bjulleten' inostrannoj kommerčeskoj informacii* and *Svět Hospodářství*.

[i] Not available.

[j] Not applicable.

has been so for the TR. Nonetheless, few PEs have succeeded in maintaining up-to-date and accurate CC quotations in the sense of preserving a proper relationship between external and local costs at least for traded goods and services. In view of the substantial fluctuations in WMPs and the much more muted target shifts in domestic prices and price policies in most PEs, it appears rather far-fetched to assume that the present commercial ERs (see Table 6.3) even approximately reflect the equilibrium dollar ER for traded goods. The Hungarian authorities, however, have followed an active ER policy since the mid-1970s in an attempt to offset on average the price increases experienced in CC trade. The Hungarian commercial ERs, especially those recently enacted, would therefore tend to approach purchasing power, perhaps with an identical bias as that present in the early 1970s.

Tourist exchange rate

The substantial dichotomy between the tourist and other noncommercial exchange regimes in TR relations does not have an immediate counterpart in CC transactions. Diplomatic expenditures and remittances from abroad are normally converted either at the official rate or at one pegged to the gold parity, as for the exchange of CC for unorganized tourist services.[43] However, unlike the ruble tourist ER, there is much greater asymmetry in CC rates applicable for resident and nonresident tourists.

The need for differentiating between areas where the official ER performs only nominal functions from areas where it has a bearing on allocatory decisions is particularly important with regard to the earning of CC from tourism.[44] Some PEs clearly seek to capitalize on their natural resources and are therefore bent on attracting tourists inter alia by declaring a favorable ER, particularly when earnings can be exchanged for "hard commodities" or CC. Other PEs deliberately seek to limit contact with foreigners and are therefore more likely to embrace all means, including overvalued ERs, to discourage tourism. In view of palpable changes in this policy stance over time, tourist ERs have exhibited fluctuations unrelated to shifts in relative costs. As with the TR regime, a sharp distinction should be drawn between organized and unorganized tourism. A country bent on promoting tourism is likely to declare a more favorable ER in the former than in the latter case, and vice versa. The argument in the former case is presumably that the gap between the black market and official organized tourist rates needs to be bridged by offering a positive premium to persuade customers of tourist services to pay for most of the local expenditures in CC directly to the state banking system.

Regarding ERs for unorganized tourism, the Soviet union has not differentiated between commerce and tourism since the 1961 currency revaluation-cum-monetary reform, the GDR does not at all differentiate, Bulgaria suspended the tourist premium between 1975 and 1978, and all other PEs provide some positive margin over the official ER but not necessarily over the commercial ER. As shown in Table 6.4, this premium can be considerable – in Poland, for example, it amounted to ten times the basic official rate until the devaluation of the złoty in January 1982.

Because the PEs normally[45] specify premiums as a percentage of the official ER, fluctuations in the latter are reflected also in the tourist ERs. It is therefore somewhat more convenient to focus on the tourist premiums than to tabulate exact ER fluctuations during the period of concern here. Because most magnitudes that one wishes to convert have an annual time dimension, Table 6.4 is a compromise: It specifies time series of average tourist rates and summarizes the premium rates in the footnotes.

The travel ER for residents

Because most PEs are chronically short of foreign exchange, they seek to discourage the CC demand by residents, especially for private trips abroad.[46] The PEs usually discourage movements abroad of their nationals through a vast network of formal and informal controls, including passport requirements and taxes, maximum CC allocations during a given time period, and other such deterrents. In addition, PEs normally allow residents to acquire CC at a vastly higher rate than either the official, commercial, or nonresident tourist ER. Thus, In Czechoslovakia the resident travel rate equals the official rate augmented with a 125 percent tax and 125 percent administrative fee. In Poland, the resident travel rate used to be the effective official rate, which was six times the official gold parity rate, augmented with a 150 percent tax.[47] In Rumania, CC is normally available to residents, naturally within the narrow limits on allocations, at twice the tourist rate for foreign residents. Finally, since late 1981, Hungary is the only PE that sells a limited amount of CC at the "commercial rate."

The exchange rate in foreign currency shops

Especially during the first half of the 1970s, virtually all PEs began to provide one outlet or another for CC purchases by nonresidents and sometimes by residents as well. Such shops normally sell mostly foreign food and other consumer goods at "duty free" prices. In most instances, the precise ER is unknown because prices are fixed directly in CC, or else they pertain only to purchases against CC or vouchers that are then converted at the tourist ER.[48] Some countries, however, also apply a special unannounced ER that one discovers only by chance.[49] It is impossible to tabulate those rates because they are not publicly quoted.

Table 6.3. *Commercial exchange rates for Eastern European currencies, 1970–1985 (local currency per U.S. dollar or ruble)*

	1970	1971	1972	1973	1974	1975	1976	1977
German Democratic Republic[a]								
Dollar	4.200	4.200	3.870	3.480	3.480	3.480	3.480	3.480
Ruble	4.667	4.667	4.667	4.667	4.667	4.667	4.667	4.667
Hungary[b]								
Dollar	[60.000]	60.000	55.257	49.165	46.753	43.973]	41.570	41.020
Ruble	[40.000]	40.000	40.000	40.000	40.000	40.000]	35.000	35.000
Poland[c]								
Dollar	[24.000]	60.000	55.200	50.475	49.800	49.800	43.160	43.160]
Ruble	[40.000]	40.000	40.000	40.000	40.000	40.000	40.000	40.000]
Rumania[d]								
Dollar	[24.000]	24.000	24.000]	20.000	20.000[e]	20.000	20.000	20.000
Ruble	[20.000]	20.000	20.000	20.000]	18.000	18.000[f]	18.000	18.000

	1978	1979	1980	1981	1982	1983	1984	1985
German Democratic Republic[a]								
Dollar	3.480	3.480	3.300	3.320	3.450	3.540	3.640	[g]
Ruble	4.667	4.667	4.667	4.667	4.667	4.667	4.667	4.667
Hungary[b]								
Dollar	37.902	35.578	32.641	34.314	36.631	42.668	48.042	50.119
Ruble	33.250	32.000	27.792	26.839	26.000	26.000	26.000	26.650

228

Poland[c]								
Dollar	[42.172]	40.235	44.211	48.575]	84.809	91.566	113.630	147.168
Ruble	[40.000]	40.000	40.000	40.000]	68.000	68.000	71.333	83.417
Rumania[d]								
Dollar	18.333	18.000	18.000	15.000	15.000	17.054	21.280	17.142
Ruble	18.000	18.000	18.000	15.000	15.000	17.000	17.167	15.500

Note: A number of rate changes occurred either at the very end or at the very beginning of the calendar year. In most cases, no adjustments were made for the few days concerned.

[a] Implied average rate between dollar data reported to the United Nations Statistical Office and official trade data in Valutamark. The ruble rate was derived by means of the official cross rate before the collapse of the BWS.

[b] Dollar and ruble rates since 1976 are the time-weighted averages of the quotations in *Magyar Közlöny* and *Népszabadság*. The rates for the period up to 1975 in the case of the dollar are inferred from the multiplier introduced in 1968 and the shifts in the official dollar rate; similarly for the ruble. Strictly speaking, of course, no commercial ERs existed before 1975, and I am therefore enclosing them in brackets.

[c] For 1970, the effective official rate was used. This differed from the tourist rate until 1 February 1978, as quoted in *Tabela Kursów*, circulated by the Polish National Bank. For later years, I have computed "commercial ERs" by relating the internal ERs discussed in Section 6.3 to the official ER. A proper commercial rate was introduced only in 1982, and I am therefore enclosing the earlier rates in brackets.

[d] More like an internal ER until 1978, when it started to be used in foreign trade accounting and, to some extent, trade decisions of selected enterprises. The dollar rates for 1970–1972 and the ruble rates for 1970–1973 are the export rates quoted in Jackson 1976, p. 129. Because these rates are not comparable to the other data, they are bracketed.

[e] Introduced on 3 December 1973.

[f] Introduced on 1 November 1974.

[g] Not available.

Table 6.4. *Average tourist exchange rates for convertible currencies, 1970–1985 (local currency per U.S. dollar)*

	1970	1971	1972	1973	1974	1975	1976	1977
Bulgaria[a]	2.000	2.000	1.843	1.689	1.574	1.161	0.966	0.948
Czechoslovakia[b]	16.200	16.200	14.900	13.264	10.253	9.767	10.106	9.924
GDR[c]	3.660	3.428	3.182	2.673	2.588	2.460	2.518	2.322
Hungary[d]	30.000	30.000	27.629	24.582	23.377	21.986	20.785	20.510
Poland[e]	40.000	40.000	36.800	33.650	33.200	33.200	33.200	33.200
Rumania[f]	18.000	18.000	16.000	14.646	13.785	12.000	12.000	12.000
USSR[g]	0.900	0.900	0.823	0.743	0.758	0.722	0.754	0.736

	1978	1979	1980	1981	1982	1983	1984	1985
Bulgaria[a]	1.024	1.298	1.286	1.383	1.427	1.753	1.818	1.858
Czechoslovakia[b]	9.476	9.305	9.399	10.294	10.665	11.013	11.622	12.000
GDR[c]	2.009	1.833	1.818	2.260	2.427	2.553	2.846	2.944
Hungary[d]	18.951	21.707	22.191	30.965	36.631	42.668	48.042	50.119
Poland[e]	32.440	30.950	30.490	33.500	84.809	91.566	113.630	147.168
Rumania[f]	12.000	12.000	12.000	11.125	11.012	13.120	14.013	12.241
USSR[g]	0.681	0.656	0.649	0.719	0.726	0.743	0.816	0.837

[a] At a 70 percent premium over the dollar ER, which was reduced on 1 November 1974 to 23.7 percent and abolished on 1 November 1975. A new premium of 50 percent was introduced on 13 June 1978 and revised to 80 percent on 1 January 1983.

[b] At a 125 percent premium until 1973. As of 1 January 1974, the premium was revised to 75 percent.

[c] No special tourist rate. However, such rates are normally quoted at parity with the West German mark. The rates listed here are the latter's average ERs to the dollar as quoted in *International Financial Statistics*.

[d] The tourist forint was set at double the value of the commercial forint until 15 February 1979, when it was reduced to 1.75. Beginning in 1980, the gap was gradually reduced and eliminated altogether as of 1 October 1981.

[e] Basically ten times the "basic rate," which is the gold parity quoted until the end of 1981.

[f] A premium of 200 percent was in effect until 28 December 1971, when it was reduced implicitly to 189.30 percent. It was further adjusted on 2 October 1974 to 141.45 percent, on 6 March 1978 to 168.46 percent, on 16 February 1981 to 146.09 percent, and on 29 December 1982 to 179.64 percent. Since 1 October 1983, the tourist exchange rate has been quoted without explicit reference to the official or commercial ERs. The data for 1983–1985 are from *International Financial Statistics*, but I have no information as to the underlying changes.

[g] No tourist ERs. Rates listed here are identical to the official gold rates.

Sources: As listed in Table 6.2.

Exchange rates for private remittances

To encourage citizens to deposit their CC holdings and foreigners to send private gifts, some PEs (including Poland, but the phenomenon appears to be more widespread) have made arrangements for special exchange facilities for private currency remittances, especially for pensioners.[50] Usually, the ER for such private remittances from abroad when converted into local currency, as distinct from special vouchers, is substantially more attractive to the holder of foreign currency than the official one, but as a rule less so than the tourist rate for foreign residents. But matters vary, as for the 100 percent bonus in Czechoslovakia, which was also applicable to diplomats. Similarly, Poland until 1978 had several special rates for remittances from abroad: Social security payments to U.S. pensioners in Poland (as well as expenditures by diplomats) could be converted at sixty złotych to the dollar until mid-1975, when it was reduced to forty-five; in February 1978, these special rates were abolished and merged with the effective official rate, which was ten times the "basic rate."

Miscellaneous rates

There are undoubtedly several other types of CC transactions that are expressed in local currency at ERs that differ from any of the several enumerated here. Three are worth mentioning. First, for many East–West ventures case by case arrangements are made for the bilateral transfer of currency at special rates that may well be only implicit in the agreement. Most of these are rather exceptional cases and ad hoc, much like organized tourism. Second, ERs in black currency markets are particularly important. They are especially volatile when regulations for private visits to CC countries are relaxed, but the restrictions on legal exchange limits remain tight; when the divergence between consumer supplies in official and other "open" retail markets and in secondary markets or in special currency shops widens; when tensions in the country rise (as during a political crisis); and other such extraordinary circumstances. The very special nature of these rates cannot commend them for conversions of any but a narrow CC demand and supply at a given time in a specific market.[51] Although Eastern European currencies are not convertible, a few Western money markets, and indeed some specialized retail shops, trade in virtually all PE currencies. The rates established here are similar to those prevailing in black local markets with the proviso that the narrow supply of such currencies is conditioned by the special circumstances under which Eastern European citizens travel to CC markets and the narrow demand by the venturesomeness of mostly nonresident tourists who, with some risk, hope to take advantage of exceptionally favorable rates.

6.6 The role of the exchange rate in adjustment

Because the scope for the transmission of adjustment incentives through the price mechanism, including ERs, is limited and not accessible in the short run (see Chapter 3), planners have recently undertaken (1) very minor changes, if at all, in the TR rates at least for pure merchandise transactions; (2) monthly, biweekly, weekly, or even daily variations in relative CC values in accordance with the weights of the currencies in the PE's imports and fluctuations in world financial markets; and (3) infrequent rescaling of the value of the CC basket against which ERs are set. In other words, a TR exchange policy has been, on the whole, nonexistent. Certainly, Hungary followed some such policy in 1978–1981 but abandoned it, possibly owing to subtle political pressures to keep the TR even in forints high and stable. It may have made a fresh start in September 1985. But the chief cause of the policy failure was undoubtedly that the institutional and organizational characteristics of the trade and payments regime within Eastern Europe obviated the practical application of a positive ER policy. Similarly, both Poland and Rumania have changed their evaluation of the TR on several occasions since the introduction of commercial ERs. The latter two de facto devaluations and the earlier revaluation of the forint were probably more inspired by considerations about price equalization than by the perceived need to induce adjustments in the external sectors.

Even in Hungary – the PE with perhaps the most liberalized price and foreign exchange regime – the ER has only marginally contributed to changes in domestic relative prices. This derives in part from the system of price determination and in part from the bargaining of enterprises with the center over the particular reference base of their domestic prices. Because domestic industrial prices are, in principle, pegged to the relevant import or export prices in CC markets (see Chapter 5), many domestic prices of traded goods move up or down uniformly in tandem with the recent depreciation or appreciation of the forint. The structural effect normally associated with a devaluation (see Chapter 3) has been minimal in Hungary. This is, therefore, an instance in which the pricing system reduces the effectiveness of the ER as an instrument of resource allocation, especially in the foreign sector.[52] Such a foreign exchange policy is unlikely to help stabilize the PE and implement adjustments under prevailing conditions. With perhaps the exception of Hungary, I find it difficult to imagine that the ER could play any substantive role in molding structural changes in the next five years or so. In sum, short of the transformation of these countries into real MPEs, the scope for active ER policies with respect to merchandise trade remains very constricted indeed.

The nature of the recent economic disequilibria in some PEs and the obstacles encountered in surmounting them, as discussed in Chapter 3, suggest that the authorities could gain considerable mileage from the removal of price distortions, including those resulting from trade impediments and improper ERs. Such a recommendation entails the formulation of a positive structural adjustment program. The majority of PEs appear to have decided that such a strategy cannot be successfully implemented without indirect coordination instruments, including an active price and ER policy. In setting up an appropriate program, it needs to be recognized that several key PEs are likely to continue to behave according to quite different rules. The most critical variables in forecasting ERs in Eastern Europe, regardless of the horizon one is willing to work with, therefore include (1) the adjustment policies that individual PEs are currently debating for near-term implementation; (2) the greatest common denominator of such policies among "important" CMEA members; (3) the differences between the contemplated policies and present realities; (4) the climate for East–West economic relations; and (5) the state of global economic and financial interdependence.

Regarding the first variable, note that the positive adjustment policies currently being contemplated range from doing relatively minor streamlining, as in the GDR, to emulating the Hungarian type of economic decentralization, as in Poland. With the exception of perhaps the USSR, all PEs can be expected to improve the significance of ERs or their surrogates in the future and to widen the areas in which these parameters influence prices, plan decisions at the micro- and/or macroeconomic level, and enterprise and actual economywide policies, possibly including intra-CMEA relations. Irrespective of desirable policy goals for the remainder of the decade, the PEs are unlikely to be able to bridge fully the sharp differences in their present economic mechanisms.

The extent to which individual PEs may be able to shorten the distance towards decentralized decision making in the next five years or so varies importantly with the degree to which CMEA partners are bent on improving their economic mechanisms. The Hungarian experience has amply demonstrated that there are formidable limits to what a small country can accomplish with indirect decisions when over half of its trade, and perhaps one fifth of its aggregate output,[53] depends on partners whose modes of behavior diverge markedly from market-type decision making.

The mileage on the road toward genuine economic reform that individual PEs may attempt to cover depends also on comprehensive transformations in CMEA institutions, behavioral rules, and policy objectives that may be in the offing. However, because the ultimate decision-making bodies in the CMEA are the individual CPs, formal changes in the CMEA cooperation mechanisms matter less than what is common in the transitions contemplated by the member countries. One major element of the answer should be how to bridge the relative distortions emerging from that market, possibly through ad hoc taxes and subsidies that move TR prices towards WMP levels or, at least, up to the level of a more operational system of domestic prices.[54] Another important component of structural adjustment might be effective production specialization within the context of the CMEA.

Inasmuch as a sizable share of each PE's total trade and the bulk of imported industrial inputs are transacted within the CMEA, where prices differ from those in domestic and East—West relations, the adjustment problem is far more complex than simply changing one or more applicable ERs. The dichotomy between TR prices and WMPs discussed earlier clearly illustrates that planning authorities cannot implement a uniform ER regime to support some overriding macroeconomic policy goal. Domestic price liberalization and harmonization of domestic with world prices are both incompatible with TR prices, unless volume and price of all three elements of the equation can be adjusted. This is evidently not the case for the bulk of TR transactions. Shifts in enterprise behavior in response to changes in foreign prices result either in the violation of CMEA trade contracts or in unfulfilled demand or supply constraints, and must be averted. Measures will therefore have to be taken to insulate against CMEA markets that continue to operate as a traditional CPE. What to do about this vexing problem is crucial with respect to policy formulations in the future. I shall revisit these issues in Chapter 12.

The implications with respect to ERs of these various determinants of Eastern Europe's economic policies in the next five years or so complicate a clear-cut forecast, especially at this unstable juncture in CMEA relations. Qualitatively speaking, the PEs are bound to improve the ER's role in management and planning, to seek a modernization of the financial and currency mechanisms of the TR zone at least up to par with the greatest common denominator of the role of money and the ER in the majority of PEs, to enhance the transferability of the TR and possibly the national currencies, and perhaps to explore partial convertibility. I turn now to these issues.

7

Eastern Europe in the world monetary system

As explained in Chapter 1, World War II and its aftermath proved to be an important watershed in profiling Eastern Europe internationally. Soon after the outbreak of the Cold War, the socialist countries severed nearly all contacts with international organizations in which also MEs participated. For the most important operational organizations, this took the form of a formal withdrawal. In others, especially those with a more intergovernmental character, including the General Agreement on Tariffs and Trade (GATT) and the United Nations and its affiliated specialized agencies, membership was not relinquished altogether. But active participation in the deliberations of these organs or in the execution of their mandate ceased for years. The PEs did so for a variety of reasons. In some cases, these organizations were not really suited to the political or economic purposes of the PEs. In others, though they could have participated in a fruitful manner, the PEs did not largely for political reasons.

A gradual rapprochement between the advanced MEs and the PEs began in some cases as early as the mid-1950s. In others, the whittling of what stood in the way of a more active involvement in the institutionalized forms of international economic affairs started later. By the mid-1970s, however, most PEs had jettisoned virtually all of their earlier inhibitions in principle to participate in international organizations, even those that had previously been characterized as archetypically capitalistic in nature. In the process, some became full members while others continued actively to reexamine their positions regarding these institutions; some even started to agitate for a reform of these organizations from without.

The degree of interest shown in particular for the multilateral financial organizations took a quantum leap with the sequence of world economic disturbances that started in 1973. Though well aware that more active intermeshing with such interdependent trading and financial regimes would not provide a panacea for their own economic and other ills, some

PEs were hoping nonetheless to derive important gains from membership. Of special interest in this evolving process of East–West economic relations are questions such as how the PEs fit into, or could participate in, the IMS and how they have viewed the chief instruments associated with the BWS, which form the subject matter of this chapter.[1]

Because few instances can be identified when the PEs as a group endorsed a common platform on the IMS and related matters, I shall first briefly clarify the evolution of the policy stances and attitudes of the PEs vis-à-vis the BWS. The reaction of the PEs to Bretton Woods is examined in Section 7.1. Some crucial incompatibilities between the PEs and the BWS, when it was created, arose largely from disagreements among the major powers over the postwar international economic and political order. But there are also genuine systemic obstacles to closer cooperation between the two, as I shall demonstrate in Section 7.2. Other problems associated with key features of the BWS that clash either with the economic characteristics of the PEs or, more likely, with their political postures or ideological precepts are investigated in Section 7.3. The official position of the PEs on an eventual reform of the BWS in the context of the fundamental international policy topics of the NIEO is discussed next. Section 7.5 examines aspects related to the participation of PEs in the IMS. Finally, specific pointers on a reformed IMS are summarized in an áttempt to arrive at a more comprehensive picture of where the PEs stand on the IMS and how they could participate more fully in such a modified system.

7.1 The socialist countries and Bretton Woods

The pillars of the IMS, as it emerged after World War II, have been the IMF, which takes care of transitory payments difficulties, and IBRD, which provides structural finance. An agreed upon exchange regime and a shared system for balance-of-payments financing administered under the guidance of the Fund as prerequisites for surmounting the conditions that led to the calamitous trade policies of the 1930s were the paramount philosophical precepts of the BWS. Key objectives of the BWS therefore concerned convertibility, multilateralism, and equilibrium ERs that function as real prices. For countries in need of reconstruction or development finance, the IBRD was designed to redeploy funds from various origins. There are other important ingredients of the BWS as conventionally understood, but the foregoing chief features suffice for now.

The PEs have traditionally been important missing actors in the BWS; but some actively participated in the debates about the Fund's creation – indeed Czechoslovakia and Poland were founding members.[2] However, by the time the key institutional and policy features of the typical CPE were fully in place, for all practical purposes, the socialist countries ignored the BWS, and Czechoslovakia and Poland formally withdrew.[3]

For many years the PEs shunned the Washington organizations and were most critical of a number of their institutional and behavioral features. The latter were felt to have been put in place chiefly for the benefit of a select few developed MEs, which were allegedly seeking dominance through currency hegemony or through the insistence upon a distribution of voting power in the management of these organizations that ran counter to the respect for greater equity in international life, on which most PEs insist as a matter of principle.[4] But attitudes have changed markedly. Certainly, the PEs do not have a clear-cut position on an IMS that they could fully support. Yet they have formulated some proposals on the matters at hand that should not be ignored, if only because some have interesting features. Furthermore, it is always worth the effort to explore ways in which the PEs could be integrated more comprehensively into the global economy. Finally, these reform proposals have been tendered not only because the PEs have some interest in integrating themselves more fully in the IMS. Some have looked more closely at the IMS once they started to feel the adverse effects of their indebtedness to Western private financial institutions at a time of rising interest rates, cutbacks in the availability of rollovers and loans, and a very soft export market. Their views on desirable reforms of the IMS should therefore not be downplayed.

The postwar history of the involvement of CMEA countries with the world's monetary system can be divided essentially into four periods: (1) the early stages that eventually led to the creation of the IMF and the IBRD, (2) the severing of most international relations outside the CMEA framework, (3) the exploration of ways of joining these monetary institutions, and (4) the experiences of the countries that did participate or continue to participate actively in the multilateral financial institutions.

Negotiations about the Bretton Woods system

Several socialist countries were important participants in the preparation, or even in the early activities, of the BWS. The USSR as the then only socialist country, aside from Mongolia, was especially active in the deliberations about the fundamental aims and prerogatives of the global institutions. In the debates that led up to the creation of the Fund, the USSR tended to favor the Keynes Plan over the White Plan. The former aimed at overcoming trade bilateralism and the deflationary bias of the gold standard by providing for the unrestricted clearing of each member's credit and debit balances, and for automatic credit financing through a clearing union (Triffin 1957, pp. 93ff.). The White Plan envisaged similar goals but without the creation of a powerful international monetary authority. It was this proposal that was adopted with some modifications.

However, in subsequent criticism the USSR did not always make clear which of the plans it considered as the lesser evil.[5]

During the initial negotiations, the USSR left the distinct impression that it would definitely be one of the founders.[6] Several of the Fund's articles were therefore drafted with a view to assuaging specific Soviet concerns, including the following. First, the quota proposed by the United States was held to be too small. The USSR wanted sufficient voting power to be able to veto a uniform change in the par value of the currencies of the member countries — hence the price of gold. Second, it contended that the gold share of the quota should be reduced from 25 to 15 percent of quotas for all, and to only 7.5 percent of quota for the then "occupied" countries. Third, the USSR argued that the ruble's ER should not be controlled by the Fund, because it did not affect the competitive position of other countries. Fourth, it insisted that rubles made available for drawings be used only for purchases from the USSR. It also contended in this connection that newly mined gold not be used for repurchases of the members' own currencies from the Fund. Fifth, the USSR objected to depositing its gold tranche for storage in the United States. Finally, it advocated that it should not provide any more economic information than it agreed with the Fund. It also proposed, more generally, that members should not be obliged to heed the Fund's views on any existing or proposed monetary or economic policy.

This formidable catalog of requests for amendments of the Fund's draft Articles of Agreement in and of itself could have deterred the USSR from joining. Nevertheless, it continued to partake actively in the shaping of the new institution and thus kept its options for membership unencumbered. During the negotiations of 1943–1944, it remained unclear whether the USSR was basically negotiating about a settlements institution. There are several pointers to the effect that it may have visualized the proposed organization more as a development institution than as an organ preoccupied with balance-of-payments and stabilization measures (see Horsefield 1969, pp. 98–9).[7]

At the Atlantic City conference of June 1944, several of the key topics mentioned about which the USSR had serious reservations were tabled and satisfactorily resolved. For instance, the USSR's quota was increased to 14 percent; France supported the Soviet view on gold subscriptions, but this did not persuade the chief negotiators; a compromise was reached on the question of information to be submitted and on the monitoring of ERs for members whose currency does not affect their international transactions; and a satisfactory resolution of the deposit of gold was found. These compromises were incorporated into the draft Articles of Agreement that were signed, by the Soviet delegation as well,[8] at Bretton Woods without any oral or written reservations at all on some of the thorniest issues (Horsefield 1969, pp. 105, 117). In spite of this endorsement, the USSR never ratified the agreement. The arguments invoked during the negotiations and the key objections to the BWS formalized later are detailed in Section 7.3. Although the USSR never formally refused to join the Fund, it decided to partake no longer in the institution's affairs after the first Board of Governors' meeting in Savannah, Ga (March 1946), where it held the status of observer. Its delegation argued that membership was pending, though more time was required to study the matter. Never since has the USSR formally contacted the IMF or the IBRD, largely for reasons that are not economic in nature.

The early experiences with and withdrawal from the Bretton Woods system

In contrast to the USSR's tacit decision not to accede to the BWS, Czechoslovakia and Poland (as well as China, Cuba, Vietnam, and Yugoslavia) were among the founders, but not for long. Poland resigned in March 1950 alleging that the Fund had failed in its original purpose and that it had become subservient to U.S. interests.[9] Czechoslovakia remained in the Fund until the end of 1954, when it was formally expelled; but in May 1955 it chose to resign voluntarily before the Board of Governors could implement the expulsion. Formally, the bone of contention was that Czechoslovakia had not consulted the Fund and had refused all information and cooperation about the June 1953 koruna devaluation and the monetary reform associated with it. Albania and Bulgaria's tentative inquiries in 1948 were without further consequence. Poland apparently approached the Fund in October 1956 (Kranz 1984, p. 32), but the latter made it then politically impossible to contemplate membership seriously (Blusztajn 1982, p. 109). At the occasion of the first session of United Nations Conference on Trade and Development (UNCTAD) in 1964, both Hungary and Rumania held exploratory talks with IMF representatives, but there was no follow-up (Kranz 1984, p. 32).

Why was the second phase discussed above so negative? There are chiefly two sets of reasons why these countries chose not to participate in the BWS and were subsequently so negative toward the Fund. One was the Cold War with its adverse climate for international relations. One should recall here Churchill's Fulton address of 5 March 1946 and subsequent rhetoric, none of which was apt to reassure the Soviet Union at the time that the spirit of cooperation of the wartime alliance had been quickly evaporating. Czechoslovakia and Poland, which were not socialist countries proper when they joined, withdrew eventually chiefly for political reasons (Blusztajn 1982, p. 109). In that respect, the actions taken by the then emerging CPEs were very similar to what motivated them to sever nearly all ties with international organizations in which East and West participated. This phase in the postwar international economic relations of the PEs lasted for about twenty years for some and endures until today for others.

Perhaps a much more crucial reason for the lack of interest in participating in the BWS was economic in nature. To understand the initial reaction of the PEs, we must look briefly at the objectives of the IMF and the IBRD and the possible interests of the PEs in the technical aspects of the BWS. Because these are discussed in detail in the next section, suffice it here to put matters bluntly in a nutshell: The Fund then had little to offer to economies that had adopted comprehensive planning with the aid chiefly of physical yardsticks, that adhered to rigid commodity and currency inconvertibility, whose ERs were not real prices and served no substantive function, and that practiced rigid bilateralism (Holzman 1976, p. 172).

The Fund's principal purpose initially was to mobilize its resources for the stabilization of agreed upon ERs with the objective of gradually eliminating foreign exchange controls for current account transactions, promoting multilateralism, the liberalization of capital flows, and other such developments that hinge essentially on the existence of real markets. The comparatively small volume of trade of the PEs and the fact that the bulk of it was conducted under balanced ex ante BTPAs between pairs of PEs left little room indeed for stabilization. This feature became very much stronger as traditional central planning was implanted throughout Eastern Europe by the end of the 1940s and commercial relations with MEs were being forcibly curtailed. Second, given the rapidly deteriorating East–West environment, the PEs decided that it was not in their best interest to provide extensive economic intelligence to the Fund that would inevitably be disseminated on a large scale. Third, they had no reason to subject their exchange regime and broader macroeconomic policies to Fund surveillance. Finally, though it was attractive to gain access to finance, this was obtainable only through Fund membership for which the price to pay was probably deemed to be too high.

Seeking out membership

A third stage in the relations between the PEs and the BWS can be dated from about the mid-1960s to the early 1970s. The more outward-looking development strategy then being explored in Eastern Europe in conjunction with the various economic reforms, the rapid increase in the volume of East–West trade and financial flows, and the attempt to introduce multilateralism within the CMEA through the creation of the TR and IBEC called for a reassessment of the IMF and the IBRD. Notably, Czechoslovakia, Hungary, Poland, and Rumania approached these institutions. Although there may have been some inducement to join the Fund because of the availability of quota drawings, the chief motive for exploring membership at the time was gaining access to IBRD loans on advantageous terms and especially qualifying to tender for projects financed by the IBRD – one of the key rationales for seeking membership also in the fourth and current phase. This exploratory period came to an abrupt end with the deterioration in East–West economic and political relations and the sudden disruptions that took place in Eastern Europe as a result of the Warsaw Pact's invasion of Czechoslovakia in August 1968 and its aftermath.

Renewed interest in the Bretton Woods system by some planned economies

The fourth phase can be dated from the early 1970s, when Rumania joined the IMF and the IBRD, to the present; Hungary and Poland have been admitted in the meantime, and China and Vietnam have become active participants. Renewed interest in the BWS emerged not only in response to the external payments position of some PEs, but also because it was held highly desirable to smooth East–West economic and financial relations. Though the USSR is not likely to join under the prevailing conditions (see Section 7.6), it has followed with keen attention the developments in the IMS and has been contemplating ways in which it might enhance its standing and role in the concert of international economic relations, including in the ongoing debates about some of the most critical of the many North–South issues. In mid-1986, prominent participants in Soviet decision making at the top echelons of the Ministry of Foreign Affairs began to test the waters for GATT membership. On several occasions in international fora, they indicated that the USSR would soon explore avenues that would enable it to participate in some form in the existing BWS.

7.2 Systemic obstacles to a fuller participation in the Bretton Woods system

The PEs spurned active participation in the BWS largely for political reasons. The rapid deterioration in East–West relations, as briefly reviewed in Chapter 1, made active participation of the PEs in institutions in which their chief adversaries held an overwhelming majority all but academic. Also very important in deciding to stay aloof were the ramifications of the particular development strategy chosen by these countries and the planning institutions and associated policy instruments put in place there (see Chapter 1). Because they minimized the role of money and external finance in fostering rapid industrialization, and severely curtailed their economic interaction with MEs, they deliberately curbed the potential benefit that could be derived from balance-of-payments financing or from financial assistance in support of structural change. A final set of deterrents that may have played a subsidiary role in shunning participation in the BWS derived from the perceived problems associated with the obligation of Fund membership to disclose sensitive economic and financial intelligence, to accept IMF and IBRD surveillance in order to benefit from the institutions' lending facilities, and the commitment to foster nonresident convertibility for current account transactions. They may have added to the arguments pleading against active participation, but they can hardly have been the chief reasons for forgoing it. Indeed, gradualism in enforcing the obligations mentioned before and others as well has been one chief feature of why the institutions are now nearly global in scope (see Section 7.5). The evenhanded enforcement of currency convertibility and strict Fund surveillance for all members have not been distinguishing marks of Fund behavior to date!

Key ingredients of the BWS until the early 1970s were fixed ERs, currencies on the gold–dollar standard, reserve creation basically through additions to the stock of monetary gold and the cumulative U.S. external deficits, convertibility at least for current account transactions and nonresidents, balance-of-payments financing to overcome transitory external payments problems, recalibration of the ER together with a stabilization package encompassing other adjustments of domestic and external policies under the Fund's auspices to weather structural payments problems, and others. In other words, the BWS was essentially designed for developed MEs, characterized by the operation of the market mechanism, private profit as the foremost incentive to economize, single equilibrium ERs, convertibility, multilateralism, and the absence of exchange restrictions as matters of course.

Perhaps paradoxically, the original features of the BWS *in se*, with perhaps only some exceptions, would have been quite acceptable to the PEs. Fixed ERs blended in rather well with the economic stability sought by these economies. Rumania and, especially, the USSR are gold producers and cling to the unique mystique of gold; they would therefore have derived direct and indirect gains from having gold as reserve backing. Even financial convertibility for nonresidents and a limited form of commodity convertibility for tourist transactions would have been palatable (Chapter 11) though with some restrictions that could have been designed to avert conflicts with Fund obligations. The most important areas in which the PEs would have encountered vexing dilemmas are the role of the U.S. dollar in the IMS, stabilization measures prescribed by the Fund, and free external convertibility. But with some goodwill, even these real obstacles could have been circumnavigated.

Unfortunately, the developed MEs that were instrumental in the creation of the BWS were, on the whole, patronizing towards the economic problems faced by the PEs and offered them conditions of membership that were humiliating in several respects. There never was a real under-standing of the particular and sometimes peculiar problems posed by the economic and institutional characteristics of the PEs. Four such logical and legitimate constituents of the economic setup of PEs (see Wilczynski 1978, p. 246) were then, and still are in most countries as follows: (1) multiple ERs are the necessary reflection of the typical two-tier price system; (2) currency and commodity inconvertibility derive from the planned allocation and utilization of resources; (3) BTPAs facilitate the planned conduct of foreign trade; and (4) pervasive exchange controls help to insulate domestic from foreign markets and thus to protect the considerable amount of policy autonomy sought by PE decision makers.

The breakdown of the gold–dollar standard and the fixed ER regime in the early 1970s have been rather perplexing for a number of PEs. Most appear to have been at a sharp loss about what should, or could, be done in terms of their own foreign exchange regime in order to come to grips with floating currencies, as examined in Chapter 6. The PEs con-tinue to prefer a regime with fixed but malleable ERs, possibly anchored to gold (see Section 7.6).

7.3 A critique of the Bretton Woods system

Although the USSR succeeded in substantially modifying the Fund's draft Articles of Agreement prepared chiefly by the U.S. State Depart-ment (the so-called White Plan), the issues then raised (especially the role of gold, the U.S. dollar, "ideal" currencies, the creation of international liquidity, the distribution of voting power, the Fund's surveillance role and the adjustment process, balance-of-payments and stabilization poli-cies, convertibility and ERs, and the disclosure of economic information) have dominated the attitude of most PEs, especially the USSR, vis-à-vis the BWS and its modifications since the early 1970s.

The role of gold in the international monetary system

The USSR's position at Bretton Woods did not challenge the mystique of gold or its role as a basic reserve. But it objected to the transfer of gold to U.S. territory, the level of the assessed gold quota for some countries, the earmarking of newly mined gold to work off quota drawings, and the disclosure of economic intelligence about gold production and stocks. Other PEs, except perhaps China, are not substantial gold producers. For this and other reasons, chiefly the role of the USSR in the socialist world, the attitude of other PEs toward the role of gold in the IMS until the breakdown of the gold-exchange standard has often mirrored the USSR's.[10]

Although one may be inclined to belittle the role of ideology in the behavior of PEs, some do have a doctrinal attachment to gold. They regard gold as a basic reserve instrument, an essential stabilizer in international economic relations, and an instrument of discipline in national monetary affairs. By virtue of gold's rarity, the emission of fiduciary money in strict proportion with gold reserves provides a strong element of discipline in domestic monetary policies and in balance-of-payments adjustment efforts. Credit money issued in only a loose relationship to its "commodity" or "reserve" backing is perceived to entail uncontrollable inflation and monetary chaos with all attending adverse consequences for employment, economic stability, and the pace at which growth can be sustained. Furthermore, of special practical importance is that the USSR is the world's second largest gold producer and thus has an obvious stake in the role of gold for monetary purposes and its price. We must keep in mind the ideological underpinnings of the attitude towards gold.

Ideological precepts play a vital role in Marxist theory, which regards money as a special commodity that serves as the universal embodiment of abstract labor and as a bearer of exchange value. With that frame of reference it is traditionally argued, especially by Soviet monetarists, that the value of money derives essentially from goods. Many goods have been money in the course of history, with precious metals gradually assuming the role of the universal backing of money; gold is said to be the culmination of that process, to be money in a worldwide sense, and to be the quasi-universal backing of national and international liquidity. Marx regarded money as a special commodity. As the all-encompassing embodiment of abstract labor, gold is considered as the crystallization of the exchange value of commodities and, hence, the bearer of exchange value.

Gold is also an ideological concern because the monetary goals that emerged in the 1970s are viewed largely as another manifestation of the more general aims of the capitalist system. Soviet commentators usually explain the global monetary crisis in either of two ways. As examined in greater detail in Section 7.6, the group of traditional commentators zeroes in on the end of the gold-exchange standard as the root of the monetary problems. The other group sees in the decline of gold more a consequence than an independent cause of the monetary crisis for both economic and political reasons.

The role of national and international reserve currencies

Most commentators of PEs stress the fundamental contradiction between the use of national currencies as international reserves and the provision of adequate liquidity backed by a "basic" international value. They also emphasize the conflict between the need for monetary stability and the exploration of purely international reserve currencies when their creation is not mainly motivated by the need for adequate liquidity as an essential ingredient of a stable economic environment.

The PEs as a matter of course have been rather contemptuous of the lack of monetary discipline and responsibility in the domestic and international monetary affairs of the leading developed MEs. The charge of laxity in monetary affairs for ulterior capitalist motives has been especially forceful since the abandonment of fixed ERs, although it had been levied well before the monetary disturbances of the 1970s, particularly at the time of the U.S.'s adventurous foreign policy of the 1960s, including in particular the Vietnam conflict. Most commentators argue that the excessive issue of currency and credit, the U.S.'s large and persistent balance-of-payments deficits to remedy the international liquidity problem and to finance U.S. investment abroad, and finally the demonitization of gold all have produced uncontrollable inflationary pressures. These policies have had adverse consequences for the PEs and need to be rectified.

The distribution of voting power

The question of voting has been raised on several occasions as the PEs object to voting by economic strength. In this they see a measure of exercising, in particular, dollar hegemony and of interfering in the internal economic affairs of sovereign states. Especially since the declaration of the NIEO, they have called for a "democratization" of the official monetary institutions. As a replacement of the present system of weighted voting, the PEs advocate that the institutions move closer to the one-country–one-vote system typical of their own organizations and of most of the United Nations system.

Surveillance and the adjustment process

Together with many developing and some developed MEs, the PEs have expressed concern over the type of adjustment processes embedded in the philosophy that is at the roots of the BWS and even more so in the guidelines gradually adopted during the period of flexible ERs. The argument is quite general: The PEs subscribe to the notion that the adjustment burden has fallen disproportionately on the countries encountering balance-of-payments deficits, although the disequilibrium usually stems from unsynchronized macroeconomic policies in surplus *and* deficit countries, or perhaps even overwhelmingly on account of mercantilist policies on the part of the surplus countries.

Balance-of-payments and stabilization policies

The authority of the Fund to prescribe stabilization policies for its members that find themselves in external payments difficulties has been another hardy objection to more active involvement with the BWS. As examined in Chapter 3, the PEs encounter considerable problems with adjustments pursued with the instruments of indirect economic control typical among the key targets of Fund recommendations (such as prices, ERs, interest rates, the compression of government expenditure, the control of money supply, and credit creation). At the same time, it is clear that the PEs may find it easier than many developing MEs to pursue adjustment policies palatable to the Fund but with their typical planning and intervention instruments. It is, then, not so much the goals and means that make for objections to stabilization measures endorsed by the Fund. The prime problem would appear to be the authority of the Fund to prescribe in principle the timing and scope of such policies, both of which the PEs contest on the ground that they constitute an inadmissible interference in their internal affairs.

Convertibility and exchange rates

The type of central planning typically embraced by PEs is incompatible with the Fund's prescriptions on commodity and currency convertibility for current account transactions. On the other hand, the PEs have never had conceptual problems with a fixed ER system anchored to gold parities, which they have embraced for themselves. But they consider their foreign exchange regime and changes therein to be intrinsic prerogatives of their own economic sovereignty, of which they hold a rather absolute view (see Spiller 1984, pp. 28–31). They maintain that the Fund should not insist on effective convertibility for PEs because that is incompatible with a number of essential operational features of strict central planning for structural change. Not only that, the PEs have traditionally refused to consult the Fund about their ER policies, as was so well demonstrated by Nicolae Ceauşescu in October 1984, when he abruptly revalued the leu in defiance of Fund recommendations. But the PEs have found it rather difficult to come to grips with a system of flexible ERs.

Information disclosure

Finally, the disclosure of sensitive economic information has been an important issue from the very start of the debates about the BWS. As noted, some mutually satisfactory solution was hammered out at Bretton Woods, because no official or other objections, either in writing or orally, were lodged by the Soviet delegation with respect to either the range or the depth of the economic intelligence to be funneled to the international monetary institutions (Horsefield 1969, p. 105). But the issue has been a hardy one in the PEs' criticism of the BWS. In the immediate postwar period, and certainly at the height of the Cold War, there were, arguably legitimate, reasons for the PEs to consider virtually all quantitative and qualitative economic information as a "state secret." Much has changed in that respect. But some PEs still do not publish sufficient information to permit a straightforward, comprehensive assessment of their economic situation.

7.4 Official position of the planned economies on the new international economic order and monetary reform

The PEs are usually quite critical of the IMS and the present monetary problems, which they view as but one facet of the more general economic crisis of capitalism. The latter's principal origin they ascribe in particular to the economic policies pursued by large developed MEs, the United States in the first instance. Rather rarely do political leaders or even informed commentators offer a positive proposal for remedying what they perceive to be the monetary disorder that ensued with the collapse of fixed ERs. Even if aired, such policy positions are rarely adopted explicitly by all PEs.[11] Such positions are usually articulated in the context of institutions or representations of which not all PEs are members.[12] It also arises as a result of their considerably different level of development and hence the varying interest in global monetary and financial affairs.

The broadest-based statements of the fundamental principles regarding the IMS by the PEs were launched on the occasion of several UNCTAD meetings, especially the Fourth Session in Nairobi in 1976 (UNCTAD 1976, pp. 152–71), the Fifth in Manila in 1979 (UNCTAD 1979, pp. 178–94), and the Sixth in Belgrade (UNCTAD 1983a, pp. 152–3). The substantive points regarding the IMS contained in all pronouncements by those who originally endorsed that part of the Nairobi declaration (UNCTAD 1976, pp. 152–4) have not been modified drastically, though several countries have rephrased their positions in response to evolving events in the world economy and international relations. Moreover, these principles are held so generally that they would appear to be shared by nearly all the conventional socialist countries.

The PEs derive their view of international economic relations in particular from a set of fundamental principles that are anchored to a clear commitment to and an interest in enhancing international interdependence when such relations are mutually advantageous and conducted on the basis of an equitable division of labor. With reference to the basic issues under review, the PEs consider "it obviously impossible to limit the process of transformation to specific fields of international economic relations" (Spröte 1983, p. 23). A reform of the IMS will therefore have to be conceived holistically within the context of "a radical restructuring of the entire system of international economic relations." This assertion refers in particular to the "international organizations whose charters and practices remain profoundly undemocratic and deprive the developing [MEs] of the opportunity of taking an equitable part in their work" (UNCTAD 1979, p. 181). The position held on subsidiary issues, when explicitly spelled out in detail, can be inferred from the preceding general assessments.

Regarding the restructuring of the IMS, the PEs officially reject the usefulness of measures aimed "at the demonitization of gold, its replacement by [SDRs] and the legalizing of 'floating [ERs]' " that "cannot provide stability and reliability for the international monetary mechanism" or "remove the basic shortcomings of the present [IMS]" (UNCTAD 1976, pp. 153–4). To normalize the international monetary situation, in principle, the PEs advocate measures "to enhance the role of gold in international liquidity and to bring about the gradual abolition and banning of the monopolistic position held by one or several national currencies in the [IMS]." They take a skeptical view of proposals aimed at reforming the IMF from within (see Section 7.6) and suggest instead that UNCTAD be "a more suitable forum for taking decisions on international monetary problems" (UNCTAD 1976, p. 154). It is these positions that have been reiterated numerous times, although in the last five years or so references to a return to gold have become rare.

Because of important shifts in the global economy since the mid-1970s, one would have expected some transformation in the policy positions of the PEs on such issues as SDR allocations, the role of gold, IBRD-lending practices, and the like. If such fundamental shifts have taken place, they have not been widely publicized to date. In *Preservation of Peace* (see Chapter 2), the PEs "advocate the regimenting of monetary–financial relations, stand against the policy of high interest rates, and champion the normalization of terms under which credits are granted and paid back so that those terms, particularly with relation to the indebtedness of the developing MEs, should not be used as a means of political pressure and interference in internal affairs" (CMEA 1984a, p. 7). They have declared themselves in favor of convening a new international conference on money and finance. In a joint statement circulated at UNCTAD VI in Belgrade, Group D outlined seven rules and principles to be observed in order to convene such a meeting. In addition to reiterating the principles touched upon earlier, some emphasis was placed on viewing monetary affairs in a global economic context, approaching all international economic issues uniformly, and allowing each country to maintain an autonomous currency and monetary regime as long as it does not disadvantage other countries (UNCTAD 1983b).

This suggests that the PEs have not yet made a clear-cut commitment on their preferred IMS. Nor are they convinced that an acceptable solution could be hammered out at a new monetary conference. In fact, although their attitude towards the convening of such a conference has become somewhat more positive in recent years, whether they will participate in it depends critically "on how the specific tasks of the conference are formulated and on the extent to which the legitimate interests of all States are taken into account during the preparatory work" (UN 1983, p. 2).

7.5 The participation of planned economies in the international monetary system

In spite of the foregoing variety of systemic, political, and institutional obstacles that may inhibit participation of PEs in the BWS, several PEs have paradoxically joined the system in recent years; others have remained active within the system or have activated their membership. In view of the peculiarities of state trading and CMEA bilateralism, not to mention the political and ideological obstacles usually brought to bear in a discussion about the BWS, one would have thought that participation by the PEs would be contingent on a host of special waivers and dispensations. That no such exceptional bargain needed to be struck, particularly on issues involving the financial disclosure and convertibility guidelines of the BWS,[13] is a testimonial to the flexibility with which the BWS institutions have been able to absorb the bulk of the developing MEs in their midst. The explanation of the paradox, then, requires a balanced evaluation of the advantages and drawbacks of participation, with particular reference to the experience of these PEs and the way in which the BWS has modified its own regulations so as to make the system universally accessible.

The significance of the requests for accession since 1972

Rumania was the first PE to join the BWS. The significance of this move lay more in Rumania's aspirations to greater economic and political independence at the time of East–West détente, and some Western countries' foreign policy ambitions to dismember the Eastern alliance, than in terms of a strictly economic confluence of interests. Indeed, Rumania's accession occurred in consequence of its decision in the mid-1960s to disengage itself, relatively speaking, from the ISDL. It may have been looking for supports to expand its external economic relations with the developing MEs, to which it has been wedded, but the chief motivation of the new foreign policy design originated elsewhere. This was reflected in the accommodating stance on the application for accession. Regarding Hungary's admission and Poland's candidature, matters have been quite different.

In contrast to the considerable political overtones of Rumania's accession in 1972, Hungary's membership is logically embedded in the economic decentralization of the NEM pursued in recent years. The further transitions toward a comprehensive, if regulated, socialist ME in which trade prices for most goods and services are fed through to a significant extent gave credence to Hungary's request for admission to the BWS in 1981. This was further buttressed by Hungary's emphasis on pursuing an outward-looking development strategy. Reaching a competitive position in world markets in products for which Hungary holds a comparative advantage now or in the near future simply requires further integration into a highly interdependent trading and financial world. It was hoped that Fund membership would give the country access to comparatively inexpensive stabilization funds and provide a powerful psychological fillip to its economic relations with MEs. The request made in late 1981 was largely motivated by the expected further deterioration in the country's terms of trade for several more years; the flagging of its export drive, especially to the developed MEs; the then imminent external financial difficulties; and the broader needs to rescale the contemplated adjustments of its economic structure to a dependence on external markets that could not have been accommodated by the traditional instruments of socialist central planning.

Poland, which also applied in November 1981, barely one week after Hungary, is a far more complex case. Its application can also be placed against the background of the economic devolution sought within its on–off incipient economic reform. The adaptation of the country's economic mechanism was slated to be an essential ingredient of a feasible long-term development strategy. Nevertheless, the immediate reasons for the move stemmed overwhelmingly from the unprecedented slide in Poland's domestic and external economic fortunes. There was at the time considerable, and growing, concern in world financial markets about the wisdom and procedures of rescheduling the debt, and the form, mode of implementation, and probable payoff of recently inaugurated or contemplated domestic economic policies. Poland therefore felt the need to reassure official as well as private financial markets abroad that its leaders were committed to heading the economy in a direction that would permit orderly servicing of its debt, perhaps after some transitory liquidity problems. The application also provided the cosmetic sheen deemed useful in the short run to promulgate internal socioeconomic reforms with the active support of all power groups in the societal crisis. Furthermore, in the medium to long run the country would have stood to benefit from access to additional financial resources, even though under mildly disciplinary international scrutiny. Of course, IBRD loans and the opportunity to bid on projects sponsored by the IBRD were also attractive inducements. As is well known, the political rifts between East and West, owing in particular to the Afghanistan syndrome and the imposition of martial law in Poland in December 1981, stalled the processing of the application until late 1984. Admission became effective on 30 May 1986.

Other PEs, including Bulgaria and Czechoslovakia, have been carefully monitoring the Hungarian and Rumanian experiments and may initiate similar, if not as far-reaching, management changes. Also these PEs could benefit in the medium to long run from refocusing the role and place of central planning in economic decision making. Inasmuch as such changes aim at directing economywide planning primarily at desirable structural adaptations and at guiding plan implementation and current managerial decisions by appropriate indirect policy instruments and supporting institutions, membership in the BWS could be most valuable.

Rationale for joining the Bretton Woods system

Because the IMF's prime task is to stabilize international finance by lending from common resources for transitory balance-of-payments reasons, it would have been logical for the Eastern European PEs to seek admission when virtually all of them were experiencing serious CC and TR balance-of-payments problems. Accession to the BWS would not have helped directly to remedy the TR deficits that emerged after 1975 because the TR not only eludes the Fund's area of authority, but the peculiar institutional and systemic problems of that currency zone, which are largely structural in origin, transcend the Fund's competence and experience. But access to fresh resources to bridge transitory payments difficulties in East–West relations or to assist in promoting exports to MEs could have aided these countries directly. Membership would also have reassured governments, bankers, and traders in MEs that the external problems of the PEs would be managed properly for at least two reasons.

For one, it would have entailed the wide-scale disclosure of macroeconomic information that the PEs have traditionally guarded rather closely. This would have enabled observers to construct a more coherent macroeconometric framework for monitoring the behavior and functioning of PEs. One key baffling problem in attaining a mutually acceptable debt-rescheduling agreement, especially for Poland, was precisely the inexperience of governments and private commercial banks of MEs to deal with a PE in external payments difficulties. Certainly, some of the obstacles may have been political. Nevertheless, the substantive issues that complicated an agreement with the banks and Western governments derived largely from a mutual lack of understanding. Western commercial banks (the London Club) and government negotiators (the Paris Club) showed only the most rudimentary knowledge of how the PEs and the CMEA really function. Agents in MEs found it rather cumbersome to negotiate against the horizon and within the framework for fundamental economic decisions that the planners normally set for themselves. Both are indeed at odds with free enterprise objectives or the obligations of democratically elected governments. Similarly, in spite of considerable savvy and sophistication acquired during the burgeoning East–West financial contacts of the 1970s, Eastern European negotiators sometimes failed to appreciate the ways in which private commercial banks and governments of MEs settle their economic obligations.

Though membership in the BWS by itself would not have affected the intrinsic creditworthiness of the PEs, it would certainly have provided a significant psychological prop. Joining the BWS would also have enabled these countries to avail themselves of the established mechanisms regarding conditionality, debt management, and macroeconomic adjustment of the IBRD and the IMF in addition to the self-discipline already presupposed upon members. That is not to say, however, that the institutions of the BWS would have come up quickly with rational policy measures suitable to the specific conditions of PEs and acceptable to them. The stabilization measures that the Fund recommended to the two CMEA members that are in the Fund as well as to Yugoslavia (Robinson, Tyson, and Woods 1984) do not appear to have been very well suited to local conditions, except when these packages, as for Hungary, were first put together in the country itself and then endorsed by the Fund's staff.

The PEs generally perceive the economic benefits of membership in the BWS to be[14] securing access to credit facilities at moderate interest rates; gaining greater financial respectability in MEs; having the option of availing themselves of the considerable store of expertise in debt management, rescheduling, and the costs and benefits of austerity policies; being entitled to bid on IBRD projects in developing MEs; and, for the poorer of the PEs, gaining the status of a developing country at the IBRD and hence obtaining access to CC funds on particularly advantageous terms. The drawbacks consist mostly of the obligation to divulge sensitive economic information and the possibility of having to submit to Fund conditionality or policy advice that may fail to blend with the precepts of the traditional PE. To the extent that the SDR may become the world's major reserve asset, countries that do not take part in the scheme are bound to suffer from a distinct disadvantage in flexibly participating in international trade and finance. Aside from alleviating the current external balance constraints and adding a degree of controlled flexibility in foreign economic policy, and thereby facilitating domestic output maintenance, membership as such is likely to affect the domestic economy only marginally. Even if limited external convertibility were to emerge (see Chapter 11), it would not be of serious consequence as far as the internal setup and external organization of these economies are concerned.

Membership in the BWS would also be most valuable as a further prop to the structural adjustment measures envisaged by the smaller CMEA members. Clearly, the Fund cannot enmesh itself directly in the economic affairs of the PEs as far as they relate to CMEA membership. However, the Fund can and does intervene for a PE encountering problems in its CC relationships. By obtaining more external flexibility, membership in the IMF and the IBRD could facilitate the transitions in economic policies and institutions that the PEs deem helpful to cope with both balance-of-payments and structural adjustment issues. Because the policy measures of the Washington institutions are normally focused on working off the external deficit, securing competitiveness of the domestic economy, and eliminating market distortions, especially in prices, the Fund's wealth of experience could be brought to bear on shaping and implementing such flexible policies in Eastern Europe. Loans for structural adjustment purposes could ease the adaptations required to make the PEs more competitive in world markets. By this indirect avenue, the policies administered with the guidance and financial assistance of the BWS could exert, though indirectly, a powerful influence on the type of SEI to be pursued with determination.

A particularly vexing issue that has led to considerable political animosity concerns the terms on which the PEs are admitted to the BWS. The PEs were not only hoping to be able to bid on IBRD-financed projects in the developing MEs, for which IMF membership is a prerequisite. They were also keen on being admitted at a per capita income level that would entitle them to soft-window loans. This particular criterion presented no big problem when the de facto accession of China and the de jure one of Rumania were being negotiated. With Hungary, however, the overwhelming majority of outside observers argued that it is a country on a medium level of development with a per capita income level well above the floor established for soft-window loans. The crucial issue revolved not so much around the computation of demographic statistics or of national income accounts but around the ER at which local values are translated into U.S. dollars. If a realistic ER had been used, Hungary would not have been eligible for the developing country status. Because Hungary insisted upon being treated like any other member, the IBRD had little choice but to use the official commercial ER, which deviates markedly from any realistic purchasing power parity (see Chapter 6). In the end, this logic prevailed and Hungary is a "developing country" for IBRD purposes. Much the same rationale was wielded to determine the terms of admission for Poland. With the recent devaluations of the commercial złoty, Poland came in well under the cutoff point.

Impact on the CMEA and Fund experience

Because Hungary and Rumania are active CMEA members, and Poland will join that group shortly, when its first standby agreement will be approved, it is legitimate to ponder the effects of their membership in the BWS on their relations with the CMEA or their positions on SEI. So far, there are no indications at all that these countries have contemplated far-reaching economic, financial, or institutional reforms simply to accommodate their participation in the IMS – quite the contrary. Certainly, some erosion of the traditional planning system, the trade and payments mechanisms, the institutional setup of the economic model and strategy, and the forms and goals of SEI held by individual PEs has taken place over the last ten years or so, and further changes are likely to be forthcoming. However, none can realistically be attributed to Fund membership or surveillance. But a further autonomous loosening of the discipline presumed in the traditional CMEA trade and payments mechanism could eventually pave the way for more PEs seeking to associate themselves with the BWS. This might take place in several different ways.

7.6 Monetary reform and the CMEA

The BWS proved to be a great benefit to the developed MEs, because it worked reasonably well for a quarter century and contributed effectively to the growth of international trade and economic development in general (Wilczynski 1978, p. 245). The IMS has obviously been going through a very difficult period since the collapse of the fixed ER system in the early 1970s. Though the BWS has proved to be resilient in spite of serious delays in formulating alternatives, the main actors in the world economy cannot forever postpone a restructuring of its key foundations without hampering the smooth functioning of global economic interdependence. It would be unfortunate if such a revamping were to materialize without taking fully into account the concerns of all participants in the world economy and without at least attempting to reflect the relative weight of the PEs in the world. It is therefore useful to look at the shared interests in fostering greater international cooperation by East and West, the possibility of there being some collusion among MEs and PEs in hammering out a more satisfactory IMS, and the key characteristics of the ways in which such international financial cooperation could be institutionalized.

The overall character of interdependence

In spite of the defects and drawbacks that the PEs normally attribute to the BWS, they generally acknowledge that the system contributed greatly to the dynamism and stability of economic development and trade in the postwar period, especially of the developed MEs (Fekete 1972, p. 154), and are therefore actively interested in a reform of the IMS. This holds even if, in the end, they were to decide not to join the BWS under current or prospective terms. A properly streamlined, smoothly functioning system, even if applicable only to MEs, is believed to inhibit trade wars and protectionism, to contribute to the stability of international financial relations, and indeed to benefit the environment of international relations (Fekete 1972, p. 160).

Common interests in a reformed BWS can emerge only if such a new system reflects the shared economic and monetary goals and prerogatives of most MEs and PEs. Issues such as influence over policy making, access to liquidity and Fund resources, a reshaped policy on surveillance and stabilization measures administered by the Fund, greater control over ER movements, precluding ER volatility, coordination of monetary and other macroeconomic policies of the key actors in the BWS, and so on, are all essential ingredients of the monetary debate. As the frustrating negotiations on the establishment of the NIEO have demonstrated with such clarity, some of the issues enumerated here cannot be satisfactorily resolved within the existing institutions. A more harmonious, less rancorous North–South relationship may then require a substantial overhaul of the BWS or the creation ab ovo of a new IMS.

Though many of the aforementioned issues also divide East and West, it would seem that a rapprochement on technical grounds would be easier to block out, if not necessarily to implement, on the grounds of reciprocal economic advantages. The shared economic interests consist of the considerable need of the PEs for technology and capital resources from abroad and the reported calls by MEs that PEs participate more and more actively in the global division of labor and attendant responsibilities for equity in development, buoyancy of economic expansion, sustainability of the development process, and stability of the global economy. Though an East–West rapprochement based on the reciprocity of interests and on respect for the fundamental characteristics of each other's system appears feasible, it does not imply that East and West will eventually be able to join forces in the BWS as it exists today or in any of the tabled reforms. This derives essentially from the key ingredients of any feasible monetary reform.

Toward a new international monetary system

At one of the rare conferences dealing specifically with the role of East and West in monetary reform, Henri Bourguinat stipulated four pivotal issues of a new IMS: (1) the universality of the reserve unit, (2) the choice of optimum exchange regime, (3) the role of gold and reserve currency, and (4) the internationalization of the monetary institutions (Bourguinat 1977, pp. 65ff.). But the fuller participation of the PEs, and incidentally a good many developing MEs, in such a system appears to require the prior resolution of several other thorny issues, which are examined later.

a. A universal reserve currency. Universality requires that a reformed IMS be anchored to a common *numéraire* as a yardstick for measuring values. It should be possible to embrace such a unit without making it dependent on any one of the major currencies. In other words, it should be an ideal currency constituted perhaps along the lines of the Bancor or the TR. The SDR might eventually become a sufficiently habitual transaction medium to be such a unit. For it to be acceptable to the PEs, however, modifications in its creation and distribution, and perhaps in several other of its features, need to be worked out.

Universalism anchored to a common *numéraire* does not forcibly preclude monetary polycentrism, for it is difficult to see how the TR – or the Soviet ruble for that matter – could be rendered compatible with a new IMS without entailing important systemic changes that might compromise the expressed interests of some PEs. Instead of having the IMS anchored solely to one dominant currency, such as the U.S. dollar, or even to a few key currencies, greater stability than presently attainable might be reached by harmonizing the global system on the basis of several, largely self-contained monetary regimes, each having a distinct monetary subsystem. Whether such a decomposition should proceed along presently existing political alliances or envisage substrata that now peg against one or a few currencies on the basis of fairly uniform, if informal, rules by which they adjust their monetary policies is still an open question (Matejka 1977, p. 113). The former would not only respect the matrix of current trade flows, particularly for CMEA members, but it would also allow a greater diversification of instruments of exchange.

b. Foreign exchange regime. Whether a reformed IMS would encompass fixed or floating ERs is a matter yet to be decided. In the equation "stable but equitable ERs" frequently suggested as one important pillar of a reformed IMS, the PEs undoubtedly accord greater weight to "stability" than to "adjustability," as emphasized in Rączkowskı 1977, pp. 94–95. These countries hold indeed that the instability and uncertainty associated with floating ERs cannot be outweighed by the degree of internal autonomy obtained in principle with such a regime.

Because the BWS was designed specifically to foster currency convertibility, multilateralism in trade, equilibrium ERs, and gradually liberalized capital markets, a realistic IMS reform cannot significantly depart from these fundamental pivots of the international economy. This may pose problems for countries not yet "ready" to pursue such goals for systemic or other reasons. But special regimes might be accommodated under either fixed or floating ERs or a combination thereof. They could be similar to those stipulated in the Fund's article VIII, although they would have to be spelled out more precisely than the "temporary" clause under which most members of the Fund have spurned convertibility for so many years.[15]

c. Gold and reserve currencies. The role of gold in the future IMS will certainly be of much concern to PEs for the reasons just examined. But there are highly likely to be other reserve instruments too. What will be the role of the SDR and the attitude of PEs towards that reserve unit? One fundamental question is whether countries will be able to participate in the SDR mechanism without becoming full members of the Fund and associated institutions. It is true that the Fund's Articles of Agreement provide for such an eventuality, but it is unclear whether this can be interpreted sufficiently flexibly to extend it to the case of PEs. Even if they were to embrace this option, the PEs would not obtain SDR allocations (Rączkowski 1977, p. 96). Although the PEs would thus not be obligated to any of the regulations linking development assistance to SDR allocations, the question of how the PEs finance their CC payments imbalances is left unanswered.

Many Eastern European monetary specialists view the SDR as an embryonic form of debt money that cannot in itself solve the prevailing monetary problems for as long as its creation is not placed under strict discipline and in line with the requirements of a stable trading and economic environment for the world as a whole. But the SDR is regarded as having an "important place" in the evolution of international currency reserves just the same (Matjuchin 1977, p. 162). The PEs have other, more fundamental problems with the SDR as a basic reserve currency, however. The SDR is regarded as credit money that has made it possible to gain some distance from the IMS based solely on national currencies. But the SDR still exhibits many problems: It is not yet sufficiently acceptable worldwide to be capable of replacing national currencies; it does not yet circulate widely, and therefore it will take a long time for it to replace national currencies; its creation is regulated by political means, and no guarantees are as yet provided to prevent the SDR from being subjected to inflationary reserve creation (see Matjuchin 1977, pp. 46–47; Matjuchin and Šenaev 1978, pp. 51–52). Because these commentators offer no alternative to the "inappropriateness of the SDR as an international currency unit," they fall back on the "necessity to strengthen the role of gold" (UNCTAD 1980, p. 3) by default.

In recent years, the PEs have been advocating the development of stable units of account for international economic agreements. They have taken a very active part in the study group of the United Nations Commission for International Trade Law (UNCITRAL) dealing with the establishment of a universal constant accounting unit. In fact, in January 1982 the USSR declared in Vienna that an indexed SDR could be acceptable as such a unit (Spiller 1984, p. 43), particularly for measuring national contributions to international organizations or international insurance conventions. Some PEs have recently also resorted to clauses in credit agreements that base the loans on a basket of currencies similar to the composition of the currencies that serve as the SDR's measurement base (Konstantinov 1982b, p. 60).[16]

d. Internationalization of the monetary institutions. The BWS's universality aim was an attempt to embrace uniform conditions throughout the world based largely on the economic institutions and behavior of developed MEs. It is quite true, formally, that the countries with the largest voting power can decide autonomously what borrowing can occur, the particular type of adjustment policies to be set by the Fund, and the conditionality conditions associated with either. Certainly, the Fund's article IV, section 3b states that the principles adopted by the Fund for purposes of surveillance "shall respect the domestic, social, and political policies of members, and in applying these principles the Fund shall pay due regard to the circumstances of members." In actual practice, more and more use has recently been made of the stipulation that the Fund pay fuller regard to domestic social and political objectives and the particular causes of balance-of-payments problems, with room for ad hoc accommodation. This more flexible approach could be suitably adapted to the particular situation of the PEs.

The PEs cannot be treated in the same way and with the same evaluation criteria as an ME experiencing financial difficulties (Lavigne 1985a, pp. 39–40). Such attempts should be avoided at all costs in designing an alternative IMS. As the past has amply demonstrated, countries seek to defend their autonomy and have remained remarkably jealous of their economic sovereignty. A globalization of the institutions of the BWS could proceed with a reasonable chance of success only if the members' interest in maintaining some degree of autonomy and economic sovereignty is explicitly recognized.

Issues of particular concern to planned economies

Other aspects of the IMS of particular interest to PEs are the distribution of votes, the shape of surveillance exercised by the Fund, the specific conditions of stabilization measures and the extent to which they can be foisted upon members, the role of gold, and the question of information.

a. Voting power. The arduous discussions about the global negotiations and the implementation of the NIEO have demonstrated that Fund members basically fall into two categories. Those with a large weight in management are unlikely to yield voluntarily all of their power. On the other hand, the large majority of developing MEs, as well as the PEs, covet a greater stake in the policy making of these institutions without necessarily being committed to absolute equality among unequals. Officially, the conflict between these two groups continues to be as rigorous as in the past. In practice, however, the voting rules have been considerably relaxed, for instance, as a result of ad hoc borrowing facilities with various kinds of majorities; on key questions, including the creation of liquidity, the majority is rather high (in some cases as high as 85 percent); the PEs as a group would have more than 15 percent of the voting power, thus giving them veto power; and most operational questions within the BWS are settled by broad consensus rather than through formal voting. The high majority applies, for instance, to the creation of liquidity such as in the form of a new tranche or in SDR allocations. Because this is a matter to which the PEs attach paramount importance, the USSR is likely to find it politically unacceptable that the United States, which possesses a fifth of the vote, has the veto power by itself, whereas the USSR would be able to muster it only on a groupwide basis.

Nevertheless, the insistence on voting equality would appear to refer chiefly to the bases of the system as a starting position that can be considerably modified through negotiations. Thus, in principle there is nothing that prevents the present members from agreeing to a variable voting allocation on issues of particular concern to the PEs. They could, in effect, be provided with a veto, for example, when it comes to Fund adjustment policies for themselves. At the same time, the developed MEs might well be entitled to safeguard their basic interests on matters that are not of vital importance to the PEs by keeping their present voting power, perhaps after allowing for some of the concerns of the developing MEs. Such could be the case, for instance, in the establishment of guidelines for ER parities and fluctuations, perhaps even for foreign exchange policies in general.

Especially if a reformed IMS were to be polycentric, such a system needs to be held together by a truly international monetary unit and by adequate global institutions. A particularly important issue in this connection, as in any alternative aspiring towards universality, is the apportionment of voting power among the various blocs. Should each group obtain sufficient votes to veto decisions, particularly with regard to liquidity creation, or should the voting power be divided equally among the blocs? The PEs would appear to favor the latter alternative (Matejka 1977, p. 111). But the question of voting power need not be settled uniformly for all decisions involving the new institutions.

b. Asymmetry. Anchoring the IMS to greater symmetry in surveillance and adjustment prescriptions is an issue that has been on the agenda of the developing MEs for many years and one about which the Fund has been seriously concerned. Also the PEs advocate greater surveillance, but not necessarily by international organizations, because economic policy in general and monetary policy in particular in many developed and developing MEs have not been managed and controlled very well at the national level. They certainly have not been up to par with the requirements for stable and sustainable economic expansion for all participants in the world economy. On the other hand, the PEs are not likely to be agreeable to this surveillance being exercised with a high degree of autonomy or to ensuing policy recommendations being foisted upon the members concerned. Especially the latter they oppose because they see in it interference in their internal economic affairs.

c. Convertibility. Because convertibility is a critical issue in any IMS, would the PE currencies have to be made convertible? Would they have to be traded in world markets and their prices be determined by the market mechanism? Would it imply that the Eastern European currencies be exchangeable into domestic commodities or services, at least in principle? The answer to this critical matter cannot possibly be provided *hic et nunc*. It must be formulated, first, with regard to a process and timetable for moving towards some minimum acceptable form of convertibility and, second, with sufficient flexibility so that modifications can be undertaken in light of emerging internal and external development conditions, including those of the PEs. The likelihood of convertibility emerging autonomously in Eastern Europe, and what particular type of convertibility this could be, will be examined in Chapter 11.

d. Information. There are several reasons that can be adduced to declare the question of information at this junction largely a nonissue for most PEs except perhaps the USSR. First, information can be provided on a confidential basis so that it will not be disseminated by the Fund. This modus has worked reasonably well up to now, but it is not likely that sensitive material for the USSR could be contained within the Fund. Second, much has changed since the time when nearly all economic information was elevated to the status of "state secret." But some PEs still do not publish sufficient information to permit a straightforward, comprehensive assessment of their economic situation. Third, it has to be recognized that the profession has sufficiently progressed and that one can now construct a fairly reliable picture of short- and medium-term macroeconomic trends. This admittedly does not yet yield fully accurate estimates of such key variables as gold stocks, foreign exchange reserves, balance-of-payments statistics, and related data, but the estimates have become quite good. Fourth, at the same time, the Fund is no longer insisting rigorously on members providing such information on a timely basis for overt publication, as explained in Section 7.5.

e. The role of gold. The only specific recommendation contained in the Nairobi declaration concerned a return to gold as the basic anchor of a reformed IMS. The Soviet Union would naturally have an interest in anything that affects the price of gold.[17] Any return of gold as an international reserve backing would increase the demand for and thus the price of gold to the benefit of gold producers. Whether a return to the gold-exchange standard is desirable from the point of view of the stability and reliability of a reformed IMS, and whether it is feasible are two different questions, however. Regarding the first, since the breakdown of the gold-exchange standard, Soviet monetary theory, and by extension most of Eastern Europe's, has been divided among two distinct academic groups with connections to government decision makers (see Lavigne 1978, pp. 373–6; Rémy 1985). For brevity's sake, I shall borrow Marie Lavigne's apt designations of "traditionalists" and "modernists."

Commentators and observers frequently associated with the Ministry of Finance and its affiliated organizations, including the financial periodical *Den'gi i kredit*, cluster their view around the traditional anchoring role of gold. They see the collapse of the gold standard as having provoked the chronic chaos of the capitalist economy. They regard the BWS as having been far from satisfactory, especially because it fostered the worldwide domination of the U.S. dollar. Nonetheless, the BWS admittedly had the merit of having based the monetary system on the dollar, itself convertible into gold and linked with all currencies through fixed parities expressed in terms of gold. Gold is viewed as a key "disciplining tool" (Bogdanov 1976, p. 116). As the priority of discipline waned, gold had to be allocated a less central role because of the "debt money" increasingly being created to finance budgetary expenditures and balance-of-payments deficits, and to buttress the internationalization of industrial and financial capital. There has been growing recognition, however, at least in academic circles associated with this traditional point of view, that the "function of gold as a universal equivalent is changing" (Krasavina 1978, p. 145).

The modernist group is usually associated with the more research-orientated institutions of the USSR and their publication outlet (in particular, *Mirovaja ėkonomika i meždunarodnye otnošenija*). Rather than treating it as the alpha and omega of the monetary crisis, the modernists argue (see Matjuchin 1978) that gold had already lost its most important historical attributes as a universal commodity and world money first within individual countries and then between them well before the onset of the crisis, in fact since the gold-exchange standard came into existence. The demonetization of gold, first after World War II and finally with the breakdown of the BWS, is seen as harmful to the stability of the IMS (Bácskai 1975, p. 22). Gold no longer retains its function as a means of payment and of circulation inside the capitalist economy, and it is even no longer a measure of value. Various explanations are invoked, including the ascent of Europe and Japan, relative to the United States, and hence the rise in international tensions stemming from economic conflicts; resentment of the exclusive role of the dollar and the policy freedom it affords the United States because of the dollar hegemony; and the conflict between monetary nationalism and the supranational tendencies built into the IMF surveillance mechanisms. The energy crisis and stagflation accelerated this demise of gold as universal money.

Monetary traditionalists see the solution to the current quagmire in the return to the gold standard or at least to the restoration of some form of gold convertibility. The modernists rarely paint a coherent position on how to surmount the contemporary monetary problems. Because they do not consider gold as the main reason underlying the volatility of the capitalist economic, trading, and financial systems, changes in socioeconomic conditions rather than in a technical tool such as gold are advocated. Nevertheless, although the modernists do not believe that the end of the gold-exchange standard totally explains the crisis of the IMS, it can be put to rest only by devising a way out in which the role of gold must necessarily be taken into account. But in what precise form remains fundamentally unclear.

There has not been any official policy statement on the gold issue since 1976, except the marginal references already quoted. It is therefore legitimate to question whether, after the experiences and fruitless debates of the past decade, the PEs still advocate a return to gold. In the absence of official pronouncements, no categorical answer can be provided, but there are three indirect indicators that a return to gold is no longer being propounded, for either doctrinal or practical reasons. First, though the debate between the traditionalists and the modernists has by no means been fully settled, a noticeable shift in favor of the position taken by those that argue against a return to gold or the gold-exchange standard has emerged. Such a reinstitution is no longer considered feasible, and it should therefore not receive further support and investigation. The strengthening of international liquidity is seen chiefly in the form of relatively stable units of accounts (including the ECU and SDR) and also by pursuing more responsible monetary policies that govern the yen and the dollar (see Krasavina and Baranova 1984, pp. 72ff.). But they remain skeptical as to the role of national currencies as international reserves.

Second, on the eve of UNCTAD VI, the organ of the USSR's Ministry of Foreign Trade contained two lengthy articles by senior ministry officials dealing, among others, with the issue of the IMS as it related to the forthcoming meeting in Belgrade. The first one, by Mr. Aleksej Manžulo, Deputy Minister of Foreign Trade, did not at all touch upon the central monetary issues beyond reaffirming the Soviet stance on UNCTAD's suitability as a "universal international organization" to devote due attention to monetary problems in addition to its other activities (Manžulo 1983, p. 17). The other one, by Mr. Aleksandr Samorodov, a senior expert of the Ministry's Department of International Economic Organizations, stated that the PEs "did not consider the attempts to restrict artificially the role of gold in the international liquid resources as substantiated especially under the persistent inflationary devaluation of paper money" (Samorodov 1983, p. 39).

The third indirect evidence is a categorical statement by Mr. Stanislav M. Borisov, Deputy Minister of Finance of the USSR. In his recent in-depth analysis of the role of gold in the world economy, he opines that it is "absolutely beyond dispute" that the discussions of a return to an official conversion of paper money into gold are utopian and unrealistic. He concludes that "The gold-standard mechanism is definitely something of the past, none of the objective economic conditions for its restoration prevails, and any attempt to agitate in that direction is in advance condemned to failure" (Borisov 1984, p. 449).

Participation in the existing system

Most of the objections to the past and present IMS made by the PEs concern basic principles or general guidelines of policy making in these countries or in the monetary institutions themselves. Their tenor is clearly on the negative side, meaning that the PEs would have several fundamental as well as operational objections to participating in the world's monetary institutions. But that has been perhaps more an ideological and political posturing than a concern motivated by more pragmatic economic and financial considerations, given that several PEs have for some time now been actively participating in both multilateral financial institutions under regular terms of agreement, including several of the usual exceptions referring to developing MEs. In addition to the issues already dealt with in Sections 7.2 and 7.5, some commentary on voting, surveillance, stabilization measures, and information may be in order.

Certainly, for Hungary, Rumania, and, to a lesser extent, Yugoslavia, the Fund has had to come to grips with the special circumstances of PEs. As the adjustment efforts of the early 1980s have amply demonstrated, the PEs can accomplish the standard expenditure-reducing and expenditure-switching policy measures recommended by the Fund rather successfully with the key operands of a traditional PE: investment reduction; a freezing, or even a compression, of private consumption; import cutbacks, if necessary, by strict denial; export promotion, if necessary, by baring domestic shelves; and other such measures. Given this, there should formally not be great incompatibility between the Fund and a PE as far as stabilization is concerned. In other words, for those PEs that politically want to participate, an appropriate adjustment regime can be worked out in consultation with the Fund. A different set of knotty issues derives from the formulation of policy goals acceptable to both the Fund and the PE, as with most MEs.

Regarding the usual objections to the past and present IMS, they appear to refer chiefly to the interpretation of the Articles of Agreement and the way in which the Fund applies them. As explained, the system has undergone a number of modifications over the years that need to be brought out in evaluating the possibility of PEs joining the Fund. Critical obstacles to forming such a system are the obligation to furnish information, the commitment to convertibility, and the weighted voting system. The first two issues have been resolved satisfactorily. The weighted voting system is a touchier issue, as examined in Section 7.5. Minor modifications of the voting structure to accommodate the special features of PEs could perhaps meet their objections on economic and technical grounds. But the present Fund members with voting clout are unlikely to yield on their acquired prerogatives.

From the point of view of international economics, then, there are not that many arguments that can be brought to bear against the PEs joining the IMS. As explained above, the major objections levied against the gold subscription, the central role of a national currency, the voting allocation, the adjustment programs, the determination of ERs, the disclosure of information, and others have nearly all been sufficiently watered down by past Fund practices with respect to the PEs that have joined and even more so with respect to many of the developing MEs. Outright membership in the IBRD and the IMF through such compromises has brought measurable benefits in terms of access to additional IBRD loans at low interest rates and drawings from the IMF to the participants and may appear increasingly attractive for several other PEs in the years ahead. But these direct financial benefits explain only one part of the rationale for seeking membership. Neither substantial quota drawings nor credits on soft terms would probably be a realistic prospect for the USSR, because its quota would inevitably be quite substantial and it could not possibly be treated as a developing country. It should therefore carefully weigh the costs associated with Fund obligations and responsibilities against the benefits of a quota.

Objections to joining the Fund are likely to emerge from two sides. On the one hand, some PEs will find the price to be paid far too high relative to the benefits to be derived in terms of drawing rights, soft loans, and contract bidding. On the other hand, it may prove to be politically undesirable to join the capitalist institutions par excellence outright. If either of these conditions were to inhibit the implementation of meaningful monetary reform, one should look for a solution that makes the PEs still part of the new IMS system without compelling them to join in a system, such as the Fund's, that is politically unacceptable.

*Attitudes of the planned economies regarding a new
international monetary system*

Because the PEs have made no clear-cut commitment to date, it might be
worthwhile to look into the possibilities of the PEs participating in a
reformed IMS. This could take on several forms, including a reshaping
of the presently existing system from within, a newly created global
monetary system, or one that would consist of several layers and be
universal only by virtue of all parts being radially centered on the global
institution.

a. A reform of the Fund from within. Given the basic objections to key
aspects of the BWS, one way in which the PEs could become associated
with it, without compromising their principles, would be through a reform of the Fund from within. The existing system would essentially be
retained in name, but some of the fundamental Articles of Agreement
could be modified and some new paragraphs added to acknowledge the
special features and needs of the PEs. The realism of this possibility is in
doubt, however, if the Nairobi declaration's statement (UNCTAD 1976,
p. 154) still holds:

The proposals made within the framework of IMF to modify the basis of the
existing [IMS] will neither ensure normal currency dealings nor establish conditions to provide stability and the necessary confidence in such an [IMS]. The
proposed modification of the Articles of Agreement of IMF would serve to en-
trench the privileged position of several Western countries in that organization.

In theory, it would be possible to establish the TR monetary region as a
subsystem linked to the IMF though a technical relationship. This could
take several forms. One would be to link the TR and the SDR directly
through a technical agreement between the IBEC and the IMF that
would offer the PEs access to SDRs. For example, an interested PE would
borrow SDRs from the IMF and contract then for a loan in TRs that
would be convertible. The CMEA as a whole would be held responsible
for the repayment of the SDR loan. The interested CMEA countries
could, as a result, have access to a new source of finance without becoming full IMF members. This might be an interesting option for some PEs,
but it would be unacceptable to others called upon to shoulder this service in analogy with the umbrella theory—the Soviet Union in the first
place. It is also doubtful whether the IMF, and the actual and potential
member PEs, would prefer such a link over direct membership.

Perhaps more useful would be the creation of a set of rules for non-
market economies (Holzman 1978a, pp. 126–7) similar to those that permitted Poland and Rumania to accede to the GATT.[18] This solution was
not acceptable to Hungary when it was negotiating in the early 1970s. It

is doubtful whether the PEs that are IMF members would be willing to replace their present direct relationship with an indirect one through the IBEC. Perhaps a more feasible policy might be to have a dual status: a special technical link between the IBEC and IMF for the PEs that do not wish to join the IMF now or in the foreseeable future, and full membership for those that wish to do so.

b. A new world monetary system. Another important issue that has received explicit emphasis in recent suggestions of how the IMS could be modified is the call of the PEs to restructure the prevailing international economic relations on a just, equitable, and democratic basis. The PEs have stressed that another international conference on money and finance be convened "with a view to democratizing the current international monetary and financial system on a just and equal basis" (UN 1983, p. 2). This would entail such a change in the Articles of Agreement that the Fund would not survive.

Exceedingly few Soviet and Eastern European observers have commented on desirable or mandatory conditions for monetary reform. For example, J. Fekete, Deputy Chairman of the Hungarian National Bank, sees the following prerequisites for a workable IMS (Fekete 1978, pp. 27ff.). There is a clear need for a universal monetary institution under the aegis of the United Nations. It should be empowered, under rules to be laid down, to issue new international money as the anchor of the new IMS. The convertibility of that new currency unit should be guaranteed not by one country, as under the gold-exchange standard, or by each country, as under the gold standard, but by all participants in the system. The role of gold is to be regularized by using the metal's value as the *numéraire* for establishing the ER of the new world currency. Third, realistic CC parities for the new world currency need to be set and should be stable yet far more flexible than those of the BWS. Finally, within this framework modalities of how to eliminate bottlenecks in international credit, to make available economically warranted long-term loan capital, or to meet other types of capital requirements in an organized way remain to be worked out. When Soviet commentators enter into positive statements, they (see Fomin 1978, pp. 108–9) frequently stress the following conditions for the emergence of a new IMS that takes into account and meets the interests of states with different socioeconomic systems and at different levels of development: (1) a healthy international political climate; (2) the prior removal of chronic payments imbalances in developed MEs and observing symmetry in adjustment by surplus and deficit countries; (3) a limit to the practice of floating ERs and the provision of compensation for losses sustained as a result of sharp ER changes of main currencies; and (4) better ways and methods of ensuring economic cooperation through more perfect forms of international liquidity. Regarding the latter, the reserve instrument must be acceptable to all participants in international exchange, neutral, sufficiently stable, and protected from the influence of ER fluctuations of all national currencies. It is uncertain whether this must necessarily be based on gold.

c. A multitier world monetary system. Another form of participation would be the explicit recognition of the de facto existence of several currency zones each with its own special needs and characteristics. The European monetary system (EMS), the dollar zone, the yen area, the Arab group, and the other developing MEs have their own peculiarities. Another one could emerge as a result of the establishment of an effective TR monetary region.[19] The interaction among the various regions, however, would be subject to common principles and a universal currency unit (Cooper 1984) to be regulated through rules acceptable to all participants. Surveillance and adjustment requirements would be confined to the interaction among currency zones. Whether this is a realistic option depends importantly on the particular features of the TR monetary system to which I turn now.

8

The CMEA's nascent monetary system and the common banks

From the earlier discussion of how PEs operate singly and within the CMEA concert, it should be clear that macro- and microeconomic planning in physical units as the chief policy instrument of these economies is nonmonetary in nature. Economic management of domestic and trade sectors, especially in CMEA relations, proceeds in good measure by way of physical planning, control, and implementation criteria. The central role of physical planning has remained largely intact in spite of various reform concepts that have been contemplated over the years. Some were partly carried out with two broad effects on the role of planning in the PE. Indirect coordination instruments have gained considerable ground as means of assisting economic agents in reaching decisions that could be dovetailed more readily with the country's overall socioeconomic objectives. At the same time, macroeconomic policies have become increasingly geared to steering economic decisions and to shifting the focus of central planning toward medium- to long-term structural development issues, although the central planning office in virtually all PEs has continued to be involved in detailed planning, but not necessarily on a daily basis.

Because there is no direct regional counterpart to the institutional base, planning instruments, and economic policy goals typical within the purview of each PE, the latter continues to exhibit a very keen interest in ensuring "equivalence" in reciprocal exchange. Although the redistribution of resources is an important feature of individual PEs, especially in the interenterprise sphere, its transposition to the CMEA level has been consistently stymied by nearly all PEs. Rather strict BTPAs that prescribe in quantum the bulk of the goods and services to be exchanged leave little room for flexibility by way of multilateral settlements, payments transfers, and other such means for fostering trade efficiency, even though they have not always been carried out to the letter and the actual needs of the CMEA participants have often diverged from those embedded in the trade protocols. Especially the developed, trade-dependent PEs have emphasized the need to explore in-depth more flexible trade and payments regimes on condition that there be no unintended redistribution of value added across the CMEA.

Another important inducement to exploring ways and means of monetizing external economic relations has emerged from East–West relations. For one, strict BTPAs could not be instituted in relations with MEs simply because these countries generally do not command actual production and trade processes the way most PEs have a habit of doing. Furthermore, most of the industrialized MEs have gradually established convertibility and are therefore not very interested in bilateral clearing, which is an archaic form of economic intercourse. In other words, the duality in regimes already observed for price formation and ERs became a distinguishing mark of the entire foreign trade and payments regime as well.

This chapter first briefly discusses what may explain the low degree of multilateralism in the CMEA, how to reconcile bilateral equilibrium with the need for multilateral exchange, and the prospects for CMEA multilateralism. The backdrop to the IBEC's creation, and the TR's meaning and precise functions in the CMEA are analyzed in the next two sections. The IBEC's evolution since the mid-1970s and its current role in the CMEA's trade and financial regimes are the focus of Section 8.4. The various ways in which third countries could participate in the TR regime are entertained next. The chapter concludes with a brief discussion of the advantages and drawbacks of the bank.

8.1 Multilateralism in the CMEA

Multilateralism in the CMEA is a complex story. The historical aspects of the evolution of bilateralism and the limited forms of multilateralism pursued in the CMEA have been addressed at length in Brabant 1977a, pp. 66–102. Here I shall point briefly to the postwar situation and the key stages in the evolution of CMEA payments cooperation until the IBEC's creation in 1964. The main focus is the present role of multilateralism as a key determinant of the direction in which the SEI mechanism might be improved.

Postwar adjustments

At the end of World War II, all countries affected by the hostilities found their economies, among other aspects, in considerable disarray. The war had wreaked havoc on their already fragile economies. In some cases, the postwar settlements envisaged possibly traumatic shifts in borders and peoples and attendant institutions on top of the devastation caused by the armed conflict. The conversion from a war-economy footing to a civilian economy under conditions of drastic shifts in resources, and sometimes geography, could have been effected by pure market forces, but only at the cost of a profound economic recession and thus the needless prolongation of the adversities encountered in the preceding five years or so. To avert this, all countries maintained or even strengthened the considerable controls over their domestic markets and even more so over the foreign sector that had been typically in force during the 1930s and the war. As a rule, capital transfers were proscribed, and current account transactions could be conducted only through government licensing.

Foreign exchange and trade controls proved to be a severe hindrance to swift recovery to full employment in MEs. Not only did it cut effective demand for each other's goods and services, it needlessly encumbered transactions and raised costs. Given the prevailing disequilibrium circumstances, the MEs decided rather soon to work off the inherited imbalances gradually but with determination. The particular type of economic and financial assistance provided under the umbrella of the Marshall Plan was instrumental in putting Western Europe back on its feet, in spurring on regional economic integration, and in laying the foundations for fostering rapid economic growth largely through the operation of markets. The bases for currency convertibility, at least in the case of current account transactions, were being firmed by multilateralizing the reciprocal exchanges of goods and services in part within the provisions and with the assistance of the resources of the European Payments Union (EPU), which started in 1950, and the already existing Bank for International Settlements (BIS). Even with these instruments, convertibility for current account transactions in most of Europe did not come about until the late 1950s or, for the German Federal Republic in particular, even the early 1960s.

The Eastern European countries *in se* faced the same problems as the European MEs and hence resorted to institutions and policy instruments that supported rather strict foreign exchange controls. But these were embraced for other reasons as well. Czechoslovakia and the eastern part of Germany, because of their level of development, may for a while have aspired to reinstituting flexible forms of trade and payments after reconstruction and reconversion to a civilian economy. But note that both economies had been exposed to considerable state regulation and external payments problems during the interwar period, Czechoslovakia did not exist as an independent state before World War I, and the GDR was altogether a new creation. The other Eastern European countries found the socialist strategy for economic growth and the strictly centralized model of central planning, as it had matured in the Soviet Union, rather congenial to overcome their economic backwardness through industrialization. Yet the desirability of following the route charted by many of the MEs surfaced as an interesting theoretical and political option in harmonizing Eastern Europe. The key issue then as now has been how to promote multilateralism, not as a means of fostering efficient markets but especially as an essential ingredient underpinning the development strategy.

Brief historical sketch

Some of the participants in the early debates advocated that regional cooperation efforts be essentially solidified on the basis of the multilateral balancing of external revenues and payments vis-à-vis the CMEA region as a whole. BTPAs would not be completely supplanted because they blended very well with the detailed planning then being actively put in place. The role of these early debates in the founding of the CMEA in 1949–1950 as well as their influence on the first phase of SEI has been summarized in Chapter 1. In short, the socialist countries had elaborated a broad document, entitled "On prices and multilateral clearing" (Hrinda and Válek 1983, p. 774), which just barely failed to be endorsed in mid-1949 but it was expected to become fully operational around 1950.

How to create multilateralism among PEs and in what particular form it might suitably assist in their ambitious development aspirations disappeared from the political agenda in the second half of 1950. It had indeed proved to be a nonstarter in laying the foundations for intra-CMEA relations and for buffering the industrialization of Eastern Europe. However, surmounting the constraints of bilateralism was as appealing to most of the CMEA participants as it had been to other economies in Europe. This derived essentially from the fact that, to be effective, the mechanism governing economic exchange needs to embody some flexibility so as not forcibly to suppress transitory imbalances over a mutually agreed period. This can be accommodated through market forces, with capital and labor mobility compensating for imbalances on account of current transactions in goods and services. Alternatively, it can be captured through the regional planning of such temporary or permanent resource transfers.

Because neither the rationale underlying the past history of multilateral payments cooperation in Eastern Europe nor the documentation of its evolution has invalidated in any substantive way the earlier comprehensive assessment (Brabant 1977a), there is no need to recount the story at length once again here. Instead, I shall place the question succinctly within the context of postwar cooperation in Eastern Europe, discuss its main stages, outline the persistent constraints within the CMEA framework, and sketch the actual and potential roles of multilateralism in fostering SEI. The characteristics of the TR regime and nonmember participation therein are taken up later.

As indicated, basically three phases can be distinguished. First, from the late 1940s on, attempts were made to overcome the obstacles posed by strict BTPAs through the triangularization and, in some cases, multi-angularization of trade and payments. This usually involved a third partner, mostly from among the Western European MEs, that was keen on obtaining goods from one PE in exchange for exports that were of interest to one or more other PEs. Although undoubtedly very useful for the particular type of commodities included in these ad hoc agreements, the very fact that they were essentially marginal appendages to the strict BTPAs in force among the PEs did not really alleviate the need for short-term payments facilities. Neither did it allow any pair of PEs to expand reciprocal exchanges far beyond the capacity to engage in that particular bilateral trade by the "weakest" partner. As a result, the PEs gradually started to advocate the adoption of a parallel settlements mechanism attached to their BTPAs that would provide for short-run financing in the form of automatic swing credits ex ante rather than ex post, as well as for the multilateral offsetting of imbalances.

The Warsaw agreement of 1957 inaugurated the second phase. It made it possible to elaborate annexes to the ex ante BTPAs in which countries declared themselves prepared to offset multilaterally some imbalances of specific goods. It also advocated that tri- or multiangular supplementary agreements be concluded with the specific objective of reaching balance at a scale larger than the various binary flows involved. To put some teeth into such arrangements, the agreement enjoined countries from maintaining deficits indefinitely by calling for settlement in selected "hard goods" that, at the time, consisted essentially of scarce raw materials and consumer goods, which for all practical purposes were identical to CC or gold. This weak form of the chiefly ex post offsetting of bilateral imbalances, either as originally formulated or for failure of compliance, had only a limited effect.

The real scarcity of the goods to be mobilized in the settlement of imbalances alerted countries to be extra careful about binary deficits, especially because at that time the potential for East–West trade, and hence for earning CC for those hard goods, had measurably improved. The problems also stemmed from the fact that it proved rather cumbersome, after national and trade plans had been worked out, to dovetail supplementary agreements with the real trade potential of partner countries. The volume involved in this type of multilateral settlement never surpassed about 1.5 percent of overall trade (see Brabant 1977a, pp. 86ff.). Although by no means altogether negligible, this limited exchange failed to imbue the CMEA trade regime with the required new vigor.

In view of these experiences and the then growing interest in fostering the ISDL, the PEs came to the conclusion that any realistic form of multilateralism compatible with their BTPAs would have to encompass regionwide negotiations in conjunction with the formulation of trade and national plans. The PEs hoped to establish a limited form of transferability because multilateral balancing ex ante is not "real transferability" (Holzman 1978b, p. 161). Transferability in this context means the ability of any holder of surplus balances to obtain supplementary deliveries from any signatory party and, after meeting certain qualifying conditions, possibly from elsewhere. Another key ingredient would be to ensure a substantial degree of homogeneity among the various bilateral prices for each product, for this would considerably lessen the incentive of participants to offset bilateral imbalances.

Multilateralism as an explicit aim of Eastern European economic cooperation was officially endorsed in late 1962 as the first follow-up to *Basic Principles*. To facilitate the implementation of this crucial policy commitment, the CMEA members decided to create the TR and to establish the IBEC, effective 1 January 1964, as the financial institution in charge of emitting the common currency and facilitating multilateral settlements. Under the provisions of the agreement to create the TR and multilaterial settlements in that unit, two types of real, if institutionalized, multilateralism could occur. It was agreed, first, to conduct a round of supplementary trade negotiations to provide for ex ante multilateralism, after the conclusion of the regular BTPAs involving the offered goods that somehow failed to be incorporated in any of the protocols. This operation might entail the creation of TR reserves if some partner could be found willing to ship goods or to perform trade-related services without insisting on immediate counterdeliveries. The IBEC would ease such transactions by granting various loans (see Section 8.3). In most cases, however, it was realized that, for lack of interest in TR deposits, this second round would initially lead to simple compensatory arrangements. The second type of multilateralism involved the violation of any of the previous contractual obligations or deliveries outside the ex ante protocols. Both were to become the subject of a year-end round of multilateral clearing negotiations organized by the IBEC to make up for uncovered bilateral imbalances or to provide for compensatory deliveries.

The IBEC's attempts to persuade its members into moving away from bilateral settlements in the CMEA have undergone some changes since 1964. The evolution of the bank's institutions, policy goals, and instruments at its disposal could be made the subject of a more refined periodization, but I shall not do so here (see Brabant 1977a, pp. 116–96). The chief reason is that the IBEC and the TR's impact on intra-CMEA multilateralism has remained very weak indeed, and no substantive changes are presently in the offing. It is therefore more useful to focus in what follows on the fundamental reasons for this lackluster performance.

Before concluding the discussion of intra-CMEA multilateralism, it may be of some interest to refer briefly to an experiment started on 1 January 1973.[1] Possibly in consequence of the consultations initiated in connection with the implementation of the provisions of section 7 of *Integration Program*, Czechoslovakia, the GDR, Hungary, Poland, and the USSR agreed to an EPU-like arrangement on an experimental basis (Drabowski 1974, pp. 104–5). Recall that the pivot of the EPU was the settlement of some predetermined, but by arrangement steadily increasing share of multilateral imbalances in CC. In the same spirit, the five participants resolved that 10 percent of the imbalances exceeding the ceiling on settlements credit or other agreed upon swing margin by more than 75 percent be liquidated in this way. Payments for above-plan deliveries and for deliveries arranged in special trade protocols at current WMPs and in CC, as the most important forms of multilateralism, were not at all affected by this arrangement.

Unfortunately, "not a single TR" (Gostomski 1979, p. 49; Kuniński 1986) was ever offset in that way, in spite of the fact that the partial CMEA arrangement was an exceedingly modest endeavor when contrasted with what had earlier been accomplished in the EPU framework. In fact, recent commentary tends to stress that any such effort at multilateralization should make provisions for the compulsory and automatic settlement of a substantial part of imbalances – Imre Vincze suggests at least 25 percent (Vincze 1984, p. 149) – at the end of the settlements period. The agreement also lacked ambition as no attempt was made to alter the nature of the bilateral balancing of trade and services endorsed in the BTPAs. It therefore would not have had much of an impact on CMEA trade and payments in any case.

In spite of its very restricted character, the attempt utterly failed just the same. The GDR withdrew from the provisions in late 1973 or early 1974 before the scheme had had a chance to take effect, and the other members subsequently suspended the partial multilateralization attempt. This failure stemmed from a variety of reasons. The agreement was introduced on the spur of the moment and lacked a stable foundation. How the IBEC was to handle transactions for which it was technically not equipped has never been discussed in the specialized literature. Perhaps most important was the fortuitous development in trade prices in world markets in 1972–1973, which apparently caused the GDR to drop out of the scheme (Ptaszek 1978, p. 24) and thus precipitated its demise (Kuniński 1986). The sharp rise in the price of raw materials and foodstuffs in the early 1970s and the unprecedented increase in WMPs of crude oil in 1973–1974, when they began to be fed into the CMEA price formula for TR transactions, induced substantial imbalances. Given the preeminently bilateral character of intra-CMEA exchanges, these imbalances could be maintained only because the USSR was willing to grant exceptional loans for a period of up to ten years. This enabled the Eastern European partners in serious regional balance-of-payments deficit to maintain a larger import quantum than they would otherwise have been able to afford. This certainly facilitated coming to grips with the external payments difficulties that would almost certainly have forced these countries into early adjustment. As discussed in Chapters 3 and 12, however, this facility has been a two-edged sword. Under the circumstances, the rather sizable surpluses accumulated earlier with the USSR were very rapidly reversed into pronounced deficits. That dampened any enthusiasm the Eastern European PEs may have had for partial settlement in CC. A final reason for its failure was its very modesty. If even an amount equal to 1.75 times the value of the swing balance mutually agreed upon would not be the subject of multilateral payments and only 10 percent of the amount of the imbalance above that trigger point could have been subjected to CC settlements, what success could have been anticipated from the agreement that was endorsed? It is true that the precise size of these ex ante clearing imbalances has never been disclosed. But that is unlikely to have been very different from the swing of 2 percent of the value of the agreed trade turnover (Wesołowski 1977, p. 174) tolerated within the IBEC and the earlier bilateral clearing arrangements (about 2–3 percent of planned trade turnover). Wesołowski suggests that an ad hoc credit ceiling could be set (Wesołowski 1977, p. 174), but I am not aware of any having been declared.

CMEA cooperation and multilateralism

As a policy goal, then, multilateralism has had a checkered history in Eastern Europe. None of the various attempts to bring about multilateralism either by political or by administrative means during the past forty years or so has contributed meaningfully to the demise of CMEA bilateralism. Whatever criterion of measuring the degree of multilateralism is used (see Brabant 1977a, pp. 73ff.), only an astonishingly small amount of CMEA trade is being settled multilaterally – perhaps up to 3 percent at most in some years (Fedorowicz 1979, p. 179). This share has remained negligible basically because the portion of trade not earmarked in a planned fashion has remained well below 1 percent of the total turnover (Konstantinov 1983b, p. 4). The institutionalization of multilateralism therefore continues to be an essentially pivotal precondition for fostering closer economic cohesion in Eastern Europe. This proposition holds even if planned regional cooperation were to be advanced as the absolute priority of SEI for as long as national sovereignty reigns supreme.

The essential explanation of why multilateralism has not yet gained a solid foothold in Eastern Europe hinges fundamentally on the BTPAs and the planning systems associated with them. Briefly, because the PEs continue to prefer comprehensive trade agreements that yield disparate prices (see Chapter 4) for a substantial part of their total trade, the transfer of bilateral imbalances, which is self-evident under normal world trading conditions, would result in the exchange of different values. The opportunities for multilateralizing this particular configuration of the regional economic intercourse are therefore rather confined.

Certainly, most observers realize that multilateralism in payments cannot easily be reconciled with bilateralism in trade: Whenever imbalances manifest themselves either because they were planned, and thus incorporated in the BTPAs, or because they violated some of the provisions of the trade protocols, they have to be worked off in subsequent trading periods and not through contemporaneous reciprocal settlements. It is primarily a question of access to markets of goods and services, which has been a most controversial subject. Given currency inconvertibility, intransferability of the TR, and deep-seated reluctance to embrace far-reaching economic reforms, no facile solution to the problem of CMEA bilateralism is in sight. The more market-oriented observers argue for a liberalization of the BTPAs. Others advocate that the problem needs to be addressed first and foremost in the context of plan provisions for the delivery of goods and services by securing primarily better adherence to BTPAs.

MTPAs may in some instances provide room for balanced deliveries of goods and services that would otherwise be eschewed. There are various ways in which MTPAs could materialize. One that could blend in with the present institutional setup of the majority of the PEs envisages the negotiation of ex ante balanced MTPAs. Provided they are carried out to the letter, no imbalances need to be "financed." Another way, short of moving into convertibility issues, would be to resort to supplementary transactions as a result of making the TR really transferable within the CMEA. Thus, "scouts" of the actual or potential creditors could survey the "markets" of any of the debtor partners and purchase whatever is available. A third solution would be to agree upon the creation of a common credit pool. Potential surplus countries reluctant to accumulate idle resources would then offset their imbalance against that of one or more other clearing members willing to hold such reserves on a temporary basis. Such a common pool of credit resources, from the technical point of view, would be quite comparable to the mechanism presently under the IBEC's supervision. Finally, and here one ventures into the issue of convertibility, the members could create a common CC pool accessible to the surplus countries. Such an external TR transferability would initially require some constraints on the disposal of those reserves so as to forestall the premature bankruptcy of the fund.

None of these solutions is likely to be implemented unless major systemic changes are inaugurated in the PEs' trade and payments regimes. Ex ante balanced MTPAs do not by themselves guarantee exact fulfillment of the contracts and are therefore bound eventually to give rise to settlement problems. Either of the two alternatives envisaging supplementary purchases is predicated on the surplus country being able to locate goods and services among the "residual resources" of debtor countries. The first alternative is further constrained by the requirement that an ex post multilateral balance emerge within a manageable time frame. Both suffer from the basic dilemma of the trade and payments model of the PEs: It is so much more difficult to attain flexibility in an orderly manner ex post when, according to the basic trade mechanism of these countries, this is believed to be superfluous and thus actively discouraged. Because the PEs are chronically short of CC reserves, the ex post settlement of imbalances in CC strikes one very sensitive chord. It is unlikely to be resorted to for lack of "hardness" of the goods for which the deficit countries have to pay in CC. Furthermore, leakage of the CC pool to East–West trade, which is quite a likely consequence of such a form of ex post multilateralism, begs the question of the continuous financing of intra-CMEA trade.

All these problems are bound to crop up in any attempt to establish ex post multilateralism. The essence of the postwar international trading and financial networks has always been anchored to ex ante multilateralism. That is, no agent in an ME is bound to decide about what to trade, where, and to what extent according to his more or less accurate evaluation of what each individual flow will bring in return. That is self-evident: A seller of goods receives CC and is entitled to acquire any product from any provenance with those balances; likewise, a purchaser of goods is bound to make payment in CC, but he or she need not necessarily obtain those financial resources from the immediate sale of goods and services. That is precisely what drives the integration processes in MEs. Suitably modified to blend in with some essential prerogatives of socialist economies, it should also be the motor conveying SEI.

8.2 The meaning and functions of the transferable ruble

To evaluate properly the significance of the TR as an international currency unit, its role, formal definition, and actual utilization need to be clarified.

A truly international currency unit?

With considerable pride the authorities of the PEs created in 1963 the TR as the first truly international currency. It is presumed to deserve this qualification ideologically because it was created in the spirit of socialist internationalism and economically because the volume of liquidity thus created would not be subject to national macroeconomic policies. Instead, it is managed by a common institution in which members have an equal voice regardless of capital subscription, size, trading interests, or level of development. It was also seen as a truly international currency unit because, by definition, it would be stable, help to foster regional multilateralism, and be instrumental in broadening the scope of SEI. In several respects, the TR resembles the SDR, but it is completely independent of national currencies and economic fluctuations. As such, it cannot be the object of speculation and its creation does not bring unjustified income in the form of internal seigniorage to the emitting country, which has been so for all capitalist monetary units, or, in principle, even of external seigniorage as has been attained by a few key world currencies.

The TR was originally seen as a vehicle for multilateralizing intra-CMEA trade, assisting in the accumulation of capital funds for joint integration projects, and providing a stable store of value. Because the TR has been slated as the pivot of commodity–money relations in support of SEI, the nature of the currency unit, its origin, how its stock can be expanded, and how its circulation is determined need to be examined carefully to avoid unwarranted inferences on the real role of the CMEA banks and the significance of the socialist capital market. Such errors have by no means been confined to "uninformed" Westerners (see Brabant 1977a, pp. 108–9). The crux of the controversy usually hinges on the role of the TR as money or the ways in which this currency unit can discharge itself of some function that is typically associated with real money. Depending upon their frame of analysis, which is unfortunately not always clearly spelled out, the TR's advocates and detractors alike may be correct, because they have chosen implicitly to formulate their arguments exclusively on incomplete, if not necessarily partial, information.

The formal role of the transferable ruble

The TR allegedly differs from any other currency unit because of its origin, source of creation, sphere of application, and purchasing power (Mazanov 1970, pp. 62 ff.). It is a currency unit established by multilateral agreement. It emanates through trade[2] as pure credit or abstract money. It applies only to the CMEA region, notably in the form of payment for intragroup imports or to generate regional credits. The TR is therefore formally detached from the "national" currencies and should not be confounded with the Soviet ruble.[3] It is alleged to be a stable currency for two reasons: It has a firm gold content (0.987412 gram of fine gold) and CMEA trade prices are supposedly by definition stable. However, because TR funds cannot be converted into gold and the official parity is only notional, the TR's value depends critically on its real purchasing power. This interpretation has been gaining strong ground in recent years (Konstantinov 1978a, p. 137). Contemporary doctrinal debates, though still divided on the issue, have been shifting noticeably in favor of viewing the relationship between the TR and gold as "practically meaningless and theoretically problematical" (Thümmler 1983, p. 441). Furthermore, CMEA prices for transactions coming under TR arrangements are not really stable, except in the short run (mostly for one year), as argued in Chapter 4. Stability of the TR is therefore a direct function of the average movement of prices for goods and services cleared under the TR regime. Because these prices are in principle derived from WMPs, if the latter are unstable the TR equivalents will be also. It is true, however, that the TR's notional parity can be changed only as a result of a new multilateral agreement, in contrast to the ability of Soviet authorities, for instance, to choose unilaterally to adjust the "value" of the domestic and *valuta* ruble.

The TR was intended to be the only currency unit used by the IBEC for intra-CMEA transactions, although its sphere of application would not forcibly be confined to the CMEA. All economic relations, including trade agreements, among the PEs are supposed to be expressed in TR. The TR is created only as accounting money as a result of temporary net receipts by members of the bank or of net transfers of such potential receipts to the bank. The latter holds in particular for the bank's capital and undistributed profits, but also for any other IEO whose own funds comprise TR contributions. Any member possessing TR balances is entitled to mobilize these funds for payment of any claim held by another member of the bank. In principle, only one account is kept for each type of transaction. Holders of current account balances that exceed regular transaction requirements are invited to open a term account at a higher interest rate. The bank's credit and interest policies are set in line with the PEs' trade and joint cooperation agreements.

With respect to its own clearing regime, on the face of it the TR, then, has all the trappings of an international currency that is "convertible into goods." In other words, it is freely transferable within the clearing region. It is not a truly CC because this giral money cannot be converted freely into other currencies and thus is financially inconvertible. Neither can it be considered a truly transferable currency because in practice, as discussed in the next section, the ostensible multilateral settlement of accounts at the IBEC is only the synthesis of the bilateral accounts. It is the latter and not the net overall balances that set rigid guidelines for subsequent negotiations about new BTPAs. The IBEC can, in principle, follow an independent credit and interest policy to foster trade, and thus influence the direction in which SEI is to be promoted in the short to medium term. These formal features are in sharp contrast to the real world in which the TR can be used even if the focus of attention is restricted to regular transactions among the PEs themselves.

The real world of the transferable ruble

Inasmuch as the TR is not convertible into other currencies, except for a limited range of noncommercial transactions (see Chapter 6), or into goods or currencies of agents who do not participate in the IBEC, it should be emphasized first of all that the TR is at best a regional currency unit. This by itself should not detract from its potential as a measure of value that determines trade prices, as a medium of exchange (or payments instrument), and as a store of value (or means of accumulation). To discuss the degree of realism of any of these attributes, and evaluate the extent to which it applies, the salient features of the trade regime of the PEs must be recalled.

As discussed, what moves goods in the CMEA lies not primarily in the financial sphere, even in the case of CC transactions, but is set by ex ante BTPAs. On the whole, the TR's role must therefore necessarily be confined to that of a unit of account. It may now be a very powerful unit of account that greatly facilitates the planning of regional economic interaction, but a unit of account it is just the same. Because it is created solely by imbalances in reciprocal regional flows of goods and services, the TR's "circulation" is necessarily a direct function not of the absolute value of intraregional trade, as it is so often mistakenly stipulated, but of the sum of the positive (or negative) imbalances in CMEA trade relations.

A bank with its own funds and deposits is normally able to create banking money in the reasonable expectation that depositors do not draw down their claims all at once and borrowers do not instantaneously exhaust their credit ceiling. But the IBEC does not expand the stock of socialist international currency by issuing TR credits, as it is so often claimed.[4] The basic explanation is rather straightforward. TR credits granted by any institution entitled to do so amount essentially to a simple redistribution of temporarily "free" financial resources accumulated by one or more clearing participants in the form of deposit accounts at the IBEC. The formidable disjunction between financial and real CMEA transactions inevitably signals that any loan obtained without the recipient having first secured concurrent commodity flows in bilateral agreements is superfluous. The emitted TR volume is therefore identical to the amount of voluntary and compulsory loans extended by the bank. It simultaneously corresponds to the sum of deposits necessarily made by the net surplus countries. In other words, the credit multipliers associated with the money "created" by the bank tend to be much smaller than unity, if perhaps not identically zero, when the loan is granted without prior agreement on the exchange of goods; otherwise, the multipliers are exactly unity.

The bank, then, fulfills primarily the role of a go-between in clearing and loan operations. As a result, new TRs are emitted only when the sum of all surpluses in regional trade rises. Any attempt to reverse imbalances, for instance, by reinforcing discipline in the framework of adherence to BTPAs, inevitably entails a reduction in the TR stock in circulation, as was clearly exhibited by the sharp deterioration of the regional terms of trade for the former CMEA surplus countries beginning in 1975 and by the call for greater discipline in recent years. The fundamental features of the CMEA trade and settlements mechanisms therefore offer a cogent explanation of why it is futile to submit credit requests without firm commodity backing. It is within the arena bounded by these parameters that the TR's real role, the two CMEA banks, and the socialist monetary system as a whole need to be evaluated.

The aforementioned characteristics of the TR refer to the theoretical definition of such a currency. The volume of TR in circulation can formally be augmented by an increase in CC or gold deposits. In practice, however, the accounts of CC deposits or credits are kept separately from TR transactions proper. Although CC transactions are an important activity of the two banks, they play a minor role in the financing of regional trade. As far as individual CMEA members are concerned, they can only create TRs by exporting more than they import in regional relations. As the gold–dollar standard so clearly illustrated, under such conditions the stock of TRs to "finance" CMEA trade can only be expanded steadily if at least one country is able and willing to run a permanent deficit in intraregional trade. The CMEA is indeed a closed entity: Nothing can be added to or withdrawn from the bank's TR funds by means available to the members, except perhaps as a result of attracting deposits and loans from outside; but these are not proper TRs.

The transferable ruble as an international currency

It is frequently stated that the TR is a full-fledged international currency not merely capable of but actually fulfilling all the functions of international money.[5] Any international currency should at the same time be a standard of value, a payments medium, and a store of value for accumulation.[6] Most Eastern European commentators claim that the TR complies with these conditions, because CMEA trade prices are expressed in that unit, payments for settlements of merchandise transactions and services (commercial and noncommercial) are effected in it, credits are transferred from TR assets, and TR current account and time deposits supposedly enlarge the bank's role in financing regional trade.

The TR is said to have a stable purchasing power because it allegedly fulfills its role as an international currency independently of the "crises" of the capitalist monetary system (Allachverdjan 1974, p. 35; Mirošničenko 1974, p. 83). The latter is only a half-truth: Because it is not yet applied in trade with third partners, the TR is by its very essence at best a regional currency. Yet its value is evidently not fully independent of changes in MEs, including their currency fluctuations, in view of the reference base of CMEA prices. Movements of WMPs over time, if not their short-term oscillations, have at least a "seismic" effect on CMEA prices.

Notwithstanding these principles, the actual value of the TR is fixed indirectly in the negotiations of BTPAs with the result that it has no uniform value, it is not fully stable in time, and it does not have the same value at any given moment to all actual or potential holders. The lack of uniformity in the TR's purchasing power is not at all a trivial matter once it is taken into account that price differences for the same goods in different bilateral relations (even the same exporting or importing country) can be very substantial. Furthermore, there is no one-to-one correspondence, not even approximately, between the WMP and the corresponding CMEA price, as underlined in Chapter 4. In view of these considerations, it is not at all obvious whether the TR meets the usual conditions of an international currency. Is it in fact a monetary unit at all? A clarification of this seemingly rhetorical question will prove useful because so much of what the CMEA and its institutions can accomplish depends on the role of the TR.

Even Eastern European economists, not least those closely associated with the international banks, uphold conflicting opinions on the issue. Some state bluntly that because the TR cannot be held in the form of banknotes, it is not money (Kulikov 1972, pp. 142–3). A Western charge has been that the TR is not money because one cannot pay anything at all with it in MEs and "payment" within the CMEA is restricted to previously contracted purchases.[7] These somewhat naive comments skirt the more fundamental issues at stake. Whether or not the TR is a real currency in the economic sense[8] depends on what it can do, not on what it cannot do.

Is the TR a standard of value? The answer must be negative, for the value of commodities and services in PEs is, in principle, a unique function of socially necessary labor expenditures (see Chapter 5). In trade, prices are set in bilateral bargaining sessions on the basis of past average WMPs, which are not at all linked with domestic wholesale prices. It is therefore difficult to see in what respect the TR could be a proper "standard of value." Moreover, it is debatable from both a philosophical and a practical point of view whether the value concept should not be defined differently. The value of a currency is determined by what can be bought with it, and this in the end depends on demand and supply conditions. Though it is not exactly the determinant of value, it is argued elliptically that the TR is a standard of value because "the foreign value of a commodity expressed in prices is determined [in TR], and therefore the [TR] is a measure of value" (Mirošničenko 1974, p. 83). Precisely because starting prices in CMEA trade negotiations are derived from nonsocialist markets, it is fairly immaterial whether such prices are converted into TR when the trade negotiations get under way (see Gadomski 1974, p. 43). It seems indisputable, then, that the TR does not "really" measure the value of commodities and services either in terms of socially necessary labor expenditures or in terms of marginal values expressed in some actual markets.

Is the TR an exchange medium? It is, but only to the extent that TRs earned by exporting prearranged volumes of goods can be mobilized solely in payment of goods resorting to a simultaneous agreement on the reverse real flow. This confined area of operation derives from the fact that a country with a positive trade balance is not in a position to mobilize it in another CMEA country without an ex ante BTPA providing for commodity flows. The fact that a surplus country can activate these balances in the next period with one or more partners who now have incurred a regional debt is not a practical solution – it certainly is not a comforting one – in a system with ostensibly multilateral settlements in a uniform payments medium. Furthermore, the transfer, now or in the future, of imbalances from one bilateral relation to another is by no means assured. This statement should not be construed as denying that individual FTOs in some PEs can order goods within the terms stipulated in the BTPAs and pay for them in TR via the IBEC (Fedorowicz 1979, p. 178). From a sheer technical, microeconomic point of view, then, the TR may act as a means of payments.[9] However, in that respect there is actually no difference between the present and the erstwhile strictly bilateral system of clearing.

Can the TR be used to finance intra-CMEA trade? Given the trade regime, to offset bilateral imbalances under the condition of a balanced regional trade pattern fixed ex ante and realized there is no need for a common currency fund. Any common unit of account would suffice. But if equilibrium of multilateral settlements is not realized ex post, if it is deemed desirable to determine regional trade ex ante in such a way that some partners have an overall claim on the region, or if the need arises to complement planned trade by market-based commerce and the claims thus generated should not be frozen temporarily, then some temporary "financing" of imbalances is required. The proper framework for an analysis of financing in this connection should not be predicated on the fact that the creditor obtains a claim that is convertible into future goods. Instead, the surplus holder should have the option to supply his or her domestic market either from within the region or from outside with the commodities that could not be procured as contracted in the agreements. Whether the creditor exerts this right or instead chooses temporarily to accumulate the funds should be left to his or her discretion. In any case, the solution most certainly should not be preempted by the settlements mechanism itself. Does the system of settlements in TR meet these conditions?

Is the TR a store of value? Certainly, TR balances can be accumulated at the IBEC. But simple legal or administrative provisions are not necessarily good evidence of their economic worth. The latter depends on whether a country willing to accumulate surpluses is motivated to do so by economic incentives. TR balances held at the IBEC can be activated sometime in the future in the same bilateral relationship where they originated. But both the low nominal and the negative real interest rates for TR deposits and, more important, the uncertainty about what precisely can be obtained for the TR, and when and where, have so far discouraged countries freely to accumulate TR balances. That the PEs have amassed at the IBEC funds to the tune of several billions of TRs neither contradicts the foregoing statement, nor does it prove that the TR is actually a good store of value.

Is the TR a good international currency unit? Does it fulfill the functions for which it was created? Should it be made convertible? Or should efforts to monetize the CMEA economies be redirected? These and similar controversial questions have been the object of speculation for more than twenty years. The real points concerning the TR appear to have been largely missed in these debates because the actual role of that unit of account lies not in the financial sphere but in that of commodity transactions. Ingrained commodity bilateralism cannot in itself be relieved through the accumulation of "real" TR funds to encourage true multilateralism, meaningful trade financing, or convertibility into national currencies or CCs. The TR has all the dispositions of a truly constructive medium for promoting multilateralism. But the effective exploitation of these potential qualities depends critically on the abandonment of bilaterally balanced trade (Nazarkin 1971, pp. 64ff.). The CMEA trade regime is predicated on equating bilateral receipts and payments, and there is therefore no need for any pool of reserves to finance intragroup trade. Only a common denominator for these transactions is required.

The TR's real worth, its instrumental role in the emergence of multilateralism, the bank's ability to finance regular trade, and the settlement of ex post bilateral imbalances would no longer be issues for debate if all members were to abandon strict trade planning and bilateral balancing, replace the present system by an agreement on clearing trade multilaterally in TR, and be willing freely to accumulate uncleared regional balances. In all this, the real issue at stake is clearly not the role and function of the TR but the willingness of the members because the TR is not sufficiently attractive to sway all PEs into adhering to the aforementioned conditions. Putting it in Machlup's words: "Money needs takers, not backers; the takers accept it, not because of any backing, but only because they count on others accepting it from them" (Machlup 1973, p. 26). By its very nature and actual functions, then, the TR does not comply with this weighty condition. Finding takers for the TR remains the crucial objective of transforming the present CMEA settlements system.

8.3 Backdrop to the bank's formation

The idea of establishing a common settlements organization similar to the Fund antedates 1964 by more than a decade. Apart from the embryonic discussions that took place in the first year or so of the CMEA's existence and earlier projects (see Chapter 1), the debates about the creation of an own settlements bank started in earnest at the first general meeting of central bankers of the PEs, which took place in May 1958 in Prague. The agreement reached in 1962 and ratified in 1963 represented the culmination of extensive top-level negotiations on the advantages and drawbacks of the various alternative ways of promulgating real multiliateralism and financial cooperation within the CMEA, and the institutional supports that would inevitably be required in the process.

The most immediate inducement to the bank's creation in 1964 was the alleged consensus on the ISDL and the establishment of a regional planning office to construct a single socioeconomic development plan according to *Basic Principles*. It is unclear whether the intention was to liberalize regional trade in the ex ante planning sense. In all likelihood the new system was designed to explore and to encourage ways of transferring national wealth across the region much more flexibly than had been permitted heretofore. However, the institution was set up without the participating authorities having really come to a clear and unambiguous consensus on the bank's mission and on how policy makers would enable the Bank Council or the SCFQ[10] gradually to assume more and more complex tasks.

Soviet decision makers particularly stressed the need for a mere technical institution entrusted especially with effectuating as smoothly as possible the trade implications of the projected common plan. There is no evidence at all that the USSR was prepared to support a freer form of multilaterialism along the basic precepts of the EPU. But not all PEs had engaged in the debates with that goal in mind. Several of the smaller ones evinced no particular loyalty toward common planning as such and therefore had quite disparate objectives when they agreed to the bank and its TR regime. They favored the establishment of a full-fledged regional bank to remedy the defects of bilateralism and the obvious shortcomings of the 1957 clearing arrangement. Poland was in the forefront of this line of argument, with strong support from Czechoslovakia and Hungary. Though others, especially Rumania, shared the adverse reaction to the suggestion of common planning, with regard to the bank they were aiming only at a refinement of the 1957 protocol. Accordingly, the process of reaching trade agreements and the settlements mechanism were to be left largely intact.

Apart from the different objectives held by the various PEs at the time, there was also a lack of solid agreement even about the more technical aspects of the institution. From the point of view of economic policy, it was quite clear that only a simultaneous change in the trade and financial mechanisms of the PEs could possibly generate significant progress toward closer cooperation. Trade organs of a number of countries tended to stress that they were not at all prepared to engage in MTPAs. But representatives of many financial institutions came out in favor of multilateral payments (see Zwass 1968, pp. 324ff.; Zwass 1971, pp. 132ff.). Most of them were arguing the case of creating an efficient international bank with a real credit system, a partially convertible or at least easily transferable socialist currency, a common fund to finance investment projects, and so on.

This diversity of views among decision makers could only be bridged through a compromise solution. Under the circumstances, the USSR apparently felt that real multilateralism and supranational planning were not mutually reinforcing or, worse, that they were incompatible. It therefore tended to favor a minimalist solution: the immediate creation of a common bank to organize smooth settlement of reciprocal trade and related claims. In other words, the USSR advocated the establishment of merely a technical institution to oversee and organize mutual settlements.

Even with this limited agreement on the establishment of a technical clearing system, there was an unambiguous expectation on the part of those participants who had argued the case for real multilateralism that a more sophisticated regional financial system would evolve in due course. Such a gradual transformation of the clearing house into a real regional banking institution would have been possible if the PEs had enacted measures to combat effectively the persistent insulation of their domestic markets, if they had gradually modified their trade mechanism, and if nonmembers had provided the bank with the financial resources to permit a smooth transition towards multilateralism. None of these possibilities seemed then to be inherently unattainable in view of the ongoing discussions about domestic economic reforms and the gradually changing climate for cooperation with other countries.

8.4 The CMEA trade regime and the IBEC

Because the IBEC's institutional and related features have not changed in any major way since Brabant 1977a was assembled, I shall focus here on the more policy-related issues of a common settlements bank. I first discuss the bank's purposes, it broad operational mechanisms, and how it has fared to date. I then examine several issues that have gained prominence over the past twenty years, although they were not of major consideration at the bank's foundation: the bank's role in other than merchandise transactions in the TR currency zone, CC operations, and its relationship to other CMEA organs.

The bank's chief tasks

Endowed with an own capital fund, the bank was set up as a regular commercial venture that would be entitled to engage in any banking operation. The introduction of a highly restrictive abstract currency unit managed solely by temporarily unbalanced reciprocal commercial transactions made the IBEC and the TR resemble Keynes's Clearing Union and Bancor, respectively, although many substantive differences should be recalled from Chapter 7. Apart from the fact that the IBEC's mission as a commercial bank far surpassed that of a clearing institution, its key official functions were those associated with the implementation of the ISDL. The bank's activities can be discussed under the headings of administration–organization, credit planning and lending, economic and financial research, operational settlements, and CC transactions. Because many of these features were adequately discussed in Brabant 1977a, I shall focus here on settlements, lending, credit planning, and CC transactions.

The TR mechanism was basically intended to perform four main tasks as set forth in the agreement. First, the bank was to perform the technical settlement of regional payments due upon the delivery of goods and services as per the BTPAs. This type of operation would normally involve the granting of very short-term (accounting, settlement, or swing) credits so as to overcome discontinuities in the reciprocal flow of payments. Such credits would not normally need the prior approval of the Bank Council. Second, the bank was to grant loans to bridge seasonal fluctuations in receipts and payments, to overcome temporary balance-of-payments problems, and to stimulate trade beyond the levels stipulated in the ex ante agreements. These would involve the issuance of short-term loans to be approved by the bank. The bank could fund these loans from its own resources, but its chief source of funds would be member deposits. To make these attractive, adequate interest rate policies for deposits and loans with a proper spread were to be formulated. Third, the bank was to seek ways and means of stimulating multilateralism not only in the simple technical sense of offsetting reciprocal bilateral imbalances but also in the area of trade and payments for which it might have to obtain means of financing such imbalances. MTPAs to be worked out with the bank's help were to be of major assistance in this endeavor. Finally, it was called upon to administer funds to create and operate common enterprises or joint investment projects. In this, it was to act mainly as custodian (of course, not as manager) of these special contributions by interested members and to take in hand the technical aspects of rendering such projects feasible. For this reason and also because the bank was apparently never called upon to exert this task, I shall largely disregard this particular task here. The only exception is the bank's role as administrator, especially of the IIB's TR funds and transactions. It is the latter that, beginning with 1971, should have become the center encouraging common enterprises and joint investment projects (see Chapter 10).

Apart from the foregoing tasks, the bank was legally authorized to enter into any normal banking operation compatible with its statutes. In particular, it was entitled to seek deposits from nonmembers and to take part in the financing and clearing of East–West trade by attracting funds from members as well as from third parties. The bank could engage in credit, accounting, clearing, arbitration, deposit, guarantee, and other types of CC operations with members and third parties. Originally, the bank's charter did not entitle it to raise money by floating loans on capital markets, but this deficiency was remedied in 1970 along with a few other, more technical features.

The bank's operational mechanisms in transferable ruble payments

The bank's operational mechanisms can best be discussed in the light of the foregoing broad goals set for the bank. Regarding the multilateralization of payments as its central task, it is necessary to separate the core issues of how to overcome bilateralism and the inevitable obstacles associated with that process, from the way in which the IBEC can or cannot discharge itself from its functions. Because this topic has earlier been discussed at length in connection with multilateralism, I shall dwell here only on the technical aspects of the regional settlement of accounts.

There is little doubt that the bank has a competent staff and by now a comprehensive infrastructure to guarantee smooth transfers of all commercial transactions. There is therefore no reason why it would not be able to do likewise for the multilateral settlement of accounts. If the bank were enabled to offset reciprocal imbalances as originally intended, it could probably considerably reduce its workload. This is especially so because, for all practical purposes, it now has to maintain dual accounts to ensure that the payments documents transmitted by the PEs are honored correctly in accordance with the trade agreements in force (Vincze 1978a, p. 50). The same is true for loans and internal accounting (Vincze 1977, p. 633). The bilateral system of accounting of all debts and credits appears to be still in effect (Farkas 1978, p. 41). Surpluses at the bank are actually only mobilizable with the same partner (Ljubskij et al. 1978, p. 60). The TR is therefore an "ideal money" that is really transferable only in the accounting sense.

The bank initially tried to foster the volume of trade coming within the scope of the two multilateral rounds, but is has hardly succeeded in boosting the degree of multilateralism above levels typical of the preceding twenty years. Though precise figures are lacking, the degree of overall multilateralism in TR settlements reportedly does not exceed 3 percent of turnover in any year, and the extent of genuine multilateralism, which cannot be equated with the share of loans in the total volume of TR settlements on average or by year-end (as in Baláẑik 1980, p. 55), would appear to be much smaller still.[11] The bank attempts to compensate ex post for bilateral imbalances, but its successful mediation efforts remain clearly contingent on the disposition of the members to engage in multilateral balancing on an ad hoc basis. To the degree that the PEs insist on the bank pursuing its settlements tasks mostly passively, the IBEC itself cannot possibly do otherwise because it has little influence over trade decisions and the execution of BTPAs.

The financing of CMEA transactions should have been an essential element of the bank's tasks. In view of what has been said, to tie over temporary differences in receipts and payments when balanced BTPAs are to be carried out, only short-term credits are required chiefly to accommodate different degrees of seasonality in reciprocal flows. For this, the bank does not need own funds because its task consists solely in recording the financial flows, calculating interest earned and due, and suggesting that in the next contract the bilateral imbalance be set exactly to pay for the interest accrued in the previous trade period. Though the precise share of credit in TR settlements is unknown, it never exceeds 40 percent of turnover for any portion at any time, and it has recently averaged out to less than 3.5 percent of turnover, though the share of gross credit in TR trade turnover is quite large – about 14 percent (Džindžichadze 1985, p. 5). But it will be in need of own funds to provide real short-term credits and to multilateralize regional trade in the likely event that the BTPAs are not fully carried out. Provided the PEs are willing automatically to "transfer" mutual balances, then, the bank need only provide short-term credits to finance planned or expected multilateral imbalances.

The bank was also to engage in financing trade on a longer-term basis. To discharge itself of such activities, it would have to mobilize its own funds and to attract temporarily free deposits or obtain loans abroad. Given the CMEA trade regime, however, such funds can be mobilized if some PE is willing to incur, on balance, a surplus by accumulating deposits in the bank that "finance" the member in deficit. In other words, the entire principle of strict BTPAs as the very essence of the CMEA trade mechanism would be called into question. Because the bank has no control over this, real financing of TR transactions has not been one of its more conspicuous operations.

To manage funds properly and to encourage members to accumulate TR deposits, the bank was to engage in an active interest rate policy and to set up an independent credit policy so as to enhance the process of SEI through the timely redeployment of free assets elsewhere in Eastern Europe. When it was founded, it was believed that the bank would be able to exert, largely autonomously, some positive impact on the CMEA settlements mechanism through its own credit and interest rate policies. As explained, no independent credit policy – as distinct from the purely formal credit planning that has been adhered to – could be developed because there has been no substantive change in the type and structure of the BTPAs that continue to regulate the pattern and intensity of commercial relations in the CMEA. It was thought for years that even within this confined space there might still be some room for an active interest rate policy. Unfortunately, this has not been the case for two reasons.

First, interest earned (due) is an asset (liability) vis-à-vis the bank on a net basis, whereas the actual pattern of intragroup exchanges is regulated bilaterally. It is now rather difficult to attribute a particular portion of the interest earned or incurred to each bilateral partner and hence to identify whence goods might be obtained for earned interest (Vincze 1977, p. 634). Because such sums can be used only in the context of BTPAs in any case, the mobilization of assets stemming from net interest earnings has posed particularly vexing problems now for over twenty years (Ljakin 1984, p. 129; Špaček 1984, p. 438). There are some claims to the effect that partly in response to the preparation and debates of the June 1984 summit and its aftermath, the SCFQ elaborated in 1984 or so (Špaček 1984, p. 438) an acceptable methodology. This has apparently been endorsed in the meantime so that the IBEC can properly apportion interest earned and incurred and thus encourage offsetting flows in the next round of BTPAs. At the same time, the IBEC has apparently been given more disciplining authority (Válek 1985, p. 10).

Second, the bank has been inhibited from activating an interest rate policy, even if had been a meaningful instrument under the circumstances, by the strictures on the level and flexibility of interest rates. Especially because the bank does not have an independent loan policy, interest rates were reset only in 1968, 1970, 1977, and 1986! There have been no changes in these posted rates for deposits since 1976, when it was agreed to lower them for current account deposits and to raise them for time deposits effective 1 January 1977. Loan rates apparently remained unchanged from mid-1970 until 1 April 1986! As a result, these interest rates (ranging between 1.5 and 4 percent for deposits and 1.5 and 5 percent for loans until 1986 and varying presently between 3.25 and 5 percent)[12] continue to be very low both by national standards of some PEs, when contrasted with capital productivity or domestic interest rates, and especially by international market levels. Given that the bulk of intragroup transactions is rather transitory or short term at best, the effective average rate on loans is very much lower.

Furthermore, the IBEC has instituted a special regime for the least developed members (until the early 1970s it had a special regime too for the European members whose trade was subject to pronounced seasonality). Interest rates for loans to these countries ranged between 0.5 and 1 percent for Mongolia and between 0.5 and 2 percent for Cuba (Konstantinov 1975, p. 94). However, this favorable rate was apparently revoked for Mongolia, who presently enjoys the same conditions as Cuba; it now applies only to Vietnam (Carevski 1982, p. 68). This continuous confounding of purely financial matters with development assistance, without making this very explicit ex ante (as it is now incurred essentially by violating BTPAs in combination with unsynchronized cyclicality in reciprocal deliveries) parallels to some extent the reprehensible mixture of economics and politics in many other aspects of the CMEA economic cooperation mechanisms.

Initially the bank had six different kinds of credit accounts, depending upon the purpose the loan was to serve, and various account types for current and term deposits. This was changed in 1970 for a variety of reasons. It had proved to be very difficult to ensure that a loan would be used specifically for the purpose for which it had been accorded, except for settlement credits. Furthermore, between 65 and 80 percent of the IBEC's loans were purely for settlements purposes. It was therefore decided henceforth to grant only settlements and other credits up to a maturity of three years. Recently, some discussions have been under way to extend the maximum maturity to five years (Válek 1985, p. 10), but this recommendation, if that, has not yet been ratified (Džindžichadze 1985, p. 5). But settlements credits continue to account for over 80 percent of the total TR loan volume.

IBEC's role in nonmerchandise transactions within the CMEA

Aside from its clearing functions, perhaps the single most successful action taken by the IBEC, naturally within the provisions elaborated by the SCFQ, has been the easing of the obstacles that have complicated the normal conduct of noncommercial transactions for many years. The direct benefits have perhaps been most visible with respect to alleviating the hindrances to CMEA tourism (see Chapter 6). Certainly, the bank cannot hope to remove political and organizational impediments until the political leadership initiates proper steps. About the second set of issues, it is not really up to the bank to deal with organizational obstructions, although it might help to coordinate its preferences with those of the entrenched bureaucracies. Once the political imprimatur has been given, passport controls have been relaxed, and other, perhaps more picayune, shenanigans have been removed, there still remains a whole array of monetary issues to be settled. The bank can accomplish something in that sphere. The questions at stake concern not only the ERs for exchanging national currencies and the sums that can be converted without much ado but also, perhaps equally important, are questions such as, how are these transactions to be balanced and at what particular coefficients can imbalances be offset against the commercial account? It is in this domain that the bank can perform yeoman work in most cases under the active supervision and guidance of other national and regional organs, particularly the SCFQ.

The issue of noncommercial settlements has as long a history as that of multilateralizing commercial transactions (see Brabant 1977a, pp. 257–78). As far as the settlements of these transactions are concerned, the members are, in principle, expected to clear such imbalances against the commercial accounts at the terms described in Chapter 6. Until 1973, this could be done once a year. Since 1974, the members have had the option of doing so quarterly and on a completely voluntary basis (Vincze 1978a, p. 22). However, the share of noncommercial transactions in total intra-CMEA settlements has remained very small – about 2 percent (Válek 1985, p. 12). This is in contrast to the almost 95 percent share for reciprocal settlements and about 3 percent for clearing on account of bilateral government credits channeled through the IBEC's accounting (Dubrowsky 1979, p. 112).

IBEC's role vis-à-vis other CMEA organs

Especially since the endorsement of *Integration Program,* the PEs have created a variety of IEOs. Some have been concerned in essence with scientific–technical coordination and the exchange of information. Their financial needs therefore do not normally surpass wage payments at a fair ER for which the standard noncommercial ERs may be quite suitable. However, other organizations – a small minority – have engaged in the production and transfer of goods or services and therefore have had a need for settling payments for intraregional transactions. From the purely technical point of view, such cross-border settlements pose no particularly involved problems, because each of these organizations normally first elaborates what precisely each member is to contribute to its establishment and operations. Because this provides "solid commodity backing," the bank only has to ensure proper bookkeeping. If one member or another reneges on the deal, however, there is little that the bank can undertake to ease the problem. Similar problems arise when such organizations, in particular the IIB, venture to allocate their own TR funds or those borrowed from the IBEC in accordance with precepts that are not fully dovetailed with those held by the member states. Such borrowing by IEOs has been possible since 1 January 1977 allegedly (see Nazarkin 1979, p. 10) in order to replenish the IIB's resources. As shown in Chapter 10, this has been the greatest hindrance to the efficient operation of the IIB and the emergence of a rational common investment policy to promote SEI.

Convertible currency transactions and the IBEC

From its very beginning, since February 1964, the IBEC has devoted quite substantial energy to fostering CC transactions. Its volume soared from TR 0.9 billion in 1964 to TR 103.3 billion in 1984 – or at an average compound growth rate of over 23 percent per year; but then it more than doubled in 1985. The comparable growth rate for 1964–1984 for TR transactions in CMEA settlements[13] was just over 10 percent, with only a slightly larger expansion in 1985. The contrast was much sharper for the first fifteen years of the bank's existence when annual growth averaged over 35 and under 11 percent for CC and TR transactions, respectively. This sharp expansion in CC transactions has been far from steady, however. Particularly conspicuous spurts occurred in 1965–1967, 1970, 1973–1974, 1977, 1983, and 1985. Seen in another relationship, whereas CC transactions in 1964 amounted to only 4 percent of the bank's volume of TR commercial settlements, a decade later the former exceeded the latter by a sizable margin for the first time ever.

Nonetheless, the absolute volume of CC transactions has declined since 1978, in some years quite dramatically, with a rebound in 1982 but another fall in 1983, owing largely to the global economic and financial problems of the early 1980s; it very sharply expanded in 1984–1985 to reach TR 219 billion in the last year for which data are available. Also their relative significance has dropped sharply both with respect to the bank's total TR turnover as well as with respect to the volume of TR settlements. The major explanation is the sharp increase in CMEA trade prices that has taken place since 1975 and the pronounced TR trade imbalances that manifested themselves intermittently during the same period. In addition, the volume of TR transactions has also been measurably inflated by the rising operations of the IEOs, most conspicuously the IIB.

Given that the bank was created primarily to foster regional settlements and SEI with the aid of the TR, the expansion of its CC transactions has been remarkable in itself and also in comparison with the optimistic expectations regarding the TR's usefulness as a regional clearing currency. However weighty all of these objections to the TR as an international currency might be, I do not wish to suggest that instead of perfecting the TR the IBEC should be provided with CC funds and all PEs should suddenly switch over to settlements in such currencies. Nevertheless, three interesting questions immediately spring to mind when looking at the sharp expansion of CC transactions: Whose resources are mobilized by the bank? What kind of transactions are involved? To what degree do these transactions benefit SEI? Unfortunately, there is not enough empirical information to provide unambiguous answers to any of these questions.

The bank has kept the precise composition and provenance of its CC resources comparatively secret. Logically, such resources must be either the bank's own capital and retained profits, or deposits by and loans extended from member banks, other IEOs, or from nonmember banks. It is true that the bank's capital has been constituted in part by CC payments,[14] but they have had little operational significance because these funds have never been put at the bank's disposal, except in a strictly legal sense. Nevertheless, the IBEC is reported to have made sizable profits in CC transactions, but it is not known to what extent these earnings were retained by it.[15]

Authorized banks may hold some CC funds at the IBEC because they need balances for current transactions in East–West trade, to settle some components of intragroup obligations, or to take advantage of favorable interest rates on deposits offered by the bank. According to the meager evidence that is available, member banks may keep some deposits on a very temporary basis, but these have probably remained quite small because each PE has jealously guarded full control over its CC resources and allocation thereof at the national level and most intragroup CC transactions are handled on a strictly bilateral basis, usually without the bank intervening even in any technical sense.[16]

Western banks may hold deposits and extend loans to the IBEC for various East–West commercial purposes. But the bulk of CC resources must have a purely financial origin, originating chiefly from funds acquired on a credit basis in Western financial markets and retained profits from CC transactions. IBEC's liquid CC resources and the volume of its transactions took a sharp leap forward in 1969 when the bank borrowed for the first time ever on a medium-term basis in Western financial markets.

Even less is known about the type of CC transactions. There are few indicators of the customer breakdown between members of the bank and other clients. The IBEC's CC operations play a crucial role, in particular, in the financing of East–West trade and especially in the bank's credit, deposit, and other activities in Western money markets. Moreover, IBEC's CC dispositions are made largely, if not exclusively, on the basis of deposits and credits from nonmember banks. Most of the bank's CC operations are on current account or for short-term lending purposes, judging from the separate year-end TR and CC balance sheets (see Brabant 1977a, pp. 143–52). Relatively little is committed in the form of loans with a longer maturity. The volume of credit transactions with member countries is traditionally assumed to be relatively small. The data suggest that the IBEC seems primarily to attract CC funds from the West and to redistribute them within the CMEA. One report states that during 1964–1975, the bank granted cumulatively TR 269.5 billion loans in CC to the members (Carevski 1977, p. 44).

The bank's participation in Western financial markets as a lender appears to have been chiefly in short-term transactions, in particular in arbitrage markets, which permit a quick return and a high turnover. But such markets are not without risk, as the bank reportedly found out rather quickly when it sustained sizable transitory losses in currency speculation in the early 1970s. These operations probably account for the bulk of CC transactions accomplished with a rather small pool of foreign exchange. Starting in 1971, the bank has also become engaged in medium-term lending and in a number of bank-consortial operations.

Although the bank clears some part of CMEA trade in CC, most of its CC transactions with members take the form of relatively short-term loans to finance East–West trade operations. The settlements conducted on behalf of other IEOs, particularly the IIB, are another possibly significant source of transactions. Most of the IIB's transactions are channeled through the IBEC as intermediary, which thus inflates the volume of its CC and TR transactions. The bank passes on the funds borrowed in the West at an interest rate that is slightly higher than what it is charged in Western markets.

8.5 Participation in the IBEC by nonmembers

The bank's charter and the agreement of 1963 stipulate that the bank is not a closed institution, membership is open to any correspondent bank willing to subscribe to the bank's principles and goals, membership is not a de jure requirement for utilizing the bank's services, and participation in the bank's activities is to be permitted according to principles to be worked out by the Bank Council. There is nothing in the bank's charter that would prevent a non-CMEA member from participating, and there is nothing that compels CMEA members from being bank participants. For example, Vietnam was a member of the bank before it joined the CMEA in 1978; similarly, Cuba was a member of the CMEA well before it joined the bank in 1974.[17]

The greater the number of countries that are willing to use a currency, other things being equal, the more valuable it becomes to its holders. The TR to date can be "transferred" within the region only to pay for goods and services debtor countries are willing to release in exchange. The more countries decide to participate in such a system, however, the wider the potential range of goods obtainable with the currency and, therefore, the more interested each country should become in holding that currency. This proposition may help to explain why the PEs have continued to agree upon the desirability of widening the circle of countries using the TR and IBEC's clearing facilities.

One of the objectives embraced in the early 1960s, when the IBEC project was under discussion, was the establishment of more intensive commercial contacts with the international financial community through the intermediary of a settlements bank. At least some members hoped for a substantial inflow of Western capital to improve East–West trade and eventually to buffer the reserves required to replace bilateralism by regional multilateralism in both real and financial terms. Other members, although basically keenly interested in acquiring foreign capital too, sought to encourage nonmember PEs as well as MEs to multilateralize clearing agreements and join the bank in one way or another. Their chief concern was to promote the respectability and acceptance of the TR in the international community rather than simply to accommodate them-selves to the rules of this "alien" community.

The project of extending the sphere in which TR funds can be circu-lated for multilateral accounting in TR to nonmembers is a hardy peren-nial at IBEC Council meetings (see Brabant 1978, pp. 80–5). Conditions for participation in TR clearing by nonmembers were worked out for the first time at the ninth meeting of the Bank Council (Sofia, 21–23 October 1965). How to implement these principles has been on the agenda ever since. The rather long-winded detail provided in IBEC's annual report (MBÉS 1965, pp. 6–7) might be cited as evidence. The members were so divided over the practical issues involved in implementing the decision that the first operational stipulations regarding the conditions of clearing with nonmembers were written out only during 1967 and adopted in May 1968 (Bień and Nosiadek 1979a, p. 19).

The lack of enthusiasm of nonmembers for the bank has stirred some concern. The 1965 principles regulating participation by nonmembers have never been disclosed in full, probably because it took such a long time to hammer out a few, seemingly innocuous stipulations. It would appear, though, that settlements between members and nonmembers could be undertaken for all kinds of transactions in which a regular international bank can be engaged. Participation could be confined to single transactions or comprise all bilateral and multilateral operations with member countries. An agreement would have to be signed between nonmembers and each of the competent bodies of the member countries (presumably the central bank or the foreign trade bank as detailed in Gančev 1979, p. 7), which would have to be submitted for approval to the Bank Council (MBÉS 1965, pp. 6–7).

Various promotional campaigns were launched after 1965 but to no avail, and for a few years the discussion quietly died down. The initial idea was revived in the late 1960s, in particular in connection with the debates on the role of monetary and financial instruments in SEI. A passus to that effect was included in *Integration Program* (Tokareva 1972, p. 64) and seems to be repeated at every appropriate and inappropriate occasion. In any case, the official discussion on extending the TR's geo-graphical sphere of operations was launched once again, and at its thirty-fourth meeting (October 1972) the Bank Council agreed on revised con-ditions for opening such accounts.

Banks of nonmember countries could make settlements with IBEC members in TR either on a bilateral or a multilateral basis (prior appro-val of the Bank Council no longer seems to be required; at least it was not stipulated in MBÉS 1972). Apparently, some safeguards regarding the "value of the currency in which transactions are made" (Nazarkin 1974, p. 63) were included, but the details have never been divulged. Transactions could cover an individual payment or comprise part or the whole of trade with one or more countries. But nonmembers were encouraged to try out such settlements initially as an experiment and, if it proved satisfactory, gradually to expand cooperation to the whole reciprocal trade and payments cycle. As an inducement, IBEC was permitted to grant TR accounting credit for up to 25 percent of the agreed transactions with a maturity of up to three years at an interest rate of only 1.5 percent – less than half the comparable transaction charges to charter members (Gräbig, Brendel, and Dubrowsky 1975, p. 122; Konstantinov 1975, p. 19).

The foregoing provisions were revised once more in October 1976 at the forty-third session of the Bank Council.[18] Although this third set of regulations parallels that of 1972 rather closely, some new modalities for participating in the TR clearing regime need to be pointed out. The bank is, in principle, entitled to issue a settlements credit for up to 100 percent of the contracted trade volume for a period up to three years. To avoid self-perpetuating credits, the precise deadline of the loan is to be stipulated in the contract. Although the bank considers it desirable to reach equilibrium in the contracted trade volumes, such is no longer an absolute prerequisite for participation. The imbalance ex ante or ex post cannot be converted into CC, but nonmember debtors may volunteer to settle their account in CC. The provisions of the 1972 set of regulations that tended already to favor nonmembers over members were further amplified in the revised 1976 rules. The bank had hoped to attract other PEs as well as a number of developing MEs. The reasons for the failure to do so need to be explored in some detail.

To appreciate the full range of issues to be considered before participating in the bank, we need further details, especially with regard to possible strings attached to the transactions. This is not so important for Western banks, but it certainly is of considerable interest to developing MEs and other PEs. Would they have to accept CMEA contract prices? Would nonmembers have to subscribe to CMEA terms and standards for the delivery of goods? Would the interest earned be transferable? Would clearing for charter members be kept separate from their clearing with other countries? Even well-placed Eastern European economists are baffled by these as yet unresolved problems (see Gräbig et al. 1975, p. 123).

With the exception of a limited form of participation by Finland and Yugoslavia, no non-CMEA country bank appears to have availed itself so far of the opportunities offered under the new regulations.[19] The other PEs (China, North Korea, Vietnam, and Yugoslavia) were the obvious candidates. Vietnam has since become a full member. China and North Korea appear to have so far shunned all contact with the bank.[20] Some developing MEs have reportedly shown interest in the bank's potential, but nothing concrete has materialized to date. The most likely candidates would have been those with bilateral clearing arrangements with CMEA members. Only one case, a failure, has become known. In late 1977, an attempt was made to exchange bananas coming within the purview of La Unión de Paises Exportadores de Banano for machinery from several Eastern European countries in TR (UNCTAD 1977, p. 14), possibly also involving the credit assistance of the IIB. It failed because the CMEA bank partners proved to be unwilling to offset bilateral imbalances. Another possibility could have emerged from the activation of the special fund for developing countries put at the disposal of the IIB, but also that avenue has remained closed (see Chapter 10).

Under the typical conditions of trade and payments within the CMEA, there has been little in the bank's operations or potential activities that could persuade MEs and private commercial banks into seeking membership or to accede to the TR accounting system. The lack of interest stems from the fact that joining the bank is unattractive because it, in principle, does not alter the broad trade opportunities for MEs. Looking at the issue from the members' point of view, the freedom of action in trade and payments with nonmembers enables some PEs to promote objectives that would be much more complex to accommodate within the multilateral settlements system.

Unlike other observers of the CMEA scene, I do not believe that the main problem resides in the possibility that outsiders may be wary of losing bargaining power if they submitted their accounts to the IBEC – after all the IBEC has so far accomplished next to nothing in regulating its members' trade flows. The primary obstacle still appears to lie with the present members, who might lose an important degree of freedom in negotiating with these developing MEs or other PEs on a multilateral, rather than a bilateral, basis. But this is a conjecture for which supporting empirical data are hard to come by.

8.6 The advantages and drawbacks of the bank

Most Eastern European observers stress that the bank has many advantages. With respect to the multilateralization of trade and the allegedly very positive role of the bank in increasing regional trade turnover, I categorize whatever claims have been made as being erroneous. These may hold if they refer exclusively to the strictly technical side of the settlements mechanism, the purely fortuitous consequence of price movements, and the phenomena associated with the endeavor of PEs to seek greater specialization and hence trade dependence. Because the bank cannot regulate regional trade flows, how could it have acted otherwise?

With regard to the settlement of accounts, there is little doubt that the system operates efficiently and has minimized the need for swing credits by speeding up the accounting of reciprocal transactions. It has undoubtedly contributed to the rationalization and standardization of the technical aspects of regional settlements. Similarly, there is no reason to doubt that the bank provides the technical framework and competence for dealing with real multilateralism should the members wish to endorse such an agreement by modifying their habitual trade and payments operations.

Related to the efficacy of the settlements mechanism is the contention that the bank has enabled the PEs to trade without having to keep CC transaction balances. This is true but only as far as it goes: Prior to the bank's creation no CC balances were needed either! This issue is directly related to the contention that the IBEC has enabled the PEs to trade in a stable environment, including in their prices, that is immune or broadly unaffected by changes taking place in CC markets. This is so, but only to the degree that CMEA trade prices for TR transactions ignore changes in relative WMPs. A related issue is that IBEC has allegedly contributed to securing greater equivalence in CMEA trade. If it has improved at all, equivalence must necessarily result from the price mechanism, over which the bank has absolutely no control because it is only a passive observer of trade negotiations and unable to influence them by its credit and interest policies.

Aside from the foregoing, I see two clear-cut advantages of over twenty years of experience. On the one hand, the bank has been a supplementary conduit for channeling financial resources from MEs to Eastern Europe at conditions that have not diverged much from those prevailing for individual PEs, provided they did not run into lending limits. In addition, the lack of flexibility in trade and payments that has characterized the system must have made it quite clear that the goals set in 1963 could not have been reached by formal means alone. Whether the members will also draw from this the conclusion that substantive changes are required in their domestic economies and in the regional integration mechanisms in a broader sense still remains to be seen. I shall return to this theme in Chapter 12.

9

Factor mobility and investment coordination

In a comprehensive analysis of CMEA cooperation in capital investments, Gerhard Kraft noted that "all previous experiences indicate that measures to enhance cooperation . . . are invariably carried out successfully when that cooperation is extended to the domain of investments" (Kraft 1977, p. 29). This observation could be generalized to virtually any type of mobility of production factors as successful specialization depends on how the patrimony of two or more countries may be organically combined. Eastern European policy makers need to devote considerably more attention to the myriad economic and other issues at stake.

In the stylized neoclassical framework of MEs not only is free trade assumed to exist, also capital and labor mobility are held to proceed without obstacles. Neither prevails fully in the real world. Nevertheless, one of the twin pillars of integration schemes in MEs, next to intragroup trade liberalization, is the provision of greater room for factor movements guided by "market" incentives. Certainly, the mechanism of factor mobility, for instance, in the European Communities (EC) is quite imperfect: Movements have remained rather small in spite of obvious differences in direct factor rewards. Nevertheless, this situation can be easily rationalized by augmenting direct factor payments by the "price" of all hindrances to the smooth operation of capital and labor markets. These are usually not within the decision-making compass of central policy makers, however.

In Eastern Europe, in contrast, the integration movement has by and large evolved with a minimum of capital and labor mobility. The variety of reasons for this state of affairs forms the subject of this chapter. Labor mobility is studied in Section 9.1. Section 9.2 briefly discusses the various kinds of capital transfers that should be considered so as to evaluate properly the role, place, and extent of capital mobility in Eastern Europe. Following this morphology, Sections 9.3–9.5 relate the role of interstate credits, the coordination of investment activities, and the place of investment loans. The chapter concludes with some pointers on the desirability of enhancing factor mobility in SEI processes.

9.1 Labor mobility and CMEA cooperation

Economic processes are *in se* quite similar in PEs and MEs, although real differences have had to be reckoned with at virtually every stage of this investigation. When the subject shifts to labor mobility, however, the similarities between MEs and PEs become exceedingly fragile and tenuous. Even if cultural inhibitions were not already forbidding, a variety of ideological, political, administrative, and economic obstacles stifle individual initiative in the PEs. Given that economics is of main concern here, the inconvertibility of the Eastern European currencies would be one prime hindrance to labor mobility, even if it were condoned legally and accommodated administratively. Severe passport restrictions, border and custom controls, visa limitations, and other circumstances provide even stronger deterrents. As a result, labor migration is normally regulated by special agreements between the two or more countries involved in the "labor exchange."

Eastern European commentators predictably object to the terminology labor-exporting and labor-importing PEs. I shall use it nevertheless but only to indicate the direction of movement. In what follows, I shall examine the general attitude towards labor mobility, the types of mobility, the motivation of such transfers, the regulation of mobility, the volume and the countries most active as recipients as well as labor shedders, the economic and financial aspects of the transfers, and the prospects for greater labor mobility in Eastern Europe.

General attitudes to migration

The free movement of people is strictly regulated in Eastern Europe. As already examined in some detail in Chapter 6, organized and unorganized tourism is severely circumscribed by myriad economic, financial, legal, and organizational obstructions. Although most types of tourism are strictly limited, the free movement of people in search of higher incomes or more satisfactory levels of living is, in principle, altogether prohibited. One of the key features of macroeconomic policies in the PEs is full employment, even if that implies disguised unemployment. Governments of many PEs have committed themselves explicitly in law, some even in their constitution, to provide secure employment opportunity to any able-bodied national of age. The socialist state therefore spurns the "guest worker" phenomenon. Similarly, the notion of gradually equalizing labor scarcities by direct policy intervention at the CMEA level is perceived to be alien.

The guaranteed right to a secure job has been a cornerstone of both economic planning and political philosophy in PEs, even though it clearly inhibits a relatively comprehensive exploration of the benefits of labor migration. Another important deterrent has been the ideological aversion to the exploitation of "cheap" foreign labor under capitalism. The phenomenon of migrant workers from within or from outside the CMEA has been considerd inimical to some basic tenets of socialism and therefore could not be entertained as a realistic option in the socialist world.

There are two broad sets of problems associated with this principle. First, although ideologically and politically the authorities may deem migration to be intolerable, job security per se does not necessarily offer sufficient satisfaction to residents; nor is it invariably consonant with economic efficiency. In other words, there may be considerable room for a more flexible approach to dealing with the labor situation in the region as a whole rather than to freeze it ab ovo at the levels sustained in each of the members. This would be beneficial not only to wax private aspirations but also to boost regional output levels. Second, although in principle frowned upon by socialist policy makers, labor migration does occur, though in a highly confined format. Its place and particular contribution to SEI therefore need to be examined to some extent.

Since the mid-1960s, it has become quite obvious that a number of CMEA members suffer from acute shortages of labor. In some, this manifestation is predominantly on account of sectoral imbalances, for instance, between the demand and supply of skilled workers. In a growing number of PEs, however, the phenomenon also has macroeconomic dimensions. Certainly, the relatively wasteful way in which PEs appropriate labor in the production process has been an important cause. To the extent that such misallocation results from systemic characteristics, however, improvements can be obtained only through changes in the underlying causes, which are part and parcel of the economic mechanism (see Chapter 12). Similarly, the levels of living of the population in the various PEs show considerable differentiation, although the slogans derived from the "equalization of levels of development," which is held to be inevitable under internationalist socialist conditions, have been high on the CMEA policy agenda for decades. Rather than strive for this policy goal of socialist internationalism in the long run by national means, it may be helpful to capitalize also on the contribution that individuals can make if they really desire to move within the CMEA.

The regulation of migration

What makes labor migration of interest to a study such as this one, dealing chiefly with financial and monetary matters, is that in the CMEA the migrant generally remains under the labor provisions of the home country, and all questions of compensation are settled at the intergovernmental level. Unlike in MEs, where migrants have to accept prevailing social, economic, cultural, and political conditions of the host country, in the CMEA and the East–West context as well workers generally move abroad under conditions set by their own country. In some cases, the labor-exporting country may share in the output produced by its labor in the host country. Such supplies are also obtained by participants in the joint financing of investment projects because each home country essentially bears the cost of its workers abroad on its own employment conditions.

The international migration of workers within the CMEA derives essentially from the national economic plans and interstate agreements as expressions of the drive to integrate the PEs into a more cohesive economic region. The bulk of labor migration in the CMEA is therefore subject to a highly organized process of temporary employment of a limited contingent of workers from one PE in another (Vajs 1982, p. 190). These movements can be better described as "planned labor transfers," and nearly all are regulated by bilateral agreements even if the venture involves the participation of more countries. That is, labor migration is dealt with in virtually the same way as any other CMEA exchange: Multilateral protocols acknowledge agreement about the general objectives and means of a common project, but all questions concerning individual contributions, payments, transfer times, and the like are regulated bilaterally. Once settled, they can be incorporated in the respective national economic and trade plans.

Usually, the provisions of the labor code as well as the work and wage regulations of the home country remain in effect for nationals on "temporary loan." This means that the length of the working day, output norms, labor protection, organization, and many other questions are regulated according to the home country's labor code. Naturally, when an individual signs a contract with a foreign company (for instance, in the case of cross-border migrants), the labor code and regulations of the host country apply to the full, but a number of more general aspects of the conditions governing such migrant workers, especially visa and income convertibility, need to be settled bilaterally.[1]

In some instances, foreign workers are employed alongside nationals, and it becomes necessary to resort to a mixture of the codes of two or more PEs. Thus, during joint construction of the Sojuz gas pipeline, questions of hiring, dismissal, remuneration, social security, trade union rights, and so on were set by the authorities of the labor-exporting countries. Working time, holidays, vacation, and labor protection, however, were regulated in accordance with the host country's norms. From an equity and efficiency point of view, this was apparently not a very satisfactory solution, although it may have been an expedient one. It led a German and Hungarian research team to comment that the Sojuz experi-

ence "points to the solution . . . : the wages of the builders should be set
on the basis of uniform and synchronized principles, and this should be
reflected in the overall cost of the project" (Poller and Tesner 1982, p.
1083). Their advocacy of a "unified policy for the utilization of labor on
integration projects" may be highly constructive, but the proposal is not
likely to be carried out soon.

Temporary workers are sent to MEs virtually only on conditions determined by the East.[2] As a rule, the governments of PEs do not allow permanent emigration, with certain exceptions usually related to family reunification. Temporary migration to MEs is usually part and parcel of the state
plans pertaining to exports or foreign aid commitments, including the
construction of capital projects, the marketing of products, the operation
of socialist-owned businesses abroad, training programs, and so on. Teams
of specialists may be sent to developing MEs to carry out agreed medical,
scientific, industrial, or agricultural schemes, or to advise on and to promote the "socialist road" to economic and social development.

Volume of migrant workers

The movement of workers within Eastern Europe and between East and
West, including East and South in some cases, has a considerable history.[3]
Intraregional mobility started soon after the end of World War II. It
involved at first mostly Bulgarian, Hungarian, and Polish workers moving to Czechoslovakia.[4] These first migrant flows were encouraged because Czechoslovakia was not only relatively depopulated as a result of
the expulsion of the Sudeten Germans after World War II, the country
also offered a working environment from which the less developed countries in the region could derive considerable benefits. Soon thereafter,
however, the volume of foreign laborers plummeted precipitously and
remained at a trickle until the mid-1960s.

In the period when significant differences existed in the labor market
situation of individual PEs, substantial migration was opposed chiefly for
ideological reasons. Later on a more pragmatic approach to economic
problems on the part of the socialist leadership resulted in a compromise
between ideological dogma and economic rationality, although it fell
short of officially promoting labor migration. The growing labor shortage in most PEs, which is currently worsening (see Chapter 3), tends to
reduce the scope for CMEA labor migration as a practicable means of
attaining a balanced labor market, but it does not erode it altogether.
However, the main factors that foster migration derive increasingly from
other concerns than labor market equilibrium.

Starting with the late 1960s, the intensification of the development
process throughout the CMEA tended to go along with greater labor
mobility (Degtjar' 1976, p. 135). The number of migrant workers reached

about 100,000 in 1973 (see Levcik 1975, 1977; Virius and Bálek 1976) and increased to perhaps 150,000 by mid-decade (Rymarczyk 1978, p. 47). Levcik's estimate of about 200,000 for 1975 has been reported also for recent years in a Polish source (Żukrowska 1984, p. 101). However, Vajs estimates a level of about 100,000 for the early 1980s and contends that Levcik's data are considerably overstated (Vajs 1982, p. 191). He places the level of "guest workers" in the total labor force of the CMEA at most at perhaps 0.1 percent,[5] which yields an upper limit at about 150,000 (Rymarczyk 1978, p. 47). Given the sharp economic and external payments shocks experienced by the PEs in recent years, the generalized labor shortage throughout Eastern Europe has probably compressed "effective migration," which may be defined as the share of man-hours from foreign workers in total man-hours used in the production process during a specific time. The number of people moving within the CMEA for short-term assignments has probably sharply risen in conjunction with trade, specialization, and production cooperation.

Only some CMEA countries are significant hosts. Czechoslovakia and the GDR lead the way, with perhaps 60,000–70,000 foreign workers in "high" years, mainly from Bulgaria, Hungary, and Poland and some developing MEs (including Algeria, Egypt, and Turkey). In the late 1970s, the share of foreign workers in total factory workers in Czechoslovakia and the GDR amounted to 0.5 and 0.8 percent, respectively (Rymarczyk 1978, p. 48). More recent estimates place the shares at 0.65 and 0.75 percent, respectively (Żukrowska 1984, p. 102). Relative to the total labor force, the proportions may have been at most half of these magnitudes. Next is the USSR with some 50,000 migrants mainly from Bulgaria, Czechoslovakia, the GDR, Hungary, Mongolia, Poland, and Vietnam. Given the large size of the Soviet labor force, however, foreign workers amounted to less than 0.05 percent of overall factory workers in the late 1970s (Rymarczyk 1978, p. 48; Żukrowska 1984, p. 102). Poland, on the other hand, has been traditionally a country with a net afflux of perhaps 0.5 percent of its factory workers. Most of these foreign workers, except those from Mongolia, Vietnam, and most developing MEs, are skilled and are engaged in specific construction projects, the operation of joint enterprises and IEOs, the training of specialists, or are participating in scientific–technical projects of one kind or another.

The Soviet Union has become the principal labor-importing country for the purpose of developing its fuel and raw material resources. There are three different types of this involvement: (1) the creation of joint organizations that possess a lease of a portion of the territory of the host country in order to develop its raw material and fuel resources by the other partner (as in the arrangement with Bulgaria concerning the exploitation of Komi's forestry resources); (2) the joint transfer of labor and capital for the construction, expansion, or remodeling of facilities for production and transportation of raw materials; and (3) the engagement of foreign workers in an activity that is completely unrelated to the one for which the labor-exporting country receives compensation.[6]

The contingents involved in East–West trade are even less certain. Especially with the emergence of political détente and the glut of foreign exchange resources in the Persian Gulf in the 1970s, the CMEA countries began to explore ways of building "turnkey" construction projects abroad in an effort to gain access to a relatively new CC source. This involves a temporary relocation of an entire construction crew, which in turn stands to benefit in terms of level and type of earnings. There are many other kinds of foreign engagement that require the temporary relocation of workers abroad, especially professionals or skilled tradesmen engaged in the construction of various industrial projects, roads, and communications, acting as advisers, or managing foreign businesses.

Motivation for labor migration

The motives of the CMEA countries to engage in a regional exchange of labor in spite of obvious obstacles can be divided into five categories. First, countries have some practical interest in balancing the demand and supply for labor nationally and regionally. With the growing scarcity of labor throughout the CMEA, this consideration has obviously receded in importance in recent years. Second, the PEs have always been interested in securing additional supplies of intermediate goods. Fuel and raw material imports can sometimes be acquired more easily through participation in the erection of production and transportation facilities in the exporting CMEA member than by other means (see Section 9.2). Third, some countries have a vested interest in exploring any means to improve their bilateral balance of payments. Fourth, especially the less developed PEs stand to benefit from skills and training for their young workers that they cannot adequately supply themselves. Finally, there is a need to develop scientific and technological cooperation within the integrating region – a mild variant indeed of the notorious brain drain in MEs.

Movements of workers in the CMEA are increasingly prompted by the need to establish international project teams to carry out "major targets in the field of science, engineering, technology, and the training of new personnel with a view to achieving maximum economies in the outlay of social labor" (Virius and Bálek 1976, p. 4). Typical for these flows is that they are in consequence of intergovernmental bilateral or multilateral agreements, within the framework of which the relevant state entities (enterprises, institutions, and planning tiers) negotiate the details of the engagements.

The motivation of migrants can be various, ranging from simple curiosity and adventure into the unfamiliar, to fundamental dedication to socialist international construction. Similarly, migrant workers may acquire skills and enhance their professional experience or credentials in the more advanced countries. Nevertheless, the principal incentive oftentimes is purely material. Workers volunteering for foreign service are guaranteed substantially larger revenues than at home and indeed access to material goods that would otherwise not be available to them without palpable hardships. Foreign workers are usually accorded preferential treatment in the allocation of housing and sometimes also of consumer goods. They also receive free or low-cost lodging on a preferential basis, inexpensive food, and free medical care. They can transfer the bulk of these earnings at an exceedingly favorable ER (see Chapter 6), send consumer durables home duty free, gain access to special shops or a priority listing for a car or housing after returning home, and other benefits. Because most of these workers are included under contracts with their own national organizations, the material dividends of accepting a temporary assignment abroad are very tangible indeed. In fewer cases (especially border workers), the agreement is signed between the enterprise and the individual foreign worker. People also want to migrate out of a sense of curiosity, adventurism, a desire to learn a foreign language, or to acquire a skill only inadequately offered, if at all, in the home market.

Types of labor migration

For some analytical purposes, it may be useful to distinguish among seven different types of labor migration in the CMEA area (Virius and Bálek 1976, p. 5): border district exchange; direct employment of foreign workers; construction crews for turnkey projects; securing supplies of primary goods; special exchange of scientists, engineers, and other specialists; hiring teams of specialists for key transportation routes; and establishing and managing joint organizations. Most of these kinds of migration involve the temporary movement of people on a short-term basis for business-related reasons or to obtain directly essential raw materials from abroad in physical terms. Among the temporary migrants it may be useful to distinguish between scientists, students, researchers, technical advisers, and the like, on the one hand, and movements of workers related to trade and specialization agreements, including specific contracts such as the construction of buildings, pipelines, jointly financed investment projects, and the like, on the other hand. The cross-border workers form a self-explanatory category: people living in border areas who are allowed to maintain their residence in one country but work nearby in another country.

Economic and financial obstacles

A particularly knotty problem from the ideological point of view has been the treatment of surplus value created by foreign workers. As argued in Chapter 5, the Marxian labor theory of value posits labor as the only source of value. Workers do not normally receive the full value of their work in terms of wage and bonus payments, or other benefits, including deferred transfers. The remainder of their total wage product performance consists primarily of the labor surplus value, which becomes the property of society as a whole and is mobilized to finance new capital projects and public consumption. Because foreign workers take part in the creation of this surplus product but do not fully benefit from it, the problem of how equitably to divide this surplus product arises.

The problem is rather complex for it includes not only intricate issues of the measurement of the surplus value and its equitable division without harming either the host country or the one whose workers have produced the surplus product to start with. Perhaps even greater difficulties stem from the fact that this surplus product is usually produced by teams from more than one country, if not in the form of live labor than in the form of embodied work (see Vajs 1976, pp. 76–79). This question may appear to be more appealing for its theoretical intricacies than for its practical merits, but this is not so (Rymarczyk 1978, p. 52). Countries have been seriously concerned about how to capture the proper surplus value created by their nationals abroad.[7]

Given that permanent migration is a rare phenomenon, eventually the earnings of foreign workers need to be transferred, which raises vexing issues of convertibility in a highly bilateralized world. The problem arises in two ways: the conversion of incomes or of labor value into TR-type goods. For example, the earnings of Bulgarian workers in Komi are administered by Bulgaria according to its wage and labor regulations. Some allowances need to be made for local expenditures, a necessity that already gives rise to an implicit convertibility problem. But those matters can be easily settled in the framework of the bilateral agreements about noncommercial exchanges. The other compensation involves evaluating the work performed by the Bulgarian workers in terms of the amount of lumber the USSR allows to be shipped to Bulgaria free of charge or at a nominal price.[8] Because at least in principle, the "value" of labor therefore ensues from the intragroup pricing principles – hence broad trends on world markets – must be disturbing. If foreign workers receive direct compensation in local currency, all the conventional convertibility issues arise in full force. Compensation probably entails transfers at the noncommercial ERs, but this solution is not without its intricate problems as examined in Chapter 6.

Labor migration and socialist economic integration

During the euphoria about the promulgation of the Target Programs as the basic device to foster SEI in the 1980s and beyond, one Soviet observer remarked that, to the extent that the ISDL is deepened, cooperation in the field of the utilization of labor resources is bound to grow and so is the mobility of the labor force (Alev 1979, p. 76). This thesis advanced the increased cooperation in the use of labor resources as but one component of the process of the jointly planned utilization of national resources with the goal of increasing the social efficiency of production in the CMEA area. Measured by that gauge, it is doubtful whether one could truly speak of integration as defined here.

This brief summary of labor mobility in Eastern Europe suggests that the scope for the employment of foreign workers in the CMEA is only a minute fraction of that in MEs. Even with the most optimistic estimates, the participation ratio of foreign workers is unlikely to exceed 0.1 percent of the combined labor force in the CMEA. It is evident from the foregoing that temporary exchanges of manpower among the PEs can only solve individual tasks and alleviate only in minor ways the constraints resulting from the level and structure of the labor resources in each individual PE (Vajs and Degtjar' 1973, p. 99). CMEA migration therefore has only a very marginal effect on ensuring labor force equilibrium in the area as a whole. The outlook for measurable changes in the near future is not very promising.

9.2 Desirability and types of capital mobility

Unlike in East–West relations or in the recent experiences of MEs, interstate capital transfers have not played a very prominent role in the postwar reconstruction, industrialization, or broad economic development of Eastern Europe as a whole. One reason has been ideological: Marx and Lenin interpreted the investment of capital abroad as another expression of the exploitation of labor and of weaker nations driven by the monopolies of the "rich" countries. Other explanations derive from economic, administrative, and organizational features of these economies.

The primary forms of capital mobility in MEs are threefold: direct foreign investment, project and financial loans from multilateral or other official financial institutions, and loans from private commercial banks that usually have a financial character, although project financing is certainly not unknown. Inasmuch as a primary feature of socialist economies is state ownership of the means of production, in most cases even including land, direct foreign investment entailing the transfer of property title to "foreigners" is frowned upon and usually forgone. There are considerable ideological and legal questions as to whether a Marxist country can

own capital in another PE or ME and whether it could tolerate a deroga-
tion of its own property in favor of foreigners. Although some countries
have recently enacted legal provisions for the emergence of direct foreign investment, usually from West to East, such flows are as a matter of
course characterized as "(direct) foreign participations" rather than as
direct foreign investment or foreign property. On the other hand, ideological obstacles to the PEs owning property in MEs have been rather
incidental. The real hub of the difficulties has emerged in the creation of
"joint property" within the CMEA by two or more of its members, possibly including nonsocialist partners.

Instead of direct foreign investment, PEs prefer socialist international
credit, which is interpreted as "not being a form of capital export" (Carevski 1977, p. 36). It is argued by some well-informed observers that
"credit is resorted to in cases in which it guarantees a higher degree of
effectiveness than internal capital investment or if sufficient internal resources are not available" (Grinev and Lebedinskas 1975, p. 40). But this
is a dubious proposition chiefly because capital effectiveness is not kept
separate from a project's financing, and there are well-known problems
with regional capital productivity comparisons. Before looking into those
questions, a brief rundown of the past record of capital movements in
Eastern Europe may be helpful.

Although limited in scope and narrowly confined to ad hoc bilateral
negotiations and implementation modalities, capital transfers have not
altogether been superfluous, as I shall show below. Intergovernmental
long-term credits other than those in CC or those pertaining to the ex
post settlement of current trade imbalances share two distinct features.
First, they are tied loans and tied debt. In other words, the borrower can
only acquire goods and services in the lender's "market" and upon maturity. Similarly, the loan recipient must transfer principal and interest by
means of excess exports to the donor country. Second, all important
loans are negotiated bilaterally even when more than two PEs participate
in the project. The absence of institutionalized provisions for organized
capital flows has severely hampered the emergence of a regional capital
market to back up current trade and specialization efforts. Needless to
add, no consistent strategy of capital mobility in support of regional
specialization has been devised to date.

A more promising basis for a regional capital market would be the
distribution of investment funds with a view gradually to equalize real
capital scarcities throughout the group. The key economic question to be
tackled is, How can a consistent, general investment strategy be formulated to remedy and eventually to forestall cyclical and chronic disequilibria in the supply of goods? However weighty the economic arguments in
favor of such a solution, the CMEA reality calls for a reduction of the
disparities in relative scarcities in selected markets of key products –

mostly fuels and raw materials – and the gradual concentration of activities that were developed in each PE as a result of the postwar industrialization strategy.

In that light, the need for a common, effective capital fund to finance investments has continued to grow, especially because some PEs have been reluctant or unable to participate effectively in specialization projects recommended by various CMEA organs without financial assistance from members who could also expect to benefit from specialization. Due to the rather odd regional price-setting principles, it has not been deemed profitable to raise the production of energy and key intermediate goods for export to member countries. The groupwide shortage of vital primary products, rising exploitation cost, and declining unit export returns add up to the result that funds appropriated for opening up new deposits or for augmenting existing facilities could be justified only if the development costs were shared with other members by means of advantageous financing. It is true that the aforementioned considerations have lost some weight after the drastic price changes since 1975. Nevertheless, the obstacles to the more efficient flow of capital in support of alleviating disparities in national scarcity levels throughout the region remain potent even today.

Pooling capital resources of two or more PEs into a common fund to promote joint investment projects is by no means a policy objective of recent origin. The aim to derive advantages from jointly allocating the region's capital funds is as old as the Council itself – in fact, it antedates it. As related in Chapter 1, the first agreements on Eastern European economic cooperation signed right after World War II envisaged both the buoyant exchange of goods and credit capital. Moreover, the cooperation schemes then contemplated for the area were anchored to a far more liberal form of capital mobility than what these countries experienced during the depression of the 1930s. Finally, the preliminary agreements underlying the elusive "founding documents" of 8 January 1949 and the Council's origins incorporated the establishment of a joint capital fund to be placed at the Bureau's disposal to finance selected projects of strategic interest to several or all CMEA members. A more or less definitive proposal was worked out during the first Council Sessions in 1949–1950 as one crucial component of a more general package of measures regarding regional trade, payments, and other types of economic interaction. This particular agreement was admittedly never implemented for a variety of reasons too intricate to be recounted here in detail (see Brabant 1974a, pp. 182ff.; Kraus 1974, pp. 218–9). Under the then prevailing conditions, this plan could not be carried out basically because regionalization became an increasingly pointless exercise when the USSR as the principal contributor (half of the fund) began to lean heavily in favor of dealing separately with the CMEA partners on an ad hoc basis. This stillborn attempt in itself showed, however, the desirability of having some type of capital mobility instituted in the area to buttress SEI.

The inability of CMEA policy makers to agree on the precise format of such an institutionalized regional fund, the reluctance to delegate a crucial and highly sensitive lever of national economic sovereignty to higher authority, or the provision in the IBEC's charter regarding the joint pooling of investment resources did not, however, stop joint funding of a sort. Nor did it inhibit the use of bilateral interstate credits to enhance various foreign policy and trade objectives. Although bilateral financial and monetary cooperation in the field of capital construction has been considerable, at least since the late 1950s, the ad hoc mechanisms used have never been transformed into a flexible, comprehensive framework within which investment coordination could be fostered as an integral part of SEI.[9]

There are several different criteria according to which credits among PEs can be categorized (see Kruliš 1979, pp. 29ff.). By form, one can distinguish between tied and financial credits, with the latter being granted either in CC or TR or both. The former could be for investment or other purposes. By type, bilateral, institutional multilateral, and other multilateral credits should be treated separately. Finally, by term structure it may be instructive to distinguish short-, medium-, and long-term credits. From this general typology, for our purposes, principally five different types of capital mobility should be distinguished: (1) short-term capital flows to accommodate temporary payments imbalances; (2) interstate credits, including those sanctioned by IBEC (see Chapter 8), that allow ex ante for annual payments imbalances; (3) interstate credits specifically related to individual projects for well-specified purposes; (4) joint financing of investment projects; and (5) multilateral coordination of investment activities through the IIB. The first two types are specifically related to temporary imbalances in bilateral payments flows and therefore belong to the arena of the settlements mechanism examined in more detail in Chapter 8. They will be touched upon here only in the context of more purposefully oriented intergovernmental credit agreements. The other three types, however, involve genuine capital mobility and are therefore examined here, although details of the IIB are deferred to Chapter 10.

9.3 Interstate credits

Of particular significance in the genesis of the IIB and in gauging its role are the special-purpose or target credits that were first granted mainly between 1957 and 1962, before the ominous controversy on the principles of the ISDL stalled SEI for most of the 1960s. After a slight surge in the mid-1960s, owing nearly exclusively to special fuel projects in the

USSR cofinanced by Czechoslovakia and the GDR (see Brabant 1984a, pp. 129–31), the issue of target credits died again until the big surge in the mid-1970s. The rationale and the forms of these credits need to be examined here. But first at least some attention should be devoted to earlier intergovernmental credit flows.

Although there is considerable uncertainty about a realistic overall value of these early intergovernmental capital flows, there is little doubt that they were important to some PEs, both lenders and borrowers. A common estimate relates that the USSR's credits to the socialist countries, not only the PEs considered here, amounted to 4.5 percent of total investment outlays in the USSR from 1947 to 1957 (Balážik 1980, p. 108). In Bulgaria, for example, the inflow of loans from the USSR is reported to have financed one quarter of all capital investments in 1944–1966 (Bass 1974, p. 85). It has apparently declined only marginally since, for Carevski reports that until 1975 the Soviet share remained in the neighborhood of 20 to 25 percent and accounted for one seventh of the Bulgarian capital stock in the productive sphere (Carevski 1977, p. 52).[10] Also, Czechoslovakia engaged in sizable interstate credits chiefly to finance the exports of investment goods to Eastern Europe, because it was originally slated to become the machine shop for the region as a whole.

Interesting features of these arrangements were their duration and low cost. A target maturity of ten to fifteen years was not uncommon, and the interest rate was a low 1–2 percent (see Špaček 1981, p. 22). Most of these loans were agreed upon in the context of the special postwar arrangements discussed in Chapter 1, genuine development assistance to socialist industrialization, and to counter the adverse trends in the socioeconomic and political environment of the mid-1950s, particularly in the GDR, Hungary, and Poland.

The net outflow of capital from the USSR or other PEs, for that matter, did not cease suddenly in 1957. But the entire character of capital flows by type as well as by lender has changed markedly since then. Thus of the total flows between 1957 and 1962, 60 percent was incurred by Czechoslovakia and 20 percent by the GDR (Balážik 1980, p. 108). Since the mid-1950s, a number of mostly bilateral and some multilateral investment projects have been jointly financed. Their overall value is unknown. A recent evaluation of these target credits estimated the total value of twenty projects financed in the 1960s (probably including the late 1950s) at TR 2 billion (Válek 1984, p. 10). The brunt of the financing has traditionally been shouldered by the more developed CMEA members (particularly Czechoslovakia and the GDR), and sometimes it was foisted upon them. Agreements were reached after laborious, mostly bilateral discussions. On the whole they left open to doubt whether a generalization of these "credits for well-defined purposes" or "target credits" could be contemplated at all. These commitments suffered from inflexibility

and were hardly undertaken with a view to improving the regional allocation of capital. Furthermore, the experience showed that these projects
could not even unambiguously safeguard the immediate interest of the
PEs directly involved. Incidentally, "interestedness" in this context was
rather narrowly confined to the import requirements of some PEs and
the reluctance of the potential exporters to divert exportables from other
client nations to the CMEA or to expand production by reshuffling domestic investments (see Brabant 1971, 1974b, pp. 175–203).

Judging from the published accounts of the controversy regarding the
economic rationale behind the target credits, the elaboration of a regional
strategy does not appear to have been faced as dispassionately as the
technical nature of the topic at hand would have warranted. The reasoning adopted was fairly straightforward, though not always sound. The
starting premise was that the enlargement of the supply of selected products must be sought regionally and cannot be financed solely by the
potential exporters. The keen self-interest of the potential importer
should suffice as motive to contribute to the financing of the output
expansion of selected products from within the region. In actual practice,
however, it turned out that the potential importer not only financed the
projects jointly with the producer. A participant also ran the risk of
subsidizing the venture, the domestic consumption of the producer, and,
by extension, the imports of such goods by other countries. This outcome
can result under certain combinations of production costs, interest rates,
trade prices, WMPs, products traded, and other "benefits" associated
with the readiness to finance (Brabant 1971, pp. 99ff.).

From the publicized experiences with these target credits, it is important to remember that several such ventures lacked an economic rationale
because they did not necessarily guarantee advantages to the lender,
borrower, and possibly potential other users of the enlarged output capacity. Under these conditions one could not really expect to bolster
"joint investment activity," not because capital is a scarce factor for all
CMEA countries anyway, but chiefly because even where capital is comparatively abundant, the owner could "earn" more by allocating disposable funds differently. Perhaps even more important is the fact that
long-term specific credits, even when well founded, can at best provide a
partial solution merely to a limited number of national economic problems because it does not induce steady and long-lasting relations between
partners in the production sphere (Belovič 1979, p. 51). For this to
emerge, different measures have to be embraced, including the establishment of common enterprises. Partly on account of the emerging economic recession in Czechoslovakia, which had been the main lender up to
the early 1960s, the search for greater efficiency in economic production
and administration, and the more general economic reforms of the mid-
1960s, "available regional investment" funds gradually dried up without

the members having remedied the fundamental causes of the disequilibria. Needless to add, no agreement was reached regarding the institutionalization of regional capital mobility as a crucial means in the promotion of SEI.

9.4 On investment coordination

The coordination of investment activities may be defined as the agreed upon establishment of new production capacities, the modernization and renovation of outmoded facilities, or the enlargement of existing production capacities by at least two countries. The agreement may involve the basic design and execution of the project or the pooling of resources from several countries, or it may be confined to assurances regarding the distribution of output once the project is on stream. The first two singly or in combination are not required for the proper coordination of investment. But the latter is absolutely mandatory in the context of CMEA cooperation. Because the PEs in principle reject direct foreign investment of whatever provenance in their economy,[11] investment coordination in the CMEA environment necessarily comprises the declared interest of two or more PEs in obtaining future deliveries of the project's output stream. As a result, the trade aspects of the investment endeavors that were motivated by the perceived need to boost SEI have always been the key element of this form of CMEA cooperation. If the country of location is reluctant, for whatever reason, to appropriate its own investment funds for the purpose, CMEA members interested in the expansion of capacity for some products are bound to fall back upon the well-tried methods of "special purpose credits" – a more apt description than joint investment. But the consistent reversion to credits in order to coordinate investments chiefly in primary goods has recently been condemned as being seriously misguided (Poller 1984, p. 23). Poller advocates that greater attention be paid to the coordination of the transmission of scientific and technological achievements into the production process.

In contrast to the traditional trade in investment goods or the classical forms of capital mobility, investment coordination among PEs in essence comprises the ratification of one or more concrete agreements about the technical and economic parameters of the projects. Such agreements are normally negotiated jointly so as to ensure that the interested partners cooperate closely not only in the implementation of the investment project but also in the later utilization of the incremental output stream. But this need not always be so.[12] The essential task of investment coordination, as it should be in harmonizing the current requirements of short-term plans, is the satisfaction of future demand for important goods and services. By dovetailing investment decisions, it becomes possible "to heed better the requirements of the reciprocal complementarity and gradual intermeshing of [the] economies in the development of the production structure, to increase the efficiency of investments, to reduce the burden of each country, and to apportion rationally the outlays among the interested countries" (Faude et al. 1984, p. 222). This agreement on sharing output may be positive as well as negative. Usually there will be an increase in trade associated with a jointly financed project, but the latter could conceivably alleviate the import requirements of the host country with the technical expertise and the financial assistance of the traditional exporter.

The coordination of investment activity, as noted, can take on several different forms that are interrelated. The key ones include (1) synchronizing investment plans, (2) implementing complementary investment projects, (3) sharing financially or materially in the outlays appropriated for investment projects, (4) jointly reconstructing, modernizing, and rationalizing enterprises, and (5) jointly creating common enterprises. The first type is the least involved, though by no means the one that is of smallest importance. It consists of reaching agreement on the degree of emphasis that individual PEs place on certain economic branches during a given time. It may be regulated in the course of coordinating national economic plans or by including projects in a Concerted Plan or Target Program, inclusive of the concurrent multilateral framework and bilateral implementation agreements. The latter are required to bring political and other general agreements on cooperation principles into fruition through the specific inclusion of their provisions, possibly after further detailed negotiations, in annual and medium-term plans.

From the economic point of view, the second form is perhaps the most crucial in the context of regional integration. It presupposes far-reaching policy concertation between at least two countries about the gradual elaboration of a de facto uniform "production complex." The third form involves participation either in the implementation of investment projects or directly in their financing. This has by now a considerable history. It is a special form of intergovernmental credit that I shall examine in greater depth in Section 9.5.

The common reconstruction, modernization, renovation, and rationalization of production processes is a very topical subject that blends in well not only with the policy concerns about economic adjustment that have dominated developments in the 1980s but also with the calls that emanated from the June 1984 economic summit. It involves the exchange of know-how and goods. The first may refer to advanced techniques or technology, organizational knowledge, or production experiences. The second may take the form of the joint development, implementation, and exchange of production processes, technologies, modern equipment, and means of rationalization. These endeavors are part and parcel of more general efforts directed at the promotion of greater standardization and specialization in production throughout the CMEA.

The last category is self-explanatory. It involves the direct transfer of investment capital in a most circumscribed form. The few existing joint enterprises[13] are all bilateral and concerned with either simple production processes: for example, textile fibers in Zawiercie (in the joint GDR–Polish enterprise Przyjaźń–Freundschaft); the processing of coal wastes in Katowice (the joint Hungarian–Polish enterprise Haldex) and in Ostrava (the joint Czechoslovak–Hungarian enterprise Haldex–Ostrava); the copper–molybdenum ore-processing and ore-enrichment plant in Érdénét (the joint Mongolian–Soviet venture Érdénét); the production of intrafirm transport equipment (the joint Bulgarian–Hungarian firm Intransmaš); Interlichter, which operates "mother" ships that facilitate the transshipment from ocean liners to river transportation on standardized barges;[14] and perhaps a few others.[15] Although they are few and share negligibly in overall production capacity, joint enterprises as a key form of SEI should not be ignored. P. Širjaev has characterized them as "the most flexible form of cooperation in the investment sphere" (Širjaev 1982, p. 72) because this form of cooperation, unlike jointly financed investment projects, is, in principle, self-sustaining.

There are two important moments in deciding for synchronizing investment decisions or even intermeshing capital projects. One derives from the general desire to enhance the process of SEI in its broadest economic, social, political, and ideological dimensions. The other set englobes issues that are more mundane, inasmuch as they all derive from the economic aspects of the proposed cooperation venture. Thus a project may fail to qualify as economically advantageous on the ground of general efficiency computations. But it may well be implemented just the same because the PEs decide it to be in their interest to do so. Important starting points for the latter, as of the former, kind of investment coordination is the preparation of jointly acceptable estimates of the evolution of future demand for a given product, the product flow from existing production capacities and the likely extentions, and efficiency calculations based on the juxtaposition of the various alternative ways of satisfying incremental future demand. In the second set of considerations, the latter criteria also encompass the variant of satisfying incremental demand through imports from third countries. Regardless of the constraints placed on the decision space, however, the trade-off must necessarily take into account the various aspects of production costs and price formation in the CMEA not only for the items to be exchanged in order to erect the projects but also for the operation of the ventures and the distribution of the future output stream.

The scope and role of investment coordination in the CMEA should have received a shot in the arm after 1975 for several reasons. First, agreement on fostering dovetailed investment programs as called for in *Integration Program,* in part supported by the newly created IIB, could in practice have had a measurable impact only with the medium-term plans for the second half of the 1970s. The main thrust of the development plans for the early 1970s had already been worked out nationally and regionally in the late 1960s. Second, by mid-decade the wide-ranging debate on the purposes and means of SEI had run its course for all practical purposes and the members began to elaborate the first Concerted Plan. Third, the sharp deterioration in internal and external development conditions heightened the need to come to grips with common tasks by better dovetailing the shrunken investment funds. Finally, the decision taken in 1975 to formulate Target Programs to be implemented starting in 1981 should have provided very considerable room for the better harmonization of investment intentions and the synchronization of capital formation throughout the CMEA.

The first Concerted Plan (1976–1980) provided for ten investment projects to be jointly financed by several PEs with a total nominal value of about TR 9 billion, of which about TR 7 billion was to be earmarked for the concurrent five-year plans, as several had already been initiated earlier or would not be completed by 1980. However, the degree of coordination went well beyond that, because the first Concerted Plan had twenty-four topics of "multilateral integration interest" in addition to the construction projects to be jointly financed (Válek 1983a, p. 845). Nevertheless, the share of overall investment outlays coordinated at the CMEA level remained very small indeed. Thus all outlays for joint construction projects in the Concerted Plan did not exceed 1.5 percent of total investments forecast for 1976–1980 (Karavaev 1979, p. 5) and ended up being well below 1 percent of actual capital outlays (Belovič, 1985, p. 115).

The Target Programs as initially conceived would have involved a total investment outlay of perhaps TR 80 to 90 billion over ten years (1981–1990). But this ambitious menu was pared sharply by the time the second Concerted Plan was finalized, and it was further pruned under impact of the external difficulties of the early 1980s. As it turned out, the second Concerted Plan envisaged only five joint investment projects valued at TR 2 billion,[16] in addition to thirteen cooperation and specialization projects, and thirteen thematic programs for scientific–technical cooperation (Válek 1983a, p. 845; Válek 1984, p. 11). The scope of this second Concerted Plan fell far short of what had been subsumed in the original Target Programs, which may be seen from the specific cooperation projects included in the programs as finally endorsed, which themselves were of perceptibly more modest scope than had been envisaged in the initial discussions.[17] Válek reports that the Target Programs envisaged 121 construction projects sited over all CMEA members to be built by 1990, of which 15 would be for fuel and energy, 12 for chemical sectors, 32 in the machine-building and metallurgical sectors, 53 in transportation, and 9 others.[18] I have no explicit aggregate values pertaining to the third Concerted Plan, but it is unlikely that more than a few joint projects and a few billion TR are involved.

One feature of this type of investment coordination in capital construction is frequently erroneously gauged. If the PEs formulate a Concerted Plan comprising a number of joint projects, it means neither that the total volume of investment flows to be coordinated is limited to that capital outlay nor that the total value would have to be moved across the region. For one, investments may be harmonized outside the boundaries of that plan and the construction values do not include other forms of investment coordination actually subsumed in the plan but that do not explicitly call for joint construction projects. Even for the sums that the CMEA members agree to pool for the erection of joint projects, the values quoted earlier normally do not all involve regional capital transferability. Thus, the construction projects of the first Concerted Plan required about TR 7 billion to be invested jointly during the five-year plan period. Because about TR 6.5 billion was appropriated for projects located in the USSR and the latter would contribute about half (TR 3.1 billion) of those expenditures (Karpič 1976, pp. 1lff.), the share of coordinated investments for common projects giving rise to capital mobility was slated at well below half of the total nominal value.

9.5 Investment loans and socialist economic integration

László Csaba recently argued with some persuasiveness that the second wave of investment credits, which started in the mid-1970s, did not involve any "special" allowances beyond the strictly businesslike agreement on the transfer of the tied loans and debts (Csaba 1985, pp. 238ff.). His is really a moot question. Although I would not venture to argue that every loan commitment automatically entails "special treatment" by the recipient, the type of package deals typical of the CMEA makes it very difficult to subscribe wholeheartedly to Csaba's thesis. One might ask, for instance, whether the USSR would have been willing to adhere to the averaging of WMPs for oil if the Eastern European countries had refused to participate in the formulation—the extent of their actual participation in its implementation continues to be a matter of dispute in any case—of the first Concerted Plan? would it have increased volumes of oil in the second half of the 1970s? or granted accommodating loans to the PEs facing severe regional payments problems in the way it apparently did? To dispel any impression that I disagree with the fundamentals of Csaba's view regarding these second-wave joint investment projects, I should like to summarize briefly the "economics" of such activities. But first a few notions of why the activities occur at all and what they really entail.

The concept of investment contribution

The predominant focus of joint investment projects by the PEs has not been joint investment at all. In the CMEA there is virtually nothing equivalent to the transfer of resources in the form of direct foreign investment, private corporate borrowing, or sovereign borrowing in general or for specific projects. The only exception perhaps is the early experience gathered with the notorious joint-stock companies established after World War II. These ventures, it will be recalled, pooled local resources owned by the newly created socialist (or the newly liberated) countries with those expropriated as war reparations (that is, local resources owned by actual or presumed collaborators, sympathizers, and residents of the axis powers and their puppet collaborators). These and other forms of unrequited transfers of capital from some of the Eastern European countries, including the wholesale dismantling of plant and equipment for reconstruction purposes in the USSR, is frequently regarded as a form of economic "exploitation" by the USSR (Marer 1974, pp. 183ff.). I find it more instructive to treat most of these capital transfers as integral parts of the USSR's war reparation claims.[19] Whether this was proper, given the new sociopolitical environments of the former German allies, and efficient from the economic point of view are altogether different questions.[20] Most, but not all,[21] of these ventures were dissolved in the early 1950s and the USSR's equity stake sold in some fashion to the home country. Needless to add that this brief experience of foreign direct investment of a sort, or even the uninterrupted one in the joint-stock companies that are still extant, could offer only few constructive pointers of how CMEA investment coordination proper ought to be tackled.

The major focus of direct cooperation in investment projects has not been "socialist direct investment" or "investment contributions," as it is usually referred to in the CMEA, but the joint financing of investment projects by the home country and one or more fraternal partner countries interested in securing incremental supplies of key products. The project remains the sole property of the home country, and it is wholly operated within its "domestic" management system. The only phase of joint participation in the project, other than its financing, is twofold: (1) in the design and, possibly, the establishment of the project, and (2) in the distribution of output, first, to pay off the debt incurred by the host country and usually also to secure an ensured volume of deliveries from the output stream over a number of years. Given that most projects include contracted deliveries of certain volumes with prices to be fixed according to prevailing TR trade prices at delivery time, the repayment is almost guaranteed to be inferior to the total volume of the committed quantities. Those excess quantities are settled within the provisions of the regular BTPAs, though the volume as such belongs to a "special" protocol. There may be other joint transactions associated with a project, but these will be discussed later.

It is useful to consider the issues involved with intergovernmental credits separately from those associated with bank credits. Although the financial and trade mechanisms of the CMEA dictate that there be a very close relationship between the two, formally as well as operationally there are important differences. This is especially the case for the criteria by which such credits are decided upon and the concrete conditions involved. Investment contributions are therefore usually handled in special bilateral loan accounts supervised by state or foreign trade banks that are external to the TR clearing and credit systems, in part because the maturity of those loans and the interest charges imposed differ from those typically provided for by the common banks (Stirtzel 1977, p. 204).

Rationale for the pooling of investment resources

It is traditionally argued that the coordination of investment decisions, possibly involving the regional redistribution of appropriated capital funds in individual member countries, is, by definition, beneficial when measured in terms of incremental returns both to the CMEA as a whole and to each participant in particular. From a strictly economic point of view, there are few problems with this proposition. But matters get less straightforward when is is argued casuistically that it is "obviously beneficial" for CMEA members interested in obtaining additional deliveries of certain products to shoulder part of the financial burden required to develop new production capacities and to maintain these additional resources on stream. In other words, the economic rationale of a given project is intricately intermeshed with its financing. I am leaving aside for now political, strategic, and ideological considerations, all of which have played an important role at one point or another.

From a technical point of view, the inherent economic merits of a given project, even if placed in the context of "strategic considerations," should be evaluated in the first instance within a framework that is independent of the ways in which the project might be financed. Bearing in mind that under prevailing conditions, most PEs can borrow financial resources from international financial markets to fund worthwhile investment projects, the decision-making process should be footed first of all on the economic merits of a proposed project as such. If a thorough economic evaluation indicated the viability of the proposed project, the go-ahead should be chiefly contingent on there not being projects that are even more profitable. If funds can be solicited from the entire world, the expected rate of total return on the capital invested should be at least as high as the rate of interest to be paid on borrowed funds or as attainable in international financial markets.[22] Both magnitudes would have to be evaluated in comparable units. Thus if funds are borrowed in CC markets, the net rate of return of the project evaluated at international prices of the goods to be exported in the future to secure, and eventually to pay off, the debt should not be inferior to the nominal interest rate. If there are other, possibly noneconomic, preferences involved in deciding upon a project, they have to be made explicit so as to add to, or to subtract premiums from the economic rate of return (or nominal interest rate) suggested earlier.

A project may not be economically more viable than another one, or it may not be economically viable at all, and yet be built because an ulterior raison d'être (such as security or strategic concern) dictates that the new output stream not be acquired from third markets. The tolerable cost associated with such a venture needs to be covered through subsidies from those PEs that feel they cannot import the goods from elsewhere. Whether the project is financed from local or foreign resources again depends critically on the opportunity cost of one alternative over another. Only by sheer coincidence can the parties interested in raising the output level of a certain product also be swayed by purely material reasons in participating in the apportionment of the total cost of the venture.

How properly to separate, or to keep carefully apart, the economic aspects of common ventures from their financing has been a baffling issue for over thirty years. It derives essentially from the absence of a real capital market in Eastern Europe, the heterogeneity of trade prices and their peculiar relationship to domestic prices, the deep-seated bilateralism in the CMEA, ideological obstacles to international property, differences in management systems, and the generally short shrift given to the economic calculus in PEs.

Costs and benefits of investment participations

If the joint financing of a project is restricted to the simple lending and repayment of funds at market terms, the benefit to the lender is the rate of interest received.[23] Because this is usually about 2–3 percent simple interest, the nominal rate of return on capital is well inferior to the marginal productivity of capital in the lender's market. It is hence frequently inferred that such capital participations must be quite disadvantageous to the lender and, conversely, highly beneficial to the borrower. There may be cases where matters are this clear-cut, but they are in all likelihood quite exceptional.

The complexity of the benefits and costs of joint investment participations for both the borrower and the lender derives from three instances.

First, capital transfers from the borrower are executed in the form of tied loans: The lender delivers goods and services for which the lender will be compensated in natura some time in the future. These goods and services are supposedly evaluated at current CMEA prices in regular TR transactions and hence diverge positively or negatively from the real scarcity of these goods in world markets and in both the borrower's and lender's economies.

Similarly, loans are normally repaid by delivering a certain amount of output coming on stream over a given period of time. These deliveries are usually priced at the CMEA terms prevailing at delivery time, although there are important exceptions. Any deliveries exceeding the amount owed for principal and interest is merged with the regular settlements mechanism, although those deliveries do not normally form a constituent part of the regular BTPA. Their prices are likely to diverge from prevailing WMPs and most certainly from real scarcities in the borrower and lender economies. There are therefore implicit costs and benefits ensuing from the two-way transfers that have to be taken into account in evaluating whether a particular project on balance proves to be an advantageous proposition.

Third, investment projects are very rarely discussed in isolation from a number of other transactions. It may be that the concrete details of joint investment participations are worked out in a strictly businesslike fashion, thus involving a simple agreement about deliveries equaling a certain TR amount (the nominal value of the loan) and the repayment of principal and interest by way of future counterdeliveries at then prevailing prices. But the decision to join in a given project almost invariably emanates in the first instance from the highest policy-making levels of government or party (or both). Though little enough is known of these political deliberations, by their very essence they involve compromises that are contracted against the backdrop of the benefits and costs of an entire sector, possibly the economy as a whole. "Benefits" have been known to be handed out, even recently (see Bagudin 1982, p. 3), at the time a country agrees to participate in a joint project. They can take on various forms: deliveries of soft goods when transferring the loan, obtaining extra-hard goods at repayment time, incremental deliveries of rather hard goods at friendship prices that would otherwise not have been available, and other compensatory transactions.

Who gains and who loses on balance? This question is often approached as if investment participation were a simple zero-sum game, in which one partner's gains are the other's losses. It most frequently is not so precisely because the economics of a project may be at great variance with its financing, regardless of how the latter is in the end arranged. The final outcome depends critically on the economic merits of the project, the possible subsidies logically required by the expressed need for relative autarky in the project, the terms at which the loans are transferred and repaid, the "extra" transactions forthcoming because an investment agreement is reached at all, and other such factors. Neither borrower nor lender may in the end gain, both may benefit, or only some participants derive profit at the expense of others.

A more specific statement of how to assess benefits and costs would be useful. But as I have shown elsewhere (Brabant 1971), the complexity of the CMEA "market" does not allow for a straightforward, relatively uncomplicated statement. Any claim to the contrary must be rejected as unrealistic. This is particularly the case for assertions based on the simple comparison of the interest rate paid and the probable productivity of capital. One such objectionable thesis is Márton Tardos's. This asserts that target credits invariably involve a price hike amounting to the "discounted value of the credit per unit of product, with the actual rate of discount corresponding to the difference between the charge on assets engaged [as] warranted by national conditions of the producer, and the cheap interest rate on the investment credit" (Tardos 1969, p. 164).

The value of a loan commitment

Many of the loans agreed upon during the first wave of commitments (about 1957–1962) involved the transfer of a combination of capital goods, services, and consumer durables. The actual goods delivered by the lender frequently had little in common with the capital requirements of the "common" project or even with operating it. In fact, getting the project under way appears to have had a higher priority than obtaining the start-up funds and getting it on stream. As it turned out in several cases, the project was funded by rechristening a "short-term transitory" surplus position on regular settlements account into a long-term loan. In that connection, the true value of the goods transferred – frequently rather soft products of marginal relevance to the requirements of the lender – was often inferior to the nominal amount of the loan, given the overvaluation of soft goods in CMEA trade (see Chapter 4).

With the second wave of investment credits since the 1970s, a noticeable shift in the direction of hardening the loans has occurred.[24] Not only are goods agreed upon in transferring the loan more directly related to the project as such, the recipient has also been insisting on higher quality goods to be shipped by the lender, frequently incorporating direct or indirect inputs from CC markets. The form of the transfer has also shifted away from the simple export of goods without immediate payment to pure credits (sometimes in CC) and construction work (Tömpe 1978, p. 315).

But it would not be accurate to claim that now all deliveries in transferring the loan are for specific projects. As an example, the Chmelnickij atomic power station, one of the projects featured in the second Concerted Plan, is half funded by several CMEA members and half by the USSR. The former transfer their contributions for 60 percent in machinery and equipment, 16 percent in metal structures and building materials, and 24 percent in the form of consumer goods (Bagudin 1983, p. 4). The hardening in terms of the CC content and quality of goods was the case most conspicuously for the construction of the Sojuz gas pipeline. For that project, the borrower also insisted upon the importation of highly skilled labor services, although that turned out to be far from a blessing in disguise (see Section 9.1). This emphasis on obtaining higher-quality goods must be seen largely in connection with the growing scarcity in world and CMEA trade of the primary goods and fuels that were nearly exclusively the object of such common efforts. Because the hardening occurred in the goods transferred in both directions, the recent shifts have not necessarily been consistently and unilaterally unfavorable to the lender.

On the evaluation of investment contributions

The economic aspects of a proposition to finance a project jointly can be unambiguously scrutinized only if there are realistic forecasts of the various components of the agreement, the terms of delivery, the commodity composition of the loan transfer, and other important parameters. In recent years, no price discounts seem to have been granted most of the time.[25] The key uncertainty in deciding rationally upon joint investment participations has therefore been the price at which the goods delivered in repayment will be invoiced. At the time of relentlessly rising prices in the late 1970s, many commentators pointed out that the investment proposition was unfavorable because its return was negative. An ostensibly crucial element of joint investment projects is the ensured stream of deliveries of goods into the future (a twenty years' horizon is not unknown!). I am not sure how valuable this security is. But given that planners are notoriously risk-averse, bent as they are on incorporating as much certainty in planning as possible, there must be a scarcity value to the security of supply, although it may be very difficult to quantify it. In any case, lowering risk must have some nonzero value to be factored into the cost-benefit calculus.

On the nominal value of a joint project

As described in Chapter 6, the constitution of joint enterprises or IEOs requiring the transfer of "capital" from at least two participants gives rise to knotty convertibility problems that have in the past been solved in an ad hoc manner. The preeminent example of this "target" computation has always been the first Haldex enterprise. This first successful joint enterprise between Hungary and Poland, leaving aside the joint-stock companies, demonstrated the complexity of arriving at a mutually satisfactory accounting for two PEs. Because the joint financing of SEI projects is, in principle, not contingent on the true evaluation of the project, it could be thought that the issue of the real value of "common property" does not arise here. This may be true in principle. But recent experience, particularly that gathered during the second wave of target credits, has shown this to be not quite so. Thus the shares of many projects included in the first and second Concerted Plans to be jointly financed were not derived by simply taking the "domestic" evaluation of the project at face value. In most cases, the distribution of the future output stream during a mutually agreed period of time was partitioned into fixed shares and the interested parties were requested to fund part of the construction project's cost in exact proportion to their future output claims. Because the transfer involves goods and services from several PEs, the question of the comparability of national trade and production data arose once again.

The first study of the joint financing of common ventures antedates the Haldex example by nearly a decade. V. Perova reports that the basic organizational ideas regarding the joint construction by two or more PEs were first formulated at the fifth CMEA Session (Moscow, 24–25 June 1954) and further developed during subsequent sessions as one of the practical measures aimed at strengthening CMEA cooperation. At that time, serious proposals on the possibilities of PEs participating in concrete construction projects as well as on how to combine the material, financial, and labor resources were apparently tabled (Perova 1984, p. 11). These initial proposals did not work out, basically owing to the rapid, unanticipated transformations then taking place in Eastern Europe.

The intricacies of converting local expenditures and trade data into a common currency unit for operational purposes can be seen from the example of establishing the common patrimony in the case of a joint enterprise (as amply documented in Georgiev et al. 1985, pp. 128–30). The difficulties involved in Haldex's creation begged for a relaxation of this tedious procedure especially if the PEs were to explore more intensively the erection of common organizations, as advocated in *Integration Program*. To compress this complexity and to enhance the establishment of common organizations within the CMEA, planners worked out the Berlin method in 1962–1963 (apparently finalized in 1964) for evaluating the costs of joint investment or construction cooperation; it has been periodically revised since (Válek 1984, pp. 73ff.). This method consists of separating a project's total cost in local currency into a wage, a trade, and a structure component. For wages, premiums, and wage-related costs (such as social benefits) the noncommercial ERs are proposed. Goods and services acquired from abroad specifically for the project are valued at their true TR cost, while CC transactions are translated at a realistic reproduction cost for the TR or at internal ERs. The value of building materials, machinery, and equipment is established by relating TR trade prices to domestic prices of the project's host country for a large sample (50–60 percent) of the products used.[26]

As related in Chapter 6, shortly after the endorsement of *Integration Program* and the euphoria it engendered, the PEs adopted "joint investment ERs," that were supposed to supplant the ad hoc computation of implicit or explicit ERs tailored to each concrete project. But they have never actually been applied. The question of how to evaluate investment in common ventures or in jointly financed projects has therefore remained on the agenda. In practice, progress has been made according to whatever determinants prevailed at the time; the SCFQ has been preoccupied with the theoretical and methodological issues involved ever since the Berlin method was first endorsed (Válek 1985, p. 11). New concerted calculation methods, whence new investment coefficients resulted, were endorsed at the sixty-first session of the Executive Committee (SĖV 1979, p. 74 and Perova 1984, p. 13) and once again at the ninety-ninth session in May 1981 (Belovič 1986a, p. 127). This latter decision apparently led in 1982 to the adoption of a concrete work program for the realization of "realistic economic indicators" for the construction and operation of joint projects (Belovič 1986a, p. 131). To the extent that these stipulations are still valid,[27] it would appear that the PEs have adopted a more flexible attitude towards the financing of joint projects than earlier versions tended to suggest. At the very least, it is explicitly recognized that partners may depart from the proposed methodology if they so wish – simply a recognition of actual practice. Nevertheless, its practical application to joint construction projects is "still rather complex . . . requiring time and effort," especially as concerns the evaluation of the local expenditure component for which there is unlikely to be a readily identifiable TR price (Perova 1984, p. 13). The CMEA's International Research Institute of Management Problems has apparently been put in charge of developing a feasible method for determining appropriate conversion factors for material expenditures. It is reported to have come up recently with a methodology that simplifies the conversion procedures and computational details, making it less labor intensive and possible to evaluate the construction cost in the TR at the stage of preparing draft agreements, but important shortcomings reportedly persist (Perova 1984, pp. 13–14).

Looking back at the past and present forms of factor mobility in the CMEA, perhaps the most conspicuous feature is the lack of transparency in transactions. Most are regulated ad hoc through special BTPAs that exhibit individualized parameters, with nonprice compensations frequently arranged to overcome interest rate inhibitions and the reluctance of PEs to relax their insistence on full control over factors of production. Precisely because of the considerable rigidities built into the economic mechanisms of PEs and the inward-oriented outlook of many policy makers, the experience with capital flows has clearly demonstrated three shortcomings. As A. Belovič recently noted, the volume of capital transfers from joint investment projects and IEOs is still far too small, too much centered on the fuel and raw material sectors instead of on attaining an optimal scale in manufacturing, and many of the agreements have not been sufficiently coordinated on a multilateral scale either in the choice of projects or in the type of production processes thus established (Belovič 1985, pp. 115–16). Such rigidity may have been desirable when the key goals of socialist economic policy were reconstruction, rapid industrialization, and the full absorption of idle resources. It may still be warranted on the basis of political, ideological, and strategic considerations, which, after all, are noneconomic factors that enter into the decision making of governments in MEs as well. Unlike in most PEs, the noneconomic costs and benefits in MEs are usually assessed, though not always explicitly. This is precisely the argument that I should like to advance in drawing meaningful conclusions from this brief examination of factor mobility: There is considerable scope for monetizing the regional exchange of production factors by setting decision-making parameters that are economically meaningful. Only when it becomes clear at which terms the services of domestic production factors can be exchanged within the region will there be some pressure from the grass roots for greater mobility to enhance SEI.

10

The International Investment Bank

The diversity of circumstances under which various types of capital movements have been accommodated in Eastern Europe (see Chapter 9) underlines the fundamental need for streamlining in that area. Greater clarity would not only create space for properly organized capital flows within the CMEA. It would also improve the transparency for potential borrowers and lenders and thus foster a more congenial disposition toward factor movements. This would come to prevail in spite of rather forbidding ideological blocks regarding property, foreign direct investment, control over the domestic economy, and others. None of these axioms of socialist economic policy or inhibitions of the political authorities needs to be compromised in any essential respect by improving the specific parameters that guide capital movements to the benefit of SEI in general and domestic economic expansion efforts in particular. A minimum requirement is the explicit recognition that capital productivity among the PEs is far from uniform, that there is considerable room for output gains, and that a strictly technical clarification of potential gains and costs of capital mobility may convince policy makers to mobilize these reserves without in any way chipping away at the foundations of socialist economic policies.

Such a regularization of a very disparate and murky decision-making sphere could have been handled at the intergovernmental level, chiefly through the coordination of nationwide plans. But with respect to investment coordination (see Chapter 9), this was never carried far beyond individual projects. Not only has there been a considerable potential for synchronizing the entire investment process against the backdrop of the needs of the region as a whole, subject to certain constraints as regards "domestic" requirements. There is even ampler room for harmonizing the various decisions involved in realizing individual projects agreed upon by the authorities of two or more PEs. Still more urgent has been the institutionalization of this process to ensure greater efficiency in the handling of dovetailed investment funds, as measured by the contribu-

330

tion of capital movements to SEI. Such a more definite organization could also make room for the target redistribution of funds attracted from outside the CMEA region and of temporarily free assets mobilized from within the region. In other words, there has been some need for establishing a specialized institution tailored to the capital needs of the group as a whole that would be able to operate both within and outside the CMEA region. Its essential mandate in third markets would be to attract funds and redeploy them for capital-formation purposes in some CMEA member(s). This was recognized implicitly in June 1970 when the members decided to establish the IIB.

The IIB is the twin of the IBEC, in principle quite similar to how the IBRD relates to the IMF. Actually the operations of these CMEA institutions have little in common with their Washington counterparts. The reasons for this state of affairs were examined in Chapter 8. Building upon the peculiarities of the TR and the settlements mechanism administered by the IBEC, I shall here sketch the backdrop to the IIB's creation, how it was set up, the instruments put at its disposal, its operations since 1971, and its relations with nonmembers. Following this, I shall briefly evaluate the IIB's contribution to SEI to date and discuss how it may evolve in the near future.

10.1 Backdrop to the bank's creation

The idea of establishing a common capital fund for the benefit of the CMEA region as a whole goes back to the very beginnings of the Council (see Chapter 1). Aside from the aborted scheme envisaged in the "founding document," a decision in principle to pool investment resources was allegedly taken during the fifth Council Session in 1954 (Timošin 1974, p. 98). But no follow-up has been reported. The CMEA charter mentions the desirability of setting up such a joint investment fund, and provisions for its creation by "interested partners" were incorporated into the settlements agreement of 1963. There appears to have been at that time little substantive public discussion about how investment coordination should proceed and what regional goals it was to serve to the benefit of all participants. Some reports mention that a proposal to pool some TR 250–500 million was on the agenda of the fourteenth meeting of the CMEA's Executive Committee in October 1964, but the communiqué (SĚV 1979, pp. 25–26) does not mention it, which presumably indicates that no broad measure of agreement – let alone unanimity among the interested participants – even on the principles involved could be mustered. The project was apparently tabled in consequence (Allen 1973, p. 38). The Polish delegate to CMEA's financial organs made at least one firm proposal to fund jointly an investment project to be supervised by the IBEC (Brabant

1977a, pp. 106–7), but no definite commitment on the part of the other members could be secured.

In the context of the discussions of the mid-1960s about reforming the CMEA organization and its integration mechanisms, several proposals for closer cooperation in investment activities were entertained. A particularly important one for the later emergence of the IIB was that made by the Polish delegation to CMEA and the SCFQ in early 1968.[1] Accordingly, the IBEC should start lending long term against a collateral of a fund composed of CCs and "hard" commodities put up by the borrower. This particular proposition was firmly embedded in a more general framework for enhancing integration objectives and instruments that both Hungary and Poland were intensively pursuing. In particular, they called for the creation of a common CC fund as the crux of the settlements mechanism and thus a pivotal integration lever. With respect to the institutionalization of long-term loans, however, it was felt that the IBEC's provisions for such investment funds had never been tested and the matters on hand were quite different from rather simple settlements tasks. It was therefore deemed expedient to create a new institution specifically designed to lend funds for joint investment purposes. Thus it was resolved in principle during the twenty-third CMEA Session (Moscow, April 1969) to set up the IIB as a complement to the IBEC. The formal agreement was signed in July 1970.[2]

At this particular juncture of the many-sided process of SEI, the IIB was seen as the center that would foster the gradual elimination of the obstacles to closer economic cooperation that were imposed upon the region nearly a quarter century before. It was then anticipated, also in conjunction with *Integration Program*'s agreed stipulations on the possible future role of money and finance in SEI, that the bank would be provided with sufficiently flexible policy instruments to discharge itself of its preeminent mission, namely, to seek greater coordination of the members' investment processes in part by granting medium- to long-term loans for projects that would be of outstanding relevance to furthering SEI. The IIB's nodal function was therefore to mobilize capital resources that could not only spearhead the SEI infrastructure but that would set the overal framework for decision making about medium- to long-term economic structures in the CMEA.

Integration Program failed to advance a bold concept of how monetary and financial relations in the CMEA were to evolve. In the absence of at least a central majority, in the short run the new institution's operational mechanisms of necessity at first had to be tailored to the then existing financial and trading regimes. It would thus have had to eschew, at least temporarily, the really formidable obstructions to the efficient planning and implementation of long-term investment loans. The timetable set for finding acceptable solutions to the CMEA's monetary and financial cooperation mechanisms, as related in Chapter 2, was seen as the boundary of the transition period.

Unfortunately, the emerging difficulties with propping up the supply of primary goods from within the region, averting unsustainable external payments problems in TR or CC relations, the lack of success with growth intensification efforts, and spreading domestic supply constraints in conjunction with flagging output performance, among other circumstances, rendered this timetable unattainable. More ominous, the goal of working out an acceptable economic mechanism with adequate indirect coordination instruments was abandoned by mid-decade – well before the coordination of investments under the IIB's aegis and guidance could possibly have been assured an unencumbered takeoff. The implications of this failure to act and then to revert back to the old ways of promoting CMEA cooperation have been dire. The system of strict BTPAs, the inconvertibility of the national currencies and the TR, the prerogatives of national decision making even over matters that intimately affect other partners, and a host of other features of CMEA cooperation have been responsible for the procrustean characteristics of this financial institution.

10.2 Organization, management, and decision making

The IIB's organizational setup parallels very closely the IBEC's. Like the latter, the IIB's does not appear to have changed markedly from its evolvement through the mid-1970s, and it need therefore not be examined here in great detail (see Brabant 1977a, pp. 203–20). It is useful to recall that the bank was endowed with a substantial subscribed capital fund (over TR 1.071 billion)[3] of which 30 percent is in CC. The members contributed 35 percent during the first two years, but no further shares have been called in since. Perhaps the thorniest issue at the time of the bank's creation was how this capital fund could be effectively mobilized in support of the bank's chief mission. It is a problem that has continued to be of central significance in CMEA affairs. To have the bank grant loans and to enable the borrower to utilize such financial resources, the problems associated with the mobilization of TR funds (see Chapter 8) had indeed to be faced squarely anew. Because no formula pledging investible resources in natura was adopted as a companion to the constitution of the capital fund, which for TR transactions[4] incidentally was handled wholly by bookkeeping entries, a member country could simply refuse to supply the capital equipment suitable for a given project, and the bank would be rendered powerless. This has had ominous consequences for the bank's operations and, more importantly, for the actual coordination of investment activities in the region (see Section 10.4).

From very early on, therefore, the bank's lending mechanism was made contingent on planned investment flows and on the "interestedness" of the bank's membership. Prior to filling the loan application, either the IIB or the potential loan beneficiary – in all likelihood chiefly the latter – would have to ensure agreement in principle of all other interested members to guarantee future deliveries as per a commonly set time schedule. This peculiar precondition arose out of the situation of the CMEA market in which money fundamentally does not command goods, except in very specific circumstances (see Chapter 8). This is even true for CC loans if earmarked within the CMEA. Matters are different if the recipient is entitled to appropriate these funds for imports from MEs. It is then mainly the availability of the funds that determines the flow of goods, although proper prior arrangements may be required here too so that prompt delivery can be ensured when the goods become needed.

An important feature of the bank's room for decision making was that, unlike in any previous multilateral arrangement in the CMEA, the IIB was entitled to manage its operational affairs with a qualified majority. Certainly, on basic issues[5] unanimity would be required just as elsewhere in the CMEA. But in most operational matters, a valid decision requires three fourths of a valid quorum. The latter depends in turn on the participation of three fourths of the members. This principle of majority voting, when introduced, had an aura of spectacular novelty attached to it. In view of the traditional unanimity of intrasocialist relations required at the time, the provisions regarding majority voting elicited a lot of commentary both in the East and the West. Although such provisions have since been emulated in some of the IEOs established in the early 1970s (see Brabant 1980, pp. 217–8), decision making by majority has been far less expedient than could have been anticipated on the strength of the principle as such, even considering the limited membership.

A sobering thought contrasting theory and practice emerges from simple arithmetic. In 1971 there were eight charter members, so for a valid quorum at the IIB, given that each member has one vote, six participants needed to be present, of which at least five had to agree on the matter up for debate. Because there are presently ten full members, a valid quorum is a minimum of eight participants, and a valid majority decision therefore requires at least six members in favor. Under present circumstances, then, there can be at most two dissenters. In other words, because all charter members usually attend Bank Council meetings, to pass muster eight PEs have to concur on key operational issues of an investment project or on the more general regulations of the IIB's involvement in the process of investment coordination. This leaves indeed only marginal room for dissension.

Although rather confined from a strictly formal point of view, the majority rule could nevertheless be applied to the bank's policy regarding the issuance of loans, the control over projects in progress, the repayment schedule for credits, the determination of interest rates, sanctions for countries violating or defaulting on the terms of their loan agreement, the establishment and utilization of special funds, and related matters. Majority decision making could therefore, in principle, be a powerful instrument to foster economically justified projects. The clear departure from all previous CMEA practices as well as from one of the much vaunted principles for undertaking actions to the benefit of all partners involved at the very least could have helped to overcome the stifling veto power wielded in earlier decades in spite of the 1967 agreement on the "interested party" principle.[6]

10.3 The bank's decision-making sphere

The bank's operational mechanisms comprise the following five areas: (1) the mobilization of loanable funds, (2) the drawing up of credit plans, (3) the evaluation of proposed projects and the monitoring of projects in progress, (4) the determination of interest rates tailored to the efficient use of resources, and (5) the bank's internal management. Because its organization and formal management do not appear to have changed measurably in recent years (see Brabant 1977a, pp. 203–20), I shall not further discuss this fifth area.

The mobilization of loanable funds

The bank's primary task is to grant medium- to long-term credits according to a set of specific guidelines concerning the scrutinizing and approval of loan requests and the follow-up during construction and repayment. Medium-term loans can be granted for up to five years (there is no minimum maturity, but anything under a three years' duration could compete and possibly conflict with the IBEC's short-term credit policies) and long-term loans with a maturity of up to fifteen years. The guiding principle in the allocation of loanable funds is the enhancement and intensification of SEI, particularly through the active promotion of production specialization according to commonly accepted economic and technical criteria of rational choice. Projects submitted for the bank's consideration can stem from any field, provided they qualify for loans according to the preceding guidelines. The evaluation of the effectiveness of loans and of each venture's regional and national repercussions is made ad hoc by the Bank Council after careful background work by the Bank Board and its specialized staff.[7] Under certain conditions ad hoc consultants may be appointed to help out with special tasks.

Although any project can, in principle, be submitted for funding, some preferred areas of common investment activity have been heavily stressed. These priorities were also enshrined, if somewhat cryptically, in the official documents of July 1970. The principal areas for which the bank is likely to grant credits are officially (article 2 in Tokareva 1972, p. 256) (1) the construction of projects and the development of sectors related to specialization and production cooperation among CMEA countries (the engineering and chemical sectors in particular); (2) the expansion of the raw material and fuel base of member countries, especially for products in short supply; (3) the construction of projects in other economic activities of common interest (this refers particularly to sectors for which the degree of regional specialization is very small, although clear possibilities for regional specialization and production cooperation exist); and (4) projects of major importance to the development of the national economies, particularly in countries that are engaged in adapting their economies to the requirements of a modern industrial society.

Loans can be granted to charter members, associated countries (such as Yugoslavia[8]), and countries entitled to draw upon special funds (such as the developing MEs). In general, banks, IEOs, and individual enterprises authorized by a country to accept international credit can submit projects for common funding by the IIB (Botos 1971, p. 651). Although most of the publicized loans to date have been extended to the charter members, some loans have been granted to the IEO Interatominstrument and Yugoslavia.

Interest rate policy

Though the bank is not mainly a profit-maximizing organization, just like the IBEC, it is to be self-financing. It must therefore ensure its own liquidity and solvability through proper credit and interest rate policies. Interest rates are a special value category in Marxist economics. As examined in Chapter 5, the interest rate in a PE is supposed to be low, and compounding is usually frowned upon. It was therefore not surprising that at the start the bank chose simple interest rates between 4 and 4.25 percent for medium-term loans (up to five years) and 4.5 to 6 percent for long-term loans (up to fifteen years) in TR. More favorable, but differentiated, conditions were granted to the non-European CMEA members. Although these rates were generally inferior to the productivity of capital in most PEs and well below international market rates, it was decided in late 1973 to lower them by one percentage point across the board (Vorob'ëv 1974, p. 12), including for the least developed members. They have remained at that level ever since. Given that the interest rate policies for loans to Cuba, Mongolia, and Vietnam are not unambiguously defined, however, there may have been some movement on that score, as discussed later in this section. As far as CC loans are concerned, the bank's interest rate policy is by necessity closely attuned to conditions in world financial markets.

Just like the IBEC, the IIB has special rates for the least developed members. These were actually 2–4 percent at the bank's inception (Apró 1972, p. 80; Dubrowsky 1973, p. 504; Větrovský 1971, p. 314). With the changeover of late 1973, they were further reduced to between 1.5 and 3 percent (Bangelska 1975, p. 10). Although these favorable conditions applied at first only to Mongolia, which was then the only privileged member, the subsequent accessions of Cuba and Vietnam extended this area of development assistance, and the rates may have dropped to 0.5 percent at the lower end (Belovič 1979, p. 48; Carevski 1982, p. 68). Current interest rates for Cuba and Mongolia are scheduled between 1.5 and 2 percent (Hájek 1980, p. 57), but those for Vietnam are probably even lower. Cuba and Mongolia are said to be able to obtain credits at the present time at from 0.5 to 2 percent,[9] and Vietnam from 0.5 to 1 percent. But I do not know when this shift was introduced.[10] In all this, the bank adheres to "no compounding" at least in the case of TR loans (Lebedinskas 1974, p. 76).

A curious footnote in this connection is the conditions at which the USSR was granted the loan for Orenburg and Sojuz (apparently between TR 1.8 and 2.4 billion, but neither its currency composition nor its borrowers are unambiguous[11]): Rather than abide by the general rules of the bank, it was granted a substantial TR credit at 2 percent, allegedly in view of the importance of the project for the advancement of SEI![12] This rate must certainly have been inferior to what the bank had to pay on TR deposits or what it was earning from the IBEC on its TR assets.[13] Because announcements of individual projects rarely list the loan terms, which are treated as a legitimate business secret, it is not known to what extent this "extraordinary" clause has been applied in other endeavors as well. The precedent of the Orenburg–Sojuz project was set allegedly because the Soviet Union objected to paying a higher than normal "socialist" interest rate as a matter of principle. Since then, projects that are considered to be of the highest importance are endorsed at the lowest interest rate – 2 percent (Brdička 1978, p. 11; Dubrowsky 1981, p. 92; Lebedinskas 1974, p. 75). Recall that "importance" is measured by the project's relevance to the advancement of SEI. Curiously enough, this qualification had in any case already been slated as the paramount lending criterion and general operational guideline for the IIB's decision making when the bank was founded.

One could examine once again how these rates were determined, how effective current interest rates are set, or how the bank's interest rate policy should be selected. The principles of liquidity and profitability in determining the bank's interest rates, although important, hardly help to explain the rates for loans denominated in TR proper. The initial interest rate schedule was justified by CMEA spokesmen on the strength of the argument that the rates then specified approximated the average productivity of capital, the rate of growth in the individual countries, and the level of international interest rates on investment credits.[14] But these considerations are not helpful in explaining the rates on medium- and long-term loans, because IBEC's short-term interest rates had already earlier been justified by this argument, and IIB's rates for such loans are lower than IBEC's! One or another of the aforementioned considerations could vaguely help to explain the rationale of the first set of interest rates. But they hardly justify the overall reduction in rates enacted in 1973. Explanations that hinge on "stimulating demand" for IIB loans (Dubrowsky 1981, p. 92) seem to miss the essence of TR credits altogether, for what is required is to foster material "supply." They are even less germane to the rationalization of why the interest rate schedule has been kept unchanged up to the present, in spite of measurable modifications in the SEI environment and productivity outlook. Probably the most likely explanation, as offered initially in justification of the 1973 reduction, is that IIB must "further activate [its TR] credit activities" (Konstantinov 1975, p. 20). But there seems to be a substantial reconsideration of this practice afoot. The June 1984 summit apparently urged a much finer differentiation of interest rates within overall limits set by the Bank Council on the basis of economically justified criteria (Garbuzov 1985, p. 35).

Interest rates on the CC portion of the loans are determined differently. Not only are the charges on CC loans substantially larger – IIB is said to levy a "profit margin" of from five eighths to a full percentage point over the rates applied in Western European financial markets, which presumably means over the rates at which IIB can borrow in Euromarkets (Kucharski 1974, p. 518) – but they also fluctuate in time and for various currency types with interest rate changes in international money markets. Such interest rates are reviewed every six months, a practice typical of the Eurocapital markets. Whereas unused portions of the loans denominated in TR are held on call without charge, unused CC loans are subject to a fixed commission charge of half a percentage point (Danov 1972, p. 8), which is also in keeping with the then Eurocapital market practices.

Project evaluation and monitoring

Although the bank is not expected to maximize profits, it must ensure its own liquidity and solvability. In addition, it is called upon to foster the optimal use of scarce capital resources, bearing in mind the other objectives of the members with respect to the bank's mission. For example, all PEs wish to draw upon the common fund, but none harbors any particular desire to promote exclusively economic efficiency. Judging by the quite substantial tasks listed, the bank simply cannot hope to cope with all problems of production specialization, the development of raw materials, and extending development aid. The IIB's own funds and those it can acquire in financial markets are manifestly far too limited to permit it to become heavily involved even in the most critical fields of coordinating and guiding the investment activities of its members. The bank's operations and persuasiveness therefore need to be closely dovetailed with "local" investment decisions. This requires that acceptable criteria be worked out to ensure the best allocation of scarce resources.

The bank's statutes specify general criteria, such as highest effectiveness, the integrational effects of the projects, and competitiveness by world market standards. The vague criterion of "high effectiveness" for the selection of projects cofinanced by the bank, as specified in article 2 of the agreement and article 15 of the IIB's statutes (Tokareva 1972, p. 267), is narrowed down in practice. It is known that the IIB members operated until early 1973 with "provisional guidelines" and thereafter with "guidelines" for project selection and evaluation (Grinev and Lebedinskas 1975, p. 40). These guidelines have been revised several times since then, including in December 1978 (Válek 1983b, p. 12) and most recently in 1984 in the context of the new "complex" set of provisions designed to improve the credit and clearing relations among the PEs (Válek 1985, p. 10).

Loans are apparently granted by looking more closely at a sequence of quantitative and qualitative features of each project submitted to the Board: achieving the highest level of technological construction, ensuring optimal redemption deadlines for a given sector, reaching optimal production scales for the given sector, producing goods consistent with worldwide parameters of costs and technology, existence of the necessary material base for the production of the goods, the potential demand for the product, and so on. This detailed enumeration of the properties each project should ideally possess may be very informative. But such evaluation criteria are clearly still far too vague and of too bewildering a variety to permit the elaboration of a consistent, generally applicable strategy for scrutinizing loan requests and ranking them according to their strictly technical merits. In the light of the information at hand (most comprehensively reviewed in Válek 1984, pp. 55–72), it appears highly doubtful that the Council has so far been able to act on the basis of a limited but uniform number of criteria that can be expressed synthetically and that complies with most of the aforementioned requirements.

Even if such an all-embracing criterion could be constructed, it would be rather unrealistic to expect that the bank will ever be enabled to evaluate projects mainly on the basis of technical and economic parameters. There are many reasons for this state of affairs, but the following may point into the right direction. Although CMEA organs can recommend investment projects to be financed by IIB loans, it is basically the project's host country that must first lodge a request for funding. It is thus up to each potential host to specify in what fields the bank could exert a lasting influence on the course of SEI through coordinated investments. Moreover, the bank disburses credits and grants loans according to a lending plan drawn up according to credit requests, expected funds, and disbursements requested by individual members. It is hardly likely that the requests in time and across sectors are solely motivated by economic efficiency. Furthermore, for political and strategic considerations, in addition to myriad economic obstacles, the bank cannot freely choose among the projects submitted for funding. Although national exclusiveness might eventually give way to regional priority objectives, the latter are hardly likely to become soon the sole or even the paramount decision-making criteria. Finally, the bank's choice is subject to a panoply of technical limitations associated with the comparability of projects, the proper assessment of costs and benefits, and the use of funds for common purposes. How does the IIB pursue its goals and exploit its control function?

The bank can choose to monitor the evolution of an investment project by comparing the actual data with the promised indices, however inadequately these reflect true scarcities. Because its supply of investment funds is limited, the bank should evaluate project conformity according to uniform criteria of effectiveness based on a few synthetic indices of its own choice that take into account all significant aspects of the projects up for deliberation. But there are measurable problems with the formulation of synthetic decision-making parameters when the underlying national expenditure and receipt data now and forecast for the future depend to such a large extent on what, from a technical economic point of view, is a heavily biased measurement base. Prices, prime cost, quality standards, planned technology, operational data, and so on, are hardly comparable across Eastern Europe. Although CMEA experts have made valuable progress in standardizing national data, the procedure they have arrived at, as noted at the bank's inception, "still has many latent and unsolved problems" (Botos 1971, p. 657). There is no reason to believe that substantial modifications over the past decade and a half have changed this fundamental constraint. A direct comparison of expected returns from the investment projects does not appear practicable. Despite these obviously knotty problems, the bank reportedly adopted uniform criteria and a common methodology for the appraisal of the economic effectiveness of the projects submitted for credit allotments soon after its inception (Gräbig et al. 1975, p. 149; Marinov 1974, p. 29).

To the best of my knowledge, no single CMEA investment criterion, or unique set of criteria, has been applied to date,[15] although several such proposals have been tendered. The recommendations recently worked out by the SCFQ, which were endorsed at the 113th session of the Executive Committee in early 1985 (Válek 1985, p. 10), reiterate the need to apply common guidelines, hopefully in conjunction with the five-year plans for the second half of the 1980s. Most of the evaluation formulae proposed are variants of the recoupment period index. The parameters that influence some part of the decision-making process are, therefore, construction time, technical production parameters, investment costs, return on investment, and so on. In economic jargon, this simply means that the real net return on borrowed funds, as conventionally measured in a PE, should not be negative; that is, the project must at least be able to service the incurred debt. If funds are short, however, some projects prove to be more profitable than others, and a rule of thumb for trading off requests that pass the above test is required. Furthermore, the mechanical application of the recoupment period index, because of its defects when placed in a strictly technical intertemporal framework (see Válek 1984, pp. 56ff.), actually could promote erroneous specialization.

To obtain a loan, the borrower must be in the possession of long-term agreements or other forms of understanding in which the bank's charter members express their interest in the construction of the project (Kucharski 1974, p. 516). Only on the strength of this declared interest is a loan application seriously entertained by the IIB. At submission time, it must be accompanied also by a form that explains the need for the given installation. Proof of interestedness in obtaining the projected output by member countries must be submitted together with justification of the economic effectiveness of the proposed project (Kucharski 1974, p. 517). Once a project is approved, a credit contract is drawn up. Although various conditions depend on the specific project, basic claims and general conditions must be fulfilled in all cases. They include, for instance, proof that the construction and sale of output is guaranteed by long-term contracts or other agreements, proof of utility and date of the commencement of operations, agreements on interest rates and repayment terms for the credit, as well as the establishment of sanctions in the event that the credit contract is violated. For this reason a standard credit contract and request document were worked out, although variations are possible, depending upon the specific conditions of the project (Behrens 1972, pp. 59–60). The credit agreement is therefore a detailed document stipulating the main technical and economic parameters of the project, the conditions of marketing the products, the performance of the project to be built, and the currency provisions (*Figyelő,* 1973:10, p. 9).

The bank is, in principle, entitled to grant credits for the full cost of the submitted project. In practice, however, it finances only a part, usually about 25–50 percent of the total value of the project.[16] The rationale for this is simple. First, the bank's statutes do not specify to what extent the IIB is entitled to supervise the construction process or the project's subsequent operations. Second, some projects are clearly of too vast a scale to commit large IIB funds without the bank running the risk of rapidly depleting its resources or overcommitting itself in Western money markets. Third, nearly every investment has some "domestic" share in the form of local labor, services, and commodities. Because, as noted in Chapters 4 and 5, internal prices are incompatible with WMPs and CMEA prices and because the bank obviously also wishes to limit possible windfall profits or losses from appropriating domestic goods at international prices, it is understandably reluctant to finance that part of the project's outlays. In this way, the bank is able to bypass the extremely knotty problem of value comparisons, and it is able to forgo detailed recomputations of the "international value" of local contributions that have no obvious international equivalent. The bank thus also prevents the credit recipient from purchasing "international" goods for other purposes than those for which the loan was designated.

From recent reports on the SCFQ's activities, it would seem that a standardized methodology for such calculations of domestic and trade values has been elaborated on several occasions (see Válek 1984, pp. 64ff.; Válek 1985, p. 10). It is not clear, however, whether all the various versions were approved by all members and to what extent they have helped the bank to judge the merits of project submissions. Persisting problems are still reported (Perova 1984, p. 14).

Credit planning

Credit disbursement and repayment of interest and principal are in principle regulated in the process of elaborating ex ante plans drawn up by the Bank Board and approved by the Bank Council. Plans are presumably formulated in several iterative phases, which eventually lead to the dovetailing of the bank's expected available funds, the borrowers' intentions to activate bank commitments, and expected disbursements on loans to be approved in the near future. These plans are not completely inflexible, although changes in the disbursement schedule are subject to special approval by the Bank Board. Any deviation not sanctioned by the bank organs (usually the Board) is subject to a penalty interest.

10.4 The bank's operations to date

The bank has two main operational tasks: to attract funds in various currencies from different sources and to mobilize them for projects that benefit SEI. Although the financing and supervision of joint investment projects is the more interesting aspect of the bank's activities, the way in which the IIB can discharge itself of its first task is sufficiently weighty for it to be dealt with first.

The bank's loanable funds

The bank's resources consist of its own funds (its capital and retained profits), deposits attracted from various sources, and borrowed funds in a number of alternative forms from members and nonsocialist financial markets. As noted, the bank would not normally seek deposits as such from members or nonmembers because the operational side of its TR transactions is in any case handled exclusively by the IBEC as it is the only institution entitled to effect TR financial flows. But it could gain access to special-purpose deposits put in the custody of the IBEC. This feature, which was already incorporated in the IBEC's founding document, is now apparently being revived (Válek 1985, pp. 11–12). I shall discuss this activation of an exceeding long-standing intention later in this section.

Although the bank's capital resource base is substantial by CMEA standards and retained profits, including 44 percent in CC at year-end 1982 (Beličenko 1983, p. 65), now add about a third to that, "own funds" could not possibly enable the bank to play directly any decisive role in the coordination of investment projects or in fostering SEI. The bank's own funds could command perhaps 2 percent of one year's investment appropriations in the CMEA as a whole as measured in the early 1970s,[17] provided it would have been fully funded. Judging from the volume of disbursements and new commitments in recent years (see the next section), the significance of its capital as a source of loanable funds has necessarily dropped very considerably. This was foreseen because it was anticipated that the bank's own TR funds would gradually assume a declining share of total disposable assets. Certainly, the importance of retained profits could rise, but the major impetus to joint investment activity was assumed to emanate from two supplementary sources of funds: the floating of securities in financial markets, and target contributions.

The bank is authorized to float bonds directly or indirectly in any financial market, including the CMEA's. For practical purposes, however, this stipulation is meant to apply chiefly to Western financial markets until real multilateralism will come about in the CMEA region (Botos 1974, p. 932). The bank explored this source of funding on several occasions in the mid-1970s, but it has not been very active in recent years, owing in part to the debt crisis in world financial markets and the adjustment problems in Eastern Europe. But a few new syndicated borrowings have been reported for 1985–1986.

The second supplementary source of funds parallels the sixth crediting form originally envisaged for the IBEC (see Chapter 8). Indeed the IIB could become the custodian of certain special capital stocks funded ad hoc by two or more PEs. Such funds could be designed to "finance" construction projects by the IIB, although the latter's role would be more that of an accountant than a financier's. But because the bank has the authority to investigate the economic significance of projects and is entitled to supervise them during the entire construction phase and the first operating years until full repayment of principal and interest is complete, it could in principle come to play a crucial role in further rounding off the common infrastructure of the CMEA, especially its transportation component. This avenue for funding has not apparently been explored to date. But the SCFQ's project that was recently endorsed by the Executive Committee may blow new vigor into this form (Válek 1985, pp. 11–12). Special funds can have a variety of origins (see VK 1986c). By their financing they may be contributed by the members, the IIB, or jointly by members and the IIB for short-term (up to five years) or long-term purposes (up to fifteen years). Their target may also vary from a well-specified single action (such as the reconstruction of a port) to a complex array of interrelated objects (such as improving the food-processing sector). In connection with the endorsement and implementation of *Scientific-technological Cooperation,* the creation of special investment funds under the aegis of the IIB has resurfaced with new vigor. By year-end 1986, none appears to have been instituted so far.

The bank's principal task has been to grant loans for investment projects that are closely associated with the mainstream of SEI processes. That is to say, at least two members must be interested in the establishment of the venture, it must be of the highest quality and technological standards, and it must yield sizable trade flows in the near future. Originally the major emphasis was placed on projects that visibly and directly advance SEI. But as revealed through its decisions, the bank has sought to promote integration-related activities in the widest sense.

The IIB was initially expected to be in a position to evaluate project requests rather autonomously, though within the policy guidelines of SEI set by the CMEA's commanding political and economic heights. Given the problems with the mobilization of TR funds, however, the bank would have to be active not only on the side of granting loans. Its activism should also ensure that the required capital and other inputs become available without delays and that the interested PEs blend the project's requirements and future output stream with the normal economic and trade planning instruments. The bank was therefore called upon to dovetail the requests for funding with the concrete supply possibilities of member countries to ensure that the inputs needed for the project would be forthcoming. As Z. Fedorowicz formulated it soon after the bank's inception, special agreements supplementary to the quotas of the regular BTPAs would have to be hammered out (Fedorowicz 1971, p. 2). This continues to be a major challenge.

The bank's basic activity is mobilizing funds to finance common investment projects, thereby helping to shape the SEI process. The bank is entitled to attract resources in gold, CC, TR, and PE national currencies. Such funds can be transferred to the bank in several ways, although each type of currency accumulation is subject to different conditions. TR funds proper can be increased only as a result of excess exports by one or more members for the specific purpose of selected investment projects. Technically speaking, the granting of TR loans can be accomplished either through deposits transferred from the IBEC to the IIB or through the IBEC's loans granted to IIB. TR deposits can also be accumulated at the IIB for longer periods than the IBEC's technical credits would permit. But none appears to have materialized thus far for reasons connected with the TR's limited raison d'être as a financial instrument.

Resources of national currencies only help to realize the IIB's tasks if they are directly tied to commodity deliveries by the lender and the utilization intentions of the borrower. In principle, one PE or another could announce its willingness to offer in general a certain fund denominated in local currency available for investment credit, and any user selected by the bank could be entitled to choose whatever is available in the "donor" country. But this would hardly be practicable even if the potential lender had a basic interest in mobilizing some part of national wealth for use abroad. Participants availing themselves of funds denominated in "local" currencies are expected to make their own separate arrangements with the bank on an ad hoc basis. In that case, the bank's role is essentially confined to the supervision of the technical transfer of these transactions (Botos 1971, p. 651). However, local funds at IIB's disposal are necessarily transformed into TR proper when utilized by other PEs, because the transfer must be arranged through regular trade channels. "National" funds could only be used for projects financed by "technical" borrowers (Dubrowsky 1981, p. 94), that is, by their own funds (Brabant 1977a, p. 219).

Neither funds in TR nor in local currencies can be expected to become the mainstay of the IIB's financial resources because they lack the essential property of transferability. The particular requirements underlying the extensive utilization of CC in CMEA trade and its essential role in East–West economic relations have been studied for a very long time. Frequent and lengthy admonishments, most recently at the joint 1984 June summit, that these flows be reconverted to the TR denomination as much as possible may be cited in evidence. In spite of this comparatively long history, how to improve the collective socialist currency to permit such a substitution at little cost remains on the policy agenda with highest priority (Garbuzov 1985, p. 35).

The bank's principal task with respect to the accumulation of disposable resources is therefore to attract CC deposits or loans. Such funds could originate in the CMEA area. In view of the generally widespread

CC shortage, however, for the time being the bank must seek to attract such funds mainly from Western financial markets. Funds in TR and CC can also be augmented from other banking activities in which the IIB is entitled to engage (such as currency speculation, interest earnings on credits, and deposits abroad). But the scope for this source of supply is likely to remain highly confined.

IIB has obtained several loans in the Eurocapital market. Publicized loans include $50 million in early 1973 with a maturity of seven years at a 0.5 percentage point over the London Interbank Offer Rate (LIBOR), the prevailing interbank rate for dollars, and $75 million in early 1974 (at about the same conditions). In 1975, IIB tapped Western financial markets for a reported total of some $420 million. This was further enlarged in 1976–1978 with loans totaling about $1.75 billion. Perhaps $300–400 million was added in 1978. The precise conditions of these loans are not known, but IIB as IBEC and individual PEs had to pay a higher margin over LIBOR than before – from 0.75 to 1.25 percentage point. Thereafter total funds borrowed abroad have remained remarkably unchanged as per the IIB's year-end balance sheets. There may have been a comparatively sharp recovery in 1985–1986, however. The abrupt rise in activity in the mid-1970s hinged on the need to make dispositions to initiate several IIB-financed projects included in the five-year plans (1976–1980), most particularly on account of Orenburg–Sojuz. Because regional funds were not mobilizable and funds in Western markets at comparatively favorable interest rates were relatively abundant, the IIB sought to attract primarily CC funds.

Projects financed by the IIB

Although the official agreement of 10 July 1970, as noted, explicitly embodies the four categories of priority projects, one or another has received disproportionate attention. The relatively advanced PEs have tended to emphasize the benefits of promoting specialization in sectors with evident parallelism and wasteful duplication across the region (mainly in those producing "soft" goods). Countries with ample natural resources to raise the output capacity and exports of raw materials, but who are reluctant to finance such projects themselves, have tended to draw attention primarily to IIB's facilities to finance such projects. Lastly, the less developed PEs, in particular Bulgaria and Rumania, have aired the view that the bank should make a significant contribution to fulfilling the basic "socialist" principle of the ISDL, namely, the equalization of development levels. Production specialization, financing of raw materials projects, and development aid have been heeded in the bank's policies, although not to the extent forecast in 1970–1971, as I shall illustrate later.

At the time of its creation, it was widely expected that the bank would be permitted to concentrate on the coordination and joint administration of selected projects especially in two fields: increasing production of chronically deficient primary goods and fuels, and the financing of advanced research and production of sophisticated manufactured products. The exploitation of new sources of raw materials and fuels by common means dominated one side of the debate concerning the investment coordination that could be attained by the activities of the newly created bank in the early 1970s. This preoccupation suggested that the IIB should essentially earmark financial resources from the smaller PEs for exploiting the USSR's abundant natural riches, thus replacing some of the ad hoc credit flows that had earlier constrained potential importers to share in the development cost of expanding output capacities. In other words, IIB credits were mainly to substitute for the "special purpose" or target credits resorted to in the late 1950s and 1960s (Beličenko 1981, p. 10). The second focus of IIB's involvement was suggested to be in remedying the chronic shortage of CMEA capacity to produce sophisticated equipment. Under the circumstances, the latter either had to be imported mostly from the West against CC or its nonavailability severely constrained growth prospects. In other words, the IIB was to be mobilized too for import substitution in complex manufacturing activities.

Neither of these two expectations was fulfilled in the early years of the IIB's existence. During the first two years of the bank's operations, not a single project for the USSR (and incidentally none for Mongolia) was approved, and none of the loans issued was appropriated for the development of fuel or raw material projects. The USSR may have submitted projects for funding but, as some observers have contended, it was rebuffed, or it was deemed politically inopportune to draw massively against the bank's resources at such an early stage. This rationalization read into the bank's activities of 1973–1975 tends to corroborate the wait-and-see attitude imputed to the USSR's borrowing activities in 1971–1972. Sharp increases in raw material and fuel prices in the early 1970s noticeably improved the real profitability of the Soviet projects that had been slated for common financing already in the late 1960s, but could not be commissioned for lack of interest, in part owing to the malaise that stemmed from the perturbations of the preludes to *Integration Program*, as discussed in Chapter 2. Thus, purely adventitious changes in WMPs removed any objection lodged on the basis of the alleged comparatively low efficiency of the USSR's projects that may have been entertained in 1971–1972. But profitability as such is hardly likely to have been of overriding concern in IIB's credit policy even during the beginning phase.[18]

As observed in Chapter 9 in connection with the more general aspects of the coordination of investments in the CMEA as called for in *Integra-*

tion Program, a key problem in promoting the IIB's involvement was that the bank had been constituted after the national five-year plans for 1971–1975 had been completed, most trade agreements had been concluded, and these aggregate and trade plans had presumably been dovetailed at the CMEA level. As a result, the room for adding new projects that would require financial and material resources not yet earmarked in the medium-term plan was not only very confined. It was also exceedingly difficult to find such a niche as the IIB's funds are supposed to enlarge, not to replace, national investment funds and regional trade (Gräbig et al. 1975, p. 150). The problems endemic to the weak mobilization capacity of the TR as such only further complicated the situation. For these and other reasons, in the early 1970s disbursements were mostly in CCs and they trailed far behind overall commitments. These circumstances could explain the relatively low ratio of disbursements to total credit commitments and the fact that the bank then had little choice but to keep most of its assets liquid. Although I have no reliable data to prove the above proposition, the following conjecture may help to support it. Before the IIB assumed sizable CC commitments in Western financial markets, in 1971–1974 total disbursements were smaller than the bank's CC funds, taking 30 percent of the contributed charter capital and the small loans obtained in MEs as a conservative estimate of the bank's CC funds.[19]

According to well-informed sources, the bank had a brisk start in 1971. Funds became available in January 1971, and the first credit requests were approved in late June (Kobak 1971, p. 21). At the very beginning of the bank's activities, the total value of the submitted projects amounted to some TR 300 million, which by year-end had risen to some TR 330 million (Dimitrov 1972, p. 21), of which TR 180 million was approved in 1971 (Garbuzov 1973, p. 12). The remaining projects were, however, not outrightly rejected: Sixteen out of twenty-eight requests were accepted, and the others were deferred pending further investigation of the creditworthiness of the requests. S. Kobak reports that in late 1971 (but before the fourth session of the Bank Council during which the second series of projects was approved), thirty projects for a total sum of TR 280 million, half in CC, were under investigation (Kobak 1971, p. 21). Judging by the bank's activities in 1972 and 1973, the initial enthusiasm cooled down remarkably fast, as the number of credit requests increased only slightly. Ju. Konstantinov reported in October 1972 that the bank had received requests for a total of thirty-six projects amounting to TR 340 million. Of these, twenty projects for more than TR 200 million had been approved (Konstantinov 1972, p. 7). There is little information available on either the type, value, or number of projects submitted for funding to the IIB.

Judging from the number of projects that have been approved in the past fifteen years, IIB's loan record appears to have leaped forward with fits and bursts. Though the total number of projects rose to ninety (VK 1985b, p. 4) or ninety-four[20] for a total value of about TR 4 billion (Beličenko 1986, p. 14) by year-end 1985, the absolute value of commitments per individual project has varied greatly over time. Most commitments for projects since the endorsement of Sojuz in 1975 have been for very small amounts, as the total value of commitments between 1976 and 1985 increased by less than 40 percent. This implies an average per project since Sojuz of about TR 22 million, with an even lower average for the projects financed in the second half of the 1970s, when the average project value was less than TR 15 million; the average value of the twenty-four projects financed during 1981–1985 amounted to TR 25 million (Stepanov and Šemakin 1986, p. 2). Data are, unfortunately, not available to permit a more accurate year-by-year investigation. Nevertheless, the number of commitments is not necessarily indicative of actual disbursements, which have trailed well behind commitments, as already indicated. Nor is it necessarily an informative gauge of the IIB's direct or indirect contribution to the advancement of SEI.

In terms of the allocation of projects over various sectors, a very skewed distribution is apparent in terms of both the total value of commitments as well as the number of projects approved. Clearly, there is no relationship between the value and the total number of commitments, not even when the extraordinary appropriations for the Orenburg–Sojuz participations are excluded from the data. Due to the relatively small numbers involved, most funds have been highly concentrated in a few economic sectors. Table 10.1 lists the cumulative sectoral composition of the projects approved to the extent that this can be pieced together from the available information. It is evident that during the first three years the bank was seriously concerned about the machine-building and metallurgical sectors, and in 1974 also the chemical industry, although commitments did not exceed TR 600 million at year-end 1974. In the first three years, more than three fourths of the loans issued went to the machine-building and metallurgical sectors, and in 1974 the chemical industry absorbed about two thirds of the allocated funds. In 1975–1976, the main focus was on the raw materials and fuel sector, especially on account of two large projects in the USSR. Since then, there has been a steady increase in the number of projects and the commitments to the machine-building and chemical sectors, which should be the premier location of production specialization. However, the sheer size of the gas pipeline project of the mid-1970s keeps tilting the overall distribution of the value of projects in favor of the fuel and energy sectors.

The geographical distribution of credits has also varied considerably over time. Whereas in 1971–1972 only six countries benefited from IIB's

Table 10.1. *Distribution of cumulative commitments, 1971–1985*

	1973	1974	1976	1978	1980	1982	1984	1985
Metallurgy	42.9	10.1	4.9	6.2	5.8	5.4	5.3	5
Machine building	33.4 ⎫	9.3	9.4	10.2	14.8	17.8	19.7	23
Electrotechnical	1.0 ⎭					1.2		
Chemical industry	11.2	77.8	1.4	2.0	2.9	3.4	3.9	5
Transportation	3.5	0.8	1.5	1.5	[a]	2.2	[a]	[a]
Fuels and energy	0	0	81.0	78.4	72.8	68.2	66.8	62
Light and food (and others)	8.0	2.0	1.8	1.7	3.7[b]	1.8	4.3[b]	5[b]

[a] Included in light and food industry.
[b] Including transportation.

Sources: 1973–1974 – Brabant 1977a, p. 238, and Konstantinov 1982a, p. 221; 1976 – Konstantinov 1978a, p. 82; 1978 – Hájek 1980, p. 54; 1980 – Dimitrov 1981, p. 4, and Dubrowski 1981, p. 91; 1982 – Alekseev 1984, p. 349; 1984 – Brunovský and Nápravníková 1986, p. 14; 1985 – Beličenko 1985, p. 38; Beličenko 1986, p. 14.

Table 10.2. *Cumulative distribution of projects by recipients, 1971–1982*

	1971	1972	1973	1974	1975	1978	1982
Bulgaria	0	4	7	9	10	11	13
Czechoslovakia	1	1	1	1	1	1	2
GDR	1	2	2	2	2	4	10
Hungary	3	3	3	3	3	9	16
Poland	5	8	10	13	13	18	18
Rumania	6	8	8	8	8	15	15
USSR	0	0	1	2	3	2?	2
Cuba	0	0	0	0	1	0?	3
Mongolia	0	0	1	1	1	1	1
Vietnam	0	0	0	0	0	0	0
Yugoslavia	0	0	0	0	0	0	1
Interatominstrument	0	0	0	0	0	0	1
Sojuz	0	0	0	0	*a*	0	0
Total	16	26	35	41	44	61	82

a The Sojuz project loan is distributed over the six Eastern European participants.
Sources: 1971–1975–Brabant 1977a, p. 240; 1978–Hájek 1980, p. 54; 1982–Válek 1983b, p. 13.

committed funds, in 1973 all members had at least one project partially financed with IIB's funds (see Table 10.2). In early 1975, a Cuban request was approved, and so all countries that were then members benefited from the bank's funds. However, the information through 1982 shown in Table 10.2 indicates that Vietnam has not yet obtained a single commitment. The information divulged in the annual reports issued since then and other materials pertaining to the IIB suggest that by year-end 1986, Vietnam had not obtained any bank loans. As noted, in 1980 the first loan to an IEO was approved and in 1982 the first to a nonmember. In sheer numbers, the less developed European PEs (particularly Bulgaria, Poland, and Rumania) have obtained funding for most projects. Because so many of these capital commitments are for relatively small-scale projects, the total funding obtained has not diverged as much as the number of projects. Nonetheless, especially the less developed European members have obtained a higher ratio of funding to capital participation than the large and developed countries. To the extent that they have been able to mobilize these loans for worthwhile purposes, at least these countries appear to have benefited from the joint investment institution.

10.5 Relations with nonmembers

The bank's relationship with nonmembers is essentially of two types. Its main correspondents are bound to be in Western financial markets, where the bank is entitled to procure additional assets to be rechanneled to the CMEA in order to promote SEI through joint investment projects. In addition, the IIB was originally intended to play an important role in arranging multilateral long-term financial development assistance to the developing MEs. The latter task is explicitly embodied in the official agreement and was further put in concrete form with the creation in 1973 of the special capital fund for developing countries.

Eastern European commentators like to stress that the bank is an open institution, that it actively seeks to promote better financial and other relations with the major financial institutions of the world, and that it hopes to lend not only to the charter members but also to nonmembers. Although it has never been explicitly stated that the bank would loan part of its charter capital and reserves to nonmembers, it should be kept in mind that such transactions would be highly illogical, for the bank's purposes are intimately related to regional integration ambitions. Only one jointly financed project with an associated member has become known. The particular project (Tang) approved for Yugoslavia is, however, closely linked to regular CMEA integration endeavors in the machine-building sector.[21] IIB's activities could, however, be extended to other areas or other economies, for example, as a result of joint operations between PEs and MEs cofinanced by the IIB or transactions on account of special funds of which the bank might be a custodian but neither the deciding nor the decisive allocator of funds.

On 11 April 1973, an agreement was reached between the IIB's Council and its members[22] to establish a special fund for development assistance amounting to TR 1 billion, with 5 percent of the total in CC and the rest in pure TR. The fund was put into operation on 1 January 1974 in the framework of IIB's general activities.[23] The signatories of the agreement were expected to contribute an initial installment of TR 100 million before the end of 1976 (Faddeev 1974, p. 320). According to the bank's balance sheets, the members have fallen far behind schedule because only one fourth of the first installment was transferred in an undisclosed proportion of TR and CC in 1975; as of year-end 1985 total contributions stood at TR 32.8 million.

The purpose of the fund is to lend to nonsocialist developing countries. Long-term credits with a maturity of up to fifteen years at low interest rates can be granted for the construction of new and the reconstruction or modernization of existing enterprises and economic organizations of the state and cooperative sectors. In exceptional cases, private firms or organizations of developing MEs could also apply for a loan from the fund (see

CMEA 1974, p. 111). No interest rate schedule has been disclosed for TR transactions. However, the IIB is likely to grant loans at interest rates similar to those used in bilateral credit agreements between PEs and developing MEs (usually between 1 and 3 percent). As far as the CC portion is concerned, however, the bank has slated a margin of three eighths to one percentage point over LIBOR (Bień and Nosiadek 1979b, p. 37).

Although a number of developing MEs have reportedly shown some active interest in the new credit fund, no project has so far been approved. One concrete funding request has become known: In the mid-1970s, Poland explored whether exports of its ships to Costa Rica and Peru could be financed through a credit from the IIB. The attempt failed because the other CMEA countries were not prepared to accept TR payment for their exportables to be incorporated in the Polish ships (Bień and Nosiadek 1979b, p. 39). They would not have been keen on obtaining more generally TR payments for their exports to developing MEs. Neither were they prepared to accept additional TR allocations for goods that could be sold for CC in world markets.

10.6 The International Investment Bank's contribution to socialist economic integration

From its very inception, it was realized by many observers versed in the practical matters of intragroup trade and finance that the new bank would at most be as good as the degree to which the intentions of policy makers, however vague at the time, could be carried out. Accordingly, the real test of the IIB would not be its ability to channel funds borrowed in Western money markets to its members for projects over which it had some control, although this source of finance could become a crucial pillar of CMEA cooperation. The twin gauges for IIB's success were realized by many to be the following. First, a critical yardstick of the IIB's participation in the coordination of investments would be the way in which it would mobilize its largely fictive assets and exhort charter members to pledge extra funds for special projects in material or other forms. Loans cannot be granted in "money" because the TR does not have command over the disposition of goods and services. Nor would the members have pledged their contributions in the form of "commodity lists" as many observers have suggested at one time or another. The first procedure would beg the question of how these funds could be mobilized. The second one would have presumed that all capital funds were already specifically appropriated for a certain number of projects in 1970 or, alternatively, that the first projects would be tailored to the commodities set aside from normal plan appropriations in the member countries. Either would have reduced the bank's role to that of a simple project overseer and accountant.

The second pivotal indicator of the IIB's success was seen in the extent to which it could persuade the charter members into subscribing on a regular basis to the coordination of their overall and sectoral investment activities to a much more involved degree than had earlier been attained. This requirement coincides with the preceding one to the extent that it involves the marshaling of funds for specific projects over which the bank hopes to exert some influence by its financial participation. In addition to this, as noted in Chapter 9, the success of SEI would in large measure be a function of the better harmonization of the PEs' investment intentions, even for projects that do not require the transfer of funds across national boundaries. But such projects, of necessity, would have to be conceived against the backdrop of distributing future output over the entire CMEA region. Hence, the critical output objective should be tailored to region-wide needs and provisions might have to be made to enable partner countries to obtain a share of the output at some future date in exchange for some participation in the conceptualization of the ventures.

The ability of the bank to mobilize its resources has been highly confined. This should not be surprising when the bank's possible room for financial maneuver is placed in the proper context of the CMEA's typical trade and payments regime: A loan becomes available only after the recipient has concluded one or more credit agreements with the countries that are willing to incur a temporary trade surplus for a very specific purpose. Such negotiations are supplementary to the regular BTPAs. It now has been particularly cumbersome to persuade countries that had paid in their capital shares from immobilized surpluses held at the IBEC, to make those funds liquid once again by enabling the countries that earlier had violated regular BTPAs to run up another deficit position, although on a special account. Hence the rather surprising, but correct, observation by a GDR economist that the IIB's loans "must be regarded as credits granted bilaterally" by any pair of members involved in the transaction (Stirtzel 1977, p. 186). This important property of TR credits is now generally acknowledged, though with reluctance in some cases. So the recipient country of a TR loan is bound to come up itself with the goods and services required for a project. Although this is a decidely suboptimal solution, it is not necessarily completely superfluous.

A capital project in which the IIB gets involved (as with the investment credits discussed in Chapter 9) has a financial angle as well as a real side. The bank is, in theory, authorized to evaluate requests for funding and to enforce certain quality standards, time limits, and other performance criteria on the project's executors. In particular, it is called upon to ensure that the project fosters SEI by contributing directly or indirectly to the stream of goods and services available for the CMEA market as a whole. The concrete trade and other negotiations associated with a request for funding are therefore of crucial importance to determine whether a project will get off the ground and thus make its, perhaps small, contribution to the advancement of SEI. Even though the loan recipient in the end may have to self-finance the project, the bank's guidance, ability to coordinate investments, and muscle to ensure that such projects emanate directly into trade and service flows that can be properly attributed to SEI might nevertheless yield palpable advantages over more conventional forms of "joint investment activities." It is in that perspective that one should view the primary potential of the IIB to contribute to the advancement of SEI. Although the bank's funding in TR does not enlarge the overall volume of financial resources that can be mustered for common purposes, the qualitatively different utilization of these same resources and the common conditions for such credits are what really count (Stirtzel 1977, p. 194).

All this suggests that the IIB's mechanisms do not in any substantive way diverge from the traditional instruments of coordinating economic policies and investment plans. They are little more than an institutionalized form of the target credit approach discussed in Chapter 9. But the bank could have made a real difference in the coordination of some concrete investment decisions directly linked to the requirements of SEI had it been delegated the authority to do so. The IIB could, for example, have become the "planning center" put in charge of key aspects of the Target Programs. Even more important would have been its galvanizing role in the concrete specifications of the Target Programs, especially the multilateral framework and the bilateral implementation agreements associated with the target programming approach. Because these instruments buttress a Concerted Plan, such an evolvement of the bank's responsibilities would have been of paramount importance in advancing the SEI process through "joint planning." This apparently has not so far happened. At any rate, it has transpired to a far smaller extent than originally anticipated by the more vocal proponents of the bank's creation in the late 1960s. In other words, credit requests and grants in reality continue to be handled nearly exclusively by the member governments.

Given the very considerable degree to which the bank's activities are circumscribed by the financial and commercial mechanisms of the CMEA, and indeed the activities of individual member governments, it is legitimate to inquire whether the bank has conducted its transactions in full compliance with the original intentions and the basic principles of SEI. Well-informed observers have argued that there continues to be cause to pay more attention to the entire cycle of a project, including, as already observed at a very early date, the "structure of the previously approved credits which not fully complies with the tasks and objectives of the bank" (Potáč 1973, p. 6).[24] Recent commentary shows that the IIB should aim its loan policy more at production specialization, cooperation, and the expansion of raw materials and fuel supplies to enhance SEI.

Central authorities of the member countries have apparently interfered too much and have failed to act with imaginative leadership in the determination of credit requests. The absence of a clear-cut methodology for evaluating project requests, controlling the implementation of projects, and following up on the promotion of SEI through bank-financed projects is recognized to be a palpable drawback (Válek 1984, pp. 63–64).

It has been proposed that central authorities henceforth confine their role in international credit matters to determining priorities and selecting applications, instead of concentrating on the formulation of detailed proposals. Similarly critical observations have recently been disclosed (see Boratyński 1975; Garbuzov 1985; Válek 1985). However, the bank itself can do very little to redress the present situation for reasons examined earlier. Although the IIB could decide not to fund projects of doubtful value, if necessary by utilizing its majority voting machinery, this might well turn out to be quite counterproductive in the long run.

11

National and regional convertibility in the CMEA

The gradual substitution of multilateralism for the presently existing forms of ex ante planning of regional cooperation by way of detailed BTPAs is one of the basic cornerstones of an effective SEI mechanism and development policy. Without endowing CMEA economic relations with considerable latitude for multilateral arrangements, there is little chance that the PEs will be able effectively to muster the supports required to nurture a number of desirable channels for deepening and broadening SEI. This is particularly so for joint ventures and direct inter-enterprise relations, regardless of whether they are planned or supervised with the aid of market-type instruments. The gradual superimposition of real transferability and, perhaps at a later stage, of convertibility as well would measurably enhance the effectiveness of SEI. They would impart greater realism to the integration policies, guidance instruments, and concomitant institutional supports that the PEs are prepared to promulgate and to adhere to as much as possible in the years to come.

This chapter examines first the broad context of convertibility. The next section is devoted to official proclamations on the subject. The most important concepts of convertibility relevant to PEs and especially their reciprocal relations are examined in Section 11.3. This is followed by an evaluation of some of the recent discussions and proposals regarding the establishment of some form of convertibility for the TR in CMEA trade, for individual countries and for the TR more generally, or for individual country currencies so as to enhance East–West trade. The most important potential benefits and drawbacks of currency and commodity convertibility are looked at in Section 11.5. Section 11.6 is concerned with the eventuality of deriving positive seigniorage in external markets. The next section devotes particular attention to the issue of purely financial convertibility because this has a bearing on the degree to which the PEs individually and the CMEA as a whole may decide to participate in East–West financial markets in preference to a more comprehensive form of convertibility. The chapter concludes with some pointers regarding the direction in which the convertibility debate may be heading.

11.1 The role of convertibility in alternative policy settings

Multilateralism, transferability, and convertibility have a direct bearing on the devolution of decision making and the possible direction of economic reforms in PEs. They are highly interdependent concepts that nevertheless can lead a separate existence under certain well-specified conditions. Thus, convertibility normally implies the existence of multilateralism and transferability. Transferability as a rule presupposes multilateralism but, from the point of view of the proper allocation of resources, it is quite inferior to convertibility. As indicated in Chapter 8, transferability could be attained by implementing full-fledged MTPAs that accommodate ex post imbalances. Under such an arrangement, in other words, positive imbalances can, but need not, be offset against negative imbalances regardless of their origin or timing. Finally, multilateralism can exist without there being scope for either transferability or convertibility. This could, for instance, emerge under conditions of comprehensive ex ante MTPAs that are adhered to as rigidly as the PEs have always intended their typical BTPAs to be carried out. These regimes are not unique. As already seen in the case of TR clearing, there is a higher degree of transferability and even convertibility of regular noncommercial transactions than there is of commercial transactions coming under the provisions of the TR clearing regime.

In the framework of the postwar economic, political, and strategic realities of Eastern Europe, the existence of an inconvertible currency and its implications with respect to the resource allocation process and external commerce permitted the USSR to exert very extensive controls over its newly acquired allies. This has also enabled it and other PEs to explore *iunctim* transactions, especially with developing MEs, and has been instrumental in warding off or in neutralizing undesirable economic and related foreign influences. Whereas the USSR could conceivably have achieved these objectives even with a convertible ruble, provided it would have been deemed worthwhile to preserve most other features of the MFT, the ruble's inconvertibility has been instrumental in isolating the smaller PEs and in immunizing the region as a whole against foreign penetration.

A convertible ruble would have considerably enhanced the chances of resuming the interwar trade ties in Europe, although Eastern Europe in all likelihood would not have neglected the potentially lucrative Soviet market to the degree these countries did in the 1920s and 1930s. Convertibility of all Eastern European currencies would have accelerated this process. It would also have facilitated the influx of ubiquitous, trade-related influences from the West. This penetration could have undermined the planned stability of the PEs, and it might conceivably have jeopardized the wholesale transplantation of an ideology that was fairly new, though by no means completely alien, to the smaller Eastern European nations. Although these unwelcome consequences could be forestalled by maintaining ruble inconvertibility, could a loyal cohesion within the region not have been enhanced through regional convertibility?

Had the ideas regarding regional integration developed in the late 1940s and early 1950s taken root, regional convertibility could eventually have become one strategic component of such a program. However, as examined in Chapter 1, the Soviet leadership at that time was not motivated, or even challenged, by such an objective, because it sought mainly to deal separately with the new partners. To the extent that the political preferences regarding SEI recently expressed by the Soviet leaders accurately reflect a firm aspiration to formulate a regional development strategy – which is by no means self-evident as yet – ruble convertibility in one form or another is bound to emerge sometime in the near future. This follows from the expressed interest in exploiting currency relations as powerful levers for selecting and managing one aspect or another of economic development.

The paramount objective of moving toward a state that is situated between the prevailing type and full convertibility would be the elimination of bilateralism and its strictures so as to accommodate new forms of cooperation that far transcend simple commercial exchange regulated through intergovernmental negotiations. It is conceptually quite clear what the PEs should do to overcome bilateralism. It would be foolhardy to maintain, or to deny for that matter, that bilateralism can be eliminated by the stroke of a pen. Though declaring legal convertibility may have useful political implications and may make for good public relations, economically meaningful convertibility as a critical lever of a country's foreign exchange regime should be the end result of the process implied in moving away from bilateralism rather than an immediate goal as such.

Certainly, the proclamation of the TR's full convertibility into CC would make intragroup bilateralism redundant. Similarly, if all PEs were to declare their currencies to be convertible either against all other currencies, the TR, or each other, it would not only suppress bilateralism in trade and commercial payments, but also the TR. But any such action would simply eliminate, not solve, the complex problem of reconciling convertibility, planning, and the TR. It indeed dispenses with the need for any particular monetary arrangement peculiar to a closely knit economic region, such as the CMEA. Suppressing the issue as such would not solve it. The particular problems would forcefully emerge as a result of the myriad adjustments called for by the institutionalization of convertibility. In other words, although a transformation of the country's currency status would be quite simple from the legal point of view, it would call for substantive modifications in economic mechanisms with wide-ranging implications for economic and political processes.

The postwar evolution of the predominant monetary system of the MEs clearly demonstrates the futility of instituting changes in the financial environment without a concomitant modification of the trade regime. The road to convertibility is arduous, paved as it is with many pits that the PEs can hardly hope to cross, let alone fill, in the short run. In that sense, comparisons between the SDR and the IBEC's TR as it exists at this stage cannot be very meaningful. Given the TR's inconvertibility and the deep-seated reluctance of key policy makers to embrace radical economic reforms, there is, as aptly opined by Franklyn Holzman, simply "no first-best solution to the problem of intra-CMEA bilateralism" (Holzman 1978b, p. 160).

Full commodity convertibility could be realistically envisaged as a policy goal only if the PEs were indeed to aspire towards shifting their economic structure, institutions, and policy instruments in the direction of a full-fledged ME. It is now highly unlikely that the PEs could realistically envisage such a move in the near future. Not only would it militate against their socialist convictions, it would also entail inequities that are simply intolerable in a socialist society. The proclamation of full convertibility of the TR into CC would make bilateralism redundant. But such action would simply eliminate the issue altogether for it dispenses with the TR as a desirable currency in support of SEI. Moreover, as argued in Chapter 3, the PEs simply cannot afford the range and depth of adjustments ensuing from declaring commodity convertibility overnight and instituting it. It is therefore necessary first to specify what the countries might be aiming at and next to outline alternative transition paths toward that coveted state. The possibility that the CMEA members may soon move toward real multilateralism, effective transferability, or some modified form of convertibility is evaluated in Chapter 12.

Convertibility can be a formidably useful instrument of economic policy under proper conditions. If not all of its parameters are fully specified, however, a call for establishing convertibility of the Eastern European currencies or of the TR may suggest very misleading interpretations of the objectives of ongoing policy discussions, feasible long-term policy goals, or emerging institutions. Such erroneous evaluations may also persuade observers into entertaining policy options for changing the model and development strategy of PEs that are quite unrealistic. It is as meaningful to maintain the hypothesis that the creation of convertibility for the ruble, forint, leu, lev, or any other PE currency will never be possible as it is to assert the converse.[1] There is indeed no "structural" or "systemic" impossibility of establishing some highly circumscribed form of convertibility by legal means (see Altman 1962, p. 367).

To maintain monetary and balance-of-payments equilibrium in an environment where the central plan acts as the pivotal regulator of economic decisions, planners may find it far easier, in several ways, to achieve and to defend currency convertibility than in an ME. The following arguments may help to clarify this paradox. The PE has the ability to defend domestic price stability and to minimize economic fluctuations. Exchange rates are stable and the state is in a position to ensure balance-of-payments equilibrium on a planned basis. Neither can be endangered by speculation. The currency issue is strictly controlled, and there is no legacy of large external liabilities on account of a lack of monetary discipline. But the facility with which PEs could operate under convertibility does not necessarily make for an economically meaningful form of convertibility.

Generally speaking, convertibility is a key instrument of economic policy because it entails free access to markets and contributes immeasurably to maintaining the proper market signals for the home country. More efficient resource allocation therefore becomes more or less a built-in feature of the economy as a whole. Although the PEs have been keenly aware of the broad advantages that could eventually be reaped, policy makers have not so far been overly preoccupied with the possible role of convertibility in promoting a more efficient allocation of resources. They have shown a keener interest in exploiting the advantageous features of convertibility in formulating trade decisions and in utilizing domestic resources in one sector or another that remains quite isolated from the rest of the economy.

Convertibility for the domestic or common currency of the PEs is a very complicated subject about which much has been written, but confusion even in the professional literature – not to mention more journalistic renditions – continues to be profuse and irritating. The cause can be traced to facile pronouncements on the part of Eastern European policy makers that, for instance, the "forint will soon be convertible" or erroneous interpretations of official policy positions such as those stated in *Integration Program*.

Observe that the concept of convertibility in the present IMS is fundamentally ambiguous. It was originally derived from the possibility of converting paper money into gold at a parity guaranteed by the emitting institution. Under this regime, convertibility was universal, total, and predictable. Especially since the demise of the fixed ER regime as the anchor of the BWS in the early 1970s, convertibility has become restrained, partial, and indirect. In view of these qualifications, it might perhaps be better, as suggested by Henri Dunajewski, to dispense with the term and replace it by "exchangeability," meaning that one currency can be turned into another on demand subject to certain limitations (Dunajewski 1979, p. 195). In what follows, I shall use the convertibility concept in that sense and specify as best as possible the full meaning of the particular variants of convertibility that have plausibly been envisaged by the PEs. Without such an exegesis, it is very difficult to gauge the relevance and bearing of the analysis for intra-CMEA cooperation or the financing of East–West trade.

11.2 Official statements regarding convertibility

Since the endorsement of *Integration Program,* much has been written about the further improvement of the TR as an international currency unit and its associated settlements mechanism, possibly even a gradual transition to convertibility. Similar speculations about the currencies of individual PEs have been made on a number of occasions. All this second guessing was induced by the particular phrasing of sequential changes stipulated in the basic document on SEI. It was aggravated to some degree also because of fundamental misunderstandings about what the program called for and what the majority of the PEs were intrinsically willing to pursue even under the most favorable of circumstances. To focus the discussion, I shall recount briefly the program's chief prescriptions regarding financial and monetary cooperation, in particular the stipulations of section 7 (Tokareva 1972, pp. 58–64).[2]

The TR was to be transformed gradually into a real international socialist currency so that it could eventually fully join on an equal footing other currencies used in global trade and finance, and reflect more adequately the global position of the PEs and the CMEA. The primary avenue to do so was seen to be the gradual but steady improvement of the economic and organizational conditions aimed at the consolidation and enhancement of the TR's role in international transactions. The initial goal was to enable the TR to perform fully the basic functions of a regional currency corresponding to the tasks arising at each stage in the evolution of SEI, given the planning context of the participants. More specifically, the PEs were actively to foster real multilateralism in CMEA trade and thus to seek to improve the basic conditions for the emergence of the TR as a really transferable currency. The program also called for the establishment of a realistic ER so as to reflect and to maintain the TR's true purchasing power. The primary backing for the TR was to remain by way of the commodities specified in ex ante trade agreements at agreed contractual prices. This would ensure the TR's independence from the instability typical of world financial markets. Although the TR's gold parity was also to be more closely scrutinized, no gold-exchange standard was actually contemplated.

Exchange rates were to become important in different endeavors. The PEs were to seek a more direct link between domestic and foreign prices either by way of formal ERs or through currency coefficients. This requirement referred to the entire array of monetary links among the individual PEs domestically as well as regionally. At a later stage, also the monetary links with third countries were to be affected. These transformations were to take on such forms that the TR could effectively serve the international economic requirements of the PEs and strengthen the basis for making economically sound decisions. Furthermore, the array of formal and informal multiple ERs was to be gradually narrowed and ultimately abandoned. By patterning the relationship between the TR and any of the members' currencies as uniformly and realistically as possible, it was hoped that a bridge toward unified effective ERs could be laid.

The program unfortunately neither unambiguously defines nor does it fully explain the particular type of convertibility envisaged. It specifies that the countries "shall establish economically well-founded and mutually agreed upon [ERs] or coefficients for the national currencies with respect to the [TR] . . . possibly to introduce in future the mutual convertibility of the [TR] into national currencies and vice versa." The members were called upon to study and prepare, in 1971, the "goals, procedures, methods, and time limits for the introduction of economically well-founded and mutually coordinated [ERs] for the national currencies with respect to the [TR] and each other on the basis of a jointly worked out and agreed upon methodology." In 1972–1974, these rates were to be introduced as formal ERs or as currency multipliers. Between 1976 and 1979, the CMEA countries were to explore the possibilities of establishing a single ER. A final decision on whether such would be implemented or not was planned for 1980.

Regarding the specific questions of convertibility, in 1971–1972 the members were to "study and prepare for implementation measures to make the [TR] convertible into the national currencies . . . and to make the national currencies mutually convertible." The conditions to do so were to be worked out jointly in 1973. This involved in particular agreement on the sphere and the forms of convertibility "according to the concrete conditions in every [PE] at the various stages of the economic cooperation between the CMEA and shall be bound up with the specific tasks and measures linked with the improvement of economic cooperation and the development of [SEI]."

These specifications are undeniably cryptic and exceedingly vague at that. At some uncertain future date convertibility between the TR and the national currencies, on the one hand, and among the national currencies, on the other, was to be envisaged. In other words, the PEs aimed above all at some form of regional convertibility that would most likely be confined to some well-defined, segmented transactions as distinct from a more comprehensive form of regional convertibility. *Integration Program* called for a reinforcement of the MFT, rather than its gradual and partial dissolution, something that would necessarily occur under most meaningful forms of convertibility. In the ensuing discussions, however, it gradually became clear that the type of convertibility aimed at was a form meant "to strengthen the role of the planned guidance of the economy" (Konstantinov 1983c, p. 12). In other words, it would be part and parcel of the "planned basis in the development of economic cooperation." Some commentators have called for the convertibility of the TR into national currencies and of the latter against each other "to proceed on the basis of plans" (Ljubskij et al. 1978, p. 63)! In more recent commentary pertaining to the ongoing changes in the "economic mechanisms," observers have emphasized that there is no need to "absolutize the trade and payments monopoly" (Kazandžieva, p. 34). It has become clearly stressed in the process that the features and characteristics of socialist production relations will be reflected in the type of convertibility that these countries may be striving for and this by necessity will make for substantive differences from convertibility in MEs (Kazandžieva 1983, pp. 30–31).

Complete convertibility in the sense of unlimited substitution of any national currency or the TR on demand by residents or nonresidents is perceived to deprive the issuing economy of protection against the unchecked monetary expansion practiced in large developed MEs. A PE rules out altogether any convertibility extending beyond current account transactions (Crăiniceanu 1977, p. 24). As argued at great length and with considerable persuasion in Fedorowicz 1975, free convertibility of the national currencies of the CMEA members into TR cannot be introduced, but many PE commentators disagree with this stance (Ondráček 1983, p. 67). It would indeed imply that the TR's creation and issuance be governed by the decision of each member country to buy TR for its currency. On the other hand, free convertibility of TR into any of the national currencies should be introduced to the full extent, if only because it would facilitate in practice the complete implementation of the regulations of noncommercial payments already in place. A PE should be interested in selling its national currency for TR, which would have real purchasing power or priority over deliveries in any partner market. These countries should also try to develop their services to attract foreign tourists. At the same time, by purchasing other currencies for TR they could better meet the demand of the local population for tourist services abroad.

Free convertibility of the TR into national currencies would increase the attractiveness of the TR as a universal means of purchase, including accumulation, in the international socialist market. It would also simplify procedures in settling noncommercial payments, which continue to be kept very much apart from trade settlements. By regulating its emission and investing it with real purchasing power in the CMEA market, the TR would gradually become convertible into the currencies of MEs on the condition that the ERs be established in proportion to the purchasing power and to the jointly established priorities of economic policy for the whole community of PEs.

At the same time, Z. Fedorowicz argues the inadmissibility of free convertibility of ME currencies into the TR because, as with unrestricted convertibility of national currencies, the TR's emission would become subject to decisions of third countries and not to those of the IBEC's authorities as *in se* the collective "authority" of the members. The guidelines for the participation of third countries in the TR regime, including its currency convertibility, however, should be improved perhaps by setting conditions that would preclude the TR's use for any speculative purpose.

Discussions of what the program may have tried to mask, when placed against the background of the high-level policy debates that took place between 1969 and 1971, have fielded the issue from doing nothing to full-fledged convertibility as a means of enhancing CMEA cooperation. Needless to add that most of the publicized debate unfolded in the West. Within the CMEA, the questions were pursued on two different fronts. The key architects of section 7 of *Integration Program* were bent on committing the members to as broad a concept of convertibility as could be harmonized with the precepts of socialist planning. The more practically minded authorities, however, saw in the program's stipulations only agreement on providing room for a few limited forms of convertibility especially in the noncommercial sphere. Seen in that context, the noncommercial ERs set in the mid-1970s, the new coefficients between the Soviet ruble and the TR scaled in 1971 and 1974, the declaration on joint investment currency coefficients in 1973, and the agreement of late 1972 regarding the free exchange of the equivalent of thirty domestic rubles for tourists (Carevski 1973, p. 507) are sometimes interpreted as instances of the successful realization of the positions stated in *Integration Program* (Válek 1985, p. 11).

11.3 Convertibility concepts

I have claimed that there is considerable misunderstanding in the professional and other literature about convertibility, particularly as it pertains to PEs individually and the CMEA as a whole. An explanation of this contention is required. Without going into a lengthy literature study, the key issues involved can best be grasped if the various parameters of the concept are first fully defined. Some Eastern European writers see in this analytical approach an attempt to solve the problem of the TR's convertibility "on two separate levels and thus from different positions" (Ondráček 1983, p. 60). In my view, however, it is of particular importance to clarify whether the discussion concerns (1) the conversion into another currency and, if so, which particular currency or currency zones are being envisaged; (2) the conversion into goods and, if so, which goods are being referred to; (3) the conversion into goods or into other currencies but only for some transactions, and which particular transactions are being contemplated; and (4) the conversion into goods or other currencies for residents or nonresidents and, if so, which particular groups of residents or nonresidents or both are being envisaged.

A few years ago, Mark Allen suggested that the "currency" of a typical PE actually consists of three different ones, owing to the alternative, noncommunicating "markets" in which this concept could be applied. He distinguished among the trade currency, the consumer currency, and the enterprise currency. Any of these three could be envisaged for four different types of convertibility: commodity or financial or both; for residents or nonresidents or both; applicable to Eastern trade or to East–West trade or to both; and for all or only some trade flows. Thus dissected into eight types of convertibility for three currencies, there is a possible combination of at least twenty-four different kinds of convertibility (Allen 1980, p. 142).[3] This is so if there is only one kind of financial or commodity convertibility applicable to residents or nonresidents and convertible or inconvertible currencies in any of the "markets." From the trade and payments regime described earlier, it should be clear that there are many more domains in which different ERs or ad hoc settlements are being resorted to. As a result, a bewildering variety of convertibility concepts has been tabled for Eastern Europe. But it may be useful at this stage to limit the discussion only to the key variants.

Perhaps the most important distinction is between commodity and financial convertibility. Commodity convertibility means that the holder of a currency is entitled to purchase any desired goods or services at prevailing prices in the currency's home market. If it requires first entering the local market, as in the case of nonresidents, the holder should be free to do so. This presupposes the existence of a local market economy that permits the free purchase of goods and services by holders of that currency, including for export. Financial convertibility means that the holder of a currency is entitled to change it into any other at the ER prevailing in the market. These rates could have been fixed previously by legal agreement or they could be the resultant of free or managed currency markets. This one variant gives rise to four combinations: financial as well as commodity inconvertibility, financial as well as commodity convertibility, financial convertibility but commodity inconvertibility, and commodity convertibility but financial inconvertibility. As Peter Wiles demonstrated years ago, the latter variant, though logical, is not a very useful one (Wiles 1973, p. 119): If commodity convertibility exists, the currency in question is de facto also financially convertible, because the holder of the money balance has the option of obtaining commodities, which he or she will normally be able to dispose of against a currency that is financially convertible. But I shall keep the redundancy for now.

The second distinction is whether either financial or commodity convertibility, or possibly both, is envisaged for residents or nonresidents. This gives eight possible combinations: financial and commodity convertibility for residents, and the same for nonresidents; financial and commodity inconvertibility for residents, and the same for nonresidents; financial convertibility and commodity inconvertibility for residents, and the same for nonresidents; and financial inconvertibility and commodity convertibility for residents, and the same for nonresidents.

The third distinction is whether either financial or commodity convertibility for either residents or nonresidents applies to all currency markets or only to some of them. This yields sixteen logical combinations if there are only two markets – the "home country" and "abroad." I shall leave it up to the reader to spell them out.

A last important distinction concerns the particular currency that is being envisaged for conversion. Given the segregated markets typical of the CMEA and its constituents, convertibility could be entertained for commercial transactions now dealt with under regular TR commercial agreements,[4] the domestic consumer currency holdings in the form of cash and savings deposits, or the domestic enterprise or producer currency balances kept at the state bank. A much greater complexity would be attained if convertibility were to be sought for some goods (for instance, consumer durables) but not for others, which at one point was under discussion in the CMEA (see Section 11.4).

Perhaps the key guide in any serious discussion of convertibility is whether reference is to commodity or to financial convertibility or possibly to both. Most currencies of developed MEs are convertible in both senses. Experience has demonstrated, however, that some degree of financial convertibility has been easiest to introduce when a large measure of commodity convertibility had previously been attained. Historically, the convertibility of current account transactions has preceded that of capital flows, if freely functioning capital markets emerged at all. But this derives exclusively from the behavior and requirements of MEs, and the precedent need not apply universally. Because there has been considerable controversy in the literature about the possibility and benefits of creating financial convertibility for the ruble or the TR, it is useful to keep the historical evidence separate from logical possibilities.

The key features of the economic model of the PEs and of their trade and payments regime illustrate the different degrees of convertibility they have already achieved in fact, though not in name. Regarding consumer money balances, excepting periods of physical allocation and rationing, there is presently a very large degree of commodity convertibility. This simply means that resident holders of domestic currency balances can command goods and services in the market without obtaining prior approval of agencies entrusted with resource allocation. Because such balances are to a considerable extent convertible into commodities, the greatest progress has been achieved in introducing some measure of financial convertibility for this consumer currency. This corroboration of the "historical path" indicated earlier simply follows from the fact, as noted in Chapter 5, that consumer sovereignty in PEs parallels that in MEs, although it is not exactly identical to it. As noted, Eastern European citizens are entitled to allocations of foreign currency from other PEs or MEs within certain restrictions and broad guidelines on the overall disposable volume (see Chapter 6). Considerable progress has been made also for nonresidents. Owing to the particular problems of maintaining consumer market balance in these economies, however, foreign exchange controls are obviously required in this sphere, especially when it concerns spending by holders of other inconvertible currencies, to avoid disruptions of domestic markets. Inadequately forecast spending sprees are invariably associated with any "liberalization" of unorganized tourism, as discussed in Chapter 6.

On the other hand, money balances in the enterprise sphere are extremely inconvertible, especially in orthodox PEs. Because economic resources are de rigueur distributed by central fiat, money cannot command goods and services within the enterprise sector of the traditional PE. Goods inconvertibility prevails because the possessor of a currency balance must generally pass through the planning hierarchy and obtain clearance prior to obtaining title to mobilize the balance. Eastern European currencies are, in principle, internally inconvertible into goods for transactions outside the consumer sphere because any producer with net bank balances can only acquire inputs with the explicit approval of the relevant planning authorities. If an enterprise commands a good, it is because it has been allocated that resource by the plan, not because it has bank balances. The plan is therefore the motive force of the movement of resources, and the associated money flows are merely an automatic response to a prior decision. The degree of commodity convertibility will remain highly restricted for as long as the planner preempts the decision-making process by inhibiting the development of some market and allocates goods directly. Internal commodity inconvertibility has been much relaxed in recent years, especially in the MPE. Nevertheless, it still remains a very important obstacle hindering the introduction of this type of convertibility.

Enterprise money is inconvertible for residents both in the financial and in the commodity sense. Just as it cannot purchase local goods, an enterprise with a money balance cannot normally acquire other currencies without obtaining the prior approval of the banking, trading, or central planning administration. Both financial and commodity inconvertibility for residents have been considerably relaxed in recent years, especially in the MPE. Those that have set a meaningful step in the direction of the devolution of decision making have by necessity created some limited range for real markets. This holds also for nonresidents. The introduction of both commodity and financial convertibility for nonresidents depends critically on the planning system in the PEs. It founders essentially on the absence of domestic markets for producer goods and on the lack of discretion of enterprise managers about the use of their money holdings.

The third currency unit introduced above is the TR. Remember that there is no central planning agency at the CMEA level and that regional trade and payments are regulated through various levels of economic bargaining about quantities traded at some prices that are not predetermined. There is therefore some potential for the emergence of convertibility into goods provided the negotiators involved can let quantities and prices move in line with shifts in the aggregate demand and supply of all participants. This has clearly not been the case to date for the well-known reasons of price heterogeneity and the inability of negotiators to bargain solely, or even mainly, on the basis of economic criteria. BTPAs stifle the potential for commodity convertibility in this sphere. TR money balances are therefore involuntary because, as noted, money as such does not command goods. The emergence of the TR's financial convertibility will proceed without a hitch once CMEA trade prices can flexibly reflect real demand and supply of the various participants.

Against the foregoing backdrop, one could now project a complicated four-dimensional matrix enveloping all possible combinations of regional and worldwide, internal and external, currency and commodity, and limited or unlimited convertibility for each possible currency and goods regime one is willing to entertain. Several of the restrictions exhibited by each entry might bear on the particular convertibility type that some PEs have possibly been envisaging. But the cases examined here can accommodate the various proposals for convertibility proffered in the CMEA over the years (see Brabant 1977a, pp. 317–42).

11.4 Convertibility proposals

I shall restrict the elaborations here to the gist of the recent discussions regarding national currency (especially forint, leu, or złoty) convertibility, some form of official convertibility for the ruble or the TR, and a greater degree of actual convertibility for the TR. But first a brief historical flashback is in order.

As discussed beforehand, in practice planning by itself cannot prevent ex post imbalances either in the framework of BTPAs or MTPAs. To avoid granting involuntary loans by the net surplus traders, from the early 1950s on several PEs began to agitate on an intermittent basis for some form of "limited convertibility." Most of these proposals have been phrased so as to restrict their scope to regular commercial transactions. Although the mechanics outlined in the alternative proposals varied, the broad goals and means put forward have always been very similar to those embraced in the early 1950s under the EPU regime.

The most common proposition is the following: Under certain conditions regarding the duration, the size, and the use of their balance, surplus countries should be entitled to convert a fraction into CC or close substitutes. The remainder would continue to be settled as in the past, although perhaps under more flexible arrangements than the strict BTPAs typical of the CMEA. Similarly for the debtor countries: Under well-specified conditions regarding the duration and size of their deficit position, they would have to amortize a certain proportion of their debt in CC. The fraction of debts and surpluses to be converted should rise over time either in accordance with a predetermined schedule or after successive rounds of multilateral negotiations until all imbalances are made fully convertible in the ex post sense. But the fractions need not be symmetrical. Thus the persistent debtor could be asked to contribute to the creation of an own fund for multilateral settlements by slating a higher CC margin for the debtor than for the creditor. A settlements bank such as the IBEC or a close competitor would be placed in charge of the practical administration of these agreements, including their enforcement. If realized, these proposals would have entailed some limited form of financial convertibility for regional transactions of official trading organs.

A variant of the proposals encompassing limited financial convertibility envisaged a restricted form of goods convertibility too, possibly in combination with a limited form of financial convertibility. That is, tradables were to be segregated into liberalized and other goods. The former would be handled in real markets with flexible quantities and prices, reflecting underlying market conditions instantaneously or intermittently (for example, on an annual basis). Some suggestions extended the liberalized trade segment to encompass also noncommercial transactions or at least their tourist component. These liberalized markets would conduct business in a new, really transferable socialist currency. Under certain conditions, as specified earlier, such balances would be settled in CC. Although nonliberalized trade would continue to be conducted as before, its share in overall transactions would be steadily compressed according to either a prearranged formula or one hammered out in successive negotiations. As a result, the TR would eventually be replaced by a socialist currency convertible into goods, but only for official traders within the CMEA.

A third group of proposals has a long history. It concerns the fuller realization of convertibility in the noncommercial sphere. The establishment of financial convertibility for noncommercial transactions would be a logical culmination of the already existing degree of goods and limited financial convertibility. This could be especially important in the sphere of tourism, where some measure of formal convertibility into the TR already exists.

A fourth group of proposals departs from efforts to attain any degree of convertibility of the TR beyond what exists now. These variants focus on some type of convertibility of individual PE currencies. Given its size, wealth, and resources, most attention has been devoted to the possibility of erecting a convertible ruble. However, in connection with the NEM, forint convertibility has been reported to be "imminent" since 1968. Hungary's accession to the IMF only reinforced this allegedly pending movement. Rumania has had the same obligation in principle since 1972, and occasionally Rumanian commentators refer to the general characteristics of a regime in which the leu could become convertible (see Crăiniceanu 1977). Now that Poland has acceded to the IMF, the question of the convertibility of the złoty, which has been debated for many years, especially in the professional Polish literature, arises in a new context.

11.5 Advantages and drawbacks of convertibility

Decision makers of PEs are well aware of the advantages of convertibility. At the same time, they are seriously concerned about its drawbacks. This ambivalent attitude arises simply because the ideal model to which PE planners aspire is not yet very well defined. Convertibility for a given economy may be a highly useful institutional support for a number of policy features if that economy is indeed organized on the basis of mainly market forces and continuous adjustments in quantities and prices are permitted. If macroeconomic managers aspire to something different, possibly only in the short to medium run, however, then the most desirable development is not necessarily free convertibility.

The advantages are normally perceived to be fourfold. First, convertibility enables the PE's currency to be accepted for trading purposes. Foreign asset holders may wish to accumulate some of their funds in that currency. This may in turn lead to the advantage of seigniorage, which means the ability of the authority in charge of a currency's emission to borrow short-term funds without having to pay the going market rate because foreigners are willing to hold balances of the home currency. Some Eastern European commentators perceive convertibility to lead automatically to a net inflow of credit for the issuing country (Kazandžieva 1983, p. 36). However, Western depositors are likely to hold PE currency balances only if they can be converted into goods directly or indirectly.

Apart from the transaction motive, such assets even if not goods convertible may be held in view of the stability and earning potential in PEs. Whether seigniorage will on balance be positive therefore depends on a number of conditions to be examined later.

Second, convertibility enables the issuer to attract other countries into participating in the CMEA's multilateral settlements mechanism and capital markets. In this, the PEs have been motivated more by concerns about obtaining flexible access to Western commercial and financial markets than by considerations involving the granting of advantageous conditions to third countries. However, it is clearly understood that any geographical widening of the TR's use in regular commerce or in capital markets is crucially contingent on transitions in economic institutions, policies, and criteria of choice that would make multilateralism a real feature of the PE's policy environment, instead of a purely formal or technical one, and that commodity convertibility will be actively sought. It is quite unlikely that any other country will join the CMEA's settlements system in TR as long as it remains purely formal (see Chapter 8).

Third, currency convertibility makes for relatively flexible commercial relations in international markets because it implies multilateralism with all other CC users. It also favorably affects the PE's access to short- and long-term capital in the form of loans, bonds, supplier credits, and so on. Furthermore, it allows for transactions now often precluded for lack of adequate foreign exchange revenues. Although such advantages can be expected from the more general salutary implications of convertibility for the allocation process, the emphasis in the literature is not primarily on the determination of the level and commodity composition of trade, but rather on the geographical distribution of a predetermined trade volume.

Finally, convertibility calls for a periodic reappraisal of the ER, which in turn could help to maintain balance-of-payments equilibrium and serve as a real measure of value linking the external economy with world markets. Closely related to the ER issue, but not necessarily identical to it in the PE context, is the advantage of maintaining a proper relationship between domestic prices (or surrogates for planning and decision-making purposes) and WMPs for those countries that perceive such a nexus as an integral element of "the instruments to be improved in perfecting the planning methods in the system of economic regulation" (Kazandžieva 1983, p. 33).

Convertibility is not, however, a one-way street. For an economy operating with real markets, subject to a minimum of control on the part of the authorities, the net effect of convertibility is likely to be positive. But its drawbacks may well outweigh the advantages. This may arise especially for economies that are characterized by pervasive administrative controls and political interferences in economic processes. The following would seem to be the most critical ones in the case of PEs.

The most frequently cited arguments in favor of creating convertibility in the PEs tend to hinge on the feasibility of minimal economic reforms. The advocates regard convertibility mainly as a convenient yardstick for reaping higher trade gains, but not necessarily as a powerful instrument to guide the formulation and implementation of development strategies in trade-dependent economies. In some contrast to the principal thrust of the alleged advantages of convertibility, the disadvantages are identified in particular in the sphere of market-type relations, which are assumed to be inevitably associated with, if not a prerequisite of, convertibility. The most frequently discussed points are summarized next.

First, a convertible TR or local currency might become the object of speculation in Western financial markets for sound economic reasons, but possibly also for political or strategic motives. Similarly, Western firms and institutions might accumulate TR balances and then suddenly decide to convert them into goods or other currencies, thereby presumably injecting an element of unwelcome volatility into the "stability" of CMEA currencies. This currency stability may by implication in turn be transmitted into the domestic economies. Under the circumstances, this eventuality raises the question of whether the PEs would be able to neutralize such speculative pressures with their present economic resources. This is an important point, for domestic stability remains one of the paramount objectives of socialist economic policies.

Because the PEs are not expected to transform their economies soon into full-fledged MEs, commodity convertibility cannot be sought without at the same time enacting formidable restrictions. The freedom to convert currency balances into goods presupposes the abolition of essential components of trade planning and the MFT. At least, it could greatly weaken central control over trade and payments. But this may shape up in two different forms. In the absence of credible macroeconomic monetary and fiscal policies, commodity convertibility will indeed weaken the MFT. Once such aggregate domestic policies are firmly in place, however, the MFT loses control over the details of day-to-day foreign exchange transactions, but its role as the center guiding decisions rises perceptibly. The mere fact that such a disintegrating development might occur at all is taken as a pointer that free convertibility is incompatible with the much vaunted socialist socioeconomic precepts. Especially with regard to price policies, negative consequences of a "socialist currency entering the capitalist markets" have been identified with the monetary pressures on prices in MEs and their trade, and the possible transmission to the PEs (Konstantinov 1983c, p. 11).

Second, currency convertibility raises the problem of how structural disequilibria in the regional or overall external payments balance can be eliminated and forestalled in the future. The only long-lasting solution seems to be fundamental adaptations in the surplus as well as in the deficit PEs to cope with disequilibria that genuinely stem from structural dislocations. Although it is admittedly not an easy task to identify the source of imbalances at each instance, this issue should be kept separate from the ability and willingness to seek such highly desirable, if not mandatory, adaptations in principle.

Third, currency convertibility or even the convertibility into goods requires the accumulation of adequate reserves. There is no precise guideline on how large "adequate" reserves should be. Regardless of their ideal volume, the PEs would have to be prepared to accumulate more reserves than heretofore to cushion balance-of-payments effects or to counter a run on their currency. The accumulation of a substantial CC or commodity reserve that can be quickly and securely monetized requires a considerable investment. Such an allocation is deemed unattainable in the short run by most PEs on account of the already widespread payments pressures on their CC trade. Furthermore, at least in the view of some authors, such a substantial investment is considered an unwarranted appropriation of scarce investment funds that drains resources from more productive activities. Even a temporary growth deceleration to permit the buildup of reserves would seem to be unacceptable to most policy makers, at least in the ex ante framework for policy formulation.

Fourth, any convertibility into Western currencies requires substantial administrative adaptations and most likely also real changes in economic structures and policies, as already noted. Apart from these changes, which themselves could induce temporarily a substantial expansion in East–West trade, convertibility may lead to a permanent expansion of East–West trade and a relative disregarding of CMEA relations. Any substantial, permanent reorientation of commerce in favor of the advanced MEs is held to be detrimental to SEI by all those keenly interested in bolstering this regional cohesion as one platform for consolidating regional power, not necessarily in the economic field.

Fifth, the willingness of agents in MEs to hold Eastern European currencies – any other direction of the monetary flows would not directly benefit the PEs – clearly depends on trade prospects and, to some extent, on what such funds earn in socialist banks. Currency convertibility necessarily leads to changes in the regional and domestic credit and interest rate policies of the PEs. This is believed to be counterproductive by nearly all Eastern European commentators, but especially by those PEs that still hope to benefit from low-cost loans from socialist partners. Western penetration of socialist financial markets could compromise the future of autonomous regional or national policies and, hence, of some sacrosanct "socialist" objectives.

11.6 The possibility of positive seigniorage

One of the attractive features of declaring convertibility for a given country's currency is that under some circumstances foreigners may be willing to hold part of their assets in that currency. As a result, the issuing country is able to extend the sphere of its domestic seigniorage to other markets, provided it can also "borrow" there at a rate below the market rate. It therefore refers not only to putting currency in circulation at home or abroad at a zero nominal interest rate, but also to other forms of private lending to the emitting authority at a rate below the market interest rate. Note, however, that this seigniorage is gross in the sense that the emitting country is bound to incur some costs in defending the currency's convertibility. It may have to hold larger reserves of gold or other acceptable international currencies to fend off a run on its currency. It may also have to open up its domestic markets or to create a sufficiently flexible market in its currency. These costs will be looked at later.

The gross advantage of being able to skim off seigniorage was qualified above with "under some circumstances." Total demand for foreign currency assets in the world equals the sum of all currency balances except those of the countries of residence. This demand must clearly be a function of relatively predictable determinants. Foreign currencies in general are held for at least four purposes (Holzman 1978b, p. 148), although there may be other reasons: (1) for intervention purposes, usually to support some central ER or to stabilize movements of the home country's ER within prespecified bounds; (2) balances of a vehicle currency are required because trade partners have accepted the currency as the denominator of their commerce, possibly in relations in which the issuing country is not even an indirect participant; (3) for pure transaction purposes on current account and possibly capital transactions; and (4) as a store of value or a medium in which foreigners want to accumulate their assets. Barring the very unusual accumulation of dollar deposits as a result of the exceptional movements of oil prices in the 1970s and the consequent accumulation of dollar assets not exchanged into goods and services, the demand for currencies used for intervention purposes and as a vehicle currency usually far exceeds that for other purposes. Given the nature of a vehicle currency and the countries that are prepared to defend their currency's ER, only the major currencies could belong to that category.

The demand for currency balances for intervention purposes and as vehicle currencies is usually heavily weighted in favor of one or a few currencies that are widely used and relatively stable in value. There are strong economic reasons for transacting one's trade in a few vehicle currencies because they are de facto the standard of value against which other currencies are measured. Vehicle currencies traditionally tend to be relatively stable in value. Their wide use in international financial transactions is therefore partly attributable to low ER risks. A vehicle currency also enables users to conserve reserves and to reduce transaction costs.

None of the currencies of the PEs under consideration here could, by any stretch of the imagination, be considered to be a vehicle currency or even a major currency in world trade and payments. If the PEs desire to establish convertibility in the hope of benefiting from the seigniorage accruing from the desire of foreigners to hold local currency balances, the latter should exceed the money balances held by a PE in excess of what it would hold at a time of currency inconvertibility. On that basis only, the outlook for positive advantages accruing from convertibility is not at all good. Perhaps of considerable importance is that, barring a movement toward goods convertibility in the PEs, the demand for PE currencies would be driven chiefly by the effective return on financial assets. Even in cases where the PE is pondering a move toward more than financial convertibility of its currency, it is not likely to lead to the emergence of unrestricted convertibility at least for current account purposes. External financial convertibility (EFC) might be a possibility, but goods convertibility is not likely to be in the offing.

Seen against this background, it is highly unlikely that there will soon be a strong demand for any PE currency that is EFC either for intervention purposes or as a vehicle currency (Holzman 1978b, p. 149). This sharply limits the value of the EFC currency that foreigners might demand or be willing to hold, all other things being equal. The experience with the adjustment period following World War II clearly demonstrated that a currency that is financially convertible but not commodity convertible tends to lose in value. This is so because a financially convertible currency that is not backed by commodity convertibility has a sharply lower value to prospective holders than one that is characterized by commodity convertibility. One might expect this to hold because, at the time in question, merchandise transactions far exceeded the volume of capital transactions, which were severely proscribed. At the present time, however, the latter are a large multiple of merchandise trade. Would this make the purely financially convertible currency more attractive? Probably not, because its value tends to be subject to a greater degree of speculation than would be the case with a currency that is goods and financially convertible. This in turn would reduce the probability of substantial seigniorage accruing from the issuance of an EFC in the CMEA. Furthermore, an EFC is likely to be associated with a larger transaction cost and to necessitate holding ampler reserves in the issuing country relative to what is now required to service East–West trade and some CMEA transactions denominated in CC.

The upshot of this elaboration is that there is nothing inherently attractive about a currency that is characterized by EFC. Hence, to encourage Western traders, banks, or treasuries to hold it, the country emitting such a currency, to be successful, needs to endow the currency with special features that create demand essentially for a store of value. Such special features include the terms of convertibility, for example, by way of guaranteed ERs, and the interest rate to be paid. Given a high enough rate of interest and guarantees against adverse currency fluctuations, EFC balances could be held as a store of value. Under these circumstances, on balance, negative seigniorage, rather than a positive benefit, might emerge. Postwar experience has demonstrated (see Holzman 1978b, p. 154) that positive seigniorage results only when the country that issues the CC possesses some monopolistic power in world financial markets. This would not appear to be the case for any PE currency any more than it is for the majority of CCs.

11.7 Financial convertibility and East–West capital flows

There has been considerable speculation in some strand of the Western literature about the CMEA and their national and regional currencies concerning the possibility of creating a financially convertible currency. Various currency units have been considered, but for the sake of analysis I shall call the abstract unit the financially convertible TR (FTR). As introduced earlier, EFC assets are held solely for financial purposes because they can be converted only into another currency on demand. Holders prefer this currency over another because of its real rate of return relative to what they can obtain on alternative financial assets. Market operators place a high value on such nonpecuniary benefits as stability and predictability, in addition to the real value of the interest earned from such investments. The variance of the nominal and real rate of return may be affected by such imponderables as political strife, military security, natural calamities, and other disasters. The only requirement for such an FTR is that investors may change their holdings on current account at any time into any desirable CC. Similarly, FTR time deposits are convertible into CC at maturity. Such convertibility could be easily created for residents as well as nonresidents, but prestige considerations may well restrict access to the emitted FTRs to foreigners.[5]

I do not at all contest the possibility of creating such an asset.[6] Any sovereign state and indeed any multilateral financial institution, such as the IBEC, can create a currency unit that is EFC. The litmus test of whether such a move would be economically warranted depends on whether the venture is cost effective, whether it can be undertaken without jeopardizing the stability of the economic system that emits the FTR, and whether nonresidents may wish to deposit their assets into such accounts.[7] Regarding cost effectiveness, at stake is what the issuer of the FTR has to pay directly and indirectly to sway CC holders into switching their assets into FTR. Apart from the administrative costs associated with such a venture, analytically the decision to emit FTR as an economic proposition hinges on the nominal interest rate, the cost of holding commodity or CC reserves, and foreign exchange risks.

Stability is closely linked with the issue of foreign exchange risk. The

FTR could be linked to gold, one national CC, oil, gas, a basket of currencies, or any other guarantee that is apt to instill potential investor confidence in the FTR. Colombatto has recently proposed that the FTR (in his view, a ruble that is EFC) be linked to a financial instrument free from accidental fluctuations and indexed to account somehow for inflation (Colombatto 1983, pp. 494ff.). Although his proposal has some special features, it is actually a variant of the suggestion originally advanced by Peter Wiles (Wiles 1973). Wiles saw in it a plausible escape from the severe inflationary pressures and ER fluctuations that were then disturbing especially the vehicle CCs. He emphasized also that it would be a highly advantageous way in which the USSR could attract foreign capital as an alternative to tapping Western financial markets.

The basic question asked by Wiles was whether the USSR or the IBEC could issue an FTR that would be only EFC for residents outside the CMEA area. He made it quite clear that reference was to a financially convertible Soviet ruble because, in his view, only the solidity of the USSR could "guarantee" the stability and reliability of such an EFC issue. However, also the IBEC's prestige in financial circles could be exploited for the issuance of an FTR, whose attractiveness could have benefited the members at large. Wiles presumably does not disagree with this contention because he argues that virtually any currency could become EFC, if at some positive explicit or implicit interest margin. I shall therefore continue to refer to the unit as an FTR. It would be a special TR, or national currency unit, inconvertible into goods but convertible into other CCs under well-specified conditions.

Wiles gave a positive answer: such speculative, nonproductive capital flows could be denominated in an attractive international unit for short- and medium-term personal savings, and "grass would grow in the streets of Zürich" (Wiles 1973, p. 123). Positive seigniorage would accrue because the issuer may tie in the FTR at all times to the major nondevaluing currencies, so its purchasing power over goods in world markets would be guaranteed by compensating for the average inflation rate that affects the issuing countries. The bank would essentially borrow short at low or no real interest rate but invest it at home or abroad at a positive real rate of return. The depositor would be guaranteed a stable asset at a predetermined ER and a value tied to the U.S. price index (Wiles 1973, p. 123).

Colombatto argues that the opportunity cost of the real rate of interest paid on FTRs is the productivity of high-quality or high-technology goods acquired with such funds. This errs on two counts. The opportunity cost is what the Eastern borrower would have to pay, say, for Euro-currency funds. As long as the latter is higher than the nominal interest rate – not the real one as Colombatto argues – paid on FTR deposits and the latter is not larger than the marginal productivity of the imports acquired in Western markets, it is sensible from a purely economic point of view to set up FTR accounts. He sees the main advantage in the fact that FTR assets may be kept forever, whereas borrowed funds have to be repaid at maturity. This is a strange way of looking at it: Depositors are not wont to maintain a given stock of FTR assets forever nor are banking consortia inhibited from calling up matured loans without rollovers. I find it therefore a non sequitur to conclude from these conditions that the FTR "*may,* and practically must, be cheaper than ordinary credit" (Colombatto 1983, p. 497). This becomes clearer once the other variables have been taken into account.[8]

Why have the PEs not so far tried to satisfy their scarcely satiable demand for Western capital by issuing an FTR? The answer is relatively simple: The real cost of operating such a scheme has exceeded what financial markets imposed in terms of real interest rates (say, nominal rates deflated by the price index of PE exports to developed MEs), except perhaps at the time of the extraordinary rise in interest rates on account of domestically oriented macroeconomic policies in the United States in the early 1980s. Wiles appeared to be arguing the case for gross positive seigniorage. He seems to have ignored two major factors. First, an FTR would be associated with considerable operating costs, as discussed. Second, it would be costly to redeem such a currency if the U.S. price level were to rise rapidly, as it did in the 1970s, thus leading to negative real interest rates in international markets. Even if the rate itself were below that of financial markets, the risk to keep reserves so as to bridge fluctuations in deposits and to prepare for the eventuality of a run on the bank, administrative and management expenses involved in operating the scheme, operational expenses to hedge against the foreign exchange risk, and other outlays would have considerably whittled that marginal advantage.

In a perfect financial market, there should be no difference between interest rates for the borrower, given equal operating costs. Similarly for the lender, although that rate is likely to be inferior to the borrower's. Because there is no difference, it might be possible for the CMEA to stretch its resources further by borrowing directly than by issuing a currency that is EFC. However, depositors must receive at least the same rate of return as available in Western financial markets. A positive margin may well be required to compensate for the uncertainty of East–West relations, the more general problems of sovereign lending, the lack of familiarity with PE markets, the lack of smooth banking contacts between East and West, and the like. Even if the nominal rate offered were to be lower than what Western financial markets normally charge, the PEs would have to immobilize additional CC reserves that thus would not be available for purchases in MEs. The borrowing PE would appear to be able to do at least as well or even better by tapping established financial markets than by issuing a currency that is EFC (see Holzman 1978b, p. 153).

11.8 Directions regarding regional convertibility

Mainly a special type of regional convertibility, if that at all, is likely to emerge in Eastern Europe in the next decade or so. This is bound to differ measurably from the limited external convertibility that may be proclaimed for residents of nonsocialist countries. It will be predominantly of a financial nature, largely planned in the context of the CMEA, with some goods convertibility in the case of noncommercial transactions, interenterprise relations concerned with special tasks, and for the transactions of IEOs broadly defined. Regional convertibility does not imply the extension of convertibility to ME currencies as well. Nor does it forcibly preclude this eventuality. Changes in the domestic economic mechanisms, by and large, determine the framework and form of regional convertibility, and whether full convertibility will eventually become a strategic aim of the economic policies of PEs. Especially during the tumultuous economic events of the 1970s and early 1980s, the PEs exhibited more resilience, if measured in terms of levels of economic activity and growth pace, in weathering the storms brought about by world market fluctuations than some observers had anticipated. These countries are not likely to forgo this feature altogether, yet the PEs cannot indefinitely remain only interested spectators in Western markets.

The introduction of a full-fledged CC in the CMEA region or in individual PEs would only make sense if certain minimum conditions were fulfilled. Obviously, there must be a minimum of CC reserves to cover any unexpected demand for foreign exchange. To the extent that large balances of domestic currencies of PEs are held abroad, the issuing country in question must build up a reserve of goods and services to ward off or to neutralize a run on the currency because of purely economic reasons. Moreover, economic growth must be ensured and yet yield an appropriate amount of competitive exportables. Furthermore, the foreign exchange and trade regimes must be made more flexible to take advantage of the demand pull of having a CC and to implement changes in the domestic economy on the basis of the demand for and the supply of the PE's currency. It would be particularly useful to establish a direct link between domestic and trade prices, to bridge the discrepancies between CMEA and world prices, and to entrust current trade decisions more and more to economic agents. Also, ERs that help to reach and to maintain balance-of-payments equilibrium need to be set. Given the discrepancies between domestic scarcity relationships and what prevails elsewhere in the CMEA and, even more so, in world markets, however, goods convertibility is not likely to be sought soon.

As noted, monetary refinements by themselves do not eliminate the barter character of CMEA trade based on a combination of state trading, shortages of some goods, and price and ER distortions. In short, the PEs could easily declare technical convertibility into any other currency. But this would not necessarily induce a useful response in terms of microeconomic trade behavior and would not entail direct real economic advantages. But it might be good public relations, lead to closer economic cooperation between East and West, and facilitate access to Western financial markets, and so might yield favorable indirect economic benefits. Note, however, that the autonomous banks in Western countries owned by PEs have already permitted the parent countries to avail themselves of the economic effects of short- and medium-term borrowing without imposing the administrative burden of having the PEs themselves cope with an EFC.

In sum, the convertibility intentions expressed in *Integration Program* are still far from being finalized. Conceptually at this stage, the introduction of convertibility must help to intermesh CMEA economic interdependence without upsetting the basic precepts of socialist planning and cooperation. Recall that in trade with MEs, the PEs already use CC. Provided they plan well, the only substantive problem is the transfer of funds from the CMEA area to the MEs, which is presently precluded for most transactions. The reverse poses no problem, but it is only infrequently exploited for other reasons. Provided the PEs really aim at implementing production integration, their main focus should be not on the issue of currency convertibility but on reaching planned regional multilateralism. Attaining this means that integration efforts need to be channeled into ways that permit the correct assessment of costs and prices, on the one hand, and a steady increase in the scope of the opportunities for plan coordination and planned cooperation in production processes, on the other. For the near future, this is likely to entail some type of "planned convertibility," however awkward this concept might sound at first.

At the heart of convertibility, as noted earlier, lies the notion that the holder of currency balances can at any time decide to accumulate, spend, or convert them. Against that backdrop, the notion of "planned convertibility" might seem a contradiction in terms, but this is not so. It requires the preservation of the present system of the central state monopoly over currency relations within the overall framework of the MFT without, however, aiming rigidly at overall, regional, or bilateral payments balance. The chief implication for CMEA relations is that ex ante MTPAs provide for a net outflow of TR planned in CC or in credit flows. Unplanned imbalances, which are bound to emerge, need to be carried over by means of credits that might be the subject of planned CC settlements in the future. A second stage of "planned convertibility" might entail controlled transferability as defined before.

Regardless of what type of institutional framework the PEs ultimately select, a key condition for any type of reform, as noted in Chapters 3 and

5, is a substantive revision in price policies. A direct dependence of internal prices in the distribution sphere on the terms at which alternatives are offered abroad is not absolutely essential, although it might be very useful to draw the correct inferences about production specialization. Thus convertibility does not necessarily entail forgoing domestic price autonomy altogether. A drastic change in external prices is clearly mandatory both for interregional and real CMEA multilateralism. The basic problem would seem to be how to avert regional imbalances. If this cannot be attained, the heart of the multilateralization issue is the question of how to settle such planned and spontaneous imbalances. As amply demonstrated by past experience, regardless of what the price policies are, ex ante planning of trade processes is by itself incapable of assuring ex post convertibility into CC.

Against this backdrop, it appears realistic to expect the following. The PEs are likely to declare soon the reciprocal convertibility of their currencies, including the TR, especially for noncommercial transactions that are not easily controlled or planned, save by stifling bureaucratic intervention. Ex post convertibility of TR balances into CC under some conditions would be a distinct possibility too, especially if the PEs do not succeed in establishing the necessary preconditions for regional commodity convertibility in production and distribution. However, regional commodity convertibility in the distribution sphere will only succeed in eliminating the most knotty balancing problems if this settlements mechanism is propped up by a significant expansion of exportable products. The realization of a limited form of external convertibility is evidently a function of the implementation of measures that spur on real regional multilateralism, which itself depends crucially on the realization of a much greater degree of harmony between CMEA and world prices than has been attained to date.

PART III

A DEVELOPMENT AND INTEGRATION SCENARIO

12

Socialist economic integration and East–West relations in the late 1980s and beyond

Having examined key aspects of Eastern Europe's postwar economic developments, it is time for me to sum up and give some indication as to what the future may hold in store for SEI and its principal participants. Chapter 3 spelled out various domestic and external constraints on the economic activity of the PEs in the years ahead. Part II provided a broad review of the most important instruments of indirect economic coordination and their supporting institutions against the backdrop of the postwar development strategies, organizational features, and managerial models of these countries. Given the current state of affairs in the PEs individually and the CMEA as a whole, realistically speaking, there should be little doubt that the PEs have only few options if they wish to resume relatively buoyant economic growth fairly soon. Yet their ideological, political, and socioeconomic preconceptions and preferences clearly argue in favor of the imperativeness of accelerating economic expansion well above the levels attained in recent years under rather unusual circumstances. Such a shift, however modest at first, would be more consonant with the societal objectives of socialist policy makers and the basic pillars of their political legitimacy.

Section 12.1 summarizes the key determinants of medium-term growth in Eastern Europe. Section 12.2 takes a closer look at the potential implications for the PEs of the recent changes in the basics of the global economic, financial, and trade framework. Although these transformations on the whole ease the prevailing external constraints for the majority of the PEs of Eastern Europe, they do not fundamentally alter the growth potential of these economies individually or in their CMEA concert. This constatation leads to a discussion of the overall development strategy for the next decade or so and the possibly important role of SEI therein as one main pillar that may actively strengthen the more general aspirations regarding growth "intensification" held by most PEs. Because it is self-evident that policy intentions as such and by themselves cannot solve the majority of the myriad problems confronting the PEs, Section

385

12.4 summarizes the groundswell of domestic initiatives and policy actions required in each PE individually and, if possible, in a CMEA-wide coordinated fashion too in order to mobilize all available forces for fostering productivity growth. These activities need to emerge not only in the field of policy design. More important, in my view, are fresh approaches to widen the variety and to clarify the reach of instruments that policy makers feel comfortable with in guiding their economic agents. Though transformations in the domestic economies of the CMEA member countries are the sine qua non for the current pursuit of real economic integration, national efforts, even if synchronized, must have a direct counterpart at the international level. It is therefore mandatory to explore with determination meaningful changes in regional economic policies, policy instruments, and institutions that buttress a more integration-minded approach to CMEA cooperation, which is presented in Section 12.5. The chapter concludes with some pointers regarding the likelihood that the transitions advocated here will be implemented and what such modifications may presage with respect to economic cooperation between East, West, and South.

12.1 Growth constraints and positive adjustment policies

The alpha and omega of economic growth in the European PEs after World War II has been more or less steady additions to the factor input stream. In some of these countries, production factors continue to be idle, are only partly mobilized, or can be redistributed in some proportions in favor of the more modern sectors, which are more productive. These PEs are therefore evidently in a position, for the time being at least, to continue to prop up extensive development policies by injecting increasing amounts of unused, underemployed, or redeployed production resources into the modern industrial sectors. However, I conjecture that this is neither a viable option for most PEs, nor is it a desirable one even for those that still possess idle or underutilized production factors for domestic as well as external reasons.

Domestic growth determinants

The internal factors that complicate the resumption of sustained growth at the rate experienced during most of the postwar period can be separated conceptually into two distinct groups. On the one hand, the volume and distribution of primary production factors in the years ahead will be quite different from how they evolved during most of the postwar period, irrespective of short- to medium-term policy decisions. On the other hand, prevailing institutions and policy instruments determine the output combinations attainable with given resource endowments. But these are not necessarily immutable. Proper and timely policy decisions in the PEs can recast the development strictures embedded in factor availabilities. Such actions may perhaps fail to bear fruit immediately. But in the medium to long run, they certainly would contribute to sustaining a higher rate of aggregate output growth than the PEs can attain under prevailing circumstances.

The exogenous growth constraints could be eased by increasing the labor force, for example, through further absorption of women, pensioners, or youngsters, or by modifying educational policies or the military draft with a view to raising the labor force. Another option would be to continue to relocate production factors from places where they are relatively underemployed or not very productive to sectors where their contribution to overall output is bound to be larger. Although some PEs can further mobilize segments of the able-bodied population into the effective labor force, the presently available leeway is not very extensive. Given the relatively low productivity of labor, say, in agriculture, one could rashly conclude that production factors could be easily relocated from that sector, as in the past. But this is only partly true. To continue the example, relatively low productivity in agriculture can be overcome by drawing labor out of the sector and channeling it into, say, manufacturing. But such a redistribution can normally be undertaken without adverse effects on output in the labor-shedding sector only if the authorities are in a position to inject considerable capital resources into it. Because the overall social and economic cost of such a strategic policy decision is quite high, it is unlikely to be borne at this juncture or even in the near future, owing to the intensifying competition of mutually exclusive claims on the scarce capital resources that can be truly reallocated without exacerbating already stringent bottlenecks. Furthermore, the agrarian labor force in many respects is *not* as malleable as it might appear at first sight, because it is dominated by the elderly and by women. Even if feasible, a redistribution of the labor force is essentially a one-shot affair. To have a lasting effect, it needs to be accompanied by other efforts to raise labor productivity. There is therefore a limit to what can be accomplished by drawing once again from the agricultural sector as the primary resource base.

In most countries, absorbing women or pensioners into the labor force might remove some of the restrictiveness of the labor supply that is presently being encountered. But it should be recalled that there are many other preferences in socialist societies than simply maximizing output. Thus social pressures may dissuade women from joining the labor force under some conditions. Similarly, owing to the well-entrenched socialist precepts of income distribution and the long-standing security associated with having completed a lifetime in the socialized production process, there are rather rigid limits to social mobilization. Current and prospective labor force pressures are on balance reducing the effective labor force. Higher educational requirements, concern about the welfare of young children, interest in lowering the work week, social pressures to lower the retirement age, and so on all militate against any significant increment in effective working hours becoming available in the production process in the foreseeable future.[1]

Matters are not very much more encouraging with other production factors, including land, natural resources, and especially capital. The vast USSR may still have room to expand its arable land, but such resources in most of Eastern Europe are fixed and perhaps already overworked. This may not prevent some countries (particularly Rumania in recent years) from eradicating established social and other infrastructures in the villages as a means of adding to its available arable resources. Significant results may be obtained in the short run. From the point of view of generating net additions to the effective service stream of such natural resources, however, the policy measures recently embraced appear to be a rather dubious way of generating lasting output gains. Although it would be rash to argue strongly against a further enlargement of the known natural resources of these countries, a cautious growth outlook would not place too much emphasis on the potential stimulus of new resource discoveries. Capital is the quintessential created factor of production. It is therefore necessary to explore in somewhat more detail what is likely to determine the future supply of capital to the material production process.

As argued in Chapter 3, Eastern Europe has gone through a period of "decapitalization" in the past decade or so. This has been one of the unintended consequences of the forced adjustment measures adopted in particular in the early 1980s. Decapitalization in the strict sense means that the stock of capital shrinks over time. What is of crucial importance in short- to medium-term considerations, however, is the economically useful stock of capital in the productive sphere. This has contracted in a number of Eastern European PEs for a variety of reasons: strictures placed on retiring obsolete plant and equipment; idling of plant and equipment for lack of maintenance, repair, and spare parts, which thus reduces the services that these assets can provide in the production process; severe constraints on net investment activity during the recent bout of externally induced adjustment policies; sluggish progress being attained with working off a still growing stock of projects in progress, some of which may never enter the effective production stream; and particularly the substantial capital "losses" deriving from cost shifts induced by changes in trade prices as well as shifts in domestic scarcities. There is therefore a very significant, and still growing, backlog demand for the renewal of existing production structures. It is true that the turbulence in investment activity stemmed chiefly from concerns about stabilizing the external payments situation and cutting aggregate domestic absorption, rather than from a sharp shift in aggregate savings behavior. The observed transformations in the level and composition of investments might therefore be temporary, although they are bound to have important implications for the medium-term production and growth potential.

External constraints have not been the only determinants of the continuing surge in investment requirements, however. This demand surge must therefore be seen in conjunction with other components of investment demand that have continued to rise in recent years. The evolution of the future demand for investment resources can be divided into (1) consumer-related services, including residential construction, education, social services, and various types of product services in the broad sense; (2) the easing of capacity constraints in transportation, energy generation, and raw material production; (3) the implementation of programs that foster factor productivity gains; (4) the enhancement of regional integration in the CMEA context; (5) the enhancement of the quality of life, including pollution control and environmental protection in a broad sense; and (6) more generally, the restructuring of output profiles quantitatively as well as qualitatively so as to strengthen the export base of these countries.

The claims on resources needed to start up new projects that may give rise directly as well as indirectly to measurable productivity gains have been steadily growing in recent years. In conjunction with the need of the PEs to improve the quality of output so as to become more competitive in international trade markets, the demand for investments in the material sphere has been steadily increasing. This has built up at a time of relatively low output growth, which has left little room for raising macroeconomic savings behavior.[2] Furthermore, it has had to compete with an even more rapidly expanding demand for capital resources, especially for infrastructure, including transportation and communication links, and sociocultural facilities in a broad sense, including housing and access to consumer service industries that have been traditionally neglected in socialist economic policies. Such "nonproductive" investments may in the end have very salutary effects, because they tend to enhance labor morale and to improve the environment within which production processes unfold and operate, and thus may lift productivity levels beyond what would otherwise have been feasible. But such benefits are unlikely to materialize overnight and, when they do, they provide chiefly a once-and-for-all shift. The outlook is therefore for an exceedingly paltry rise in the physical supply of capital funds particularly in the productive sphere. This would imply only a moderate recovery from the rather anemic investment experience of the early 1980s (see Chapter 3).

This not very promising outlook for the buoyancy of factor supply in the productive sphere provides only a one-sided view of what determines efficiency in an economy. It needs to be counterbalanced at the very least through reference to the room for maneuver that can be gained by modifying existing policy instruments and their supporting institutions. It is their eventual transformation that determines to some degree the effectiveness with which a given supply of inputs can be mobilized for productive purposes. The recent bout of externally induced adjustments has clearly underlined the limited reach of weak market-type signals in bringing about desirable structural changes through target shifts in the behavior of economic agents.

The instruments and institutions typical of the traditional CPE that were still at the disposal of central authorities in Eastern Europe during the recent crises were very useful. After the "reforms" of the 1960s and 1970s, they were evidently accessible to a smaller degree and could be activated only by exerting greater precaution so as to avert dysfunctional social reactions. When fully engaged, however, they were instrumental in quickly reversing the worrisome external imbalances and slashing domestic absorption to levels that could be sustained in the short term. As the backbone of the resilience of the PEs and the CMEA as a whole to domestic and external shocks, those CPE legacies have not so far lifted most of the PEs concerned out of the doldrums of slow growth, and they are probably not apt to surmount this congenital syndrome in the near future. The pace of aggregate economic growth may be stepped up prospectively with the given institutions and policies chiefly through the encouragement of external trade and financial flows, as was attempted by some PEs in the early 1970s. This will be examined in the next section. Alternatively, it can be greatly cushioned by selective and timely changes in the domestic economic mechanisms, which are studied in Section 12.4.

External development constraints

Under some circumstances, the domestic supply could evidently be augmented by attracting labor and capital from markets facing less stringent factor supply conditions. As discussed in Chapter 9, there is not likely to be great scope for a sharp increase in the volume of labor and capital that the PEs want to or can obtain from within the CMEA area so as to equilibrate relative factor scarcities throughout the region. The possibility of mobilizing additional resources need therefore be seen chiefly in non-CMEA markets. But the limits on incremental resource flows from outside the area are perhaps even more stringent, albeit to a different degree for each PE. Seen against their respective factor endowments, there are strong economic reasons to foster capital movements from West to East and labor movements the other way around. Labor migration is as a rule proscribed for the reasons discussed in Chapter 9. Capital inflows into Eastern Europe are not actively sought by global financial markets as a more or less stable component of a policy aimed at equalizing relative factor scarcities because of severe limitations on access to CMEA markets. Though it has recently been provided for in the modified joint venture laws of several CMEA countries, direct foreign investment is unlikely to take a quantum leap and thus maintain a buoyant pace of growth unless essential components of the decision-making mechanisms of these countries are restructured so as to render them more compatible with those typical of MEs. Although this may prevent the emergence of equity participation on any significant scale, some obstacles could be circumvented through the creation of various kinds of joint ventures.

The experience with joint ventures in Eastern Europe over the past fifteen years has not been very favorable for a number of reasons, some of which are touched upon in Section 12.5. This effectively delimits the narrow arena for capital inflows from third markets to various kinds of loan capital. Policy makers of the PEs are reluctant to encourage rapid capital inflows because growing CC debts might constrain their economic sovereignty to a dysfunctional degree, as events of the past few years have clearly demonstrated. This is not to say that the PEs will henceforth be completely averse to borrowing in world financial markets. Indeed the setbacks in the implementation of envisaged output and distribution targets incurred in 1985–1986 have to some degree been mitigated for now through new borrowing in Western markets on quite favorable terms. Moreover, individual countries face different self-imposed as well as external constraints. Thus the ability of Poland and Rumania to attract new capital is highly limited for reasons that are unique to these countries. The opportunities available to the GDR, Hungary, and the USSR are ampler, although policy makers may wish to minimize their external vulnerability. The latter's prospect has made Bulgaria and particularly Czechoslovakia apprehensive about taking up substantial loan capital. Borrowing abroad to bridge the present economic doldrums is not likely to provide more than a temporary escape valve unless economic mechanisms are modified to bolster the export potential of PEs or to make it attractive for foreigners to "invest" in the area. Under present circumstances, the PEs clearly prefer in particular so-called self-liquidating capital inflows because they can be dovetailed comprehensively with other proportions in the national economic plans. But this severely confines the scope for using Western financial resources for long-term growth purposes in the PEs.

Are the prospects for boosting merchandise trade better than those underlying factor mobility? On the strength of their resource endowment, the comparative advantage of the PEs will continue to move away from fuels, basic industrial materials, foodstuffs, and standard, labor-intensive manufactures in favor of processed products that already embody a considerable level of technological maturity. Clearly, the industrial sophistication and innovative potential of these countries is far from identical. Structural change along the basic guidelines emanating from comparative advantage indicators would therefore lead to a diversified production pattern. A shift in the gap from the present to a more desirable composition of exports is promising for the most developed members of the group. The GDR has recently made some changes in this direction, and Czechoslovakia might potentially do the same. But for the least developed CMEA members, such as Rumania, there is less scope for such transformations.

Because of the decision-making processes and organizational features typical of these economies, structural changes in response to or in anticipation of shifts in real comparative costs cannot emerge spontaneously, but have to be planned. This is one legacy of the long struggle between the "market" and "plan" in economic discourses. Some countries clearly still insist on "planned commodity–money relations," but others may in the end sway opinion sufficiently to provide room for indirect coordination instruments. A major dilemma arises here, for planned structural change can in the end succeed only if the authorities devolve some of the detailed prerogatives traditionally vested in a limited number of central decision makers. They therefore need to yield some measure of economic sovereignty with a view to enhancing the degree to which their economies can participate in the international division of labor. Opening up such communication channels may entail other transitions that some high-level policy makers still perceive to be inimical to the basics of a socialist society.

In addition to the overall external economic outlook, the conditions for CMEA cooperation in the medium term will be affected importantly by regional output constraints for basic materials, in the Soviet Union in particular, and by limitations on boosting export revenues from traditional manufactures – the backbone of the intragroup commodity exchange pattern in the postwar period. Because world demand is more exacting and subject to stiffer competition than demand in the CMEA, even more so after the transformations in both world and CMEA markets since the mid-1970s, it is more difficult to earn CC than to raise an equivalent TR amount at prevailing ERs. Recent experiences in East–West trade have demonstrated that these constraints are particularly pronounced on account of the competition provided by the NICs. Inability or unwillingness to accommodate to the demands prevailing in developed MEs is perhaps the key explanation for the declining market shares of PEs in Western Europe in contrast to what some developing countries have accomplished.[3] But the loss in market share could stem also from two other factors. First, supply problems in the PEs may have limited their ability to take advantage of ME demand developments. Second, it is difficult to identify this decline with a loss in inherent "competitive edge," given that the PEs are usually in disequilibrium. Furthermore, the ability of the NICs to capture a substantial share of the export market of manufactures is not indicative of the import needs of the vast majority of developing MEs, which may still mesh better with the real comparative advantage of the PEs than with the supply of the NICs as the latter is largely keyed to consumer demand in Japan and the United States. Nevertheless, restrictions of whatever nature in accessing markets in MEs compound the already substantial difficulties of shifting economic structures and trade patterns especially of the Eastern European PEs, unless major transformations take place in the regional cooperation and trading arrangements.

The CMEA area is not likely soon to become a homogeneous planning region in which members voluntarily redistribute value added in ways that parallel domestic redistribution policies, which have been at the very center of the individual socialist society and principal development strategy. Regional economic cohesion therefore needs to be solidified chiefly on the basis of the economic calculus. Even in cases where the countries decide to render development assistance or to promote factor transfers for other reasons than strict material gain, the economic calculus needs to be embraced much more vigorously so that the direct and indirect costs of political decisions can be placed in their proper perspective. More attention to the economic benefits and losses of macro- and microeconomic decisions may be achieved through various institutions. But their *chozrasčët* implications evidently cannot altogether be ignored, even if the CMEA members were to agree wholeheartedly on a measurable intensification of the scope and depth of plan coordination. At the very least, the economic calculus needs to be refined as a technical tool even to formulate the plans and certainly to ensure proper implementation throughout the planning process. As Nikolaj F. Fedorenko recently remarked, "even though there is a tradition of viewing planning primarily as the core of the management system, it makes sense to begin with problems of organization. The fact is that the functions of planning depend on the organization of management, and its methods depend on the economic mechanism" (Fedorenko 1984, p. 6). Such a proper use of the economic calculus would enable policy makers to distinguish more clearly between resource appropriation and output results, to weed out what is not up to par, and to foster those processes that are quite profitable either from a strictly economic point of view or, given the political preferences for relative self-sufficiency, from the raisons d'être of the integrating region.

What are the chances of boosting East–West trade ties? It is difficult to assess with any degree of confidence the possibilities that the PEs appear to have to boost their merchandise trade with developed and developing MEs. It is undoubtedly true that the PEs have to offer a wide range of products on an intermediate technological level that may well suit a variety of capital needs of the developing MEs. The latter in turn still have ample room to expand their exports of primary goods. At the same time, on the supply side the PEs are facing increasing competition from developing MEs, particularly the NICs, owing to their superior marketing abilities and financial acumen. Not only do these countries compete very aggressively for outlets in other developed as well as developing MEs, but they do not normally maintain buoyant trade ties with the PEs for economic and other reasons. But one of the prime deterrents is precisely that the planning environment is not particularly suited to the market-minded approach to economic growth and the profitability guidelines encouraged in these economies. The PEs have therefore but meager chances of partaking in that dynamic trade expansion, either as importer or as exporter, and need to counter the competition it provides in their traditional markets outside the CMEA. The developing MEs capable of measurably lifting their exports of foodstuffs and primary goods are now precisely the countries whose room for policy maneuver remains constrained for the foreseeable future, owing in part to their precarious external payments balance in the years ahead. In other words, those countries could sustain an inflow of capital goods only on credit terms, something that the PEs are not keenly interested in.

A "normalization" of trade between the developed MEs and the PEs is impeded by a variety of circumstances. Growing protectionism in these MEs on account of their parlous employment situation and much more intensive competition on the part of developing MEs, in the first instance the NICs, for outlets that the PEs would like to explore particularly in Western Europe hem in the potential demand for CMEA products in developed MEs. Though the demand for imports of manufactures from the PEs in advanced MEs is still marginal at best and the PE share in demand in MEs for most products remains trivial, it has already been subjected to various formal and informal quantitative restrictions (including in clothing, footwear, steel, and textiles). Furthermore, it is rather problematic whether the MEs will eventually tolerate a much bolder participation of the PEs in their markets on a "fair" basis.

A particularly important question in this respect is the easing of the present tensions in the overall framework of East–West economic cooperation. Systemic and other features of the Eastern European economies may hinder or slow down their integration with MEs. But there are also constraints arising from the limited ability of the PEs to exploit their comparative advantage in a range of semistandard manufactures of intermediate technological sophistication. Ingrained obstacles to proper quality control, inability to cater to consumer demand, relatively unsophisticated marketing and financing skills, and other determinants of success in the market place obviously restrain using trade dynamically. Also important are physical limits on the amounts of foodstuffs, fuels, and raw materials that these countries can divert to CC markets. Domestic capacity limitations place strict bounds on the potential exports of these countries. In addition, the developed MEs harbor political preferences that lead them to seek to diversify their procurements of key products to counteract recent price and quantum volatility, especially in energy markets. On the other hand, demand in the PEs for a range of products from MEs, involving primary goods and advanced production processes, continues to be very intensive and outstrips the supply of CC. Even with moderately flexible foreign borrowing facilities, the PEs will eventually encounter difficulties to finance such flows, unless the domestic supply of competitive exportables can be raised significantly.

If the foregoing analysis in a nutshell of the near-term growth conditions of the PEs within the CMEA context is correct, the conclusion is inescapable that extensive growth ambitions should be thrown overboard and replaced by a variety of policies and instruments that foster productivity growth. Accomplishing this may be placed very highly on the policy agenda of individual PEs, and some of them will undoubtedly reap considerable benefits in the years to come. Given the highly confined markets of all CMEA members, save perhaps the Soviet Union's, however, it is difficult to envision how a strong and lasting, self-sustaining boost to the pace of productivity growth might be engineered only on the basis of national productive and reproductive forces. Trade in general and economic intercourse within the context of the primary integrating region of these PEs in particular will have to be accorded special attention.

12.2 The current global economic environment and the planned economies

The recent global economic environment has sustained several important quasi-structural shifts, and more appear to be in the offing. Some of these have been simply in attitudes and concerns of key policy makers. Others have already yielded measurable changes in crucial decision-making parameters. Of particular importance has been the movement away from benign neglect of the global repercussions of domestically oriented fiscal and monetary policies in major participants in the global economy. The impacts on exchange and interest rates of the particular combination of the macroeconomic policy mix pursued by the United States in the early 1980s and the generally anti-inflationary policy stance maintained by other major developed countries stand out in this respect. Several important shifts in these policy precepts have surfaced since late 1985. At the economic summit in Tokyo in May 1986, these concerns culminated in a broad, if vague, agreement about policy coordination through mutual surveillance among the major industrial countries, particularly the so-called major seven (Canada, France, Germany, Italy, Japan, the United Kingdom, and the United States). As a result of this

more congenial attitude toward policy concertation and the major concrete actions enunciated in September 1985, and February and May
1986, nominal and real interest rates have declined by several points and
the misalignment in the ERs of major currencies has been narrowed
considerably, largely in an orderly fashion. A third important component
of the evolving global environment in recent months concerns the large
shifts in oil markets.

If these major trends can be sustained into the future and, as far as ERs
and interest rates are concerned, perhaps further improved, there is
hope for greater stability in global economic and financial affairs. From
them, also a positive influence would emanate for maintaining the international trading framework. With the new GATT round under way, they
may even help to extend this framework and reverse some of the more
glaring protectionist measures enunciated since the early 1970s. Are such
features of a renovated global environment apt to exert a positive influence on the PEs? Indeed might they change the fundamentals of the
medium- to long-term development picture drawn in Section 12.1?

The declines in interest rates and oil prices, and the realignment of ERs
are bound to benefit the CMEA countries with substantial CC debts or
with large CC oil import bills. This appraisal needs to be tempered by the
constatation that the crucial economic variables in PEs are not mainly
driven by the type of demand forces that make for a much more favorable outlook in the developed MEs, and to a lesser extent also in the
developing MEs, at this juncture of the troubled 1980s. For the PEs,
however, the shifts in the global environment may yield somewhat more
room for domestic and regional policy flexibility. This would ease the
need to maintain strict external surpluses even though they might considerably curtail short- and medium-term domestic growth opportunities.
Because these countries are only partially integrated in world trading and
financial markets, the benefits of substantial shifts in the latter affect the
PEs mainly indirectly, if at all. Especially important in this regard are the
favorable repercussions of the anticipated upswing in economic activity in
Western Europe on the external demand for Eastern European exports.

As far as the most important direct benefits of the oil price slide are
concerned, the recent changes in the global energy markets, if sustained,
are a two-edged sword for the CMEA members. Clearly, the net energy
exporters are bound to lose a considerable amount of export revenue in
their global markets. For the USSR, the loss in 1986 might range from $3
billion at $20 per barrel to $7 billion at $10 per barrel, provided 1985
quantities can be maintained, which is not at all assured.[4] The downward
slide of the dollar relative to European currencies, in which the bulk of
the East–West trade of the PEs is invoiced, can only exacerbate the negative impact of the terms-of-trade effect on the PEs. The net energy importers, on the other hand, can benefit only to the extent that they

procure their petroleum imports from world markets. CMEA energy prices will eventually decline too, but with considerable delays and at a pace that is very muted as compared to the transformations in world markets. Estimates are that in 1986 oil prices in the CMEA, in current dollar terms, may decline by perhaps 5 percent; in 1987, they might drop by 11 percent (assuming that the average WMP in 1986 declines by about 35 percent relative to 1985).

It is well known that the impact of the price and supply fluctuations in world energy markets since the mid-1970s on the PEs has had a different character from that experienced by most MEs. The net energy exporters undoubtedly benefited substantially in terms of current CC export revenues on account of both volume increases and favorable terms-of-trade movements. But the gains obtained from within the CMEA were much more gradual, far more muted as a result of the institutional and pricing provisions typical of CMEA relations, and in part offset by sizable surpluses in their overall TR payments that they had permitted a number of energy importers to run up in the second half of the 1970s (and Poland even more recently). These were allowed to emerge in spite of the continuing adherence in principle to the rather strict bilateral balancing of accounts on an annual basis within the CMEA. Furthermore, several PEs were able to divert oil imports produced at TR, usually after transformation, to CC markets at a substantial premium. The only major exception has been Rumania, which has not relied extensively on oil procurements from the CMEA and certainly not at conventional TR prices.

Now that world oil prices have dropped markedly, the situation is the reverse of the one that prevailed especially in the early 1980s. But there are several major differences. Whereas the net energy exporters started to partake in world trade in energy products in a major way only after the first oil price shock, and therefore initially gained relatively modestly in absolute terms from the price rise, they have recently depended to a very large extent on such CC earnings to finance a sizable share of imports. It is difficult to evaluate precisely what share of CC earnings can be attributed to petroleum and products for most European countries. For the USSR, however, this share in total exports to all MEs amounted to 68.4 percent in 1983 and to 65.5 percent in 1984; the corresponding data for oil and product exports to developed MEs were as high as 75.2 and 72.1 percent, respectively. These magnitudes signal a slight drop from the early 1980s, when the share was about four fifths. But it should be recalled that prices of other traded fuels usually move in tandem with petroleum prices. The overall dependence of the Soviet Union on CC earnings from fuel exports is therefore even larger than suggested here.

In the short run, the loss in CC revenues especially in the USSR can probably be offset by borrowing in financial markets, provided the climate for this remains ambient. Although the USSR can still borrow at favorable rates, a sustained decline in world oil prices in combination with a lackluster output performance in the USSR would adversely affect assessments of its short-term creditworthiness, and might complicate the external financing of its temporary payments deficits. On the other hand, the net importers of energy from within the CMEA do not stand to gain much in the short run from the drop in oil prices, because CMEA prices in 1986 are based on WMPs of 1981–1985. They could, in principle, divert a substantial component of their oil import demand toward world markets. But this is not likely to materialize soon, owing to the persisting tight external payments situation of the majority of these countries and the fact that the "real cost" of oil prices in TR is probably below the "real domestic cost" of earning CC for oil imports at WMPs exceeding roughly fifteen to twenty dollars per barrel.

Given the current socioeconomic situation of the majority of the Eastern European CPEs, the overriding policy concerns in the short run remain conditioned by the state of the CC current accounts of these countries; the importance of offsetting any major shortfalls, such as in agriculture, through imports; the need to correct the magnitude of intra-CMEA current account imbalances and, as already indicated, to work off the unusual and rather skewed accumulation of debt in TRs, which will have to be repaid soon, except perhaps in the case of Poland; and the unfavorable outlook for a speedy resumption of more expansive domestic input policies, owing to deep-rooted and sizable adjustment problems.

The current situation in world energy markets underlines, if ever a need there was, that the Soviet Union cannot indefinitely sustain its present trade policies. It may therefore agitate for significant shifts in intra-CMEA economic relations. These are likely to take the form of a further hardening in the goods that the USSR normally procures from CMEA partners, even if the local price in real terms were not to exceed the current CC price. If it were to do so, it would heighten the pressure on Eastern Europe to undertake meaningful structural changes. Recent shifts in global markets, then, may ease somewhat the short-term adjustment requirements of the PEs. But they neither change their nature or magnitude, nor do they by themselves justify in any way a more positive outlook for SEI. Emphasis on the latter does not, of course, entail advocacy of regional self-sufficiency per se. A resumption of relatively rapid growth in Eastern Europe is contingent on the availability of primary inputs. These can be acquired either from within the CMEA at conditions that are unique or from world markets. To engage in the latter, the PEs must earn the means to pay for such imports now or in a relatively near future, something that is not yet guaranteed. From a realistic point of view, then, there is no alternative to the PEs pursuing steady improvements in their productive structures so as to maintain reciprocal interest in the regional exchange of goods and services with only gradual modification in the traditional patterns of CMEA cooperation.

12.3 A feasible strategy for the next decade or so

The foregoing analysis suggests that the room for maneuver with regard to the formulation of concrete remedial policies in the individual countries is highly limited. But circumstances vary to some degree among the countries. The range of feasible alternatives is by and large bounded by prolonging the traditional pattern of CMEA commercial exchanges in the near term in conjunction with the simultaneous, though gradual, restructuring of the component economies in an effort to solidify the very foundations of SEI. For this to be feasible and to emerge in fact, the Eastern European PEs must make the main CMEA producer of hard goods, especially energy, sufficiently interested in upgrading its related production capacities, if necessary also by redirecting its trade from MEs to the CMEA.

As argued, the USSR cannot possibly forgo its CC revenues derived from liquid fuel exports without reshaping its import pattern in a dramatic way. In this connection, I find it nonetheless naive to pretend that there are absolutely no ways by which the Soviet Union could be persuaded to divert its exports of key products from MEs to the CMEA, provided that neither the real domestic production cost nor the external opportunity cost is ignored, as has so often been the case. The USSR, in my view, is at worst indifferent between acquiring identical goods from the nonsocialist area if cost conditions are invariant. In other words, if the Eastern European partners were prepared to pay current WMPs in CC or in equally "hard" goods, food being a particular case in point, the USSR would probably be amenable to rerouting a substantial component of most primary goods earmarked for MEs. The country may actually be prepared to pay a certain premium to acquire the goods from within its primary trading area rather than from MEs. But there must be a limit to the opportunity cost that the USSR is willing to take in stride in order to maintain and advance regional economic cohesion in the CMEA. Similarly, a certain proportion of goods now reserved for "fraternal" countries outside the traditional CMEA region (including Angola, Cuba, Kampuchea, Laos, and Vietnam) could be redirected to the CMEA only at a margin to be incurred by Eastern Europe, as there is a limit to the diversion of trade for strictly economic reasons. The precise magnitude of price concessions or protective taxes could usefully be made more explicit and transparent with a view to clarifying the microeconomic aspects of SEI to all concerned.

If this assessment is correct, it would seem to be erroneous to posit the inherent impossibility of a prolongation of the traditional trading patterns within the CMEA. If tackled as outlined in the preceding paragraphs, the outlook for more buoyant growth in Eastern Europe is not as bleak as suggested in some recent analyses that advance the trade diversion thesis: Essentially minimize CMEA commitments so as to intensify

East–West ties and thus gain access to competitive markets both as exporters and importers. In contrast to this scenario, I should like to propose an alternative that is fundamentally anchored to a reinforcement of SEI.

It is evidently a daunting exercise to forecast for the next decade or so with any degree of confidence. Nonetheless, when seen against the backdrop painted throughout this monograph and the review of more general crucial development conditions in these countries in the years ahead, the strategy that may raise the feasible pace of economic growth without kindling rather stringent internal and external imbalances now or in a more distant future would appear to consist of five principal layers. This structure is invariant to the type of economic reform that these countries may be willing to entertain in the near future. But if the objective of near-term economic policies is to foster a measurable increase in factor productivity and a nontrivial acceleration in the overall pace of output growth, the precise weights to be allotted to each of these layers, and indeed their concrete bearings on the macroeconomic policy outlook, are not invariant to the type of reform that may be in the offing. This issue is revisited in Section 12.4.

First, the PEs need to commit themselves with greater conviction and firmness to the encouragement of SEI so that the USSR as the main net supplier of key primary goods may be found willing to uphold, and thus "harden," the traditional security of supply from within the region. This could be accomplished initially by diverting potential exports from third markets to Eastern Europe. Conditions may improve to such an extent that the USSR might even be prepared to raise autonomously its export capacity of such hard goods at competitive prices or that the client partners may voluntarily choose to participate in the creation or cofinancing of incremental capacities.

Second, as a necessary corollary of the first proposition, the scope and depth of specialization in the production of manufactures need to be greatly enlarged (see Gavrilov and Sadovskij 1985). This is required simply to generate export possibilities. In addition, specialization is needed to modernize economic structures, particularly in industry. This would accelerate the production of high-quality goods, including those needed to meet the real future requirements of the USSR. Ideally, these two first sets of policy actions ought to be carefully intertwined, but measurable progress could be achieved in other configurations too.

Third, to buttress the modernization drive, specialization in manufactures in Eastern Europe needs to be harmoniously meshed with the selective acquisition of goods from the West that are not available, or not in sufficient quantities, from CMEA markets. This is particularly the case for the transfer of technology from developed MEs.

Fourth, all CMEA partners should exhibit a greater proclivity toward boosting regional production capacities of fuels and other primary and intermediate inputs that are crucial to utilizing available capacities as completely as physically advisable, particularly in industry. The benefit of the long-coveted "security of supply" may materialize only at an extra outlay simply to guarantee future output levels. The protective cost that may thus be implied must remain acceptable to all members involved and needs to be funded equitably. Otherwise, the PEs should explore more intensively alternative sources of supply, particularly in developing MEs.

Finally, the substitution of imports for domestic and regional production processes intensive in labor and primary goods needs to be vigorously promoted so that the PEs can gradually, but steadily, intensify their participation in the world economy and enable also developing MEs to step up their trade without greatly exacerbating their external payments difficulties.

One basic pillar of this overall concept of the direction in which the CMEA region could – and indeed should – be heading for concerns East–West exchanges. I am certainly not advocating that the PEs disengage themselves from Western markets simply to beef up their regional economic cooperation. To produce themselves the kind of manufactures required for modernization, including the efforts of the net exporter of fuels and raw materials, the Eastern European PEs must continue selectively to import technology and, in some cases, goods and services that cannot otherwise be procured. This hardening of the products offered may require even more CC imports than are already embodied at this time. Whether that share is already "too" high is a moot issue. Complaints of Eastern European observers that their present exports to the CMEA contain a substantial component of CC imports, and are therefore quite hard, may well rest on fact, but the very basis of that contention is hardly germane to the economics of intragroup transactions. The real issue is not the origin of these products but their cost relative to TR returns. Any misalignment in relative TR prices stemming from a different degree of hardness of reciprocal exports should indeed be rectified by shifts in policy instruments – relative prices in the first instance – rather than through administrative intervention.

In other words, the prime requirement of a more buoyant near-term growth pattern at an acceptable rate of expansion rests on finding ways and means of sustaining the exchange of the bulk of primary goods and fuels required by most participants against manufactures that most of them can produce with some degree of comparative advantage. At the same time, the underlying real cost structures for these primary goods need to be adequately reflected either in explicit prices or in terms of high-quality goods obtained from modernized manufacturing sectors in return. This is a demanding agenda and no easy way out of the implied dilemmas is at hand. To preserve the attractiveness of this very traditional pattern of regional trade within the CMEA, some countries need to enact measures that induce some producers to maintain output levels and, where possible, to raise them for strictly economic reasons. Thus, although the USSR might presently not be very keen on switching its actual and potential exports from developed MEs to Eastern Europe, the USSR's investment requirements are not quite such that the bill of goods cannot at all be filled by the Eastern European PEs even if this "investment participation" were to be placed on a strictly economic footing. Eastern Europe must come to grips more fully with the notion that the era of the easy exchange of below-standard manufactures for hard fuels and primary goods is a relic of a distant past and that the type of exchange they wedded themselves to in the postwar period cannot be further perpetuated.

Increasingly critical Eastern European commentators argue the following case. The USSR's predilections with respect to the organization of Eastern Europe played an instrumental role – in some cases it was pre-eminent – in the emergence of the typical Eastern European economic structures in the postwar period. In retrospect and with the present hindsight, that particular configuration has proved to be not very well suited to the resources and traditions of these countries. The *primus inter pares* is hence "blamed" for Eastern Europe's structural deficiencies. Two comments are warranted in this respect. First, Eastern European policy makers at the time were cognizant of the emerging gross bias toward extensive development; at the very least, they should have been! I suspect therefore that inept leadership there was at least of equal importance in framing a grid out of this traditional type of exchange, in viewing it increasingly as being permanent, and indeed in utilizing it as the foundation of extensive growth ambitions of their own. More important, however, is that ascribing historical blame as such is not very useful to overcome the prevailing growth obstacles and other deficiencies in the CMEA. The argument leading up to a plea for development assistance in reverse may be a useful reference point in political debates, but it is not likely to rectify what is structurally unsound in the CMEA. Second, similar comments apply to the observations frequently voiced that an acceleration of SEI would force Eastern Europe to cater largely to Soviet demands. As a result, Eastern Europe would thus be forced to ignore world market standards and their rapid development. This may certainly be a valid argument when placed in the context of the area's relative isolation of the 1950s and 1960s. It is probably not an acute issue now that the demand for advanced technological products can be, and is partly being, satisfied through CC imports.

The proposal advocated here involves a quadrilateral exchange: intensified relations within Eastern Europe, strengthening of the traditional ties between Eastern Europe and the USSR, and more comprehensive exploitation of relations with the developed and the developing MEs on the basis of real comparative advantage indicators. The reason why I am advocating this type of medium- to long-term strategy is relatively straightforward. The PEs can realistically hope to compete effectively with the advanced MEs in terms of technological sophistication, marketing skills, and financial facilities only after profound alterations in their present and near-term economic situation. At this stage, most PEs have one decisive advantage: a relatively cheap, well-disciplined, rather highly skilled labor force that cannot migrate. But Eastern European labor may need further incentives to capitalize on its innate qualifications. Current production technologies in Eastern Europe may well fail to be close enough to the cutting edge of the knowledge frontier to outcompete most MEs in the foreseeable future in their own markets. But I contend that the main producer of hard primary goods and fuel carriers does not have a compelling need to import invariably products and processes that embody the most advanced technology from MEs. A significant proportion of its "appropriate" technological requirements could thus be filled at a lower cost from "fraternal" countries if the latter were left no alternative but to pursue positive structural adjustment to accommodate real economic integration.

This does not mean that I am advocating regional self-sufficiency at any cost. A resumption of relatively rapid economic growth in Eastern Europe is contingent on the availability of economically warranted levels of primary inputs. These can be acquired either from within the primary trading region at conditions that are unique or from world markets at prevailing conditions, including whatever real trade discrimination may still hamper this interbloc exchange. To choose the latter road, the PEs must be in a position to earn the means to pay for such imports now or in a relatively near future. Such conditions are not yet guaranteed and hence need to be supported prospectively. There would therefore not seem to be any alternative under realistic conditions to the PEs pursuing steady improvements in their productive structures so as to support reciprocally the traditional patterns of CMEA economic cooperation.

12.4 Feasible domestic economic reforms

There are various ways in which the above agenda can be implemented. Especially as regards the promotion of intragroup ties, traditional central planning may well succeed in lifting output levels, in improving the quality and range of products, and in fostering greater specialization in manufactures. Whether it will also be capable of generating goods of sufficiently high quality that can hold their ground in world markets, sustain production in quantities adequate to support steady revenue gains, and place these goods on markets abroad with a degree of marketing and financial flexibility typical of the ME environment, are different matters, however. To strengthen the very basis of SEI and to exploit CC exports at the same time, the PEs need to embrace shifts in their economic mechanisms to dovetail decision making; to let agents react to demand and supply forces as they perceive them and on the basis of unambiguous, sufficiently accurate criteria of choice; and to regulate all this macroeconomically so that agents at the lower rungs of the planning hierarchy do not lose sight of basic socialist precepts and central planners can maintain the desired strategic growth momentum in the medium to long run (see, for instance, Abalkin 1985; Evstigneev 1986; Fedorenko 1984; Matlin 1985).

As argued in Chapter 3, the PEs need to put in place a positive structural adjustment policy to foster productivity growth. Whether this is accomplished through central planning or not amounts to one set of very important issues. The other side of the coin is that any renovation requires considerable capital commitments in the years to come. A crucial component of any positive adjustment policy is the rational exploitation of the room for maneuver as regards economic structures embedded in investment requirements, opportunities, and overall appropriations. Decapitalization in Poland since the late 1970s, although admittedly extreme,[5] is by no means unique especially if official capital and investment data of PEs are corrected for a number of statistical problems[6] and the full requirements of broad sectors in the material as well as the nonmaterial spheres are taken as crucial delimiters.

Current policy concerns in Poland may nevertheless help to focus attention on the more general aspects of the problem. Though a renewal of the economic structures requires investment and the country is now able to muster more funds than it could in recent years, the flexibility that Poland will have in the second half of the 1980s is subject to several constraints. The first and foremost is on the latitude for maneuver in the volume of savings. There is little hope presently of raising significantly the share of net capital formation in aggregate output without jeopardizing present consumption levels or the external balance (Krauss 1985, p. 3). The second constraint emerges from the funds tied up in incomplete projects that were started in earlier years and are still deemed to be worthwhile from an economic point of view. The latter criterion is presumably that the return that can be achieved by appropriating the incremental capital sums required to finish up the projects, when appropriately discounted, is positive and exceeds the yield on projects yet to be initiated. But, as recently noted, "these investment projects are becoming increasingly obsolete as time passes" (Krauss 1985, p. 3). It is therefore necessary to complete them now or to scrap them altogether. Present requirements to bring such "worthwhile" ongoing projects into the production stream are estimated to amount to as much as one third of total available funds in 1986–1990 and about 85 percent of the funds earmarked for 1986–1987! A third crucial constraint emerges from decapitalization in its strict economic sense. Over the past several years, particularly since 1980, the production facilities routinely "consumed" in the course of the normal utilization of buildings, machinery, equipment, and so forth, have not been replaced or properly maintained in good working order for lack of funds. Checking the process of decapitalization in combination with commissioning still worthwhile ongoing projects is estimated to require more than three fourths of the capital fund earmarked for the current five-year plan. There is therefore little flexibility left beyond, as Krauss puts it, what has already been "administratively captured." A far-ranging restructuring of the economy will hence not be possible until the next five-year plan cycle in the 1990s. However, this rather bleak picture deserves a counterweight at the least.

Whereas policy makers may have few options about a radical restructuring of their economies at this point in time, there is considerable room for the rational planning of capital replacement investments, for speeding up the investment process, for ensuring the optimal use of existing production facilities, for properly maintaining available facilities, and for reappropriating existing facilities to the extent that productive capacity is fungible at all. As Krzysztof Krauss notes, these goals could be pursued most appropriately by "indirect management methods" rather than through the centralization of funds.

As argued in Section 12.1, there is little hope for accelerating the pace of aggregate growth on the strength of factor availability. Nor is the mileage attainable from factor redistribution, including of capital spending, very considerable. As matters stand, it will be very difficult in fact to slow down the redistribution already required by a variety of social and other commitments that the leadership of most PEs has continued to emphasize in the past fifteen years, although recently in a much more nuanced format. It is doubtful that the adverse impact of unfulfilled expectations on effective factor availability for the production process can be reversed soon. The only way out, then, is through gradual change in the room for maneuver. This can be enlarged by steadily improving economic performance possibly as a result of altering the conventional methods for carrying out economic policies, which themselves could usefully be revamped.

The recent attempts in a number of PEs, particularly the USSR, to boost productivity by insisting upon greater discipline on the shop floor, antialcohol abuse measures, cutting out slack, mobilizing reserves, countering inappropriate use of resources and shirking, adhering better to preset schedules for delivery of materials and new production facilities, and so on, may have a very salutary effect even in terms of output growth for a while. Such an aggregate "Gorbačёv effect," however, provides essentially a temporary lift unless it is accompanied by other, lasting productivity incentives for the labor force. There may be various ways in which such material and other incentives can be implanted. But, in my view, most critically hinge on shifts in the "economic mechanisms."

The economic mechanism essentially consists of (1) the procedures for planning production and investments, (2) the allocation of goods through the channels of material supply and interenterprise contacts, (3) the performance indicators by which the activities of enterprises, associations, and ministries are evaluated, (4) the incentives to managers and workers to strive for good performance, (5) the financial flows accompanying the movement and use of resources, and (6) the prices at which goods and services are valued. Clearly, the economic mechanism as defined here is only one aspect of the "economic system," which includes, in addition, the arrangements for the ownership of the means of production and the organizational structure to administer and conduct economic activity.[7]

Of the policy instruments and supporting institutions discussed here, several would appear to offer some chance for sensitizing the development environment to factor productivity growth. Some of the requirements are necessarily contingent on changes in the regional organization of the PEs and depend essentially on what is likely to occur in the East–West economic environment. These issues are discussed in the next two sections. Looking at the individual PE, the most important levers to be activated are wholesale prices, anchoring wholesale prices to trade prices, effective ERs, interest rates, wage compensation according to performance, a much more active consumer price policy, greater parametrization of the economy as a whole according to social profitability criteria, and more active credit policies. Prices that accurately reflect real economic scarcities so as "to orient producers in the development of production and consumers in resource conservation" (Fedorenko 1984, p. 10) are the most critical of the various levers that need to be thoroughly reviewed (Zsolnai and Gavrilov 1985). Perhaps of the utmost importance would be the gradual institutionalization of "rule certainty" for all economic agents. By this I mean that the room for decision making needs to be unambiguously delineated and that the declared rules of the game are fashioned in such a way that economic agents can act upon them in their own interest. Capricious injunctions on the part of central planners or political leaders should be banned.

Clearly, it would be foolhardy to advocate a greater parametrization of the PEs' economic environment without at the same time addressing the need to transform domestic and regional institutions. Of the institutions to be remodeled in each PE, the planning center is of prime importance. Medium- to long-term structural policy issues should become the primary concern of each planning center. That includes topics such as income distribution, aggregate savings and investment, the nonmaterial sphere, the productive infrastructure, and especially the evolving situation of the economy. Most other decisions can be reached at the enterprise level under macroeconomic guidance, including income, monetary, and fiscal policies. In this connection, it would also be crucial to foster greater competition if not within each economy, owing to the highly concentrated nature of production in most of the smaller economies, at least among CMEA members and, where possible, also among enterprises belonging to MEs. Trade guidance can be provided through indirect instruments, including an effective tariff policy, the abolition of widespread nonparametric subsidies and taxes that buffer domestic from foreign prices, and an active ER policy.

I am not advocating in this connection the establishment of convertibility soon. A highly limited form of ex post settlement of imbalances in CC or a modified EFC could be realized, but it would not necessarily enhance the development opportunities of the countries under discussion. Certainly, a convertible forint, for example, might provide an important psychological fillip to Hungary's standing in international financial markets and improve its rating by Western commercial banks. Whether such convertibility with all its necessary restrictions would soon induce greater rationalization of the PE remains to be seen, however. The likelihood of meaningful convertibility being created in any other PE is even dimmer.

How likely is it that some of the modifications advocated here will be realized soon? Given the uncertainty created by M. Gorbačëv's reportedly highly dynamic and cost-conscious leadership, it would not appear to be too far-fetched to claim that some of these "reforms" are likely to emerge, although perhaps piecemeal rather than in a radical format. A telltale sign of the "changing mood" was recently evoked by V. Syčëv, otherwise a most cautious participant in the integration debate. In an interview preceding the fortieth CMEA Session (Warsaw, June 1985), he argued that

The question of perfecting the mechanism of cooperation within the framework of the CMEA is a very important one. It is necessary, and this was stressed at the [June 1984 summit], for the mechanism to be more active, to respond to the task of the [ISDL] and raising its efficiency, organically combining cooperation in [planning] with the active utilization of commodity–money relations, in order to perfect an active system for price formation in mutual trade, as well as instruments for [CC] and financial cooperation. Work on these questions is now actively taking place in the CMEA (Syčëv 1985, p. 8).

12.5 Feasible regional economic reforms within the CMEA area

Although most PEs have experienced substantial – in some cases, critical – adjustment problems since the mid-1970s, the CMEA institutions, policies, and policy instruments have on the whole remained intact. This is paradoxical, for some of the key foreign sector problems stemmed at least in part from the special features of the CMEA trade and financial regimes. Although some modifications could have been enacted, the chances for a complete or partial overhaul of the SEI mechanism (see Chapter 2) were mostly ignored. The outlook for substantive changes in the near future is not very encouraging. The various kinds of dichotomies attributable to there being two "world" markets, therefore, remain crucial to a better comprehension of the feasibility of introducing structural and institutional changes in Eastern Europe.

It is almost self-evident that any meaningful shift in the economic mechanism or development strategy aimed at improving factor productivity growth, save under strict coercion, in individual PEs will have to rely, at least partly, on indirect coordination instruments and supporting institutions (see, for instance, Bakoveckij and Grinev 1985; Bogomolov 1985, pp. 92–93; Dimova 1986). Some undoubtedly depend in the first instance on domestic policy measures. But others hinge prominently on what materializes in the foreign economic relations of these countries. This is especially important for countries that depend for a substantial proportion of their aggregate national output on economic relations with partners that do not directly support such reforms. Thus, a PE in isolation may seek to restructure its prices and possibly bring them in line with WMPs. In others, however, trade prices and ERs do not even approximately reflect the terms on which alternatives are effectively offered, and goods and services can be procured. Because of the importance of CMEA partners to the reforming PE, the latter needs to erect formidable buffers to neutralize the effects of these unsympathetic forces on the macroeconomic level and thus prevent detracting the reform movement. For example, if prices are to be used effectively in decentralized decision making, the pricing authorities need to institute offsetting taxes and subsidies to bridge the gap between CMEA and world prices. This can be accommodated to some degree for some goods, given the rather different commodity composition of CMEA and East–West trade, and that enterprises frequently operate for "different" markets. It is doubtful, however, that any PE could come up with a comprehensive set of buffers to bridge the dysfunctional impact of the CMEA's present obstacles in that respect. Nor would it be desirable for enterprises to act upon different rules and incentives, especially when policy makers are molding, possibly major, adjustment efforts to improve overall factor productivity. The only exception is perhaps the highly centralized decision making in the GDR's *Kombinate*.

Even more important are indirect coordination instruments and supporting institutions over which the economy in isolation has little control. Thus, the emergence of multilateralism, transferability, and convertibility depends in large measure on there being key trading partners that pursue the same course towards the institutionalization of such a policy framework and to whom a substantial component of foreign economic intercourse may be relocated. Likewise, market-type decision making depends importantly on the availability of foreign exchange reserves for a variety of purposes. Engaging such funds from one region, say, Western financial markets, directly or indirectly to acquire goods and services from the "odd" partner group is not very attractive if it may impair the borrower's ability to secure sufficient future funds to repay the loan. Similarly, participation in a worldwide IMS that ignores major trading partners cannot but bestow only partial benefits.

Reforms of the CMEA as an institution meant to foster SEI could englobe three overlapping types of issues. One set concerns the ability to reach basic decisions, and therefore involves high-level bodies such as the summit, the CCS in charge of economic affairs, the Executive Committee and its subcommittees, and the Council Session. It might also affect the jurisdiction of the Secretariat, although this matter appears to resort more appropriately under the second set of issues. It concerns in particular the delegation of authority from the highest decision-making tiers to the executive and secretarial levels. Finally, CMEA reforms may be approached from without by following up on measures undertaken in one or more key members. This would essentially amount to making the entire, formal as well as informal, CMEA bureaucracy more effective.

Starting with the eventuality of renewing the CMEA organization from within, since the ascent of Michail S. Gorbačëv a new wind has undeniably been blowing through the CMEA corridors. His scathing remarks on the "armchair administration" exercised by the CMEA organs and adhered to in most policy meetings included in his address to the Twenty-seventh Congress of the USSR's CP in February 1986 (see Gorbačëv 1986, p. 104) can hardly be interpreted otherwise. When seen in conjunction with the increasingly critical comments on the CMEA's operations made in recent years by a number of high-level officials also of other PEs, at first sight, there would appear to be considerable room for optimism regarding, possibly fundamental, changes in the CMEA's organization and operations. There is certainly something to be said for this interpretation, but recall that the several attempts at reforming the CMEA from within and from without launched during the nearly forty years of the CMEA's existence, particularly since the late 1950s, have thus far led to comparatively trivial results at best.

These endeavors have taken on various forms, ranging from simple changes in the organizatinal makeup of the CMEA to successively more ambitious and lengthy draft policy documents. The former have indeed entailed measurable progress but only when confined to very concrete projects in the microeconomic sphere (such as in the case of the existing joint enterprises). The latter have not altogether been without a measure of success, especially as concerns cooperation on detailed projects that affect supplies and transaction terms for critical industrial materials. The PEs have also experimented with changing the CMEA from within by altering, for example, the stifling unanimity provisions or by coaching the Standing Commissions into binding agreements. Let us look at the critical role of the unanimity rule in CMEA affairs.

Endeavors to change the CMEA were on the policy agenda throughout most of the 1970s, even though *Integration Program* had stipulated that the CMEA as an organ designed to galvanize the movement towards SEI would remain unchanged for the next fifteen to twenty years. This was especially prevalent after the calamitous changeover from the market outlook of the early 1970s to the post-1974 emphasis on various types of plan coordination and joint planning. Rumors to the effect that major changes in the CMEA's charter and the procedures and methods of the various CMEA agencies were to be on the forthcoming Session's agenda surfaced repeatedly in the discussions around several meetings of the Council Session held during the second half of the 1970s. They allegedly, once again, led to major opposition on the part of Rumania chiefly because the replacement of the sacrosanct unanimity principle with majority decison making was said to be the centerpiece of the proposed revision. These rumors were particularly persistent at the time of the thirty-second Council Session, which apparently debated a draft of the charter's changes and of modifications in procedures and methods that had been in preparation at least since 1975. The communiqué of that Session (see *Ėkonomičeskaja gazeta*, 1978:28, p. 13) indeed states that agreement had been reached on such a document.[8]

The precise bearing of this document, which was not released at the time and is not included in any of the official and quasi-official compendia of CMEA documents, has remained in doubt. L. Štrougal at the time endorsed the draft principles but he called upon the Executive Committee to provide the concrete follow-up (see Bratislava's *Pravda*, 29 June 1978, p. 6). M. Mănescu, however, asserted at the end of the meeting that "it is not necessary to modify CMEA's rules and its other basic normative documents" (*Agerpress*, 29 June 1978; Stancu 1978, p. 26). On the basis of this and other evidence, I concluded at the time (Brabant 1980, pp. 216–18) that another failure had been registered. The Rumanians apparently succeeded in enshrining in the document itself a number of their reservations with respect to "undertakings," the role of the CMEA in international agreements, the delegation of functions to the CMEA, and the harmonization of policy stances vis-à-vis third countries or other international organizations (Uschakow 1983a, p. 175).

The aforementioned document has recently been published (Uschakow 1983a, pp. 164–80).[9] In another contribution (Uschakow 1983b, p. 199), the compiler has interpreted it as having entailed major changes in fact as well as in articles IV,3 and IV,4 of the CMEA charter. As discussed, the latter certainly does not obviously amount to a major change[10] for countries that are not keen on participating in a particular project can still declare their interest and then stall implementation from within. Furthermore, the unanimity rule remains in effect officially as well as in practice, in spite of a streamlining of the interestedness principle in the charter's revision – most recently in June 1979 (Vel'jaminov 1986). Understandings and concertations are useful "modifiers" of the CMEA's traditional action instruments comprising recommendations and decisions on organizational matters. They certainly are not additional to the latter two, as suggested in Uschakow 1983b, p. 199. Given that they are essentially taken by the member countries, understandings and concertations are far from revolutionary. They do not really empower the Secretariat with a great deal of discretion on what should be vital SEI issues. Because this document may still be on the CMEA debating table, it might be indicative of things to come under the new Soviet leadership. It may therefore be instructive to examine briefly its portent and see whether, if indeed fully agreed upon and implemented in the CMEA, it might amount to a "quiet revolution," perhaps without this being as yet adequately reflected in the organization's constitution.

The document consists essentially of two parts. It first presents a broad declaration on the shortcomings in the organization, decision-making procedures, and implementation modalities of the CMEA. The second part has five substantive components that deal respectively with (1) priorities of CMEA organs and improvements in the planning of their activities; (2) speeding up of the examination and decision about questions submitted to CMEA organs; (3) ascertaining the implementation of agreements reached by CMEA organs and of the protocols worked out on their basis; (4) ensuring the general steering of the activities of the IEOs by the CMEA and increasing the effectiveness of its deliberations; and (5) improving the organization of cooperation in the CMEA with respect to third countries and international organizations, and the cooperation of the CMEA with these countries and organizations.

The document is a very broad statement on how to improve the role of the Secretariat and its subsidiary organs; how to hand over concrete responsibilities of agreed upon assignments or programs to the various organs, especially the Council Committees, Standing Commissions, and the IEOs; how to delegate authority to the CMEA organs; and how these organs should organize themselves better so as to ensure swift implementation of decisions worked out by the legislative bodies, to improve the functioning of these organs, and to become more efficient and effective. In not one single instance did the members agree on concrete measures. The document is strewn with "shoulds" and "coulds," but not even a timetable is set for any of the concrete follow-up suggestions. Furthermore, the reservations of Rumania enshrined in the document cast doubt as to the degree to which the CMEA's charter could be affected by *Basic Directions.*

In this interpretation, the 1978 protocol amounts essentially to another failed attempt to inspire the CMEA into more productive and effective work with a view to prompting SEI. The CMEA therefore continues to function broadly as it was created in early 1949. There have admittedly been a number of extensions in breadth and in depth together with the organizational expansion of the official and other CMEA organs (see Chapter 2). But as experience has amply documented, the results obtained have been rather disappointing. It would therefore seem advisable to maintain a healthy degree of skepticism as to the transformations that may emanate in the near future from within the CMEA.

Although there is only weak ground for optimism as regards the renovation of the "SEI mechanism" from within the CMEA organization, the possibilities of achieving measurable progress towards the same result by a different route appear to be more promising. This is especially true regarding the potential response to the "ambiance" engendered by the ongoing groundswell of shifts in economic policies, instruments, and institutions at the grass roots, and even more so in reflection of those that may be in the offing. There are two broad reasons for this position. First, the reforms since the 1960s have demonstrated the strict limits to what a small PE can accomplish by itself. Not only does such a small country need a "favorable environment" for its reforms to take off, but it also stands to gain considerably from having syncretic support from and a favorable resonance in main partners, particularly if the latter's importance is slated to grow sharply. Admittedly, these conditions were not completely ignored in the past reforms. But two reasons may have been at the core of a lack of response in the CMEA. The reforms of the various PEs came at a time when the CMEA was passing through a major political and economic malaise engendered by the rather astounding failure of *Basic Principles* to act as a major guideline of SEI in the 1960s. Furthermore, the reform experiments were essentially formulated in isolation and in response chiefly to domestic priorities. They therefore germinated in isolation, largely in view of local conditions and development concerns, although their fate was in the end decided by rather crude, peremptory political interference. These circumstances are in my view not present at this juncture. The recent external adjustment measures and the lingering, domestic as well as external, adjustment desiderata act as the common lever that may sway those countries into adopting bolder reforms in a dovetailed manner.

The second explanation of why the current environment may be more receptive to sympathetic reform experimentation and constructive feedbacks throughout Eastern Europe hinges on a critical feature of the reforms of the 1960s. It is related to the last point mentioned, but it deserves separate treatment. Unlike in the early 1960s, when the USSR was recovering from the 1957 administrative reorganization and the replacement of Chruščëv in late 1964, the current Soviet leadership appears to be seriously preoccupied with how to surmount lethargic, if presently not flagging, output growth and how to rectify a number of economic ills. I am not arguing that the USSR may soon embrace a transition mechanism to a market-type socialist environment. But it is arguably less likely to oppose such systemic experimentation and the exploration of indirect coordination instruments throughout the European CMEA. Similarly, to improve the quality and range of output in Eastern Europe without measurably weakening the economic potential of the CMEA region in the short to medium run, the USSR will need to show greater concern and flexibility and thus be more accommodating with respect to the future organization of production and distribution in the CMEA.

In this connection, it may be useful to revive the notion of an Eastern European common market consisting of at least two distinct tiers: the smaller PEs and the latter's relations with the USSR.[11] Under some conditions, however, it might even be constructive to entertain a further disaggregation with the more developed Central European[12] PEs (say, Czechoslovakia, the GDR, and Hungary) pursuing a slightly more integrative course than Bulgaria, Rumania, and, indeed, Poland,[13] whose economic problems of the early 1980s are bound to bear importantly on what may be feasible in the near future. The emergence of such partial integration schemes would depend critically on the USSR's attitude towards SEI. These various integration tiers need to be synchronized, possibly in analogy with the role of Benelux in the early stages of the EC or of the erstwhile "currency snake" countries in the EMS. That is, PEs that desire to move ahead with broad-based integration faster than the pace contemplated by other partners should not be inhibited from doing so, provided their activities do not prejudice in a major way the interests of the other integrating partners.

On purely economic grounds there would seem to be ample justification for such a decentralized approach to SEI. On the one hand, the commodity composition of Eastern Europe's trade differs measurably from the Soviet Union's, and the former is indeed compelled to seek much greater intraproduct specialization particularly in manufacturing activities. On the other hand, the smaller PEs are generally more favorably predisposed towards decentralized decision making, owing in part to their trade dependence, level of development, and industrial maturity. This is certainly the case for some of the countries of the highest integration tier. Finally, the growth intensification strategy that these countries have endeavored to nurse along since the late 1960s depends critically on the all-around improvement of the level and composition of their trade, not only with the CMEA but with all countries. However, their "natural" competitiveness in certain branches would appear to argue strongly for intensifying in the first instance their reciprocal economic and financial relations.

The foregoing arguments run conspicuously counter to one strand of recent Western economic thought on the future of SEI. Marie Lavigne, for example, has argued in several instances (see Lavigne 1983, 1984) that regaining a more rapid pace of growth in Eastern Europe depends critically on forging trade relations with the West and the Soviet Union.[14] Others have emphasized the paramount importance of fostering ties with European MEs. If it were true that Eastern Europe can pursue serious measures to enhance productivity growth only if cooperation primarily with the developed MEs is sharply intensified, the outlook for rapid economic expansion in the region would be very bleak indeed.

If the PEs were in a position to divert their trade to the West without incurring severe balance-of-payments problems, they would have re-aligned their foreign commerce long ago, there would be no malaise in the CMEA, and the outlook for relatively rapid economic expansion in the region would be more encouraging. It is precisely because of the sharp dichotomy between the fairly insular CMEA region and the keen competition that prevails in developed MEs that a sharp and substantial switch in trade from Eastern to Western markets is simply not feasible in the foreseeable future. Because ensuring steady increases in per capita national output levels provides one of the prime legitimations of the political regime of a socialist economy, an alternative to the present moderate growth expansion needs to be activated soon. It can be based neither on domestic demand and supply nor primarily on an expansion of economic and financial ties with the West. The fundamental dilemma for the PE leadership is that modernization of these economies is an urgent necessity, if these countries wish to stave off falling further behind other countries. But this cannot be based on extensive cooperation with the West or on Western resources. Yet modernization without active links with the West is unthinkable (Hardi 1986, p. 389). There then does not appear to be a realistic alternative to fostering SEI with great determination. That, I submit, is precisely the lesson of the June 1984 CMEA economic summit and one central guideline underlying the recent policy discussions, including those at the CP congresses of early 1986: to commit the PEs to a broad-based search for such an alternative economic structure in order to restore more buoyant growth.

The question of how to shape SEI therefore remains on the agenda. For SEI to become a strategic force in the design and implementation of revamped development policies, the PEs need to put in place bold initiatives that can simultaneously expand the regional supply of basic industrial inputs and more effective specialization in manufactures that are, or will soon be, competitive in world markets. Such an industrial restructuring could be hardened in regional trade, nursed along within the protected regional shelter, and then gradually upgraded to bolster Eastern Europe's capacity to earn CC.

12.6 Policy implications and impact on East–West relations

There are a host of geopolitical and reform deterrents associated with being a CMEA member. But there are other good reasons why Eastern European leaders are unlikely to choose radical economic reforms that must hinge on a relative disengagement from the CMEA in the near term. One set of deterrents stems from the geopolitical and reform barriers associated with being a CMEA member. Policy makers are likely to test on an experimental basis the trade-offs between economic benefits of further integrating themselves within the global commercial and financial fabric and the costs of becoming too dependent on forces completely beyond their control. But they are likely to do so gingerly over time. The gap between the precepts of socialism per se and economic rationality needs to be narrowed to a point where socialist policy makers can state explicitly their ideological preferences. Once set, it would enable them to zero in on creating greater scope for the pursuit of economic rationality on the basis of firm rules governed by suitable, and credible, macroeconomic policies. This was the principal motivation for the analysis of key aspects of monetary cooperation presented in Part II.

Though I have serious reservations about the realism of any policy advice that posits a direct and incontrovertible trade-off between SEI and East–West trade, or suggestions that the future of the PEs lies unassailably in a sharp expansion of East–West ties, as noted, the route advocated here has clear-cut implications for East–West trade. The propositions presuppose from the outset a proclivity for measurably raising the level of commercial and financial interactions between the two trading blocs. Not only would the pace of expansion advocated here fall considerably short of that endorsed by many observers, it would serve quite different goals. Commercial and financial links between East and West would be blended much more harmoniously with the development course of the PEs themselves as well as with the possibly staggered acceleration of SEI in the CMEA context as a whole or with reference to several integration tiers.

The most important commercial and financial partners of the PEs outside their primary trading region are the developed MEs in Western Europe, chiefly the EC members. Though relations between the EC and the CMEA are by necessity laden with political overtones, one can build up a case for the reciprocal recognition of and the "normalization" of relations between these two groups at least on economic grounds. As argued earlier, different factor endowments in the developed MEs and the PEs provide a prima facie argument for the transfer of resources from West to East. Failing such a boost on account of political and other obstacles, the apparent economic room for factor mobility could be filled in part by a sharp expansion of trade in goods and some services. This would benefit both groups of countries. For the MEs, this could provide an additional stimulus to outside demand and thus help to shore up their flagging growth performance of the past decade or so. For the East, a measurable expansion of trading relations with the MEs would be the funnel to prop up the technical sophistication and marketing know-how that the PEs so desperately need to pursue a meaningful positive adjustment policy as sketched earlier. A more formalized approach to cooperation between the two economic blocs might provide a useful start. Such a regularization of economic and financial ties appears to require first a measurable change in political attitudes and diplomatic goodwill. A broad, even if vague political framework agreement of mutual recognition could open the way for the PEs to negotiate individually, possibly even separately, with the EC. This is especially important because the Commission of the EC is the sole arbiter of external trade negotiations, and it can also exert a measurable influence on financial relations with outside markets. A more formalized approach to cooperation between the two economic blocs might therefore provide a useful start.

For a very long time, the EC's existence was all but ignored by the PEs, because they regarded market integration essentially as another means to amass greater monopoly power under capitalist conditions so as to exploit labor. Furthermore, though the EC obtained the power eventually to take charge of all foreign trade regulations also with nonmember countries, when this came into force virtually all EC members had bilateral agreements with the PEs that could not be abrogated. But these agreements ran out at the end of 1974 at the latest. Owing to the refusal of the PEs to negotiate with the EC on a country-by-country basis, trade relations between the two European blocs since 1974 have developed essentially without there being a set of framework trade and payments agreements.

Given the then imminent transfer of treaty-making power from the member countries to the Commission of the EC, the PEs gradually began to change their attitude vis-à-vis the role and function of the EC, starting in the early 1970s. A landmark shift was launched when Brežnev on 20 March 1972 declared for the first time ever that the "USSR does not at all ignore the real situation in Western Europe, including also the existence of an economic grouping of capitalist countries such as the [EC]."[15] He went on to call for the reciprocal recognition of the two economic blocs, a gambit to which the EC Commission reacted positively in late 1972. Ever since then, negotiations about reciprocal recognition have been on and off, with the main stumbling block to date remaining the EC Commission's contention that the CMEA does not have the power to negotiate concretely about the real trading interests of its members, and that there is therefore no point in discussing only framework agreements, with the real meat being added in bilateral negotiations with individual CMEA members. It would amount to a formal recognition by MEs of an institution that is not very well understood.

The latest rumble about a framework agreement was initiated by the declaration of the June 1984 summit, which suggested that the CMEA is no longer bent on negotiating comprehensively with the EC. This point has since been buttressed by *sub rosa* diplomatic overtures by both sides. A broad, vague political declaration of mutual recognition could open the way for CMEA's individual members to negotiate separately with the Commission. But even that step forward is bound to take time and to be little more than a prelude to the easing of tensions between East and West that would appear to be required to "normalize" economic relations between the two blocs.

The foregoing reflections indicate that East–West economic integration is unlikely to be advanced at an accelerated pace in the next quinquennium or so. The division of Europe, even in economics, will not differ very much in 1990 from what can be observed now. This pessimistic note may, however, be offset by gazing into the crystal ball at how the Eastern European PEs will be operating in the medium term. I would be very surprised if by the beginning of the next decade several PEs had not enacted major changes in their economic policies, including development goals, modes of operation, and planning outlook. They are already at this juncture being examined in preparation for the medium-term planning cycle for the first half of the 1990s (Zsolnai and Gavrilov 1985). In any case, indirect instruments of economic coordination are likely to play a much more important role in determining economic decisions in the late 1980s than they do now, and they are bound to incite changes in the organization and policy instruments typical of the CMEA. Given the wide dispersion of economic policy precepts in the various CMEA members and the continuing importance of that group for each individual PE, however, a uniform situation is not likely to emerge soon, certainly not during this decade.

Notes

Introduction

1 For the sake of completeness, there are three other forms of involvement with the CMEA aside from full membership: associate membership (Yugoslavia since 1964); cooperant status (Finland since 1973, Iraq and Mexico since 1975, Nicaragua since 1984, and Angola, Ethiopia, and Yemen since 1986); and observer status, which is open to other socialist countries, developing MEs, or organizations invited by the Council. For details, see Brabant 1980, pp. 176–9.

2 The same is not the case for bilateral cooperation (for instance, the economic dependence of Cuba, Mongolia, and Vietnam on the Soviet Union). But these intercountry relations are so specific that they should properly be kept separate from the objectives of this study.

3 The official title reads: *Comprehensive program for the further extension and improvement of cooperation and the development of socialist economic integration by the CMEA member countries*. I shall refer here to the version reproduced in Tokareva 1972, pp. 29–103.

4 Whether this notion can be applied also to the period preceding *Integration Program*, when the PEs reserved it exclusively to MEs and called their own endeavor the ISDL, is a moot question. For a broader discussion, see Brabant 1980, pp. 5–6.

5 This very involved question of the relationship between the superstructure and the base of society in Hegelian and Marxian philosophy, and the orthodox political ideology based thereon, cannot be addressed in detail here. For a lucid statement, see Carrère d'Encausse 1985, pp. 74–9.

6 An instructive elaboration is in Carrère d'Encausse 1985, pp. 372ff.

7 I have dealt with these "laws" in greater detail in Brabant 1980, pp. 61–9. Their bearing on the topics selected here for in-depth exploration is clarifed later in this introduction.

8 This has been clarified in a broader setting in Brabant 1980 and is briefly restated in Chapter 1.

9 Especially relevant in this context are Brabant 1977a regarding "commodity-money" relations in the CMEA and Brabant 1980 for the broader features of the evolution of SEI, the organization of the CMEA, and the economics of SEI.

10 It should be stressed that the CMEA members hope to advance their regional cooperation directly in the production process, in contrast to market-type integration schemes. One should therefore explore in detail, as Sobell does (Sobell 1984, pp. 14ff.), sectoral and subsectoral production specialization modes. However, these microeconomic elaborations need to be synthesized in a "macroeconomic view of integration." Some aspects of the latter are explored in this book.

11 These researchers, including Lavigne (1983, 1984), contend that one can find the essence of this strategy in recent CMEA documents of SEI to be discussed in more detail in Chapter 2.

12 With respect to *Integration Program*, this thesis is buttressed in Brabant 1980, pp. 229–44.

1. Socialist economic integration in perspective

1 As Michel Tatu recently phrased it, "the 'cold war' is in reality nothing but a slightly more crystalline form of the initial situation" (Tatu 1985, p. 75).

2 These elements are dealt with in greater logical and empirical detail in Brabant 1974a, pp. 182ff.

3 No unequivocal founding date has so far been adopted. For details about when the decision to set up the Council was taken, see Brabant 1974a, pp. 192–4. I have surveyed the circumstances of the CMEA's creation on several other occasions (especially Brabant 1979, 1980), but "new" founding dates keep surfacing.

4 Some of the recent Soviet literature (for instance, Faddeev 1974; Lukin 1974), in addition to other Eastern European sources referenced in Brabant 1974a, 1979, frequently refer to basic documents that were drawn up by 8 January 1949, when the Council's founding conference allegedly closed. According to well-placed CMEA officials, the Secretariat's library holds a full set of archival materials, but access is restricted to a handful of CMEA officials and policy makers. Karel Kaplan claims to possess documents from the Czechoslovak CP archives, from which he has quoted extensively (Kaplan 1977, 1978, 1979). Sláma (1979) also depends on this information.

5 An English translation and commentary is in Brabant 1979, pp. 253–65.

6 The historiography about the Cold War is far from unanimous about who is to be held responsible for provoking and kindling the political animosity. The revisionist school blames shortsighted American foreign policy, while the conservative branch cites true perception of Stalin's strategy regarding Eastern Europe, or the rest of the world for that matter, as having been instrumental in firming the American posture. Whether one or the other comes closer to the truth will not be investigated here. For two stimulating accounts with diametrically opposite views, see Carrère d'Encausse 1985 and Yergin 1977.

7 It is instructive to reassess these deliberations now that the sting of the first Cold War has lost most of its potency. For the Soviet position, see, for example, Molotov 1949, pp. 461–8. The various options reviewed by the American government are summarized in Yergin 1977.

8 Especially important in this context were the widely discussed Czechoslovak–Polish cooperation program and the various variants of a Balkan federation, in

which Bulgaria and Yugoslavia were to join as initiators; other potential participants were various combinations of Albania, Greece, Rumania, and Turkey. References to the pertinent literature are in Brabant 1974a, 1976, 1979.

9 I do not dispute that the political animosity engendered by Soviet moves foiling participation in the Marshall Plan and scuttling subregionalization endeavors were central in the Council's establishment. Neither do I question that the types of reciprocal assistance envisaged by these schemes were crucial topics in the early Council debates (for references, see Brabant 1974a, pp. 186–8; Kaplan 1977, 1979; Kiss 1972, p. 15).

10 There are at least three different series of hastily improvised attempts to bolster regional economic cooperation, including the CMEA's creation, which have been labeled the Molotov Plan in the West. Some observers (especially Carrère d'Encausse 1985, pp. 21ff.) have sketched these projects as manifestations of a much grander design on the subjugation of the region that Stalin had hatched well before the balance of forces in World War II had turned in favor of the allies. I find this point of view rather disagreeable because its interpretation reads too much into historical events well after the facts. For a comprehensive review of most of the agreements hammered out at that time, see Hegemann 1974.

11 Incidentally, though the designation Comecon is an alternative contraction for CMEA, it was coined essentially in parallel to the Communist International or Comintern and the Cominform. It is therefore a politically loaded term that I shall avoid here.

12 How much economic and financial assistance the USSR really provided at the time has never been very clear. Eastern European accounts generally favor the position that the USSR tranferred a subztantial volume of capital to Eastern Europe, but it also captured large assets from the region (see Chapter 9).

13 To eliminate more confusion than is warranted, I shall refer to the initial "working apparatus" as the Bureau of the Council, which is now largely standard terminology for whatever organizational secretariat was set up in 1949. This Bureau was endowed with a technical secretariat, encompassing officers and supporting personnel to assist the Bureau in its mandate, especially the preparation of the official Council Session. The Bureau was rechristened "Secretariat" in 1954, when the PEs set out to revive the idea of fostering regional cooperation on the basis of production specialization through the coordination of plans and for that purpose sought to reinvigorate the institutional bearings of intragroup cooperation.

14 Kaplan (1979), in particular, contains highly useful extracts of what are purported to be genuine documents on the "internal embassy" system.

15 But whatever new light has been thrown on the matter confirms the overall picture drawn in Brabant 1974a, 1979. Complementing the sources cited in the latter two articles are two quasi-official histories of the CMEA (Faddeev 1974; Lukin 1974) and the details quoted from archives of the Czechoslovak CP in Kaplan 1977, 1978, 1979. Wolfgang Seiffert (particularly in Seiffert 1983, pp. 46–55) arrogates to himself to have accomplished the same with the counterpart archives of the GDR, but several of his claims (including on p. 46 regarding the founding documents) simply do not at all pan out because they are patently off the mark.

16 Brabant (1979) examined this document against the historical record and in its proper CMEA setting in an effort to clarify some of the many problems faced in attempting to harmonize goals and instruments in the service of radically transforming comparatively backward economies.

17 There is a tendency in some of the Eastern European literature on SEI to suggest that the idea of founding the Council was endorsed when the conference opened on 5 January (Lukin 1974, p. 44; Menžinskij 1971, p. 83). Faddeev (1974, p. 64) writes that on 8 January preliminary statutes (*položenie*) were adopted. This might suggest that the Council was established on 8 January, when the conference closed. It bears stressing that the first source (see Faddeev 1967) that disclosed the concrete dates of the conference appeared nearly twenty years after the Council's creation!

18 There is an extensive list of possible founding dates (see Brabant 1974a, pp. 192–4; Brabant 1979, pp. 251–2), and new conflicting dates appear from time to time in the specialized Eastern European literature. An amusing one is given by Margot Hegemann, otherwise a CMEA historian of repute (Hegemann 1971, p. 6). She advocates 28 January 1949–well after the Council's announcement of 25 January in *Pravda!*

19 Kaplan (1977, 1979) divulges the most useful details, but the puzzle is far from complete!

20 This was perhaps the reason why some Western observers regarded the CMEA as an institution designed to bring about uniformity in Eastern Europe's response to the West's embargo (Alexandrowicz 1950). Its ostensible purposes were to disrupt world markets and to sow the "seeds of unrest" in MEs.

21 Especially in Čížkovský 1966, 1970, 1971; Faddeev 1974; Hegemann 1980; Kaplan 1977, 1979; Loščakov 1984; Lukin 1974.

22 At the official ER then in force, the fund would have amounted, in terms of pre-1971 U.S. dollars, to about $18.9 million. At the rate introduced in March 1950, it would have equaled some $25 million if all contributions had earlier been properly converted into rubles.

23 This is perhaps one of the reasons why, since the Council's revival in the second half of the 1950s, a key theme of SEI has been that the CMEA is manifestly not a supranational organ.

24 The best sources to date are Čížkovský 1970, pp. 246ff. and Čížkovský 1971, pp. 59ff. These and other treatments are examined in some detail in Brabant 1974a, pp. 194ff.

25 This is not the proper place to block out the traditional model at great length. For details, the reader is referred to the specialized literature on the traditional model (see, for instance, Bergson 1964; Kornai 1959; Wellisz 1964; Wilczynski 1970; Wiles 1962). For a synoptic survey contrasting old and new in the Eastern European model, see Campbell 1974; Marczewski 1973; Wilczynski 1972.

26 I doubt that such action was taken in full awareness of the cost implicit in the policy choice as argued, for example, in Gudac 1983.

27 For some hilarious cases of faulty specifications in the traditional CPE, see, for instance, Granick 1954; Kornai 1959.

28 For a comprehensive survey of the reforms, see, for instance, Bornstein 1973, 1975; Höhmann, Kaser, and Thalheim 1972; JEC 1974, 1977; Marczewski

1973; Selucký 1972; Wilczynski 1972. For a detailed discussion of individual reforms, consult the specialized country literature.

29 Comprehensive surveys of such indicators as elaborated during the reforms of the 1960s are in Boltho 1971, pp. 62ff.; ESE 1965, pp. 43ff.; Marczewski 1973, pp. 160ff. A useful Soviet source is Zacharov 1975.

30 For a more comprehensive discussion, see, in particular, Allen 1982a; Gudac 1983, 1984b; Wolf 1985a.

2. The CMEA's organization and policy programs

1 I can outline only the barest beams of the CMEA edifice here. For more details, see Brabant 1980, pp. 172–217.

2 For the summit's impact on the Session until the early 1970s, see Savov 1973, p. 54. For a broader setting, see Brabant in press, a.

3 Earlier versions of the charter stipulated a semiannual periodicity, whereas the "founding documents" called for a quarterly schedule. But neither this nor the other periodicity has been attained, with few exceptions for the biannual meetings (in 1962 and 1969, for instance).

4 There have been four secretaries: Aleksandr I. Loščakov (1949–1950?), Aleksandr A. Pavlov (1950?–1958), Nilolaj V. Faddeev (1958–1983), and Vjačeslav V. Syčëv (1983–present).

5 I have borrowed this particular translation of *administratirovanie* from the unofficial Tass translation of the speech as transmitted on the English newswire (Gorbačëv 1986).

6 For an unusually revealing recollection, see Seiffert 1983, pp. 12ff.

7 Some of these agreements were first recommended in 1954 in part on the basis of the preparatory work of the Bureau and its Secretariat not only before mid-1950 but also during the doldrums of 1950–1953 (Góra and Knyziak 1974, p. 33). In the wake of the political events of the mid-1950s, however, they were revised in 1957–1958 and then nearly completely ignored.

8 "Interestedness" has been a hotly debated topic in Eastern Europe. For some useful comments, see Franzmeyer and Machowski 1973, pp. 47ff. and Machowski 1970, pp. 285ff. I shall return to the issue in Chapter 12.

9 The full title reads *Basic principles of the international socialist division of labor*. It is reproduced in Tokareva 1967, pp. 23–39.

10 These are the conventional stipulations that have since been enshrined in the *Charter of the economic rights and duties of states* (see United Nations General Assembly resolution 3281 (XXIX) of 1974).

11 "Normalization" from within or from without as the expression of socialist solidarity is an awkward translation of the Soviet doctrine regarding *ozdorovlenie*, literally the process of returning to health.

12 Vietnam was then not a full member. Albania had already become inactive. But Cuba's omission is curious, to say the least.

13 It would have the force of law also with respect to the medium-term plans in the countries that still pass such a "plan law." Hungary, for example, no longer does.

14 The official communiqué of the summit (*Pravda*, 15 June 1984, p. 1) suggests

that other documents were agreed upon. This may explain some of the more obscure statements in the published declarations (see CMEA 1984a, 1984b). Recent commentary tends to equate current policy thinking on SEI in a number of countries, especially in the USSR under M. Gorbačёv's dynamic leadership, with the summit's achievements. Some of the quotations currently cited in the literature do not at all stem from the published declarations (for details, see Brabant in press, b)!

15 *Declaration of the main directions of further development and deepening of economic, scientific, and technological cooperation of the CMEA member countries* (henceforth *Main Directions*) and *Declaration of the CMEA member countries on the preservation of peace and international economic cooperation* (henceforth *Preservation of Peace*).

16 The price issue was raised publicly by Boris Gostev, a high-level Soviet spokesman, in a post-summit interview on 14 June 1984 without clarifying when and how new price guidelines were to be implemented. In January 1985, the Executive Committee at its 113th session (*Pravda*, 18 January 1985) decided that trade prices during the new five-year plan cycle (1986–1990) would continue to be established according to the reformulated WMP reference mechanism adopted in 1975. For more details, see Chapter 4.

17 Reports around the summit suggested agreement on holding a regular summit at five-year intervals, but the available documents do not disclose any preset periodicity. In fact, another summit was convened on very short notice, just after the forty-second Council Session, in Moscow, 10–11 November 1986.

18 Its full title reads *Comprehensive program to promote the scientific and technological progress of the member countries of the Council for Mutual Economic Assistance up to the year 2000.* It was published in all main CP papers of 19 December 1985.

19 Soon after the adoption of the document, in a report to the CCO, Ceauşescu emphasized that there was need to return to the "provisions of the program we adopted in 1984" (*Scînteia*, 28 December 1985, p. 1).

20 Some were already negotiated in detail in the course of the bilateral cooperation programs that most Eastern European countries have recently signed with the USSR.

21 A detailed discussion of this mechanism since its endorsement in *Integration Program* is in Brabant 1980, pp. 231–9.

22 Whether the PEs explicitly decided to forgo for the time being the creation of a limited form of convertibility, or whether they did so by inaction only, is something I cannot answer for lack of reliable source material. More on this question is in Chapter 11.

23 It is true that, strictly speaking, one of the key problems in the CMEA stems from physical restrictions on volumes available for exports, including exports to the preferential region. However, a volume limitation, say, of imports from the USSR could be offset by importing additional volumes from elsewhere. It is in this sense that the CMEA volume restrictions are *in se* payments restrictions.

24 In 1984, it varied between 14.6 and 19.6 percent for Rumania's exports and imports, respectively, and 55.7 and 59.3 percent for Bulgaria's exports and imports, respectively.

3. Adjustment policies in perspective

1 Macroeconometric models (see Brada 1982 and Portes 1984) that assume an unbounded response of labor to real rewards tend to overstate their case.

2 Hungarian public utilities have recently marketed bonds publicly on an experimental basis.

3 It does not exist in Cuba, Hungary, and Mongolia.

4 Polish enterprises, for example, were authorized to borrow in the 1970s in order to circumvent U.S. bank regulations that place a ceiling on lending to one entity of at most 10 percent of the bank's capital.

5 Recent commentary has tended to stress the similarity of adjustment in MEs and PEs. This may be so if the economies were in equilibrium before the disturbance. Because this is unlikely to be in the "permanent shortage economy," conventional adjustment processes of MEs differ from those in PEs.

6 The Western literature sometimes assumes that this contraction of the reserve base may automatically entail a reduction in the domestic money supply in view of set reserve ratios. But this formality is rarely adhered to.

7 These official data are subject to various measurement biases as compared to standard statistical methodologies utilized by most MEs. However, the trends that can be identified should not markedly be affected by them.

8 Rough estimates indicate that Eastern Europe's terms of trade with the developing MEs declined by about 50–60 percent between 1970 and 1980. With the developed MEs, however, they increased in some cases and otherwise declined, but not by very much. The major impact was felt particularly in trade with the CMEA, mainly the USSR, of course, where the terms of trade for Eastern Europe declined by 30–45 percent, an erosion that has continued since.

9 *Külkereskedelmi statisztikai évkönyv, 1984* (Budapest, Központi Statisztikai Hivatal, 1985), p. 395. The comparison with 1970 as base is less shrill because the ruble terms of trade declined to 88.5 and the dollar to 77.8 in 1975 (*Külkereskedelmi árstatisztikai adatok, 1959–1977* (Budapest, Központi Statisztikai Hivatal, 1978), p. 5).

10 Poland experienced the price explosion only in a very limited sense, TR prices in 1973–1974 were fixed and the share of nonsocialist imports of energy increased from nil in 1972 to 5.1 and 7.8 percent in 1973 and 1974, respectively [*Rocznik statystyczny handlu zagranicznego, 1974* (Warsaw, GUS, 1974), p. 112 and *Ibid., 1976* (Warsaw: GUS, 1976), pp. 92–3]. In fact, Poland's terms of trade improved in every year of the first half of the 1970s (see *Rocznik statystyczny handlu zagranicznego, 1984* (Warsaw: GUS, 1984), p. 5), except in 1973 for nonsocialist trade (-4.75 percent) and 1974–1975 for socialist trade (-0.89 and -3.73 percent, respectively). Since 1979, however, the terms of trade have declined steadily at annual rates of between 0.8 (in 1982) and 4 percent (in 1983), especially in trade with socialist partners.

11 Thus between 1978–1984 the ratio of Hungary's export to import volumes of CC relations steadily increased to 161.9 but it dropped to 147.4 in 1985. The corresponding evolution of the net barter terms of trade was 103.4 in 1978 to 106.1 in 1981, with a drop to 104.9 in 1982, 102.3 in 1983, 99.8 in 1984, and 100.1 in 1985. The decline in 1982–1984 probably stemmed largely from the

contraction of petroleum prices in world markets and the generally soft economic situation in key Eastern European markets.

12 Female participation in the PEs is roughly in the 75–95 percent range – well above rates in advanced MEs. Some PEs have been seriously concerned about the adverse impacts of oversaturation. The GDR and Hungary, among others, have recently enacted legislation that on balance reduces the effective labor force participation of married women with young families.

13 Plausible forecasts of demographic trends in the region as well as of social and other determinants of employment indicate that the labor force is likely to expand by an average annual 0.5 percent in the next ten to fifteen years – less than half the rate of expansion of 1.3 percent attained through the 1960s and most of the 1970s (for the derivation of the data, see UN 1981, p. 351).

14 For a thoughtful evaluation of the inward-turning and outward-looking policy options of PEs, see Köves 1981, 1985.

15 For a broader framework of analysis of structural adjustment and stabilization, see Allen 1982a, 1982b; Gudac 1983, 1984a, 1984b; Wolf 1980, 1984, 1985a, 1985b.

4. Socialist trade prices and CMEA cooperation

1 Note that the composition of this group has changed over time, and it is unclear when and to what extent the specifics discussed here have indeed been applied to all members. I shall therefore primarily illustrate the trade experience of the active European CMEA members.

2 Some trilateral agreements existed, usually involving at least one ME. These exceptional arrangements were as a rule internally balanced and did not comprise a significant share of intra-CMEA trade. For pertinent details with references, see Brabant 1977a, pp. 73–78.

3 This was set low – at $1.25 per ton it was apparently even below the actual transportation charges incurred by Poland (Machowski 1969, p. 99) – in part because it was designed to be the transfer mechanism for Soviet reparation claims on Germany and its wartime allies. It was argued that the German territory with all appurtenances ceded to Poland at the USSR's behest was more valuable than the Polish territory kept by the USSR. It could therefore be treated as a legitimate German asset on which reparation claims could be levied.

4 Hegemann sees the reverse movement – a loss in the terms of trade of commodity exporters (*sic!*) among the PEs – as the principal force that promulgated the establishment of an own price system (Hegemann 1980, p. 59)!

5 Some writers argue that the "price stop" preceded the commodity price boom of the early 1950s (Kiss 1971, p. 219), but this is rather implausible.

6 There are different versions of the base and application of stop prices in 1950. In principle, the reference was to be January 1949 to June 1950 inclusive (Hegemann 1980, p. 60), but practice undoubtedly deviated from this, if only because of new goods not yet included in formal trade agreements.

7 The issue was on the draft agenda of the Council Session due in mid-1950, but it was not convened until November. Hegemann (1980, p. 59) is unambiguous about the adoption of stop prices in the summer of 1950, but it is not clear which body made such a decision.

8 Two documents were apparently drafted and approved in June 1958. They are variously referred to as "General principles for the determination of prices in foreign trade among socialist countries" or "Principles for the determination of prices," and "Methods for the determination of world prices" or "Methods for the computation of world prices" (see Neustadt 1974, p. 10; Pěnkava 1975, p. 650; Západocký 1977, pp. 85–88).

9 Especially important are the 1960 documents about the concrete methods for establishing reference prices for new products (particularly engineering goods), modernized machinery and equipment, and durable investment goods; and the 1972 (1975 revised) document about the formation of prices in specialization and cooperation agreements (Západocký 1977, p. 89). They have since been revised (VK 1985a, p. 1), but none has been published.

10 Perhaps the most complete discussion is in Ausch and Bartha 1969; Ausch 1972, pp. 72–137; Tarnovskij and Mitrofanova 1968, which has been reviewed in detail in Hewett 1974, pp. 31–37; Žukov and Ol'sevič 1969, pp. 26–28.

11 At the time, only Eastern European countries could be and were members. Many sources actually include the qualifier "socialist countries" in the title of the documents, but I have no solid evidence that these PEs may have been bent on extending their price rules also to other PEs.

12 This Commission was superseded in 1971 by the higher-level Committee for Cooperation in the Field of Planning Activity (see Chapter 2).

13 It is crucial to recall this unspecified parameter of the Bucharest principles in interpreting the 1975 shift. As I. Garamvölgyi stressed it (*Figyelő*, 1975:10, p. 7), this switch was neither a contravention of the spirit or the actual specifics of the Bucharest agreement, nor did it signal the introduction of a new price system, unlike what may be in the offing for the future (see Chapter 5).

14 This interpretation of the Bucharest rules emerged first during the early debates on the basic principles of the ISDL and the creation of an IPS in the late 1950s (see Západocký 1977, p. 88).

15 J. Rutkowski reports, for example, that in the negotiations of the prices in Poland's agreements for 1971–1975 only 2 percent of exports and 13 percent of imports with Bulgaria, 24 and 18 percent with the GDR, and 34 and 19 percent with Hungary, respectively, were subject to price negotiations at all (Rutkowski 1977, p. 4). These data presumably refer to the number of products specified in the trade agreements. Prices for other goods were simply copied from earlier medium-term trade agreements.

16 This rule does not apply to Cuba at least since 1972 (Hegemann 1980, p. 295), when Cuba joined the CMEA. But it is not clear whether the phantom transport charges were levied before.

17 The adjustment for actual transportation costs in the case of noncontiguous countries was apparently first introduced at the behest of the GDR in 1962 as a means of containing the negative impact of price negotiations that might have emerged from the Varna conference (Hewett 1974, p. 34). It will be recalled that that meeting was the first broad exchange of views on the desirability and feasibility of the establishment of an IPS.

18 More recently, however, the transport rule has been justified as a way of sharing the differential rent (Koz'menko 1986, p. 25).

19 Popov relates, for example, that Bulgaria agreed during 1958–1965 to base prices of steel from Poland and the Soviet Union on average 1956 prices of the European Coal and Steel Community, which happened to be lower than those of 1957. Bulgaria also requested, and obtained, a 10 percent discount from the USSR (Popov 1969, p. 147). "Complexity" in Czechoslovak–Soviet relations in the mid-1960s is discussed in Brabant 1984a.

20 Admittedly, the literature on CC transactions in CMEA trade is even less clear-cut than that regarding general price formation. The bulk of such transactions is probably cleared on special accounts. The remainder and the substantial indirect transactions through an actual or formal Western intermediary, however, involve actual CC payments.

21 For instance, Rumania's purchases of unplanned oil deliveries from the Soviet Union in 1979 or Hungary's diversion of planned meat exports from the markets of the European Community to the USSR in 1974.

22 They have been very important too relative to the evolution of the more ideological precepts of value and price, commodity relations, and other such categories. However, these issues are all but ignored here because they would carry the present analysis too far afield.

23 The reasoning parallels that pertaining to the evaluation of the benefits and costs of guaranteeing security of supply through special purpose credits. For a formal analysis, see Brabant 1971 and Chapter 9.

24 The only positive confirmation of the use of the TR's average annual ER of each reference year known to me is in Špaček 1984, pp. 438–9. This reference is said to reflect a decision of the CMEA's SCFQ probably dating from late 1978 (Konstantinov 1982a, p. 128), but further details are lacking.

25 In virtually all cases in which "good" fits are obtained, particularly for the long period, the average December rate of each reference year appears to do slightly better than the one of the negotiation year, but the differences are generally not statistically significant. With regard to the short period, however, the statistical features are, without exception, at least as good for the conversions at average December rates of the negotiation year than for those at average December rates of each reference year. This would appear to conflict with what Špaček reported as the official policy pursued within the TR clearing mechanism of the IBEC (Špaček 1984). However, as noted, these inferences can be confirmed robustly only after testing a consistent series of end-year ERs.

26 This admittedly poses restrictions, given the comparatively small size of Hungary, its atypical resource endowment, and not very competitive position in world markets. However, no other PE publishes data that permit a duplication of the methods applied to the Hungarian foreign trade data.

27 This is frequently mentioned parenthetically; see, in particular, Kraus 1985, p. 10; Kuznecova 1985, p. 158; Matějček 1984, pp. 11ff.; Mitrofanova 1982, pp. 141ff; Svěrák 1985, p. 10; VK 1985a, p. 1; Weiss 1979, p. 31.

28 But strong evidence was found against the contention that the pricing principles were shifted to three-year averaging in 1980, as contended, for instance, in Bethkenhagen 1983, p. 628; Cornelsen 1983, p. 17; Haendcke-Hoppe 1983, pp. 1069–70.

5. Domestic prices, structural adjustment, and economic reform

1 Soviet economists at one point were proscribed even to discuss price-formation principles because, as Molotov is reported to have warned (see Wilczynski 1970, p. 127), "prices concerned politics not economics," and could therefore not be the subject of a technical public debate.

2 Recall that all of these countries experienced very great difficulties with controlling money and inflation after both world wars.

3 If placed within the concrete context of Soviet developments (and also in that of some of the Eastern European countries), this argument is not as odd as it may appear at first glance. For more detailed argumentation, see Brabant 1980, pp. 76–78. However, I find it rather far-fetched to employ this rationalization as an overt manifestation of the explicit awareness of the cost of such policies, as argued in Gudac 1983, pp. 4–5.

4 For a summary of the relationship between internal and external prices in various PEs at the height of the reforms, see Mitrofanova 1973, pp. 90ff.; Mitrofanova 1974, pp. 41ff.; UN 1968, pp. 43ff.; UN 1973, pp. 36ff.

5 It might be useful to recall that until 1967 and since 1970 only a fraction of prices in Czechoslovakia have been set by economic units; between 1967 and 1969, however, close to half of all prices were set in this way (Górczak 1985, p. 9).

6 The most vocal proponent of this approach has been Richard Portes (for a summary, see Portes 1984). A useful analysis is also presented in Brada 1982. Perhaps the sharpest critique has been made by János Kornai (see, for instance, Kornai 1980, p. 479 and Kornai 1982, pp. 111ff.).

7 The Polish situation continues to be in considerable flux, however. Even though price devolution sharply rose in 1981–1982, recentralization occurred in 1983–1984. There are presently once again strong signs of the willingness of the authorities to devolve price formation (Górczak 1985, p. 9).

8 For a recent survey of the relationships in Eastern Europe, see Aristov 1978, 1980; Čerkasov and Malafeev 1985, pp. 98ff; Mitrofanova 1986.

9 This is the case for the bulk of primary and intermediate goods traded in market exchanges, whence publicly quoted prices can be utilized. As argued in Chapter 4, CMEA prices in these sectors probably approximate average WMPs. If so, it is a real irony now that all efforts to eradicate noncompetitive forces would appear to reduce in the end to the introduction of precisely these reprehensible features into the CMEA cooperation mechanism!

10 The SCEP was replaced in 1971 by the newly created CMEA Committee for Cooperation in the Field of Planning Activity. The latter does not appear to have concerned itself greatly with the details of an IPS. But it clearly has not been able to skirt the matter altogether and is likely to be called upon to play a more activist role soon, as argued later. At the time of the decision to maintain the modified Bucharest formula for the entire period 1981–1985, the Executive Committee in January 1981 requested the SCFT to include the price issue in its work program (Čerkasov and Malafeev 1985, p. 83). Because the modified Bucharest principles were confirmed for 1986–1990, one may surmise that no satisfactory solution has been found to date.

11 Lidvanova (1985, p. 76) reports that in 1984 more than 4,000 enterprises of CMEA countries were in direct contact. But Bakoveckij and Grinev (1985 p. 97) quote this magnitude as applying to enterprises and associations combined. For an ebullient evaluation of direct relationships, see Epštejn 1985.

12 Note that not all countries, including Bulgaria, Hungary, and Poland, avoid the terminology (Kazandžieva 1983, p. 27).

6. Exchange rates and foreign exchange policies

1 For a broad analytical approach to the role of the ER in recent stabilization efforts of four PEs, see Wolf 1984, 1985a, 1985b. An even more skeptical view is presented in Brabant 1984b, 1984c.

2 To the extent that the balance of payments in foreign currency prices is in equilibrium, the ER does not at all influence the size of the net subsidies or taxes incurred by the government budget. If that balance is not in equilibrium, however, the ER will codetermine the precise volume of the budgetary transfers (see Brabant 1977a, pp. 247–57).

3 Some observers (see Wolf 1984, 1985a, 1985b) stress that planners may recently have fostered export-revenue maximization by the FTOs. I strongly doubt that this intention is now widespread or even the main norm, except perhaps in Hungary.

4 This does not suggest that CPEs necessarily aim at a zero balance of payments for any predetermined period of time and allows for the implementation of an ex ante intertemporal equilibrium by the planner.

5 For example, the Hungarian internal ERs (5.111 domestic forints per *deviza* forint in dollar transactions and 3.067 for TR transactions) introduced in 1968 were computed on the basis of average price relations of exports, mostly of manufactures, in 1960–1964. They remained unchanged until 1976 in spite of palpable movements in domestic and trade prices, the direction and commodity composition of trade, and relative trade and domestic wholesale prices. Similarly in Poland: Until 1970, transactions of the foreign trade enterprises were effected at a special ER that was approximately six times the official one. Internal ERs (ten for TR, thirteen for other clearing currency (per dollar equivalent), and fifteen per dollar for CC transactions) were introduced in 1971 on the basis of the average relationship between the domestic cost of exports and export revenues in 1967–1968. Policy makers intended to keep these rates in place for the entire five-year plan cycle 1971–1975, although the clearing currency rate was eliminated already in 1973. Further changes have occurred intermittently since then (for details, see Böhm 1983, pp. 207ff.; Böhm 1985, pp. 98ff.; Kulczycki 1979, pp. 177–8; Rewkiewicz and Tekielski 1981, pp. 3ff.; Wesołowski 1974, pp. 83–85).

6 This includes Czechoslovakia and Poland; Hungary and Rumania in effect also revised internal ERs by changing the taxes and subsidies that buffered domestic from trade prices. Other PEs, however, have held on to the coefficients as originally established with only infrequent revisions.

7 Hungary's domestic wholesale prices have gradually been patterned after competitive WMPs. Because of the dichotomy between CC and TR prices, however, the latter are buffered by ad hoc taxes and subsidies.

8 In the CMEA framework, such an action could have been contemplated only in conjunction with a host of other measures (see Section 6.5).

9 Actually, until early 1976 the dollar multiplier and the official *deviza* forint rate were pegged to movements in the value of the dollar relative to other CCs. The commercial ER for the dollar has apparently been adjusted according to changes in the value of the dollar relative to other CCs of importance in Hungary's nonsocialist trade (normally a basket of nine currencies weighted with trade shares of some reference period).

10 Until recently, the effective internal ERs differed by sector or type of commodity, as they do in other PEs where such rates exist separately from the official ER or even the nominal commercial ER (as in the GDR).

11 Comments regarding transactions with other PEs, except those effected in CC (some or all of the transactions with China, Cuba, and Yugoslavia), are quite similar to those pertaining to the TR regime in the CMEA.

12 I use TR and CC here as shorthand notation for all PE currencies and all developed ME currencies, respectively.

13 The official value of the forint since 1976, the złoty since 1982, and the leu since early 1983 is no longer quoted by these PEs. However, since there has not been an official realignment of the gold parity, some of the other CMEA partners that quote individual official ERs keep pegging the forint, leu, and złoty at the levels in force before the Hungarian, Polish, and Rumanian authorities suspended quotation. The official parity of the leu is quoted, for example, in *International Financial Statistics*.

14 For example, Czechoslovakia pegged the koruna's gold parity to the dollar's on the basis of the relationship between prices in Czechoslovakia and those prevailing in the United Kingdom, the United States, Sweden, and Switzerland evaluated at the official dollar parities. The new gold parity of the koruna in May 1953 was not, however, a reflection of a careful price comparison. For details, see Vencovský 1979, pp. 814–15.

15 Until 1965, the Soviet *valuta* ruble was used to record trade. Internal accounting proceeded at the gold parity rate until 1958. As of 1 January 1959, the special Valutamark rate was introduced at par with the West German mark of 1959, but no convincing rationale for this decision has ever been presented (see Nattland 1972, pp. 127–33).

16 Note that Rumanian organs continued to publish the official ERs based on the gold parity until 29 January 1983 in *România Liberă*. Since then, Rumania's quotations are, however, only available through IMF publications.

17 In the case of Hungary, for example, the ruble's commercial rate has been adjusted infrequently since 1976. These redefinitions have probably been undertaken in an attempt to reduce the average effect of the medium-term movement in CMEA trade prices on the domestic price level.

18 Because Rumania does not publicly quote its commercial ERs and *International Financial Statistics* reports only the dollar rate, it is not clear whether the leu's devaluations of 1983 against the dollar were also applied to the ruble, thus preserving the cross rate introduced in 1981. From informed sources it would appear that the Rumanian authorities preserved unity until 1 July 1983 (see Table 6.3), when the devaluation against the dollar was not applied to the ruble.

19 In addition to the internal ERs implied in the commercial rates quoted in

Table 6.3, Czechoslovakia in 1968 introduced average internal ERs that were slightly modified in later years. It had, however, introduced a reproduction coefficient–something akin to a multiplier–already in 1954 (at 14.9 koruny to the dollar), which had gradually declined to 21.3, although this was at considerable variance with rates based on wholesale (13.43 koruny per dollar) and retail prices (at 11.82 koruny per dollar). This reproduction coefficient apparently played some role in planning (Ondráček 1970, p. 65). The dollar internal ER in 1970 was set at 3.75 and the ruble's at 2.25. According to reliable sources, these rates were kept intact until the end of 1980, when the dollar rate was reduced to 2.2. Sectoral rates, however, were modified much more frequently, at least for the dollar. For possible clues, see Durčáková 1983a, pp. 196ff. But these rates differed considerably from the internal ERs calculated as "reproduction coefficients." For ruble and dollar reproduction coefficients, see Durčáková 1983b, pp. 225ff. and Durčáková 1986, pp. 106ff. The Polish internal ERs are discussed in Section 6.2.

20 For some sectoral calculations for Hungary, see Brabant 1977b, pp. 242–55.

21 Insurance and commercial transportation charges were settled at the official ER by way of special tariff schedules patterned after rate schedules of comparable MEs (such as the Western European passenger and freight rates, which were periodically averaged to guide CMEA transportation charges). For details, see Koz'menko 1986, pp. 25ff. and Šanina 1976, pp. 151ff.

22 Relative to overall IBEC transactions, the share of TR tourist earnings dropped from 2 percent before the mid-1970s to 1.5 percent in recent years. For the smaller PEs, however, the share is much larger (3 to 3.5 percent for Czechoslovakia), but well below the share of CC tourist earnings in total CC revenues (over 10 percent for Czechoslovakia). For details, see Špaček 1986, p. 4.

23 Obviously, there are no intra-CMEA prices for most consumer services, so ad hoc solutions were adopted (Brabant 1977a, pp. 264–7).

24 The 1971 and subsequent protocols were agreed upon only by the active CMEA members, including Cuba since the mid-1970s and Vietnam since the late 1970s. The Prague agreement remained in force for China, and presumably the other Asian PEs, until 1978, when China chose not to renew it; other PEs concluded bilateral agreements (Špaček 1986, p. 2).

25 This is still continuing although countries now have the ability to apply a wide band around the central rates for noncommercial transactions. For example, Czechoslovakia and Hungary used a coefficient of 1.6 from 1 January 1981; since 1 January 1985 they use 1.5. In relations with the GDR, Czechoslovakia has been using a coefficient of 1.7 (Špaček 1986, p. 10).

26 The new coefficients should have come into effect on 1 January 1975. However, Poland and Rumania's equanimity and practical problems with the exact calculation of these rates delayed their application. In fact, new rates were announced with some intervals throughout the beginning of that year. I have indicated 1 March 1975 because it was then that Hungary announced a complete set and that the new agreement was signed by the six members.

27 Špaček (1986, p. 10) reports that this coefficient was introduced in 1976. But the source mentioned in Table 6.1 is probably more reliable.

28 Starting in early 1982, one PE after another announced relatively frequent

changes in the noncommercial ERs, especially for the złoty. However, no strong confirmation for an overall changed system of central rates emerged, but it is clear that the linking ruble coefficient was reduced to 1.7. Wesołowski (1983a, p. 17) and Špaček (1986, p. 10) mention that this was instituted on 1 January 1981, but the source referred to in Table 6.1 indicates that the new coefficient was agreed to only in late 1981. Perhaps it was introduced retroactively. The information in Table 6.1 is therefore tentative.

29 This considerably complicates the computation of the internal ER between noncommercial and commercial units. The rates in Table 6.1 are those given in most sources, except the value of the złoty which has been determined by the Polish devaluation of 55 percent enacted in February 1982. Changes between then and 1 January 1985 are ignored in the tabulation.

30 The only exception was the comparatively free tourist zone for the GDR and Poland that was agreed upon in 1972 but abolished in late 1977 because of severe imbalances in favor of Poland. These emerged soon after the establishment of the free zone as Polish citizens crossed the border in far greater number than anticipated and went on buying sprees in the GDR. With the growing dislocations in Poland and the tightening of consumer supplies in the GDR, the situation became intolerable in the mid-1970s, and the unique experiment with the free reciprocal access to each other's market was gradually curbed and finally abolished by administrative means.

31 This was set in the agreement of 8 December 1972 at the equivalent of thirty domestic rubles per traveler – up from ten rubles (Carevski 1973, p. 507). This is woefully inadequate for any but the most trivial out-of-pocket expenses. No official change in that allocation appears to have been enacted since.

32 This development is reported in Hrinda and Válek 1983, p. 780; Pachta 1980, p. 16; Špaček 1986, p. 13; and Wesołowski, 1983a, p. 17, unfortunately without details beyond the fact that the agreement was reached on 25 January 1980.

33 As in the case of Haldex, which emerged from Hungary's lack of interest in transferring a technology at the "free" price called for by the 1949 Sofia principles regarding the transfer of technology within the CMEA and Poland's reluctance at the time to breach these principles openly.

34 An English translation of the purported agreement ("Rates or coefficients of the national currencies with respect to the collective currency [the TR] and among themselves") has been available for some time. Follow-up agreements, however, are not.

35 This is a verbatim quotation of part of the preamble of the English translation, which is unfortunately very crude. It is not known who did the translation and from which original, but it is said to be highly reliable.

36 In most cases, however, such goods would otherwise not be offered, and it is therefore difficult to speculate about the ER applied here.

37 For details for Polish workers in the USSR see Brabant 1985d. Poland is the only country that publicly quotes such rates. But similar arrangements are likely to prevail in other PEs, although no systematic information on the subject has been disclosed to date.

38 Even such bilateral agreements are not always adhered to, as was demonstrated rather spectacularly by Rumania's unilateral decision in the summer of

1980 that gasoline purchased by residents of other CMEA members be paid for in CCs or be offset by special oil deliveries. Several PEs obliged not only to help out stranded tourists and save the vacation season, but also because, although exceptional in its publicity, Rumania's stance intrinsically did not differ from the overall precepts that determine the framework for the formulation of tourist policies in Eastern Europe.

39 As an illustration, in late 1981 Czechoslovakia's demand for tourist forints threatened to get out of hand. The remedy adopted by the Czechoslovak authorities, with at least tacit Hungarian approval, was to suppress the availability of tourist services altogether, on a temporary basis (*Práca*, 2 December 1981, p. 2). This situation recurred at least in 1985 and 1986.

40 The rates listed in Table 6.2 are for the most part simple averages of the weighted monthly average quotations with the number of days for which the rates remained valid as weights. This is not really the proper average because of the well-known seasonality of trade volume. In most cases, however, no proper trade weights are available for the period as a whole and it would therefore be rather useless to adopt further inconsistencies in an attempt to correct the already inconsistent data manipulations. More refined weighted average rates of some PE currencies are published regularly in *Monthly Bulletin of Statistics*, Nos. 3, 6, 9, and 12.

41 This is a summary of various accounts, none of which is unambiguous as to the exact practices followed in IBEC's exchange quotations. For some useful points, see Konstantinov 1982a, pp. 124–8; Konstantinov 1983a, p. 24; and Mironjuk 1983, p. 8. Komissarov 1976, p. 103 states that the basket in the early phase consisted of 11 currencies, a reference that is repeated in the more recently published Beličenko and Matjuchin 1983, p. 103. However, Svĕrák 1985, p. 10 states that the basket comprises thirteen currencies. The IBEC's ER tables regularly quote thirteen CC. Note that in July 1985, the bank started quoting the European Currency Unit (ECU), in October the Finmark, in November the Singapore dollar, and in December the Norwegian kroner so that there may now be sixteen national currencies and one international currency unit in the basket.

42 For those that rely chiefly on multiple internal ERs by commodity group or trade direction, even the average internal ER, as with Czechoslovakia and for a long time also Hungary, has not kept pace with developments in relative prices.

43 In Czechoslovakia, for example, diplomats can avail themselves of the same rate as that applicable to private remittances from abroad. This was less favorable than the tourist rate until 1973 (a premium of 100 percent as against 125 percent), but the relation has since been reversed (a premium of 100 percent as against 75 percent).

44 The policy regarding the sale of CC to residents in order to procure tourist goods and services abroad is a different matter altogether, and this will be dealt with separately in Section 6.5.

45 When Rumania revalued the leu against the dollar in 1978, the premium rate of 12 was maintained until 1981, and the quotation of the tourist rate as a percentage premium over the basic rate was suspended. This is indicated in Table 6.4 as an implicit premium.

46 The demand for foreign currency on the part of own diplomats and trade representatives abroad is normally controlled by volume (usually a daily subsistence allowance in dollars or the equivalent), and the precise ER plays a role only as a bookkeeping device in the parent organization concerned.

47 Thus, while foreigners in the early 1970s acquired local currency at the rate of forty złotych to the dollar, residents paid at least sixty.

48 However, Poland had a PKO premium until 1 January 1975 with a rate of fifty-six złotych to the dollar.

49 For example, Cepelia shops in Poland, where mostly handicraft articles and souvenirs can be bought also with the domestic złoty, used to offer about twice the tourist rate if the customer paid directly in CC. Similarly, whenever a Western tourist offered fifty dollars or more in any CC to be exchanged into złotych, a premium of fifteen złotych per dollar or its equivalent was offered.

50 In 1980–1981, Poland actively promoted special privileges to private capital flows by aliens of Polish origin. This policy is still in force at this time, but I do not know to what extent it is actually utilized.

51 Such rates are periodically tabulated in *Pick's currency yearbook* (see, for example, Steve 1981), but the exact provenance, and therefore bearing, of these rates is a bit ambiguous.

52 Wolf (1985c) contests this rather pessimistic interpretation. But his misconception of how the Hungarian price system actually works and current commentaries by Hungarian observers would appear to lend more credence to the pessimistic than the optimistic view.

53 Wolf (1985c) argues that less than 7 percent of Hungarian overall output depends on TR trade. But I find this very hard to reconcile with the facts of trade.

54 If the PE were a price taker in both CMEA and world markets, acting only upon actual trade prices would induce it to redeploy production structures perhaps wholly to the price arbitrage business: Acquire low-priced fuels and raw materials from the CMEA in exchange for overpriced soft manufactures from world markets! The problem with this proposition is that the PE is not really a "small country" and that there are pronounced discontinuities in the demand and supply schedules typical of CMEA markets.

7. Eastern Europe in the world monetary system

1 Some perspective on the evolution of their relationship with the IMS will be provided too, but it would be too tedious to do so here from a strictly historical point of view.

2 Other countries that existed at the time and became founder members – although they were not then quite "socialist" – include Cuba and Yugoslavia. The People's Republic of China could not have been a founder because it came into being only in October 1949. In the early 1950s, Czechoslovakia agitated on its behalf for the expulsion of the Republic of China, which failed. But China did not actively covet the chair held by the Republic of China until the early 1970s. The Socialist Republic of Vietnam assumed the membership obligations of the Republic of Vietnam after reunification.

3 So did Cuba in 1964 ostensibly because it could not meet its financial obliga-

tions. The real reason for the severing of relations stemmed, however, from Cuba's revolution and societal changes of the early 1960s.

4 This lofty socialist principle of interstate relations has not always been a guiding beacon in the behavior of PEs in international life!

5 It is worth recalling here for later reference that the CMEA's own regional monetary unit and settlements bank, both established in 1964, basically embody important ingredients molded along the fundamental formal lines of the Bancor and the Clearing Union as advocated by Keynes. But essential elements thereof, including global control of liquidity creation, purely "ideal" money creation, symmetric penalization of debtors and creditors, and others have not yet been emulated in the CMEA. Unlike the Bancor, which was conceived as a pure credit currency unit, the PEs decided to set up a bank with an own capital fund. For a brief comparison of the Keynes Plan with the IBEC, see Zwass 1974, pp. 128–9.

6 For a wide-ranging documentation of this early history, see Horsefield 1969, pp. 77–117; Lavigne 1978, pp. 367–72; Mikesell 1951, pp. 101–16.

7 At the time the USSR did not distinguish between stabilization, which was to become the focus of the Fund, and development assistance, which was to be the center of attention of the IBRD. But a central motivation of Soviet involvement with the Atlantic partners was aid for reconstructing its war-devastated economy. This was perhaps also the prime obstacle in the negotiations about the eventual conclusion of a peace agreement and the exacerbation of the Cold War.

8 Nevertheless, important Soviet observers still argue that the basic principles embodied in the Articles of Agreement "combined a number of articles which were totally unacceptable to them" (Fomin 1978, p. 106). These allegedly included the allocation of votes, the reporting on gold and exchange reserves, the transfer of gold to U.S. territory, convertibility for current account purposes, and the conditionality provisions associated with drawings.

9 But recent commentary singles out politics and the Cold War as the overwhelming deterrents to active participation (Blusztajn 1982, p. 109).

10 For a comprehensive review of the evolution of the USSR's stance on gold, see Rémy 1981, 1985.

11 There has not been a common policy stance on issues of concern here by the entire group in the strict sense since the late 1950s. Such policy positions have been formulated on occasion in general statements about international affairs in the context of full-scale meetings of the Warsaw Treaty Organization, CMEA declarations, or major UNCTAD conferences. But some PEs submerge their policy standpoints on matters of active interest to the Group of 77 with the latter's or those of its geographical components. At least five socialist countries (Cuba, North Korea, Rumania, Vietnam, and Yugoslavia) are active members of the Group of 77. Also China favors many positions enunciated by the Group of 77, although it is not formally a member thereof.

12 In UNCTAD, for example, the majority of PEs form Group D, which includes Byelorussia, Eastern Europe (including Albania), Ukraine, and the USSR. Cuba and Mongolia usually join with Group D's statements, and they are full CMEA members.

13 But it must be pointed out that Hungary had already earlier provided ample

macroeconomic information, including information on its external financial transactions, on a voluntary basis or under prodding of private commercial banks. Rumania's submissions to the IMF and the IBRD, however, are not only furnished on a confidential basis, they are also highly incomplete, and most of them cannot be reproduced even in regular statistical compilations.

14 For a recent discussion of benefits and drawbacks of membership for Poland, see Głuchowski 1981, pp. 62–64 and Kranz 1984, pp. 38–40.

15 This clause was incorporated in the Articles of Agreement because none of the major Fund members, save the United States, was ready to declare full convertibility soon after the war.

16 The USSR has, for example, recently signed two agreements on the financing of Swedish exports of capital goods that are anchored to the ECU (*The Financial Times*, 12 September 1985, p. 6).

17 Indeed at the time that gold was still the official anchor of the BWS, the position of the PEs in international fora was to raise the price of gold (see UNCTAD 1966, 1970).

18 Rather than to negotiate over tariffs and most favored nation (MFN) treatment by the PEs, it was decided to agree upon a minimum rate of growth for the trade of these PEs with GATT signatories in exchange for MFN treatment accorded by MEs. This positive growth has not been attained in recent years. I do not know how the GATT has been able to paper over this ostensible breach of contractual obligations.

19 Matjuchin and Šenaev (1978, p. 50) note with some interest that the present IMS "does not preclude regional agreements on fixed [ERs]."

8. The CMEA's nascent monetary system and the common banks

1 Most accounts say 1973, but some (for instance, Ptaszek 1978, p. 24) refer to 1 January 1974.

2 The term "trade" is used here in a broad sense and includes all regional transactions insofar as they imply payments now or in the future.

3 M. Wyczalkowski's statement, for example, that "All that the IBEC does is to make the Soviet ruble a unit of account and to permit multilateral trade" (Wyczalkowski 1966, p. 190) is wrong, at least formally. It is equally misleading to speak of the "convertible ruble" as J. Pinder does when he refers to the TR (Pinder 1972, pp. 55–56).

4 For instance, Allen 1975, p. 15; Bartha 1975, p. 15; Ribi 1970, p. 361.

5 But some authors are more succinct and state that the TR fulfills all the functions incumbent on an *socialist* international currency unit (Allachverdjan 1974, pp. 35–36). Because the tasks of this particular currency are left unspecified, the problem at hand needs to be addressed first within the scope of the functions of an international currency in general. The conclusions can then be applied to the special conditions of the CMEA.

6 Some observers add that it should also be a "circulation medium," which the TR is claimed to be too (Izrjadnov and Kirillov 1973, p. 32). It is not clear what this means. If it refers to "bank notes," the TR does not comply with this function. If it refers to a "coefficient" for converting other values into a com-

mon unit, then the TR obviously fulfills this function, but this is of little more than formal significance.

7 This led the chairman of the bank to countercharge that neither can one pay the check of a Moscow restaurant in dollars (Nazarkin 1973, p. 82)!

8 It can be nicely debated whether a "currency" created solely by legal means is indeed also a currency in any other meaningful sense.

9 This is sometimes seen as demonstrating the transferability of the TR. It is true that enterprises may well be unaware of whether the goods they demand are stipulated in the BTPA. If they are included, then the TR is transferable. If they are not, then the demand will simply not be honored.

10 This was created in late 1962 with the specific mission of rendering CMEA transactions more flexible.

11 1977 and 1978 year-end TR balances attributed to multilateral deals amounted to 1.6 and 1.5 billion TR. (Beličenko and Matjuchin 1983, p. 23).

12 Based on Brdička 1978, p. 10; *Ėkonomičeskaja gazeta,* 1986:22, p. 20; Garbuzov 1977, p. 73; Kuraň 1978, p. 13. The upper rate for loans up to three years is 5 percent, for deposits 4 percent. As of 1 April 1986, the rates for loans with a maturity of between 3 months and 2 years were raised by between 0.5 and 0.75 percentage point.

13 I distinguish here between TR transactions on account of intragroup settlements and overall TR operations. The former pertain to regional settlements for trade, credit, and noncommercial transactions. The latter include in addition all other TR transactions arising from the operations of a number of IEOs, particularly the IIB, the growing expenditures of the CMEA organization *strictu sensu* (the Secretariat in the first instance), and a host of other transactions whose precise nature is somewhat of an enigma. The latter type of TR operations has risen very rapidly over the last decade.

14 Half of the funded capital (about TR 120 million in 1984), although at the bank's founding no provisions for CC contributions of the subscribed capital (TR 300 million in 1964, which has since been raised to TR 305.3 million in consequence of Cuba's and Vietnam's accessions) were made.

15 In Brabant 1977a, p. 149, I conjectured that the larger share of the CC profits is retained by the bank. But experts disagree about this feature. An accurate estimate for the IIB in 1982 is discussed in Chapter 10.

16 Konstantinov (1983b, p. 47) discloses that the trade contracts for 1982 as signed through April 1982 embodied a planned exchange with less than 1 percent to be settled in CC. The proportion for 1981 is given as 0.6 percent. Because this cannot possibly refer to the CC share in total intra-CMEA trade, which is more likely to be on the order of 10–15 percent, it may be indicative of the negligible role of CC in CMEA clearing effected through the IBEC.

17 But the bulk of Cuba's transactions did not come under IBEC's rules until 1976, and Vietnam has effectively participated in it only since 1982 (Garbuzov 1985, p. 3). There is reason to believe that a substantial part of Cuba's transactions with its CMEA partners continues to be handled outside the bank's framework because of the sizable CC component of these trade relations and because they are often utilized to transmit concealed development assistance or price subsidies granted by the European PEs.

18 See Moscow Narodny Bank, *Press Review,* 1976:788 (8 December 1976), pp.

14–17 and *IBEC Economic Bulletin*, 1977:5, pp. 2–6. I have examined this in greater detail in Brabant 1978, pp. 83–85.

19 Zwass (1979, p. 131) reports that at the end of 1976 clearing arrangements in TR "for a small volume of transactions" existed between the USSR, Czechoslovakia, Morocco, Iraq, Finland, and "some other" developing MEs, but this may refer to the currency unit of the agreement rather than to the clearing itself. In a letter dated 25 October 1977, the IBEC stated that no nonmembers were participating (Clement, Altmann, and Sláma 1977, p. 20). This is also the point argued in Vincze 1984, p. 149. J.-P. Saltiel (Saltiel 1978, p. 140) reports that some Western banks explored with the IBEC ways of utilizing the TR in the framework of industrial cooperation projects, to finance local expenditures of construction works, to pay for aviation transportation, or for tourist services all only within the area of the CMEA. But no positive response could be elicited.

20 Yugoslavia started TR accounting at the IBEC on 1 January 1981 (Konstantinov 1983a, p. 27). But this is probably exclusively on account of the one IIB loan, channeled in part through IBEC, that was granted to Yugoslavia in 1980.

9. Factor mobility and investment coordination

1 For useful details of the Polish workers employed in the GDR, see Oschlies 1983, pp. 1086–91.

2 Since 1983, Hungarian nationals are entitled to accept foreign employment on their own terms, but a share of foreign earnings has to be mandatorily repatriated on a regular basis together with social security and pension contributions.

3 For a comparative perspective on labor migration in East and West, see Vajs 1982, pp. 189ff. and Wilczynski 1983, pp. 195–243.

4 The first agreement signed in 1945 concerned the employment of Polish workers in Czechoslovak border areas. A year later, a similar agreement was reached with Bulgaria and several other countries (Vajs 1974).

5 Virius and Bálek (1976, p. 5) report that in the mid-1970s the comparable ratio for Czechoslovakia was perhaps 0.25 percent.

6 The latter kind, which has been practiced chiefly between Bulgaria and the USSR, especially appears to be a simple form of labor export in exchange for selected primary goods.

7 It has been suggested that the USSR transfers to Bulgaria an amount equivalent to 1.2 times the earnings of Bulgarian workers in the Soviet Union (Vajs 1982, p. 204). Even given the generally low wages in PEs, I find this proposition rather implausible, unless it is simply an apparent accounting identity. Remember that the compensation of Bulgarian workers, including hefty foreign assignment premiums, is regulated by Bulgaria. On the other hand, the "value" to the Soviet authorities of the work performed by Bulgarian citizens in Komi, for example, must be measured in terms of Soviet work and wage regulations. It would therefore seem more likely that the USSR compensates Bulgaria for the surplus product according to the base applicable in the USSR rather than according to that set by Bulgaria. This would imply that the transfer occurs according to the value of the work performance as measured by Soviet standards. The losses or gains accruing from this "wage product equalization" are borne by Bulgaria.

8 Bulgaria receives three sevenths of the lumber output from the Komi operation in accordance with the 44 and 56 percent participation shares of Bulgaria and the USSR, respectively (Rymarczyk 1978, p. 50).

9 Note that investment coordination is but one form of cooperation in the allocation of capital funds and may or may not involve capital mobility. It usually does not in the CMEA context, a matter explored in greater detail in Section 9.5.

10 I do not know to what extent these credits resulted from explicit interstate agreements. Some of them may have emanated from regular trade agreements that could not be balanced ex post.

11 I am aware that several PEs in recent years have enacted measures that allow for direct foreign investment, usually from West to East.

12 For an interpretation that treats the foregoing case as "usual," see Faude et al. 1984, p. 221. In my view, this is overly restrictive.

13 From the published literature, it is rarely unambiguous whether a joint venture is really a common enterprise with an own capital fund, joint management, *chozrasčët* operations, and distribution of profit based on real economic transactions. For more details, see Brabant 1980, pp. 204–25.

14 This is apparently the only truly multilateral joint enterprise with Bulgaria, Czechoslovakia, Hungary, and the USSR as founders.

15 Válek reports on eight joint enterprises (Válek 1983a, p. 848; Válek 1984, pp. 23–29). In addition to those listed, he includes Mongolčechoslovakmetall and Mongolsovcvetmet, which are Czechoslovak–Mongolian and Soviet–Mongolian joint ventures, respectively, concerned with nonferrous ores and metal processing in Mongolia. Válek (1984, p. 56) asserts that two antedate *Integration Program* (presently Haldex–Katowice and Intransmaš) and that six were created since the early 1970s. That is leaving aside the Mongolian–Soviet enterprises created in the interwar period. But other observers quote figures as high as 20. Belovič (1985, p. 114) states that as of 1 January 1985, there were twelve joint enterprises, but he apparently includes some IEOs operating only on a *chozrasčët* basis.

16 VK 1983, p. 1 and Belovič 1985, p. 115. Over three fourths of that sum (TR 1.512 billion) was appropriated for the Chmelnickij atomic power station (VK 1981b, p. 3).

17 For example, the machine-building program originally envisaged 140 multilateral specialization agreements calling for joint construction or investment coordination (Lidvanova 1985, p. 80).

18 Of the 121 bilateral and multilateral projects, 19 were slated for the non-European members (11 in Cuba, 7 in Mongolia, and 1 in Vietnam). The bulk of the remainder (36 projects) would be sited in the USSR. The distribution over Eastern Europe was envisaged as follows: 12 in Bulgaria, 9 in Czechoslovakia, 7 each in the GDR and Hungary, 16 in Poland, and 15 in Rumania (Válek 1983a, p. 850; Válek 1984, p. 120).

19 Since the Western powers prevented the USSR from collecting a portion of the $10–20 billion claimed from the Western occupied parts of Germany and legitimate German property in countries under the control of the Western allies, the USSR attached eventually what it could get from its own sphere of influence.

20 But it seems improper to treat this transfer as reverse Marshall aid to be offset by Soviet magnanimity (see Marer 1974, pp. 183ff.).

21 Virtually all Central European PEs possess uranium ores that used to be explored jointly with the USSR. The Czechoslovak (the Jáchymov complex) and German (A. G. Wismuth) joint-stock companies are apparently still extant, though little is known about their operations (see Pounds 1965, p. 452). The Hungarian uranium ores were discovered later and are therefore exploited only by Hungary, although the USSR has exclusive use of the resource for enrichment purposes and apparently receives ore at very favorable prices (Holzman 1976, p. 76). Earlier there had been a Rumanian-USSR uranium company (Sovromcvarţ), but this was dissolved and sold back to Rumania in the mid-1950s. There are Mongolian–Soviet ventures dating back to the 1920s and 1930s not included here (as acknowledged in Válek 1984, p. 56).

22 This is presumably the meaning of Tömpe's rule that the nominal rate of return should at least equal the rate at which funds can be borrowed in financial markets (Tömpe 1978, p. 318).

23 In the context of central planning, the security of supply might be perceived as a benefit too. Except for some special products, current economic conditions exhibit sufficient flexibility for the long-term contracting of the selected goods that are commonly the object of investment projects financed by more than one PE.

24 A broader perspective on this "hardening" is offered in Csaba 1985, pp. 234ff. and Tömpe 1978, pp. 315ff.

25 Hungarian authors contend that no discounts have recently been granted (Csaba 1985, p. 235; Tömpe 1978, p. 319), but I am not convinced. An agreement to supply at a constant price may, but need not, imply "discounts" or "surcharges" that become apparent only at the time of repayment. This is so because the apparent offer prices in TR pertain to restricted contingents only; they are certainly not the terms at which anyone can solicit deliveries with any degree of realism.

26 Until 1972, a 60 percent sample had to be evaluated. Since 1973, only a 50 percent sample appears to be required. For sources and details, see Brabant 1977a, pp. 279–93.

27 These rules and regulations are the most recent known to this observer. A new set may have been agreed upon in the meantime in order to improve the bases for the elaboration of joint investments in conjunction with the introduction of the new five-year plans for 1986–1990 and the concurrent third Concerted Plan. The topic was apparently very high on the agenda of the meeting of the CCS in charge of economic affairs in May 1985 (Belovič 1986b, p. 118), which was concerned with the joint financing of the provisions of the scientific–technical cooperation program endorsed in late 1985 (see Chapter 2). Incidentally, the role of this "sherpa" organ has risen very sharply since the debate on holding the 1984 summit and is apparently to be the key preparatory committee of high-level policy decisions in the years to come.

10. The International Investment Bank

1 It was first proposed by Henryk Kisiel (Kisiel 1968, p. 11). For a lucid summary of the debate, see Misiak 1969, pp. 18ff.

2 Rumania initially chose not to participate allegedly because of the majority voting procedures (see Section 10.2). But it reviewed this stance and soon

reversed this decision; it was admitted on 1 January 1971. For a backdrop, see Brabant 1974b, pp. 88–90, 98–100 and Brabant 1977a, pp. 199–200.

3 The original capital fund was set at TR 1 billion. But the subsequent accessions of Cuba, Rumania, and Vietnam augmented it.

4 The "hardness" of the bank's TR capital has been debated for many years in the literature (see Brabant 1977a, pp. 127–40). The very logic of the TR (see Chapter 8) precludes such a characteristic being attached to the settlements regime itself. No "supplementary" measures were envisaged, so the TR capital has essentially remained fictive.

5 For details see Brabant 1977a, pp. 210–11. The official stipulations are reproduced in Tokareva 1972, pp. 261, 269.

6 As explained in Chapter 2, this still permits a member to declare its interest "in principle" and yet obstruct the project's implementation. For a detailed legal examination, see Fiumel 1984.

7 Note that the Board itself can decide on project funding provided the sums involved are "small." In the mid-1970s, the Bank Council set the limit at TR 2 million. Although there have been sizable upward price changes in the PEs in the meantime, including in their reciprocal trade, I am not aware of any revised decision of the Bank Council since then.

8 An agreement on cooperation between the IIB and Yugoslavia was signed in April 1974 (Vorob'ëv 1974, pp. 7–8), although the country is not formally a bank member. It obtained the first loan only in 1982.

9 Carevski (1982, p. 68) reports these rates together with the officially posted 1.5–2 percent range without explanation.

10 The one loan to Mongolia to date was granted at 0.5 percent in view of the project's "importance" (Carevski 1982, p. 68; Dubrowsky 1981, p. 92).

11 Belovič (1979, p. 49) lists TR 1.8 billion, Carevski (1982, p. 65) states TR 2 billion, Alchimov (1978, p. 12) quotes TR 2.27 billion, of which TR 1.867 billion in CC, and Beličenko (1986, p. 15) lists TR 2.4 billion. However, the bulk of it was distributed among the six Eastern European PEs involved as full or, in the case of Rumania, partial participants in the construction of the trunk line, compressor stations, and wellhead equipment. Local expenditure for construction of housing and related amenities, pocket expenses of foreign workers, bonus and other "hardship" payments, and related costs of participation in the Orenburg venture were, of necessity, borne by each participant and are therefore not at all reflected in these loan data. The total loan extended by the Eastern European PEs apparently amounted to TR 3.2 billion or 67 percent of the total expenditure for the project (Válek 1984, p. 108).

12 It is often stated that this 2 percent applied to the entire loan. This led me (Brabant 1977a, p. 238) to speculate that the bulk of the loan must have been TR denominated. However, subsequent disclosures and the IIB's activities in world financial markets have made it abundantly clear that the largest part by far of the loan was in CC. If the low interest rate is applicable for that part of the credit too, the remaining CMEA members are undoubtedly subsidizing the USSR's de facto borrowing. Konstantinov (1975, p. 94) indicates that the low rate applies only to the TR portion.

13 The only deposit rates known to me are those reported in a Western source (Amundsen 1973, p. 84). This relates that the IIB granted initially 3.75 per-

cent for TR deposits with a term up to five years and 4.15 percent for deposits with a longer maturity. Because such deposits by their very nature must remain at the IBEC, however, the IIB's rates for deposits cannot diverge from the IBEC's unless some subsidization takes place, as argued later in this chapter. The IIB receives 2 percent on current account balances at the IBEC and between 2.5 and 4 percent for time deposits, unlike "regular" customers for which the corresponding magnitudes are 1.5 and 1.5 to 4 percent (Vasin 1980, pp. 70ff.).

14 For the argument, see Wiesel 1973, p. 398. I have examined the bearing of this contention in Brabant 1977a, pp. 176–9, 228–30.

15 The IIB apparently adopted the standard methodology recommended by the SCFQ in the early 1970s with subsequent revisions. This document is frequently referred to in the literature (Danov 1975, pp. 82–83) but, to my knowledge, has not so far been published.

16 For the projects approved through 1980, the average share of loans in the overall construction value, as conventionally measured (see Chapter 9), amounted to 38 percent (Carevski 1982, p. 65). Jordanov (1985, p. 40) gives the range as 22–50 percent for loan commitments through 1984.

17 Given the obstacles of converting national currency values into a comparable unit, no precise estimate can be prepared. The magnitude cited here is based on a comparison with total Polish investment activity in 1970 reported by Leonard Siemiątkowski, then president of the Polish National Bank, in *Życie Gospodarcze*, 1970:26, pp. 1, 10.

18 In assessing the bank's policies of the past fifteen years or so, one must not forget that the USSR has been able to secure important concessions from CMEA partners, among others, in the form of credits at more favorable interest rates than IIB's along the basic conditions of the special purpose credits of the late 1950s and early 1960s (see Chapter 9).

19 This does not, however, mean that no deliveries from the TR area were made. For instance, Hungary reportedly acquired locomotives and railroad equipment for the electrification of the transit line between Czechoslovakia and Rumania "paid" for by IIB's loan in TR.

20 It is important to bear in mind that there is considerable confusion about counting the projects accepted for financing. This stems from the fact that several credits for one project are sometimes counted as one (such as in "the number of projects cofinanced by IIB") and at other times separately (such as in "the number of loans committed"). In what follows, I have endeavored to adhere to the first definition, but sparsity of information may well entail some mixup.

21 Yugoslavia actively cooperates with the CMEA members in this and a number of other sectors through its associate status. This permits it to participate in the work of CMEA organs, especially a number of Standing Commissions, of its own choice.

22 Cuba and Vietnam were then not members and apparently have not acceded to the agreement.

23 See *Izvestija*, 12 April 1973 and *Vnešnjaja torgovlja*, 1973:7, p. 45.

24 See also the commentary by S. Potáč, then the president of the Czechoslovak state bank and presently chairman of the planning commission, in *Svět Hospodářství*, 1973:27, p. 3.

11. National and regional convertibility in the CMEA

1 Colombatto polemicizes on this issue (Colombatto 1983, p. 488), in my view, quite inappropriately.

2 For a summary with references, see Brabant 1977a, pp. 55–62.

3 Incidentally, this number of possible combinations has a downward bias. Every single combination must necessarily include what happens to *each* of the three currencies and *each* of the four different convertibility types, allowing for logical, though practically redundant, alternatives. The reader can easily verify that there are necessarily more than twenty-four combinations even with Allen's set of four variants and three currency units.

4 Commercial agreements settled in CC are already convertible in some sense, although holders of CC balances are not necessarily entitled to enter local markets without prior permits from planning agencies.

5 Note that PE policy makers in recent years have considerably relaxed their aversion to admitting openly that CCs play some role as parallel currency in their markets. Thus any holder of CCs in most PEs can acquire coupons or vouchers (for example, Tuzex vouchers in Czechoslovakia or PKO notes in Poland), which are easily reconverted into CC or local currency (see Chapter 6).

6 Colombatto attributes to me and Marie Lavigne the contention that such a move would not be possible at all (see Colombatto 1983, p. 488). I categorically reject this interpretation.

7 The authorities could reap additional seigniorage by letting residents hold FTR instead of CC balances.

8 T. Bácskai recently argued that Hungary could attract CC deposits by offering "a rate equivalent to the market interest rates of short-term deposits . . . of foreign currencies of a similar steady value" (Bácskai 1984, p. 129). The experiences with private CC deposit accounts in Hungary by nonresidents, which are reportedly more solid than Swiss bank accounts, would seem to militate against this, however.

12. Socialist economic integration and East–West relations in the late 1980s and beyond

1 A reduction of the size and duration of conscription is essentially determined in the political arena. An increase in the work week has recently been tried out in some PEs, including Poland and Rumania. Because such decisions amount to major reversals of acquired or pledged benefits and social rights, and the marginal productivity of a longer working day, under the circumstances, is at any rate inferior to average productivity, the results achieved to date have not at all been very encouraging.

2 In spite of some deceleration in recent years, the savings rate has continued at a relatively high level by international standards of comparison.

3 For some useful measurement, see Poznanski 1985a, 1985b, and 1986. I agree with most of the conclusions reached by Poznanski and indeed have little trouble accepting his careful empirical analysis. But some inferences appear to suffer from several erroneous assumptions, which I shall clarify in Section 12.5.

4 In 1985, net Soviet exports of oil and products to nonsocialist markets amounted to about 56 million tons. For every drop in the world oil price by one dollar per barrer, therefore, Soviet CC revenues decline by about 400 million dollars. Given that the average price in 1985 was around twenty-seven dollars per barrel, a drop in oil prices to a range of ten to twenty dollars per barrel in 1986 would entail a loss of CC revenue of about $6.8 billion to $2.9 billion, respectively, provided total export volume can be maintained.

5 If this example were to be generalized for all of Eastern Europe without serious modifications, it would admittedly present a highly skewed picture.

6 Including far too low physical retirement rates and capital losses incurred as a result of the changed cost of primary inputs, as argued earlier.

7 For a highly instructive analysis of these categories with special references to the USSR, see Bornstein 1985.

8 Its title reads *Basic directions for the further improvement of the organization of multilateral cooperation of the CMEA member countries and the Council's operations.* I shall abbreviate this here to *Basic Directions.*

9 Uschakow gives as source a special CMEA publication that is not otherwise identified. The document is said to be annex 7 of the protocol of the thirty-second Council Session.

10 The revised charter is available in Tokareva 1981, pp. 13–25.

11 This notion has been discussed at some length in Brabant 1976, pp. 4–9 and Machowski 1973, pp. 18–19.

12 For a recent discussion of such a two-tier SEI strategy, see Nyers 1982, pp. 402–3.

13 The original suggestion for a Central European economic union envisaged also Poland (see Machowski 1973, p. 18). The latter's profound socioeconomic and political crises since the late 1970s would clearly argue for a revision of the concept, however.

14 For a critical analysis of this thesis as argued in Lavigne 1984, p. 34, see Brabant 1984a.

15 From a speech to the fifteenth congress of Soviet trade unions as reported in *Izvestija,* 21 March 1972, p. 1.

Bibliography

Abalkin, L. (1985). "Intensifikacija i ékonomičeskij rost," *Planovoe chozjajstvo* 5: 18–26.

Abolichina, G. and O. Bakoveckij (1986). "Razvitie prjamych svjazej v socialističeskom sodružestve," *Ékonomičeskie nauki* 3: 52–9.

Alchimov, Vladimir S. (1978). "Rol' bankovskoj sistemy v razvitii Sovetskogo sojuza," *Vnešnjaja torgovlja* 6: 10–16.

Alekseev, Aleksandr M., et al., eds. (1984). *Meždunarodnye valjutno-finansovye i kreditnye otnošenija* (Moscow: IMO).

Alev, F. (1979). "Ispol'zovanie trudovych resursov stran SĖV v uslovijach socialističeskoj ékonomičeskoj integracii," *Izvestija akademii nauk – serija ékonomičeskaja* 6: 74–82.

Alexandrowicz, Charles H. (1950). "Comecon: the Soviet retort to the Marshall Plan," *World Affairs* 1: 35–47.

Allachverdjan, Derenik A. (1974). "Tovarno-denežnye otnošenija i razvitom socialističeskom obščestve," *Finansy SSSR* 2: 24–36.

Allen, Mark (1973). The socialist international finance system (New Haven, CT: Yale Center for Russian and East European Studies), mimeographed.

(1975). The evolution of the International Bank for Economic Cooperation, 1964–1973 (Washington, DC: International Monetary Fund), Department Memorandum DM/75/12.

(1980). "Discussion," in *East European integration and east–west trade,* edited by Paul Marer and John M. Montias (Bloomington, IN: Indiana University Press), pp. 142–4.

(1982a). Prices, the exchange rate and adjustment in planned economies (Washington, DC: International Monetary Fund), Department Memorandum DM/82/34.

(1982b). "Adjustment in planned economies," *Staff Papers* 3: 398–421.

Altman, Oscar L. (1962). "L'or russe et le rouble," *Economie Appliquée* 3/4: 354–72.

Amundsen, Gunnar L. (1973). *Problèmes de coordination monétaire dans la région du CAEM (Comécon) – exigences fondamentales et implications théoriques* (Oslo: Utenrikspolitisk Institut).

Apró, Antal (1972). *Meždunarodnye organizacii stran-členov SĖV v uslovijach socialističeskoj ékonomičeskoj integracii* (Moscow: Ėkonomika).

447

448   *Bibliography*

Aristov, Gennadij V. (1978). "Optovye i rozničnye ceny na potrebitel'skie tovary v evropejkich stranach-členach SĖV," *Ėkonomika i organizacija promyšlennogo proizvodstvo* 6:129–39.

(1980). *Rol' cen v upravlenii socialističeskoj ėkonomiki – iz opyta zarubežnych stran SĖV* (Moscow: Nauka).

Ausch, Sándor (1972). *Theory and practice of CMEA cooperation* (Budapest: Akadémiai Kiadó).

Ausch, Sándor and Ferenc Bartha (1969). "Theoretical problems of CMEA intertrade prices," in *Socialist world market prices*, edited by Tamás Földi and Tibor Kiss (Budapest: Akadémiai Kiadó and Leyden: Sijthoff), pp. 101–25.

Bácskai, Tamás (1975). "Währungspolitische Diskussionen in den sozialistischen Ländern," *Europäische Rundschau* 4:21–26.

(1984). "Hungarian rate of exchange policy," *The New Hungarian Quarterly*, No. 96:117–29.

Bagudin, Pavel (1982). "Sotrudničestvo stran SĖV v oblasti kapitalovloženij i vnešnjaja torgovlja," *Vnešnjaja torgovlja* 8:2–7.

(1983). "Soglasovannyj plan mnogostoronnich integracionnich meroprijatij stran SĖV na 1981–1985gg., ego realizacija i svjaz' so vzaimnoj torgovlej," *Vnešnjaja torgovlja* 3:2–6.

Bakoveckij, O. D. and G. Abolichina (1986). "Prjamye svjazi: kursom integracii," *Ėkonomičeskaja gazeta* 25: 21.

Bakoveckij, O. D. and V. S. Grinev (1985). "Problemy razvitija prjamych proizvodstvennych svjazej v socialističeskom sodružestve," *Izvestija akademii nauk SSSR – serija ėkonomičeskaja* 2:97–106.

Balážik, Milan (1980). *Medzinárodné menovo-finančné vzťahy v RVHP* (Bratislava: VTEL).

Bangelska, Velička (1975). "Kreditnata dejnost na Meždunarodnata investicionna banka," *Vŭšna tŭrgovija* 12:10–12.

Bartha, Ferenc (1975). "Gondolatok a KGST-országok közötti sokoldalú elszámolási rendszer megteremtéséről," *Külgazdaság* 1:14–22.

Basiuk, Jerzy, Mirosława Jaroszyńska, and Bolesław Krawczyk (1975). *Ceny handlu zagranicznego na rynku krajów RWPG* (Warsaw: PWE).

Bass, L. A. (1974). "Voprosy sotrudničestvo SSSR i NRB v uslovijach ėkonomičeskoj integracii," in *Voprosy razvitija i sotrudničestva socialističeskich stran*, vol. 2, edited by A. I. Petrov (Moscow: Akademija nauk), pp. 33–42.

Bautina, Ninel' V. (1972). *Soveršenstvovanie ėkonomičeskich vzaimootnošenij stran-členov SĖV* (Moscow: Ėkonomika).

Behrens, Harald and Harry Bornkessel (1972). "Ein Jahr Internationale Investitionsbank," *Sozialistische Finanzwirtschaft* 16:59–60.

Beličenko, Al'bert N. (1981). "Meždunarodnyj investicionnyj bank – važnyj instrument ravitija socialističeskoj ėkonomičeskoj integracii," *Vnešnjaja torgovlja* 11:8–13.

(1983). "Ob ėffektivnosti kreditov MIB v razvitii proizvodstva stran-členov banka," *Ėkonomičeskoe sotrudničestvo stran-členov SĖV* 10:65–70.

(1985). "Kredity MIB na službe sodružestva," *Ėkonomičeskoe sotrudničestvo stran-členov SĖV* 12:38–41.

(1986). "Meždunarodnyj investicionnyj bank – 15 let plodotvornoj dejatel'nosti," *Den'gi i kredit* 2:13–22.

Beličenko, Al'bert N. and Georgij G. Matjuchin (1983). *Kreditnye otnošenija meždu stranami-članami SĚV* (Moscow: Finansy i statistika).

Belovič, Alexander (1979). "Základné formy medzinárodného socialistického investičného úveru," *Finance a Úvěr – Čtvrtletní Příloha* 1:34–53.

(1985). "Koordinacija investicij stran SĚV," *Voprosy ėkonomiki* 7:113–22.

(1986a). "Problémy zdokonalování zbožně-peněžních nástrojů investiční spolupráce členských států RVHP," *Finance a Úvěr* 2:124–31.

(1986b). "Zdokonaľovanie koordinácie investícií členských krajín RVHP," *Nová Mysl* 3:118–28.

Bergson, Abram (1964). *The economics of Soviet planning* (New Haven, CT: Yale University Press).

Bethkenhagen, Jochen (1983). "Erdöl und Erdgas im RgW-Intrablockhandel," *DIW Wochenbericht*, 22 December 1983: 625–32.

Bień, Andrzej and Gregorz Nosiadek (1979a). "Doskonalenie funkcji rubla transferowego jako waluty międzynarodowej (część I)," *Handel Zagraniczny* 2:19–21.

(1979b). "Doskonalenie rubla transferowego – część II: fundusz specjalny Międzynarodowego banku inwestycyjnego," *Handel Zagraniczny* 3:37–40.

Biskup, Józef and Gregorz Nosiadek (1978). "Formy współpracy krajów RWPG w ramach międzynarodowych organizacji ekonomicznych," *Handel Zagraniczny* 1:10–11.

Blusztajn, Mieczysław (1982). "Polska a Międzynarodowy fundusz walutowy," *Bank i Kredyt* 4/5:105–10.

Bogdanov, Oleg S. (1976). *Valjutnaja sistema sovremennogo kapitalizma (osnovnye tendencii i protivorečij)* (Moscow: Mysl').

Bogomolov, Oleg T. (1967). *Teorija i metodologija meždunarodnogo socialističeskogo razdelenija truda* (Moscow: Mysl').

(1980). "Meždunarodnyj rynok stran SĚV," *Voprosy ėkonomiki* 4:113–21.

(1985). "Soglasovanie ėkonomičeskich interesov i politiki pri socializme," *Kommunist* 10:82–93.

Böhm, Edward (1983). "Die Wechselkurse im polnischen Westhandel 1971–1982," *Osteuropa-Wirtschaft* 3:204–16.

(1985). *Die Krise des polnischen Außenhandelssystems* (Hamburg: Weltarchiv).

Boltho, Andrea (1971). *Foreign trade criteria in socialist economies* (Cambridge: Cambridge University Press).

Bonin, John P. (1977). "The visible hands, quantity targets as coaxing tools," *Journal of Comparative Economics* 1:278–308.

Boratyński, Zbigniew (1975). "Jak MBI finansuje inwestycji," *Życie Gospodarcze* 20:13.

Borisov, Stanislav M. (1979). "Meždunarodnoe valjutno-finansovoe sotrudničestvo stran socializma," *Finansy SSSR* 3:3–14.

(1984). *Zoloto v ėkonomike sovremennogo kapitalizma*, 2nd ed. (Moscow: Finansy i statistika).

Bornstein, Morris, ed. (1973). *Plan and market – economic reforms in Eastern Europe* (New Haven, CT: Yale University Press).

(1975). *Economic planning, east and west* (Cambridge, MA: Ballinger).

(1985). "Improving the Soviet economic mechanism," *Soviet Studies* 1:1–30.

Botos, Katalin (1971). "A Nemzetközi beruházási bank és a szocialista integráció," *Pénzügyi Szemle* 6:646–58.

450   Bibliography

(1974). "A beruházáspolitikák koordinációja," *Külgazdaság* 12:923–32.

Bourguinat, Henri (1977). "The international payments crisis and the foundation of east–west cooperation," in *The international payments crisis and the development of east–west trade* (Brussels: Establissements Emile Bruylants), pp. 17–70.

Brabant, Jozef M. van (1971). "Long-term development credits and socialist trade," *Weltwirtschaftliches Archiv* 107/1:92–122.

(1973). *Bilateralism and structural bilateralism in intra-CMEA trade* (Rotterdam: Rotterdam University Press).

(1974a). "On the origins and tasks of the Council for Mutual Economic Assistance," *Osteuropa-Wirtschaft* 3:182–209.

(1974b). *Essays on planning, trade and integration in Eastern Europe* (Rotterdam: Rotterdam University Press).

(1976). "Die Rolle Mitteleuropas im RgW," *Osteuropa-Wirtschaft* 1:1–20.

(1977a). *East European cooperation – the role of money and finance* (New York: Praeger).

(1977b). "The relationship between domestic and foreign trade prices in centrally planned economies – the case of Hungary," *Osteuropa-Wirtschaft* 4:235–58.

(1978). "Le rouble transférable et son rôle dans le commerce est–ouest," in *Unités et monnaies de compte*, edited by Jean-Louis Guglielmi and Marie Lavigne (Paris: Economica), pp. 77–105.

(1979). "Another look at the origins of East European economic cooperation," *Osteuropa-Wirtschaft* 4:243–66.

(1980). *Socialist economic integration – aspects of contemporary economic problems in Eastern Europe* (Cambridge: Cambridge University Press).

(1984a). "The USSR and socialist economic integration – a comment," *Soviet Studies* 1:127–38.

(1984b). Exchange rates and macroeconomic adjustments in Eastern Europe – a comment (paper presented to the Conference on the Soviet Union and Eastern Europe in the World Economy, Washington, DC, 18–19 October).

(1984c). CMEA institutions and policies versus structural adjustment – a comment (paper presented to the Conference on the Soviet Union and Eastern Europe in the World Economy, Washington, DC, 18–19 October).

(1985a). "Eastern European exchange rates and exchange policies," *Jahrbuch der Wirtschaft Osteuropas – Yearbook of East-European Economics*, vol. 11/1, pp. 123–72.

(1985b). "The relationship between world and socialist trade prices – some empirical evidence," *Journal of Comparative Economics* 3:233–51.

(1985c). "World prices and price-formation in intra-CMEA trade – selected empirical evidence," *Osteuropa-Wirtschaft* 3:163–80.

(1985d). *Exchange rates in Eastern Europe – types, derivation, application* (Washington, DC: World Bank Staff Working Paper No. 778).

(In press, a). "The CMEA summit and socialist economic integration – a perspective," *Jahrbuch der Wirtschaft Osteuropas – Yearbook of East-European Economics*.

(In press, b). "Economic adjustment and the future of socialist economic integration," *Eastern European politics and economics*.

(In press, c). "Socialist and world market prices – an in-growth?" *Journal of Comparative Economics*.

(In press, d). *Regional price formation in Eastern Europe – on the theory and practice of trade pricing* (Dordrecht: Kluwer Academic Publishers).

Brada, Josef C. (1980). "Discussion," in *East European integration and east–west trade*, edited by Paul Marer and John M. Montias (Bloomington, IN: Indiana University Press), pp. 111–18.

(1982a). "Real and monetary approaches to foreign trade adjustment mechanisms in centrally planned economies," *European Economic Review* 2:229–44.

Brdička, Květoslav (1978). "Výsledky zasedání bankovních rad – Mezinárodní banky spolupráce a Mezinárodní investiční banky," *Zahraniční Obchod* 1:10–11.

Brendel, Gerhard and Eugen Faude (1973). "Wesenszüge und Entwicklungstendenzen des RGW-Preisbildungssystems," *Wirtschaftswissenschaft* 9:1283–97.

Brunovský, Ján and Helena Nápravníková (1986). "Mezinárodní investiční banka jako faktor stimulace rozvoje socialistické ekonomické integrace," *Zahraniční Obchod* 7:13–15.

Caffet, Jean-Pierre and Marie Lavigne (1985). "Les pays à économie centralement planifiée sont-ils protectionnistes?" in *Le protectionisme – croissance-limites-voies alternatives*, edited by Bernard Lassudrie-Duchêne and Jean-Louis Reiffers (Paris: Economica), pp. 283–92.

Campbell, Robert W. (1974). *Soviet-type economies – performance and evolution* (London: Macmillan).

Carevski, Nešo V. (1973). "Problemi na konvertiruemostta na valutite pri socializma," *Trudove na viššija ikonomičeski institut "Karl Marks"* 3:489–524.

(1977). *Valutno-finansovite otnošenija v uslovijata na integracijata* (Varna: G. Bakalov).

(1982). "Meždunarodnijat socialističeski kredit – dinamičen element na ikonomičeskata integracija," *Meždunarodni otnošenija* 1:57–69.

Carrère d'Encausse, Hélène (1985). *Le grand frère – l'Union soviétique et l'Europe soviétisée* (Paris: Flammarion).

Čerkasov, N. A. and A. N. Malafeev (1985). *Razdelenie truda i tovarno-denežnye otnošenija v uslovijach internacionalizacii socialističeskogo proizvodstva* (Leningrad: Leningradskij universitet).

Chadžiev, Stanislav, Georgi Dimitrov, and Velian Džambazov (1978). *Socialističeskata ikonomičeska integracija i razvitieto na stroitelstvoto v stranite-členki na SIV* (Varna: G. Bakalov).

Chodov, Leonid (1976). "Auf dem Wege zu gemeinsamen Strategien," *Die Wirtschaft* 19:23.

Cipiur, Jan (1984). "Trudne prognozy," *Rzeczpospolita*, 4 November: 8.

Čížkovský, Milan (1966). "K některým rysům hospodářské spolupráce mezi europejskými socialistickými státy v letech 1945–1953 (informativní přehled)," *Acta Universitatis Carolinae – Economica* 2:145–78.

(1970). "Internationale Koordinierung der Volkswirtschaftspläne im Comecon," in *Planung IV*, edited by J. H. Kaisser (Baden-Baden: Nomos), pp. 243–264.

(1971). *Mezinárodní plánování – zkušenost a možnosti RVHP* (Prague: Academia).

Clement, Hermann, Franz-Lothar Altmann, and Jiří Sláma (1977). *Neue Entwicklungen im Bereich des transferablen Rubels* (Munich: Osteuropa-Institut), mimeographed.

CMEA (1974). *Sovet ėkonomičeskoj vzaimopomošči – 25 let* (Moscow: Sekretariat SĖV).

(1984a). "Deklaracija stran-členov Soveta ėkonomičeskoj vzaimopomošči 'Sokranenie mira i meždunarodnoe ėkonomičeskoe sotrudničestvo,' " *Ėkonomičeskaja gazeta* 26:6–7.

(1984b). "Zajavlenie ob osnovnych napravlenijach dal'nejšego razvitija i uglublenija ėkonomičeskogo i naučno-techničeskogo sotrudničestva stran-členov SĖV," *Ėkonomičeskaja gazeta* 26:4–5.

Colombatto, Enrico (1983). "CMEA, money and ruble convertibility," *Applied Economics* 4:479–506.

Cooper, Richard N. (1984). "A monetary system for the future," *Foreign Affairs* 1:166–84.

Cornelsen, Doris (1983). "Die Wirtschaft der DDR unter dem Einfluß weltwirtschaftlicher Veränderungen," *FS-Analysen* 6:5–30.

Crăiniceanu, Gh. (1977). "Moneda națională în schimburile economice externe şi cerințele convertibilității," *Era Socialistă* 12:23–25.

Csaba, László (1985). "Joint investments and mutual advantages in the CMEA – retrospective and prognosis," *Soviet Studies* 2:227–47.

Cvetkov-Golubarev, Cvetan (1974). "Problemi na cenite na mašinostroitelnata produkcija v tŭrgovijata meždu stranite-členki na SIV," *Planovo stopanstvo* 7:53–66.

Danov, Krŭstju S. (1972). "Dejnost na Meždunarodnata investicionna banka," *Finansi i kredit* 10:5–12.

(1975). "Kredit Meždunarodnogo investicionnogo banka," *Den'gi i kredit* 11:78–86.

Degtjar', Ljudmila S. (1976). *Problemy racional'noj zanjatosti pri socializme* (Moscow: Nauka).

Dembinski, Paweł H. (1985). "L'inconvertibilité est-elle un obstacle aux échanges entre les économies planifiées de l'Europe de L'Est et les économies de marché?" *Revue d'Etudes Est-Ouest* 4:109–29.

Dimitrov, Dimitŭr (1972). "Kreditnata dejnost na Meždunarodnata investicionna banka," *Finansi i kredit* 8:16–32.

(1981). "Deset godini Meždunarodna investicionna banka," *Finansi i kredit* 10:3–6.

Dimova, Ruska (1986). "Sŭštnost i rolja na prekite vrŭzki meždu stranite ot socialističeskata obštnost," *Ikonomika* 2:26–38.

Dochia, Aurelian (1984). "Resources management and the system of prices in a socialist economy," *Revue Roumaine des Sciences Sociales* 2:137–47.

Drabowski, Eugeniusz (1974). "Problemy wymienalności walut krajów RWPG," *Handel Zagraniczny* 2:94–97.

Dubrowsky, Hans-Joachim (1973). "Internationale Investitionsbank – Vereinigung finanzieller Ressourcen sozialistischer Länder," *Einheit* 4:500–4.

(1979). "15 Jahre IBWZ," *Deutsche Aussenpolitik* 1:110–17.

(1981). "Zehn Jahre Internationale Investitionbank der RGW-Länder," *Wirtschaftswissenschaft* 1:88–94.

Dŭlbokov, Sava (1965). *Ikonomičeskoto sŭtrudničestvo i finanso-kreditnite otnošenija meždu socialističeskite strani* (Sofia: BKP).

Dunajewski, Henri (1979). "Quelques observations sur la fonction internationale des monnaies des pays de l'Europe de l'Est," *Revue d'Etudes Comparatives Est-Ouest* 4:195–204.

Durčáková, Jaroslava (1983a). "Problémy využívání korigovaného kursu kčs při stimulaci efektivnosti vývozu a dovozu – 1. část," *Finance a Úvĕr – Čtvrtletní Příloha* 196–200.

(1983b). "Problémy využívání korigovaného kursu kčs při stimulaci efektivnosti vývozu a dovozu – 2. část," *Finance a Úvĕr – Čtvrtletní Příloha* 4:222–41.

(1986). "Nĕkteré možnosti zpřesnĕní výchozího základu kursu v ohledem na dovoz," *Finance a Úvĕr* 2:101–13.

Džindžichadze, Važa G. (1985). "MBĖS na novom ėtape socialističeskoj ėkonomičeskoj integracii," *Den'gi i kredit* 9:3–11.

Editorial (1986). "Soveršenstvovani mechanizma sotrudničestva," *Ėkonomičeskoe sotrudničestvo stran-členov SĖV* 5:18–24.

Epštejn, D. (1985). "Protivorečija neposredstvenno obščestvennogo proizvodstva i soveršenstvovanie upravlenija ėkonomikoj," *Ėkonomičeskie nauki* 9:9–13.

ESE (1965). *Economic survey for Europe in 1962, part II* (New York: United Nations).

Evstigneev, Rubin M. (1986). "Chozjajstvennye mechanizmy stran SĖV i integracija," *Voprosy ėkonomiki* 1:138–45.

Faddeev, Nikolaj V. (1967). "Mnogostoronnee ėkonomičeskoe sotrudničestvo – važnyj faktor razvitija socialističeskich stran," in *Mnogostoronnee ėkonomičeskoe sotrudničestvo socialističeskich gosudarstv – sbornik dokumentov*, edited by Praskov'ja A. Tokareva, Michail D. Kudrjašov, and Vasilij I. Morozov (Moscow: Juridičeskaja literatura), pp. 3–12.

(1974). *Sovet ėkonomičeskoj vzaimopomošči – XXV let* (Moscow: Ėkonomika).

Farkas, György (1978). "A transzferábilis rubel fejlődési lehetőségei, *Külgazdaság* 12:39–50

Faude, Eugen, Gerhard Grote, and Christa Luft, eds. (1976). *Sozialistische Außenwirtschaft* (Berlin, GDR: Die Wirtschaft).

(1984). *Sozialistische Aussenwirtschaft – Lehrbuch* (Berlin, GDR: Die Wirtschaft).

Fedorenko, Nikolaj F. (1984). "Planirovanie i upravlenie – kakimi im byt'?," *Ėkonomika i organizacija promyšlennogo proizvodstva* 12:3–20.

Fedorowicz, Zdzisław (1971). "Międzynarodowy bank inwestycyjnyj," *Bank i Kredyt* 1:1–2.

(1975). *Podstawy teorii pieniądza w gospodarce socialistycznej* (Warsaw: PWE).

(1979). "La convertibilité du rouble transférable," *Revue d'Etudes Comparatives Est–Ouest* 4:177–83.

Fekete, János (1972). "Some connections between the international monetary system and east–west economic relations," *Acta Oeconomica* 2:153–65.

(1978). "Monetary and financial problems in east and west," in *Money and finance in east and west*, edited by Christopher T. Saunders (New York: Springer-Verlag), pp. 15–29.

Fitzgerald, E.V.K. (1985). "The problem of balance in the peripheral socialist economy: a conceptual note," *World Development* 1:5–14.

Fiumel, Henryk de (1984). "Réflexions sur le principe de l'intérêt dans les statuts du Conseil d'Assistance Economique Mutuelle (C.A.E.M.)," *Polish Yearbook of International Law*, vol. 13, pp. 69–75.

Földi, Tamás and Tibor Kiss, eds. (1969). *Socialist world market prices* (Budapest: Akadémiai Kiadó and Leyden: Sijthoff).

Fomin, Boris S. (1978). "Monetary and financial aspects of east–west economic cooperation," in *Money and finance in east and west*, edited by Christopher T. Saunders (New York: Springer-Verlag), pp. 99–110.

Franzmeyer, Fritz and Heinrich Machowski (1973). "Willensbildung und Entschei-
dungsprozesse in der Europäischen Gemeinschaft und im Rat für gegenseitige Wirtschaftshilfe," *Europa-Archiv* 2:47–60.

Gadomski, Marian (1974). "Rubel transferowy–miernikiem wartości?," *Finanse*
10:42–48.

Gančev, Todor (1979). "15 godini dejnost na MBIS v služba na meždunarodnoto
razdelenie na truda i socialističeskata integracija," *Finansi i kredit*, 3:3–14.

Garbuzov, Vasilij F. (1973). "Soveršenstvovanie valjutno-finansovych otnošenij
stran-členov SÈV," in *Meždunarodnaja socialističeskaja valjuta stran-členov SÈV*
(Moscow: Finansy), pp. 5–13.

  (1977). "Meždunarodnaja valjutno-finansovaja sistema stran-členov SÈV na sovremennom ´etape," *Èkonomičeskoe sotrudničestvo stran-členov SÈV* 3:70–74.

  (1985). "Valjutno-finansovye otnošenija–na uroven' novych zadač," *Èkonomičeskoe sotrudničestvo stran-členov SÈV* 4:32–37.

Gavrilov, V. N. and D. A. Sadovskij (1985). "Problemy i perspektivy sotrudničestva
stran SÈV v oblasti mašinostroenija," *Izvestija akademii nauk–serija ékonomičeskaja* 5:95–104.

Georgiev, Georgi S., Vasil Kalčev, and Stojan Enev (1985). *Mechanizŭm za kolektivno
upravlenie na socialističeskata ikonomičeska integracija* (Sofia: Nauka i izkustvo).

Głuchowski, Jan (1981). "Międzynarodowy fundusz walutowy a członkostwo Pol-
ski," *Sprawy Międzynarodowe* 12:55–64.

Góra, Stanisław and Zygmunt Knyziak (1974). *Międzynarodowa specjalizacja produkcji
krajów RWPG* (Warsaw: PWE).

Gorbačëv, Michail S. (1986). *Političeskij doklad central'nogo komiteta KPSS XXVII
s´ezdu kommunističeskoj partii Sovetskogo sojuza* (Moscow: Tass wire in Russian 25
February 1986).

Górczak, Tomasz (1985). "Modele cenowe w krajach RWPG," *Życie Gospodarcze*
29:9.

Górska, Urszula (1978). "System cen w obrotach wzajemnych państw RWPG,"
Rynki Zagraniczne 14:3, 6

Gostomski, Eugeniusz (1979). "Stosunki walutowo-finansowe w procesie integracji
gospodarczej krajów RWPG," *Zeszyty naukowe wydziału ekonomiki transportu uni-
wersytetu gdańskiego* 4:39–56.

Gräbig, Gertrud, Gerhard Brendel, and Hans-Joachim Dubrowsky (1975). *Ware-
Geld-Beziehungen in der sozialistischen Integration* (Berlin, GDR: Die Wirtschaft).

Granick, David (1954). *Management of the industrial firm in the USSR* (New York:
Columbia University Press).

Grinberg, Ruslan S. and Michail S. Ljubskij (1985). "Ceny i valjutnye otnošenija v
sotrudničestve stran SÈV," *Voprosy ekonomiki* 6:99–107.

Grinev, V. S. and A. A. Lebedinskas (1975). "Opredelenie éffektivnosti privlečenija
inostrannych kreditov pri sozdanija na territorii SSSR proizvodstvennych
moščnostej," *Planovoe chozjajstvo* 6:39–47.

Gudac, Toma (1983). Policy responses to external disequilibria in the planned
economies: factors affecting pricing and exchange rate policies (Washington,
DC: International Monetary Fund), Department Memorandum DM/83/47.

  (1984a) "Pricing and exchange rates in planned economies," *Finance and Development* 9:40–43.

  (1984b) The role of credit and interest rate policies in modified planned economies (Washington, DC, International Monetary Fund), Department Memorandum DM/84/52.

Haendcke-Hoppe, Maria (1983). "DDR Außenhandel im Zeichen schrumpfender Westimporte," *Deutschland Archiv* 10:1066–71.

Hájek, Karel (1980). "Světová socialistická bankovní soustava," *Plánované Hospodářství* 2:49–57.

Hardi, Peter (1986). "Die Bedeutung der Ost-West-Zusammenarbeit für die osteuropäischen Länder," *Europa-Archiv* 13:383–92.

Hegemann, Margot (1971). "Die Entwicklung der Zusammenarbeit im RGW," *Zeitschrift für Geschichtswissenschaft* 1:5–33.

(1974). "Gemeinsame Interessen und gemeinsame Aktionen der Sowjetunion und der Volksdemokratien als Faktor für die Entstehung der sozialistischen Staatengemeinschaft," *Jahrbuch für Geschichte der sozialistischen Länder Europas* 1:57–84.

(1980). *Kurze Geschichte des RGW* (Berlin, GDR: VEB Deutscher Verlag der Wissenschaften).

Hewett, Edward A. (1974). *Foreign trade prices in the Council for Mutual Economic Assistance* (Cambridge: Cambridge University Press).

Höhmann, Hans-Heinrich, Michael C. Kaser, and Karl C. Thalheim, eds. (1972). *Die Wirschaftsreformen Osteuropas im Wandel* (Freiburg i.B.: Rombach).

Holzman, Franklyn D. (1976). *International trade under communism – politics and economics* (New York: Basic Books).

(1978). "Comments," in *Money and finance in east and west,* edited by Christopher T. Saunders (New York: Springer-Verlag), pp. 126–7.

(1978) "CMEA's hard currency deficits and rouble convertibility," in *Economic relations between east and west,* edited by Nita Watts (New York: St. Martin's Press), pp. 144–70.

(1979). "Some systemic factors contributing to the convertible currency shortage of centrally planned economies," *The American Economic Review* 2:76–80.

Horsefield, Keith J. (1969). *The International Monetary Fund 1945–1965 – twenty years of international monetary cooperation. vol. I: chronicle* (Washington, DC: International Monetary Fund).

Hrinda, Vasil and Vratislav Válek (1983). "Místo a úloha devizově finančních vztahů při rozvoji hospodářské a vědeckotechnické spolupráce členských států RVHP," *Finance a Úvěr* 11:773–83.

Huschke, Thomas (1984). "Die Börsenpreise als Hauptwarenmarktpreise," *Wissenschaftliche Zeitschrift der Hochschule für Ökonomie "Bruno Leuschner"* 4:42–46.

Ivanova, Vera and Aleksandŭr Zacharčev (1974). *Ekvivalentnost i vzaimna izgoda na meždunarodnija socialističeski pazar* (Sofia: Bŭlgarska akademija na naukite).

Izrjadnov, V. S. and V. N. Kirillov (1973). "Valjutno-finansovye otnosěnija na službe razvitija ėkonomičeskich svjazej meždu stranami-členami SĚV," *Vestnik moskovskogo universiteta – ėkonomika* 6:31–35.

Jackson, Marvin (1976). "Prices and efficiency in Romanian foreign trade," in *Quantitative and analytical studies in east–west economic relations,* edited by Josef C. Brada (Bloomington, IN: IDRC), pp. 117–33.

Janota, Oldřich (1985). "Development of foreign exchange relations among the CMEA countries," *Czechoslovak Foreign Trade* 11:10–12.

JEC (1974). *Reorientation and commercial relations of the economies of Eastern Europe,*

456 *Bibliography*

edited by U.S. Congress, Joint Economic Committee (Washington, DC: Government Printing Office).

(1977). *East European economies post-Helsinki.* edited by U.S. Congress, Joint Economic Committee (Washington, DC: Government Printing Office).

Jordanov, Georgi (1981). "Kreditirane na kapitalni vloženija ot Meždunarodnata investicionna banka," *Finansi i kredit* 3:3–10.

(1983). "Problemi na funkcioniraneto na kredita v prevodni rubli na Meždunarodnata investicionna banka," *Finansi i kredit* 10:38–42.

(1985). "Podobrjavane kreditnata dejnost na Meždunarodnata investicionna banka," *Ikonomika* 11: 34–40.

Kalčev, Vasil (1974). "Teoretičeski problemi na socialističeskata ikonomičeska integracija," *Planovo stopanstvo* 1: 66–71.

Kaplan, Karel (1977). Die Entwicklung des Rates für gegenseitige Wirtschaftshilfe (RgW) in der Zeit von 1949 bis 1957 – zu einigen Fragen der Kontinuität in den Integrationsproblemen und—tendenzen (Ebenhausen: Stiftung Wissenschaft und Politik), typescript.

(1978). *Dans les archives du comité central – 30 ans de secrets du bloc soviétique* (Paris: Albin Michel).

(1979). The Council for Mutual Economic Aid /1949–1951/ –/excerpts of documents with commentary/ (Frankfurt a.M.), mimeographed.

Karavaev, Valerij P. (1979). *Integracija i investicii: problemy sotrudničestva stran SĚV* (Moscow: Nauka).

Karpič, Vilen I. (1976). "Proizvodstvenoto sŭtrudničestvo meždu stranite ot SIV – osnova za progressivnoto razvitie na technija stokoobmen," *Vŭnšna tŭrgovija* 9:9–12.

Kazandžieva, Kina (1983). "Konvertiruemost na socialističeskite valuti pri sŭvremenite uslovija," *Finansi i kredit* 8:27–37.

Kerner, Antonín and Jan Trubač (1975). "Základní rysy metodologie společného plánování," *Acta Universitatis Carolinae–Oeconomica* 2:101–15.

Kisiel, Henryk (1968). "O nową rolę Międzynarodowego banku współpracy gospodarczej," *Życie Gospodarcze* 21:11.

(1974). "Mechanizm rozliczeń międzynarodowych w zakresie wymiany towarów," in *Integracja ekonomiczna krajów socjalistycznych*, 2nd ed., edited by Paweł Bożyk (Warsaw: Książka i Wiedza), pp. 227–62.

Kiss, Tibor (1971). *International division of labour in open economies – with special regard to the CMEA* (Budapest: Akadémiai Kiadó).

(1972). *Hol tart a KGST integráció?* (Budapest: Kossuth).

Klawe, Andrzej J. (1976). "Ceny w handlu międzynarodowym krajów RWPG," *Sprawy Międzynarodowe* 2:90–98.

Klepacki, Zbigniew M. (1975). "Membership and other forms of participation of states in the activities of the socialist economic, scientific and technical intergovernmental organizations," *Polish Yearbook of International Law*, vol. 7, 45–64.

Knyziak, Zygmunt (1974). "Ceny w handlu wzajemnym krajów RWPG a ceny krajowe," in *Integracja ekonomiczna krajów socjalistycznych*, 2nd ed., edited by Paweł Bożyk (Warsaw: Książka i Wiedza), pp. 174–88.

Kobak, Stanislav (1971). "Tätigkeit der Internationalen Investitionsbank," *Die Wirtschaft* 47:21.

Köhler, Heinz (1965). *Economic integration in the Soviet bloc – with an East German case study* (New York: Praeger).

Komissarov, Vasilij P. (1976). *Meždunarodnye valjutno-kreditnye otnošenija SSSR i drugich socialističeskich stran* (Moscow: IMO).

Konstantinov, Jurij A. (1972). "Valjutno-finansovye otnošenija stran SĖV," *Vnešnjaja torgovlja* 10:2–8.

——— (1975). "Prevodnata rubla – integrirana valuta na stranite-členki na SIV," *Finansi i kredit* 7:3–19.

——— (1977). "Meždunarodnaja valjutno-finansovaja sistema stran-členov SĖV na službe socialističeskoj integracii," *Vnešnjaja torgovlja* 12:2–8.

——— (1978a). *Den'gi v sisteme meždunarodnych ėkonomičeskich otnošenij stran SĖV* (Moscow: Finansy).

——— (1978b). "Valjutnaja sistema stran SĖV," *Meždunarodnaja žizn'*, 6:23–34.

——— (1982a). *Meždunarodnaja valjutnaja sistema stran-členov SĖV* (Moscow: Finansy i statistika).

——— (1982b). "Valjutno-kreditnye otnošenija stran-členov SĖV v razvivajuščimisja stranami," *Finansy SSSR* 3:53–60.

——— (1983a). "K voprosu o povyšenii roli perevodnogo rublja, razvitii ego funkcij," *Den'gi i kredit* 3:21–28.

——— (1983b). "Prevodnata rubla v sistemata na meždunarodnite ikonomičeski otnošenija na stranite-členki na SIV," *Finansi i kredit*, 4:32–48.

——— (1983c). "Vzaimodejstvie na nacionalnite valuti s meždunarodnata socialističeska valuta," *Finansi i kredit* 2:3–15.

——— (1984). "Valjutnaja sistema socialističeskogo gosudarstva," *Finansy SSSR* 2:28–35.

Kormnov, Jurij F. (1972). *Specializacja i kooperacja proizvodstva stran SĖV v uslovijach ėkonomičeskoj integracii* (Moscow: Ėkonomika).

——— (1977). "Dol'gosročnye celevye programmy sotrudničestva stran SĖV," *Voprosy ėkonomiki* 1:86–94.

Kornai, János (1959). *Overcentralization of economic administration* (London: Oxford University Press).

——— (1971). *Anti-equilibrium* (Amsterdam: North-Holland).

——— (1972). *Rush versus harmonic growth* (Amsterdam: North-Holland).

——— (1980). *Economics of shortage* (Amsterdam: North-Holland), vols. 1, 2.

——— (1982). *Growth, shortage and efficiency* (Oxford: Blackwell).

Kotábová, Éva (1980). "Směry úvěrové činnosti," *Hospodářské Noviny* 47:11.

Koval'cev, G. (1975). "Socialističeskaja integracija i planirovanie," *Meždunarodnaja žizn'* 7:14–22.

Köves, András (1981). "Befelé vagy kifelé fordulás – gondolatok a KGST-országok külgazdasági stratégiájáról," *Közgazdasági Szemle* 7/8:878–95.

——— (1985). *The CMEA countries in the world economy: turning inwards or turning outwards* (Budapest: Akadémiai Kiadó).

Kozlov, Viktor I. (1978). *Kapital'noe stroitel'stvo i ego rol' v razvitii socialističeskoj ėkonomičeskoj integracii stran-členov SĖV* (Moscow: Strojizdat).

Koz'menko, Vasilij (1986). "Transportnyj faktor i cenoobrazovanie na rynke stran SĖV," *Vnešnjaja torgovlja* 1:25–28.

Kraft, Gerhard (1977). *Die Zusammenarbeit der Mitgliedsländer des RGW auf dem Gebiet der Investitionen* (Berlin, GDR: Akademie-Verlag).

Kranz, Jerzy (1984). "Państwa socjalistyczne w MFW i Banku światowym," *Sprawy Międzynarodowy* 11:27–44.

Krasavina, Lidija N. (1978). "Diskussija o roli zolota v meždunarodnych ėkonomičeskich otnošenijach," *Voprosy ėkonomiki* 2:145–49.

Krasavina, Lidija and E. Baranova (1984). "Aktual'nye problemy meždunarodnych valjutno-kreditnych otnošenija," *Den'gi i kredit*, 6:72–78.

Kraus, Ján (1974). "Ulohy a miesto menovo-finančnej problematiky v 25-ročnej činnosti RVHP," *Finance a Úvěr* 4:217–26.

Kraus, Josef (1985). "Cenová tvorba zemědělsko-potravinářských výrobků v obchodě zemí RVHP," *Zahraniční Obchod* 9:9–12.

Krauss, Krzysztof (1985). " 'Sprawiedliwie' czy w oparciu o rachunek?" *Trybuna Ludu*, 4 July:3.

Kruliš, Zdeněk (1979). *Mezinárodní socialistický úvěr ve společenství RVHP* (Prague: Academia).

Kucharski, Paweł (1974). "Zagadnienia kredytowania i rozliczeń w Między-narodowym banku inwestycyjnym," *Bank i Kredyt* 12:16–19.

Kulczycki, Marek (1979). *Kurs walutowy w systemie kierowania handlem zagranicznym* (Warsaw: PWE).

Kulikov, Vsevolod V. (1972). *Tovarnye otnošenija v mirovom socialističeskom chozjajstve* (Moscow: Moskovskij gosudarstvennyj universitet).

Kuniński, Robert (1986). "Wymienalność rubla transferowego," *Rynki Zagraniczne* 105: 3.

Kunz, Willy, ed. (1982). *Sozialistische ökonomische Integration* (Berlin, GDR: Die Wirtschaft).

Kuraň, Zdeněk (1978). "Za další zvýšení účinnosti úvěrové soustavy Mezinárodní banky hospodářské spolupráce a Mezinárodní investiční banky," *Finance a Úvěr* 1:12–16.

Kuznecova, S. (1985). "Formirovanie cen vo vzaimnoj torgovle stran SĖV," *Meždunarodnaja žizn'* 4:157–8.

Lavigne, Marie (1978). "The International Monetary Fund and the Soviet Union," in *International economics—comparison and interdependencies*, edited by Friedrich Levcik (New York: Springer-Verlag), pp. 367–82.

——— (1983). "The Soviet Union Inside Comecon," *Soviet Studies* 2:135–53.

——— (1984). The evolution of CMEA institutions and policies and the need for struc-tural adjustment (paper presented to the Conference on the Soviet Union and Eastern Europe in the World Economy, Washington, DC, 18–19 October).

——— (1985a). "Les pays socialistes européens et le Fonds Monétaire International," *Le Courrier des Pays de l'Est*, No. 291:29–42.

——— (1985b). *Economie internationale des pays socialistes* (Paris: Armand Collin).

Lebedinskas, A. A. (1974). "Kreditnye otnošenija stran-členov SĖV pri sovmest-nom sooruženii chozjajstvennych ob'ektov," *Den'gi i kredit* 12:74–81.

Lemoine, Françoise (1973). "La fixation des prix du commerce international dans les économies socialistes," *La Documentation Française—Notes et Etudes Documen-taires*, No. 4002:5–30.

——— (1977). "Les prix des échanges à l'intérieur du Conseil d'aide économique mutu-elle," in *Comecon—progrès et perspectives* (Brussels: Nato-Directorate of Eco-nomic Affairs), pp. 135–76.

Lér, Ondřej (1985). "Nástroj úvěrové politiky," *Svět Hospodářství* 83:1.

(1986). "Komplexní program vědeckotechnického pokroku zemí RVHP – význam organizací-koordinátorů," *Svět Hospodářství* 42:1.

Levcik, Friedrich (1975). "Migration und Ausländerbeschäftigung in Osteuropa," *Europäische Rundschau* 4:125–36.

(1977). "Migration and employment of foreign workers in the CMEA countries and their problems," in *East European economies post-Helsinki*, edited by U.S. Congress, Joint Economic Committee (Washington, DC: Government Printing Office), pp. 458–78.

Lidvanova, L. (1985). "Soveršenstvovanie ėkonomičeskogo mechanizma sotrudničestva stran-členov SĖV pri razvitii ich proizvodstvennoj kooperacii," *Ėkonomičeskie nauki* 5:75–80.

Ljakin, Valerij V. (1984). "Meždunarodnyj bank ėkonomičeskogo sotrudničestva (k 20-letniju dejatel'nosti)," *Voprosy ėkonomiki* 1:127–34.

Ljubskij, Michail S., Lilyja Ch. Suljaeva, and Vladimir M. Šastitko (1978). *Valjutnye i kreditnye otnošenija stran SĖV* (Moscow: Nauka).

Loščakov, Aleksandr I. (1984). "Interv'ju glavnoj redakcii – 35 let SĖV: istoki i sovremennost'," *Ėkonomičeskoe sotrudničestvo stran-členov SĖV* 5: 33–36.

Lukin, Lev I. (1974). "Pervoe desjatiletie Soveta ėkonomičeskoj vzaimopomošči," *Voprosy istorii* 4:39–57.

Machlup, Fritz (1973). "The expanded role of SDRs and the possibilities of an SDR standard," in *Europe and the evolution of the international monetary system*, edited by Alexander K. Swoboda (Leyden: Sijthoff), pp. 25–34.

Machowski, Heinrich (1969). "Zur Preisbildung im RgW-Intrablockhandel: das Beispiel der polnischen Steinkohle," *Osteuropa-Wirtschaft* 2:89–112.

(1970). "Organisatorische Probleme der wirtschaftlichen Zusammenarbeit im Rat für gegenseitige Wirtschaftshilfe," *Vierteljahrshefte zur Wirtschaftsforschung* 4:279–89.

(1973). "Die Funktion der DDR im RgW," *Deutschland Archiv*, Special October Issue on the GDR, pp. 3–19.

(1983). "Rat für gegenseitige Wirtschaftshilfe," in *Handbuch der Finanzwirtschaft*, vol. 4, 3rd ed., edited by Fritz Neumark (Tübingen: J. C. B. Mohr (Paul Siebeck), pp. 365–92.

Manžulo, Aleksej (1983). "Šestaja sessija JUNKTAD: celi i zadači," *Vnešnjaja torgovlja* 4:15–20.

Marciszewski, Jerzy, and Jerzy Rutkowski (1976). "Ceny w ekonomicznym mechaniźmie współpracy krajów RWPG," *Handel Zagraniczny* 7:10–14.

Marczewski, Jean (1973). *Crise de la planification socialiste?* (Paris: Presses Universitaires de France).

Marer, Paul (1974). "Soviet economic policy in Eastern Europe," in *Reorientation and commercial relations of the economies of Eastern Europe*, edited by U.S. Congress, Joint Economic Committee (Washington, DC: Government Printing Office), pp. 135–63.

Marer, Paul and John M. Montias, eds. (1980). *East European integration and east–west trade* (Bloomington, IN: Indiana University Press).

Marinov, Velko T. (1974). "Meždunarodnijat investicionen kredit i socialističeskata ikonomičeska integracija," *Planovo stopanstvo* 1:16–29.

Marrese, Michael and Jan Vaňous (1983). *Soviet subsidization of trade with Eastern Europe – a Soviet perspective* (Berkeley, CA: Institute of International Studies).

Matějček, Petr (1984). "Tvorba kontraktních cen zemědělských produktů ve vzájemném obchodě členských státu RVHP," *Zahraniční Obchod* 1:11–14.

Matejka, Harriet (1974). "Convertibility in East Europe," *Annales d'Etudes Internationales – Annals of International Studies* 5:175–90.

——— (1977). "Conclusion of the colloquium," in *The international payments crisis and the development of east–west trade* (Brussels: Etablissements Emile Bruylants), pp. 107–19.

Matějka, Karel (1986). "Pro nás klíčový úkol," *Hospodářské Noviny:* 26, 1, 4.

Matjuchin, Georgij G. (1977). "Novaja forma mirovych deneg," *Mirovaja ėkonomika i meždunarodnye otnošenija* 4:38–47.

——— (1978). "The role of gold in the future monetary system," in *Money and finance in east and west,* edited by Christopher T. Saunders (New York: Springer-Verlag), pp. 243–49.

Matjuchin, Georgij G. and V. Šenaev (1978). "Novaja valjutnaja sistema i uroki Bretton–Vudsa," *Mirovaja ėkonomika i meždunarodnye otnošenija* 6: 43–52.

Matlin, A. (1985). "Zakon stoimosti i planovoe cenoobrazovanie," *Voprosy ėkonomiki* 11: 76–87.

Mazanov, Gennadij G. (1970). *Meždunarodnye rasčěty stran-členov SĖV* (Moscow: Finansy).

MBÉS, *Meždunarodnyj bank ėkonomičeskogo sotrudničestva* (Moscow: MBÉS), annual reports starting with activity year 1964.

Medvedev, Roy A. (1972). *Let history judge – the origins and consequences of Stalinism* (New York: Knopf).

Menžinskij, Viktor I., ed. (1971). *Meždunarodnye organizacii socialističeskich stran* (Moscow: Meždunarodnye otnošenija).

Miastkowski, Lech (1980). "Zmiany struktury i poziomu cen detalicznych w gospodarce socjalistycznej," *Ekonomista* 4:893–915.

Mikesell, Raymond F. (1951). "Negotiating at Bretton Woods," in *Negotiating with the Russians,* edited by Raymond Dennett and Joseph E. Johnson (Boston: World Peace Foundation), pp. 101–16.

Mironjuk, Michail A. (1983). "Perevodnyj rubl'. Praktika ispol'zovanych rubljach," *Bjulleten' inostrannoj kommerčeskoj informacii* 105:1,8.

Mirošničenko, K. G. (1974). "Za dal'nejšee ukreplenie kollektivnoj socialističeskoj valjuty – perevodnogo rublja," *Finansy SSSR* 2:83–87.

Misiak, Marek (1969). "A blueprint for closer CMEA integration," *Polish Perspectives* 2:18–28.

Mitrofanova, Nina M. (1973). "O vzaimosvjazi vnutrennich i vnešnetorgovych cen v evropejskich socialističeskich stranach," *Planovoe chozjajstvo* 9:90–97.

——— (1974). "Perspektivy dal'nejšego soveršenstvovanija vnešnetorgovych cen socialističeskich stran," *Planovoe chozjajstvo* 4:41–49.

——— (1977). "Ob ėkonomičeskoj priorode kontraktnych cen vo vzaimnom sotrudničestve stran SĖV," *Izvestija akademii nauk SSSR – serija ėkonomičeskaja* 5:116–24.

——— (1978). *Ceny v mechanizme ėkonomičeskogo sotrudničestva stran-členov SĖV* (Moscow: Nauka).

——— (1982). "O kontraktnych cenach na prodovol'stvie," *Voprosy ėkonomiki* 9:140–6.

——— (1986). "Sistema kontrolja cen v stranach SĖV," *Voprosy ėkonomiki* 7:109–118.

Molotov, Vjačeslav M. (1949). *Problems of foreign policy – speeches and statements* (Moscow: Foreign Languages Publishing House).

Možin, A. (1986). "Prjamye vzjazi: uslovija, problemy, perspektivy," *Ėkonomičeskaja gazeta* 37:20.

Mrňa, Dušan (1986). "Aktivní roli měnovým vztahům," *Hospodářské Noviny* 24: 3.

Mujżel, Jan (1974). "Zmiany poziomu cen w gospodarce socjalistycznej," *Ekonomista* 4:817–45.

Nattland, Karl-Heinz (1972). *Der Außenhandel in der Wirtschaftsreform der DDR* (Berlin: Duncker und Humblot).

Nazarkin, Konstantin I. (1971). "Rol' MBĖS v ėkonomičeskom sotrudničestve stran SĖV," *Meždunarodnaja žizn'* 6:64–71.

(1972). "Kompleksnaja programma integracii i zadači Meždunarodnogo banka ėkonomičeskogo sotrudničestva," *Meždunarodnaja žizn'* 7:28–36.

(1973). "Kompleksnaja programma integracii i zadači Meždunarodnogo banka ėkonomičeskogo sotrudničestva," in *Meždunarodnaja socialističeskaja valjuta stran-členov SĖV* (Moscow: Finansy), pp. 76–87.

(1974). "MBĖS v valjutnoj sisteme socialističeskogo sodružestva," *Meždunarodnaja žizn'* 2:60–67.

(1979). "The role of the IBEC in the international socialist system," *IBEC Economic Bulletin* 9:2–14.

Němeček, Edvard (1972). "K otázce sjednocení kursu československé mény," *Acta Universitatis Carolinae – Oeconomica* 2:3–18.

(1975). "Funkce kursu socialistické měny," *Acta Universitatis Carolinae – Oeconomica* 2:71–86.

Neustadt, Alojz (1974). "Svetové ceny v socialistickom obchode," *Hospodářské Noviny* 23:10.

Nove, Alec (1971). "Inflation, integration and convertibility in Eastern Europe," *International Currency Review* 5:15–20.

Nyers, Rezső (1977). "A KGST többoldalú integrációs intézkedéseinek hatása a magyar népgazdaságra az 1976–1985–as években," *Közgazdasági Szemle* 4:423–9.

(1982). "Hagyomány és újítás a KGST-együttműködésben," *Közgazdasági Szemle* 4:385–403.

Ondráček, Mojmír (1970). "Individualizaci reprodukčních podmínek a reálný kurz mény," *Finančné Študie* 4:57–78.

(1983). "Přístupy ekonomů socialistických zemí k řešení měnové problematiky RVHP – úloha měnových kursů (koeficientů) v plánovitě řízené ekonomice," *Finance a Úvěr* 1:60–69.

Oschlies, Wolf (1983). "Polnische 'Gastarbeiterzy' in der DDR – Rechtsgrundlagen und Alltag," *Deutschland Archiv* 10:1084–91.

Pachta, Pavel (1980). "Rozvoj spolupráce členských států RVHP v oblasti neobchodnich platů," *Zahraniční Obchod* 7/8:15–17.

Pécsi, Kálmán (1977). *A KGST termelési integráció közgazdasági kérdései* (Budapest: Közgazdasági és Jogi Könyvkiadó).

Pěnkava, Jaromír (1975). "Zdokonalování cenové tvorby v procesu socialistické ekonomické integrace členských států RVHP," *Finance a Úvěr* 10:649–57.

Perova, Viktorija (1984). "Sotrudničestvo stran-členov SĖV v sooruženii proizvodstvennych ob'jektov," *Vnešnjaja torgovlja* 4:10–14.

Petřivalský, Jiří (1972). "Zdokonalování devizových vztahů zemí RVHP," *Plánované Hospodářství* 2:38–45.

Pilat, Vasile and Daniel Dăianu (1984). "Some problems of the development of European socialist economies," *Revue Roumaine d'Etudes Internationales* 3:245–61.

Pinder, John (1972). "An Ostpolitik for the Community," in *The European Community in the world – the external relations of the enlarged European Community*, edited by Ph. P. Everts (Rotterdam: Rotterdam University Press), pp. 37–68.

Poller, Roland (1984). "Einige Aspekte der langfristigen Investitionskoordinierung der RGW Länder," *Wissenschaftliche Zeitschrift der Hochschule für Ökonomie 'Bruno Leuschner'* 1:22–6.

Poller, Roland and István Tesner (1982). "A KGST-országok beruházási együttműködése a szocialista gazdasági integráció folyamatában," *Közgazdasági Szemle* 9:1072–84.

Popov, Konstantin I. (1969). "Modern theories of building up price systems in trade between socialist countries," in *Price formation in various economies*, edited by Douglas C. Hague (London: Macmillan), pp. 145–50.

Portes, Richard (1984). The theory and measurement of macroeconomic disequilibrium in centrally planned economies (paper presented to the Conference on the Soviet Union and Eastern Europe in the World Economy, Washington, DC, 18–19 October).

Potáč, Svatopluk (1973). "Erfolgreiche Tätigkeit der Internationalen Investitionsbank," *Aussenhandel der Tschechoslowakei* 12:6.

Pounds, Norman J.G. (1965). *Eastern Europe* (London-Harlow: Longmans).

Poznanski, Kazimierz (1985a). Competitiveness of Polish industry (paper presented at the Workshop on the Polish Economy and Debt, Washington, DC, 21–22 October).

  (1985b). "Les investissements directs des firmes multinationales et le progrès technique en Europe de l'Est et en Amérique latine," *Revue d'Études Est–Ouest* 3:17–46.

  (1986). "Competition between Eastern Europe and developing countries in the western market for manufactured goods," in *East European economies: slow growth in the 1980s*, vol. 2, edited by Joint Economic Committee, Congress of the United States (Washington, DC: Government Printing Office), pp. 62–90.

Prybyla, Jan S. (1986). "China's economic experiment: from Mao to market," *Problems of Communism* 1:21–36.

Ptaszek, Jan (1978). "Współpraca w ramach międzynarodowego systemu walutowo-finansowego krajów RWPG," *Handel Zagraniczny* 9:23–25.

Rączkowski, Stanisław (1977). "The international monetary crisis and the socialist countries," in *The international payments crisis and the development of east–west trade* (Brussels: Etablissements Emile Bruylants), pp. 71–105.

Radev, Stojan (1978). "Kreditni otnošenija ot nov tip," *Ikonomičeska život* 32:6.

Rémy, Alain (1981). Le rôle de l'or dans l'économie monétaire occidentale: analyses soviétiques (Paris: Université de Paris I – Panthéon-Sorbonne), Thèse de 3ème cycle, mimeographed.

  (1985). *Un retour à l'or? Analyses soviétiques sur le système monétaire international* (Paris: Economica).

Rewkiewicz, Jan and Maciej Tekielski (1981). "Kontrowersje wokół kursu walutowego," *Rynki Zagraniczne* 143:3–6.

Ribi, Rolf C. (1970). *Das Comecon – eine Untersuchung über die Problematik der wirtschaftlichen Integration der sozialistischen Länder* (Zürich: Polygraphischer Verlag).

Robinson, Sherman, Laura d'Andrea Tyson and Leyla Woods (1984). Conditionality and adjustment in socialist economies: Hungary and Yugoslavia (paper presented to the Conference on the Soviet Union and Eastern Europe in the World Economy, Washington, DC, 18–19 October).

Rutkowska, I. and Józef Rutkowski (1977). *Problemy współczesnej gospodarki światowej* (Warsaw: Książka i Wiedza).

Rutkowski, Jerzy (1977). "Stabilność i elastyczność cen w obrotach wzajemnych krajów RWPG," *Handel Zagraniczny* 1:3–8.

Rymarczyk, Jan (1978). "Współpraca krajów RWPG w wykorzystaniu zasobów ludzkich a procesy integracji gospodarczej," *Sprawy Międzynarodowe* 4:42–52.

Šagalov, Gennadij L. (1986). "Voprosy povyšenija effektivnosti vnešneėkonomičeskich svjazej," *Planovoe chozjajstvo* 2:115–20.

Saltiel, Jean-Pierre (1978). "Le rôle éventuel du rouble transférable dans le commerce est-ouest," in *Unités et monnaies de compte*, edited by Jean-Louis Guglielmi and Marie Lavigne (Paris: Economica), p. 140.

Samorodov, Aleksandr (1983). "JUNCTAD-VI i valjutno-finansovye problemy," *Vnešnjaja torgovlja* 5:37–44.

Šanina, Valentina A. (1976). *Transportno-ėkonomičeskie svjazi stran-členov SĖV* (Moscow: Nauka).

Savov, Michail N. (1973). "Sovet ėkonomičeskoj vzaimopomošči (osnovnye celi, principy, funkcii i struktura)," *Izvestija akademii nauk SSSR – serija ėkonomičeskaja* 4:49–62.

Seiffert, Wolfgang (1983). *Kann der Ostblock überleben? – Der Comecon und die Krise des sozialistischen Wirtschaftssystems* (Bergisch Gladbach: Gustav Lübbe Verlag).

Selucký, Radoslav (1972). *Economic reforms in Eastern Europe: political background and economic significance* (New York: Praeger).

SĖV (1979). *Kommjunike o zasedanijach ispolnitel'nogo komiteta Soveta ėkonomičeskoj vzaimopomošči* (Moscow: SĖV Sekretariat).

Silvestrov, Sergej (1986). "Podnik v integraci? dosud mnoho překážek!" *Hospodářské Noviny* 29:3.

Širjaev, Jurij S. (1986a). "Mechanizm sotrudničestva – novye kriterii," *Ėkonomičeskaja gazeta* 30:20.

(1986b). "Naučno-techničeskij progress i socialističeskaja integracija," *Voprosy ėkonomiki* 5:129–36.

Širjaev, P. (1982). "Investicionnoe sotrudničestvo – faktor intensifikacii proizvodstva v stranach-členach SĖV," *Ėkonomičeskie nauki* 5:67–74.

Sláma, Jiří (1979). Die politische und wirtschaftliche Integration Osteuropas in der Stalinära (1945–1953) (Munich: Osteuropa-Institut München), typescript.

Sobell, Vladimir (1984). *The red market – industrial co-operation and specialisation in Comecon* (Aldershot: Gower).

Špaček, Petr (1981). *Platebně úvěrový mechanismus v RVHP* (Prague: Academia).

(1984). "MBHS – základní článek platebního a úvěrového mechanismu členských států RVHP," *Finance a Úvěr* 7:433–40.

(1985). "Posílit úlohu kolektivní měny," *Svět Hospodářství* 17:1.

(1986). "Kursové aspekty efektivnosti zahraničního cestovního ruchu v členských státech RVHP," *Finance a Úvěr – Čtvrtletní Příloha* 1:1–19.

Spiller, Hans, ed. (1984). *Finanz- und Währungsbeziehungen zu nichtsozialistischen Ländern* (Berlin, GDR: Staatsverlag).

Spröte, Wolfgang (1983). "The socialist countries' position on international economic relations," in *The transformation of the international economic order*, special issue of *Asia, Africa, Latin America*, II, p. 23.

Stancu, Ştefan (1978). "Un eveniment remarcabil în dezvoltarea colaborării şi cooperării economice dintre ţările membre ale C.A.E.R.," *Revista Economică* 27:24–26.

Stepanov, V. V. and A. Ju. Šemakin (1986). "Dejatel'nost' Meždunarodnogo investicionnogo banka," *Bjulleten' inostrannoj kommerčeskoj informacii* 73:2, 8.

Steve, G.T., ed., *Pick's currency yearbook* (New York: Pick), various issues.

Stirtzel, Rosemarie (1977). Zum Einfluß welwirtschaftlichen Strukturveränderungen auf dem Prozeß der planmäßigen Gestaltung der sozialistischen ökonomischen Integration under Beachtung des internationalen sozialistischen Kredits (Halle (Saale), Martin-Luther-Universität), doctoral dissertation, mimeographed.

Svěrák, Vladislav (1985). "Devizově finanční vztahy RVHP – předpoklady pro zavedení kriteriálního kursu," *Hospodářské Noviny* 10:10.

Syčěv, Vjačeslav V. (1985). "Novi široki chorizonti," *Ikonomičeski život* 28:8–9.

(1986a). "Novye rubeži naučno-techničeskogo sotrudničestva," *Ėkonomičeskoe sotrudničestvo stran-členov SĖV* 1:14–19.

(1986b). "Novye rubeži naučno-techničeskogo progressa stran-členov SĖV, *Planovoe chozjajstvo* 4:41–51.

Tardos, Márton (1969). "A model of intra-regional foreign trade," in *Socialist world market prices*, edited by Tamás Földi and Tibor Kiss, (Budapest: Akadémiai Kiadó and Leyden: Sijthoff), pp. 145–66.

Tarnovskij, Oleg I. and Nina M. Mitrofanova (1968). *Stoimost' i cena na mirovom socialističeskom rynke* (Moscow: Nauka).

Tatu, Michel (1985). *Eux et nous – les relations est–ouest entre deux détentes* (Paris: Fayard).

Teichmanowa, Eufemia (1976). "Koszt transportu w obrotach towarowych między krajami RWPG," *Handel Zagraniczny* 11:37–9.

Thümmler, Wolfgang (1983). "Geldtheoretische Aspekte der kollektiven Währung der Mitgliedsländer des RGW – transferabler Rubel," *Wissenschaftliche Zeitschift der Humboldt-Universität zu Berlin* 4:441–5.

Timošin, Viktor G. (1974). *Razvitie otnošenij planomernosti v mirovoj socialističeskoj sistema chozjajstva* (Moscow: Moskovskij universitet).

Tokareva, Praskov'ja A., ed. (1981). *Mnogostoronnee ėkonomičeskoe sotrudničestvo socialističeskich gosudarstv – dokumenty 1975–1980* (Moscow: Juridičeskaja literatura, 4th edition).

Tokareva, Praskov'ja A., Michail D. Kudrjašov, and Vasilij I. Morozov, eds. (1967). *Mnogostoronnee ėkonomičeskoe sotrudničestvo socialističeskich gosudarstv – sbornik dokumentov* (Moscow: Juridičeskaja literatura).

(1972). *Mnogostoronnee ėkonomičeskoe sotrudničestvo socialističeskich gosudarstv – sbornik dokumentov*, 2nd ed. (Moscow: Juridičeskaja literatura).

Tömpe, István (1978). "On the economic nature of investment contributions between CMEA countries," *Acta Oeconomica* 4:313–23.

Triffin, Robert (1957). *Europe and the money muddle—from bilateralism to near-convertibility, 1947–1956* (New Haven, CT: Yale University Press).

UN (1968). "Note on the institutional developments in the foreign trade of the Soviet Union and Eastern European countries," *Economic Bulletin for Europe* 1:43–52.

(1973). "Recent changes in the organization of foreign trade in the centrally planned economies," *Economic Bulletin for Europe* 1:36–49.

(1981). "Exploration of growth determinants and patterns," *Economic Bulletin for Europe*, 3:345–433.

(1983). Joint statement of Group D and Mongolia regarding the launching of global negotiations (New York: United Nations), document A/38/479.

UNCTAD (1966). *International monetary issues and developing countries—report of the group of experts* (New York: United Nations), publication No. E.66.II.D.2.

(1970). *International monetary reform and co-operation for development—report of the expert group on international monetary issues* (New York: United Nations), publication No. E.70.II.D.2.

(1976). *Proceedings of the United Nations, Conference on Trade and Development, fourth session, vol. I—reports and annexes* (New York: United Nations), publication No. E.76.II.D.10.

(1977). *Multilateral system of payments in transferable roubles of the member countries of the Council for Mutual Economic Assistance* (Geneva: UNCTAD), document TD/B/AC.23/5 of 19 April 1977.

(1979). *Proceedings of the United Nations Conference on Trade and Development, fifth session, vol. I—reports and annexes* (New York: United Nations), publication No. E.79.II.D.14.

(1980). Position paper submitted by experts from Group D on the requirements of an international monetary system which would foster world trade and development, Geneva: TD/B/AC.CRP.1.

(1983a). *Proceedings of the United Nations Conference on Trade and Development, sixth session, vol. I—reports and annexes* (New York: United Nations), publication No. E.83.II.D.6.

(1983b). *The world economic situation with special emphasis on development: proposal submitted by the German Democratic Republic on behalf of Group D*, Document TD/L.230 of 18 June 1983, reproduced in German in *Gemeinsame Erklärungen sozialistischer Staaten zu Fragen der Umgestaltung der internationalen Wirtschaftsbeziehungen auf demokratischer Basis* (Berlin, GDR: Ministerium für Auswärtige Angelegenheiten), pp. 1–16.

Uschakow, Alexander (1983a). *Integration im RGW (COMECON) — Dokumente* (Baden-Baden: Nomos).

(1983b). "Probleme der politischen Kooperation und Integration in Osteuropa," in *Moderne Welt—Jahrbuch für Ost—West Fragen 1983*, p. 191–206.

Usenko, E. T. (1985). "Ėkonomičeskoe soveščanie stran-členov SĖV i nekotorye pravovye problemy socialističeskoj integracii i sochranenija mira," *Sovetskoe gosudarstvo i pravo* 6:90–8.

Vajs, Tiberij A. (1974). "Sotrudničestvo stran SĖV v ispol'zovanii rabočej sily," *Ėkonomičeskie nauki* 7:67–73.

(1976). *Problemy sotrudničestva stran SĖV v ispol'zovanii trudovych resursov* (Moscow: Nauka).

466   Bibliography

(1982). "Cooperation of the CMEA countries in the sphere of employment," in *Employment policies in the Soviet Union and Eastern Europe*, edited by Jan Adam (New York: St. Martin's Press), pp. 189–208.

Vajs, Tiberij A., and Ljudmila S. Degtjar' (1973). "Sotrudničestvo stran SĚV v ispol'zovanii trudovych resursov," *Planovoe chozjajstvo* 12:95–100.

Válek, Vratislav (1981). "Financial and monetary relations within the CMEA," *Czechoslovak Foreign Trade* 9:9–12.

(1983a). "Význam a postavení společné investiční činnosti členských států RVHP v procesa socialistické ekonomické integrace," *Politická Ekonomie* 8:843–52.

(1983b). "Efektivnost výstavby integračních objektu v rámů RVHP," *Zahraniční Obchod* 10:10–14.

(1984). *Společná investiční činnost členských států* RVHP (Prague: SNTL).

(1985). "Zdokonalování devizově finančního mechanismu v rámi RVHP," *Zahraniční Obchod* 8:10–14.

Vasin, Jurij F. (1980). "V interesach realizacii kompleksnoj programmy," *Den'gi i kredit* 1:70–76.

Vel'jaminov, Georgij M. (1986). "Pravovye osnovy sotrudničestva stran-členov SĚV na sovremennom ètape," *Vnešnjaja torgovlja* 2:18–21.

Vencovský, František (1979). "Funkce zlata v historii československé měny," *Finance a Úvěr* 12:802–817.

Větrovský, Jiří (1971). "Změny v mezinárodní bankovní soustavě zemí RVHP," *Finance a Úvěr* 5:306–15.

Vincze, Imre (1972). "World market prices and domestic prices," in *Reform of the economic mechanism in Hungary–development 1968–1971*, edited by Otto Gadó (Budapest: Akadémiai Kiadó). pp. 131–45.

(1977). "A KGST közös valutájáról és nemzetközi elszámolási rendszeréről," *Közgazdasági Szemle* 6:627–43.

(1978a). *A KGST nemzetközi valutarendszere* (Budapest: Közgozdasági és Jogi Könyvkiadó).

(1978b). "Multilaterality, transferability and exhangeability: their content and conditions of their realization within the CMEA," *Acta Oeconomica* 1/2:127–45.

(1984). *The international payments and monetary system in the integration of the socialist countries* (The Hague: Martinus Nijhoff).

Virius, Miroslav and Jaroslav Bálek (1976). "Pohyb pracovních sil mezi zeměmi Rady vzájemné hospodářske pomoci," *Zahraniční Obchod* 9:4–8.

VK (1981a). "Další zdokonalování finančné devizových vztahů," *Svět Hospodářství* 101:5.

(1981b). "Čs. účast na společných investicích zemí RVHP," *Svět Hospodářství* 116:3.

(1983). "Impuls pro rozvoj zahraničního obchodu," *Svět Hospodářství*, 45:1,5.

(1985a). "Tvorba kontraktních cen," *Svět Hospodářství* 117:1.

(1985b). "Mezinárodní investiční banka: významný faktor spolupráce v investicích," *Svět Hospodářství* 153:1,4.

(1986a). "RVHP–za lepší finanční mechanismus," *Svět Hospodářství* 32:4.

(1986b). "RVHP–pro lepší spolupráci ve vědě," *Svět Hospodářství* 71:5.

(1986c). "Rada vzájemné hospodářské pomoci: tvorba společných finančních fondů," *Svět Hospodářství* 70:4.

Vorkauf, H. (1977). "Studie zu Problemen der Entwicklung des abgestimmten Planes mehrseitiger Integrationsmaßnahmen zu einer qualitativ neuen Form der Planungszusammenarbeit der RGW-Länder," *Volkswirtschaftsplanung – Beiträge zur Theorie und Praxis* 4.

Vorob'ëv, V. A. (1974). "Kompleksnaja programma socialističeskoj ékonomičeskoj integracii i Meždunarodnyj investicionnyj bank," *Den'gi i kredit* 9:6–13.

Weiss, W. (1979). *Sozialistische internationale Produktionskooperation und Intensivierung – Zum 30. Jahrestag der Gründung des RGW* (Jena: Friedrich-Schiller-Universität).

Wellisz, Stanisław (1964). *The economics of the Soviet bloc* (New York: McGraw-Hill).

Wesołowski, Jerzy (1974). "Kierunki rozwoju systemu walutowego w Polsce," *Studia Finansowe*, vol. 16 pp. 81–96.

(1977). *System walutowy krajów RWPG* (Warsaw: PWE).

(1983). "Kursy niehandlowe – przeszłość czy przyskłość?" *Handel Zagraniczny* 5:16–19.

(1983). "Problemy kursu i wymienalności," *Finanse* 6:1–10.

Wiesel, Iván (1973). "A kamat szerepe a szocialista valutáris rendszerben és a KGST tagállamok gazdasági együttműködésében," *Pénzügyi Szemle* 5:387–99.

Wilczynski, Jozef (1970). *The economics of socialism* (London: Allen and Unwin).

(1972). *Socialist economic development and reforms – from extensive to intensive growth under central planning in the USSR, Eastern Europe and Yugoslavia* (London: Macmillan).

(1978). *Comparative monetary economics – capitalist and socialist monetary systems and their interrelations in the changing international scene* (New York: Oxford University Press).

(1983). *Industrial relations in planned economies, market economies and the third world – a comparative study of ideologies, institutions, practices, and problems* (New York: St. Martin's Press).

Wiles, Peter J. (1962). *The political economy of communism* (Oxford: Blackwell).

(1968). *Communist international economics* (Oxford: Blackwell).

(1973). "On purely financial convertibility," in *Banking, money and credit in Eastern Europe*, edited by Yves Laulan (Brussels: Nato Directorate), pp. 119–25.

Wojciechowski, Bronisław (1982). "Kurs złotówki," *Handel Zagraniczny* 1/2:6–7.

Wojciechowski, Henryk (1977). *Problemy integracyjne krajów socjalistycznych* (Poznań: Akademia Ekonomiczna w Poznaniu).

Wolf, Thomas A. (1980). "On the adjustment of centrally planned economies to external economic disturbances," in *East European integration and east–west trade*, edited by Paul Marer and John M. Montias (Bloomington, IN: Indiana University Press), pp. 86–111.

(1984). The role of exchange rates in economic stabilization and structural adjustment in four centrally planned economies (paper presented to the Conference on the Soviet Union and Eastern Europe in the World Economy, Washington, DC, 18–19 October).

(1985a). "Economic stabilization in planned economies – towards an analytical framework," *Staff Papers* 1:78–131.

(1985b). "Exchange rate systems and adjustment in planned economies," *Staff Papers* 2:211–47.

(1985c). Devaluation in modified planned economies: a preliminary model for Hungary (Washington, DC: International Monetary Fund), department memorandum DM/85/59.

Wyczalkowski, Marian (1966). "Communist economics and currency convertibility," *Staff Papers* 2:155–97.

Yergin, Daniel (1977). *Shattered peace – the origins of the cold war and the national security state* (Boston: Houghton Mifflin).

Zacharov, Stanislav N. (1975). *Rasčëty èffektivnosti vnešneèkonomičeskich svjazej (voprosy metodologii i metodika rasčëtov)* (Moscow: Ėkonomika).

Zápotocký, Evžen, et al. (1977). *Mezinárodní hospodářské vztahy – II. socialismus* (Prague: SPN).

Žolobov, Vadim (1986a). "MIB: orientacija na uskorenie naučno-techničeskogo progressa," *Ėkonomičeskaja gazeta* 23:21.

(1986b). "MIB i sovremennye zadači sotrudničestva stran SĖV," *Vnešnjaja torgovlja* 5:19–21.

Zsolnai, András and Evgenij Gavrilov (1985). "Sbliženie chozjajstvennych mechanizmov," *Ėkonomičeskoe sotrudničestvo stran-členov SĖV* 12:45–48.

Žukov, V. N., and Jurij Ja. Ol'sevič (1969). *Teoretičeskie i metodologičeskie problemi soveršenstvovanija cenoobrazovanija na rynke SĖV* (Moscow: Nauka).

Żukrowska, Katarzyna (1984). "Zasoby pracy krajów RWPG a współpraca międzynarodowa," *Sprawy Międzynarodowe* 11:91–102.

Zwass, Adam (1968). *Pieniądz dwóch rynków – zarys rozwoju i kierunków reform* (Warsaw: PWN).

(1971). "Aufgaben und Funktionen der Internationalen Bank für wirtschaftliche Zusammenarbeit," *Vierteljahrshefte zur Wirtschaftsforschung* 2:132–47.

(1974). *Zur Problematik der Währungsbeziehungen zwischen Ost und West* (Vienna: Springer-Verlag).

(1979). "Inwieweit transferierbar sind die RGW-Währungen?" *Kredit und Kapital* 1:121–38.

Index

accumulation, definition of, 44
adjustment mechanisms, 91
adjustment policies
  and CMEA prices, 187–95
  in CPE, 88, 117–23
  definition of, 14
  in early 1980s, 16, 70, 92–105
  and imbalances, 88–92, 110–15; cures for, 112–15; symptoms of, 111–12
  and indirect coordination, 103–5, 113–17
  in ME, 88, 115–17, 164, 425
  in mid-1980s, 72–3, 84, 105–10, 403
  in MPE, 88, 123–6
  in PE, 102–5, 425
  and price formation, 186–7
Afghanistan, 251
agreed specialization, 9–11
  see also bilateralism; plan coordination; specialization; structural bilateralism; trade model and prices
agricultural growth, 93, 95, 96, 99, 178
Albania, 1, 421, 423
Alchimov, Vladimir S., 442
Allen, Mark, 366, 444
Angola, 399, 419
antimercantilism, 92, 106
arbitrage, 134, 137, 146, 197, 295, 435
  see also bilateralism; East–West trade; structural bilateralism
autarky, 36, 42, 43, 45, 48, 69, 137, 190, 193, 325
  see also autonomy in economic policy; bilateralism; Council for Mutual Economic Assistance (CMEA) prices; economic model; economic reform and strategy; socialist economic integration (SEI); specialization; trade model and prices; world market prices (WMPs)
autonomy in economic policy, 6, 187, 190, 198–9, 202, 382
  see also economic model; strategy of growth; socialist economic integration (SEI)

Bácskai, Tamás, 444
Bakoveckij, O. D., 430
Bálek, Jaroslav, 439
Balkan federation, 92, 420
  see also Council for Mutual Economic Assistance (CMEA) founding; federalism in Eastern Europe; integration, approaches to
Bancor, 288, 436
Bank for International Settlements (BIS), 271
Banking School, 90
Basic Directions, see under Council for Mutual Economic Assistance (CMEA) documents
Basic Principles of the International Socialist Division of Labor (Basic Principles), see under Council for Mutual Economic Assistance (CMEA) documents
Beličenko, Al'bert N., 442
Belovič, Alexander, 329, 440, 442
Berlin method, 327
  see also capital mobility; International Investment Bank (IIB); joint enterprises; joint investment
bilateralism, 48, 63, 82–3, 85–6
  and capital transactions, 146, 155
  and clearing credits, 146, 155
  and economic model, 153–6, 269–70
  and integration in 1980s, 73, 86
  and prices, 131, 137, 142, 146–8, 153–6, 188
  and reexports, 146, 155
  and specialization, 155, 188
  and strategy of growth, 63, 153–6
  see also capital mobility; clearing; economic model; plan coordination; structural bilateralism; swing credits; trade and payments agreements
Borisov, Stanislav M., 264
Bourguinat, Henri, 256
Bretton Woods system (BWS), 17, 207, 222, 361, 409
  benefits of, 253–4
  conditions for membership in, 243–4, 256
  and convertibility, 243, 247, 253, 257, 259, 261, 265, 266
  and economic reform in PEs, 241
  and exchange rates, 237, 239, 243–4, 249, 256, 257
  and gold, 243, 244–5, 249, 257–8, 259, 261–4, 267, 437
  and ideal currency, 244, 257, 258–9, 267, 436

469